Wages, Welfare Costs and Inflation in Classical Athens

Wages, Welfare Costs and Inflation in Classical Athens

William T. Loomis

Ann Arbor

THE UNIVERSITY OF MICHIGAN PRESS

Published in the United States of America by
The University of Michigan Press
Manufactured in the United States of America
∞ Printed on acid-free paper

2001 2000 1999 1998 4 3 2 1

A CIP catalogue record for this book is available from the British Library.

Library of Congress Cataloging-in-Publication Data

Loomis, William T.
Wages, welfare costs and inflation in classical Athens / William T. Loomis.
p. cm.
"This book is a revised and augmented version of a 1993 Harvard Ph.D. thesis in Classical Philology"—P. .
Includes bibliographical references and index.
ISBN 0-472-10803-4 (cloth)
1. Wages—Greece—Athens—History. 2. Cost and standard of living—Greece—Athens—History. 3. Inflation (Finance)—Greece—Athens—History. 4. Public welfare—Greece—Athens—History. I. Title.
HD5061.83.Z9A45 1998
331.2′9385—dc21 98-11372
CIP

For Leslie

Acknowledgments

This book is a revised and augmented version of a 1993 Harvard Ph.D. thesis in Classical Philology. Originally, I had intended to defer publication until this revised version could benefit from the inevitable additions and corrections that I expect to turn up in producing a related work, *Talents to Chalkoi: A Catalogue of Athenian Monetary Figures*, which will collect the figures in *all* categories (i.e., not just labor, transport and welfare costs). But for various reasons, having mostly to do with my frequent geographical moves, I have not been able to complete the *Talents* book as quickly as I had hoped, and further delay in the publication of this book now seems undesirable. The *Talents* book will include a list of addenda and corrigenda to this book, but I do not expect that its major conclusions will be materially altered.

In finally bringing this project to completion, I want to express my enormous gratitude to a number of individuals and institutions, in the (roughly) chronological order of their benefactions:

The late Sterling Dow, for first interesting me, as a college freshman, in the drachmas and talents in Aristophanes' *Acharnians*, and for suggesting that I explore Athenian monetary figures further as a graduate student.

The Department of the Classics of Harvard University, for its award to me, in 1989–1990, of the Charles Eliot Norton Fellowship to the American School of Classical Studies at Athens, where I collected most of the data for this book; and the School itself, for enabling me, as an Associate Member that year, to make use of the extraodinary resources of its Blegen Library.

Ernst Badian, my thesis adviser, whose great interest in this subject, and prompt and careful scrutiny of the details as well as the argument of the thesis version, resulted in numerous improvements. It was a unique privilege to be able to work under the guidance of this erudite, energetic and trenchant critic: I cannot imagine a better thesis adviser.

John P. Bodel and Alan L. Boegehold, members of my thesis committee, for their careful readings and helpful suggestions at both the earliest and the latest stages of the thesis version.

Kevin Clinton, for prompt and enlightening responses by letter to a number of questions about Eleusinian inscriptions.

The Senior Fellows of the Center for Hellenic Studies, and in particular its Directors, Deborah Boedeker and Kurt A. Raaflaub, for providing a congenial and supportive atmosphere in which, as a Junior Fellow in 1994–1995, I was able to correct, revise and amplify the thesis version.

Stephen V. Tracy, for reading and commenting on the penultimate version of Chapter 8.

The University of Michigan Press, and in particular Ellen Bauerle, Acquiring Editor for Classical Studies, and Christina Milton, Managing Editor, for their efficient and professional management of all phases of the publication of this book.

Leslie C. Becker and Katharine T. Loomis, for putting up with me during all phases of the production of this work.

In a book of this kind, with literally tens of thousands of details, it is inevitable that there will be errors of both omission and commission—omission of the figures that I have failed to report, and commission in the date, description, interpretation or source citation of the figures that I do discuss. In the list of addenda and corrigenda that I plan to publish in the *Talents* book, I shall gratefully acknowledge all corrections, which should be sent to me in care of the University of Michigan Press.

Contents

Abbreviations

Apart from the usual inconsistencies in the English spelling of *different* Greek words, there are (consistent) inconsistencies in the spelling of the names of some Greek authors and their works, which generally are transliterated in the main text but Latinized in citations in the footnotes and appendices, e.g., Isokrates in the main text but Isoc. in citations, the latter to preserve consistency with the format in *Talents*. Inscriptions are cited from *IG*, even if a later edition has appeared, unless that later edition provides a different text of the relevant passage; later editions are cited from *Agora* where applicable and otherwise from *SEG* unless it fails to report, or misreports, the text of the later edition. Scholia to Aristophanes are cited from the edition of W. J. W. Koster et al. (Groningen 1960–), to the extent that it has appeared, and otherwise from the edition of F. Dübner (Paris 1877). All such citations, as well as the citations from *PA*, are by inscription, line or item number (as the case may be), rather than by page number(s). All other citations should be self-explanatory. I use the following abbreviations:

AA	*Archäologischer Anzeiger*
ABSA	*Annual of the British School at Athens*
AD	Ἀρχαιολογικὸν Δελτίον
AE	Ἀρχαιολογικὴ Ἐφημερίς
Agora	*The Athenian Agora: Results of Excavations Conducted by the American School of Classical Studies at Athens* (Princeton 1953–)
Aig.	Aiginetan
AJA	*American Journal of Archaeology*

AJAH	*American Journal of Ancient History*
AJPh	*American Journal of Philology*
amt.	amount
AncSoc	*Ancient Society*
AncW	*Ancient World*
ap.	apud
ARV	J. D. Beazley, *Attic Red-figure Vase Painters*^{2} (Oxford 1963), as supplemented by J. D. Beazley, *Paralipomena* (Oxford 1971), and T. H. Carpenter, *Beazley Addenda*^{2} (Oxford 1989)
ASAA	*Annuario della Scuola Archeologica di Atene*
ASNP	*Annali della Scuola Normale Superiore di Pisa*
Ath. Pol.	*Athenaion Politeia* (Aristotle's unless otherwise specified)
BCH	*Bulletin de correspondance hellénique*
BMCRev	*Bryn Mawr Classical Review*
Böckh, *SdA*	A. Böckh, *Die Staatshaushaltung der Athener*^{3} (M. Fränkel rev.), 2 vols. (Berlin 1886)
Buchanan, *Theorika*	J. J. Buchanan, *Theorika: A Study of Monetary Distributions to the Athenian Citizenry during the Fifth and Fourth Centuries B.C.* (Locust Valley, New York 1962)
Bugh, *Horsemen*	G. R. Bugh, *The Horsemen of Athens* (Princeton 1988)
Burford, *Craftsmen*	A. Burford, *Craftsmen in Greek and Roman Society* (London 1972)
Burford, *GTBE*	A. Burford, *The Greek Temple Builders at Epidauros* (Liverpool 1969)
Burford, "Heavy Transport"	A. Burford, "Heavy Transport in Antiquity," *Economic History Review* (2nd ser.) 13 (1960) 1–18
c.	century or circa
CAH	*Cambridge Ancient History* (1st ed. 1923–1939, 2nd and 3rd eds. 1970–) (Cambridge 1923–)

CGFPR	C. Austin, ed., *Comicorum Graecorum fragmenta in papyris reperta* (Berlin 1973)
ch.	chalkous/chalkoi
Chambers, *ASdA*	M. Chambers, *Aristoteles Staat der Athener* (Berlin 1990)
CID	*Corpus des inscriptions de Delphes* (Paris 1977–)
Clinton, "Ins. Eleusis"	K. Clinton, "Inscriptions from Eleusis," *AE* (1971) 81–136
Clinton, "Review"	K. Clinton, Review of Lawton, *ADR*, *BMCRev* 7 (1996) 743–751
CPG	E. L. von Leutsch and F. G. Schneidewin, eds., *Corpus paroemiographorum Graecorum*, 2 vols. (Göttingen 1839–1851)
CPh	*Classical Philology*
CR	*Classical Review*
CSCA	*California Studies in Classical Antiquity*
Davies, *APF*	J. K. Davies, *Athenian Propertied Families, 600–300 B.C.* (Oxford 1971)
dr.	drachma(s)
Ehrenberg, *People*	V. Ehrenberg, *The People of Aristophanes*[2] (Oxford 1951)
epist.	epistulam
FGrH	F. Jacoby, ed., *Die Fragmente der griechischen Historiker* (Leiden 1923–1958)
FHG	C. Mueller, ed., *Fragmenta historicorum Graecorum* (Paris 1841–1870)
fr.	fragment(s)
Gabrielsen, *Financing*	V. Gabrielsen, *Financing the Athenian Fleet: Public Taxation and Social Relations* (Baltimore 1994)
Gabrielsen, *Remuneration*	V. Gabrielsen, *Remuneration of State Officials in Fourth Century B.C. Athens* (Odense 1981)
Gallo, "Salari"	L. Gallo, "Salari e inflazione: Atene tra V e IV sec. A.C.," *ASNP* (ser. 3) 17 (1987) 19–63
Gow, *Machon*	A. S. F. Gow, ed., *Machon* (Cambridge 1965)

Griffith, *MHW*	G. T. Griffith, *The Mercenaries of the Hellenistic World* (Cambridge 1935)
G-S	A. W. Gomme and F. H. Sandbach, *Menander: A Commentary* (Oxford 1973)
Guthrie, *HGP*	W. K. C. Guthrie, *A History of Greek Philosophy*, 6 vols. (Cambridge 1962–1981)
Hansen, "Misthos"	M. H. Hansen, "Misthos for Magistrates in Classical Athens," *SO* 54 (1979) 5–22
HCT	A.W. Gomme, A. Andrewes and K. J. Dover, *A Historical Commentary on Thucydides*, 5 vols. (Oxford 1945–1981)
Himmelmann, "Entlohnung"	N. Himmelmann, "Zur Entlohnung künstlerischer Tätigkeit in klassischen Bauinschriften," *JDAI* 94 (1979) 127–142
ID	*Inscriptions de Délos* (Paris 1926–)
IG	*Inscriptiones Graecae* (Berlin 1873–)
inc.	figure incomplete
JDAI	*Jahrbuch des Deutschen Archäologischen Instituts*
JHS	*Journal of Hellenic Studies*
Jones, *Ath. Dem.*	A. H. M. Jones, *Athenian Democracy* (Oxford 1957)
K-A	R. Kassel and C. Austin, eds., *Poetae comici Graeci* (Berlin 1983–)
Kraay, *ACGC*	C. M. Kraay, *Archaic and Classical Greek Coins* (London 1976)
Kroll, "Archive"	J. H. Kroll, "An Archive of the Athenian Cavalry," *Hesperia* 46 (1977) 83–140
K-T	A. Koerte and A. Thierfelder, eds., *Menandri quae supersunt*[2], 2 vols. (Leipzig 1959)
Kyz.	Kyzikene
Lawton, *ADR*	C. L. Lawton, *Attic Document Reliefs* (Oxford 1995)
Lex. Seg.	*Lexica Segueriana*, in I. Bekker, ed., *Anecdota Graeca* I (Berlin 1814) 1–476
loc. unst.	location unstated

LSJ	H. G. Liddell and R. Scott, *A Greek-English Lexicon*[9] (1940 9th ed. by H. S. Jones, with 1996 rev. suppl. by P. W. Glare) (Oxford 1996)
Maier	F. G. Maier, ed., *Griechische Mauerbauinschriften*, 2 vols. (Heidelberg 1959–1961)
MDAI(A)	*Mitteilungen des Deutschen Archäologischen Instituts (Athenische Abteilung)*
min.	minimum
min. inc.	minimum possible of a figure that is or may be incomplete
misc.	miscellaneous
M-L	R. Meiggs and D. Lewis, eds., *A Selection of Greek Historical Inscriptions to the End of the Fifth Century B.C.*, rev. ed. (Oxford 1988)
mn.	mna(s)
NAC	*Quaderni ticinesi di numismatica e antichità classiche*
NC	*Numismatic Chronicle*
Nolan, *Inscribing Costs*	B. T. Nolan, *Inscribing Costs at Athens in the Fourth Century B.C.* (Ph.D. diss., Ohio State University, 1981) (Ann Arbor 1981)
ob.	obol(s)
OCD	S. Hornblower and A. Spawforth, eds., *Oxford Classical Dictionary*[3] (Oxford 1996)
Osborne	M. J. Osborne, *Naturalization in Athens*, 4 vols. (Brussels 1981–1983)
PA	I. Kirchner, *Prosopographia Attica*, 2 vols. (Berlin 1901–1903)
p.a.	per annum
P&P	*Past and Present*
p.d.	per day
ΦΟΡΟΣ	D. W. Bradeen and M. F. McGregor, eds., ΦΟΡΟΣ: *Tribute to Benjamin Dean Meritt* (Locust Valley, New York 1974)

Pickard-Cambridge, *DFA*	A. Pickard-Cambridge, *The Dramatic Festivals of Athens*² (1968 rev. 2nd ed. with 1988 supp., both by J. Gould and D. M. Lewis) (Oxford 1988)
p.m.	per month
p.pr.	per prytany
Pritchett, *GSW*	W. K. Pritchett, *The Greek State at War*, 5 vols. (Berkeley 1974–1991)
quan. unst.	quantity/quantities unstated
Randall, "Erechtheum Workmen"	R. H. Randall, Jr., "The ErechtheumWorkmen," *AJA* 57 (1953) 199–210
RBN	*Revue belge de numismatique et de sigillographie*
RE	G. Wissowa, W. Kroll et al., eds., *Paulys Realencyclopädie der classischen Altertumswissenschaft* (Stuttgart 1894–)
REG	*Revue des études grecques*
RFIC	*Rivista di filologia e di istruzione classica*
Rhodes, *CAAP*	P. J. Rhodes, *A Commentary on the Aristotelian* Athenaion Politeia (Oxford 1981)
Σ	scholion/scholia
Schwenk	C. J. Schwenk, *Athens in the Age of Alexander: The Dated Laws & Decrees of 'the Lykourgan Era,' 338–322 B.C.* (Chicago 1985)
SEG	*Supplementum Epigraphicum Graecum* (Leiden 1923–)
SO	*Symbolae Osloenses*
st.	stater(s)
Stewart, *Greek Sculpture*	A. Stewart, *Greek Sculpture: An Exploration*, 2 vols. (New Haven 1990)
Supp. Hell.	H. Lloyd-Jones and P. Parsons, eds., *Supplementum Hellenisticum* (Berlin 1983)
SVF	H. F. A. von Arnim, ed., *Stoicorum Veterum Fragmenta* (Leipzig 1903–1924)
T.	talent(s)

Talents	W. T. Loomis, *Talents to Chalkoi: A Catalogue of Athenian Monetary Figures* (Ann Arbor forthcoming)
TAPhA	*Transactions and Proceedings of the American Philological Association*
Tod	M. N. Tod, ed., *A Selection of Greek Historical Inscriptions*, 2 vols. (vol. 1^2) (Oxford 1946–1948)
Tracy, *ADIT*	S. V. Tracy, *Athenian Democracy in Transition: Attic Letter-Cutters of 340 to 290* B.C. (Berkeley 1995)
Tracy, *ALC*	S. V. Tracy, *Attic Letter Cutters of 229 to 86* B.C. (Berkeley 1990)
v.	versus
vel sim.	vel similiter
Westermann, "Ephodia"	W. L. Westermann, "Notes upon the Ephodia of Greek Ambassadors," *CPh* 5 (1910) 203–216
Whitehead, *Demes*	D. Whitehead, *The Demes of Attica 508/7–ca. 250* B.C.*: A Political and Social Study* (Princeton 1986)
ZPE	*Zeitschrift für Papyrologie und Epigraphik*
>	more than
<	less than
→	increase or decrease in amount, or chronological change
[ ]	letters restored by editors of epigraphical and papyrus texts, or suppressed by editors of manuscript texts
{ }	letters suppressed by editors of epigraphical and papyrus texts
< >	letters added or substituted by editors
?	no preserved classification, date, amount or description

Athenian Monetary Denominations

1 talent	=	60 mnas	=	6,000 drachmas	=	36,000 obols	=	288,000 chalkoi
		1 mna	=	100 drachmas	=	600 obols	=	4,800 chalkoi
				1 drachma	=	6 obols	=	48 chalkoi
						1 obol	=	8 chalkoi

Introduction

Goals and Scope of Inquiry

The goals of this book are (a) to collect all ancient Athenian wages, salaries, transport costs, and travel and welfare allowances, and to organize these figures by category and date, (b) to evaluate each figure critically in order to determine what people were paid for various kinds of work or allowances, and (c) to consider three general questions: (i) Was there a "standard wage" at Athens?, (ii) Was there inflation and deflation in Athens?, and (iii) What are the implications of the answers to (i) and (ii) for the hotly debated question of whether Athens was an "embedded" or a "market" economy? Although the figures range from the sixth century B.C. to the second century A.D., more than 95% of them are from the years 450 to 320 B.C., and the main focus of this book accordingly is on pay and allowances in the classical period.

One may reasonably ask why prices, and price inflation and deflation, are not included in this book. The answer is that most prices are "apples and oranges," i.e., they are not obviously and directly comparable to one another in the way that wages and allowances clearly are.[1] When we look at the wages of soldiers or stonemasons or dikasts at various periods in the fifth and fourth centuries, in each case we clearly are dealing with the same commodity—a single day's labor of a man doing a particular task. But when we turn to the prices, say, of houses, we are not told enough about the size, condition, location and other distinguishing characteristics of the houses to know whether 500 drachmas for an οἰκία before 322 would have bought the same kind of house as [4]50 drachmas for an οἰκία in c. 414.[2] The two categories of prices that *might* be thought to be useful for comparative purposes—for grain and livestock

1. For analogous observations resulting from a recent study of wages and prices on Delos, see G. Reger, *Regionalism and Change in the Economy of Independent Delos, 314–167 B.C.* (Berkeley 1994) 9–10.

2. See *IG* I^3 426. 68 ([4]50 dr. min. inc. for οἰκία in c. 414); Arist. *E.N.* 1133b 24 (5 mn. for οἰκία before 322).

(e.g., so many drachmas for a medimnos of wheat or a female sheep in various years)—are unusually dependent on temporary weather conditions (most of the fourth-century grain figures cluster around the famine of c. 330) or religious conservatism (most of the prices for livestock come from sacred calendars),[3] and thus are not as indicative of long-term trends—or as reliably comparable to one another—as daily wages and allowances. Finally, apart from the lack of comparability of most prices, they usually reflect a significant investment of capital as well as labor, and thus do not fit well in a study of wages, salaries, transport costs, and travel and welfare allowances, where the labor of a single individual is the only, or at least the most important, component.

Prior Scholarship

Athenian labor and welfare costs, and most other monetary figures, were collected comprehensively for the first (and last) time by August Böckh for the first edition (1817) of his *Die Staatshaushaltung der Athener*. This collection was updated in some respects by Böckh for the second edition (1850) and by Max Fränkel for the third edition (1886). It was, and is, a remarkable book, primarily because of its breadth: it pulled together almost all evidence then available for the functioning of the Athenian economy—not only wages, prices and other monetary figures, but also population figures, the machinery of public financial administration, taxation, and other sources of public revenue. It has never been superseded, and is still widely consulted as a reference work. It is still the only place, for example, where one can turn for a collection of all categories of labor and welfare costs.

Obviously, however, a book of this age has serious limitations. First of all, the evidence has increased enormously: there have been some very significant additions by papyri—notably Aristotle's *Athenaion*

3. For the temporarily inflated price of wheat in c. 330 (from 5 to 16 dr. per medimnos), see *IG* II^2 360. 9, 30, 56, 68; 408. 13; 1672. 287–288, 297–298; [Dem.] xxxiv. 39. For the (consequent) price increases for livestock in the same period, see *IG* II^2 1672. 120, 128, 289–290. For the remarkable stability in the prices of sacrificial animals, perhaps reflecting a religious conservatism that placed a higher value on uniform religious expenditures than on the uniform quality of religious victims, see "Priests, Oracles and Seers" p. 86 with n. 29.

Politeia—and hundreds of new inscriptions. Second, Böckh was inclined to treat all the evidence as if it were equally valid: Aristophanes is cited as if he were as reliable as an inscription,[4] and writers of the Roman imperial period are given the same weight as a classical author.[5] Finally, Böckh tended to assume that wages and prices were stable from the beginning of the sixth century right through the Hellenistic and Roman periods.[6]

Since Böckh's great work, there have been studies on individual categories of figures, notably Pritchett's on military pay,[7] Nolan's on inscribing costs,[8] and Buchanan's on welfare allowances.[9] In addition, Gallo recently has considered the general question of inflation.[10] But because these modern studies have focused on individual categories or questions, they have not benefited from the comparative approach that an examination of all labor costs makes possible—this comparative approach is especially helpful for labor costs, where the useful evidence is relatively meager and secure evidence in one category often can shed light on the much more spotty evidence in another category. Moreover, the modern studies have not been based on an up-to-date collection of the evidence: most of them rely on Böckh's collection, supplemented by random references to newer material.[11] Finally, although the modern studies often have expressed a theoretical awareness of the uneven quality of the sources and the possible effects of inflation, they have not always allowed for these problems in practice.[12]

---

4. E.g., Böckh, *SdA* I 303. Cf. "Travel Allowances" ##4, 6, 15.

5. E.g., Böckh, *SdA* I 154–155. Cf. "Doctors, Lawyers and Professors" ##2–5, 12.

6. This is especially apparent in his discussion of manual laborers (*SdA* I 148–149), where figures ranging from the fifth century to the Ptolemaic period are compared solely on the basis of the task performed, without any consideration of their dates.

7. Pritchett, *GSW* I 3–29.

8. Nolan, *Inscribing Costs*.

9. Buchanan, *Theorika*.

10. Gallo, "Salari."

11. See, e.g., "Soldiers and Sailors" n. 2 for the (relatively few) missing items from Pritchett's catalogue, and "Inscribers" n. 234 for the more numerous omissions from Nolan's catalogue. Gallo's article, which has very full and up-to-date bibliographical references, does not refer to any comprehensive collection more recent than Böckh's and does not itself purport to collect, or to be based on, all the relevant data.

12. E.g., Pritchett, *GSW* I 3–29, does not address the question of diachronic changes in military pay. In that category, the "weaker" sources present fewer difficulties than in his work on prices, for which see, e.g., W. K. Pritchett, "The Attic Stelai, Part II," *Hesperia* 25 (1956) 178–328 at

Method and Sources

The foundation of this book is the catalogue of "Athenian Labor, Transport and Welfare Costs" contained in Appendix 1. A catalogue of "Non-Athenian Labor, Transport and Welfare Costs in Literary Sources [only]" is contained in Appendix 2. Both catalogues are excerpted from larger catalogues (which I shall publish separately in *Talents*) of *all* monetary figures, i.e., not only wages and salaries, but also prices of all kinds (for food, livestock, tangible personal property [including clothing, jewelry, furniture, pottery, books, sculpture and paintings], armor, building materials, precious metals, slaves, houses and other real estate), interest rates, business profits, foreign exchange rates, loans, bribes, embezzlements, dowries, fortunes, estates, funeral costs, liturgies, ransoms, tax revenues, war booty, war costs, festival expenses, judicial fines and judgments, the costs of religious sacrifices, etc. The computer-assisted method used in collecting these figures, and the relatively modest omissions from the catalogues occasioned by this method, are discussed in the Introduction to the Appendices (pp. 259–260). Within each catalogue, the figures are arranged by category, and within each category, by date.

Chapters 1–10 examine various categories of wages and salaries, Chapter 11 deals with transport costs, and Chapters 12 and 13 with travel and welfare allowances. Within each chapter, I consider the figures individually. If there are any problems with the interpretation of the Greek or Latin text (or, in one case, the painting), or with the date, I deal with these initially. I then consider the extent to which the figure is credible and useful. At the end of each chapter, I try to establish what people in the particular category really were paid at various periods, and offer preliminary observations on the relevance of these figures to the general questions (discussed in Chapters 14–16) concerning a standard wage, inflation and deflation, and the embedded or market nature of the economy.

204, where he reports shoe prices from sources as varied as Ar. *Plut.* 983 (8 dr., 388 B.C.), *IG* II^2 1672. 105 (6 dr., 329/8 B.C.) and Lucian *D. Meretr.* xiv. 2 (2 dr., A.D. 2nd c. but referring to 4th/3rd c. B.C.?), without any discussion of the possible effects of comic exaggeration or inflation and deflation on these figures.

The sources for the various figures vary widely in character. The principal sources are, in order of importance, (1) inscriptions, (2) roughly contemporary historians and philosophers, (3) comic poets, (4) orators, and (5) later writers of the Hellenistic and Roman periods, including scholiasts and grammarians.

1. Inscriptions are the most reliable source. They usually are contemporary with the transactions that they record, and thus are not subject to errors caused by inaccurate memory, or by the sorts of manuscript corruption that affect literary texts. More importantly, they are unbiased in the sense that they usually record public expenditures for archival purposes without regard to the interests of particular payees or other interested parties.[13] Finally, they contain precise figures rather than vague approximations. Even inscriptions, however, have potential weaknesses: they are subject to inscribing errors (the ancient equivalent of typographical errors),[14] their dates may be uncertain, they may be incompletely preserved, and (as a result) their printed texts frequently contain restorations or editorial comments that are at best unsupported and at worst impossible.[15] Moreover, epigraphical evidence is not available for most categories.[16] But, where it is available, an accurately dated and adequately preserved inscription is our most reliable source.

2. Roughly contemporary historians and philosophers are generally reliable, although with the passage of time their memory and research are subject to errors. Thucydides, as a contemporary source for the pay of soldiers, sailors and public officials, had personal experience of the figures and no incentive to distort them, so his information should be accepted.[17] Similarly, the *Ath. Pol.* should be reliable for the figures that

---

13. Of course, the mere fact of inscribing, e.g., a public building account, reflects a cultural bias prevalent in fifth- and fourth-century Athens, but not earlier or later. Cf. R. MacMullen, "The Epigraphic Habit in the Roman Empire," *AJPh* 103 (1982) 233–246.

14. E.g., "Construction and Other Manual Workers" #8 (with n. 26); "Inscribers" #45 (with n. 49).

15. E.g., "Overseers, Architects and Other Salaried Construction Personnel" #1; "Inscribers" ##106, 176, 185 and 224 with n. 248; "Travel Allowances" #2.

16. Inscriptions are the principal sources for "Priests, Oracles and Seers," "Overseers, Architects and Other Salaried Construction Personnel," "Construction and Other Manual Workers," "Inscribers," "Transport Costs," and "Travel Allowances," but they are rare or non-existent for all other categories.

17. E.g., "Soldiers and Sailors" ##5, 12–13, 15–16, and further discussion at pp. 55–57.

it gives for the third quarter of the fourth century,[18] but its information for earlier periods should be tested, if possible, against more contemporary sources.[19] Of course, historians and philosophers, like all literary sources, are subject to manuscript corruption.[20]

3. Comic poets are full of monetary figures, just as they are full of political and sexual allusions, no doubt because money, like sex and politics, was such an important part of the daily fabric of Athenian life. As such, it was subject to all sorts of comic horseplay. Indeed, where we have attested figures in the same category from more sober sources, it is usually clear that the comic poets have exaggerated their figures upwards or downwards to get a laugh.[21] Even where we lack reliable comparanda, the context often makes it clear that a figure is intended to seem especially high or low.[22] On the other hand, there are figures, such as the triobol pay for dikasts, which clearly are accurate "background facts" that provide a realistic setting for the play.[23] In dealing with figures from comic sources, therefore, I am inclined to judge them (a) as exaggerated where more reliable sources or the context indicate that they are (in the later case, even where there is no more reliable source, the figures can be useful in indicating what is beyond the limit of plausibility),[24] (b) as "background facts" where they are confirmed by more reliable sources, and (c) as uncertain where they do not obviously fall into either class (a) or class (b)—in that case, their plausibility in relation to analogous, though not precisely comparable, figures from more reliable sources becomes relevant.

4. Orators also provide monetary figures, though less frequently for labor costs than for other categories, such as fortunes, dowries, bribes and public revenues and expenditures. Because orators usually take a strongly adversarial position on the issues in controversy, we should be very hesitant to accept any figure which, if true, would help an orator's

---

18. E.g., "Public Officeholders" ##30 (a)–(g).

19. E.g., "Public Officeholders" ##17–19.

20. E.g., "Public Officeholders" #7.

21. E.g., "Soldiers and Sailors" #7 (upwards); "Prostitutes and Pimps" #2 (downwards).

22. E.g., "Doctors, Lawyers and Professors" #6.

23. See "Public Officeholders" #11. Cf. the much less certain "Priests, Oracles and Seers" #7.

24. See "Miscellaneous Workers" #2.

case or hurt his opponent's.[25] On the other hand, where he refers to a contemporary figure whose accuracy does not affect his case, it may be accepted as an innocuous "background fact."[26] Even where his case does to some extent depend on the accuracy of the figure, if it is a contemporary basic wage or allowance within the everyday knowledge of his audience or is plausible in relation to better attested analogous figures, it is entitled to some weight, since the orator's credibility with the audience would be adversely affected by obvious inaccuracies and the figure is in any event plausible.[27] But statements about much earlier figures, unless supported by reliable documentary or comparative evidence, are less likely to be reliable because of the orator's biases or inaccuracies in his memory and research—faults that would not be so apparent to his audience.[28]

5. Later writers of the Roman imperial period, such as Plutarch, Diogenes Laertius and Lucian, as well as scholiasts and grammarians, must be used with great caution. They lived so long after the events in question that their comprehension of ancient monetary figures was necessarily vague (just as ours is when we read early nineteenth-century dollar or pound sterling figures, to say nothing of even earlier figures cast in terms of ducats or florins). Their information obviously is (at best) only as good as their underlying source (provided that they did not misunderstand the source, or misremember it when they wrote), and often the source is not identified, so in each case the plausibility of their figures must be tested against more contemporary figures. Sometimes the figure is easy to confirm,[29] sometimes it is clearly wrong,[30] sometimes it is plausible enough to be probable though not absolutely certain,[31] and

---

25. See S. Dow, "The Athenian Calendar of Sacrifices," *Historia* 9 (1960) 270–293 at 280, n. 6: "In respect to the orators, is it not the proper rule to be slow to believe any unsupported extreme statement made by them which if true would help their case?" For an example, see "Public Officeholders" #22.

26. E.g., "Doctors, Lawyers and Professors" #12.

27. E.g., "Soldiers and Sailors" #19; "Welfare and Support Allowances and Distributions" #10.

28. E.g., "Welfare and Support Allowances and Distributions" #5.

29. E.g., Lucian *Bis Acc.* 12 (3 ob. dikast pay, for which see "Public Officeholders" #11 with n. 25). Even where the figures are accurate, the other details may not be, e.g., "Soldiers and Sailors" #18 with n. 53.

30. E.g., "Doctors, Lawyers and Professors" #2.

31. E.g., "Public Officeholders" #10.

sometimes there are no reliable analogous figures and judgment must suspended.[32]

Apart from these general principles, the other point to keep in mind is that we lack almost all of the evidence that must have existed at one time, e.g., temporary records on papyrus or on clay or wax tablets, which would have recorded pay in the "private sector"—an area about which we now know very little. On the whole, therefore, the private sector is excluded from this book except in the categories of lawyers, professors and prostitutes (an interesting combination!), where the evidence does permit some general observations.

Although we have a great many figures for wages and allowances, my conclusions, after prolonged critical study, are that many of them are not credible and that most of them are not useful for comparative purposes. The first conclusion may come as a surprise to scholars who have long accepted the handful of figures that are relevant to their own area, but I hope that they will be persuaded when they see all of the figures together. In any event, because I supply all of the figures, along with my reasons for acceptance or rejection, those who want to disagree will have all the relevant material at hand.

Only after (a) all of the evidence has been collected, and (b) the maximum possible accuracy has been achieved in assessing its meaning, date and credibility, is it possible (c) to try to answer, or at least to discuss, the general questions concerning a standard wage, inflation and deflation, and the embedded or market nature of the economy.

32. E.g., "Travel Allowances" #1.

Chapter 1
Public Officeholders

Böckh discussed this category,[1] as he did most others, but he was at a great disadvantage compared to us in that Aristotle's *Athenaion Politeia*, which is the most important source, had not yet been discovered. Rhodes and Chambers, in their 1981 and 1990 commentaries on the *Ath. Pol.*,[2] collected most of the work of subsequent scholars, which is noted at the appropriate places. Public religious officials are discussed under "Priests, Oracles and Seers" and travel allowances for ambassadors under "Travel Allowances."

1. late 460s. Dikast pay introduced by Perikles: 1 or 2 ob. p.d.? The sources are unanimous that it was Perikles who introduced pay for jury service, and the *Ath. Pol.* and Plutarch narrow the date further by referring this innovation to Perikles' rivalry with Kimon.[3] If they are right, dikast pay probably was introduced *before* Kimon's ostracism in 461, although some scholars have assigned the introduction to the period of Kimon's exile, when (as a result of the reforms of Ephialtes in 462/1) the law courts, having assumed many of the Areiopagos' responsibilities, needed more dikasts "and the

---

1. Böckh, *SdA* I 287–308.
2. Rhodes, *CAAP*; Chambers, *ASdA*.
3. Pl. *Gorg*. 515e: ταυτὶ γὰρ ἔγωγε ἀκούω, Περικλέα πεποιηκέναι Ἀθηναίους ἀργοὺς καὶ δειλοὺς καὶ λάλους καὶ φιλαργύρους, εἰς μισθοφορίαν πρῶτον καταστήσαντα; Arist. *Pol.* 1274a 8–9: τὰ δὲ δικαστήρια μισθοφόρα κατέστησε Περικλῆς; Arist. *Ath. Pol.* xxvii. 3–4: ἐποίησε δὲ καὶ μισθοφόρα τὰ δικαστήρια Περικλῆς πρῶτος, ἀντιδημαγωγῶν πρὸς τὴν Κίμωνος εὐπορίαν. . . . κατεσκεύασε μισθοφορὰν τοῖς δικασταῖς; Plut. *Per.* ix. 1–3: ἄλλοι δὲ πολλοὶ πρῶτον ὑπ' ἐκείνου (Perikles) φασὶ τὸν δῆμον ἐπὶ κληρουχίας καὶ θεωρικὰ καὶ μισθῶν διανομὰς προαχθῆναι. . . . πρὸς τὴν Κίμωνος δόξαν ἀντιτατόμενος ὑπεποιεῖτο τὸν δῆμον, . . . Περικλῆς καταδημαγωγούμενος τρέπεται πρὸς τὴν τῶν δημοσίων διανομήν. . . . καὶ ταχὺ θεωρικοῖς καὶ δικαστικοῖς λήμμασιν ἄλλαις τε μισθοφοραῖς καὶ χορηγίαις συνδεκάσας τὸ πλῆθος; Ael. Arist. iii. 98 (Behr): Περικλῆς. . . . πρῶτος γὰρ εἰς μισθοφορὰν κατέστησε τὰ πράγματα.

memory of his [Kimon's] generosity was fresh."[4] None of the early sources gives the amount of pay, but since it was raised from 2 to 3 ob. p.d. in 425 (#10 below), i.e., only four years after Perikles' death, it seems likely that it had reached the 2 ob. level during his lifetime. Because 2 ob. for dikasts seems reasonable in comparison with 4 ob. for Eleusinian epistatai as far back as c. 449–447? (#4 below), it is possible that 2 ob. p.d. was the original rate, but a rate of 1 ob. p.d. (which is explicitly, though not well, attested)[5] cannot be excluded, particularly if pay was introduced before the reforms of Ephialtes (if 1 ob. was the original rate, it could have been raised after more dikasts were needed as a result of the reforms).

2. c. 450. Athena Promachos officials paid 1–9 ob. p.d.? As discussed in greater detail under "Overseers, Architects and Other Salaried Construction Personnel" #1, it is impossible to determine what the epistatai, secretary and assistant in the Athena Promachos accounts (*IG* I³ 435. 81–82) were paid, although (to judge from other roughly contemporary documents [##4 and 6 below]), the epistatai and secretary probably were paid between 4 ob. and 1 dr. p.d. An important distinction between administrative officials like the epistatai, on the one hand, and dikasts (and later, ekklesiasts), on the other hand, is that administrative officials seem to have been paid every day of the year, including holidays, i.e., whether or not they were working,[6] while dikasts and ekklesiasts were paid only for the court or ekklesia session that they attended.

3. 450/49? Athenian? officials? (or rowers or soldiers?) sent to Miletos, or Milesian soldiers? paid 4 ob. (p.d.?). As discussed in

4. Rhodes, *CAAP* 339–340; see also Chambers, *ASdA* 267–268. For a suggested chronology, see E. Badian, *From Plataea to Potidaea* (Baltimore 1993) 13, 69–70, 101.

5. The only indication that the rate ever was as low as 1 ob. p.d. is Poll. viii. 113: καὶ τὸ δικαστικόν, ὅπερ καὶ τριώβολον καὶ δύ' ὀβολὼ καὶ ὀβολὸς ἦν 'Αττικός (doubted by G. Busolt and H. Swoboda, *Griechische Staatskunde* II [Munich 1926] 898, n. 4). I agree with A. H. Sommerstein (*Aristophanes Clouds* [Warminster 1982] 202–203) that Ar. *Nub.* 863 (ὃν πρῶτον ὀβολὸν ἔλαβον ἡλιαστικόν) means simply the first money that Strepsiades earned as a dikast, rather like our expression "the first cent/dollar that I earned." Hesych. δ 1813 (Latte) (δικαστικόν . . . τριώβολόν . . . οὐ μέντοι ἕστηκεν, ἀλλ' ἄλλοτε ἄλλως ἐδίδετο) could be based on the fact that the rate once had been 2 ob. p.d. *Com. Adesp.* fr. 941 (K-A) (quoted in n. 43 below) obviously is about ekklesiast pay, notwithstanding the confused reference by Zenobios to dikasts as well.

6. For the evidence, see "Overseers, Architects and Other Salaried Construction Personnel" ##4, 7, 8.

greater detail under "Soldiers and Sailors" #2, there are many uncertainties about the fragmentary *IG* I^3 21. If the date is at least approximately right, if the 4 obols is pay, and if the payees are Athenian officials, their pay would be paralleled by that of the Eleusinian epistatai in #4 below, but the evidence of this #3 obviously is quite uncertain.

4. c. 449–447?[7] Epistatai of Eleusinian funds paid 4 ob. (p.d.), apiece. This decree provides for five epistatai (one acting as a secretary) to manage the funds of the Eleusinian goddesses. The epistatai are to collect past debts, take care of the annual offerings, recover lost property, and make expenditures, not only at Eleusis itself, but also at Athens (apparently for construction at the city Eleusinion) and at Phaleron.[8] These duties obviously were thought to require some ability since the epistatai were elected rather than chosen by lot. Their compensation of 4 ob. (almost certainly p.d.) therefore

---

7. I here follow the Corpus date of c. 449–447, rather than 432/1 suggested by Mattingly and Clinton (see Corpus edition plus addenda at p. 938 and *SEG* XXXVIII 2 for the arguments on each side).

8. *IG* I^3 32. 7–17, 20–30:

ἄ[νδρας δὲ hελέσ]θ̣[αι 'Α]θεναίο-
ν πέ[ν]τε, τούτ[ος δὲ φέρεν τέττ]αρας ὀβολὸ-
[ς] hέκασ[τ]ον π[α]ρὰ τõν κολ[ακρ]ετõν, hένα δ[ὲ]
[τ]ούτον [γρ]αμμ̣α̣τε[ύ]ε[ν κατὰ] φσε͂[φ]ον̣· τούτο-
[ς] δὲ ἐπισ[τε͂]ναι [τ]οῖς χρέμασι τοῖς τοῖν θ-
[ε]οῖν καθάπερ hοι ἐπὶ τοῖς ἐμ πό[λ]ει ἔργ[ο]-
[ι]ς ἐπ̣ε̣στ[ά]το[ν] τõι νεõι καὶ τõι ἀ[γ]άλματι·
[ἐχ]σομοσίαν δὲ μὲ ε͂ν[α]ι· [τὸς δὲ] hειρεμένο-
[ς] προσιόντας πρὸς τὲν βολέν, ἐάν τι ὀφελ-
ό[μ]ενον ε͂[ι] τοῖν θεοῖν, φρά[ζ]εν καὶ ἀ[ν]απρά-
[τ]τεν·
ἐπιμελε͂σθαι δὲ καὶ τõν ἐπετε-
ίον hὰ λαμβάνεται τ̣οῖ[ν θ]εοῖν καὶ ἐάν τι
[ἀ]πολολὸς πυνθάνονται [ἀ]νασόι[ζε]ν· τὸς δ-
ὲ λογιστὰς λογίζεσθαι 'Ελευσῖνι μὲν τὰ
'Ελευσῖνι ἀνελομένα, ἐν ἄστει δὲ τὰ ἐν ἄσ-
τει ἀνελομένα ἀνακαλõντας τὸν αρχιτέ-
κτονα Κόροιβον καὶ Λυσανίαν ἐν τõι 'Ελε-
υσινίοι, Φαλεροĩ δὲ ἐν τõι hιεροĩ hὰ Φαλ-
ερόνδε ἀνέλοται· ἀναλίσκεν δὲ ὅ τι ἄν [μά]-
λιστα δέει μετὰ τõν hιερέον καὶ τε͂ς β[ολ]-
ε͂ς βουλευομένος τὸ λοιπόν·

The reference to the architect in lines 25–26 indicates that the expenditures of the epistatai included construction at the city Eleusinion. For this entry, see also "Overseers, Architects and Other Salaried Construction Personnel" #2.

seems appropriate in comparison with the 2 ob. p.d. probably paid at this time to dikasts (#1), who were chosen by lot.

5. 447–432. Parthenon officials paid uncertain amounts. As discussed in greater detail under "Overseers, Architects and Other Salaried Construction Personnel" #3, it is not certain that elected epistatai and secretaries were among the persons included in payments for monthly salaries in the Parthenon accounts (*IG* I^3 436–449), and in any event the amount of their individual salaries is not ascertainable.

6. c. 440–432.[9] Overseers of the public water supply paid 1 dr. p.[d.] apiece?[10] Although the inscription that provides this figure is very fragmentary, the preserved portion does seem to involve the water supply, and the interpretation of the [d]rachma as the pay decreed for officials (not expressly called "epistatai") overseeing the water supply is plausible, though obviously not certain.

7. pre-431. More than 20,000 men were supported by the state, including 6,000 dikasts, 500 bouleutai, 500 dockyard guards, 50 Akropolis guards, 700 local and 700? overseas officials, plus (just prior to 431?) 2,000 men selected by lot who were carried on (i.e., rowing?) ships collecting tribute; also (an unspecified number of) prison guards.[11] The question marks in the foregoing paraphrase indicate a few of the many uncertainties about the text, chronology and

---

9. This is the date given in the Corpus for the so-called Springhouse Decree, on the basis of its lettering and references (in lines 13–14) to the sons of Perikles. See the Corpus edition for references to scholarly discusssions, including W. E. Thompson's slightly later date of c. 430 and, more recently, A. G. Woodhead's date of 435/4.

10. *IG* I^3 49. 3–7:
ἐκαστο[- - - - - - - - - - - - ^{35} - - - - - - - - - - - - - - - μισθὸν λαμβάνειν δ]-
ραχμὲν τε̑[ς hεμέρας hεκάστες, ἐπιμέλεσθαι δὲ αὐτὸς καὶ τε̑ς κρένες κα]-
ὶ τε̑ς ἀγογε̑ς [τõ hύδατος - - - - - - - - - ^{23} - - - - - - - - Νικόμαχος εἶπε· τ]-
[ὰ] μὲν ἄλλα καθ[άπερ τε̑ι βολε̑ι, - - - - - - - - - - - ^{33} - - - - - - - - - - - - -]
ει, hόπος ἂν ῥέοσ[ι. . . .

11. Arist. *Ath. Pol.* xxiv. 3: συνέβαινεν γὰρ ἀπὸ τῶν φόρων καὶ τῶν τελῶν καὶ τῶν συμμάχων πλείους ἢ δισμυρίους ἄνδρας τρέφεσθαι. δικασταὶ μὲν γὰρ ἦσαν ἑξακισχίλιοι, . . . βουλὴ δὲ πεντακόσιοι, καὶ φρουροὶ νεωρίων πεντακόσιοι, καὶ πρὸς τούτοις ἐν τῆι πόλει φρουροὶ ν̄, ἀρχαὶ δ' ἔνδημοι μὲν εἰς ἑπτακοσίους ἄνδρας, ὑπερόριοι δ' εἰς †ἑπτακοσίους†· πρὸς δὲ τούτοις ἐπεὶ συνεστήσαντο τὸν πόλεμον ὕστερον, . . . ἄλλαι δὲ νῆες αἱ τοὺς φόρους ἄγουσαι ⟨καὶ⟩ τοὺς ἀπὸ τοῦ κυάμου δισχιλίους ἄνδρας, ἔτι δὲ . . . δεσμωτῶν φύλακες· ἅπασι γὰρ τούτοις ἀπὸ τῶν κοινῶν ἡ διοίκησις ἦν.

meaning of this passage.[12] For purposes of this study, the passage is useful only in that it indicates that even before 431 there were many paid public officials doing a wide variety of jobs. Unfortunately, however, the passage does not tell us how much they were paid.

8. 425. Ambassadors to Persian King, 2 dr. p.d. μισθός for 11 years—pay or ἐφόδια? In Aristophanes' *Acharnians*, an ambassador says that he and (an unspecified number of) his fellow ambassadors had been sent to the Persian King eleven years before, drawing μισθός of 2 dr. p.d.[13] Dikaiopolis' apoplectic reaction suggests that the rate probably, and the term certainly, have been exaggerated for comic purposes but, in the absence of any more reliable evidence that ambassadors received μισθός in the fifth century and, if so, what its amount was, this passage is best considered in connection with ambassadorial ἐφόδια, for which see "Travel Allowances" #4.

9. 425. Ambassadors or taxiarchs to Thrace?, 3 dr. (p.d.) pay (μισθοφοροῦντας) or ἐφόδια? In the *Acharnians* there also is a reference to some public officials serving in the "Thraceward" region and drawing pay of three drachmas, presumably per day: τοὺς μὲν ἐπὶ Θρᾴκης μισθοφοροῦντας τρεῖς δραχμάς (602). From the context,[14] it is not clear whether they are military officers or

---

12. On which see Rhodes, *CAAP* 300–309, and Chambers, *ASdA* 254–256. For this entry, see also "Soldiers and Sailors" #6.

13. Ar. *Ach.* 65–7, 90 (Πρεσβευτής and Δικαιόπολις):

Πρ. ἐπέμψαθ' ἡμᾶς ὡς βασιλέα τὸν μέγαν,
μισθὸν φέροντας δύο δραχμὰς τῆς ἡμέρας,
ἐπ' Εὐθυμένους ἄρχοντος·—
Δι. οἴμοι τῶν δραχμῶν.

Δι. ταῦτ' ἄρ' ἐφενάκιζες σὺ δύο δραχμὰς φέρων.

Euthymenes had been archon in 437/6, and the *Acharnians* was produced in 426/5.

14. Ar. *Ach.* 593–619 (Δικαιόπολις and Λάμαχος):

Λα. ταυτὶ λέγεις σὺ τὸν στρατηγὸν πτωχὸς ὤν;
Δι. ἐγὼ γάρ εἰμι πτωχός;
Λα. ἀλλὰ τίς γὰρ εἶ;
Δι. ὅστις; πολίτης χρηστός, οὐ σπουδαρχίδης,
ἀλλ' ἐξ ὅτουπερ ὁ πόλεμος, στρατωνίδης·
σὺ δ', ἐξ ὅτουπερ ὁ πόλεμος, μισθαρχίδης.
Λα. ἐχειροτόνησαν γάρ με—
Δι. κόκκυγές γε τρεῖς.
ταῦτ' οὖν ἐγὼ βδελυττόμενος ἐσπεισάμην,
ὁρῶν πολιοὺς μὲν ἄνδρας ἐν ταῖς τάξεσιν,
νεανίας δ' οἵους σὺ διαδεδρακότας,

ambassadors. Dikaiopolis is angry that young men who shirk duty and danger (διαδεδρακότας) draw fat salaries while grey-haired citizens serve in the ranks as soldiers (600–602). One of the former is Lamachos, who here is apparently an elected (598, cf. 607) taxiarch[15] and called by Dikaiopolis a μισθαρχίδης (597) who μισθοφορεῖν (608) and μισθοφορῇ (619). But also in the category of young shirkers are ambassadors to the Persian King at Ekbatana and to Chaone in Epiros (613), the sorts of places that the old soldiers never have seen as ambassadors (610, 613), and Lamachos also is said to be the sort that gets that job (614). The reference to the Chaonians in 604 probably is to an embassy (as in 613), but the references to Kamarina and Gela in 606 could be to the recent military expedition to Sicily.[16] The reference to the Thraceward region (602) probably also is to a military expedition, but it could be to an embassy.[17] My

---

τοὺς μὲν ἐπὶ Θρᾴκης μισθοφοροῦντας τρεῖς δραχμάς,
Τεισαμενοφαινίππους, Πανουργιππαρχίδας,
ἑτέρους δὲ παρὰ Χάρητι, τοὺς δ' ἐν Χάοσιν,
Γερητοθεοδώρους, Διομειαλαζόνας,
τοὺς δ' ἐν Καμαρίνῃ κἀν Γέλᾳ κἀν Καταγέλᾳ.
Λα. ἐχειροτονήθησαν γάρ.
Δι. αἴτιον δὲ τί
ὑμᾶς μὲν ἀεὶ μισθοφορεῖν ἁμηγέπῃ,
τωνδὶ δὲ μηδέν'; ἐτεόν, ὦ Μαριλάδη,
ἤδη πεπρέσβευκας σύ, πολιὸς ὢν ἔνῃ;
ἀνένευσε· καίτοι γ' ἐστὶ σώφρων κἀργάτης.
τί δαὶ Δράκυλλος κεὐφορίδης καὶ Πρινίδης;
εἶδέν τις ὑμῶν τἀκβάταν' ἢ τοὺς Χάονας;
οὔ φασιν. ἀλλ' ὁ Κοισύρας καὶ Λάμαχος,
οἷς ὑπ' ἐράνου τε καὶ χρεῶν πρώην ποτέ,
ὥσπερ ἀπόνιπτρον ἐκχέοντες ἑσπέρας,
ἅπαντες "ἐξίστω" παρῄνουν οἱ φίλοι.
Λα. ὦ δημοκρατία, ταῦτα δῆτ' ἀνασχετά;
Δι. οὐ δῆτ', ἐὰν μὴ μισθοφορῇ γε Λάμαχος.

15. Cf. line 593 (στρατηγόν) with lines 1073–1074 (Lamachos ordered by στρατηγοί to move λόχους). See also J. A. O. Larsen, "The *Acharnians* and the Pay of Taxiarchs," *CPh* 41 (1946) 91–98 at 92, 95–96; Pritchett, *GSW* II 126; and A. H. Sommerstein, *Aristophanes Acharnians* (Warminster 1980) 185–186.

16. See Thuc. iii. 86 (in 427, Athenians send twenty ships to Sicily to aid Leontinoi and its allies [including Kamarina], who had sent an embassy to Athens); iii. 90, 103, 115 (Athenians fighting in Sicily in 426 and 425). But embassies in connection with the expedition also are possible.

17. See Thuc. ii. 29. 1, 4 (in 431, Athenians request Nymphodoros of Abdera to act as their proxenos to persuade Sitalkes to help them subdue τὰ ἐπὶ Θρᾴκης χωρία); ii. 58. 1 (in 430, Athenians send expedition against Chalkidians ἐπὶ Θρᾴκης and Poteidaia); ii. 79. 1–2 (in 429,

own view is that it would be a mistake to try to pin Aristophanes down here: he probably is not thinking of a specific military expedition or embassy but rather of cushy public jobs in general, and the 3 dr. p.d.—three times the highest attested non-comic figure for fifth-century public officeholders (#6)—probably is exaggerated for comic effect. As such, it should not be taken seriously as independent evidence of the μισθός or ἐφόδια of a taxiarch or ambassador,[18] but instead should be compared with other evidence in those categories, to shed light on the extent of (probable) comic exaggeration here: see "Soldiers and Sailors" #8 and "Travel Allowances" #6.

10. 425. Dikasts raised by Kleon from 2 to 3 ob. (p.d.).[19] The only sources for this raise are four scholia to Aristophanes, plus Ar. *Ach.* 657 (Kleon ὑποτείνων μισθούς), but the scholiast's very specific statement—that Kleon did this "as general when the war was going well" (i.e., after the capture of the Spartan hostages at Pylos)—is a credible detail, which the scholiast is unlikely to have made up as an inference from #11 below. Moreover, a modest beginning of 2 ob. p.d., followed by an increase to 3 ob., seems reasonable and plausible.

Athenians send expedition against Chalkidians ἐπὶ Θρᾴκης and Spartolos); ii. 95. 1–2 (also in 429, Sitalkes aids Athenians by marching against Chalkidians ἐπὶ Θρᾴκης). Apart from Nymphodoros, who was not an Athenian, we hear of no ambassador to the Thraceward region, but there may have been one or more; Aristophanes (*Ach.* 137) says that a theoros to Sitalkes had drawn μισθὸν . . . πολύν.

18. See W. J. M. Starkie, *The Acharnians of Aristophanes* (London 1909) 125, for a helpful statement of the problem. He was inclined (126) to see the 3 dr. as referring to ambassadors, as did Ehrenberg, *People* 230, n. 1, and 229, n. 6 (where he disagreed with the conclusion of Larsen [as in n. 15] 97–98, that it refers to taxiarch pay). Gallo, "Salari" 48 with n. 77, apparently finds 3 dr. p.d. credible.

19. Σ Ar. *Vesp.* 88a: ἦσαν δὲ ἡλιασταὶ τὸν ἀριθμὸν φʹ [500]· ἐδίδοτο δὲ αὐτοῖς χρόνον μέν τινα δύο ὀβολοί, ὕστερον δὲ Κλέων στρατηγήσας τριώβολον ἐποίησεν ἀκμάζοντος τοῦ πολέμου τοῦ πρὸς Λακεδαιμονίους; Σ Ar. *Vesp.* 300b: ἦν μὲν γὰρ ἄστατον τὸ τοῦ μισθοῦ· ποτὲ γὰρ διωβόλου ἦν, ἐγίνετο δὲ ἐπὶ Κλέωνος τριώβολον; Σ Ar. *Av.* 1541e: οὐχ εἱστήκει δὲ αὐτοῖς τὸ τριώβολον· πολλάκις γὰρ καὶ δύο ὀβολοὺς εἰλήφασιν; Σ Ar. *Ran.* 140: τὸν δικαστικὸν μισθὸν, ὅτι δύο ὀβολῶν ἦν. . . . καὶ ὅτι τὸ δικαστικὸν μισθάριον δύο ὀβολοὶ ἦσαν. . . . ἦν δὲ καὶ τριώβολον, τοῦτο τῶν στρατηγῶν κολακείας χάριν προστιθέντων (for continuation, see n. 28). For the possibility that the rate originally had been 1 ob. p.d., see #1 and Poll. viii. 113 (quoted in n. 5). Σ (*vet.*) Ar. *Plut.* 330b (quoted in n. 48) obviously confuses Kleon's increase in dikast pay with the early fourth-century increase in ekklesiast pay. K. J. Dover, *Aristophanes Clouds* (Oxford 1968) 205, says of the increase in dikast pay: "it is not certain that this is more than a rash inference from passages of Ar. The evidence collected by Busolt-Swoboda [as in n. 5—scholia quoted above (except Σ *Ran.* 140) plus Ar. *Ach.* 657, quoted in main text], is of unequal value." For more on Kleon's raise, see "Inflation and Deflation" pp. 240, 243–244, 250.

In any event, the contemporary evidence (#11) shows that by 424 the 3 ob. p.d. rate had been established.

11. 424–pre-322. Dikasts paid 3 ob. (p.d.). The earliest contemporary evidence of this rate is Aristophanes' *Knights*, produced in 424.[20] There are numerous other Aristophanic references in the *Wasps*, produced in 422,[21] in the *Horai* (c. 421–414),[22] and in the *Birds*, produced in 414.[23] In 411, dikast pay was suspended (see #17 below), but it probably was restored soon after the democracy itself was restored later that year; certainly there is evidence that in and before 405 dikasts were being paid, and in one instance that pay is said to be 3 ob.[24] There are a number of references, which cannot be dated more closely than "4th c.," to the dikastic triobol.[25] Pseudo-Lucian, in speaking of Demosthenes'

---

20. Ar. *Eq.* 51, 255–256 (ὦ γέροντες ἡλιασταί, φράτερες Τριωβόλου, οὓς ἐγὼ [Paphlagon = Kleon] βόσκω), 800. The "oracles" give humorous expression to hopes for further increases in pay under an expanded Athenian empire in *Eq.* 797–798: ἔστι γὰρ ἐν τοῖς λογίοισιν | ὡς τοῦτον [sc. Δῆμον] δεῖ ποτ' ἐν Ἀρκαδίᾳ πεντωβόλου ἡλιάσασθαι.

21. Ar. *Vesp.* 609, 684, 690, 788, 791, 1121; Σ Ar. *Vesp.* 300b–c, 389c, 663, 684a–b. For purposes of this study, there is no need to consider the accuracy of Aristophanes' statement that the total annual cost of 6,000 dikasts was 150 T. (Ar. *Vesp.* 663 et Σ). Lines 684–685,

σοὶ δ' ἥν τις δῷ τοὺς τρεῖς ὀβολούς, ἀγαπᾷς, οὓς αὐτὸς ἐλαύνων
καὶ πεζομαχῶν καὶ πολιορκῶν ἐκτήσω πολλὰ πονήσας,

where Bdelykleon speaks of the three obols that Philokleon "acquired by much toil, rowing and infantry-fighting and besieging," have sometimes been taken to mean 3 obols earned as a soldier or sailor, but I agree with the scholiast (Σ Ar. *Vesp.* 684a: τοὺς τρεῖς ὀβολούς: τὸν δικαστικὸν μισθόν), Dover (*HCT* IV 293), and Pritchett (*GSW* I 17–18 with n. 56), that it refers to the 3 ob. p.d. dikast pay that Aristophanes is saying the demos itself (αὐτός) has acquired by military operations.

22. Ar. fr. 588 (K-A): Hesych. δ 1813 [Latte] δικαστικόν· Ἀριστοφάνης ἐν Ὥραις τριώβολόν φησιν εἶναι. For the date, see K-A III.2 296.

23. Ar. *Av.* 1541: τὰ τριώβολα. Σ Ar. *Av.* 1541d: ἅπερ ἐλάμβανον οἱ κριταὶ οἱ ἐν ἡλιαίᾳ κρίνοντες εἰς μισθόν.

24. Phryn. Com. fr. 70 (K-A): τριώβολον | ὅσουπερ ἡλιάζομαι. I assign this a date of "pre-405?" since Phrynichos' last datable play was the *Muses*, for which he won second prize after the *Frogs* in 405 (Ar. *Ran.* Hypothesis I [c]). Ar. *Ran.* 1466 (δικαστὴς αὐτὰ [revenue produced by the fleet] καταπίνει μόνος) shows that dikasts were being paid in 405.

25. Lucian *Bis Acc.* 12: οἱ δικασταὶ ἐξ ἁπάντων Ἀθηναίων· ὁ μισθὸς τριώβολον ἑκάστης δίκης (a humorous exaggeration, at least on days when more than one case was heard); Poll. viii. 20: δικαστικόν· ἦν δὲ τοῦτο τριώβολον ὁ τῷ δικαστῇ διδόμενος μισθός; Poll. viii. 113 (quoted in n. 5); Lib. *Decl.* xxxiii. 5: ὦ δικασταί, . . . ἀποίσεσθε τὸ τριώβολον; *Suda* β 49 (Adler), βακτήρια καὶ σύμβολον: τὸ μέντοι σύμβολον ⟨μετὰ⟩ τὴν κρίσιν ἀποδιδοῦντες ἐκομίζοντο τριώβολον· ὅπερ καὶ δικαστικὸν γέγονεν; *Suda* η 214 (Adler), ἡλιασταί: . . . οἵτινες ὑπὸ τῶν δημοτῶν ἐτρέφοντο τριώβολον λαμβάνοντες μισθὸν δικαστικὸν μετὰ τὸ κρῖναι. . . . συγγενεῖς δὲ αὐτοὺς εἶπε τοῦ τριωβόλου, οἷον προσῳκειώμενοι καὶ προσπεφυκότες τῷ τριωβόλῳ· λέγει γάρ, ὡς γέροντες ἡλιασταὶ φράτορες

public career (c. 355–322), says that he used to awaken the city's sense of honor, which long had been prostrated in pursuit of the 1 dr. (presumably ekklesiast) fee and the 3 ob. (presumably dikast) fee.[26] (Dem. xxxix. 17 indicates that jury pay, and therefore jury trials, were suspended in 350/49 during the financial crisis arising from the invasion of Euboia.) Finally, the 3 ob. p.d. rate is confirmed for the period prior to 322 by the *Ath. Pol.*[27] In the context of so many contemporaneous attestations of the 3 ob. rate, I regard the late references to dikast pay of 2 ob., 4 ob. and 1 dr. p.d. as mistakes, sometimes arising from confusions with pay for ekklesiasts and soldiers.[28]

12. pre-422. Theoros or rower? to Paros paid 2 ob. (p.d.), μισθός or ἐφόδιον? Philokleon says that he had "never been on a state delegation anywhere, except to Paros, and then I was only paid two obols."[29] The translation is Sommerstein's, who comments, "(sc. per day): this low remuneration suggests that Philocleon was an oars-

---

τριωβόλου; Eust. ad *Il.* xviii. 490–540 (van der Valk IV 229. 5): καὶ οἱ δικασταὶ δὲ Ἀθήνησι μισθὸν λαμβάνουσιν, εἰ καὶ τριώβολον ἐκεῖνο; Eust. ad *Od.* i. 156 (Stallbaum I 41. 21): καὶ τριώβολον, μισθὸς δικαστικός (for continuation, see n. 28). For a mythical dikast, see Zenob. v. 2 (*CPG*), Λύκου δεκάς: Ἐπειδὴ Λύκος ὁ ἥρως πρὸς τοῖς ἐν Ἀθήναις δικαστηρίοις ἵδρυτο. . . . Ἀφώριστο δὲ αὐτῷ τριώβολον τῆς ἡμέρας.

26. [Lucian] *Dem. Enc.* 36: (Demosthenes) ἐγείρει δ' ἐρριμμένον ἤδη χρόνου πρὸς τὴν δραχμὴν καὶ τὸ τριώβολον τὸ τῆς πόλεως ἀξίωμα. For other possible interpretations of this passage, see #23 below with n. 54.

27. Arist. *Ath. Pol.* lxii. 2: Μισθοφοροῦσι. . . . τὰ δικαστήρια τρεῖς ὀβολούς, discussed in #30 (b) below.

28. Σ Ar. *Vesp.* 658: καὶ ἡ ἔξω διδομένη τοῖς δικασταῖς δραχμή; Σ Ar. *Ran.* 140 (on δύ' ὀβολώ, which probably refers to the διωβελία dole ["Welfare and Support Allowances and Distributions" #7 with n. 13]): τὸν δικαστικὸν μισθὸν, ὅτι δύο ὀβολῶν ἦν. . . . καὶ ὅτι τὸ δικαστικὸν μισθάριον δύο ὀβολοὶ ἦσαν. . . . ἦν δὲ καὶ τριώβολον, τοῦτο τῶν στρατηγῶν κολακείας χάριν προστιθέντων· ἐπὶ δὲ Ἀριστοφάνους καὶ δραχμὴν ἦν λαβεῖν (Hansen, "Misthos" 13 with n. 30, thought that the 2 obols referred to dikast pay that had been restored, at a reduced level, after 411); Eust. ad *Od.* i. 156 (Stallbaum I. 41. 21–23): καὶ τριώβολον, μισθὸς δικαστικός. καὶ οἱ ἁπλῶς τρεῖς ὀβολοί. ἐξ ὧν τριωβολιμαῖος, ὁ εὐτελής. καὶ τετρωβολίζειν, τὸ λαμβάνειν δικαστικὸν τετρώβολον. ἐγένετο γὰρ φασι καὶ τοσοῦτον ποτέ; Phot., τετρωβολίζων: τὸ δικαστικὸν τετρώβολον λαμβάνων· ἐγένετο γὰρ καὶ τοσοῦτόν ποτε. As discussed in greater detail under "Soldiers and Sailors" #20, Theopomp. Com. fr. 56 (K-A) seems to concern the διωβελία (2 ob.) dole (or possibly soldier's pay), rather than dikast pay.

29. Ar. *Vesp.* 1188–1189:

ἐγὼ δὲ τεθεώρακα πώποτ' οὐδαμοῖ,
πλὴν εἰς Πάρον, καὶ ταῦτα δύ' ὀβολὼ φέρων.

man in the state trireme which took the delegates to Paros."[30] If so, it should refer to a time (much earlier than 422) when Philokleon would, as a young man, have been able to do the rowing, and it would indicate that the daily wage of a rower in the pre-Poteidaia period (i.e., pre-432) was 2 ob. p.d. (see "Soldiers and Sailors" #10).[31] The other possibility is that the 2 ob. was paid to Philokleon as a theoros.[32] I incline to this second alternative, for three reasons: (a) the language (τεθεώρακα . . . δύ' ὀβολὼ φέρων) on its face suggests that the two obols were earned as a theoros, (b) insofar as #3 above is good evidence, 2 ob. p.d. would be too low for a rower even in an earlier period, but (c) it would accord well with the earlier pay for non-strenuous public office, viz., the 2 ob. p.d. paid to dikasts prior to 425 (#10).[33] If the payment was to a theoros, there remains the question whether it was μισθός or ἐφόδιον, on which see "Travel Allowances" #7.

13. 422. Public prosecutor paid 1 dr. (p.d.). In another passage in the *Wasps*, it is said that if a dikast arrives late, he will not collect his triobol, but the public prosecutor (called ξυνήγορος in line 482), even if he arrives late, will collect a 1 drachma συνηγορικόν, which the scholia interpret as his fee.[34] A 1 dr. fee for a prosecutor, who had to

---

30. A. H. Sommerstein, *Aristophanes Wasps* (Warminster 1983) 226. Service as a sailor-rower also was the interpretation of Σ Ar. *Vesp.* 1189d: ⟨ἀπ'⟩ ἰκρίων θεωροῦντες τοὺς δύο ὀβολοὺς παρεῖχον.

31. So D. M. MacDowell, *Aristophanes Wasps* (Oxford 1971) 285. Cf. "Soldiers and Sailors" #5 (sailors at Poteidaia drawing 1 dr. p.d.).

32. As Böckh, *SdA* I 271, seems to have been the first to suggest. Ehrenberg, *People* 228, n. 2, thought the figure too low for a theoros. See Pritchett, *GSW* I 18–19, for references to the opinons of various scholars and two other interpretations (soldier on expedition to Paros and soldier-escort of theoroi, supported by Σ Ar. *Vesp.* 1189a: ἔπαιξεν. ἀντὶ τοῦ "ὅτε εἰς Πάρον ἐστρατευσάμην"; Σ Ar. *Vesp.* 1189b: ἀντὶ τοῦ "μισθωτὸς ὢν στρατιώτης").

33. In any event, there does not seem to be comic distortion of the *figure*. Since Philokleon is contrasting his modest service with the pretentious theoriai of Androkles and Kleisthenes, he would be less likely to minimize his own compensation than to exaggerate theirs, as Dikaiopolis did in ##8 and 9.

34. Ar. *Vesp.* 689–691:

"ὡς ὅστις ἂν ὑμῶν
ὕστερος ἔλθῃ τοῦ σημείου, τὸ τριώβολον οὐ κομιεῖται."
αὐτὸς δὲ φέρει τὸ συνηγορικόν, δραχμήν, κἂν ὕστερος ἔλθῃ.

Σ Ar. *Vesp.* 691a: ὑπὲρ τοῦ συνηγορῆσαι. ἐλάμβανον γὰρ οἱ ῥήτορες δραχμήν, ὅτε ἐδημηγόρουν ὑπὲρ τῆς πόλεως ἢ ὑπὲρ ἄλλου τινός; Σ Ar. *Vesp.* 691b: φαίνεται, ὅτι μισθοφόρος ἡ ἀρχή. On the various kinds of συνήγοροι, see MacDowell (as in n. 31) 198. For this entry, see also "Doctors, Lawyers and Professors" #7.

prepare and argue his case, certainly seems plausible and reasonable in relation to the triobol for the dikast, who merely had to sit and listen.

14. 421/0. Hieropoioi (overseers of sacred rites) of the Hephaistaia paid the same as ?[35] If they were to be paid the same as the bouleutai (so the Corpus edition), we do not know how much that was (##16, 17 below). If they were to be paid the same as the dikasts (so Wilamowitz), they would have been paid 3 ob. p.d. All that can be said for certain is that hieropoioi did receive pay at this time.

15. c. 420. 1,000 dr. for the demarch of Plotheia? This has been interpreted by Whitehead as a capital sum, whose interest (estimated by Whitehead at 120 dr.) was to be administered by the demarch for deme cults.[36] Whatever the actual available interest may have been, I agree with Whitehead that it is not the demarch's salary, since the rest of the inscription is concerned exclusively with cult finances and there is no suggestion elsewhere in the abundant deme evidence that deme officials received *any* salary.

16. pre-411. Until the revolution of the 400, bouleutai were being paid.[37] But the amount is not known, nor is the date when such pay was instituted. I follow Rhodes in thinking that that bouleutic pay "is likely to have been instituted before rather than after the outbreak of the Peloponnesian War,"[38] partly on the evidence of #7, and partly because the introduction of pay for bouleutai seems more likely in

---

35. *IG* I³ 82. 17–21:
[- 7 - hι]ιεροποιὸ[ς] δὲ hοίτινες hιεροποιέσοσ[ι τὲν θυσίαν δέκα ἄνδρας δι]-
[α]κλ<u>ε</u>[ρο͂σαι] ἐκ το͂ν δ[ικα]σ̣το͂ν hένα ἐκ τε͂ς φυλε͂ς ἐκ το͂ṿ [- - - - 19 - - - - α]-
[ρ]χοι <u>δ</u>[ιακλ]εροσάντ[ον μ]ετὰ το͂ν τε͂ς βολε͂ς· διακλεροσ[άντον δὲ hοῦτοι ἐναντί]-
ον τε͂ς βολ[ε͂]ς· hοι δὲ λ[αχ]όντες μισθοφορόντον καθάπερ ḥ[οι βολευταί, hέος ἂν ἐ]-
πιμέλοντα[ι] τούτον· h[ο]ι̣ δὲ κολακρέται ἀποδιδόντον αὐτ̣ο[ῖς τὸ ἀργύριον.
Near the end of line 20, Wilamowitz suggested hοι δικασταί.

36. *IG* I³ 258. 2: [δη]μάρχωι X. This is the first item in a list of expenses entitled (line 1) [κεφ]άλαια. See Whitehead, *Demes* 161 (with n. 79), 165–169.

37. Thuc. viii. 69. 4: (The 400) ἐπέστησαν τοῖς ἀπὸ τοῦ κυάμου βουλευταῖς οὖσιν ἐν τῷ βουλευτηρίῳ, καὶ εἶπον αὐτοῖς ἐξιέναι λαβοῦσι τὸν μισθόν· ἔφερον δὲ αὐτοῖς τοῦ ὑπολοίπου χρόνου παντὸς αὐτοὶ καὶ ἐξιοῦσιν ἐδίδοσαν.

38. Rhodes, *CAAP* 304. But war expenses evidently had *not* been an obstacle to the dikasts' raise in 425 (#10); see also "Inflation and Deflation" pp. 240, 243–244, 250.

peacetime than in war, when there would have been other, more pressing, demands on the public treasury.

17. 411. Under the 400, pay for public officials was abolished, except for the nine archons and the prytaneis, who drew 3 ob. p.d.[39] Since we do not know how much bouleutai had been paid before (#16), we cannot say whether the 3 ob. p.d. for the bouleutai who were serving as prytaneis was their usual pay or a reduced rate during an emergency, when the other bouleutai were not being paid at all. Because (a) the bouleutai had been receiving μισθός (n. 37), (b) the public officials who no longer were paid are called ἀμίσθους (n. 39), (c) there is no suggestion of a distinction between μισθός and ration-money (e.g., σιτηρέσιον), and (d) such a distinction does not appear for soldiers until the fourth century,[40] I interpret the 3 ob. p.d. for archons and prytaneis as μισθός = gross pay.

18. 411. No pay for public officials under the 5,000.[41] The blanket wording of Thucydides' and Aristotle's statements probably should not be taken literally since the 5,000 are unlikely to have been more opposed than the 400 to pay for the archons and the prytaneis (#17), which presumably continued.

19. pre-403/2–c. 393. Ekklesiasts raised from nothing to 1 ob. to 2 ob. to 3 ob. (p.d.). Although pay for dikasts had been instituted very early (#1), and various officials (including members of the Boule) were receiving pay before 431 (##7, 16), pay for attending the Ekklesia probably was not introduced until after the restoration of the democracy in 403/2—certainly it is unlikely that Athens could have

---

39. Thuc. viii. 65. 3: οὔτε μισθοφορητέον εἴη ἄλλους ἢ τοὺς στρατευομένους . . . ; 67. 3: ἐνταῦθα δὴ λαμπρῶς ἐλέγετο ἤδη μήδε ἀρχὴν ἄρχειν μηδεμίαν ἔτι ἐκ τοῦ αὐτοῦ κόσμου μήτε μισθοφορεῖν; Arist. *Ath. Pol.* xxix. 5: τὰ μὲν {χρήματα} προσιόντα μὴ ἐξεῖναι ἄλλοσε δαπανῆσαι ἢ εἰς τὸν πόλεμον, τὰς δ' ἀρχὰς ἀμίσθους ἄρχειν ἁπάσας ἕως ἂν ὁ πόλεμος ᾖ, πλὴν τῶν ἐννέα ἀρχόντων καὶ τῶν πρυτάνεων οἳ ἂν ὦσιν· τούτους δὲ φέρειν τρεῖς ὀβολοὺς ἕκαστον τῆς ἡμέρας. I follow Rhodes, *CAAP* 379–382, and Chambers, *ASdA* 279–280, in referring all of these accounts to the same occasion, and in seeing the payments to archons and prytaneis as a specific exemption from the general rule stated by Thucydides.

40. For the μισθός-σιτηρέσιον distinction in military pay, see "Soldiers and Sailors" pp. 33–34. Hansen, "Misthos" 13, asserts that the 3 ob. for archons and bouleutai in 411 was εἰς σίτησιν, but the *Ath. Pol.* does not say this. Cf. ##30 (a) and (c) with n. 58.

41. Thuc. viii. 97. 1: ἐψηφίσαντο . . . μισθὸν μηδένα φέρειν μηδεμιᾷ ἀρχῇ; Arist. *Ath. Pol.* xxxiii. 1: ψηφισάμενοι μηδεμίαν ἀρχὴν εἶναι μισθοφόρον.

afforded to institute a new paid office during the last years of the war. The *Ath. Pol.* informs us that Agyrrhios, who was one of the secretaries of the Boule in that year,[42] instituted the first payment, of 1 ob. (presumably per day),[43] and that this later was raised to 2 ob. by Herakleides of Klazomenai and to 3 ob. by Agyrrhios.[44] This sequence is confirmed in part by Aristophanes' *Ekklesiazousai*,[45]

---

42. *IG* II^2 1. 41–42; *IG* II^2 2 + *SEG* XXXII 38. 6–7 (name restored); *SEG* XXVIII 45. 77 (name restored). Of course, Agyrrhios need not have introduced ekklesiast pay in the year in which he was secretary.

43. Cf. *Com. Adesp.* fr. 941 (K-A): ὀβολὸν εὗρε †Παρνοίτης†. The source of this fragment is Zenobios (ii. 91 Buehler), who goes on to explain: Καλλικράτης Ἀθήνησι πολιτευσάμενος, ἐπικαλούμενος δὲ †Παρνύτης†, μισθὸν ἔταξε τοῖς δικασταῖς καὶ τοῖς ἐκκλησιασταῖς· ὅθεν σκωπτόντων αὐτὸν τῶν κωμικῶν τὸ γελοῖον εἰς παροιμίαν ἦλθεν. (Καλλικράτης was Meineke's emendation of the manuscripts' variant readings Καλλιστράτης and Καλλίστρατος.) In addition to confusing the name, and the (still corrupt) nickname, Zenobios also confused ekklesiastic with dikastic pay.

44. Arist. *Ath. Pol.* xli. 3: μισθοφόρον δ⟨ὲ τὴν⟩ ἐκκλησίαν τὸ μὲν πρῶτον ἀπέγνωσαν (the Athenians) ποιεῖν· οὐ συλλεγομένων δ' εἰς τὴν ἐκκλησίαν, ἀλλὰ πολλὰ σοφιζομένων τῶν πρυτάνεων ὅπως προσιστῆται τὸ πλῆθος πρὸς τὴν ἐπικύρωσιν τῆς χειροτονίας, πρῶτον μὲν Ἀγύρριος ὀβολὸν ἐπόρισεν, μετὰ δὲ τοῦτον Ἡρακλείδης ὁ Κλαζομένιος ὁ βασιλεὺς ἐπικαλούμενος διώβολον, πάλιν δ' Ἀγύρριος τριώβολον.

45. Ar. *Eccl.* 183–188, 300–310:

ἐκκλησίαισιν ἦν ὅτ' οὐκ ἐχρώμεθα
οὐδὲν τὸ παράπαν· ἀλλὰ τόν γ' Ἀγύρριον
πονηρὸν ἡγούμεσθα. νῦν δὲ χρωμένων
ὁ μὲν λαβὼν ἀργύριον ὑπερεπῄνεσεν,
ὁ δ' οὐ λαβὼν εἶναι θανάτου φήσ' ἀξίους
τοὺς μισθοφορεῖν ζητοῦντας ἐν τἠκκλησίᾳ.

ὅρα δ' ὅπως ὠθήσομεν τούσδε τοὺς ἐξ ἄστεως
ἥκοντας, ὅσοι πρὸ τοῦ
μέν, ἡνίκ' ἔδει λαβεῖν
ἐλθόντ' ὀβολὸν μόνον,
καθῆντο λαλοῦντες
ἐν τοῖς στεφανώμασιν,
νυνὶ δ' ἐνοχλοῦσ' ἄγαν.
ἀλλ' οὐχί, Μυρωνίδης
ὅτ' ἦρχεν ὁ γεννάδας,
οὐδεὶς ἂν ἐτόλμα
τὰ τῆς πόλεως διοι-
κεῖν ἀργύριον φέρων·
ἀλλ' ἧκεν ἕκαστος
ἐν ἀσκιδίῳ φέρων
πιεῖν ἅμα τ' ἄρτον αὐ-
τῷ καὶ δύο κρομμύω
καὶ τρεῖς ἂν ἐλάας.
νυνὶ δὲ τριώβολον

which also provides a *terminus ante quem* of c. 393[46] for the final (3 ob.) stage. Both the *Ath. Pol.* and Aristophanes make it clear why pay for ekklesiasts was introduced in the first place, and why it was twice increased: without pay, the prytaneis could not obtain a quorum; with pay, they could—although the pay soon had to be doubled and then tripled in order to provide an adequate inducement for citizens to attend the Ekklesia.[47]

20. 388. Ekklesiasts paid 3 ob. (p.d.). A passage in Aristophanes' *Plutus*, produced in 388, shows that in that year ekklesiast pay still was 3 ob. p.d.[48]

21. c. 379–377. 40 dr. (min. inc.) for secretary (of board having something to do with Delos?), μισθός for what period?[49] In this brief, and incompletely published, inscription, the uncertain amount of the μισθός, and its uncertain time period, make it a difficult figure to use.

22. pre-c. 360. Aischines as junior clerk in public offices drawing 2–3 dr. (p.m. or p.pr.?). In reviewing Aischines' early career, Demosthenes says that after serving in his youth (παῖδ') as an

ζητοῦσι λαβεῖν, ὅταν
πράττωσί τι κοινὸν ὥσ-
περ πηλοφοροῦντες.

This pay is effectively described as μισθός in line 188. For other references to the triobol ekklesiast pay, see Ar. *Eccl.* 292b, 380, 392.

46. For the date of the *Ekklesiazousai*, see R. G. Ussher, *Aristophanes Ecclesiazusae* (Oxford 1973) xx–xxv (c. 393) and compare R. Seager, "Thrasybulus, Conon and Athenian Imperialism, 396–386 B.C.," *JHS* 87 (1967) 95–115 at 107, n. 110 (391 or 390).

47. This explanation furnished by the ancient sources, which is both explicit and plausible, seems preferable to the modern hypothesis that "the *ekklêsiastikon*, and its subsequent increases in the 390s, was meant to help subsidize the income of some of those for whom service as rowers was no longer regularly available" (E. M. Burke, "The Economy of Athens in the Classical Era," *TAPhA* 122 [1992] 199–226 at 223–224).

48. Ar. *Plut.* 329–330:
Δεινὸν γὰρ εἰ τριωβόλου μὲν οὕνεκα
ὠστιζόμεσθ' ἑκάστοτ' ἐν τἠκκλησίᾳ. . . .

See also Σ (*vet.*) Ar. *Plut.* 171bα: διαβάλλει τὸ ἐπὶ φιλονεικίᾳ τῶν Ἀθηναίων τριώβολον. Evident confusion with the increase in *dikast* pay prior to 424 is shown by Σ (*vet.*) Ar. *Plut.* 330b: τούτους οὖν τοὺς ἐκκλησιαστὰς ἐποίησαν φανερόν τι λαμβάνειν ἀπὸ τῶν τῆς πόλεως προσόδων οἱ δημαγωγοὶ πείσαντες τὴν πόλιν· ὕστερον δὲ ὁ Κλέων ἐποίησεν αὐτὸ τριώβολον.

49. *SEG* XXXIX 170. 3–5: γρα[μματεῖ Χ]αιρενέωι Λαμπ(τρεῖ) μισ[θός . . .]ΔΔΔΔ (numerals and line numbers derived from photograph published in O. Alexandri, "Χρονικά," *AD* 25 B.1 [1970] 40–91 at 60 with pl. 56a). For the date, see *SEG* XXXIX 170, XL 152. R. Develin, *Athenian Officials, 684–321 B.C.* (Cambridge 1989) 224, records Chaireneos "as a secretary of some sort" under 378/7.

assistant in his mother's foreign cult practices he was an undersecretary in the public offices at (a salary of) two or three drachmas.[50] This raises at least three questions: When was Aischines an undersecretary, what was the time period for the salary, and how reliable is this evidence? As to the date, I presume that any such service as undersecretary would have occurred before Aischines was 30 years old, and thus I have assigned this entry the date "pre-c. 360."[51] As for the salary period, 2–3 drachmas per *day* would be too large in relation to (a) dikast and ekklesiast pay of 3 ob. p.d. and (b) Demosthenes' obvious intention to characterize this as a low salary, so he must be saying that it was 2–3 dr. per month or prytany, i.e., 12–18 ob. for 30–37 days or c. 1/3 to 3/5 ob. p.d. This absurdly low figure effectively answers the third question: because Demosthenes wants to make Aischines' background as squalid as possible, he gives a figure that is at once low and imprecise—enough to create a poor impression while leaving himself plenty of room to fudge![52]

23. c. 355–322. Ekklesiasts(?) paid 1 dr. (p.d.) and dikasts(?) 3 ob. (p.d.). A phrase from one of Demosthenes' *Prooimia* excoriates his opponents for keeping the people in a state of weakness "with the drachma and chous [grain distribution] and the four obols," and in a similar vein pseudo-Lucian says that Demosthenes used to arouse the city's sense of honor, which long had been prostrated in pursuit of "the drachma and the triobol."[53] Although it is not said what the drachma, four obols and three obols are for, the most economical hypothesis is to attach all of these figures to securely attested rates: ekklesiast pay (#30 [a]), the theoric distribution for two days ("Wel-

---

50. Dem. xix. 199–200: οὐκ ἴσασιν οὗτοι τὸ μὲν ἐξ ἀρχῆς τὰς βίβλους ἀναγιγνώσκοντά σε τῇ μητρὶ τελούσῃ, καὶ παῖδ' ὄντ' ἐν θιάσοις καὶ μεθύουσιν ἀνθρώποις καλινδούμενον; μετὰ ταῦτα δὲ ταῖς ἀρχαῖς ὑπογραμματεύοντα καὶ δυοῖν ἢ τριῶν δραχμῶν πονηρὸν ὄντα;

51. For Aischines' birth in c. 390, see E. M. Harris, "When was Aeschines Born?," *CPh* 83 (1988) 211–214. The age of 30 seems a conservative upper limit for Aischines' service as ὑπογραμματεύς since it followed his youth (παῖδ').

52. Cf. E. M. Harris, *Aeschines and Athenian Politics* (New York 1995) 29: "two or three drachmas a day." E. Badian suggests to me that 2–3 dr. is like "two or three bucks" in American English.

53. Dem. *Prooem.* lii. 4: νῦν δὲ δραχμῇ καὶ χοῒ καὶ τέτταρσιν ὀβολοῖς ὥσπερ ἀσθενοῦντα τὸν δῆμον διάγουσιν; [Lucian] *Dem. Enc.* 36 (quoted in n. 26). See also #11 above.

fare and Support Allowances and Distributions" ##14–16) and dikast pay (##11, 30 [b]), respectively.[54]

24. 352/1. 5 dr. apiece for citizens chosen to decide disputed boundaries of the sacred orgas. As discussed in greater detail under "Travel Allowances" #17, the 5 dr. in *IG* II^2 204. 64 may have been thought of as a kind of replacement wage, more like our jury pay than a travel allowance, for a period that was indefinite but probably was estimated at two to five days, i.e., c. 1–2 dr. p.d.?

25. c. 337. [2 epistatai?] for repairs to Peiraieus fortifications and Long Walls paid 3 ob. p.d. apiece, and also [1 ob.?] p.? to look after the harbor fortifications? As discussed in greater detail under "Overseers, Architects and Other Salaried Construction Personnel" #6, (a) the status of the elected officials (epistatai?) in *IG* II^2 244. 28–45 is not certain, (b) the pay of 3 ob. p.d. probably (but not certainly) applies to them, but (c) the restoration of 1 ob. for the second part of their work has no basis on the stone.

26. c. 335–322. Sophronistai given 1 dr. p.d. and ephebes 4 ob. (p.d.) εἰς τροφήν.[55] As discussed in greater detail under "Soldiers and Sailors" #30, I interpret the 4 ob. as ration-money for young men during the two years that they were training for their future responsibilities as citizens and soldiers. The 1 dr. for the (elected) sophronistai is called μισθός by the later sources, and the 2 ob. (50%) increment over the ephebes' rations allowance seems plausible.[56]

---

54. Buchanan, *Theorika* 27, n. 1 (cited with caution in M. H. Hansen, *The Athenian Assembly* [Oxford 1987] 153, n. 317), speculates that the figures in the *Prooimion* are both for ekklesiast pay—4 ob. for a regular session and 1 dr. for an ἐκκλησία κυρία—and thus represent a mid fourth-century transitional stage between #20 and #30 (a). That is possible, but (as Buchanan concedes) the pseudo-Lucian passage "tends to confound even this inference."

55. Arist. *Ath. Pol.* xlii. 3: δίδωσι δὲ καὶ εἰς τροφ[ὴν] τοῖς μὲν σωφρονισταῖς δραχμὴν ᾱ ἑκάστωι, τοῖς δ' ἐφήβοις τέτταρας ὀβολοὺς ἑκάστωι· τὰ δὲ τῶν φυλετῶν τῶν αὑτοῦ λαμβάνων ὁ σωφρονιστὴς ἕκαστος ἀγοράζει τὰ ἐπιτήδεια πᾶσιν εἰς τὸ κοινόν, συσσιτοῦσι γὰρ κατὰ φυλάς; Phot., σωφρονισταί: ἄρχοντές τινες χειροτονητοὶ δέκα τὸν ἀριθμὸν ἑκάστης φυλῆς ⟨εἷς⟩· ἐχειροτόνει μὲν ὁ δῆμος, ἐπεμελοῦντο δὲ οἱ χειροτονηθέντες τῆς τῶν ἐφήβων σωφροσύνης, μισθὸν λαμβάνοντες ἕκαστος παρὰ τῆς πόλεως καθ' ἡμέραν δραχμήν; *Lex. Seg.* 301. 7–10, σωφρονισταί: ἄρχοντές τινες χειροτονητοί, δέκα τὸν ἀριθμόν, ἑκάστης φυλῆς εἷς. ἐπεμελοῦντο δὲ τῆς σωφροσύνης τῶν ἐφήβων, μισθὸν παρὰ τῆς πόλεως λαμβάνοντες ἕκαστος καθ' ἡμέραν δραχμήν. For the date, see Rhodes, *CAAP* 51–58, 494.

56. Cf. Rhodes, *CAAP* 507: "The instructors . . . were presumably paid a salary higher than these maintenance grants." Note that the sophronistai received, apparently every day of the year,

27. 333/2? Salaries at Eleusis: 2 dr. p.d. for elected architect, 3 ob. p.d. for elected scribe. As discussed in greater detail under "Overseers, Architects and Other Salaried Construction Personnel" #7, these payments (in *IG* II^2 1673 + *SEG* XXXIV 122. 60–62) all seem to be μισθός, and no payments are recorded for the Eleusinian epistatai themselves.

28. 329/8. 250 dr. to Eleusinian spondophoroi (number not stated), sent "to the islands," for what period? An account of the Eleusinian epistatai records the payment of 250 dr. to the spondophoroi,[57] the messengers who were sent throughout Greece to proclaim the celebration of the Eleusinian Mysteries. In the absence of any specific information as to how many spondophoroi there were, how long they were to be away, and whether the amount appropriated was in the nature of μισθός, ἐφόδια, τροφή, other things or a combination thereof, not much can be made of this figure.

29. 329/8. Salaries at Eleusis: 2 dr. p.d. for (probably elected) architect, 1 ob. p.d. for elected scribe. As discussed in greater detail under "Overseers, Architects and Other Salaried Construction Personnel" #8, it is virtually certain that all of these payments (in *IG* II^2 1672. 12, 44, 119, 143) are μισθός, and again there is no record of payments for the Eleusinian epistatai themselves.

30. pre-322. The *Ath. Pol.* lists a number of payments to public officeholders:[58]

(a) Ekklesiasts drew 1 dr. (p.d.) at regular sessions, and 9 ob. (p.d.) at the principal (κυρία) ekklesia. Sometime between 388 (#20) and 322,[59] their daily pay had been raised from 3

---

the same pay that the ekklesiasts and prytaneis received only on the days that they were sitting (##30 [a] and [c] below).

57. *IG* II^2 1672. 4: [σ]πο[ν]δοφόροις ἐπὶ νή[σ]ων εἰς μυστήρια τὰ μεγάλα HHΠ. For this figure, see also "Travel Allowances" #21.

58. Arist. *Ath. Pol.* lxii. 2: Μισθοφοροῦσι δὲ πρῶτον ὁ δῆμος ταῖς μὲν ἄλλαις ἐκκλησίαις δραχμήν, τῆι δὲ κυρίαι ἐννέα ⟨ὀβολοὺς⟩. ἔπειτα τὰ δικαστήρια τρεῖς ὀβολούς· εἶθ' ἡ βουλὴ πέντε ὀβολούς· τοῖς δὲ πρυτανεύουσιν εἰς σίτησιν ὀβολὸς προστίθεται {δέκα προστίθενται}. ἔπειτ' εἰς σίτησιν λαμβάνουσιν ἐννέ' ἄρχοντες τέτταρας ὀβολοὺς ἕκαστος καὶ παρατρέφουσι κήρυκα καὶ αὐλητήν, ἔπειτ' ἄρχων εἰς Σαλαμῖνα δραχμὴν τῆς ἡμέρας. . . . ἀμφικτύονες εἰς Δῆλον δραχμὴν τῆς ἡμέρας ἑκάστης ἐκ Δήλου ⟨λαμβάνουσι⟩. λαμβάνουσι δὲ καὶ ὅσαι ἀποστέλλονται ἀρχαὶ εἰς Σάμον ἢ Σκῦρον ἢ Λῆμνον ἢ Ἴμβρον εἰς σίτησιν ἀργύριον.

59. Gallo, "Salari" 52–53, suggests the Lykourgan period.

ob. (presumably at all sessions). The word μισθοφοροῦσι indicates that these payments, as well as the 3 ob. for the dikasts and the 5 ob. for the bouleutai in (b) and (c) below, were μισθός (see n. 60).

(b) Dikasts drew μισθός of 3 ob. (p.d.). There had been no change since 425 (see #11).

(c) Bouleutai drew μισθός of 5 ob. (p.d.), and those serving as prytaneis received an additional 1 ob. (p.d.) εἰς σίτησιν. This is our first attested figure for regular members of the Boule, although we know that they had been paid as early as 411, and probably before 431 (##7 and 16). #17 tells us that in 411 bouleutai who were serving as prytaneis were receiving 3 ob. p.d. (which I interpreted as μισθός = gross pay), so the 6 ob. here represents a doubling of their gross compensation. The 1 ob. p.d. εἰς σίτησιν is low in comparison with the c. 2–4 ob. p.d. ration-money allowances for soldiers in the fourth century ("Soldiers and Sailors" ##29–30 with additional discussion at pp. 57–58) and the 4–6 ob. p.d. payments εἰς σίτησιν for sophronistai, archons and other officials (##26, 30 [d]–[g]), and it therefore probably takes account of the fact that bouleutai also drew μισθός of 5 ob. p.d.[60]

(d) The nine archons drew 4 ob. (p.d.) εἰς σίτησιν, but collectively they had to support a herald and a piper, probably out of these funds (παρατρέφουσι). 4 ob. is just 33 1/3% more than the 3 ob. p.d. μισθός that the archons had received in

60. Gabrielsen, *Remuneration* 67–81 and 151–155, argues that the author of the *Ath. Pol.* and other fourth-century writers use μισθός, εἰς τροφήν and εἰς σίτησιν interchangeably. In fact, the evidence adduced by him indicates only that τροφή sometimes is used in the sense of μισθός (as in the fifth century; see "Soldiers and Sailors" pp. 33–34 with n. 9), but the *Ath. Pol.*'s specification of 5 ob. bouleutic μισθός and 1 ob. εἰς σίτησιν for bouleutai who served as prytaneis indicates that there was at least a theoretical distinction between these payments, probably rooted in their respective histories. By the third quarter of the fourth century, however, the focus may have been less on labels and more on gross pay—certainly the great differences in σίτησις allowances (1–6 ob.) are diminished when one compares the much narrower range of gross compensations: 9 ob. for ekklesiasts at principal sessions (only ten days per year); 6 ob. for ekklesiasts at regular sessions, bouleutai serving as prytaneis, the governor of Salamis, the amphiktyons sent to Delos, and the sophronistai; 5 ob. for other bouleutai; 4 ob. for archons; and 3 ob. for dikasts. Presumably, archons and bouleutai drew additional pay as ekklesiasts on the four days per prytany that the Ekklesia was in session, so the proportional differences in their pay were further diminished.

411 (#17)—even less if they had to support the herald and piper out of the extra obol. The low raise might be explained, at least in part, by the fact that it is only for σίτησις, but I suspect that the gross compensation of the archons was less than that of the bouleutai because only nine were needed and there was an adequate supply of citizens willing to accept relatively low pay for this relatively prestigious office; indeed, it is possible that the label εἰς σίτησιν for their compensation enhanced their image as honorable volunteers in the service of the state.[61]

(e) The governor of Salamis was paid 1 dr. p.d. (it is unclear whether the words εἰς σίτησιν for [d] and [g] apply here). In the absence of comparative figures, there is not much that one can say about this.

(f) The amphiktyons to Delos were paid 1 dr. p.d., by Delos, probably εἰς σίτησιν.[62] In the absence of comparative figures, I consider this figure also under "Travel Allowances" #25.

(g) There was unspecified pay (εἰς σίτησιν ἀργύριον) for whatever officers were sent to Samos or Skyros or Lemnos or Imbros.[63]

31. pre-322.[64] Arbitrator paid 1 dr. (a) as a deposit by prosecuting party and (b) by party seeking (for reasons sworn to under

61. For the self-selection of allotted officials such as archons, see n. 74 below. For the potentially pejorative implications of μισθός as compared to σῖτος or σίτησις, see "Soldiers and Sailors" #11 with n. 38.

62. The δὲ καί in the immediately following clause makes it likely that the amphiktyons also took σίτησιν. For a possible precedent earlier in the century (377–374 B.C.), see *IG* II^2 1635. 49–50, 74–75 (payments to the amphiktyons and their secretaries εἰς τὰ ἐπιτήδεια) with the comment of D. M. Lewis, Review of Gabrielsen, *Remuneration*, *JHS* 102 (1982) 269.

63. Hansen ("Misthos" 7, 15–19) argues that, except for the σίτησις grants of ##30 (c)–(g), magistrates (as distinguished from dikasts, ekklesiasts and bouleutai) received no pay after 411, even though they had been paid earlier (#7 above). I agree with Rhodes, *CAAP* 695, that "these stipends ought to be provided in the fourth century no less than in the fifth" (this also is the major conclusion of Gabrielsen, *Remuneration*). ##21, 24–29 and possibly 31 (only #26 is cited by Rhodes and Gabrielsen) are concrete evidence of fourth-century payments (some clearly μισθός) to public officials (some clearly elected), although none holds an obviously prestigious office. Cf. Lewis (as in n. 62 above).

64. As Jacoby, *FGrH* IIB (Kommentar) 648, observes, the reference in Harpokration (n. 65) to the *Ath. Pol.* gives us a *terminus ante quem* of 322.

oath) to postpone arbitrator's judgment. The contemporary sources are known to us only through Harpokration, repeated by the *Suda*,[65] but they are confirmed by Pollux and Photios, who seem to be relying on different sources.[66] The only item in our catalogue that is remotely comparable (in terms of job responsibilities) is the 1 dr. p.d. for the ξυνήγορος in 422 (#13), but it would be hazardous to speculate, on the basis of these two slender pieces of evidence, that the pay of public lawyers had not changed in one hundred years. For this entry, see also "Doctors, Lawyers and Professors" #27.

32. late 4th. c.? Bouleutai paid 1 dr. p.d. It is difficult to date Hesychios' statement.[67] I have labeled it "late 4th c.?" on the ground that his ultimate source is likely to have been a fourth-century orator or a compilation like the *Ath. Pol.*, but this is necessarily uncertain. In any event, the 1 dr. p.d. represents either (a) a conflation of the *Ath. Pol.*'s information about bouleutai who also were serving as prytaneis[68] or (b) a further increase (which would fit with #33) in the pay for attendance at the Boule.

---

65. Harp., παράστασις: Ἰσαῖος ἐν τῷ περὶ τοῦ Πύρρου κλήρου [iii. 47]. τοὔνομα παρὰ πολλοῖς ἐστιν Ἀττικοῖς, ἔστι δὲ δραχμὴ καταβαλλομένη ὑπὸ τῶν δικαζομένων τὰς ἰδίας δίκας· Μένανδρος Μισογύνῃ [fr. 278 K-T] "ἕλκει δὲ γραμματείδιον | ἐκεῖσε δίθυρον καὶ παράστασις, μία | δραχμή." [K-T print Bentley's emendation ἐκεῖ σε.] Ἀριστοτέλης δ' ἐν Ἀθηναίων πολιτείᾳ [lix. 3] περὶ τῶν θεσμοθετῶν λέγων φησὶν ὅυτως "εἰσὶ δὲ γραφαὶ πρὸς αὐτούς, ὧν παράστασις τίθεται. . . ." Δημήτριος δὲ ὁ Φαληρεὺς [228 *FGrH* 7] ἐν τοῖς περὶ νομοθεσίας τοὺς διαιτητάς φησι λαμβάνειν τὰς δραχμάς μίαν μὲν ἀπὸ τῆς λήξεως, ἥν παράστασιν ἐκάλουν, ἑτέραν δὲ καθ' ὑπωμοσίαν ἑκάστην; *Suda* π 443 (Adler), παράστασις: τοὔνομα πολὺ παρὰ τοῖς ῥήτορσιν. ἔστι δὲ δραχμὴ καταβαλλομένη ὑπὸ τῶν δικαζομένων τὰς ἰδίας δίκας with substantially identical citations to Men., Arist. *Ath. Pol.* and Dem. Phal.

66. Poll. viii. 39: ἡ δὲ παράστασις δραχμὴ ἦν, ἣν ὁ διώκων παρὰ διαιτητῇ προσεισέφερεν; viii. 127: ἐλάμβανον δὲ οἱ διαιτηταὶ δραχμὴν παρὰ τοῦ κρίνοντος, τὴν καλουμένην παράστασιν, ἐγγράψαντος αὐτοῦ ἐν γραμματείῳ τὸ ἔγκλημα καὶ τὸ τίμημα. . . . ἐλάμβανον δὲ καὶ ἑτέραν ὑπὲρ τῆς ἀντωμοσίας; Phot., παρακατάστασις: ἀργυρίδιον ἦν μία δραχμὴ ὑπὸ τῶν ἰδίας δικαζομένων δίκας τοῖς διαιτηταῖς καταβαλλόμενον· ἔτι δὲ καὶ παρὰ τῶν ὑπομνυμένων αὐτάς· κατεβάλλετο δὲ καὶ τοῖς θεσμοθέταις ἐπί τισι γραφαῖς; *Lex. Seg.* 290. 19–22, παρακατάστασις: ἀργυρίδιόν ἐστιν ἐν μιᾷ δραχμῇ καταβαλλόμενον ἐν τοῖς διαιτηταῖς ὑπὸ τῶν δικαζομένων ἰδίας δίκας καὶ ἐπὶ τῶν ὑπομνυμένων αὐτάς. καὶ τοῦτο ἐκαλεῖτο παρακατάστασις. For these fees, see D. M. MacDowell, *The Law in Classical Athens* (London 1978) 208–209.

67. Hesych. β 931 (Latte), βουλῆς λαχεῖν: τὸ λαχεῖν βουλευτήν, καὶ δραχμὴν τῆς ἡμέρας λαβεῖν.

68. As Rhodes, *CAAP* 692, points out, J. E. Sandys, *Aristotle's Constitution of the Athenians*[2] (London 1912) 246, had suggested that Hesychios' figure was a conflation.

33. 161–108. Bouleutai paid 1 dr. p.d.? Four decrees honor agonothetai of the Theseia festival. Among their other benefactions, these officials contributed sums of money to the Boule as a καθέσιμον, or fee for attending the Theseia.[69] In the three inscriptions where the figure is preserved, it is either 1,200 drachmas (twice) or 600 drachmas, and this has been interpreted as 1 dr. p.d. for each of the (then) 600 bouleutai, since the Boule on festival days was ἀφέσιμος.[70] Either the καθέσιμον was equivalent to what the bouleutai would have earned had they been sitting in the Boule (and thus their compensation had risen 1 ob. p.d. since the 320s), or the donors were more generous than the state at festivals.

As a group, what can be said about these figures? Pay for public office seems to have been introduced in the late 460s, for dikasts, who were chosen by lot and paid either 1 or 2 ob. p.d. (#1). Soon thereafter, probably in the early 440s, we find at least one set of *elected* officials (#4, cf. ##2, 3) being paid 4 ob. p.d. and, a bit later, other supervisory officials who may have been paid 1 dr. p.d. (#6). Before 431, we are told of the existence of a great many other paid public officeholders (#7), but unfortunately nothing about their rate of pay. In 425, dikasts were raised from 2 to 3 ob. p.d. (##10, 11) and remained there for the rest of the classical period (#30 [b]): this job may have "appealed only to those rich enough not to be deterred by the loss of a day's earnings, and to those so poor that they would regard 3 obols as better than nothing at all."[71] For other officials in the fifth century, we are less well informed: members of the Boule

69. *IG* II^2 956 (161/0). 14–15: ἔδωκεν δὲ καὶ τεῖ βουλεῖ καθέσιμον [δρ]αχμὰς ^{v}ΧΗΗ^{v}; *IG* II^2 957 (157/6). 9–10: [ἔδωκεν δὲ καὶ τεῖ βουλεῖ καθέ]σιμον δραχμὰς ^{vv}𐅅Η^{v} (I depart from the Corpus text by restoring *epsilon* rather than *eta* in τεῖ βουλεῖ, to conform to the spelling of the other inscriptions in this group); *IG* II^2 958 (153/2 or 149/8?). 12: ἔδω[κεν δὲ κ]αὶ τε[ῖ] βουλε[ῖ καθέσ]ιμον δραχμὰς ^{v}ΧΗΗ^{v}; *IG* II^2 959 + 1014 + *SEG* XL 121 (109/8). 18–19: [ἔδωκεν δὲ καὶ τεῖ βουλεῖ καθέσιμο]ν δ[ραχμὰς - - -] (for the dates of these last three inscriptions, see Tracy, *ALC* 183–185, 240–241, 261).

70. See commentary on *IG* II^2 956, citing Arist. *Ath. Pol.* xliii. 3. See also Rhodes, *CAAP* 521.

71. Rhodes, *CAAP* 691. In addition, as S. Todd, "*Lady Chatterley's Lover* and the Attic Orators: The Social Composition of the Athenian Jury," *JHS* 110 (1990) 146–173 at 168–169, argues, jury pay of 3 ob. p.d. may have appealed to small farmers, whose farm income would not have been diminished by a few days' absence from the farm, at least in certain seasons.

were paid, but we are not told how much (#16); ambassadors probably were not paid as much as the 2–3 dr. p.d. alleged by Aristophanes (##8, 9); a theoros was perhaps paid 2 ob. p.d. (#12); and a public prosecutor quite plausibly was paid 1 dr. p.d. (#13).

In 411, pay for all officeholders was abolished (except for the nine archons and the prytaneis, who received 3 ob. p.d. [##17, 18]), but it probably was resumed after the restoration of the democracy later that year, and after the final restoration of the democracy in 403 pay was instituted for the first time for attendance at the ekklesia (rapidly increasing, between c. 403 and c. 393, from 1 to 3 ob. p.d. [#19]).

By the 330s or 320s, pay rates had changed, but not uniformly. Dikasts, who had been the first to receive any pay, had no increase at all (#30 [b]), and public lawyers also may have had no raise (#31). The nine archons had a very modest increase (from their 3 ob. p.d. rate under the 400 [#17]) to 4 ob. p.d. (#30 [d]), labeled εἰς σίτησιν, but they probably had to support a herald and piper out of this. Members of the Boule who served as prytaneis doubled their pay, from 3 ob. (#17) to 6 ob. p.d. (including 1 ob. εἰς σίτησιν [#30 (c)]). Also doubled, in an even shorter period, were ekklesiasts, from 3 to 6 ob. p.d., with an extra 3 ob. for attendance at the principal ekklesia (#30 [a]). One can speculate about the reasons for these disparities, with varying degrees of certainty. It evidently was difficult to get a quorum of 6,000 in the Ekklesia,[72] and possibly also of 500 in the Boule, without paying close to the local equivalent of the minimum wage (see "Construction and Other Manual Workers" #7). On the other hand, there may have been an adequate supply of dikasts to meet a (presumably) much smaller (though more frequent) demand, and there may have been a feeling that pay for dikasts never should be as high as that for able-bodied men employed in military service or other active occupations.[73] Service as an archon may have carried

72. This is explicitly stated by Arist. *Ath. Pol.* xli. 3 and Ar. *Eccl.* 300–310 (quoted in notes 44–45).

73. Cf. M. M. Markle, "Jury Pay and Assembly Pay at Athens," in P. A. Cartledge and F. D. Harvey, eds., *Crux: Essays in Greek History presented to G. E. M. de Ste. Croix on his 75th Birthday* (Exeter 1985) 265–297 at 285: "I suggest that the adversary situation of the courts and its dramatic interest attracted the poor in considerable numbers at low pay, but the pay had to be

with it prestige significant enough to persuade a few relatively wealthy citizens to serve (only nine were required), and thus there may have been no need to pay them as much as ekklesiasts.[74]

increased to induce them to attend the comparatively boring assemblies. . . ." This strikes me as inherently implausible: if they were really poor, they could not have afforded to forego the double pay of 6 obols in the ekklesia, however boring the sitting.

74. Although dikasts and archons were selected by lot, "lots were drawn, as a rule only amongst such citizens as presented themselves for allotment" (M. H. Hansen, *The Athenian Democracy in the Age of Demosthenes* [Oxford 1991] 230–231, citing Isoc. xv. 150; Lys. vi. 4, xxxi. 33), so the allotment pool for a particular office would have included only those willing to accept the specified payment.

Chapter 2
Soldiers and Sailors

Collected here are payments to military personnel, variously called ὁπλῖται, ναῦται, ἱππεῖς, etc. The subject of military pay, both inside and outside of Athens, has been studied relatively recently by Pritchett,[1] whose collection of the relevant evidence (made before the era of computer word searches) is only slightly smaller than mine.[2] Although I agree for the most part with his description of individual figures,[3] our interpretation of the evidence as a whole differs in some important respects.

1. Pritchett, *GSW* I 3–29. At 2, Pritchett says that his "manuscript was completed in July, 1970." For Böckh's collection and discussion, see *SdA* I 340–358.

2. The only precise figures in my Athenian catalogue that were not collected by Pritchett are ##2, 7, 8 and 30. On the other hand, he collected a number of figures from non-Attic inscriptions (Pritchett, *GSW* I 21–23, to which may be added further figures from non-Attic inscriptions and papyri in Griffith, *MHW* 300–307) that are outside the scope of my (exclusively literary) non-Athenian catalogue (Appendix 2), while omitting *Hist. Alex. Magni* (α, β and γ) iii. 26 (Amazon cavalry before 323), Polyb. xiii. 2. 3 (Skopas and soldiers in 205) and later Greek literary evidence of military pay.

3. The only items that I describe differently are the following: (a) the 3 Chian tessarakostai paid by the Chians in 411 to each sailor in the Peloponnesian fleet (Thuc. viii. 101. 1) was not necessarily a "rate per day" (Pritchett, *GSW* I 16) since we have "no materials for guessing how many days' pay this represents" (Andrewes, *HCT* V 347), although (on the basis of ##16 and 18) N. Hardwick, "The Solution to Thucydides VIII 101.1: The 'Chian Fortieths'," *NAC* 25 (1996) 59–69, argues that it was for 3 1/2 days [plausible but necessarily speculative since we cannot be sure (i) that a "fortieth" = 1/3 Chian stater, (ii) that the Peloponnesian sailors were paid by the Chians at the then-current Athenian rate of 3 Attic ob. p.d., and (iii) that there was no deduction for provisions (the νῆες were ἐπισιτισάμεναι δυοῖν ἡμέραιν)]; (b) the 5 dr. furnished by Chios to each Peloponnesian sailor in 406 (Xen. *Hell.* i. 6. 12) is said expressly to be for traveling expenses (ἐφοδιασάμενος, for what period?) rather than "ten days' pay" (Pritchett, *GSW* I 40); (c) the 1 daric p.m. paid by Cyrus to his Greek mercenaries in 401 (Xen. *Anab.* i. 3. 21 [#21]) was worth 20 rather than 25 dr. (*Anab.* i. 7. 18), i.e., 4 rather than 5 ob. p.d. (Pritchett, *GSW* I 20, and see n. 63 below), and payments in Kyzikene staters (Xen. *Anab.* v. 6. 23, vii. 2. 36, vii. 3. 10) were not necessarily equivalent to payments in the same number of darics (Pritchett, *GSW* I 20, and see n. 64 below); (d) the 4 ob. p.d. soldier's pay in Plut. *Mor.* 233c (#33) refers to Lysimachos' army in the early third century rather than to Lysander's navy in c. 408 (Pritchett, *GSW* I 19, n. 66).

As Pritchett recognized, the threshold question is one of terminology: how is military pay described and what is it for?[4] He noted the "conventional view . . . that payment was made under two different terms: μισθός, or wages for service, which, with the exception of expenses for weapons and clothing, the soldier could lay up; and σιτηρέσιον which refers to rations or to their equivalent in money."[5] He demonstrated, however, that Thucydides uses the words μισθός and τροφή "synonymously" to refer to the same payment, covering the "soldier's entire monetary allowance," without "the later distinction between pay and rations,"[6] and he also noted that Thucydides uses the word σῖτος "in the sense of payment for food."[7] He con-

---

4. In 1935, Griffith already had remarked (*MHW* 264) that "even the word μισθός, indicating the basis of every transaction between a soldier and his employer, is to be regarded as a preliminary hazard, to be mastered indeed if possible, but at all events to be approached with care."

5. Pritchett, *GSW* I 3 (notes omitted). In his n. 2, Pritchett observed that in "Hellenistic times, *opsonion* [pay] became the usual word for *misthos* of classical times. Similarly, *sitonion* became more common than *siteresion* or *sitarchia* for a cash allowance in lieu of rations. The word *sitometria* was used for rations in kind." The Athenian evidence refers almost entirely to the classical period, and does not include any specific monetary figures described as ὀψώνιον, σιτώνιον or σιταρχία. As to whether the soldier was expected to provide his own weapons and clothing, see pp. 58–59 below.

6. Pritchett, *GSW* I 4–5, citing (a) for the 60 talents furnished by the Segestans for 60 Athenian ships, Thuc. vi. 8. 1 (μισθόν) and 47. 1 (τροφήν), and (b) for Tissaphernes' payments to the Peloponnesian fleet, Thuc. viii. 5. 5 (τροφήν), 29. 1 (τροφήν), 29. 2 (μισθοῦ), 36. 1 (μισθός) and 45. 6 (τροφὴ . . . μισθόν); to these may be added (c) for Perdikkas' payments to Brasidas' troops, Thuc. iv. 80. 1 (τρέφειν), 80. 5 (μισθῷ) and 83. 6 (τροφῆς), and (d) for the pay demanded by the Athenian fleet at Samos, Thuc. viii. 83. 3 (μισθὸν . . . τροφήν) and 86. 6 (τροφήν). Pritchett also noted instances where τροφή explicitly = χρήματα (Thuc. vi. 93. 4, vii. 48. 5 and viii. 58. 6), to which may be added the following passages from Book viii, either alone or in combination with viii. 80. 1 (Tissaphernes' provision of χρήματα): 43. 4, 46. 5, 57. 1–2, 58. 5, 78. 1, 80. 2, 81. 3, 87. 1, 87. 3, and 99. 1. In addition to the foregoing instances, Thucydides describes payments by Tissaphernes to sailors as μισθός in the following passages in Book viii: 45. 2, 46. 1, 48. 3, 50. 3, 83. 2, 84. 2, and 85. 3.

7. Pritchett, *GSW* I 6, citing Thuc. v. 47. 6 for the 1/2 to 1 Aiginetan dr. to be paid as σῖτος to allied troops by parties to the Athens-Argos-Mantineia-Elis alliance of 420 (#11). Since Thucydides is here quoting from a treaty (whose text, apparently identical in this respect, is partially preserved in *IG* I^3 83. 22–24), it is not clear that in his own words he would have described this payment as σῖτος; certainly there are no other instances where he uses σῖτος to mean a monetary payment of any kind (elsewhere he uses σῖτος to mean "food" or "grain," e.g., ii. 19. 1 and vi. 71. 2, and σιτία to mean "rations," e.g., i. 48. 1 and vii. 43. 2; cf. Pritchett, *GSW* I 3, n. 2, and Griffith, *MHW* 294). Pritchett also (*GSW* I 6, n. 7) noted *IG* I^3 375. 4, 8–9, 11–12, and 24 (410/9 B.C.), where monetary payments are recorded for σῖτος for cavalry horses; since the horses would not have received a salary in addition to fodder (!), σῖτος here clearly means ration-money and nothing more. Although Griffith (*MHW* 294, n. 4) reasonably remarked that it "seems

cluded that in the fifth century, at least for Thucydides, μισθός = τροφή = σῖτος = ration-money only: "Just as dikastic pay was for maintenance, so the stratiotic pay made to citizens in the fifth century was for purchase of rations. . . . The vocabulary drawing a sharp distinction between pay and money for rations does not seem to have been developed until the rise of large mercenary armies in the fourth century."[8]

There is, however, another possibility, viz., that μισθός/τροφή represented gross pay, i.e., ration-money *plus* pay. I think that this alternative is more likely, for four reasons:

1. There is no affirmative reason why μισθός/τροφή should be ration-money alone. Without actually saying so, Pritchett seemed to assume that τροφή was the ancestor of σιτηρέσιον, i.e., he seemed intuitively to give weight to its narrower meaning of "food" rather than to its broader meaning of "means of support,"[9] but this is not necessary and indeed, given the fact that τροφή is used synonymously with μισθός, the broader meaning arguably is *more* likely.

2. The σῖτος allowance provided by the Athens-Argos-Mantineia-Elis alliance (see n. 7 above and #11 below) does not resolve this question.[10] I suggest below (#11) that it also is gross pay, but even if I am wrong about that and the (primarily Peloponnesian) parties to this

---

to put too great a strain upon the capacity of the word σῖτος, which is sufficiently strained by being used for ration-money only," to have it include pay (Hellenistic μισθός) as well, I suspect that it may do just that in the alliance of 420; see #11 with n. 36.

8. Pritchett, *GSW* I 6, 4 (notes omitted). For other expressions of his conclusion that in the fifth century military pay was ration-money only, see *GSW* I 23–24, 27–28, 35, 40, 51. With respect to maintenance for dikasts, Pritchett's n. 8 (p. 6) cites "εἰς σίτησιν: Aristotle *Ath. Pol.* 62. 2," but these words apply to the extra obol for the prytaneis and the 4 ob. for the nine archons, rather than to the 3 ob. μισθός for dikasts (see "Public Officeholders" #30 with notes 58 and 62).

9. See LSJ, *s.v.* τροφή. Gabrielsen (*Remuneration* 67–81, 151–155) argues that in the fourth century as well as the fifth μισθός = εἰς τροφήν = εἰς σίτησιν, but the 15 passages cited by him show only that, as in the fifth century, τροφή was sometimes used in the sense of μισθός (but see #29 and n. 92 below); none of them uses μισθός interchangeably with σῖτος or σίτησις. (The σῖτος allowance for the cavalryman's horse in Arist. *Ath. Pol.* xlix. 1 is not necessarily the same as the μισθός for the cavalryman himself in Xen. *Hipparch.* i. 23 [quoted in n. 107 below]; see n. 7 above and #27 below.)

10. Pritchett, *GSW* I 6, argued that μισθός/τροφή in the negotations of 412 (n. 6 [b] above) and σῖτος in the alliance of 420 (n. 7 above) were "the only monetary payments negotiated by the parties concerned. It seems reasonable to conclude that this usage reflects common fifth-century practice" (i.e., to negotiate for rations only).

alliance were agreeing about ration-money only, σῖτος obviously is a different word from, and cannot control the meaning of, μισθός/τροφή in Athens.

3. Thucydides' use of the word μισθός for *mercenary* pay suggests that it means more than ration-money.[11] Mercenaries are unlikely to fight for someone else, i.e., without a patriotic motive, unless they expect to "net" some money over and above whatever they have to pay for food.[12] If μισθός means more than ration-money for mercenaries, it ought to have the same meaning for Athenian soldiers and sailors.

4. Other per diem figures for the second half of the fifth century indicate that rations alone would have been covered by 2–3 ob. p.d. or less, and thus that the 1 dr. p.d. received by soldiers and sailors before c. 412 was gross pay—the *sum* of what later came to be known as μισθός and σιτηρέσιον. The most pertinent figures are (a) for dikasts, who were paid 2–3 ob. p.d. down to 411,[13] i.e., during the period that soldiers and sailors were getting 1 dr. p.d. (##4–5, 12–13, 15 below), and (b) for dole recipients, who were paid 1–2 ob. p.d. in the last decade of the fifth century,[14] when the attested pay for sailors was 3 ob. p.d. (##16, 18 below). If the 1–2 ob. payments to dole recipients were intended to cover rations, the 3 ob. payments to dikasts would have covered a bit more, and the 3 ob. to 1 dr. payments to soldiers and sailors certainly covered more. Pritchett argued that food costs may have been higher in Poteidaia or Sicily.[15] That is possible, but the opposite is at least as likely: in the countryside, closer to the

11. For Thucydidean references to μισθός as the pay of mercenaries fighting alongside Athenian soldiers, see Thuc. i. 121. 3, i. 143. 1–2, iv. 129. 2, v. 6. 2, vi. 22. 1, vi. 43. 1, vi. 90. 3, vii. 13. 2, vii. 25. 7, and vii. 57. 3, 9, 11. For μισθός as the pay of other mercenaries, see Thuc. i. 31. 1, i. 35. 4, i. 60. 1, ii. 96. 2, iii. 109. 2, iv. 52. 2, iv. 76. 3, iv. 80. 5, iv. 124. 4, v. 6. 4, vii. 58. 3, and viii. 100. 3.

12. Certainly the μισθός/τροφή paid by Perdikkas to Brasidas' Peloponnesian troops (Thuc. iv. 80. 1, 80. 5, 83. 6) must have included more than ration-money to induce them to journey all the way to Macedon. Note also the Athenian bakers ἐμμίσθους (vi. 22. 1), the Athenians' expectation that Sicily would be a source of ἀίδιον μισθοφοράν (vi. 24. 3) and the μισθός for the divers at Syracuse (vii. 25. 7): in all three of these instances, μισθός clearly is more than just ration-money.

13. "Public Officeholders" ##10, 11, 17.

14. "Welfare and Support Allowances and Distributions" ##7–10.

15. Pritchett, *GSW* I 23.

source of supply (e.g., in Sicily), food might have been cheaper than in the city. In any event, at Athens itself, one year after dikasts are recorded as receiving 3 ob. p.d.,[16] Thracian peltasts were being paid 1 dr. p.d. (#15 below), so it is pretty clear that this drachma covered more than ration-money.

I conclude, therefore, that μισθός/τροφή means gross pay (pay plus ration-money), and now turn to individual figures. I examine non-Athenian as well as Athenian figures where they seem relevant.

1. c. 477–441. Introducton of military pay, by Aristeides, Kimon or Perikles? After reviewing all of the evidence,[17] Pritchett concluded that "general military pay . . . was introduced before the beginning of the Peloponnesian War" and perhaps as early as the 460s or 450s.[18] I agree with that conclusion, but would raise the lower date since (a) the accounts for the Kerkyraian Expedition (#4 below) and the *Ath. Pol.*'s statement about paid armed forces (#6 below) give us a *termi-*

16. Ar. *Av.* 1541 et Σ 1541d ("Public Officeholders" #11 with n. 23).

17. Pritchett, *GSW* I 7–11, citing [Xen.] *Ath. Pol.* i. 13 (δῆμος is paid for sailing in ships, at the uncertain date [c. 443–423?] of this *Ath. Pol.*); Ion Chius 392 *FGrH* 13 (Kimon obtained four months' τροφή for ships from booty in c. 477); Arist. *Ath. Pol.* xxiv. 1 (Aristeides advised Athenians that there would be τροφή for all public employees, including those στρατευομένοις), xxvii. 2 (when war broke out in 432/1 δῆμος "had become accustomed to earning pay on their military expeditions" [συνεθισθεὶς ἐν ταῖς στρατιαῖς μισθοφορεῖν]); Plut. *Cim.* xi. 2 (Kimon gave μισθός supplied by allied tribute to Athenian crews), *Per.* xi. 4 (Perikles sent out 60 triremes every year, in which many citizens used to sail ὀκτὼ μῆνας ἔμμισθοι), xii. 5 (military expeditions furnished able-bodied [soldiers] "abundant resources from the common funds" [τὰς ἀπὸ τῶν κοινῶν εὐπορίας]); Σ Dem. xiii (Dilts 167. 24–25) (Perikles πρῶτος . . . ἔταξε μισθοφορὰν καὶ ἔδωκε τῷ δήμῳ στρατευομένῳ). As Pritchett (*GSW* I 10–11) observed, Plut. *Them.* x. 5 (Troizenians vote 2 ob. p.d. support [τρέφειν] to Athenian refugees ["Welfare and Support Allowances and Distributions" #4]) and x. 6–7 (citizens embarking on ships at Salamis given 8 dr. ἐφόδια ["Travel Allowances" #1] do not involve military pay. Similarly, Phanias Eres. *FHG* II 295, fr. 7 ap. Plut. *Them.* vii. 7 (Themistokles gives 1 T. to Athenian trierarch Architeles [bribe to remain at Artemision or wages for crew?]) probably does not involve wages, but, even if it does, the pay period is not specified.

18. Pritchett, *GSW* I 12–13. Pritchett suggested that military pay would have followed soon after the introduction of dikast pay (late 460s, see "Public Officeholders" #1), in order to make military service a realistic and attractive alternative to jury service, but Rhodes, *CAAP* 306, rightly points out that "payment for service in the army and navy . . . could well be earlier than payment for performance of a citizen's civilian duties."

nus ante quem of 433,[19] (b) the Samian War accounts (#3 below) push that back to 441, and (c) the "Regulations for Miletos" (#2 below) may push it back further, to c. 450.

2. 450/49? Athenian? rowers, soldiers or officials? sent to Miletos?, or Milesian soldiers?, paid 4 ob. (p.d.?).[20] Bradeen and McGregor reported that this fragmentary inscription, "which mentions triremes (or trierarchs), transports, four obols in pay, and soldiers," had been understood by some scholars "as arranging for Milesian military aid to Athens," but they followed Lewis in seeing the "details of the transportation of the new board [of Athenian officials to Miletos] and the reorganization of the garrison. . . . The four obols in pay ought surely to be ascribed to the Athenians."[21] The earlier commentators cited by Bradeen and McGregor also interpreted the four obols as pay (to the extent that they commented at all), even though nothing explicit is preserved that labels it as μισθός or τροφή. In addition to this uncertainty, there are a number of others:

(a) The date is not certain. Most commentators have favored 450/49, but Fornara suggested a slightly later date (post-442?) and Mattingly has urged 426/5 or 425/4.[22]

(b) If the four obols is pay, it is not clear that it is pay per day.

(c) If the four obols is pay, it also is not clear if it is for Athenian rowers to Miletos, Athenian soldiers garrisoned there, Athe-

---

19. The references to military μισθός in *IG* I^3 138. 4, 8 and 9 (dated "ante a. 434") are all restored.

20. *IG* I^3 21. 10–15:
[- - ^{11} - -] τριερ̣[- ^{8} -] τ̣ο̂ν στρατιο[τ]ί̣δ[ον - - ^{19} - -]
[- - ^{22} - -] ὅπλα παρέχεσθαι κ̣[- - ^{21} - -]
[- - ^{22} - -]ε· ὑπερετε̂ν [δ]ὲ τού[τοις - - ^{18} - -]
[- - ^{20} - - τέ]τταρας ὀβο[λὸ]ς π[- - ^{23} - -]
[- - ^{21} - -]ον hεκ⟨ά⟩στο [τ̂ο] σόμ̣[ατος - - ^{20} - -]
[- - ^{16} - - 'Αθέν]α̣ζε τοι̂ς στρ̣[α]τιό[τεσι - - ^{21} - -]
For this entry, see also "Public Officeholders" #3.

21. D. W. Bradeen and M. F. McGregor, *Studies in Fifth-Century Attic Epigraphy* (Norman, Oklahoma 1973) 40, with references.

22. See Bradeen and McGregor, *Studies* 24–25, n. 3 (for prior discussions of the date), to which add C. W. Fornara, "The Date of the 'Regulations for Miletus'," *AJPh* 92 (1971) 473–475; H. B. Mattingly, *The Athenian Empire Restored: Epigraphic and Historical Studies* (Ann Arbor 1996) 338–340, 453–460, 481–485; additional bibliography collected in *IG* I^3 p. 937 and *SEG* XLII 6.

nian officials sent there, or (as thought earlier) Milesian soldiers.

On the date, I am inclined to accept the Corpus date of 450/49.[23] On the pay period, I am inclined to think that the four obols is pay per day since it is paralleled by the pay for the Eleusinian epistatai and secretary, which is usually dated to c. 449–447, although it has been dated as late as 432/1 (see "Public Officeholders" #4). As for the payees, I am inclined to agree with Bradeen and McGregor that they are Athenians, although it is impossible to tell whether they are rower-soldiers or officials.[24] But obviously nothing is certain in this text: it is possible that this is our earliest evidence of Athenian military pay rates, but it may be nothing of the kind!

3. 441–439. 1 dr. p.d. for sailors in the Samian War? Fornara linked the recorded expenditures for this war with ship figures provided by Thucydides, and allocated the linked figures to approximate time periods in particular years as follows: (a) 128 T. (min.) for 40 ships in the initial campaign of just over three months in 442/1, (b) 368 T. (min.) for 60 ships in the second campaign of 3 1/2 months in 441/0 (aided in the last 2 1/2 months by 40 ships and in the last month by 60 more ships), and (c) 908 T. (min.) for these 160 ships in the continuation of the second campaign for more than 5 1/2 months in 440/39.[25] If this linkage and allocation are approximately

23. See Bradeen and McGregor, *Studies* 65–70, for the arguments. For the most recent discussions of the dating problems of fifth-century Attic inscriptions, see Mattingly (as in n. 22) and A. Henry, "The Sigma Enigma," *ZPE* 120 (1998) 45–48.

24. See Bradeen and McGregor, *Studies* 40, with references to other views; for later bibliography, see n. 22 above. It is unclear whether the word ὑπερετε̃ν in line 12 refers to rowers or to servants, but if the former, rowers also could function as soldiers. If the payees were Milesian soldiers, the 4 ob. would be useful comparanda for Athenian military pay.

25. C. W. Fornara, "On the Chronology of the Samian War," *JHS* 99 (1979) 7–19 at 12–14 (at 12 "two to three months" for the first campaign is probably a slip). The talent figures are provided by *IG* I^3 363. 5 (HΔΔ𐅃TTT---), 12 (HHH𐅄Δ𐅃TTT---), 17 (𐅅HHHH𐅃TTT---), 19 (XH[H]HH--- [total of the first three figures]). Cf. Isoc. xv. 111 (1,<2>00 T.); Diod. Sic. xii. 28. 3 (<1,>200 T.); Nep. *Timoth.* i. 2 (1,200 T.). The ship figures are provided by Thuc. i. 115. 3 (40), 116. 1–2 (60 + 40), 117. 2 (60 more). For the chronology, see Thuc. i. 115. 2, i. 117. 3 (siege of Samos lasts into ninth month). For doubts about the allocation of payments to particular years, see D. M. Lewis, "Chronological Notes (10)," *CAH* V^2 (1992) 498–505 at 502 (first payment in 441/0 and the second two in 440/39, on either side of the Panathenaia). Gabrielsen's calculation (*Financing* 115) that "the cost per ship per month would be about 2.3 talents" seems to be a slip, based on the premise that there were only 60 (rather than 160) ships.

correct, the expenditure works out to about one talent per ship per month, or one drachma per day for each member of a crew of 200 sailors.[26] But since the linkage and allocation are to some extent based on circular reasoning, i.e., they assume (rather than prove) the 1 T. p.m. figure for ships' crews, I place a question mark after the figure (1 dr. p.d.) in my catalogue.

4. 433. 1 dr. p.d. for sailors on the Kerkyraian Expedition? In the account of expenditures for this expedition, the smallest restorations that are epigraphically possible support a minimum rate of 1 dr. p.d. for the rowers.[27] Because this figure recurs repeatedly in the immediately following years, I feel confident that it (rather than some higher figure) is the correct figure, but since we are not told this explicitly, I also place a question mark after this figure in my catalogue.

5. 432–430. 1 dr. p.d. μισθός for hoplites and sailors at Poteidaia. Each hoplite at Poteidaia was drawing 2 dr. p.d. (1 dr. for himself and 1 for his servant [ὑπηρέτῃ]), and the sailors were drawing "the same μισθόν," i.e., 1 dr. p.d.[28] Although doubt was once expressed about the authenticity of this passage, the recent trend has

---

26. The standard size of a trireme's crew was 200 sailors (Hdt. vii. 184. 1, viii. 17; Xen. *Hell.* i. 5. 4–7; Pl. *Critias* 119a–b; Dem. iv. 28 [quoted in n. 86 below]). 1 dr. p.d. x 200 sailors x 30 days = 6,000 dr. or 1 T. p.m., so that (a) c. 128 T. would be required for 40 ships for just over 3 months, (b) c. 368 T. would be required for (i) 60 ships for 3 1/2 months (= 210 T.), (ii) 40 ships for 2 1/2 months (= 100 T.), and (iii) 60 ships for 1 month (= 60 T.), and (c) c. 908 T. would be required for 160 ships for a little more than 5 1/2 months.

27. *IG* I^3 364. 12, 23 with Thuc. i. 45. 1, 50. 5, 51. 4: [ΔΔ]𐅉 T (min.) for 10 ships and [𐅊] (min.) for 20 ships for a campaign that took place in a single summer. At 1 T. p.m. per trireme (so Dover, *HCT* IV 293; Andrewes, *HCT* V 97; see also n. 26 above), 26 T. would be required for 10 ships for just over 2 1/2 months, and 50 T. would be required for 20 ships for precisely 2 1/2 months. Pritchett did not use this inscription as evidence for pay rates but he seemed to agree that a rate lower than 1 dr. p.d. would require the fleet to be away from Athens much longer than Thucydides' account leads us to expect (*GSW* I 9, n. 25).

28. Thuc. iii. 17. 4: τήν τε γὰρ Ποτείδαιαν δίδραχμοι ὁπλῖται ἐφρούρουν (αὑτῷ γὰρ καὶ ὑπηρέτῃ δραχμὴν ἐλάμβανε τῆς ἡμέρας). . . . νῆές τε αἱ πᾶσαι τὸν αὐτὸν μισθὸν ἔφερον. The commentators are unanimous in interpreting νῆές, by metonymy, as the *sailors* on the ships, and in believing that the sailors had no servants, and thus were paid only 1 dr. p.d. See J. Classen and J. Steup, *Thucydides* III^3 (Berlin 1892) 33; Gomme, *HCT* II 275–276; Andrewes, *HCT* V 97 (who interpreted νῆές τε αἱ πᾶσαι as *all* Athenian ships on duty that year [not just those at Poteidaia], "i.e. this is a general rule"). Thuc. iii. 17. 4 is probably the source for Poll. iv. 165: δίδραχμοι ὁπλῖται.

been strongly in favor of accepting it.[29] For purposes of this study, it is not important whether the servant was a slave or not, or whether he received all or part of the drachma paid to the hoplite for him.[30] What is important is that this is the earliest explicit evidence for a daily wage for soldiers and sailors, and that this wage was set at 1 dr. p.d. per man.

6. pre-431. Paid army and navy. More than 20,000 men were supported by the state, including 1,600 archers and 1,200 cavalrymen, plus (just prior to 431?) 2,500 hoplites, (4,000 men rowing in?) 20 guard ships and 2,000 men selected by lot who were carried on (i.e., rowing?) ships carrying tribute.[31] The question marks in the foregoing paraphrase indicate a few of the many uncertainties about the text, chronology and meaning of this passage.[32] For purposes of this study, the passage is useful only in that it indicates that before 431 there was a substantial paid army and navy. Unfortunately, however, the passage does not tell us how much soldiers and sailors were paid.

7. 425. 2 dr. μισθός (p.d.) proposed for Thracian mercenaries.[33] Is this meant to be taken seriously? I think not. There is a joke here,

---

29. Gomme, *HCT* II 272–277; Pritchett, *GSW* I 14–16; S. Hornblower, *A Commentary on Thucydides* I (Oxford 1991) 400–401; L. Kallet-Marx, *Money, Expense, and Naval Power in Thucydides' History 1–5.24* (Berkeley 1993) 130–134. Pritchett and Kallet-Marx supply very full references to earlier discussions.

30. See Pritchett (*GSW* I 16–17 [n. 50], 50) on the question of whether the servant was a slave. If he were a slave, I should think that it would have been within the hoplite's discretion whether to pay him any part of the drachma, and if he were free, that it might have been a matter of negotiation between the two of them or the state might have set the terms; at the very least, the hoplite would have been responsible for feeding and clothing his servant. See also pp. 58–59 below on the question of whether the hoplite had to provide his own armor.

31. Arist. *Ath. Pol.* xxiv. 3: συνέβαινεν γὰρ ἀπὸ τῶν φόρων καὶ τῶν τελῶν καὶ τῶν συμμάχων πλείους ἢ δισμυρίους ἄνδρας τρέφεσθαι. . . . τοξόται δ' ἑξακόσιοι καὶ χίλιοι, καὶ πρὸς τούτοις ἱππεῖς χίλιοι καὶ διακόσιοι. . . . πρὸς δὲ τούτοις ἐπεὶ συνεστήσαντο τὸν πόλεμον ὕστερον, ὁπλῖται μὲν δισχίλιοι καὶ πεντακόσιοι, νῆες δὲ φρουρίδες εἴκοσι, ἄλλαι δὲ νῆες αἱ τοὺς φόρους ἄγουσαι ⟨καὶ⟩ τοὺς απὸ τοῦ κυάμου δισχιλίους ἄνδρας. . . . ἅπασι γὰρ τούτοις ἀπὸ τῶν κοινῶν ἡ διοίκησις ἦν. For 4,000 as the crew of the 20 guard ships, see n. 26.

32. On which see Rhodes, *CAAP* 300–309, and Chambers, *AdSA* 254–256. For this entry, see also "Public Officeholders" #7.

33. Ar. *Ach.* 159–161:

Θε. τούτοις [Odomantoi] ἐάν τις δύο δραχμὰς μισθὸν διδῷ,
καταπελτάσονται τὴν Βοιωτίαν ὅλην.
Δι. τοισδὶ δύο δραχμὰς τοῖς ἀπεψωλημένοις;

namely that the Thracians would be grossly overpaid, as indeed they would be in relation to the Athenian hoplites at Poteidaia, as well as the Thracian mercenaries of 413 (#15 below).

8. 425. Taxiarchs or ambassadors to Thrace, 3 dr. (p.d.) pay (μισθοφοροῦντας) or ἐφόδια? As discussed in greater detail under "Public Officeholders" #9 (see also "Travel Allowances #6), line 602 of the *Acharnians* could be interpreted as referring to the pay or ἐφόδια of an ambassador or a taxiarch, but it probably should not be taken seriously as independent evidence of any of these things. [Xen.] *Ath. Pol.* i. 3 might suggest that generals and hipparchs (chosen by election rather than lot) were not paid at all, but even if they were, or if (although generals and hipparchs were not paid) elected taxiarchs were paid (as suggested by Ar. *Ach.* 597, 608 and 619; cf. ##21, 32 below), we have no other evidence of rates of pay for Athenian taxiarchs or other officers with which we can compare this passage, to determine the extent of (probable) comic exaggeration.

9. pre-422. Rower-soldier or dikast? paid 3 ob. (p.d.). As discussed in greater detail under "Public Officeholders" #11 (with n. 21), I interpret the 3 ob. in *Wasps* 684 as dikast pay that Aristophanes is saying has been *funded* by military operations.

10. pre-422. Rower or theoros? to Paros paid 2 ob. (p.d.). As discussed in greater detail under "Public Officeholders" #12, I am inclined to interpret the 2 ob. in *Wasps* 1189 as pay for a theoros.

11. 420. 3 Aig. ob. p.d. to hoplites, light-armed soldiers and archers, 1 Aig. dr. to cavalrymen. Athens, Argos, Mantineia and Elis agreed to furnish armed assistance to one another. After the first 30 days, the summoning state was to provide σῖτος of 3 Aiginetan obols per day to hoplites, light-armed soldiers and archers, and 1 Aiginetan drachma to cavalrymen.[34] The Attic equivalents are 4.325 and 8.650

Of course, if the Odomantian soldiers each had a servant, they would not be overpaid in relation to the Athenian hoplites at Poteidaia (#5), but then the joke would be spoiled, so I think that Aristophanes intends us to take this as 2 dr. p.d. for *one* mercenary soldier. An additional element of the joke may be that the absurd figure is proposed by an ambassador who so far has achieved nothing on his lengthy mission to Thrace!

34. Thuc. v. 47. 6: ἡ πόλις ἡ μεταπεμψαμένη διδότω σῖτον, τῷ μὲν ὁπλίτῃ καὶ ψιλῷ καὶ τοξότῃ τρεῖς ὀβολοὺς Αἰγιναίους τῆς ἡμέρας ἑκάστης, τῷ δ' ἱππεῖ δραχμὴν

obols, respectively.[35] Since these figures are higher than what would have been needed for ration-money alone in Athens (see pp. 35–36 above with notes 13 and 14), I am inclined to interpret σῖτος here in the same way as Thucydidean τροφή, i.e., as gross pay (the equivalent of Hellenistic μισθός + σιτηρέσιον).[36] It is possible that the lower figure (than 1 dr. p.d.) reflects lower labor and living costs in the more rural Peloponnese, where locally-produced food was more likely to be available.[37] Perhaps the Peloponnesians used σῖτος in the same way that the Athenians used τροφή and/or perhaps they also wanted, in this mutual assistance treaty, to avoid any suggestion of μισθός for mercenary troops.[38]

12. 415. Sailors paid 1 dr. p.d.? The Segestans brought the Athenians 60 talents "as one month's pay [μισθόν] for sixty ships."[39] If there were 200 sailors per trireme, that would work out to 1 dr. p.d. for the sailors.[40]

Αἰγιναίαν. The surviving portions of *IG* I^3 83. 22–24 correspond exactly with Thucydides' text of this treaty.

35. See Kraay, *ACGC* 329 (Aiginetan dr. weighs 6.1 grams and Attic dr. 4.3 grams); P. Marchetti, "Les cours de l'attique et l'éginétique et les rapports or-argent dans les comptes de Delphes," in D. Knoepfler, ed., *Comptes et inventaires dans la cité grecque (Actes du colloque international d'epigraphie tenu à Neuchâtel du 23 au 26 septembre 1986 en l'honneur de Jacques Tréheux)* (Neuchâtel 1988) 103–110 (with references). Cf. Griffith, *MHW* 294: "3 Aeginetan (= 4 Athenian) obols."

36. In this, I follow O. Schulthess, "Σιτηρέσιον," *RE* (2. Reihe) 3 (1927) 382–388 at 384 ("offenbar Verpflegungsgeld und Sold zugleich bezeichnet"). Griffith, *MHW* 294, and Pritchett, *GSW* I 6, interpreted the σῖτος allowance as ration-money alone. I concede that my interpretation is inconsistent with the probable meaning of σῖτος as money for (horse-) rations only in *IG* I^3 375 (n. 7 above), but the figures seem too high for (human) rations alone. For horse-rations as part of the cavalryman's compensation, see ##19, 25, 27 and 29 below.

37. So Andrewes, *HCT* V 97, and see pp. 35–36 above. Gallo, "Salari" 38, remarks that the figures may reflect a compromise among the treaty participants. Kraay, *ACGC* 98, observes that the "heavy emphasis [in the coinage of the Arkadian League] on a single denomination, the triobol, strongly suggests that this was not a coinage designed for the purposes of retail trade, but rather for large numbers of payments at a standard rate; it is probably not a coincidence that in the treaty made in 420 . . . the daily pay of an infantry-man is stipulated as three Aeginetan obols." For the implications for Athenian pay rates, see p. 56 below.

38. For the potentially pejorative connotations of μισθός, see E. Will, "Notes sur ΜΙΣΘΟΣ," in J. Bingen, G. Cambier and G. Nachtergael, eds., *Le monde grec: hommages à Claire Préaux* (Brussels 1975) 426–438 at 437–438.

39. Thuc. vi. 8. 1: οἱ Ἐγεσταῖοι μετ' αὐτῶν ἄγοντες ἑξήκοντα τάλαντα ἀσήμου ἀργυρίου ὡς ἐς ἑξήκοντα ναῦς μηνὸς μισθόν.

40. For 200 as the conventional size of a trireme's crew, see n. 26 above. This probably also was the number for the Sicilian Expedition since Thuc. vi. 31. 3 (quoted in n. 41 below) says that sailors were paid 1 dr. p.d., which for a crew of 200 works out to 200 dr. p.d. x 30 days =

13. 415. Sailors paid 1 dr. p.d. The public treasury provided 1 dr. p.d. μισθός to sailors, and the trierarchs gave an (unspecified) extra amount to the *thranitai* (rowers with the longest oar).[41]

14. 415. Peltasts or archers paid 4 ob. (p.d.)?[42] As with the Miletos inscription (#2), interpretation of this fragmentary text necessarily is uncertain: the distance between μισ[θ-] in line 27 and the four obols in line 32 prevents the certain identification of the latter as pay, there is no helpful phrase like τε̃ς ἐμέρας, and the payees (if such they be) are not clearly the peltasts (in the dative case) or the archers (in the accusative case).[43] About all that can be said is that 4 ob. p.d. may have been the pay of the peltasts or archers, but if so, why were they paid less than the 1 dr. p.d. recorded for all other soldiers and sailors in this period?[44] In the end, not much can be made of this figure.

6,000 dr. = 1 T. p.m. See also Dover, *HCT* IV 228, 293. As Andrewes (*HCT* V 97) observes, the 1 T. per ship indicates that the Segestan envoys knew what the "normal" rate was. Although it is possible that there were pay differentials within the crew (i.e., that some sailors received more than 1 dr. p.d. and some less but that the average was was 1 dr. p.d.), #13 points to a standard wage of 1 dr. p.d. Cf. n. 100 below.

41. Thuc. vi. 31. 3: τοῦ μὲν δημοσίου δραχμὴν τῆς ἡμέρας τῷ ναύτῃ ἑκάστῳ διδόντος . . . τῶν ⟨δὲ⟩ τριηράρχων ἐπιφοράς τε πρὸς τῷ ἐκ δημοσίου μισθῷ διδόντων τοῖς θρανίταις τῶν ναυτῶν. . . . See also Thuc. vi. 31. 5: ἐκ τοῦ δημοσίου μισθοῦ, and Dover, *HCT* IV 293.

42. *IG* I^3 93. 27–32.

[- - 22 - -]μένας μισ[θ - - - - - - -]
[- - 21 - - τ]ετταράκον[τα - - - - -]
[- - 19 - - πελ]τασταῖς χρ[- - - - - -]
[- - 22 - - τ]οχσότας π[- - - - - -]
[- - 23 - -]δεει ἐκ το[- - - - - -]
[- - 21 - - τ]έτταρας ὀβο[λὸς - - - -]
[- - 17 - - κυβε]ρνέτας δὲ καὶ [- - - -]

I add pairs of square brackets at the ends of the Corpus edition's text of lines 29, 30, 31 and 33.

43. The δέ in line 33 suggests that the [κυβε]ρνέτας were *not* the payees. Cf. B. Jordan, *The Athenian Navy in the Classical Period* (*University of California Publications: Classical Studies* 13) (Berkeley 1975) 115.

44. Might they be mercenaries, and if so would that account for their lower wages? All peltasts recorded by Thucydides as fighting for the Athenians are foreigners (Thuc. ii. 29. 5, ii. 79. 4, iv. 28. 4, iv. 32. 2, iv. 129. 2, vii. 27. 1), but (as argued by D. W. Bradeen, "An Athenian Peltast?," ΦΟΡΟΣ 29–35 at 33–35) *IG* I^3 60. 17–18 indicates that there were Athenian peltasts as well. Archers recorded by Thucydides as fighting for the Athenians include both citizens and foreigners (see passages collected by Gomme, *HCT* II 41, to which add iv. 129. 4, v. 52. 2, vi. 101. 6, vii. 42. 1, vii. 60. 4, vii. 62. 2, plus *IG* I^3 60. 17–18). On the Sicilian Expedition, many archers were foreigners; compare vi. 25. 2 and 43. 1 (Athenians and Cretans); vi. 22. 1, 69. 2 and 101. 6 (Athenians and foreigners not distinguished); and vii. 42. 1, 60. 4 and 62. 2 (all foreigners). But the

15. 413. 1 dr. p.d. for Thracian peltasts.[45] This is what each of them actually was drawing (ἐλάμβανεν). Apparently, that would have been acceptable if they had arrived in time to go to Sicily, but it was thought to be too expensive for the Dekeleian War. Although the payment is not called μισθός, τροφή or anything else, I am inclined to see it as gross pay (μισθός/τροφή) like all the other payments in this period.[46]

16. 411. 3 ob. (p.d.) μισθοφορά for sailors. Alcibiades advised Tissaphernes to cut the pay of the sailors in the Peloponnesian fleet to 3 ob. p.d., which also was the rate for the Athenian fleet.[47] When had the reduction from 1 dr. p.d. taken place? Presumably it happened after the Thracian peltasts were sent home in 413, and most probably after news of the Sicilian disaster reached Athens, very late in 413.[48] That would have been an appropriate time for belt-tightening, but the actual cut probably did not come until 412 since that was when Tissaphernes also reduced the pay in the Peloponnesian fleet from "the standard Athenian rate"[49] of 1 dr. to 3 ob.+ p.d.[50]

---

one attested figure for mercenary pay—1 dr. p.d. for Thracian mercenaries in 413 (#15)—shows that, in that instance at least, mercenaries received the same pay as citizen soldiers. See also p. 60 below.

45. Thuc. vii. 27. 1–2: Ἀφίκοντο δὲ καὶ Θρᾳκῶν τῶν μαχαιροφόρων . . . ἐς τὰς Ἀθήνας πελτασταὶ. . . . οἱ δ' Ἀθηναῖοι, ὡς ὕστεροι ἧκον, διενοοῦντο αὐτοὺς πάλιν ὅθεν ἦλθον ἐς Θρᾴκην ἀποπέμπειν. τὸ γὰρ ἔχειν πρὸς τὸν ἐκ τῆς Δεκελείας πόλεμον αὐτοὺς πολυτελὲς ἐφαίνετο· δραχμὴν γὰρ τῆς ἡμέρας ἕκαστος ἐλάμβανεν.

46. Griffith, *MHW* 295, agreed that this 1 dr. was the equivalent of μισθός plus σιτηρέσιον, but he had different views (from mine) about the gross compensation of the Athenian hoplites in this period (see notes 111 and 113 below).

47. Thuc. viii. 45. 2: τήν τε μισθοφορὰν ξυνέτεμεν (Alcibiades), ἀντὶ δραχμῆς Ἀττικῆς ὥστε τριώβολον καὶ τοῦτο μὴ ξυνεχῶς δίδοσθαι, λέγειν κελεύων τὸν Τισσαφέρνην πρὸς αὐτοὺς ὡς Ἀθηναῖοι ἐκ πλέονος χρόνου ἐπιστήμονες ὄντες τοῦ ναυτικοῦ τριώβολον τοῖς ἑαυτῶν διδόασιν. Alcibiades is urging Tissaphernes to tell the Peloponnesian sailors that the Athenians "with their longer experience of naval matters [ἐκ πλέονος χρόνου goes with ἐπιστήμονες ὄντες rather than διδόασιν; cf. Andrewes, *HCT* V 97–98] are [at this moment] paying their own men 3 obols." Their alleged motive for paying so little is of course fictitious: Alcibiades did not want Tissaphernes to say that the Athenians could not *afford* more, since Tissaphernes clearly could—hence the moral motive.

48. Thuc. viii. 1 and Andrewes, *HCT* V 450. It is unlikely that the Athenians would have been paying the Thracians 1 dr. p.d. in 413 if they had already cut the pay of their own soldiers to 3 ob. p.d.

49. Andrewes, *HCT* V 97, and see n. 98 below.

50. (From my non-Athenian catalogue) Thuc. viii. 29. 1–2: καὶ μηνὸς μὲν τροφήν, ὥσπερ ὑπέστη (Tissaphernes) ἐν τῇ Λακεδαίμονι, ἐς δραχμὴν Ἀττικὴν ἑκάστῳ πάσαις ταῖς ναυσὶ διέδωκε, τοῦ δὲ λοιποῦ χρόνου ἐβούλετο τριώβολον διδόναι, ἕως ἂν

17. 411. Under the 400, when pay for almost all public officials was abolished, Athenian soldiers and sailors continued to be paid.[51] We are not told how much, but the figures for earlier in 411 (#16) and for c. 408 (#18) point strongly to a wage of 3 ob. p.d.[52]

18. c. 408. 3 ob. (p.d.) μισθός for sailors. Alcibiades was paying Athenian sailors 3 ob. (p.d.) while Lysander had raised the pay of the Peloponnesian sailors from 3 to 4 ob.[53]

19. 403/2. Cavalrymen's μισθός was reduced from 1 dr. to 4 ob. (p.d.), and mounted archers' from 2 dr. to 8 ob.,[54] i.e., both took a 33 1/3% pay cut. Since we have no exclusively Athenian evidence for cavalry pay in prior years, we cannot say when, and by what stages, cavalrymen had come to be paid 1 dr. p.d. and mounted archers 2 dr. p.d. In #11, I interpreted the treaty provisions of 420 as a (primarily Peloponnesian) agreement to pay (σῖτος = μισθός/τροφή?) cavalrymen twice as much as hoplites, light-armed troops and archers. If the same pay ratio (i.e., cavalryman:hoplite = 2:1) were in force in

---

βασιλέα ἐπέρηται· ἢν δὲ κελεύῃ, δώσειν ἔφη ἐντελῆ τὴν δραχμήν. . . . ὅμως δὲ παρὰ πέντε ναῦς πλέον ἀνδρὶ ἑκάστῳ ἢ τρεῖς ὀβολοὶ ὡμολογήθησαν. ἐς γὰρ πέντε ναῦς καὶ πεντήκοντα τριάκοντα τάλαντα ἐδίδου τοῦ μηνός· καὶ τοῖς ἄλλοις, ὅσῳ πλείους νῆες ἦσαν τούτου τοῦ ἀριθμοῦ, κατὰ τὸν αὐτὸν λόγον τοῦτον ἐδίδοτο. See Andrewes, *HCT* V 70–72, for the arithmetical difficulties posed by the second part of this passage (reflecting a pay differential that Thucydides did not bother to explain fully), and 96–97 on the question whether the reductions here and in viii. 45. 2 (quoted in n. 47) are the same or represent different stages in the Spartans' negotiations with Tissaphernes. On the timing of the cuts by the Athenians and Tissaphernes, see also n. 98 below.

51. Thuc. viii. 65. 3: οὔτε μισθοφορητέον εἴη ἄλλους ἢ τοὺς στρατευομένους; Arist. *Ath. Pol.* xxix. 5: τὰ μὲν {χρήματα} προσιόντα μὴ ἐξεῖναι ἄλλοσε δαπανῆσαι ἢ εἰς τὸν πόλεμον, τὰς δ' ἀρχὰς ἀμίσθους ἄρχειν ἁπάσας ἕως ἂν ὁ πόλεμος ᾖι. . . . See also "Public Officeholders" ##17–18.

52. So Andrewes, *HCT* V 97.

53. Plut. *Alc.* xxxv. 5: Λυσάνδρου γὰρ ἐπὶ τὴν ναυαρχίαν ἀποσταλέντος ὑπὸ τῶν Λακεδαιμονίων καὶ τετρώβολον ἀντὶ τριωβόλου τῷ ναυτῇ διδόντος, ἐξ ὧν ἔλαβε παρὰ Κύρου χρημάτων, αὐτὸς (Alcibiades) ἤδη γλίσχρως χορηγῶν καὶ τὸ τριώβολον, ἀπῆρεν ἀργυρολογήσων ἐπὶ Καρίας. See also Xen. *Hell.* i. 5. 4–7 and Plut. *Lys.* iv. 5–6 (Athenian crews defect to Lysander's fleet for the extra obol—query whether this really happened). For the date of c. 408, see P. Krentz, *Xenophon, Hellenika I–II.3.10* (Warminster 1989) 11–14.

54. Lys. *In Theozotidem*, lines 75–79 (Gernet-Bizos fr. vi + *ZPE* 107 [1995] 230–236): τοὺς μὲν ἱππέας ἀντὶ δραχ|μῆς τέσσαρα[ς ὀβ]ολοὺς μισ|θοφορεῖν, το[ὺς δ' ἱπ]ποτο|ξότας ὀκτὼ ὀ[βολοὺς] ἀντὶ δυοῖν | [δ]ρ[α]χμαῖ⟨ν⟩. The word μισθοφορεῖν makes it clear that the figures were, at least in origin, μισθός/τροφή (gross pay) rather than σῖτος or σιτηρέσιον (ration-money only), whether for horses or men. Cf. the contrary view of Bugh (*Horsemen* 131–132, 154), following the very tentative suggestion (expressed with reservations) by Kroll ("Archive" 97–98, n. 36), and see also n. 59 below.

Athens, we might conjecture that, prior to the reduction of c. 412, Athenian cavalrymen were paid 2 dr. while hoplites were receiving 1 dr. p.d., and that both suffered a 50% cut in c. 412, to 1 dr. and 3 ob. p.d., respectively. But since the disparity in cavalry and hoplite pay presumably was occasioned, at least in part, by the fact that the cavalryman had to feed his horse, and usually an attendant and the attendant's horse,[55] as well as himself, the reductions may not have been proportional: it appears that in 351 (#29 below) it cost twice as much to feed the horse(s) (plus attendant?) as the cavalryman himself, and if that were so in c. 412, the (putative) reduction for a cavalryman might have been to 1 dr. 3 ob. (i.e., 3 ob. for the cavalryman and 1 dr. for the horse[s] and attendant), but this hypothesis would require a further reduction to 1 dr. before 403/2. At each stage of this reduction, the more prestigious mounted archers would have been paid more than cavalrymen because they would have been responsible for bows and arrows in addition to all of the other regular cavalry equipment, and they would have needed additional attendants (possibly with additional horses) to look after the bows and arrows.[56] It is possible that in 403/2, after the war had ended and the treasury was depleted,[57] everyone took a 33 1/3% cut: mounted archers from 2 dr. to 8 ob., cavalrymen from 1 dr. to 4 ob., and hoplites, sailors, light-armed troops, and archers from 3 ob. to 2 ob.[58] It is also possible, as a practical matter, that the reduced μισθός covered rations only, leaving no actual μισθός for the soldiers themselves.[59]

---

55. See Bugh (*Horsemen* 37, 64, 102, 123, 223–224) for references to the (sometimes mounted) *akolouthoi*, *hippokomoi*, *hypêretai* and *therapontes*. See also I. G. Spence, *The Cavalry of Classical Greece* (Oxford 1993) 284–285.

56. The continuing double pay of mounted archers in relation to cavalrymen is clear evidence of their greater expenses and prestige, on which see W. T. Loomis, "Pay Differentials and Class Warfare in Lysias' *Against Theozotides*: Two Obols or Two Drachmas?," *ZPE* 107 (1995) 230–236 at 232–234.

57. These cuts would fit well with the cuts in 403/2 in the eligibility for welfare benefits, and possibly also in the amount of those benefits, from 2 to 1 ob. p.d. See "Welfare and Other Support Allowances and Distributions" ##8, 10.

58. See #20 below for possible support for a reduction for hoplites et al.

59. As suggested by Kroll, "Archive" 97–98, n. 36, although he is aware of the difficulty of extracting a "peacetime fodder allowance" from the word μισθοφορεῖν. It seems to me that the way out of this difficulty is to interpret μισθοφορεῖν in its fifth-century sense, viz., as pay + rations, for the cavalryman and his horse(s) and attendant. His earlier pay of 2 dr. and 1 dr. 3 ob. (if I am right about them) would have covered pay and rations, but the reduction to 1 dr. might

20. Late 5th c.? 2 ob. (p.d.) for soldier or dole recipient?, or 4 ob. (p.d.) for soldier?[60] The lack of context and precise date make it impossible to interpret this comic fragment with certainty. Since Pollux says that it comes from a play called Στρατιώτιδες, the 2 ob. has been thought to refer to soldier's pay, the notion being that if women also served as soldiers a military couple could double its income,[61] but there is no independent evidence that soldier's pay had in fact fallen to 2 ob. p.d., even in 403/2 (see #19 and n. 58 above). A second possibility is that someone who had been taking 2 ob. p.d. on the dole could live in luxury on 4 ob. p.d. as a soldier, which might have been a military wage at the very end of the century (#21 below). Perhaps the easiest interpretation is that Theopompos' man was on the dole (διωβελία), and the joke here would then be that the family would do quite well if it could get a double dole.[62] But all of this is necessarily speculative.

21. 401–399. Cyrus' mercenaries in Asia raised from 1 to 1 1/2 darics per month. The effect of this was to increase their μισθός from 4 ob. to 1 dr. per day.[63] This seems to have been a temporary

---

have covered rations only (2 ob. for the cavalryman and 4 ob. for his attendant and horses?; see #29 with n. 88 below), and the further reduction to 4 ob. would have put soldier, attendant and horses on even slimmer rations. Mounted archers would have suffered similar cuts for themselves, their horses, their attendants, and their attendants' horses. If so, μισθός had been converted to σῖτος, but the original label had not been changed. See also n. 54 above.

60. Theopomp. Com. fr. 56 (K-A):
καίτοι τίς οὐκ ἂν οἶκος εὖ πράττοι τετρωβολίζων
εἰ νῦν γε διώβολον φέρων ἀνὴρ τρέφει γυναῖκα;

61. See Pritchett, *GSW* I 19, and K-A ad loc. for citations to earlier views on this passage. Although, in the absence of context, the 2 obol earner could be anyone, I agree with Pritchett that it probably is not a dikast, not so much because the title of the play suggests female soldiers as because dikast pay had not been as low as 2 ob. since c. 425 and, as K-A observe, dikast pay of 4 ob. is not otherwise securely attested (see "Public Officeholders" ##10–11 with n. 28). At this early date, it probably would be too early to think of the 2 ob. as μισθός that would be supplemented by σιτηρέσιον, as K-A suggest (with references to earlier scholarship), and in any event we might expect the proportions to be reversed: 4 ob. μισθός and 2 ob. σιτηρέσιον.

62. For the διωβελία, attested from 410–404, see "Welfare and Support Allowances and Distributions" ##7, 9. Awareness of the διωβελία may have prompted the suggestion (without discussion) in J. M. Edmonds, *The Fragments of Attic Comedy* I (Leiden 1957) 868, that the fragment dates from the Ionian War, i.e., 412–404.

63. (From my non-Athenian catalogue) Xen. *Anab.* i. 3. 21: προσαιτοῦσι δὲ μισθόν· ὁ δὲ Κῦρος ὑπισχνεῖται ἡμιόλιον πᾶσι δώσειν οὗ πρότερον ἔφερον, ἀντὶ δαρεικοῦ τρία ἡμιδαρεικὰ τοῦ μηνὸς τῷ στρατιώτῃ. From *Anab.* i. 7. 18, we learn that 1 daric = 20 Attic drachmas, so that the raise was from (the equivalent of) 20 to 30 dr. p.m., or 4 to 6 ob. p.d.

increase, given by an extraordinary leader in an extraordinary situation, since soon thereafter, in 400 and 399 (when Cyrus had died and the army was in a very different position), the rate returned to 1 daric or 1 Kyzikene stater per month, with double pay for λοχαγοί and quadruple pay for στρατηγοί.[64] Griffith argued that, in addition, the mercenaries received rations in kind or σιτηρέσιον,[65] and if we assign this allowance a value of c. 2 ob. p.d.,[66] we arrive at gross pay (fifth-century μισθός/τροφή or fourth-century μισθός + σιτηρέσιον) of c. 1 dr. p.d.[67] As Griffith pointed out, this is the first time that we hear of σιτηρέσιον.[68]

22, 23 and 24. 4th c.? 4 ob. (p.d.) for soldiers and sailors. For purposes of my catalogue, I have assumed that the 4 ob. soldier's pay

---

Griffith, *MHW* 295 (followed by J. Roy, "The Mercenaries of Cyrus," *Historia* 16 [1967] 287–323 at 310, n. 87, and Pritchett, *GSW* I 20), thought that 1 daric = 25 Attic drachmas, i.e., 5 rather than 4 ob. p.d., although Pritchett elsewhere (*GSW* I 47–48, n. 101) expressed awareness of the 1:20 exchange rate.

64. (From my non-Athenian catalogue) Xen. *Anab.* v. 6. 23; vii. 2. 36, 3. 10, 6. 1, 7. The payments in Kyzikene staters (*Anab.* v. 6. 23; vii. 2. 36, 3. 10) were not necessarily precisely equivalent (but seem in any event to have been close) to payments in the same number of darics; cf. Pritchett, *GSW* I 20, with Kraay, *ACGC* 262–263, and R. Bogaert, "Le cours du statère de Cyzique à Athènes aux Ve et IVe siècles avant J.-C.: état de la question," *RBN* 123 (1977) 17–39 (with references to prior scholarship). For the pay of Athenian officers, see ##8, 32.

65. Griffith, *MHW* 265–266, 295, pointing to (a) Cyrus' detailed arrangements for stocks of food (Xen. *Anab.* i. 4. 19, 5. 9–10, 10. 18) and (b) the fact that he paid μισθός only once, and then mostly for arrears (Xen. *Anab.* i. 2. 11–12), to which could be added (c) Xenophon's use of the word σιτηρέσιον (n. 68 below). Griffith's further argument (295, n. 3), that when Xenophon "wrote μισθός he meant μισθός, and neither more nor less," probably should not be pressed too far in this transitional period from μισθός/τροφή to μισθός + σιτηρέσιον.

66. I choose 2 ob. as (a) the amount of the διωβελία and its fourth-century successors ("Welfare and Support Allowances and Distributions" ##7, 22) and (b) the σιτηρέσιον in #29 below. In the fifth century, the amount was 1–2 ob. (see pp. 35–36 above with n. 14).

67. Griffith, *MHW* 295–297, after valuing μισθός at 5 rather than 4 ob. (n. 63 above), seems to have valued rations at 2–3 ob. to arrive at "composite pay (μ[ισθός] + σ[ιτηρέσιον])" of 7 or 8 ob.

68. Griffith, *MHW* 267–268, citing Xen. *Anab.* vi. 2. 4 (soldiers complain that they are not furnished σιτηρέσιον). The fact that on one occasion *discharged* mercenaries were not given μισθός and had no other *accumulated* money to buy provisions (Xen. *Anab.* vii. 1. 7) does not seem to me to indicate that Xenophon did not observe "the distinction between pay and rations" (Pritchett, *GSW* I 6). For less regular provision of rations in kind, see Xen. *Anab.* vii. 3. 10 (Seuthes promises the mercenaries pay and tells them to take σῖτα δὲ καὶ ποτὰ ὥσπερ καὶ νῦν ἐκ τῆς χώρας).

given by Pausanias Attikos[69] and Eustathios,[70] and the 4 ob. pay for rowers on the Paralos given by Harpokration,[71] are derived from sources that refer to some period in the fourth century; certainly Harpokration and Pausanias draw primarily on the orators and one of Eustathios' comments is derived from Pausanias. Moreover, 4 ob. seems too low for most of the fifth century (except for the end, when it may be too high [##16–19]), while being consistent with most of the fourth-century figures below, as well as with #21. Because σιτηρέσιον already had appeared in Asia (#21), and is attested at Athens in 351 (#29), I am inclined to interpret all of these figures as μισθός alone, which would be supplemented by rations in kind or a rations allowance.[72] Since the Athenians evidently felt that they could afford to introduce pay for ekklesiasts soon after the war, and to raise that pay to 3 ob. p.d. by c. 393,[73] they also would have been able to raise the pay of soldiers from the low figures of 403/2 (#19). As in the fifth century, soldiers should have been paid considerably more than dikasts, as an incentive and reward for their more time-consuming and dangerous work. It is probable, therefore, that by 393 the gross pay (however denominated and allocated between μισθός and σιτηρέσιον) of footsoldiers had been restored to 1 dr. p.d.

25. 383. 3 Aig. ob. (p.d.) for (infantry-)men and 2 Aig. dr. (p.d.) for cavalrymen. These were the amounts that Sparta's allies were permitted to supply in lieu of soldiers, the Attic equivalents being 4.325 and 17.3 ob., respectively.[74] Since the allies were not asked

---

69. Paus. Att. τ 25 (Erbse), τετρωβόλου βίος· στρατιωτικὸς μισθός.

70. Eust. ad *Il.* xiii. 637 (van der Valk III 529. 18–19): κεῖται παρὰ τοῖς παλαιοῖς καὶ τετρώβολον, στρατιωτικός τις μισθός; Eust. ad *Od.* i. 156 (Stallbaum I 41. 23–24): καὶ τετρωβόλου βίος παρὰ Παυσανίᾳ, ἀντὶ τοῦ στρατιώτου μισθός.

71. Harp., Πάραλος: Δημοσθένης Φιλιππικοῖς. μία τῶν παρ' Ἀθηναίων πρὸς τὰς δημοσίας χρείας διαπεμπομένων τριήρων. . . . οἱ δὲ ἐπιβεβηκότες αὐτῆς . . . διὰ ταύτην τὴν ὑπηρεσίαν τέτταράς τε ὀβολοὺς ἐλάμβανον καὶ τὸ πλεῖον μέρος τοῦ ἐνιαυτοῦ οἴκοι ἔμενον, ἄλλα τέ τινα ὑπῆρχεν αὐτοῖς παρὰ τῆς πόλεως, ὥς φησιν Ὑπερείδης ἐν τῷ κατ' Ἀρχεστρατίδου. . . .

72. Griffith, *MHW* 301–302, thought that the 4 ob. p.d. figures given by Eusthathios (#23) and Menander (##31–32 below) were too low for the fourth century (especially the end of the century), but he seems to have interpreted them as gross pay rather than as μισθός alone.

73. "Public Officeholders" #19.

74. (From my non-Athenian catalogue) Xen. *Hell.* v. 2. 21–22: λόγοι δὲ ἐγένοντο ἀργύριόν τε ἀντ' ἀνδρῶν ἐξεῖναι διδόναι τῇ βουλομένῃ τῶν πόλεων, τριώβολον Αἰγιναῖον κατὰ ἄνδρα, ἱππέας τε εἴ τις παρέχοι, ἀντὶ τεττάρων ὁπλιτῶν τὸν μισθὸν τῷ

also to provide rations or ration-money and since the large amount for cavalrymen suggests that it included a generous allowance for horses and attendants, I interpret these figures as gross pay, the equivalent of fifth-century μισθός/τροφή.[75] We have no direct evidence as to what Athenian military pay rates were at this time, but their gross pay should have been higher than the 4.325 obols that was established in the more rural Peloponnese, where living costs presumably were lower (see #11).

26. pre-368. 1 dr. p.d. for hypaspist (shield-bearing footsoldier) in army of Alexander II of Macedon.[76] Tronson, rejecting the *communis opinio* that this inscription refers to Alexander the Great and thus should be dated to 336/5, argued (persuasively in my view) that it was part of a bilateral treaty between Athens and Alexander II providing that his hypaspists would be paid 1 dr. p.d. (presumably by Athens in the event that it required assistance from Alexander).[77]

ἱππεῖ δίδοσθαι. εἰ δέ τις τῶν πόλεων ἐκλίποι τὴν στρατιάν, ἐξεῖναι Λακεδαιμονίοις ἐπιζημιοῦν στατῆρι κατὰ τὸν ἄνδρα τῆς ἡμέρας. Cf. Diod. Sic. xv. 31. 2, under 377/6: ὁπλίτης πρὸς δύο ψιλοὺς τεταγμένος, ὁ δ' ἱππεὺς πρὸς τέτταρας ὁπλίτας ἰσαζόμενος. For the Attic equivalents, see n. 35 above, and cf. Griffith, *MHW* 296: "3 Aeginetan (4 Attic) obols." The Aiginetan stater was a didrachm (Kraay, *ACGC* 329). It is interesting that μισθός for Peloponnesian footsoldiers had not changed since 420 (#11 above), while cavalrymen's had doubled (see n. 115 below).

75. Griffith, *MHW* 296, added a rations allowance of 2–3 Attic obols (why not 4 ob. as he did for the hoplites at Poteidaia at 294?; see n. 111 below) to this μισθός of "4 Attic obols" (but see n. 74 above) to reach the conclusion "that the rate of composite pay (μ. + σ.) in 383 was perhaps an Attic drachma or 7 obols a day. . . ." Although Xenophon speaks only of μισθός (for which see n. 65), the Spartans are not likely to have provided ration-money for mercenaries out of their own pockets.

76. *IG* II² 329. 8–10:

. . . ος π . . . ου Ἀλέξανδρον παρ[ε - - - - - - - - - - - - - - - - - -]
[. . ὑ]πασπιστῆι δραχμὴν καὶ τοῖ[ς - - - - - - - - - - - - - - - - - -]
. . ׀ ἑκάστης τῆς ἡμέρας· ἀποπέμ[πειν - - - - - - - - - - - - - - - -]

77. A. Tronson, "The Relevance of *IG* II² 329 to the Hellenic League of Alexander the Great," *AncW* 12 (1985) 15–19, with references to the earlier scholarship, including A. J. Heisserer, *Alexander the Great and the Greeks: The Epigraphic Evidence* (Norman, Oklahoma 1980) 3–26. Heisserer (21–22) already had pointed out that the connection between this inscription and Arrian *Anab.* vii. 23. 3 was speculative (Griffith, *MHW* 299 [anticipated by Böckh, *SdA* I 342–343], had suggested that if Alexander the Great's ordinary soldier, on the authority of this inscription, had received 30 dr. p.m., Arrian's "ten stater man" [δεκαστάτηρον] would have received 40 dr. p.m. [1 stater = 4 dr.], and Arrian's "double pay man" [διμοιρίτην] would have received 2 dr. p.d. or 60 dr. p.m.).

Griffith[78] already had urged that this was μισθός alone, since (a) reference is made elsewhere in the inscription (lines 4, 7 and 12) to σῖτον, which must mean rations in kind (σιτηρέσιον by then being established as the term for ration-money) and (b) 1 dr. would be too high for ration-money (see n. 66). If the rations were worth a minimum of 2 ob. p.d. (n. 66), the soldier's gross compensation would be at least 8 ob. p.d.[79]

27. 360s. The Athenians were said to be spending nearly 40 talents per year on the cavalry.[80] That would be consistent with daily μισθός for men, or σῖτος for horse-rations, of 4 ob. for 1,000 cavalrymen, 6 ob. for less than c. 667, 12 ob. for less than c. 334, or 17.3 ob. (#25 above) for less than c. 231.[81] Since we do not know (a) whether Xenophon was using "the conventional maximum figure that assumes a cavalry at ideal strength [of 1,000]" or some other figure,[82] and (b) whether he was referring to μισθός or σῖτος or both, the significance of the 40 T. is necessarily uncertain. I suspect that it refers to σῖτος of 4 ob. p.d. for a putative 1,000 horses (plus attendants?), since that would be consistent with the 4 ob. (out of a gross σιτηρέσιον of 1 dr. for cavalrymen) that seems to have been allotted to cavalry rations in 351 (#29 below),[83] but obviously this is uncertain.

28. c. 359. 30 dr. for sailors, for what period?[84] Although this sum has been variously interpreted as "a month's pay in advance at the rate of one drachma per man per day" and "three months'

---

78. Griffith, *MHW* 297–8, who, however, connected the inscription with Alexander the Great.

79. Griffith, *MHW* 301, n. 4, estimated "3 ob. σῖτος" for "composite pay" of "1 1/2 drachmae a day."

80. Xen. *Hipparch.* i. 19: ἡ πόλις ἀνέχεται δαπανῶσα εἰς τὸ ἱππικὸν ἐγγὺς τετταράκοντα τάλαντα τοῦ ἐνιαυτοῦ. See also n. 9 above. For the date of the *Hipparchos*, see J. K. Anderson, *Xenophon* (New York 1974) 184.

81. 40 T. = 1,440,000 ob. ÷ 360 = 4,000 ob. p.d., which, when divided by 4, 6, 12 and 17.3 ob., yields the number of cavalry. For earlier cavalry μισθός rates, see ##11, 19 and 25, and see also pp. 60-61 below.

82. Kroll, "Archive" 97–98, n. 36.

83. In this I follow Kroll, "Archive" 97–98, n. 36. See also Bugh, *Horsemen* 154–156, and n. 88 below.

84. Dem. li. 11: θαυμάζω δ' ἔγωγε, τί δή ποτε τῶν μὲν ναυτῶν τοὺς ἀπολειπομένους, ὧν τριάκοντα δραχμὰς ἕκαστος ἔχει μόνας, δοῦσι καὶ κολάζουσιν οὗτοι, τῶν δὲ τριηράρχων τοὺς μὴ συμπλέοντας, ὧν τριάκοντα μνᾶς εἰς ἔκπλουν εἴληφεν ἕκαστος, οὐ ταὐτὰ ποιεῖθ' ὑμεῖς.

rations at two obols a day,"[85] we are not told the time period to which the 30 dr. applies, and in fact 30 *drachmas* may may be no more than a sum arbitrarily selected by the orator as an effective rhetorical contrast to the 30 *mnas* taken by each of the trierarchs.

29. 351. 2 ob. p.d. rations allowance for footsoldiers and sailors, 1 dr. p.d. for cavalrymen. Demosthenes proposed that as "ration-money only" (τροφή, σιτηρέσιον μόνον) Athenian and mercenary infantry soldiers and sailors be given 10 dr. p.m., and cavalrymen 30 dr. p.m.; these amounts are said expressly *not* to be "full pay" (μισθὸν ἐντελῆ), since Demosthenes said the soldiers could make up "the rest" (τὰ λοιπά) "from the war," i.e., in raiding expeditions.[86] Evidently, this proposal was made at a time when the Athenians were unwilling or unable to appropriate full military pay, and it does not tell us what μισθός was, or should have been.[87] It does, however, give us (presumably bare minimum) amounts for σιτηρέσιον, it tells us that a cavalryman had to cover rations expenses that were three times those of an infantryman (probably for the cavalryman, his attendant and his horse[s]),[88] and it shows that τροφή now was (at least in this

85. Gabrielsen, *Financing* 113 (1 dr. p.d. pay) citing A. Kirchhoff, "Über die Rede 'vom trierarchischen Kranze'," *Philologische und historische Abhandlungen der Königlichen Akademie der Wissenschaften zu Berlin aus dem Jahre 1865* (1866) 65–108 at 92 (2 ob. p.d. rations).

86. Dem. iv. 28: χρήματα τοίνυν· ἔστι μὲν ἡ τροφή, σιτηρέσιον μόνον, τῇ δυνάμει ταύτῃ τάλαντ' ἐνενήκοντα καὶ μικρόν τι πρός, δέκα μὲν ναυσὶ ταχείαις τετταράκοντα τάλαντα, εἴκοσιν εἲς τὴν ναῦν μναῖ τοῦ μηνὸς ἑκάστου, στρατιώταις δὲ δισχιλίοις τοσαῦθ' ἕτερα, ἵνα δέκα τοῦ μηνὸς ὁ στρατιώτης δραχμὰς σιτηρέσιον λαμβάνῃ, τοῖς δ' ἱππεῦσι διακοσίοις οὖσιν, ἐὰν τριάκοντα δραχμὰς ἕκαστος λαμβάνῃ τοῦ μηνός, δώδεκα τάλαντα. εἰ δέ τις οἴεται μικρὰν ἀφορμὴν εἶναι, σιτηρέσιον τοῖς στρατευομένοις ὑπάρχειν, οὐκ ὀρθῶς ἔγνωκεν· ἐγὼ γὰρ οἶδα σαφῶς ὅτι, τοῦτ' ἂν γένηται, προσποριεῖ τὰ λοιπὰ αὐτὸ τὸ στράτευμ' ἀπὸ τοῦ πολέμου, οὐδένα τῶν Ἑλλήνων ἀδικοῦν οὐδὲ τῶν συμμάχων, ὥστ' ἔχειν μισθὸν ἐντελῆ.

87. Griffith, *MHW* 271–272, argued that τὰ λοιπά was *all* of the μισθός, σιτηρέσιον by then having become established as a separate payment. The observation of R. S. Stroud, "Theozotides and the Athenian Orphans," *Hesperia* 40 (1971) 280–301 at 299, n. 57, that "[a]t some time before *ca.* 350 the pay of the Hippeis was restored to its previous rate of one drachma per day; Demosthenes, IV, 28" seems to assume that the σιτηρέσιον payment here was of the same character as the (pre-reduction 1 dr. p.d.) μισθός of #19 (as a *practical* matter, it may have been; see n. 59 above).

88. If it cost 6 ob. to feed a cavalryman (plus [2?] horse[s] and an attendant) and 2 ob. to feed a soldier or sailor, presumably it cost 2 ob. to feed the cavalryman and 4 ob. for his horse(s) and attendant (for the [sometimes mounted] attendants, see n. 55 above). Kroll, "Archive" 97–98, n. 36, supposes that the 4 ob. is for the cavalryman's (single) horse only, but (as E. Badian points out to me), even if the horse "ate like a horse," it probably ate hay and barley rather than wheat,

instance) the equivalent of σιτηρέσιον rather than μισθός. More importantly, it indicates that there was a general perception that *normally* soldiers received significant μισθός in addition to σιτηρέσιον. What would that μισθός have been if the Athenians had been able to pay for it or, put another way, how much would the troops need to make up on their own? To judge from the ekklesiast pay of 393 ("Public Officeholders" #19), the Spartan figures of 383 (#25 above), and the figures for the end of the century (##31–33 below), I should think that μισθός would have to be at least 4 ob. p.d. in addition to the 2 ob. σιτηρέσιον, for gross pay of 1 dr. p.d. And it may have been higher, to judge from the net μισθός of 1 dr. p.d. in #26: as a practical matter, the troops would not have been restrained from taking at least this much from their booty.[89]

30. c. 335–322. Ephebes given 4 ob. (p.d.) apiece εἰς τροφήν. Their sophronistes, who was given 1 dr. εἰς τροφήν ("Public Officeholders" #26), took the money for the ephebes of his tribe and bought a common stock of provisions for all of them, since they took their meals together by tribes.[90] Although the ephebes had nominal military duties, serving as a national guard, they really were *training* for their future responsibilites as citizens and soldiers; certainly their work was neither as strenuous nor as dangerous as that of soldiers in *combat*. Since the ephebes received their arms, and may have received their clothing, from the state,[91] and since the sophronistai had actual custody of the money, their 4 ob. p.d. appears to have been a

---

dried figs, etc., and therefore the rations of two horses might not have cost any more than a single man's.

89. Griffith, *MHW* 296–297, thought that 2–4 ob. p.d. had to be added as μισθός to the 2 ob. σιτηρέσιον, so that they "received at least 4 obols a day composite pay (μ. + σ.); but a composite pay of a drachma a day may be nearer the truth, though this must be regarded as a maximum figure. This means that between 400 and 350 B.C. the rate has fallen, perhaps as much as from 8 to 4, and certainly from 7 to 5 or 6 obols." But if the daily composite pay of Cyrus' mercenaries was 6, rather than 7 or 8 ob. (see #21 and n. 67 above), the rate may not have fallen at all, and indeed it actually increased whenever μισθός was closer to 1 dr., as in #26. For supplements to military pay, over and above μισθός and σιτηρέσιον, see n. 103 below.

90. Arist. *Ath. Pol.* xlii. 3: δίδωσι δὲ καὶ εἰς τροφ[ὴν] τοῖς μὲν σωφρονισταῖς δραχμὴν ᾱ ἑκάστωι, τοῖς δ' ἐφήβοις τέτταρας ὀβολοὺς ἑκάστωι· τὰ δὲ τῶν φυλετῶν τῶν αὑτοῦ λαμβάνων ὁ σωφρονιστὴς ἕκαστος ἀγοράζει τὰ ἐπιτήδεια πᾶσιν εἰς τὸ κοινόν, συσσιτοῦσι γὰρ κατὰ φυλάς. . . . For the date, see Rhodes, *CAAP* 51–58, 494.

91. Arist. *Ath. Pol.* xlii. 4–5: λαβόντες ἀσπίδα καὶ δόρυ παρὰ τῆς πόλεως . . . φρουροῦσι δὲ τὰ δύο ἔτη χλαμύδας ἔχοντες, καὶ ἀτελεῖς εἰσι πάντων.

σιτηρέσιον, not intended to leave them the surplus spending money that an additional μισθός would have provided, and Rhodes interprets this τροφή as "maintenance grants" rather than μισθός, i.e., not τροφή in the Thucydidean sense.[92]

31. 314/3. 4 ob. p.d. for sailor. A fragment from Menander's *Olynthia* seems to say that a sailor serving with the Athenian admiral Aristoteles was paid 4 ob. p.d.,[93] presumably (at this date) μισθός alone, to which at least 2 ob. p.d. (n. 66 above) would have to be added for rations, for a minimum gross pay of c. 1 dr. p.d.

32. 4th/3rd c. 4 ob. (p.d.) for soldiers, 4 dr. for officers? Two passages from Menander's *Perikeiromene* have been read as indicating such pay (again, presumably, μισθός alone). The repeated allusions to pay suggest that these men are mercenaries, and the implication seems to be that 4 ob. is considered a low rate.[94] In the absence of more context, interpretation of these passages (the two here and #31) obviously cannot be certain, but all three Menander passages suggest that at the end of the fourth century 4 ob. p.d. was the standard military μισθός, to which at least 2 ob. p.d. would have to be added for rations, for a minimum gross pay of 1 dr. p.d. (cf. n. 72 above). The 4 dr. p.d. for officers finds no corroboration elsewhere, and (if textually sound) may be a humorous exaggeration (but cf. the

---

92. Rhodes, *CAAP* 507, 695. This would be further confirmation (in addition to #29) that τροφή no longer (necessarily) meant μισθός.

93. Men. fr. 297 (K-T): μετ' Ἀριστοτέλους γὰρ τέτταρας τῆς ἡμέρας | ὀβολοὺς φέρων. The date is supplied by Diod. Sic. xix. 68. 3.

94. Men. *Peric.* 379–382, 392–394 (slaves Σωσίας and Δᾶος):

(Σω.) πότερα νομίζετ' οὐκ ἔχειν ἡ[μᾶς χολὴν]
οὐδ' ἄνδρας εἶναι;
(Δα.) ναὶ μὰ Δία, τε[τρω]β̣ό[λους.]
ὅταν δὲ τετράδραχμος τοιούτ[ους] λα[μβάνηι,] 381
ἢ ῥαιδίως μαχούμεθ' ὑμῖν.

(Σω.) οἱ παῖδες οἱ τὰ πελτί' ο̣ῦ̣τ̣ο̣ι̣ πρὶν πτύσαι
διαρπάσονται πάντα, κἂν τετρωβόλους 393
καλῇς.

I follow the interpretation of G-S 497, and, in line 381, their preferred reading τετράδραχμος (Jensen's emendation, taking it as the pay of an officer) rather than τετραδράχμοις (C) or τετραδράχμους (Sudhaus), taking it as the increased pay of the soldiers. Sandbach's revised Oxford text (1990, with addenda at p. 345), surprisingly in view of the commentary, prints τετραδράχμους.

3 dr. p.d. in #8 and the double and quadruple pay for λοχαγοί and στρατηγοί in #21).

33. Early 3rd c. 4 ob. (p.d.) for soldiers in Lysimachos' army. But one such soldier indicated that no Spartan would serve for that amount.[95] It is difficult to know how much weight to give to this story, but the 4 ob. p.d. (again, at this date, presumably μισθός alone) is consistent with the roughly contemporary figures in Menander, and we likewise probably should suppose minimum gross pay of c. 1 dr. p.d.

As a group, how are these figures to be interpreted?

For the period prior to 433, the fragmentary #2 could be interpreted as indicating that soldiers or rowers were paid 4 ob. p.d., and #3 is consistent with pay for sailors of 1 dr. p.d., but neither figure is certain.

For the period 433 to 412, Pritchett collected "the diversity of opinions about the amount of misthos"—2 ob., 3 ob., and 1 dr. p.d.—and remarked that these "conjectures . . . cannot all be correct."[96] After considering all of the evidence, he concluded that 3 ob. p.d. was standard and 1 dr. exceptional.[97] Dover, Andrewes and Rhodes disagreed, thinking that 1 dr. was normal.[98] In my view, the evidence strongly indicates that 1 dr. p.d. was the usual rate. This is

95. (From my non-Athenian catalogue) Plut. *Mor.* 233c: Τῶν παρὰ Λυσιμάχῳ στρατευομένων ἐρωτηθείς τις ὑπ' αὐτοῦ, μήτι τῶν εἱλώτων ἐστί, "σὺ δ'οἴει" ἔφη "ἐπὶ τὸ παρὰ σοῦ τετρώβολον Λάκωνα ἥξειν;"

96. Pritchett, *GSW* I 14, 23, citing among others Böckh, *SdA* I 341, 344 ("In der Regel . . . nur drei Obolen"); Gomme, *HCT* II 42, 275–276 (1 dr. p.d "clearly a special rate . . . double the ordinary rate" of 3 ob. p.d.); Ehrenberg, *People* 228 (2 ob. p.d. the "usual payment"); Jones, *Ath. Dem.* 7 (n. 27), 32 (n. 54) (1 dr. p.d. "the rate till the Sicilian disaster . . . when it was halved"). P. Gauthier, "Les clérouques de Lesbos et la colonisation athénienne au Ve siècle," *REG* 79 (1966) 64–88 at 75–76, suggested that 4 ob. p.d. was "la règle" before 413.

97. Pritchett, *GSW* I 23–24.

98. Dover, *HCT* IV 293 (1 dr. p.d. "had been customary for a generation" prior to 415, though it seemed "unusually high . . . in retrospect"); Andrewes, *HCT* V 97–98 ("[o]utside this passage [Thuc. viii. 45. 2 (#16 above)], the evidence supports Dover. . . . Similarly it is more likely that Tissaphernes first offered the standard Athenian rate (at [Thuc. viii.] 29, 45. 6), then reduced it when the Athenian rate dropped to 3 ob., than that he began by offering double the standard rate"); Rhodes, *CAAP* 306 ("more probably a higher rate [than 3 ob.] was normal until after the Sicilian expedition"). Hornblower (as in n. 29) 402 reserves judgment until his (yet to appear) notes on Thuc. viii. 45.

the figure consistently reported by Thucydides. If there were only one such report, there might be some force to Pritchett's argument that Thucydides recorded "the rate [only] when it was exceptional."[99] But in fact, he records it eight times, at widely spread dates: 432–430 (three rates in one passage [#5]), 415 (three rates in two passages [##12–13]), 413 (Thracian peltasts [#15]) and 412 (Peloponnesian sailors paid by Tissaphernes [#16]). Moreover, a rate of at least 1 dr. p.d. is required for 433 by the accounts of the Kerkyraian Expedition (#4), and a rate well in excess of 3 ob. p.d. is supported by the alliance of 420 (#11): it is hard to see how the equivalent of 4.325 ob. p.d. could be the standard rate in the rural Peloponnese if 3 ob. were the standard in urban Athens. In none of these instances is there any indication that 1 dr. p.d. is "exceptional." On the contrary, so many instances of that rate in so many years for so many different payees suggest that this was the normal rate.[100] Pritchett's view was based in part on his interpretation of μισθός/τροφή as ration-money only, the notion being that since soldiers would have needed no more for rations than dikasts (except in unusual circumstances), they should have received the same rations allowance. But it appears that for dikasts as well as soldiers and sailors, μισθός/τροφή meant gross pay (covering the fourth-century equivalent of μισθός plus σιτηρέσιον), and that the soldiers and sailors were paid twice as much as the dikasts. This is not surprising, since soldiers were employed 24 hours per day in dangerous work, while dikasts had a relative sinecure for only a few hours per day.

In c. 412, after the Sicilian Disaster, the rate fell drastically, to 3 ob. p.d. (##16, 18). It seems to have remained there until after the

---

99. Pritchett, *GSW* I 24.

100. Jordan (as in n. 43) 113–115, argues that 1 dr. p.d. was standard only for the highest class of sailors, the *nautai*, and that the *hyperesia* (consisting of "slaves, freedmen, and occasional foreign mercenaries") must have received less. This argument has an intuitive appeal, but such evidence as there is does not support it: it is true that Thucydides, in speaking of the Sicilian Expedition, says that the *nautai* were paid 1 dr. p.d. (vi. 31. 3, quoted in n. 41), but he also says that the μισθός for a trireme crew was 1 T. per month (vi. 8. 1, quoted in n. 39), and if there were 200 men (of all ranks) in the crew (n. 26), the *hyperesia* also must have received 1 dr. p.d. on average (see n. 40). Perhaps this is less surprising when one remembers that slaves working on the Erechtheion were paid as much as citizens and metics for the same work (see "Construction and Other Manual Workers" #3 with n. 12). Moreover, the *thranitai* did receive an (unspecified) extra payment (#13).

Peloponnesian War, when it may have fallen further, to 2 ob. p.d., but this last stage is not attested (##19, 20). In the same period, cavalrymen's pay no doubt also fell; I have reconstructed the stages as (a) a drop from 2 dr. to 1 dr. 3 ob. in c. 412, (b) a further drop to 1 dr. before 403/2, and (c) a final cut from 1 dr. to 4 ob. in 403/2—but only the last stage is attested (#19).

For the fourth century, the figures are fewer and less well dated. Moreover, unlike the fifth-century figures, they usually are not for gross pay, so it is harder to interpret them, and Pritchett expressed no general view at all with respect to them.[101] I am inclined to think that for most of the century there was a minimum standard rate of 4 ob. p.d. μισθός plus 2 ob. p.d. σιτηρέσιον, for a minimum gross pay of 1 dr. p.d. This rate fits well with the 4 ob. p.d. μισθός of the mercenaries in 401–399 (#21), the 3 ob. p.d. μισθός for ekklesiasts in c. 393 ("Public Officeholders" #19), the 4.325 ob. p.d. for Peloponnesian soldiers in 383 (#25), the 2 ob. p.d. σιτηρέσιον in 351 (#29), the three 4 ob. p.d. figures (presumably μισθός) of c. 300 (##31–33), and the three 4 ob. p.d. figures (again presumably μισθός) vaguely dated to the fourth century (##22–24). Of course, as *minimum* standard rates, these figures could be exceeded, as they certainly were by the 1 dr. p.d. (apparently μισθός) stipulated in the early 360s (#26) and the 4 ob. p.d. τροφή (apparently σιτηρέσιον) for the ephebes of c. 335–322 (#30), and Demosthenes doubtless would have been glad to have μισθὸν ἐντελῆ exceed 4 ob. in 351 (#29), whether from raiding expeditions or from the contributions, loans and exactions by generals and trierarchs that had become an increasingly prominent feature of naval finance in the fourth century.[102] In any event, there seems to have been a general expectation, not always attainable (as in #29, at least initially), that soldiers would net a minimum of 4 ob. p.d. above their costs for rations. Taken together, these figures certainly show that military pay rates rebounded from their lows of 3 ob. p.d. in the last decade of the fifth century (and possibly 2 ob. p.d. in 403/2), and that they fairly soon reached their pre-c. 412 level of 1 dr.

101. See Pritchett, *GSW* I 19–23.

102. For this "privatization of naval finances," see Gabrielsen, *Financing* 117–118, 121–125.

p.d., sometimes exceeding that figure. That fact is not instantly obvious because μισθός/τροφή had been replaced by μισθός plus σιτηρέσιον, the figures for each of which were usually less than 1 dr. p.d.

In the category of "Military Bonuses," there are only two figures in my Athenian catalogue[103] and, since the number of soldiers is not stated in either case, they do not shed any light on rates of pay.

I leave open five questions that do not directly bear on the rates of military pay discussed above:

1. Did Athens provide its soldiers and sailors with clothing and armor? Pritchett collected some evidence.[104] In c. 510–500, Athenian [cleruchs?] in Salamis were required to furnish themselves with arms worth 30 drachmas.[105] In 421, there are comic references to arms dealers and their prices, suggesting that individuals (rather than the state) were the buyers.[106] In the 360s, cavalrymen apparently were required by law to acquire their own arms with their μισθός.[107] In c. 335–322, the state furnished each ephebe with a shield and spear (and possibly a *chlamys*), and some wealthy Athenians donated arms to the state.[108] In the late third century, a general was praised for furnishing money for clothing for his men.[109] From these isolated pieces of evidence it seems that originally soldiers of some wealth (i.e., cavalrymen and hoplites) were required to furnish their own arms, and presumably their clothing as well; rowers would not have needed armor and thus

103. Both in 335, when it is alleged that Demosthenes would not pay (a) 5 T. to an unstated number of mercenaries to give up the citadel of Thebes (Aeschin. iii. 240) and (b) 9 or 10 T.? to an unstated number of Arkadian mercenaries to liberate Thebes (Aeschin. iii. 240; Dinarch. i. 20–21).

104. Pritchett, *GSW* I 3–4, n. 3.

105. *IG* I^3 1. 8–10: [τ]ὰ δὲ [h]όπλα π[αρέχεσ]θ̣α[ι αὐτὸς : τ]ριά[κ]οντα : δρ[αχμο̃ν ⁝]

106. Ar. *Pax* 1224–1263: before Peace, 10 mn. for a cuirass (θώρακος), 60 dr. for a trumpet (σάλπιγγι), 1 mn. for 2(?) helmets (κράνεσιν); after Peace, 1 dr. for 50 spears (δόρατα).

107. Xen. *Hipparch.* i. 22–23: τοὺς ἱππέας οἱ φύλαρχοι. . . . δυνατοὶ δ' εἰσὶ . . . τῷ μισθῷ ἐπαναγκάζοντες κατὰ τὸν νόμον ὁπλίζεσθαι. As noted under #27, we do not know what that μισθός was.

108. For the ephebes, see n. 91; for arms donations, see Dem. xviii. 116, xlv. 85.

109. *IG* II^2 1304. 34–35: ἐν πᾶσι τοῖς ἔτεσι[ν αὐ]τοῖς προδιδοὺς ἀργύριον εἰς | ἐσθῆτα.

would not have had to supply any, but if a thete served as a hoplite, Dover reasonably suggested that the state would have furnished him arms while hoplites ἐκ καταλόγου would have been expected to provide their own.[110] By the fourth century, however, the state was distributing at least some arms, and possibly some clothing, free of charge. The only exclusively Athenian wage listed in my catalogue that might have been offset by an obligation to buy arms is that of the hoplites at Poteidaia (#5). Although it is conceivable that part of the 1 dr. p.d. for their servants was deemed to be (indirect) compensation for arms expenses, I suspect that hoplite armor was an accepted burden that accompanied the privilege of hoplite status, and that the 1 dr. p.d. was deemed to be a standard per capita wage, applying to hoplites, servants and sailors alike.

2. What portion of the soldier's pay was for rations in the era before σιτηρέσιον? Griffith tried to determine this on the basis of the figures provided for σῖτος in the alliance of 420 (#11).[111] But apart from mistakes and uncertainties about details, this approach was anachronistic because it posed the question, for the fifth century, in terms that did not assume a distinctly separate (and technical) significance until the fourth century. In the fifth century, μισθός or τροφή was a single amount, and how a soldier chose to allocate it was his business. A less complicated and hazardous approach would be to subtract from the soldier's μισθός/τροφή the amount that was being paid in the same period as a dole (1–2 ob. p.d.): the difference should be the soldier's minimum "net pay," i.e., when μισθός/τροφή was 1 dr. p.d. the soldier was netting at least 4 ob., but when it fell to 3 ob. p.d. (and the diobelia was in force), he may not have been netting much more than 1 ob. p.d.

---

110. Dover, *HCT* IV 264, 310, and cf. M. H. Hansen, *Demography and Democracy: The Number of Athenian Citizens in the Fourth Century B.C.* (Copenhagen 1986) 83–89. For Cyrus' mercenaries, see Roy (as in n. 63) 310.

111. Griffith, *MHW* 294–295, converted the 3 Aiginetan ob. to 4 Attic ob. (but see n. 35), and assumed that the entire amount was for rations only (but see #11). He then applied that amount to the μισθός/τροφή figures given by Thucydides. From the 2 dr. gross pay of the hoplite at Poteideia (#5), he deducted "σιτηρέσιον" of 4 ob. for the hoplite and 2–3 ob. for the servant, leaving "5 obols or 1 drachma as a hoplite's daily μισθός," and for the Thracian peltasts (#15) he seems to have subtracted 2 ob. from their 1 dr. (like the servant at Poteidaia?), leaving net "μισθός" of [4 ob., or] "two-thirds of what the hoplites at Potidea received."

3. Was part of military pay withheld until the end of the campaign? Pritchett collected some evidence that led him to conclude that it was, and Andrewes agreed, but the evidence cited may describe exceptional measures.[112]

4. Were mercenaries paid at the same rate as citizen soldiers? Griffith was inclined to think not,[113] but there is not much hard evidence. The 1 dr. p.d. paid to the Thracian mercenaries in 413 (#15) shows that on at least one occasion mercenaries were paid at the same rate as citizens. In the fragmentary #14, it is not certain that the 4 ob. (p.d.?) (which was less than the 1 dr. p.d. for citizen sailors in ##12 and 13) was pay or that it was for mercenary peltasts and/or archers.

5. How did cavalrymen fare in relation to hoplites? We have several figures, but they are not easy to compare and only one is from Athens itself. In 420 (#11) the ratio of cavalryman to hoplite pay in the Peloponnese was 2:1, and in 383 (#25), also in the Peloponnese, it was 4:1. In Athens in 351 (#29), the ratio was 3:1, but that was for σιτηρέσιον only.[114] The only two ratios that are clearly comparable are ##11 and 25, both from the Peloponnese and both (I think) for μισθός + σιτηρέσιον; the jump from 2:1 to 4:1 is striking (expecially since the pay for hoplites continued, after 37 years, to be 3 Aig. ob. p.d.), and Griffith was perhaps right in thinking that it reflects a scarcity of cavalry in the Peloponnese.[115] As for Athens itself, it is

112. Pritchett, *GSW* I 24–29; Andrewes, *HCT* V 98. Pritchett cited inter alia Ar. *Eq.* 1366–1367 (μισθὸν . . . 'ντελῆ promised at end of voyage); Thuc. viii. 45. 2 (quoted in n. 47 above: Tissaphernes urged by Alcibiades to withhold pay to prevent dissipation and desertion); Polyaenus iii. 9. 51 (Iphikrates normally withheld one-fourth of pay as security against desertion).

113. Griffith, *MHW* 294–297, suggested that after deduction of σιτηρέσιον from their 1 dr. p.d., the Thracian peltasts (#15) received net μισθός of 4 ob. p.d. as compared to 5 ob. to 1 dr. for the hoplites at Poteidaia (#5), but see n. 111; with respect to the mercenaries paid for by Sparta's allies (#25), he was uncertain as to whether they were paid less than citizen soldiers; although both Athenian citizens and mercenaries took the same σιτηρέσιον in 351 (#29), he thought that the μισθός for the citizens might have been greater. All of this, of course, is speculative.

114. From non-Attic inscriptions Griffith, *MHW* 302, reported 5:2 in 303 and 2:1 in c. 270, to which add, from my non-Athenian literary catalogue, 2:1 in 168 (Liv. xliv. 26. 4; App. *Mac.* 18. 2).

115. Griffith, *MHW* 302: "It is just possible that the very high ratio in 383 B.C. may reflect an increase in the value of cavalry (particularly scarce in the Peloponnese), as the best weapon against the new peltasts, who began to make their name about 10 years earlier; e.g. Xenophon's

possible that #29 reflects the same costs and ratios (viz., 2 obols for the cavalryman and 4 obols for his horse[s] and attendant) as the pre-reduction 1 dr. p.d. for cavalrymen in #19 (see n. 59), but this is necessarily uncertain. Because cavalry pay was subject to a number of variables that did not affect hoplite pay (the availability of horses and bulky horse fodder), because we have so few figures, and because the figures that we do have are not really comparable, I refrain from generalizing at all about trends in cavalry pay, either alone or in relation to that of hoplites.

---

account of the famous engagement in which the Spartan *mora* was destroyed by peltasts, makes it clear that a good cavalry charge would have saved the situation (Xen. *Hell.* iv. 5. 16)."

Chapter 3

Doctors, Lawyers and Professors

Collected here are amounts paid to what we would call "professional" persons—physicians, advocates and academics. There seems not to have been any treatment of these figures since Böckh's (partial) collection and very brief discussion.[1] All professors' fees, except those in #4 below, apparently are for a course rather than for individual lessons.

1. pre-c. 522. 100 mn. p.a. to physician Demokedes from Athenians.[2] This story, which has Demokedes receiving substantial raises in successive years in different locations, has a fairy-tale quality. In addition, a 10,000 dr. annual salary in the sixth century is incredible on its face, at least when the employer is someone other than the Persian King, so I do not take this figure seriously.

2. c. 470–420. 100 mn. to Protagoras for instruction (per student).[3] As with #1, 10,000 dr. for Protagoras, as well as for Zeno and Gorgias (##3 and 5), seems incredibly large. None of the sources is contemporary. Even for Plato (n. 7 below), Zeno was a quasi-legendary figure, almost a century in the past, and thus his fee may have grown with this legend. The other sources for these 100 mn. fees are much later, and it is

---

1. Böckh, *SdA* I 153–155.

2. Hdt. iii. 131. 1–2: Ὁ δὲ Δημοκήδης οὗτος ὧδε ἐκ Κρότωνος ἀπιγμένος Πολυκράτεϊ ὡμίλησε· πατρὶ συνείχετο ἐν τῇ Κρότωνι ὀργὴν χαλεπῷ· τοῦτον ἐπείτε οὐκ ἐδύνατο φέρειν, ἀπολιπὼν οἴχετο ἐς Αἴγιναν. καταστὰς δὲ ἐς ταύτην πρώτῳ ἔτεϊ ὑπερεβάλετο τοὺς ἄλλους ἰητρούς, ἀσκευής περ ἐὼν καὶ ἔχων οὐδὲν τῶν ὅσα περὶ τὴν τέχνην ἐστὶ ἐργαλήια. καί μιν δευτέρῳ ἔτεϊ ταλάντου Αἰγινῆται δημοσίῃ μισθοῦνται, τρίτῳ δὲ ἔτεϊ Ἀθηναῖοι ἑκατὸν μνέων, τετάρτῳ δὲ ἔτεϊ Πολυκράτης δυῶν ταλάντων. I assign the payment by the Athenians to pre-c. 522 since Polykrates died in c. 522.

3. Diog. Laert. ix. 52: οὗτος (sc. Πρωταγόρας) πρῶτος μισθὸν εἰσεπράξατο μνᾶς ἑκατόν; Σ Pl. *Rep*. 600c: Πρωταγόρας Ἀρτέμωνος, Ἀβδηρίτης. οὗτος φορτοβαστάκτης ἦν, ἐντυχὼν δὲ Δημοκρίτῳ ἐφιλοσόφησεν καὶ ἐπὶ ῥητορείαν ἔσχεν, καὶ πρῶτος λόγους ἐριστικοὺς εὗρεν, καὶ μισθὸν ἔπραξεν τοὺς μαθητὰς μνᾶς ρ´; Quintilian iii. 1. 10: . . . Abderites Protagoras, a quo decem milibus denariorum [i.e., drachmas?] didicisse artem quam edidit Euathlus dicitur. For Protagoras' dates (c. 490–420), see Guthrie, *HGP* III 262–263; from this, I derive his period of activity of c. 470–420.

possible that the figure for Zeno was simply repeated in similar contexts (cf. a similar repetition for Demosthenes in ##17 and 18). Böckh suggested that these fees were possible when there were few teachers of the caliber of Protagoras, Zeno and Gorgias, but that later, when teachers became more numerous, the standard fee dropped to 5 or 10 mn. (##12 and 19).[4] This seems unlikely to me since the general wage level rose from c. 450 to c. 330, and there is specific evidence that professors' fees rose in the fourth century.[5] I am prepared to believe that Protagoras, Zeno, Prodikos, Gorgias and Hippias commanded very high fees from very wealthy students, but I think that 100 mn. is an exaggerated sum.[6]

3. c. 450. 100 mn. to Zeno, for teaching Pythodoros and Kallias, apiece.[7] For the reasons stated under #2, I am inclined to think that this sum is exaggerated.

4. c. 450–395. 1/2 dr., 1 dr., 2 dr., 4 dr., 50 dr. to Prodikos for lessons, apiece.[8] Although the evidence of the late commentators (espe-

---

4. Böckh, *SdA* I 155.

5. See ##12 and 19 below, and "Inflation and Deflation" p. 241.

6. For Zeno, Prodikos and Gorgias, see ##3, 4 and 5 below. For Hippias (more than 150 mn. from Sicily, of which more than 20 mn. came from the small town of Inykos), see Pl. *Hp. Ma.* 282e (from my non-Athenian catalogue). This 150 mn. is less incredible than the 100 mn. from individual students in ##2, 3 and 5, since the amount (only one and one-half times as large) seems to come from a relatively large number of students spread over Sicily.

7. Pl. *Alc.* I 119a (Sokrates speaking): Ἀλλὰ τῶν ἄλλων Ἀθηναίων ἢ τῶν ξένων δοῦλον ἢ ἐλεύθερον εἰπὲ ὅστις αἰτίαν ἔχει διὰ τὴν Περικλέους συνουσίαν σοφώτερος γεγονέναι, ὥσπερ ἐγὼ ἔχω σοι εἰπεῖν διὰ τὴν Ζήνωνος Πυθόδωρον τὸν Ἰσολόχου καὶ Καλλίαν τὸν Καλλιάδου, ὧν ἑκάτερος Ζήνωνι ἑκατὸν μνᾶς τελέσας σοφός τε καὶ ἐλλόγιμος γέγονεν. This was quoted almost verbatim by Ael. Arist. iv. 31 (Behr): Ἀλλὰ τῶν ἄλλων Ἀθηναίων δοῦλον ἢ ἐλεύθερον εἰπὲ ὅστις αἰτίαν ἔχει διὰ τὴν Περικλέους συνουσίαν σοφώτερος γεγονώς, ὥσπερ ἐγὼ ἔχω σοι διὰ τὴν Ζήνωνος Πυθόδωρον τὸν Ἰσολόχου καὶ Καλλίαν τὸν Καλλιάδου· ὧν ἑκάτερος Ζήνωνι ἑκατὸν μνᾶς τελέσας σοφός τε καὶ ἐλλόγιμος γέγονεν. Since the office of στρατηγός was held by Kallias in 432/1 (Thuc. i. 61. 1, 63. 3) and by Pythadoros in 426/5 (Thuc. iii. 115. 2, iv. 2. 2), I assign a date of c. 450 to their instruction by Zeno.

8. Pl. *Crat.* 384b (Sokrates speaking): εἰ μὲν οὖν ἐγὼ ἤδη ἠκηκόη παρὰ Προδίκου τὴν πεντηκοντάδραχμον ἐπίδειξιν, ἣν ἀκούσαντι ὑπάρχει περὶ τοῦτο πεπαιδεῦσθαι, ὥς φησιν ἐκεῖνος (sc. Πρόδικος), οὐδὲν ἂν ἐκώλυέν σε αὐτίκα μάλα εἰδέναι τὴν ἀλήθειαν περὶ ὀνομάτων ὀρθότητος· νῦν δὲ οὐκ ἀκήκοα, ἀλλὰ τὴν δραχμιαίαν· οὔκουν οἶδα πῇ ποτε τὸ ἀληθὲς ἔχει περὶ τῶν τοιούτων; [Pl.] *Ax.* 366c (Sokrates speaking): καὶ ταῦτα δὲ ἃ λέγω, Προδίκου ἐστὶν τοῦ σοφοῦ ἀπηχήματα, τὰ μὲν διμοίρου ἐωνημένα, τὰ δὲ δυοῖν δραχμαῖν, τὰ δὲ τετραδράχμου. προῖκα γὰρ ἁνὴρ οὗτος οὐδένα διδάσκει, διὰ παντὸς δὲ ἔθος ἐστὶν αὐτῷ φωνεῖν τὸ Ἐπιχάρμειον, "ἁ δὲ χεὶρ τὰν χεῖρα νίζει·" δός τι, καὶ λάβε τι; Arist. *Rhet.* 1415b 15–17: τοῦτο δ' ἐστίν, ὥσπερ ἔφη Πρόδικος, ὅτε νυστάζοιεν οἱ ἀκροαταί, παρεμβάλλειν ⟨τι⟩ τῆς πεντηκονταδράχμου αὐτοῖς; Anon. Comm. ad Arist. *Rhet.* 1415b 16: ἡ πεντηκοντάδραχμος εἶδός ἐστι βοτάνης, ὃ προσφερόμενοι οἱ ἄνθρωποι διατελοῦσιν· ἔλεγεν οὖν ὁ Πρόδικος, ὅτι, ὅτε νυστάζουσιν οἱ ἀκροαταί, δεῖ παρεμβάλλειν αὐτοῖς ἀπὸ τῆς πεντηκονταδράχμου καὶ προσφέρειν, ὡς ἂν δια-

cially Tzetzes) is remote, the figures themselves seem reasonable, and the combined authority of Plato and Aristotle indicate that Prodikos' "50 dr. exhibition" was well known: a wealthy student certainly could have afforded it.

5. post-427? 100 mn. to Gorgias for instruction in rhetoric, per (single?) student.[9] For the reasons stated under #2, I am inclined to think that this sum is exaggerated.

6. pre-423. 1 T. to Sokrates?, from Hyperbolos, for instruction in forensic speaking.[10] As Sommerstein observes, "this conveys to Strepsiades that it will be possible, but very difficult and very expensive, to make an orator of Pheidippides; to the audience, that Hyperbolus was totally devoid of natural oratorical ability; to both alike, that the training Socrates can offer must be a valuable asset, since Hyperbolus was prepared to pay so heavily for it and it has made him such a successful prosecutor and politician."[11] Although Hyperbolos may have paid for lessons in forensic speaking, Aristophanes probably invented the fee, or at least exaggerated it, for comic effect.

7. 422. Public prosecutor paid 1 dr. (p.d.). As discussed in greater detail under "Public Officeholders" #13, this figure (in Ar. *Vesp.* 691) seems plausible.

8. c. 410–399. 20 mn. sent to Sokrates by Aristippos (in gratitude for prior instruction?) but not accepted.[12] The point of this story seems

---

τελῶσι διυπνιζόμενοι ὑπ' αὐτῆς καὶ διεγειρόμενοι εἰς τὸ προσέχειν. εὗρον δὲ σχόλιον εἰς τὴν πεντηκοντάδραχμον τοιοῦτον· "ἀναμνήσθητε, ὅτι λαμβάνετε πεντήκοντα δραχμάς"; *Suda* π 2366 (Adler), Πρόδικον: . . . πρῶτος δὲ οὗτος τὴν πεντηκοντάδραχμον ἐπίδειξιν ἐποιήσατο; Σ (Tzetzes) Ar. *Nub.* 358a: οὗτος ὁ Πρόδικος μετὰ πολλῶν αὐτοῦ συγγραμμάτων ἐξέθετο καὶ λόγον, ᾧ κλῆσις Πεντηκοντάδραχμος, ἐν ᾧ εἰσάγει τὸν Ἡρακλέα ἐντυγχάνοντα τῇ Ἀρετῇ καὶ Κακίᾳ. . . . For Prodikos' long period of activity (c. 450–395), see Guthrie, *HGP* III 274–275.

9. Diod. Sic. xii. 53. 2: οὗτος (sc. Γοργίας) καὶ τέχνας ῥητορικὰς πρῶτος ἐξεῦρε καὶ κατὰ σοφιστείαν τοσοῦτο τοὺς ἄλλους ὑπερέβαλλεν, ὥστε μισθὸν λαμβάνειν παρὰ τῶν μαθητῶν μνᾶς ἑκατόν; *Suda* γ 388 (Adler), Γοργίας: . . . ἔπραττε δὲ τῶν μαθητῶν ἕκαστον μνᾶς ρ´. I am inclined to accept the *Suda*'s interpretation of these as fees per *single* student, and assign this entry to "post-427?" on the (unprovable) assumption that the fees were charged after Gorgias' first visit to Athens in 427 (Diod. Sic. xii. 53. 1).

10. Ar. *Nub.* 874–876 (play produced in 423, Sokrates speaking):
πῶς ἂν μάθοι ποθ' οὗτος [sc. Φειδιππίδης] ἀπόφευξιν δίκης
ἢ κλῆσιν ἢ χαύνωσιν ἀναπειστηρίαν;
καίτοι ταλάντου τοῦτ' ἔμαθεν Ὑπέρβολος.

11. A.H. Sommerstein, *Aristophanes Clouds* (Warminster 1982) 203.

12. Phanias Eres. *FHG* II 299, fr. 21 ap. Diog. Laert. ii. 65: Ἀρίστιππος τὸ μὲν γένος ἦν Κυρηναῖος, ἀφιγμένος δ' Ἀθήναζε, καθά φησιν Αἰσχίνης, κατὰ κλέος Σωκράτους. οὗτος σοφισ-

more to extol Sokrates for his well known immunity from financial temptation than to report an actual offer, and I therefore am inclined to think that, although Aristippos probably could have afforded a 20 mn. gift (see ##22–23 below), he may not have actually sent it. In any event, it is a gift rather than a fee, so it tells us nothing about standard charges by professors of philosophy, rhetoric, etc.

9. 5th/4th c. "1 T. illnesses": weight or physician's fee for curing?[13] Like Pollux, we must remain uncertain as to the meaning of this partial line, but even if it does refer to physicians' fees for serious illnesses, in this comic context it doubtless was exaggerated.

10. 5th/4th c. "3 ob. fever": negligible value or physician's fee for curing?[14] Here the meaning really does seem to be that the fever was annoying but only worth "two bits."

11. 5th/4th c.? 3 ob. to common advocate.[15] Three obols seems a bit low for real advocates (cf. #7 above), and it probably demeans the quality of representation that Μέθη, in this comic setting, is likely to find.

12. pre-399. 5 mn. to Euenos of Paros for instruction (for one student, or for two?), paid by the "man who has spent more money on soph-

---

τεύσας, ὥς φησι Φανίας ὁ περιπατητικὸς ὁ Ἐρέσιος, πρῶτος τῶν Σωκρατικῶν μισθοὺς εἰσεπράξατο καὶ ἀπέστειλε χρήματα τῷ διδασκάλῳ. καί ποτε πέμψας αὐτῷ μνᾶς εἴκοσι παλινδρόμους ἔλαβεν, εἰπόντος Σωκράτους τὸ δαιμόνιον αὐτῷ μὴ ἐπιτρέπειν. If Aristippos was "a little older than Plato" (Guthrie, *HGP* III 491), i.e., if he was born c. 430, he probably did not come to Athens before c. 410, and he would have had to send his gift before Sokrates' death in 399. Hence my dates c. 410–399.

13. Alcaeus Com. fr. 12 (K-A) ap. Poll. ix. 53: τὸ δὲ ἐν ταῖς Κράτητος Τόλμαις . . . ταλαντιαῖος . . . ἄδηλον εἴτε τιμὴν εἴτε ῥοπὴν λέγει, ὥσπερ ὅταν Ἀλκαῖος ὁ κωμικὸς ἐν Ἐνδυμίωνι εἴπηι "νοσημάτων ταλαντιαίων." K-A quote their predecessors ad loc., Meineke ("dicit fortasse morbos pro quorum medela talentum medico numerandum erat") and Kock ("fortasse νοσημάτιον ταλαντιαῖον, i.e. veternus Endymionis, ad quem curandum Gorgias medicus arcessitus morbulum levem esse dicit, cuius curatio constet non plus talento"), and give "saec. V/IV" as Alkaios' floruit.

14. Nicophon fr. 20 (K-A):

ἐὰν δὲ γ' ἡμῶν σῦκά τις μεσημβρίας
τραγὼν καθεύδηι χλωρά, πυρετὸς εὐθέως
ἥκει τρέχων, οὐκ ἄξιος τριωβόλου·
κᾆιθ' οὗτος ἐπιπεσὼν ἐμεῖν ποιεῖ χολήν.

K-A give "saec. V/IV" as Nikophon's floruit.

15. Lucian *Bis Acc.* 15: Οὐκοῦν συνήγορον ἀναβιβασάσθω (sc. the defendant, ἡ Μέθη "Intemperance") τῶν κοινῶν τούτων τινά· πολλοὶ γὰρ οἱ κἂν ἐπὶ τριωβόλῳ διαρραγῆναι ἕτοιμοι. This (fictitious) trial before the Areiopagos seems to be set in the fifth or fourth century B.C.

ists than all others."[16] This is our first reliable figure, stated in (what purports to be) a lawcourt speech to a jury that would know whether it was credible, and it shows what a very rich man could and would spend for the best possible instruction for his sons. It may be that in the last decade of the fifth century, when wages (at least in the public sector) generally had fallen,[17] professors' fees also were slightly lower than they had been, or would be later (#19 below).

13. c. 390. 3–4 mn. to sophists for instruction (per student).[18] Since these figures appear in a speech "Against the Sophists," we might suspect that they have been exaggerated, but they do not seem wildly out of line with the 5 mn. in #12, and I therefore am inclined to accept them as amounts charged by "average" sophists.

14. 388. 3 T. to advocates for Ergokles.[19] The allegations in this speech and its companion (Lys. xxviii) are that Ergokles, allegedly once a "poor man," acquired "the largest fortune in the city," "more than 30 talents,"[20] by personally pocketing tribute-like contributions made by the cities of Asia Minor. If this were true, Ergokles would have had the means—and the incentive—to pay his lawyers 3 T., and in the circumstances this would be a credible fee. On the other hand, because the allegations of the 3 T. fee and 30 T. fortune give dramatic force to the prosecution's case, *both* may be exaggerated. Since the jury voted to impose the death penalty on Ergokles,[21] it evidently believed the gist of the prosecution's case. But even if Ergokles was guilty, we are not in a position

---

16. Pl. *Apol.* 20a–b (Sokrates speaking): ἔτυχον γὰρ προσελθὼν ἀνδρὶ ὅς τετέληκε χρήματα σοφισταῖς πλείω ἢ σύμπαντες οἱ ἄλλοι, Καλλίᾳ τῷ Ἱππονίκου· τοῦτον οὖν ἀνηρόμην—ἐστὸν γὰρ αὐτῷ δύο ὑεῖ—"Ὦ Καλλία, . . . τίνα αὐτοῖν ἐν νῷ ἔχεις ἐπιστάτην λαβεῖν; τίς τῆς τοιαύτης ἀρετῆς, τῆς ἀνθρωπίνης τε καὶ πολιτικῆς, ἐπιστήμων ἐστίν; οἶμαι γάρ σε ἐσκέφθαι διὰ τὴν τῶν ὑέων κτῆσιν. ἔστιν τις," ἔφην ἐγώ, "ἢ οὔ;" "Πάνυ γε," ἦ δ' ὅς. "Τίς," ἦν δ' ἐγώ, "καὶ ποδαπός, καὶ πόσου διδάσκει;" "Εὔηνος," ἔφη, "ὦ Σωκράτες, Πάριος, πέντε μνῶν."

17. See "Inflation and Deflation" pp. 240–241.

18. Isoc. xiii. 3: Οὗτοι τοίνυν εἰς τοῦτο τόλμης ἐληλύθασιν, ὥστε πειρῶνται πείθειν τοὺς νεωτέρους ὡς, ἢν αὐτοῖς πλησιάζωσιν, ἅ τε πρακτέον ἐστὶν εἴσονται καὶ διὰ ταύτης τῆς ἐπιστήμης εὐδαίμονες γενήσονται. καὶ τηλικούτων ἀγαθῶν αὐτοὺς διδασκάλους καὶ κυρίους καταστήσαντες οὐκ αἰσχύνονται τρεῖς ἢ τέτταρας μνᾶς ὑπὲρ τούτων αἰτοῦντες. For c. 390 as the date of this speech Κατὰ τῶν σοφιστῶν, see G. Mathieu and E. Brémond, *Isocrate Discours* I (Paris 1929) 139.

19. Lys. xxix. 6: Τίς δ' οὐκ οἶδεν Ἀθηναίων τρία τάλαντα περὶ Ἐργοκλέους μεσεγγυηθέντα τοῖς λέγουσιν, εἰ δύναιντο αὐτὸν σῶσαι; For this speech's date of 388, see L. Gernet and M. Bizos, *Lysias Discours* II (Paris 1926) 151.

20. Lys. xxviii. 2, 4; xxix. 2.

21. Lys. xxix. 2.

to know precisely how much he stole or how much he really paid his lawyers, and in any event their fee in this case would hardly be typical.

15. c. 373. 20 T. to Isokrates from Nikokles for speech.[22] Nikokles, as king of Cypriot Salamis, probably could have afforded 20 T., but we have no way of knowing whether Pliny or pseudo-Plutarch, writing more than 400 years after the event, got the figure right. In any event, it is hardly a typical figure for speech-writing, and more probably was a patronage gift.

16. c. 367–360. More than 80 T. to Plato from Dionysios (II) of Syracuse (in gratitude for prior instruction?).[23] The figures in this story (100 mn. for three books and more than 80 T. for Plato) both seem high. No doubt Dionysios, like Nikokles (#15), could have afforded the 80 T.+, but the actual figure may have been smaller, and in any event it seems to have been more of a patron's gift in gratitude for Plato's presence in Syracuse than a fee for instruction.

17. c. 366–364. 10,000 dr. to Isaios from Demosthenes for instruction in public speaking.[24] Although Demosthenes alleged that his father had left an estate of nearly 14 T.,[25] Davies has shown that he ended up with "something [more] in the region of 3 *tal.*"[26] (= 18,000 dr.), and thus he could not have afforded (before he even acquired the c. 18,000 dr.) to pay Isaios and Neoptolemos (#18) 10,000 dr. apiece. There are other indications that it would have been difficult for Demosthenes to pay even

---

22. Plin *N.H.* vii. 110: viginti talentis unam orationem Isocrates vendidit; [Plut.] *Mor.* 838a: εὐπόρησε (sc. Ἰσοκράτης) ⟨δ'⟩ ἱκανῶς οὐ μόνον ἀργύριον εἰσπράττων τοὺς γνωρίμους, ἀλλὰ καὶ παρὰ Νικοκλέους τοῦ Κυπρίων βασιλέως, ὃς ἦν υἱὸς Εὐαγόρου, εἴκοσι τάλαντα λαβὼν ὑπὲρ τοῦ πρὸς αὐτὸν γραφέντος λόγου. For the date of c. 373, see Davies, *APF* 246 ("soon after [the death of Evagoras in] 374/3").

23. Satyrus *FHG* III 163–164, fr. 16 ap. Diog. Laert. iii. 9: Λέγουσι δέ τινες, ὧν ἐστι καὶ Σάτυρος, ὅτι Δίωνι ἐπέστειλεν (sc. Πλάτων) εἰς Σικελίαν ὠνήσασθαι τρία βιβλία Πυθαγορικὰ παρὰ Φιλολάου μνῶν ἑκατόν. καὶ γὰρ ἐν εὐπορίᾳ, φασίν, ἦν παρὰ Διονυσίου λαβὼν ὑπὲρ τὰ ὀγδοήκοντα τάλαντα, ὡς καὶ Ὀνήτωρ φησὶν ἐν τῷ ἐπιγραφομένῳ "εἰ χρηματιεῖται ὁ σοφός." For the dates of Plato's second (c. 367–365) and third (c. 361–360) trips to Syracuse (then under Dionysios II, who [unlike his father, Dionysios I] cultivated Plato), see Guthrie, *HGP* IV 24–28.

24. [Plut.] *Mor.* 839f: καθηγήσατο (sc. Ἰσαῖος) δὲ Δημοσθένους, ἀποστὰς τῆς σχολῆς, ἐπὶ δραχμαῖς μυρίαις· διὸ καὶ μάλιστα ἐπιφανὴς ἐγένετο. Presumably, Demosthenes' rhetorical training took place in the interval between his attaining majority in c. 366 and the trial of his guardians in 364 (see Dem. xxx. 15, 17, and Davies, *APF* 125).

25. Dem. xxvii. 4, 9–11, 59; xxix. 59.

26. Davies, *APF* 133.

1,000 dr.[27] No doubt he paid Isaios a substantial fee, perhaps as much as Isokrates' standard 1,000 dr. (#19), but certainly not 10,000 dr.

18. c. 366–364. 10,000 dr. to actor Neoptolemos from Demosthenes for teaching him to speak whole paragraphs (periods) without taking a breath.[28] See #17 for the inability of Demosthenes to pay so high an amount.

19. c. 366–338. 10 mn. to Isokrates (usual fee for instruction in public speaking).[29] The allegation by Demosthenes that Lakritos paid this sum *could* be an exaggeration, designed to impugn his innate rhetorical abilities and suggest that he had paid a lot to learn how to "make the worse argument appear the better," and Demosthenes' figure could in turn be the source of the statements by Plutarch and pseudo-Plutarch that 10 mn. was Isokrates' regular fee. But since the figure itself does not seem wildly out of line with the well attested 5 mn. for pre-399 (#12 above), I am inclined to accept it.

20. c. 366–338. 10,000 mn. Isokrates would give this sum for instruction in self-confidence and a good voice.[30] The story indicates on its face that this amount never was intended to be paid.

---

27. Plut. *Demosth.* v. 6: ἐχρήσατο (sc. Δημοσθένης) δ' Ἰσαίῳ πρὸς τὸν λόγον ὑφηγητῇ, καίπερ Ἰσοκράτους τότε σχολάζοντος, εἴθ' ὥς τινες λέγουσι τὸν ὡρισμένον μισθὸν Ἰσοκράτει τελέσαι μὴ δυνάμενος τὰς δέκα μνᾶς δία τὴν ὀρφανίαν, εἴτε μᾶλλον τοῦ Ἰσαίου τὸν λόγον ὡς δραστήριον καὶ πανοῦργον εἰς τὴν χρείαν ἀποδεχόμενος; [Plut.] *Mor.* 837d–e: καὶ Δημοσθένη δ' ἔτι ῥητορεύοντί φασι μετὰ σπουδῆς προσελθεῖν αὐτῷ (sc. Ἰσοκράτει), καὶ χιλίας μὲν ἃς [μόνας] εἰσπράττετο οὐκ ἔχειν φάναι παρασχεῖν, διακοσίας δὲ ⟨μόνας⟩ δώσειν, ἐφ' ᾧ τε τὸ πέμπτον μέρος ἐκμαθεῖν· τὸν δ' ἀποκρίνασθαι ὡς "οὐ τεμαχίζομεν, ὦ Δημόσθενες, τὴν πραγματείαν· ὥσπερ δὲ τοὺς καλοὺς ἰχθῦς ὅλους πωλοῦσιν, οὕτω κἀγώ σοι, εἰ βούλοιο μαθητεύειν, ὁλόκληρον ἀποδώσομαι τὴν τέχνην."

28. [Plut.] *Mor.* 844d–f: λέγουσι. . . . τοῦ δὲ πνεύματος αὐτῷ (sc. Δημοσθένει) ἐνδέοντος Νεοπτολέμῳ τῷ ὑποκριτῇ μυρίας δοῦναι, ἵν' ὅλας περιόδους ἀπνεύστως λέγῃ. For the date, see n. 24 above.

29. Dem. xxxv. 15, 42: Λάκριτος Φασηλίτης, μέγα πρᾶγμα, Ἰσοκράτους μαθητής. . . . ἐπεὶ δ' οὖν δεινός ἐστιν (sc. Λάκριτος) καὶ πιστεύει τῷ λέγειν καὶ ταῖς χιλίαις δραχμαῖς αἷς δέδωκεν τῷ διδασκάλῳ (for the date of this speech in "c. 351?," see L. Gernet, *Démosthène Plaidoyers Civils* I [Paris 1954] 179); Plut. *Demosth.* v. 6 (quoted in n. 27 above); [Plut.] *Mor.* 837d–e (quoted in n. 27 above); [Plut.] *Mor.* 838e: εἰώθει (sc. Ἰσοκράτης) δὲ καὶ πρὸς τοὺς γνωρίμους αὐτοῦ λέγειν, ὡς αὐτὸς μὲν δέκα μνῶν διδάσκοι, τῷ δ' αὐτὸν διδάξοντι τόλμαν καὶ εὐφωνίαν δώσειν δεκακισχιλίας. Since the earliest reported potential payer of this amount is Demosthenes, and since Isokrates could have charged this amount until his death in 338, I date this entry c. 366–338.

30. [Plut.] *Mor.* 838e (quoted in n. 29). I assign #19's date also to this entry.

21. c. 365. 1 T. to Isokrates from Timotheos for writing letters to the Athenians.[31] From the spoils of Samos, Timotheos would have had the resources, and perhaps the incentive, to pay this amount, which (as 6,000 dr.) was six times Isokrates' standard fee for instruction (#19). It is difficult for us to judge whether Timotheos actually did give this amount, which in any event would have been an extraordinary reward—probably a patronage gift—for "public relations."

22. pre-360. 1 T. to Aristippos from one student for instruction in rhetoric and philosophy.[32] This figure, appearing in a comedy, is obviously an exaggeration, as #23 below makes clear.

23. pre-360. 500 or 1,000 dr.?, charged by Aristippos for instruction, per student.[33] Although these figures are credible in relation to the 10 mn. of #19, they appear in a story whose point is the value of a philosophical and rhetorical education in relation to the cost of a slave, so that the figures were not, perhaps, intended to be precise.

24. 335. 5 T. to Demades, from Demosthenes et al. to negotiate with Alexander for their safety.[34] Demosthenes et al. would have had the in-

---

31. [Plut.] *Mor.* 837c: ἀκροαταὶ δ' αὐτοῦ (sc. Ἰσοκράτους) ἐγένοντο εἰς ἑκατόν, ἄλλοι τε πολλοὶ καὶ Τιμόθεος ὁ Κόνωνος, σὺν ᾧ καὶ πολλὰς πόλεις ἐπῆλθε, συντιθεὶς τὰς πρὸς Ἀθηναίους ὑπὸ Τιμοθέου πεμπομένας ἐπιστολάς· ὅθεν ἐδωρήσατο αὐτῷ τάλαντον τῶν ἀπὸ Σάμου περιγενομένων. Since Timotheos captured Samos in 366/5 (Diod. Sic. xviii. 18. 9), I assign this gift to c. 365.

32. Alexis fr. 37 (K-A):

ὁ δεσπότης οὑμὸς περὶ λόγους γάρ ποτε
διέτριψε μειρακίσκος ὢν καὶ φιλοσοφεῖν
ἐπέθετο. Κυρηναῖος ἦν ἐνταῦθά τις,
ὥς φασ', Ἀρίστιππος, σοφιστὴς εὐφυής,
μᾶλλον δὲ πρωτεύων ἁπάντων ⟨τῶν⟩ τότε,
ἀκολαστίαι τε τῶν γεγονότων διαφέρων.
τούτωι τάλαντον δοὺς μαθητὴς γίγνεται
ὁ δεσπότης, καὶ τὴν τέχνην μὲν οὐ πάνυ
ἐξέμαθε, τὴν δ' ἀρτηρίαν συνήρπασεν.

Since Aristippos is said to have been still living in 366 (Diod. Sic. xv. 76. 4), I assign a date of pre-360 to this and the following entry.

33. Plut. *Mor.* 4f–5a: καὶ Ἀρίστιππος οὐκ ἀκόμψως ἀλλὰ καὶ πάνυ ἀστείως ἐπέσκωψε τῷ λόγῳ πατέρα νοῦ καὶ φρενῶν κενόν. ἐρωτήσαντος γάρ τινος αὐτὸν πόσον αἰτοίη μισθὸν ὑπὲρ τῆς τοῦ τέκνου παιδεύσεως, "χιλίας" ἔφησε "δραχμάς." τοῦ δ' "'Ηράκλεις" εἰπόντος, "ὡς ὑπέρπολυ τὸ αἴτημα· δὺναμαι γὰρ ἀνδράποδον χιλίων πρίασθαι" "τοιγαροῦν" εἶπε "δύο ἕξεις ἀνδράποδα, καὶ τὸν υἱὸν καὶ ὃν ἂν πρίῃ."; Diog. Laert. ii. 72: συνιστάντος τινὸς αὐτῷ υἱὸν ᾔτησε πεντακοσίας δραχμάς· τοῦ δ' εἰπόντος, "τοσούτου δύναμαι ἀνδράποδον ὠνήσασθαι," "πρίω," ἔφη, "καὶ ἕξεις δύο."

34. Diod. Sic. xvii. 15. 3–5: Ἐπὶ τελευτῆς δὲ Δημάδης, πεπεισμένος ὑπὸ τῶν περὶ Δημοσθένην, ὥς φασι, πέντε ταλάντοις ἀργυρίου, συνεβούλευε μὲν σώζειν τοὺς κινδυνεύοντας,

centive to pay this amount, but it is difficult for us to judge whether it really was so high, and in any event it would have been an extraordinary *fee*—the context and the use of the word πεπεισμένος with a sum of money suggest that it was in fact a *bribe*.

25. c. 335–323. 800 T. to Aristotle from Alexander for research on animals.[35] This amount, although within Alexander's means, seems enormous, more credible as a gift than a fee. Since it is attested only in a late source, and only as a λόγος, I am not inclined to place much reliance on it.

26. c. 335–323. 50 T. (or 30 gold T.?) sent to philosopher Xenokrates by Alexander, 30 mn. accepted.[36] The *Suda*'s 30 gold T. obvious-

---

παρανέγνω δὲ ψήφισμα γεγραμμένον φιλοτέχνως· περιεῖχε γὰρ παραίτησιν τῶν ἀνδρῶν καὶ ἐπαγγελίαν τοῦ κολάζειν κατὰ τοὺς νόμους, ἂν ὦσιν ἄξιοι τιμωρίας. ὁ μὲν οὖν δῆμος ἀποδεξάμενος τὴν ἐπίνοιαν τοῦ Δημάδου τό τε ψήφισμα ἐκύρωσε καὶ τὸν Δημάδην μεθ' ἑτέρων ἀπέστειλε πρεσβευτὴν πρὸς τὸν βασιλέα, δοὺς ἐντολὴν καὶ περὶ τῶν Θηβαίων φυγάδων ἀξιῶσαι τὸν 'Αλέξανδρον συγχωρῆσαι τῷ δήμῳ τοὺς πεφευγότας Θηβαίους ὑποδέχεσθαι. ὁ δὲ Δημάδης πρεσβεύσας καὶ τῇ τοῦ λόγου δεινότητι πάντα κατεργασάμενος ἔπεισε τὸν 'Αλέξανδρον ἀπολῦσαι τοὺς ἄνδρας τῶν ἐγκλημάτων καὶ τἄλλα πάντα συγχωρῆσαι τοῖς 'Αθηναίοις; Plut. *Demosth.* xxiii. 6: ὁ Δημάδης λαβὼν πέντε τάλαντα παρὰ τῶν ἀνδρῶν ὡμολόγησε πρεσβεύσειν καὶ δεήσεσθαι τοῦ βασιλέως ὑπὲρ αὐτῶν, εἴτε τῇ φιλίᾳ πιστεύων, εἴτε προσδοκῶν μεστὸν εὑρήσειν ὥσπερ λέοντα φόνου κεκορεσμένον. Diodoros' account appears under the archonship of Euainetos (33<u>5</u>/4).

35. Athen. ix. 58 (398e): νομίζων (sc. Λαρήνσιος) δὲ καὶ παρὰ τῷ πολυμαθεστάτῳ 'Αριστοτέλει μνήμης ἠξιῶσθαι τὸ ζῷον [sc. τόν τέτρακα (type of bird)] ἐν τῇ πολυταλάντῳ πραγματείᾳ (ὀκτακόσια γὰρ εἰληφέναι τάλαντα παρ' 'Αλεξάνδρου τὸν Σταγιρίτην λόγος ἔχει εἰς τὴν περὶ τῶν ζῴων ἱστορίαν) ὡς οὐδὲν εὗρον περὶ αὐτοῦ λεγόμενον, ἔχαιρον ἔχων ἐχεγγυώτατον μάρτυρα τὸν χαρίεντα 'Αριστοφάνη. I date this gift between the peace arranged in #24 and Alexander's death in 323.

36. Cic. *Tusc.* v. 91: Xenocrates, cum legati ab Alexandro quiquaginta ei talenta attulissent, quae erat pecunia temporibus illis, Athenis praesertim, maxima, abduxit legatos ad cenam in Academiam; iis apposuit tantum quod satis esset, nullo apparatu. Cum postridie rogarent eum cui numerari iuberet, "Quid? vos hesterna," inquit, "cenula non intellexistis me pecunia non egere?" Quos cum tristiores vidisset, triginta minas accepit, ne aspernari regis liberalitatem videretur; Val. Max. iv. 3. ext. 3: legatos ad eum [sc. Xenocratem] cum aliquot talentis miserat [sc. Alexander]. quos in academiam perductos solito sibi, id est modico, apparatu et admodum paruulis copiis excepit. postero die interrogantibus cuinam adnumerari pecuniam uellet, "quid? uos" inquit "hesterna cena non intellexistis ea me non indigere?" ita rex philosophi amicitiam emere uoluit, philosophus regi suam uendere noluit; Plut. *Alex.* viii. 5: ὁ μέντοι πρὸς φιλοσοφίαν ἐμπεφυκὼς καὶ συντεθραμμένος ἀπ' ἀρχῆς αὐτῷ (sc. 'Αλεξάνδρῳ) ζῆλος καὶ πόθος οὐκ ἐξερρύη τῆς ψυχῆς, ὡς ἡ περὶ 'Ανάξαρχόν τε τιμὴ καὶ τὰ πεμφθέντα Ξενοκράτει πεντήκοντα τάλαντα καὶ Δάνδαμις καὶ Καλανὸς οὕτω σπουδασθέντες μαρτυροῦσι; Plut. *Mor.* 181e: Ξενοκράτει δὲ τῷ φιλοσόφῳ πεντήκοντα τάλαντα πέμψας (sc. 'Αλέξανδρος), ὡς οὐκ ἐδέξατο μὴ δεῖσθαι φήσας, ἠρώτησεν εἰ μηδὲ φίλον ἔχει Ξενοκράτης· "ἐμοὶ μὲν γάρ" ἔφη "μόλις ὁ Δαρείου πλοῦτος εἰς τοὺς φίλους ἤρκεσεν"; Plut. *Mor.* 331e: Ξενοκράτει δὲ τῷ Πλάτωνος συνήθει πεντήκοντα τάλαντα δωρεὰν ἔπεμψεν (sc. 'Αλέξανδρος); Plut. *Mor.* 333b: Ξενοκράτην, πεντήκοντα τάλαντα δωρεὰν 'Αλεξάνδρου πέμψαντος, ὅτι οὐχ ἔλαβε θαυμάζομεν; Themistius xxi. 252a: πότε χρημάτων

ly is a mistake for the 50 T. attested by all of the earlier sources (except for Valerius Maximus' "aliquot talentis"). Again, 50 T. could have been paid by Alexander, but the point of this story, like that in #8, seems to be Xenokrates' immunity from financial temptation, so *any* large sum would suffice for purposes of the story. In any event, it is more in the nature of a patronage gift than a fee, and thus tells us nothing about stan-dard fees at this time.

27. pre-322. Arbitrator paid 1 dr. (a) as a deposit by prosecuting party and (b) by party seeking (for reasons sworn to under oath) to postpone arbitrator's judgment. As discussed in greater detail under "Public Officeholders" #31, this figure, which is plausible on its face, is supported by a variety of contemporary and later sources.

28. c. 307–270. 120 dr. p.a. to Epicurus from each (student?).[37] The context for this figure is too brief for us to determine the status of the payers or the precise consideration for their payment.

29. c. 300–250. 7 dr. to "philosopher" (i.e., actor) hired for one show. As discussed in greater detail under "Actors, Artists, Musicians and Writers" #20, this figure (in Lucian *Icar.* 29) obviously has nothing to do with philosophers.

30. c. 285. 1 mn. to Hippomachos the gymnastic trainer, for course?[38] Gow summarizes: "Gnathaena said that the mina was not, as it might be to an athletic trainer, a subscription for a course. The def. art.

διδομένων κρείττων ἐφάνης, ὥσπερ Ξενοκράτης ἐκεῖνος τῶν πεντήκοντα παρ' Ἀλεξάνδρου ταλάντων; *Suda* ξ 42 (Adler), Ξενοκράτης: . . . καὶ πέμψαντος αὐτῷ τοῦ Μακεδόνος Ἀλεξάνδρου χρυσοῦ τάλαντα λ´, αὐτὸς ἀπέπεμψεν, εἰπών, βασιλέα δεῖσθαι χρημάτων, οὐ φιλόσοφον. Like Alexander's gift to Aristotle (#25), I date this gift between the peace arranged in #24 and Alexander's death in 323.

37. Epicurus *Ep.* fr. 121. 3–9 (Arrighetti):

[. . . ἣν οὖ]ν ἔταξα τιμὴ[ν]
ἐμαυτῶ[ι] κἂν ἐν Ὑπερβο[ρ]είοις ὦ-
σιν ἀποστέλλ[ε]ιν, ταύτην καὶ
ὑμῖν συντάττω· [ἑ]κατὸν γὰρ
καὶ εἴκοσι [δ]ρ[αχ]μὰ[ς μόν]ας κα-
τ' ἐνιαυτὸν βούλομα[ι] παρ' ἑκα-
τέρου λαμβάνειν.

For Epicurus' residence in Athens c. 307–270, see D. J. Furley, "Epicurus." *OCD* 532–534 at 533.

38. Lynceus ap. Athen. xiii. 47 (584c): ὡς δ' ὁ τὴν μνᾶν τῇ θυγατρὶ δοὺς αὐτῆς οὐδὲν ἔτι ἔφερεν, ἀλλ' ἐφοίτα μόνον, "παιδίον," ἔφη (sc. Γνάθαινα), "ὥσπερ πρὸς Ἱππόμαχον τὸν παιδοτρίβην μνᾶν δοὺς οἴει αἰεὶ φοιτήσειν;" Gow, *Machon* 9, places Gnathaina's birth c. 330 and floruit c. 310. That suggests that her daughter's corresponding dates might be 25 years later: birth c. 305, floruit c. 285. For more on this passage, see "Prostitutes and Pimps" #41.

τὴν μνᾶν suggests that it was, at any rate at some period of Gnathaenium's life, a standard fee."[39] But it is not clear that Hippomachos' fee for his course would have been the same as Gnathainion's for one night!

31. c. 270–226. 9 ob. p.m. tuition at Lyceum under Lykon (inadequate for extravagant entertainment costs).[40] This figure seems very low, unrealistically so, and perhaps it was created to dramatize the misfortune of the older students who had to pay entertainment costs that vastly exceeded these 9 ob. contributions.

32. c. 232–207. 1 T.: for this a sophist will even turn three somersaults.[41] This obviously is intended as a joke.

33. c. 160–152. 1 mn. customary fee of teachers of Stoic dialectic.[42] This fee seems reasonable, and Cicero was close enough to the period that some reliance can be placed on his testimony. Since it would take more than one lesson to learn dialectic, the fee certainly was for a course. This figure may indicate that professors' fees had dropped from their fourth-century levels (cf. ##12, 13, 19, 23).

---

39. Gow, *Machon* 120.

40. Antigonus Carystius ap. Athen. xii. 69 (547d–f): καὶ Λύκων δὲ ὁ περιπατητικός, ὥς φησιν Ἀντίγονος ὁ Καρύστιος. . . . ὕστερον δὲ καὶ τοῦ περιπάτου προστὰς ἐδείπνιζε τοὺς φίλους ἀλαζονείᾳ καὶ πολυτελείᾳ πολλῇ χρώμενος. χωρὶς γὰρ τῶν παραλαμβανομένων εἰς αὐτὰ ἀκροαμάτων καὶ αργυρωμάτων καὶ στρωμνῆς ἡ λοιπὴ παρασκευὴ καὶ ἡ τῶν δείπνων περιεργία καὶ ὁ τῶν τραπεζοποιῶν καὶ μαγείρων ὄχλος τοσοῦτος ἦν ὥστε πολλοὺς ὀρρωδεῖν καὶ βουλομένους προιέναι πρὸς τὴν διατριβὴν ἀνακόπτεσθαι, [καὶ] καθάπερ εἰς πολίτευμα πονηρὸν καὶ χορηγιῶν καὶ λειτουργιῶν πλῆρες εὐλαβουμένους προσάγειν. ἔδει γὰρ ἄρξαι τε τὴν νομιζομένην ἐν τῷ περιπάτῳ ἀρχὴν (αὕτη δ' ἦν ἐπὶ τῆς εὐκοσμίας τῶν ἐπιχειρούντων) τριάκονθ' ἡμέρας, εἶτα τῇ ἕνῃ καὶ νέᾳ λαβόντα ἀφ' ἑκάστου τῶν ἐπιχειρούντων ἐννέα ὀβολοὺς ὑποδέξασθαι μὴ μόνον αὐτοὺς τοὺς τὴν συμβολὴν εἰσενεγκόντας, ἀλλὰ καὶ οὓς παρακαλέσειεν ὁ Λύκων, ἔτι δὲ καὶ τοὺς ἐπιμελῶς συναντῶντας τῶν πρεσβυτέρων εἰς τὴν σχολήν, ὥστε γίνεσθαι μηδὲ εἰς τὸν μυρισμὸν καὶ τοὺς στεφάνους ἱκανὸν τὸ ἐκλεγόμενον ἀργύριον. For Lykon's headship of the Lyceum for 44 years until his death in c. 226 (hence my date c. 270–226), see J. Glucker and R. W. Sharples, "Lyco," *OCD* 895.

41. Chrysippus *SVF* III fr. 688 ap. Plut. *Mor.* 1047f: καὶ τὸν μὲν σοφὸν ἐν τοῖς περὶ Βίων καὶ βασιλεῦσι συνέσεσθαί φησιν ἕνεκα χρηματισμοῦ καὶ σοφιστεύσειν ἐπ' ἀργυρίῳ, παρ' ὧν μὲν προλαμβάνοντα πρὸς οὓς δὲ συντιθέμενον τῶν μαθητῶν, ἐν δὲ τῷ ἑβδόμῳ ⟨περὶ⟩ τοῦ Καθήκοντος καὶ κυβιστήσειν τρὶς ἐπὶ τούτῳ λαβόντα τάλαντον. For Chrysippos' assumption of the headship of the Stoa in 232 and his death in 207, see J. Annas, "Chrysippus," *OCD* 329.

42. Cic. *Acad.* ii. 98: sic ludere Carneades solebat: "Si recte conclusi, teneo; sin uitiose, minam Diogenes reddet"; ab eo enim Stoico dialecticam didicerat, haec autem merces erat dialecticorum. J. Annas, "Diogenes (3)," *OCD* 474, gives Diogenes' dates as c. 240–152. G. Striker, "Carneades," *OCD* 293–294, gives Carneades' dates as 214/3–129/8, with his headship of the Academy "some time before 155" to 137/6. Accordingly, I assign a date of c. 160–152 to this entry.

34. A.D. 2nd c. 2 ob.–2 T. for various philosophies or philosophers (Cynic 2 ob., Sceptic 1 mn., Epicurean 2 mn., Pythagorean 10 mn., Stoic 12 mn., Peripatetic 20 mn., Academic 2 T.).[43] These figures are all obviously intended as jokes.

35. A.D. 2nd c. 2 mn. proposed for every self-proclaimed philosopher, 2 T. claimed by Academic.[44] These figures also are obviously not intended to be taken seriously.

36. A.D. late 2nd c. 1 T. (p.a.?) to Apollonios for chair of political oratory.[45] In the absence of much other information about Athenian wages and prices at this period, or the number of students Apollonios had, it is difficult to evaluate this figure, which (coming from a contemporary source) could be plausible.

37. c. A.D. 190–230. 100 dr. to Proklos for lectures for all time, per auditor.[46] This could be plausible, for the reasons stated under #36.

---

43. Lucian *Vit. Auct.* (Ἀγοραστής and Ἑρμῆς)—6: Ἀγ. πόσου τοῦτον (sc. Πυθαγόραν) ἀποκηρύττεις; Ἑρ. Δέκα μνῶν. Ἀγ. Ἔχω τοσούτου λαβών; 11: Ἀγ. ναύτης δ' ἂν ἴσως ἢ κηπουρὸς ἐν καιρῷ γένοιο (sc. Διογένης), καὶ ταῦτα, ἢν ἐθέλῃ σε ἀποδόσθαι οὑτοσὶ τὸ μέγιστον δύ' ὀβολῶν. Ἑρ. Ἔχε λαβών; 18: Ἀγ. φέρε ἴδω τί καὶ πράξεις με ὑπὲρ αὐτοῦ (sc. Σωκράτους) σύ; Ἑρ. Δύο τάλαντα. Ἀγ. Ὠησάμην ὅσου φῄς; 19: Ἀγ. Τίς ἡ τιμή (sc. τοῦ Ἐπικουρείου); Ἑρ. Δύο μναῖ. Ἀγ. Λάμβανε; 25: Ἀγ. πόσον ὑπὲρ αὐτοῦ (sc. Χρυσίππου) καταβαλῶ; Ἑρ. Μνᾶς δώδεκα. Ἀγ. Λάμβανε; 26: Ἀγ. πόσου δέ ἐστιν (sc. ὁ Περιπατητικός); Ἑρ. Εἴκοσι μνῶν; 27: Ἀγ. πόσου τοῦτον (sc. τὸν Σκεπτικὸν) ἄξιον χρὴ φάναι; Ἑρ. Μνᾶς Ἀττικῆς; Lucian *Pisc.* 15 (Plato to Παρρησιάδης "Frankness"): πρῴην δὲ τὸ ἀτιμότατον Φιλοσοφίαν ἀπέφαινες ἐν τοσούτῳ θεάτρῳ ἀποκηρύττων κατὰ μέρη δύ' ὀβολῶν ἕκαστον εἶδος αὐτῆς τῶν λόγων; 23 (Diogenes speaking): καὶ ἄλλως ὑπὲρ ἅπαντας ὕβρισμαι δύ' ὀβολῶν πρῴην ἀποκεκηρυγμένος; 27 (Diogenes speaking): ὃς (sc. Παρρησιάδης) καθάπερ τὰ ἀνδράποδα παραγαγὼν ἡμᾶς ἐπὶ τὸ πωλητήριον καὶ κήρυκα ἐπιστήσας ἀπημπόλησεν, ὥς φασιν, τοὺς μὲν ἐπὶ πολλῷ, ἐνίους δὲ μνᾶς Ἀττικῆς, ἐμὲ δὲ ὁ παμπονηρότατος οὗτος δύ' ὀβολῶν; 48 (Παρρησιάδης speaking): πόσου ἄξιον αὐτὸν (sc. Κυνικὸν) χρὴ φάναι; ἐγὼ μὲν γὰρ δύ' ὀβολῶν πρῴην αὐτὸν ἐτιμησάμην. It is not certain that this entry or #35 are set in Athens (as distinct from some other part of the Roman Empire).

44. Lucian *Pisc.* 41–43 (Παρρησιάδης, Φιλοσοφία and Ἀκαδημικός): Πα. Ἄκουε, σίγα. ὅσοι φιλόσοφοι εἶναι λέγουσιν καὶ ὅσοι προσήκειν αὐτοῖς οἴονται τοῦ ὀνόματος, ἥκειν εἰς ἀκρόπολιν ἐπὶ τὴν διανομήν. δύο μναῖ ἑκάστῳ δοθήσονται καὶ σησαμαῖος πλακοῦς. . . . Φι. Βαβαί, ὅσοι· πλήρης μὲν ἡ ἄνοδος ὠθιζομένων ἐπὶ τὰς δύο μνᾶς, ὡς ἤκουσαν μόνον. . . . Ἀκ. Ποῦ τὰ δύο τάλαντα;

45. Philostr. *V.S.* 600: ὁ δὲ Ἀπολλώνιος ὁ Ἀθηναίος ὀνόματος μὲν ἠξιώθη καθ' Ἕλληνας, ὡς ἱκανὸς τὰ δικανικὰ καὶ τὰ ἀμφὶ μελέτην οὐ μεμπτός, ἐπαίδευσε δὲ Ἀθήνησι καθ' Ἡρακλείδην τε καὶ τὸν ὁμώνυμον τοῦ πολιτικοῦ θρόνου προεστὼς ἐπὶ ταλάντῳ. For the date, see [author unstated], "Apollonios (88)," *RE* 2 (1896) 144.

46. Philostr. *V.S.* 604: Τὰ δὲ τῆς μελέτης πάτρια τῷ ἀνδρὶ τούτῳ (sc. Πρόκλῳ) διέκειτο ὧδε· ἑκατὸν δραχμὰς ἅπαξ καταβαλόντι ἐξῆν ἀκροᾶσθαι τὸν ἀεὶ χρόνον. For the date, see R. Hanslik, "Proklos (1)," *RE* 23 (1957) 183.

As a whole, what can be said about these figures? The most useful way of sorting them is to look at them by category:

(a) For doctors, we have only three figures (##1, 9 and 10), and the first seems to be a fairy-tale exaggeration while the last two are, on their faces, jokes. So we are left with the dismal conclusion that we have *no* reliable figures for doctors.

(b) For lawyers, we have a few more figures (##7, 11, 14, 15, 21, 24 and 27). #7 (1 dr. for a public prosecutor) and #27 (1 dr. for an arbitrator) both seem plausible, while #11 (3 ob. for a common advocate) probably suffers from comic deflation. The other figures (3 T. from Ergokles [#14], 20 T. from Nikokles [#15, probably a gift], 1 T. from Timotheos [#21, also probably a gift], and 5 T. from Demosthenes et al. [#24, probably a bribe]) are all immense, but in each case affordable by the client, and for Ergokles and Demosthenes the services rendered (saving their lives) would have been worth the sum paid. I am inclined, therefore, to regard all of these figures with caution: they are possible, even plausible, but unverifiable—and certainly not typical.

(c) For professors, we have the most figures (##2–6, 8, 12–13, 16–20, 22–23, 25–26, 28–37). Of these, some were clearly jokes or otherwise not intended to be taken seriously (##6, 20, 22, 32, 34 and 35). One, on closer inspection, has nothing to do with professors (#29), and another lacks sufficient context to be used with confidence (#28). Others are almost certainly exaggerations in a later period of sums paid to or by legendary figures (##2, 3, 5, 17 and 18). Four others, while possible, seem to be careless background for a story whose point was not to convey precise monetary figures, at least about professors (##8, 23, 30 and 31). Some are more in the nature of gifts by grateful patrons or students, and thus give no indication of standard fees (##8, 16, 25 and 26). That leaves us with a very few professors' fees that may be taken seriously (##4, 12, 13, 19, 33, 36, 37, and possibly 23): 1/2 to 50 dr. in the fifth century (#4), 500 dr. about 400 (#12), 300 to 400 dr. in c. 390 (#13), 500–1,000 dr. in the mid-fourth century (##19 and 23), 100 dr. in the second century (#33), and still 100 dr. in the second century A.D. (per student [#37], with 6,000 dr. being paid to a professor [#36] by or for an unstated number of students)—and all of these post-fourth-century figures are difficult to evaluate because of the paucity of other figures for these later periods. The earlier figures are consistent with the general rise in wages from the fifth to the fourth centuries that we observe elsewhere,[47] but since we are dealing here with exceptional individuals, the figures themselves may be exceptional (except #13), and we therefore should be slow to draw general conclusions that are not supported by figures from other categories.

47. See "Inflation and Deflation" pp. 241–242.

Chapter 4

Priests, Oracles and Seers

Collected here are amounts paid to priests, oracles and seers, including emoluments (variously called ἀπόμετρα or ἱερ[ει]ώσυνα) paid in money, but excluding those that consist of choice portions of sacrificial victims and other offerings; sums appropriated for sacrifices and religious charges (to persons making a sacrifice, etc.) are excluded except where (as in #19) they arguably comprised part of a priest's ἱερ(ει)ώσυνα. This category seems never to have been discussed before, not even by Böckh.

1. 450–430. (a) 3 ob. ἀπόμετρα and (b) [4 dr.?] hιερ[ε]όσ[υνα] for Paiania deme (priest or priestess?).[1] Although, in this sacred calendar of the deme Paiania, most of the ἀπόμετρα consist of portions of the sacrificial victim, in A. 28 and B. 32 there are cash ἀπόμετρα of 3 ob. In B. 22, the text is very poorly preserved: the 12 dr. seem to be the cost of an adult victim, but the restoration of [4 dr.?] for ḥι̣ε̣ρ[ε]ọσ̣[υνα] is entirely speculative.

2. c. 448. 50 dr. (p.a.) for priestess of Athena Nike.[2] In the absence of a label like ἀπόμετρα, hιερεόσυνα or μισθός, we should probably take this as general compensation for the year (see n. 7 below).

---

1. *IG* I^3 250 A. 26–28, B. 21–22, 31–32:

ἐς τὸ Ἐλευσίνιον ⁝ Χλοα-
ῖα χοίρο ἄρρεν καὶ θέλει- A. 27
α ⁝ ἀπόμετρα ⁝ τρε͂ς ⁝ |||^{vv}

τέ | λ̣εον
Δ̣⊢̣⊢̣ ḥι̣ε̣ρ[ε]ọ́σ̣[υνα ⊢⊢⊢⊢ ?] B. 22

Χλοα̣[ῖα χοί]ρọ θέ̣λεια ⁝ ἄρρε-
ν ⁝ ἀπό[με]τρα ⁝ τρε̣͂ς ⁝ |||^{vvv} B. 32

In B. 21–22, all letters except for λ̣εον are in a rasura.

2. *IG* I^3 35. 3–12:

[τε͂ι]
['Αθεναίαι τε͂ι Νί]κ̣ει hιέρεαν hὲ ἂγ̣ [κλ]-

3. c. 440–430? 1 dr. lunch for Thorikos deme (priest or guard?, and attendants?), apiece.[3] As shown in n. 3, the interpretation of this fragmentary inscription is very uncertain.

4. c. 440–430 or c. 400–375? [1 dr.] p.d. for polis priest ἐς σιτία.[4] The 1 dr. p.d. restoration fits well with the later date but seems a bit high for the mid fifth century, when we might expect something closer to 4 ob. p.d.[5] Because of the double uncertainties about the date and figure, I am not inclined to place much reliance on this figure.

[εpομένε λάχε]ι ἐχς 'Αθεναίον hαπα[σο͂]-
[ν καθίστα]σθαι καὶ τὸ hιερὸν θυρο͂σα-
ι καθ' ὅ τι ἂν Καλλικράτες χσυγγράφσ-
ει· ἀπομισθο͂σαι δὲ τὸς πολετὰς ἐπὶ τ-
ε͂ς Λεοντίδος πρυτανείας. φέρεν δὲ τ-
ὲν hιέρεαν πεντέκοντα δραχμὰς καὶ
τὰ σκέλε καὶ τὰ δέρματα φέρεν το͂ν δε-
μοσίον·

I accept the Corpus date, which was based on letter forms and later was strengthened by the argument that they were inscribed by the same hand as the Athena Promachos accounts (*IG* I^3 435), "which must belong to the 450s" (M-L 311, citing S. V. Tracy, "Hands in Fifth-Century B.C. Attic Inscriptions," in *Studies Presented to Sterling Dow on His Eightieth Birthday* [*Greek, Roman and Byzantine* Monograph 10] [Durham, North Carolina 1984] 277–282 at 281–282). Cf. H. B. Mattingly, *The Athenian Empire Restored: Epigraphic and Historical Studies* (Ann Arbor 1996) 522: the date might be "twenty years later."

3. *IG* I^3 256 bis (= *SEG* XXXIII 147). 1–5:

[. . . . . .19. . . . . 'Εκ]ατομβαιῶν-
[ος . . . . .19. . . . .]ΑΚΙ καὶ τοῖ-
[ς . . . . .18. . . . . ἄ]ριστομ παρέ-
[χεν . . . . . . .14. . . . . . . δρα]χμὴν ἑκατερ̣-
[ο. . . . . .19. . . . .]

For the date, see *IG* I^3 256 bis (p. 958). In lines 2–3, Daux (see *SEG* XXXIII 147, p. 44) tentatively suggested the restoration [τῶι φύλ]ακι καὶ τοῖ[ς ἀκολούθοις αὐτο͂ πᾶσι ἄ]ριστομ. As Whitehead observes (*Demes* 194, n. 101), "the connection, if any, between the latter clause and δρα]χμὴν ἑκατερ[ο or ω (lines 4–5) is not clear."

4. *IG* I^3 48 bis. 3–7:

τ⟨ὸ⟩ν ἄνδρα ε͂ναι ἱερ - - - - c. 11–12 - - - -
καὶ λητοργε͂ν τῆι θεῶι ὅ τι ἂν ἡ πόλι[ς κελεύηι - - c. 6–7 - -]
εχεται καὶ ⟨λ⟩ίθο καὶ ξύλο· καὶ οἴκησιν δ[οναι καὶ δραχμὴν τῆ]-
ς ἡμέρας ἐς σιτία· τὸ δὲ ἀργύριον διδό[ναι τὸς ταμίας ἀπὸ το͂]
τῆς θεο͂ ἀργυρίο·

Of line 6, Lewis reported: "suppl. ed. dubitanter." He dated the inscription on its letter forms to c. 440–430, in disagreement with the date in the first quarter of the fourth century proposed by the original editor, D. Peppa-Delmousou, "Χαλκῆ ἐπιγραφὴ τοῦ Μουσείου 'Ακροπόλεως," *AE* (1971) 137–145.

5. See "Inflation and Deflation" p. 240.

5. c. 430. Payments for local (trittys?) cults: (a) 10 dr. ἀπόμετρα, (b) 1 dr. for priestess?, (c) 1 dr. for (priest or priestess?).[6] As shown in n. 6, the last two figures are uncertain.

6. 424/3. 50 dr. (p.a.) for priestess of Athena Nike.[7] As with #2, this probably is general compensation for the year.

7. 422. 2 ob. (p.d.?) for dream interpreter.[8] MacDowell comments on the two obols: "the normal minimum payment for any small service

---

6. *IG* I^3 255 B. 10–13, 20–23:

- - - - - - - - - - - - - - - - ṭαι ἐς ἀπόμετρα ⁝ Δ ᵛ
- - - - - - - - - - - - - - - - - - ας hιέρεια λαμβα-
[νέτο - - - - - - - - - - - -]αι ⁝ ⊦ ⁝ κατὰ τὸ hιερọ-
[ν hέκαστον · - - - - - - - - - -]

[- - - - - - - - - - - λαμβα]νέτο καθάπερ ἑ τες 'Αρτέ-
[μιδος - - - - - - - - - - - λα]μβανέτο τῦν δεμοσίον h-
[- - - - - - - - - - - - - - - -] ⁝ ⊦ ⁝ κατὰ τὸ hιερὸν ἕκασ-
[τον · -]

The Corpus editor, M. H. Jameson, reported: "Ad cultus trittyis cuiusdam rettulit Wilhelm, quem plerique secuti sunt." It is not certain that the ⊦ in line 12 goes with the priestess in line 11, or that the ⊦ in line 22 goes with λαμβανέτο in line 21 or (if it does) who the subject is of λαμβανέτο.

7. *IG* I^3 36. 4–11:

. . . τ-
ε͂ι hιερέαι τε͂ς 'Αθενάας τε͂ς Νί-
κες ᵛ πεντήκοντα δραχμὰς τὰ-
ς γεγραμμένας ἐν τῆι στήλ[ηι]
ἀποδιδόναι τὸς κωλακρ[έτας],
[ο]ἳ ἂν κωλακρετῶσι τõ Θ̣[αργηλ]-
[ιῶ]νος μηνός, τῆι ἱερ[έαι τῆς 'Α]-
[θην]αίας τῆς Νίκη[ς . . . .⁸. . . .]

This text is inscribed on the opposite side of the stele which carries the inscription quoted in n. 2. Because the payments in this later inscription are to be made in Thargelion, I assume that that means once per year, and that the earlier payments (τὰς γεγραμμένας ἐν τῆι στήλ[ηι]) also had been made once per year.

8. Ar. *Vesp.* 42–53 (slave Sosias recounts dream to slave Xanthias):

Σω. ἐδόκει δέ μοι Θέωρος αὐτῆς πλησίον
χαμαὶ καθῆσαι, τὴν κεφαλὴν κόρακος ἔχων.
εἶτ' 'Αλκιβιάδης εἶπε πρός με τραυλίσας·
"ὁλᾷς; Θέωλος τὴν κεφαλὴν κόλακος ἔχει."
Ξα. ὀρθῶς γε τοῦτ' 'Αλκιβιάδης ἐτραύλισεν.
Σω. οὔκουν ἐκεῖν' ἀλλόκοτον, ὁ Θέωρος κόραξ
γενόμενος;
Ξα. ἥκιστ', ἀλλ' ἄριστον.
Σω. πῶς;
Ξα. ὅπως;
ἄνθρωπος ὢν εἶτ' ἐγένετ' ἐξαίφνης κόραξ·
οὔκουν ἐναργὲς τοὔτο συμβαλεῖν, ὅτι
ἀρθεὶς ἀφ' ἡμῶν ἐς κόρακας οἰχήσεται;

in Athens; cf. *Frogs* 140–2 [Charon's fee for transport across Acheron]."[9] Sommerstein adds: "per day, presumably; hardly a living wage, but a professional interpreter of dreams might well be contracted to several employers simultaneously, though a rich man like Nicias or Alcibiades (Plut. *Nic.* 4.2., 13.1) might retain the exclusive services of one or more seers or soothsayers."[10] MacDowell and Sommerstein may possibly be right in seeing the 2 ob. as an accurate "background fact"—what a dream interpreter normally would earn: certainly the 2 ob. is not out of line with the 3 ob. p.d. for dikasts or 1 dr. p.d. for soldiers and sailors in this period.[11] But in the absence of other, more reliable, figures for dream interpreters, we should be slow to accept this one uncritically.

8. 408/7. 3 dr. 3 ob. (inc.) for Eumolpids (for Eleusinian mysteries).[12] In this context (of miscellaneous expenses for the Eleusinian Mysteries), it is impossible to tell whether the figure is for emoluments or expenses, and in any event it is incomplete.

9. c. 403–399. Polis sacred calendar figures: ἀπόμετρα of (a) 100 dr. for priestess of Demeter and (b) 10 dr. for priestess of Athena Polias, ἱερεώσυνα of (c) 16 dr. and (d) 4 dr. 2 ob. for tribal (priests or priestesses?) and (e) 2 ob. (inc.) for (priest of?) Hermes in Lykeion.[13]

Σω. εἶτ' οὐκ ἐγὼ δοὺς δύ' ὀβολὼ μισθώσομαι
οὕτως ὑποκρινόμενον σοφῶς ὀνείρατα;

9. D. M. MacDowell, *Aristophanes Wasps* (Oxford 1971) 134–135. In fact, Charon's charge normally was said to be 1 ob. (see "Transport Costs" #3), so the *Frogs* passage is a clear example of comic exaggeration. In any event, the standard (mythological) charge for a ferry ride to Hades is not good evidence for the (real-life) charges for small services in Athens.

10. A. H. Sommerstein, *Aristophanes Wasps* (Warminster 1983) 156.

11. "Public Officeholders" #11; "Soldiers and Sailors" ##4–5, 12–13.

12. *IG* I^3 386. 161–164:

- -ΔΔ _σανίδια ἐν ο[ἶ]ς τὸς μύστας κ[αταγ]ράφ[οσι]
- -⊦⊦⊦III_Εὐμολπίδαις 162
⊦⊦ ἐφ' ἱερᾶι συκε̂ι κέραμον
_σκε[υά]ντι

13. *IG* II^2 1357 b. 1–6 + *Hesperia* 4 (1935) 19, no. 2. 30–39, 44–52, 75–76 (lines 75–76 = *SEG* XL 146. 258–259; all lines are part of a single inscription):

ἱερέαι 'Αθηναί-
ας Πολιάδος
Δ ___ἀπόμετρα
'Ερμῆι ἐλ Λυκείο
⊦/// οἶς
/// II ___ἱερεώσυνα

The 100 dr. for the priestess of Demeter is substantial, both in relation to the other figures and to the 50 dr. for the priestess of Athena Nike (##2 and 6 above), and it indicates the importance that the polis attached to the Eleusinian cult.

10. early 4th c. (a) 5 dr. for ἱερεώσυνα and (b) 3 dr. in lieu of skin of singed sacrificial victims, in each case for various local (deme or tribe?) priestesses.[14]

Τάδε τὸ ἕτερον ἔτος θύεται Ἀ[θήνησιν]
Ἑκατομβαιῶνος
πέμπτηι ἐπὶ δέκα
ἐκ τῶν φυλο-
βασιλικῶν
Γλεόντων φυλῆι
Λευκοταινίων
τριττύϊ οἶν
⊦⊦⊦⊦ λειπογνώμονα
⊦⊦⊦⊦ΙΙ ἱερεώ[σ]υνα

ἕκτηι ἐπὶ δέκα
ἐκ τῶν φυλο-
βασιλικῶν
Γλεόντων φυλῆι
Διὶ Φρατρίωι καὶ
Ἀθηναίαι Φρα-
τρίαι βόε δύο
𐅄 [λ]ειπογνώμονε
:ΔΠ⊦ ἱερεώσυνα

ἱερέα[ι Δήμητρος]
Η ἀπόμ̣[ετρα]

14. *IG* II^2 1356. 2–24 (labeled by Kirchner "Lex demi vel tribus de eis quae sacerdotibus tribuenda sunt"):

[.........18......... πυρῶν ἡμιέκτε]ω : ΙΙΙ : μέ[λι]τος [κοτ]-
[ύλης : ΙΙΙ : ἐλαίο τριῶν κοτυλ]ῶ[ν : ΙC : φ]ρυγάνων : ΙΙ : ἐπὶ δὲ τ[ὴν]
[τράπεζα]ν κω[λῆν, πλευρὸν] ἰσχίο, ἡμίκραιραν χορδῆ-
[ς· ᵛ Ἡρώ]ινης ἱε[ρείαι ἱερε]ώσυνα :Π:, τὰ δέρματα ἐκ τῶν
[Ἡρ]ωινίων?, ἅπαν[τος εὐστō] τελέο : ⊦⊦⊦ :, δεισίας κρεῶν,
πυρῶν ἡμιέκτεω [: ΙΙΙ : μέλιτο]ς κοτύλης : ΙΙΙ : ἐλαίο τριῶν κ-
οτυλῶν : ΙC : φρυγάνω[ν : ΙΙ : ἐπὶ δὲ] τὴν τράπεζαν κ[ω]λῆν, πλε-
υρὸν ἰσχίο, ἡμίκρα[ιραν χορδ]ῆς· ᵛ Διονύσ[ο] Ἀν[θίο] ἱε-
ρείαι ἱερεώσυνα :Π: τ[ὸ δέρμα τō τελέ]ο· ἐπὶ[δ]ὲ τὴν τρά-
πεζαν κωλῆν, πλ̣ευρὸν [ἰσχίο, ἡμίκραιραν] χορδῆς ᵛ Ἥ-
ρας ἱερείαι ἱερεώσυν[α :Π: τὸ δέρμα?, ἅπαντ]ος εὐστō τ-
ελέο : ⊦⊦⊦ :, δεισίας κρεῶν, [πυρῶν ἡμιέκτεω : ΙΙΙ :] μέλιτος
κοτύλης : ΙΙΙ : ἐλαίο τριῶν κο[τυλῶν : ΙC : φρυγάν]ων[: ΙΙ :]· ἐ[πὶ δ]ὲ
τὴν τράπεζαν κωλῆν, πλευρ[ὸν ἰσχίο, ἡμίκραιραν χο]-
ρδῆς· ᵛ Δήμητρος Χλόης ἱερε[ίαι ἱερεώσυνα :Π: δεισί]-

11. 4th c.? 1 dr. for Apollo's oracles, apiece.[15] "For Apollo once gave a drachma oracle / made a drachma loan to Kronos, and then did not get it (paid) back. Being enraged at that, he gave another oracle / made another loan, no longer worth drachmas, nor (consisting of) pots and pans, by Zeus, and not property either, but expulsion from his kingdom by his own child." The implication in this comic fragment is that the oracles once cost 1 dr. apiece, but this is in an entirely fictional context, so it provides no reliable information on amounts paid to oracles or seers.

12. c. 400–350. 1 dr. 2 ob. ἱερειώσυνα for Teithras deme (priest or priestess?).[16]

13. 396/5. ἱερεώσυνα of (a) 3 ob. and (b) 1 dr. for Demotionidai phratry priest.[17]

ας κρεῶν, πυρῶν ἡμιέκτεω : ΙΙΙ : μέ[λιτος κοτύλης : ΙΙΙ : ἐλαί]-
ο τριῶν κοτυλῶν : ΙϹ : φρυγάνων : ΙΙ : ἐ[πὶ δὲ τὴν τράπεζαν κ]-
ωλῆν, πλευρὸν ἰσχίο, ἡμίκραιρα[ν χορδῆς· ^{v}....^{7}...]
ας ἱερείαι ἱερεώσυνα :Π: τὸ δέρμ[α τô τελέο, δεισίας]
κρεῶν, πυρῶν ἡμιέκτεω : ΙΙΙ [: μέλιτος κοτύλης : ΙΙΙ : ἐλαίο τ]-
ριῶν κοτυλῶν : ΙϹ : φρ[υγάνων : ΙΙ : ἐπὶ δὲ τὴν τράπεζαν κωλ]-
ῆν, πλευρὸν ἰσ[χίο, ἡμίκραιρα[ν χορδῆς· - - - - - - - ἱ]-
ερείαι ἱερε[ώσυνα :Π: -]

15. *Com. Adesp.* fr. 1062. 9–13 (K-A):
ἔχρησε γὰρ Κρόνωι ποθ' Ἀπόλλων δραχ[μήν,]
κᾆιτ' οὐκ ἀπέλαβε. ταῦτα δὴ θυμὸν πνέ[ων]
ἑτέραν ἔχρησε[ν οὐκέτι] δρα[χ]μῶ[ν ἀ]ξ[ίαν,]
οὐ σκευάρια, μὰ τὸν Δί', οὐδὲ χρήματα,
ἐκ τῆς βασιλείας δ' ἐκπεσεῖν ὑπὸ π[αιδίου.]

In the prior edition (*CGFPR* fr. 215), Austin quotes (Gilbert) Murray as follows: "The word χρᾶν means both 'to lend money' and 'to give an oracle': 2 ways of helping people in an emergency."

16. *SEG* XXI 542 A. 2–6:
Βοηδ[ρομιῶνος]
τετρ[άδι - - - - - - - - -]
Διὶ : ἐντ̣ - - - - - - - - - - - -
ΔΠ⊦⊦ οἶν : ἄρρεν - - - - - - - - - -
⊦ΙΙ ἱερειώσυνα

17. *IG* II^{2} 1237 + *SEG* XL 132. 1–8:
Δ ι ὸ ς Φ ρ α τ ρ ί ο
ἱερεὺς ⟦Θεόδωρος⟧ Εὐφα⟦ντίδο⟧ ^{vv} ἀν-
έγραψε καὶ ἔστησε τὴν στήλην. ^{v}
ἱερεώσυνα τῶι ἱερεῖ διδόναι τ-
άδε· ἀπὸ τô μείο κωλῆν, πλευρόν, ὂ-
ς, ἀργυρίο ΙΙΙ. ^{v} ἀπὸ τô κορείο κωλῆ-
ν, πλευρόν, ὀς, ἐλατῆρα χοινικια-
ῖον, οἴνο ἡμίχον, ἀργυρίο ⊦. ^{vvvv}

In line 8, C. W. Hedrick, Jr., *The Decrees of the Demotionidai* (Atlanta 1990) 7, prints Ι, but since he translates this (14) as "one *drachma*," I presume that Ι is a misprint for ⊦, which Kirchner had printed

14. 377/6–375/4. 1 T. for Delian ἀρχεθέωροι (emoluments or expenses?).[18] In the context of other expenses of the Delian Amphiktyons, it looks as if this enormous disbursement was for various expenses incurred by the archetheoroi. Possibly the talent includes their (own) pay, but if it does, it is impossible for us to isolate its amount.

15. 363/2. Salaminioi clan priests: for priest of Herakles, (a) 30 dr. for ἱερεώσυνα and (b) 3 dr. for πελανός (sacrificial cake); for priest of Eurysakes, (c) 6 dr. for ἱερεώσυνα, (d) 7 dr. for πελανός (for both cults), (e) 13 dr. in lieu of leg and skin of sacrificial victim.[19] The figures for πελανός are presumably an advance for expenses rather than compensation.

16. 352. [30 dr.] for hierophant and priestess of Demeter, apparently together rather than apiece, (emoluments or expenses?) for performing sacrifices in connection with Eleusinian orgas boundary dispute.[20] Even if this is for emoluments, the restored figure is necessarily uncertain.

17. pre-350. 22 dr. to Eleusinian priestess for favorable sacrifices?[21] It is not clear that the 22 dr. go to the priestess, or (if they do) that they

---

(see also *SEG* XL 132). At 30, Hedrick comments on the cash ἱερεώσυνα: "The relative importance of each sacrifice is clearest in the amounts of money allotted to the priest: from the *meion* he receives only three obols, but from the *koureion* he receives a full drachma."

18. *IG* II² 1635. 32–35:
τάδε ἀνηλώθη· στέφανος ἀριστεῖον τῶι θεῶι, καὶ τῶι ἐργασαμένω-
ι μισθός, Χ𐅅 · τρίποδες νικητήρια τοῖς χοροῖς, καὶ τῶι ἐργασαμέν-
ωι μισθός, Χ[.]· ἀρχεθεώροις Τ· εἰς κομιδὴν τῶν θεωρῶν καὶ τῶν χορῶ-
[ν] Ἀντιμάχωι Φίλωνος Ἑρμείωι τριηράρχωι ΤΧ ⁝

19. *SEG* XXI 527. 27–30, 34–36:
τοῖς δὲ ἱερεῦσι καὶ ταῖς ἱερείαι-
ς ἀποδιδόναι τὰ γέρα τὰ γεγραμμένα· τῶι δὲ τõ Ἡρ-
ακλέος ἱερεῖ ἱερεώσυνα ΔΔΔ δραχμάς· εἰς πελαν-
ὸν δὲ ⊦⊦⊦ δραχμάς·

τῶι δὲ τõ Εὐρυσάκος ἱερεῖ ἱερεώσυνα Π⊦ δραχμά-
ς· εἰς πελανὸν ἀμφοτέρωσε Π⊦⊦ δραχμάς· σκέλος κ-
αὶ δέρματος ἐν Εὐρυσακείωι Δ⊦⊦⊦ δραχμάς·

20. *IG* II² 204. 57–60:
θῦ-
[σαι δὲ καὶ ἀρεστήριον] το[ῖν θεοῖν] τὸν ἱ[ε]ροφάντην καὶ τὴν ἱέ-
[ρειαν τῆς Δήμητρος, δοῦναι δ' αὐτοῖς] τὸν ταμίαν τοῦ δήμου τὸ
[ἀργύριον τριάκοντα δραχμάς]·

21. *IG* II² 1540. 57–58:
ἱερέαι καλ-
[λιερῆσαι? - - - - - - -]ίοις ΔΔ⊦⊦·

are for personal emoluments, rather than sacrificial expenses. One wonders whether ordinary, or unfavorable, sacrifices would cost less!

18. c. 350. 1 1/2 ob. to 7 dr. 1 1/2 ob. for Marathon deme ἱερώσυνα (20 preserved or partially preserved figures).[22] There seems to be some

---

22. *IG* II^2 1358. 1–52 (column 2):
- - - - ιο[- - - - - - - τάδε ὁ δήμαρχος]
[ὁ Μα]ραθωνίων θύει ἐ[ν - - - - - - - -]
ηνται δέκα ἡμέρων· ἥρωι : [χοῖρος ⊢⊢⊢, ἡρώινηι]
χοῖρος ⊢⊢⊢. ᵛ τράπεζα τῶι ἥρω[ι καὶ τῆι ἡρώινηι ⊢].
Βοηδρομιῶνος· πρὸ μ[υ]στ[η]ρ[ίων - - - - - - -]
β<u>ο͡ῦ</u>ς 𐅄ΔΔΔΔ, οἶς Δ⊢⊢. ᵛ Κουροτρόφω[ι - - - -]
δευτέρας ᵛ τριμήνο· ᵛ Ποσιδεῶ[νος - - - - - -]
βοῦς Ḥ𐅄 /// ///, οἶς Δ⊢⊢, ἡρώινηι [οἶς Δ⊢, ἱερώσυνα]
Π⊢⊢. ᵛ Γῆι ἐγ Γύαις βοῦς κύουσα 𐅄ΔΔ[ΔΔ, ἱερώσυνα . . .]
Τελετῆι : σπυλια : ΔΔΔΔ. *vacat*
τρίτης τριμήνο· Γαμηλ[ιῶ]νος·
Δαίραι οἶς κύουσα ΔΠ⊢, ᵛ ἱερώσυνα ⊢.
Γῆι ἐπὶ τῶι μαντείωι ᵛ οἶς Δ⊢. ᵛ Διὶ ὑπ[άτωι - -]
Ἰόλεωι οἶς Δ⊢⊢. Κοροτρόφωι χοῖρο[ς ⊢⊢⊢, τράπε]-
ζα ⊢, ἱερώσυνα ⊢⊢IC. ᵛ ἥρωι Φηραίωι [οἶς Δ⊢⊢,]
ἡρώινηι ᵛ οἶς ᵛ Δ⊢, ἱερώσυνα ⊢⊢⊢. *vacat*
Ἐλα[φη]βολιῶνος δεκάτηι ἱσταμένο· [Γῆι ἐπὶ τῶι]
μαν[τε]ίωι τράγος παμμέλας ΔΠ. ᵛ ἱε[ρώσυνα ⊢].
τετάρτης τριμήνο· Μουνιχιῶνος· Ἀρ . . . c. 5 . .
Νέχωι? βο͡ῦς ᵛ 𐅄ΔΔΔΔ, οἶς Δ⊢⊢, ἡρώινι οἶς Δ⊢, ἱε[ρώσυ]-
να Π⊢⊢. Νεανίαι βο͡ῦς 𐅄ΔΔΔΔ, ᵛ οἶς Δ⊢⊢, χοῖρο[ς ⊢⊢⊢]
ἡρώινηι ᵛ οἶς Δ⊢, ᵛ ἱερώσυνα ᵛ Π⊢⊢IC. *vacat*
τάδε ὁ δήμαρχος ὁ Μαραθωνίων θύει· ἥρωι ἐν
. ρασιλείαι : οἶς ᵛ Δ⊢⊢, ᵛ τράπεζα ⊢, ἡρώινηι οἶς ᵛ Δ⊢.
ἥρωι παρὰ τὸ Ἑλλώτιον ᵛ οἶς ᵛ Δ⊢⊢, τράπεζα ⊢, ᵛ ἡρώι-
νηι οἶς Δ⊢. *vacat*
Θαργηλιῶνος· Ἀχαίαι κριὸς Δ⊢⊢, ᵛ θήλ[ε]α Δ⊢,
ἱερώσυνα ⊢⊢⊢. ᵛ Μοίραις ᵛ χοῖρος ᵛ ⊢⊢⊢, ᵛ ἱερώ[σ]-
υνα IC. *vacat*
Σκιροφοριῶνος· πρὸ Σκίρων· Ὑττηνίωι τὰ ὡρα[ι]-
α ᵛ οἶς ᵛ Δ⊢⊢. ᵛ Κοροτρόφωι χοῖρος ⊢⊢⊢, ἱερώσυνα ⊢⊢I.
Τριτοπατρεῦσι οἶς, ἱερώσυνα ⊢⊢. ᵛ Ἀκάμασιν
οἶς Δ⊢⊢, ἱερώσυνα ⊢⊢.
τάδε τὸ ἕτερον ἔτος· προτέρα δραμοσύνη· Ἑκα-
τ[ο]μβαιῶνος· Ἀθηναίαι Ἑλλωτίδι βο͡ῦς 𐅄ΔΔΔΔ,
οἶες τρεῖς ΔΔΔ⊢⊢, ᵛ χοῖρος ⊢⊢⊢, ᵛ ἱερώσυνα ΠΗ . . . ,
Κοροτρόφωι οἶς Δ⊢, χοῖρος ⊢⊢⊢, ἱερώσυνα ⊢ . . . ,
δαφνηφόροις Π⊢⊢.
τάδε τὸ ἕτερον ἔτος θύεται μετὰ Εὔβουλον ἄρχ[ο]-
ντα Τετραπολεῦσι· ὑστέρα δραμοσύνη·
Ἑκατομβαιῶνος· ᵛ Ἀθηναίαι Ἑλλωτίδι οἶς Δ[⊢],
Κοροτρόφωι χοῖρος ⊢⊢⊢, ᵛ ἱερώσυνα ⊢IC.
Μεταγειτνιῶνος· ᵛ Ἐλευσινίαι ᵛ βο͡ῦς ᵛ 𐅄ΔΔ[Δ],

rough relationship between the cost of the sacrifice and the amount of the ἱερώσυνα, i.e., all ἱερώσυνα in excess of 5 dr. (lines 9, 21, 22, 36 and 45) are for sacrifices costing more than 100 dr., while the smallest ἱερώσυνα, of 1 1/2 ob. (line 29), is for the cheapest sacrifice (3 dr.). But the ἱερώσυνα are not based precisely on the prices of the sacrificial victims: in lines 48 and 50, for example, the victim costs 20 dr. and the ἱερώσυνα are 1 dr. 1 ob. and 1 dr., respectively, while in lines 33 and 47 the victim costs 12 dr. but the ἱερώσυνα are 2 dr., and Quinn showed that the ἱερώσυνα in fact are based on the *type* of victim: 1 1/2 ob. for a 3 dr. χοῖρος, 1 dr. for an 11 dr. οἶς or a 16 dr. οἶς κυοῦσα or a 20 dr. ὗς κυοῦσα (all for female divinities), 2 dr. for a 12 dr. οἶς or a 12 dr. κριός (both for male divinities), and 4 dr. for a βοῦς.[23]

19. c. 350–300. ἱερειώσυνα include καταρχήν (sacrifice charge?) of (a) [3 ob.] for [adult victim] and (b) 1 1/2 ob. for [suck]ling (victim)?[24] These restorations are obviously uncertain, as is the status of the payments as ἱερειώσυνα.

20. 334/3. 4 dr. for priestess at Cholargos deme Thesmophoria—emoluments or expenses?[25] Because such detailed provision is made for

---

Κόρηι κριὸς Δ⊢⊢, ^{v} χοῖροι τρεῖς Π⊢⊢⊢⊢, ^{v} ἱερώ[σ]-
υνα Π⊢ΙΙΙΙC, ^{v} ἀλφίτων ἑκτεὺς ΙΙΙΙ, ^{v} οἴνο χ̣ο̣[ς . .],
Κοροτρόφωι οἶς Δ⊢, ^{v} ἱερώσυνα ⊢. *vacat*
Διὶ 'Ανθαλεῖ οἶς Δ⊢⊢, ἱερώσυνα ⊢⊢. *vacat*
'Ανθεστηριῶνος· 'Ελευσινίαι ὗς κύουσα : ΔΔ,
ἱερώσυνα ⊢Ι. Χλόηι παρὰ τὰ Μειδύλου ὗς κύου[σα]
ΔΔ, ^{v} ἱερώσυνα ⊢, ^{v} ἀλφίτων ἑκτεὺς ΙΙΙΙ, ^{v} οἴνο χ[ο̂ς]
Σκιροφοριῶνος· πρὸ Σκίρων· ^{v} Γαλίωι κριὸς Δ[⊢⊢],
ἱερώσυνα ⊢⊢, ^{v} φρέατος Π⊢

For the reasons stated at p. 84 with n. 23, G. M. Quinn, "The Sacrificial Calendar of the Marathonian Tetrapolis" (Ph.D. diss., Harvard University, 1971) 23, restored ⊢⊢Ι⟨C⟩ at the end of line 31, Π⊢[⊢Ι]⟨C⟩ at the end of line 36, and ⊢[ΙC] at the end of line 37. In line 9, where we would expect ἱερώσυνα of ⊢⊢⊢⊢, Quinn 66 stated that there would have been space for Π "and not much more." For the date of c. 350 (rather than the Corpus' 400–350), see S. Dow, "Six Athenian Sacrificial Calendars," *BCH* 92 (1968) 170–186 at 174, 178.

23. Quinn (as in n. 22) 92–103.

24. *IG* II^{2} 1359 + *SEG* XXV 166. 2, 6–7.
ἱερειώσυνα τάδε [διδόναι. . . . 2
καταρχὴ[ν δὲ διδόναι τελείου :ΙΙΙ: γαλα]- 6
θηνοῦ :ΙC:

25. *IG* II^{2} 1184. 1–7, 15–18:
τοὺς ἱε[ρ]-
[ο]μνήμονας.
τὰς δὲ ἀρχούσας κοινεῖ ἀμφοτ-

other items that cost money (beginning with barley and ending with torches), I am inclined to think that the priestess would not have had to spend any money herself, and that this sum is therefore an emolument. Its size is comparable to the deme and clan ἱερ(ε)ώσυνα in ##10 (a), 15 (c) and 18.

21. c. 330–270. Eleusis sacred calendar figures: (a) 1 dr. 3 ob. for lunch for hierophant and herald (apparently together), (b) 20 dr. for ἱερεώσυνα and other items, (c) 10 dr. for ἀπόμετρα for priestess.[26] We may compare the 1 dr. 3 ob. for lunch for two individuals with the putative 1 dr. per individual in #3. It is impossible to isolate the portion of the 20 dr. that went for ἱερεώσυνα—less than half if, as is likely, 10–12 dr. went for the goat.[27] The ἀπόμετρα are identical to those in ##5 (a) and 9 (b) above.

ἔρας διδόναι τῆς ἱερείας εἰς
τὴν ἑορτὴν καὶ τὴν ἐπιμέλεια-
αν τῶν Θεσμοφορίων ἡμιεκτεῖον
κριθῶν....

καὶ δᾳδ-
[α] μὴ ἐλάττονος ἢ δυεῖν ὀβολοῖν καὶ
ἀργυρίου ⊢⊢⊢⊢ δραχμάς· ταῦτα δὲ δι-
δόναι τὰς ἀρχούσας·

Kirchner ad loc., citing Isaios viii. 19, identified τὰς ἀρχούσας in line 2 as the two women chosen to preside over the deme Thesmophoria, and he reported that Michon thought that τῆς ἱερείας in line 4 had been inscribed in error for τῆι ἱερείαι.

26. *IG* II² 1363 + *SEG* XXIII 80 A. 3–13, B. 23:

πένπτει ἱσταμένου
ἱεροφάντηι καὶ κήρυκι
ε[ἰ]ς ἄριστον τὴν ἑορτὴν
προαγορεύουσιν τῶν
[ᵛ]⊢ΙΙΙ Προηροσίων
ἑβδόμει ἱσταμένου
ΔΔ Ἀπόλλωνι Πυθίωι ⟨α⟩ἶξ
καὶ τὰ ἐφ' ἱεροῖς, προγόνιον
καὶ τὰ μετὰ τοῦτου,
τράπεζαν κοσμῆσαι
τῶι θεῶι, ἱερεώσυνα ἱερεῖ

Δ εἰς τὰ ἀπομετρα τῆι ἱερείαι 23

The figure ΔΔ also appears in lines A. 34 and A. 41, without enough context to indicate whether it covered the same items as the 20 dr. in line A. 9.

27. For the prices for normal goats, all of them 10–12 dr., see *IG* I³ 426. 63 (67 goats plus offspring for [7]10 dr. in c. 414); *IG* II² 1357 + *Hesperia* 4 (1935) 19, no. 2. 81, 84 (= *SEG* XL 146. 264, 267) (10 dr. for [αἶξ] in c. 403–399); *SEG* XXI 527. 85 (10 dr. for goat in 363/2); *SEG* XXI 541 A. 36, 51, 56, B. 13, 51, Γ. 12, 37, Δ. 12, 40, E. 43, 46 (10–12 dr. for goats in c. 360–350); *IG* II²

22. 329/8. 49 dr. 2 ob. to Eleusinian priest for πελανός.[28] This seems to be an advance for the cost of an enormous number of sacrificial cakes.

Not much can be said about these figures as a group. Our two figures for oracles and seers (##7, 11) are either uncorroborable or clearly unreliable. For priests and priestesses, a number of figures should be put to one side since they (or their contexts) are incompletely preserved (##3, 5 [b] and [c], 8, 9 [e], 17, 19 [a] and [b]), speculative restorations (##1 [b], 4, 16), or uncertain because we cannot isolate a net figure for priests (##14, 21 [b]) or tell whether the figure is for the priests or their (usually sacrificial) expenses (##8, 17; cf. ##15 [b] and [d], 22). That still leaves a number of credible figures (##1 [a], 2, 5 [a], 6, 9 [a]–[d], 10 [a] and [b], 12, 13 [a]–[b], 15 [a], [c] and [e], 18, 20, 21 [a] and [c]), but about all that we can say about them is that priests received relatively small amounts of money, in addition to their emoluments in kind: unspecified compensation of 3 ob., ἀπόμετρα of 3 ob. to 100 dr., ἱερ(ει)ώσυνα of 1 1/2 ob. to 30 dr., general compensation of 50 dr. (p.a.), and 1 dr. 3 ob. for two lunches. In at least some cases, these emoluments seem to have some relationship to the cost of sacrifices and the importance of the divinity, but I cannot discern any general inflationary or deflationary trends, comparable to what we see in other areas: in the fifth century, the priestess of Athena Nike was paid the same amount in 424 that she had been paid in c. 448 (##2, 6), and in the fourth century, as Dow remarked, the prices of sacrificial animals in sacred calendars were remarkably stable, perhaps reflecting a religious conservatism that placed a higher value on uniform religious expenditures than on the uniform quality of religious victims.[29]

1358. 26, 30, 34, 45, 48, 50 (12 dr. for goat in c. 350). Cf. Isaeus vi. 33 (13 mn. for goats, quant. unst., and [slave] goatherd before 364); *SEG* XXI 541 Γ. 47 (5 dr. for kid in c. 360–350); *IG* II^2 1358. 18 (quoted in n. 22 above) (15 dr. for a τράγος παμμέλας in c. 350); *IG* II^2 1672. 289–290 (30 dr. for goat during famine in 329/8).

28. *IG* II^2 1672. 290–291:

Ἱπποθῶ[ν]-

τος ἱερεῖ πελανὸν ΔΔΔΔΠ⊦⊦⊦⊦ΙΙ·

29. S. Dow, "The Law Codes of Athens," *Proceedings of the Massachusetts Historical Society* 71 (1953–57) [1959] 3–36 at 15: "[T]he Athenians knew perfectly well that not all ordinary rams cost fifteen drakhmai even in the most normal years. All sorts of small variations would take place. The law could disregard these. What the law plainly meant, though modern scholars have not

realized it, was reasonable enough. In buying ordinary rams, fifteen drakhmai were to be paid; for that sum the best that could be had ought to be bought. In good seasons, the victim would be a plump one; in poor seasons, lean. In times of disaster, sacrifices might be curtailed or omitted. Whatever happened, the gods, being Greek gods, would be reasonable and would understand. The only dread of the officials was the very human audit of their accounts."

Chapter 5
Actors, Artists, Musicians and Writers

Collected here are amounts paid to actors, artists, musicians and writers for their artistic products. Excluded are amounts paid to persons other than the creating artist (e.g., subsequent owners of a painting)[1] or to what we would call craftsmen (e.g., encaustic painters of the kymatia mouldings or gilders of rosettes in the Erechtheion).[2] Since Böckh's initial collection and very brief discussion,[3] the payments for sculpture have been discussed by Stewart.[4]

1. c. 475. 10,000 dr. to Pindar for one line of poetry praising Athens as the "bulwark of Greece."[5] Although there was a related tradition that the Thebans had fined Pindar for this line and that the Athenians gave him double reimbursement,[6] the figure seems incredibly high, especially for this early date,[7] so I am inclined to see the entire story as one of a

---

1. For which see *Talents*, "C. Tangible Personal Property: Pottery Containers," "Sculpture," and "Paintings." Prices preserved as graffiti on painted pots seem to have been paid to dealers rather than to painters.

2. For which see "Construction and Other Manual Workers," especially pp. 117–119 with n. 44.

3. Böckh, *SdA* I 135–136, 153–154.

4. Stewart, *Greek Sculpture* 65–67.

5. Isoc. xv. 166: . . . Πίνδαρον μὲν τὸν ποιητὴν οἱ πρὸ ἡμῶν γεγονότες ὑπὲρ ἑνὸς μόνον ῥήματος, ὅτι τὴν πόλιν ἔρεισμα τῆς 'Ελλάδος ὠνόμασεν, οὕτως ἐτίμησαν ὥστε καὶ πρόξενον ποιήσασθαι καὶ δωρεὰν μυρίας αὐτῷ δοῦναι δραχμάς. . . .

6. [Aeschin.] *Epist.* iv. 3: . . . ἐζημίωσαν αὐτὸν Θηβαῖοι τοῦτο ποιήσαντα τὸ ἔπος, οἱ δὲ ἡμέτεροι πρόγονοι διπλῆν αὐτῷ τὴν ζημίαν ἀπέδοσαν. . . . If this story were true, the Theban fine would have been 5,000 dr.

7. Compare, at the other extreme, Σ Pind. *Nem.* v. 1a: φασὶν ὅτι τοῦ Πυθέου (sc. Αἰγινήτου) οἰκεῖοι προσῆλθον τῷ Πινδάρῳ παρακαλοῦντες ὅπως εἰς αὐτὸν γράψῃ ἐπινίκιον. Πινδάρου δὲ αἰτήσαντος τρεῖς (codd.) δραχμὰς ἔφασαν ἐκεῖνοι κάλλιον εἶναι χάλκεον ἀνδριάντα ποιῆσαι τῆς αὐτῆς τιμῆς ἢ τὸ ποίημα. χρόνῳ δὲ ὕστερον γνωσιμαχήσαντες ἐπανῆλθον τὸ αὐτὸ διδόντες. Schmid's emendation of τρεῖς to τρισχιλίας seems to have been universally accepted; I agree that 3 dr. seems low, but I suspect that Schmid based his 3,000 dr. on prices for bronze statues in the Hellenistic period (##15, 18 below).

number of fourth-century fabrications of decrees that refer to the period 490–450.[8]

2. c. 450. Less than [6,]600 dr. 2 ob. for sculptors of Athena Promachos statue in year (VI?), less than 10,100 dr.+ in year (VIII?). As discussed in greater detail under "Construction and Other Manual Workers" #1, these amounts (in *IG* I[3] 435. 76–77, 111–112) are gross wages for *all* workers, not just sculptors, and in any event the number of workers and days worked are not stated, so that it is impossible to isolate the pay of individual workers.

3. c. 430s. 100 T. Eleans agree to return Pheidias to Athens, or pay this sum.[9] Strictly speaking, this is a bail figure, but I include it as indicating what some people might have thought was the value of a distinguished sculptor. At this early date (and even in later periods), the figure itself is impossibly large. No doubt Seneca is reporting the details of a fictitious case, devised for purposes of a rhetorical exercise in the Roman imperial period.

4. 434/3. 16,392 dr. annual wages for Parthenon pediment sculptors, number unstated.[10] Because we are not told the number of sculptors, the number of days each worked and the amount of sculpture completed, this gross figure also is not a useful indication of sculptor wages, although a number of (very different) suggestions have been made.[11]

5. pre-425. 10 T. to Herodotos for flattering Athens.[12] Plutarch obviously had some doubts about this story, and Jacoby ad loc. does not

8. See #5 below and "Welfare and Support Allowances and Distributions" ## 4–5 (with notes 8 and 10) for other examples and bibliography, to which add, for this case, M. B. Walbank, *Athenian Proxenies of the Fifth Century B.C.* (Toronto 1978) 77–78.

9. Sen. *Contr.* viii. 2: Elii ab Atheniensibus Phidian acceperunt ut his Iovem Olympium faceret, pacto interposito ut aut Phidian aut centum talenta redderent. Perfecto Iove Elii Phidian aurum rapuisse dixerunt et manus tamquam sacrilego praeciderunt, truncatum Atheniensibus reddunt. Petunt Athenienses centum talenta. Contradicunt.

10. *IG* I[3] 449. 401–402:

M𐅇XHH		
H𐅄ΔΔΔ	ἀγ[αλματοπο]ιοῖς	401
Δ𐅂𐅂	ἐνα[ιετίον μι]σθός	402

11. See "Construction and Other Manual Workers" pp. 116–117 with n. 37.

12. Diyllus 73 *FGrH* 3 ap. Plut. *Mor.* 862a–b: ἀλλὰ τοῦτό γε βοηθεῖ τῷ Ἡροδότῳ πρὸς ἐκείνην τὴν διαβολήν ἣν ἔχει κολακεύσας τοὺς Ἀθηναίους ἀργύριον πολὺ λαβεῖν παρ' αὐτῶν. εἰ γὰρ ἀνέγνω ταῦτ' Ἀθηναίοις, οὐκ ἂν εἴασαν οὐδὲ περιεῖδον ἐνάτῃ τὸν Φιλιππίδην παρακαλοῦντα Λακεδαιμονίους ἐπὶ τὴν μάχην ἐκ τῆς μάχης γεγενημένον, καὶ ταῦτα δευτεραῖον

comment at all on the figure. In the absence of any indication (other than #1 above) that Athens bestowed enormous monetary rewards (as distinct from olive wreaths, etc.) on writers, I am inclined to regard this story, and certainly the 10 T., as a later invention.

6. 421/0–416/5. Less than 5 T. 3,310 dr. for, inter alia, bronze workers on statues of Athena and Hephaistos.[13] That gross figure also includes raw materials (copper, tin, lead, wood, firewood and charcoal), as well as wages for a table-maker and movers, so it is impossible to determine what individual bronze sculptors were paid.

7. 413. 50 dr. to Hegemon of Thasos, for singing epic parody of the Gigantomachia when news of Sicilian Disaster reached Athens.[14] This relatively modest figure is not excessively disproportionate in relation to the 1 dr. p.d. that was being paid to soldiers and sailors at this time,[15] and it is not implausible that the Athenians tendered it as a token of their

---

εἰς Σπάρτην ἐξ Ἀθηνῶν, ὡς αὐτός φησιν, ἀφιγμένον· εἰ μὴ μετὰ τὸ νικῆσαι τοὺς πολεμίους Ἀθηναῖοι μετεπέμποντο τοὺς συμμάχους. ὅτι μέντοι δέκα τάλαντα δωρεὰν ἔλαβεν ἐξ Ἀθηνῶν, Ἀνύτου τὸ ψήφισμα γράψαντος, ἀνὴρ Ἀθηναῖος οὐ τῶν παρημελημένων ἐν ἱστορίᾳ Δίυλλος εἴρηκεν. A. J. Bowen, *Plutarch: The Malice of Herodotus* (Warminster 1992) 125, thinks "[t]he sum is possible; the circumstances are problematic."

13. *IG* I[3] 472. 146–148, 166:
μισθὸς τοῖς ἐργασαμένοις τὸ ἄνθ̣εμον hυπ̣[ὸ] 146
τὲν ἀσπίδα καὶ το̂ν πετάλον τὸν hύ[σ]τ̣ε̣ρον
προσμισθοθέντον.

[ἀναλόματ]ος κεφάλαιον ΡΧΧΧΗΗΗΔ 166

14. Hegemon fr. 1 (Brandt) ap. Athen. xv. 55 (698e–f):
εἰς Θασίους ⟨δὲ⟩
μηδένα πημαίνων κλυτὸν ἄργυρον ἐγγυαλίξω,
μή τίς μοι κατὰ οἶκον Ἀχαιϊάδων νεμεσήσῃ,
πεσσομένης ἀλόχου τὸν ἀχάϊνον ἄρτον ἀεικῶς,
καί ποτέ τις εἴπῃ σμικρὸν τυροῦντ' ἐσιδοῦσα,
"ὦ φίλη, ὡνὴρ μὲν παρ' Ἀθηναίοισιν ἀείσας
πεντήκοντ' ἔλαβε δραχμάς, σὺ δὲ μικρὸν ἐπέψω."

For the likely circumstances and date of this award, see Athen. ix. 72 (407a–b): εὐδοκίμει δ' ὁ ἀνὴρ μάλιστα ἐν ταῖς παρῳδίαις καὶ περιβόητος ἦν λέγων τὰ ἔπη πανούργως καὶ ὑποκριτικῶς καὶ διὰ ταῦτα σφόδρα παρὰ τοῖς Ἀθηναίοις εὐδοκίμει. ἐν δὲ τῇ Γιγαντομαχίᾳ οὕτω σφόδρα τοὺς Ἀθηναίους ἐκήλησεν, ὡς ἐν ἐκείνῃ τῇ ἡμέρᾳ πλεῖστα αὐτοὺς γελάσαι, καίτοι ἀγγελθέντων αὐτοῖς ἐν τῷ θεάτρῳ τῶν γενομένων περὶ Σικελίαν ἀτυχημάτων. οὐδεὶς ἀπέστη καίτοι σχεδὸν πᾶσι τῶν οἰκείων ἀπολωλότων. ἔκλαιον οὖν ἐγκαλυψάμενοι, οὐκ ἀνέστησαν δ', ἵνα μὴ γένωνται διαφανεῖς τοῖς ἀπὸ τῶν ἄλλων πόλεων θεωροῦσιν ἀχθόμενοι τῇ συμφορᾷ· διέμειναν δ' ἀκροώμενοι καίτοι καὶ αὐτοῦ τοῦ Ἡγήμονος, ὡς ἤκουσε, σιωπᾶν διεγνωκότος. A. Körte, "Hegemon (3)," *RE* 7 (1912) 2595–2596, suggests that the 50 dr. was second prize in a parody competition, but there is no support for that in these passages.

15. See "Soldiers and Sailors" ##12, 13, 15.

gratitude at this moment of great national grief. But the source requires that we be at least somewhat skeptical. Hegemon has returned to Thasos, where he has fallen on hard times, and in an effort to bolster his standing he recalls the honor in which he had been held by the Athenians: the 50 dr. *could* be an embellishment for his more general point.

8. 408/7. 60 dr. to Erechtheion sculptors per standard-sized figure (calculated as 60 days' work at 1 dr. p.d.?). As discussed in greater detail under "Construction and Other Manual Workers" (pp. 117–119 with n. 38), 60 dr. seems to have been the price for a standard-sized figure, and it is possible that it was based on the assumption that such a figure should take 60 days to carve. Because we know that the sculptures were marble, it is likely that the entire 60 dr. went to the sculptor.[16]

9. c. 407–400? 1 gold st. to Choirilos for poem celebrating Athenian victories over Xerxes, per line.[17] Although Jacoby enclosed the words "ἐφ' οὗ ποιήματος κατὰ στίχον στατῆρα χρυσοῦν ἔλαβε" in double square brackets (= "zusätze des ausgeschriebenen autors"),[18] he did not say where the addition came from nor, for this portion of *FGrH*, did he live to provide a commentary. The most likely chronological setting for this payment is in the years between 407/6 (when Athens melted down the golden Nikai to produce Athens' first and only gold coinage, including staters)[19] and 400/399, when Archelaos died. In this period, Athens was in economic crisis, reflected not only in the melting of the golden Nikai but also in cuts in soldiers' pay and the diobelia dole,[20] so it is very improbable that the Athenians would have wanted, or could have afforded, to indulge in the extravagance of paying a poet one gold stater per line of poetry, even if he did celebrate a distinguished ancient victory.

---

16. Marble seems to have been supplied without cost to the epistatai of public works from (state-owned?) quarries on Mount Pentelikos: that conclusion is suggested, at any rate, by the absence of any charge for this marble in the otherwise very detailed Erechtheion and Eleusinian building accounts.

17. *Suda* χ 595 (Adler), Χοιρίλος, Σάμιος: . . . τελευτῆσαι ἐν Μακεδονίᾳ παρὰ 'Αρχελάῳ, τῳ τότε αὐτῆς βασιλεῖ. ἔγραψε δὲ ταῦτα· τὴν 'Αθηναίων νίκην κατὰ Ξέρξου, ἐφ' οὗ ποιήματος κατὰ στίχον στατῆρα χρυσοῦν ἔλαβε καὶ σὺν τοῖς 'Ομήρου ἀναγινώσκεσθαι ἐψηφίσθη.

18. 696 *FGrH* 33a.

19. Kraay, *ACGC* 68–69. Although it would fit the story nicely if the gold stater were a daric (!), the fifth-century sources always seem, for the Persian coin, to specify that it is a δαρεικός στατήρ, e.g., *IG* I³ 383. 17–18, 44–46; Hdt. vii. 28. 2; Thuc. viii. 28. 4.

20. See "Inflation and Deflation" pp. 240–241, 244–245.

10. post-403/2. 7 ob. μισθός for trumpeter-fish.[21] In this comic fragment, (a) it is not clear whether the "trumpeter" is a musician or a fish, (b) the payment may have been exaggerated, and, in any event, (c) we are not told the time period of this service, so that it is impossible to judge its accuracy, or to use it for comparative purposes.

11. c. 366–364. 10,000 dr. to actor Neoptolemos from Demosthenes for teaching him to speak whole paragraphs (periods) without taking a breath. As discussed in greater detail under "Doctors, Lawyers and Professors" ##17 and 18, it is highly unlikely that Demosthenes could or did pay this high amount (in [Plut.] *Mor.* 844f).

12. 365. Less than 16 mn. to sculptor Leochares for "Apollo" and one other statue (sum also used for food and *eisphorai*).[22] Although this letter is usually regarded as a forgery,[23] the figure is not implausible. But even if it is accurate, we cannot isolate how much of the 16 mn. went to Leochares, what each statue cost, and (if either or both was of bronze) what the net payment to Leochares was.

13. 350–320. [160?] dr. to sculptor [Menekrates the Boi]otian for restoring statue of Athena Nike?[24] This text, as restored, is almost

---

21. Archippus fr. 16 (K-A):

ἐκήρυξεν βόαξ
σάλπης δ' ἐσάλπιγξ' ἕπτ' ὀβολοὺς μισθὸν φέρων

For the date, see K-A II 542.

22. Pl. *Epist.* xiii 361a–b (Plato to Dionysios): Περὶ δὲ ὧν ἐπέστελλές μοι ἀποπέμπειν σοι, τὸν μὲν 'Απόλλω ἐποιησάμην τε καὶ ἄγει σοι Λεπτίνης, νέου καὶ ἀγαθοῦ δημιουργοῦ. ὄνομα δ' ἔστιν αὐτῷ Λεωχάρης. ἕτερον δὲ παρ' αὐτῷ ἔργον ἦν πάνυ κομψόν, ὡς ἐδόκει· ἐπριάμην οὖν αὐτὸ βουλόμενός σου τῇ γυναικὶ δοῦναι, ὅτι μου ἐπεμελεῖτο καὶ ὑγιαίνοντος καὶ ἀσθενοῦντος ἀξίως ἐμοῦ τε καὶ σοῦ· δὸς οὖν αὐτῇ, ἂν μή τι σοὶ ἄλλο δόξῃ. πέμπω δὲ καὶ οἴνου γλυκέος δώδεκα σταμνία τοῖς παισὶ καὶ μέλιτος δύο. ἰσχάδων δὲ ὕστερον ἤλθομεν τῆς ἀποθέσεως, τὰ δὲ μύρτα ἀποτεθέντα κατεσάπη· ἀλλ' αὖθις βέλτιον ἐπιμελησόμεθα. περὶ δε φυτῶν Λεπτίνης σοι ἐρεῖ. 'Αργύριον δ' εἰς ταῦτα ἕνεκά τε τούτων καὶ εἰσφορῶν τινων εἰς τὴν πόλιν ἔλαβον παρὰ Λεπτίνου, λέγων ἅ μοι ἐδόκει εὐσχημονέστατα ἡμῖν εἶναι καὶ ἀληθῆ λέγειν, ὅτι ἡμέτερον εἴη ὃ εἰς τὴν ναῦν ἀναλώσαμεν τὴν Λευκαδίαν, σχεδὸν ἑκκαίδεκα μναῖ. τοῦτ' οὖν ἔλαβον, καὶ λαβὼν αὐτός τε ἐχρησάμην καὶ ὑμῖν ταῦτα ἀπέπεμψα.

23. See L. Edelstein, *Plato's Seventh Letter* (Leiden 1966) 131–133, with references to earlier work.

24. *IG* II^2 403 + *SEG* III 85. 23–31:

[. . . καὶ] ἐπ[ε]ιδ[ὴ ὁ ανδ]ρ[ι]αν[το]π[οι]ὸ-
[ς ἐπεσκεύασε]ν [ε]ὖ ἡμ̣[ιρραγῆ (*sic*) κ]α̣[ὶ τὰ] ἄλ[λα,]
[τὴν πρυταν]είαν [πρυτανεύουσαν] μ[ερ]-
[ίσαι αὐτῶι δρα]χμ[ὰς ἑξή]κ̣[ο]ν̣[τα? καὶ ἑκα]-
[τόν?, καὶ προσαγ]αγε[ῖ]ν τὴν̣ προτ[ανείαν?,]
[ἥτις ἂν προτ]ανε[ύ]ηι ο. ν. ς εἰ[ς τὸν δῆμ]-
[ον αὐτὸν?] 'Αθηναίων τὰ πρ[ῶτα . . .^{5}. .]

entirely fanciful,[25] and obviously wrong in one place,[26] so it must be ignored, as non-existent evidence.

14. pre-336. 1 T. or "sufficient change"?, to (60?) Athenian humorists, to write down and to send humorous sayings to Philip of Macedon.[27] Jacoby, commenting on the Telephanes fragment, suggests that this text was a work of the Roman imperial period on the city (ἄστυ) of Athens. How reliable, at that late date, Telephanes' source would have been is difficult to say, but the emphasis of his own work would not have given him any incentive to be critical about the one talent, which would have been incidental to his main focus (note that Hegesander terms the amount ἱκανὸν κερμάτιον). One talent is an amount that Philip could have afforded, but we may doubt whether he would have been so frivolous or extravagant.

15. pre-323. 3,000 dr. for (bronze?) portrait statue.[28] See #18 below for speculations on what portion of this amount might have gone to the sculptor.

16. pre-322. 2 dr. max. to girls who played the reed-pipes, harp or lyre (presumably apiece and per performance).[29] Rhodes says that "no

---

[. · ἐπαινέσαι] δὲ τον ἀνδρια[ντοποιὸν Με]-
[νεκράτη Βοι]ώτιον, ὅτι [τ]ὴν [ἐπισκευὴν - -]

25. As indicated not only by the restorer's question marks but also by the odd formulations, such as πρυτανείαν πρυτανεύουσαν μερίσαι.

26. As indicated by *SEG*'s *sic*.

27. Telephanes 371 *FGrH* 1 ap. Athen. xiv. 3 (614d–e): Ἱππόλοχος δ' ὁ Μακεδὼν ἐν τῆι Πρὸς Λυγκέα ἐπιστολῆι γελωτοποιῶν μέμνηται Μανδρογένους κὰι Στράτωνος τοῦ Ἀττικοῦ. πλῆθος δ' ἦν Ἀθήνησι τῆς σοφίας ταύτης· ἐν γοῦν τῶι Διομέων Ἡρακλείωι συνελέγοντο ξ´ ὄντες τὸν ἀριθμόν, καὶ ἐν τῆι πόλει διωνομάζοντο ὡς "οἱ ξ´ τοῦτ' εἶπον" καὶ "ἀπὸ τῶν ξ´ ἔρχομαι." ἐν δὲ τούτοις ἦσαν Καλλιμέδων τε ὁ Κάραβος καὶ Δεινίας, ἔτι δὲ Μνασιγείτων καὶ Μέναιχμος, ὥς φησι Τηλεφάνης ἐν τῶι Περὶ τοῦ ἄστεος· τοσαύτη δ' αὐτῶν δόξα τῆς ῥαιθυμίας ἐγένετο, ὡς καὶ Φίλιππον ἀκούσαντα τὸν Μακεδόνα πέμψαι αὐτοῖς τάλαντον, ἵν' ἐγγραφόμενοι τὰ γελοῖα πέμπωσιν αὐτῶι; Hegesander *FHG* IV 413, fr. 3 ap. Athen. vi 76 (260a–b): ἱστορεῖ δὲ περὶ αὐτοῦ καὶ τάδε Ἡγήσανδρος ὁ Δελφός, ὡς τοῖς Ἀθήνησιν εἰς τὸ Διομέων Ἡράκλειον ἀθροιζομένοις τοῖς τὰ γέλοια λέγουσιν ἀπέστελλεν (sc. Φίλιππος) ἱκανὸν κερμάτιον καὶ προσέτασσέ τισιν ἀναγράφοντας τὰ λεγόμενα ὑπ' αὐτῶν ἀποστέλλειν πρὸς αὐτόν.

28. Diog. Laert. vi. 35: τὰ πολλοῦ ἄξια τοῦ μηδενὸς ἔλεγε (sc. Διογένης) πιπράσκεσθαι καὶ ἔμπαλιν· ἀνδριάντα γοῦν τρισχιλίων πιπράσκεσθαι, χοίνικα δ' ἀλφιτῶν δύο χαλκῶν. I assign this a date of pre-323 because Diogenes is said to have died on the same day as Alexander the Great (Diog. Laert. vi. 79).

29. Arist. *Ath. Pol.* l. 2: καὶ τάς τε αὐλητρίδας καὶ τὰς ψαλτρίας κ[αὶ] τὰς κιθαριστρίας οὗτοι (sc. οἱ ἀστυνόμοι) σκοποῦσιν ὅπως μὴ πλείονος ἢ δυοῖν δραχμαῖν μισθωθήσονται, κἂν πλείους τὴν αὐτὴν σπουδάζωσι λαβεῖν, οὗτοι διακληροῦσι καὶ τῶι λαχόντι μισθοῦσιν.

doubt they might also be called on to provide sexual entertainment,"[30] but if they were, I should think that that would be a matter of separate negotiation! The 2 dr. ceiling is quite plausible in the context of 1 dr. 1 1/2 ob. to 2 dr. 3 ob. p.d. paid to construction workers in 329/8.[31]

17. pre-322. 1 T. for actor (Aristodemos or Polos?), for one play or two days?[32] This figure comes to us in three versions of what is almost certainly the same story, viz., that when an actor (either Aristodemos or unnamed or Polos) boasted to a public speaker (either Demosthenes or Demades) that he had been paid 1 T. (either without further specification or for one play or for two days), the public speaker replied that he had been paid more (either an unstated amount or 10 T. or 5 T.) as a bribe to keep silent. In each case, the point of the story is more the bribery of the public speaker than the pay of the actor: the kernel of truth is probably that the public speaker was bribed, but the figures, which vary and are all like our "million dollars," sound like embellishments to a popular rumor, and as such they should not be given any weight.

18. c. 307–303. 3,000 dr. for bronze statue of Asklepiades of Byzantion—how much for sculptor?[33] Stewart comments as follows:

---

30. Rhodes, *CAAP* 574. See also "Prostitutes and Pimps" #20.

31. See "Construction and Other Manual Workers" #7.

32. Critolaus *FHG* IV 373, fr. 3 ap. Gell. *N.A.* xi. 9. 2: Ipse etiam Demosthenes, ut idem Critolaus refert, non id postea concelavit, quin gloriae quoque hoc sibi adsignavit. Nam cum interrogasset Aristodemum, actorem fabularum, quantum mercedis, uti ageret, accepisset, et Aristodemus "talentum" respondisset: "at ego plus" inquit "accepi, ut tacerem." C. Gracchus fr. 44. 20–23 (Malcovati): Graecus tragoedus gloriae sibi ducebat talentum magnum ob unam fabulam datum esse, homo eloquentissimus civitatis suae Demades ei respondisse dicitur: "mirum tibi videtur, si tu loquendo talentum quaesisti? ego, ut tacerem, decem talenta a rege accepi." [Plut.] *Mor.* 848b: Πώλου δέ ποτε τοῦ ὑποκριτοῦ πρὸς αὐτὸν (sc. Δημοσθένην) εἰπόντος, ὅτι δυσὶν ἡμέραις ἀγωνισάμενος τάλαντον λάβοι μισθόν "ἐγὼ δ'" εἶπε "πέντε τάλαντα, μίαν ἡμέραν σιωπήσας."

33. *IG* II^2 555. 9–16:

ὅπως (δ') ἂν εἰδῶ[σι ἅπαντ]-
[ες ὅτι] ὁ δῆμος ὁ 'Αθηναίων μέμνηται κα[ὶ χάρι]-
[ν ἀποδ]ίδωσιν ὑφ' ὧν ἂν εὖ πάθει καὶ τιμ[ᾶι ἐν]
[παντὶ] κ[αι]ρῶι ἀξίως τῶν εὐεργεσιῶν, στῆσ[α]-
[ι τὸν δ]ῆμον εἰκόνα χαλκῆν ἐν Βυζαντίωι 'Ασ-
[κληπι]άδου ἀπὸ τρισχιλίων δραχμῶν καὶ στ-
[εφανῶ]σαι αὐτὸν χρυσῶι στεφάνωι ἀπὸ χιλί]-
[ων δρα]χμῶν·

Kirchner does not print a left square bracket to match the last right square bracket in line 15.

A bronze two m. high with walls around 8 mm. thick weighs about 300 lbs., approximately 300 minae (5 talents) in Greek parlance, giving a price of 10 drs. per pound/mina. Material costs would be about 1.8 drs. per mina, or 550 drs. in total, extrapolating from fifth-century rates and allowing for the halving of the silver:bronze ratio when Persian silver flooded the market after Alexander's conquests. Adding incidentals such as charcoal, metal inlays, and stone for the base, this would still leave over 2,000 drs. for sculptor and apprentices, a tidy sum by any standards."[34]

Perhaps, but on their face the premises for this conclusion (size and weight of statue, silver:bronze ratio, cost of "incidentals") are all uncertain, and therefore make the conclusion itself speculative.

19. 4th/3rd c. 60 T. offered to painter Nikias for "Nekyomanteia of Homer," (Attalos' or Ptolemy's?) offer rejected.[35] This offer and its rejection are plausible enough, but the 60 T. seems impossibly large, and therefore is probably an embellishment of the core story.

20. c. 300–250. 7 dr. to "philosopher" (i.e., actor) hired for one show.[36] This figure (which obviously has nothing to do with philosophers) has a certain plausibility, but, in the absence of much other wage and price information for the third century, it is hard to evaluate.

21. mid 3rd c. 1 T. to Amoibeus the citharode, for one day's performance.[37] This figure seems impossibly high for one day's work.

---

34. Stewart, *Greek Sculpture* 67.

35. Pliny *N.H.* xxxv. 132: . . . Athenis necyomantea Homeri. hanc vendere Attalo regi noluit (sc. Nicias) talentis LX potiusque patriae suae donavit, abundans opibus; Plut. *Mor.* 1093e: . . . Νικίαν γράφοντα τὴν Νέκυιαν. . . , Πτολεμαίου δὲ τοῦ βασιλέως ἑξήκοντα τάλαντα τῆς γραφῆς συντελεσθείσης πέμψαντος αὐτῷ, μὴ λαβεῖν μηδὲ ἀποδόσθαι τὸ ἔργον. . . .; Plin. *N.H.* xxxv. 133 is doubtful as to whether this Nikias, or another, should be dated to the 112th Olympiad (332–329 B.C.), probably because that would not fit with Attalos. In any event, I date this episode more broadly to the 4th /3rd c.

36. Lucian *Icar.* 29: οὗτοι τοίνυν εἰς συστήματα διαιρεθέντες καὶ διαφόρους λόγων λαβυρίνθους ἐπινοήσαντες οἱ μὲν Στωϊκοὺς ἑαυτοὺς ὠνομάκασιν, οἱ δὲ Ἀκαδημαϊκούς, οἱ δὲ Επικουρείους, οἱ δὲ Περιπατητικοὺς καὶ ἄλλα πολλῷ γελοιότερα τούτων. ἔπειτα δὲ ὄνομα σεμνὸν τὴν ἀρετὴν περιθέμενοι και τὰς ὀφρῦς ἐπάραντες καὶ τὰ μέτωπα ῥυτιδώσανες καὶ τοὺς πώγονας ἐπισπασάμενοι περιέρχονται ἐπιπλάστῳ σχήματι κατάπτυστα ἤθη περιστέλλοντες, ἐοικότες μάλιστα τοῖς τραγικοῖς ἐκείνοις ὑποκριταῖς, ὧν ἢν ἀφέλῃ τις τὰ προσωπεῖα καὶ τὴν χρυσόπαστον ἐκείνην στολήν, τὸ καταλειπόμενόν ἐστι γελοῖον ἀνθρώπιον ἑπτὰ δραχμῶν ἐς τὸν ἀγῶνα μεμισθωμένον. I assign the narrator Menippos' dates of c. 300–250 to this entry, for which see also "Doctors, Lawyers and Professors" #29.

37. Aristeas ap. Athen. xiv. 17 (623d): τοῦ παλαιοῦ Ἀμοιβέως, ὅν φησιν Ἀριστέας ἐν τῷ περὶ Κιθαρῳδῶν ἐν Ἀθήναις κατοικοῦντα καὶ πλησίον τοῦ θεάτρου οἰκοῦντα, εἰ ἐξέλθοι

22. A.D. 2nd/3rd c. 1,000 dr. to painter for the finest painting.[38] This is only a rhetorical example. Perhaps it reflects what was thought to be plausible for a good painting, but in the absence of specific information, not much reliance can be placed upon it.

23. Date? 1 dr. to Arabian flute player to play, 4 dr. to stop![39] It is not certain that this information comes from a line of comedy, or if it does, that it is from an Attic comedy, but it obviously is a joke. Quite possibly, the 1 dr. for playing is an authentic "background fact" (compare #16 above), against which the 4 dr. for stopping would then be an intentional, comic distortion.

As a whole, these figures are disappointing. Many of them are more or less incredible (##1, 3, 5, 9, 10, 11, 14, 17, 19, 21). At least one does not really purport to be an actual figure (#22), and one is nothing more than the creation of a modern scholar (#13). Others are effectively useless because they are gross payroll figures (##2, 4, 6). A few more are hard to evaluate because they do not break down the cost of materials and labor (#12, 15, 18). That leaves only five credible (or partially credible) figures that are also usable: the 50 dr. to Hegemon for singing an epic parody in 413 (#7), the 60 dr. to the Erechtheion sculptors for a standard-sized figure in 408/7 (#8), the 2 dr. for female musicians sometime before 322 (#16), the 7 dr. for the actor in c. 300–250 (#20), and the 1 dr. for the Arabian flute player of uncertain date (#23). We are thus left with a parodist, some sculptors, some musicians, and an actor, all the figures for writers and painters having been eliminated. The only observation that I can make with confidence from these five figures is that sculptors (#8) and musicians (#16) were paid at about the same level as contemporary construction workers.[40]

ᾀσόμενος, τάλαντον Ἀττικὸν τῆς ἡμέρας λαμβάνειν. For Amoibeus' floruit in the mid 3rd century, see Plut. *Arat.* xvii. 4–5

38. Σ Herm. *Stat.* (Walz V 3. 7–12): φιλοσόφου δὲ ζητήματος παράδειγμα τόδε· ζωγράφῳ τις ὑπέσχετο δώσειν χιλίας δραχμὰς, εἰ τὸ κάλλιστον γράψας εἴη· ὁ δὲ ἀπαιτεῖ τὰς χιλίας κύκλον γράψας· φιλόσοφον οὖν τὸ ζήτημα, ζητοῦμεν γὰρ, εἰ κύκλος ὁ κόσμος, καὶ εἰ ὁ κόσμος ζῶν.

39. *Com. Adesp.* fr. *920 (K-A): δραχμῆς μὲν αὐλεῖ, τεττάρων δὲ παύεται. The earliest surviving source seems to be Steph. Byz. *Ethn.* (Meineke 108. 1–2), Ἀραβία: ὁ Ἀράβιος αὐλητής, ὃς "δραχμῆς μὲν ηὔλει, τεττάρων δ' ἐπαύετο." See also Zenob. ii. 58 (*CPG*), Ἀράβιος ἄγγελος: Εἴρηται δὲ ἐπὶ τοῦ Ἀραβίου αὐλητοῦ, ὃς ηὔλει μὲν δραχμῆς, ἐπαύετο δὲ τεττάρων.

40. See "Construction and Other Manual Workers" ##3, 7.

Chapter 6

Overseers, Architects and Other Salaried Construction Personnel

Collected here are payments to epistatai, architects and other salaried construction personnel who were paid every day of the year, including holidays, i.e., even when they were not actually working (see ##4, 7 and 8 below). Since Böckh's brief discussion,[1] the principal work has been done by scholars working on individual inscriptions (see notes 3–5 and 13 below).

1. c. 450. 1–9 ob. p.d. for epistatai (number unstated), secretary and assistant for Athena Promachos statue? The building accounts give the total of the annual salaries (μισθοί) of these people as 1,963 dr. 2 ob.[2] Three attempts have been made to extract per diem salaries for individuals from this figure:

(a) Meritt calculated that the aggregate daily rate was 31 ob. p.d. (based on a 380-day year), and suggested that there were *two* epistatai, each paid 2 dr. p.d., and a secretary, who was paid 7 ob. p.d.[3] This is unlikely since (i) no provision is made for the assistant ([hυπερ]έτει), whom Meritt did not read originally,[4] and (ii) a salary of 2 dr. p.d., or even 7 ob. p.d., has

---

1. Böckh, *SdA* I 149.

2. *IG* I³ 435. 81–82:

X𐅅HHHH μ[ισθοὶ ἐπισ]τάτεσι κα[ὶ γραμμα]-
𐅃ΔꜰꜰꜰII τ[εῖ καὶ hυπερ]έτει

The restoration of the all words except μ[ισθοί] is assured by identical words in lines 21–22, 28–29, 54–55, 87–88 and 114–115. For this entry, see also "Public Officeholders" #2.

3. B. D. Meritt, "Greek Inscriptions," *Hesperia* 5 (1936) 355–430 at 376. Meritt found that 380 was the only number between 330 and 400 that yielded a daily rate denominated in whole, half or quarter obols. If Year VI? had 380 days, the Corpus restoration of the same gross figure in lines 114–115 (Ẋ[𐅅HHHH𐅃ΔꜰꜰꜰII]) would require that year VIII? also had 380 days, but (as far as I can determine) there is no evidence to support another 380-day year two years after Year VI?.

4. Meritt later deduced [hυπερ]έτει from a new fragment. See E. Schweigert, "Inscriptions from the North Slope of the Acropolis," *Hesperia* 7 (1938) 264–310 at 267.

no attested parallel until the second half of the fourth century.

(b) Schweigert (as in n. 4) proposed 9 ob. apiece for the two epistatai, with the residue (13 ob.) "allocated on a graduated scale between the secretary and the general factotum." Again, 9 ob. p.d. has no attested parallel until the second half of the fourth century.

(c) Raubitschek drew attention to the five Eleusinian epistatai (including a secretary) in (roughly contemporary) #2 below. Since they were to serve καθάπερ hοι ἐπὶ τοῖς ἐμ πό[λ]ει ἔργ[οι]ς ἐπε̣στ[ά]το[ν] τôι νεôι καὶ τôι ἀ[γ]άλματι, Raubitschek suggested that there also were *five* epistatai here, including the secretary, and that they were paid 1 dr. p.d., with 1 ob. p.d. left over for the assistant.[5] But 1 dr. p.d. for the Athena Promachos epistatai seems a bit high in relation to the 4 ob. p.d. for the Eleusinian epistatai,[6] and in any event 1 ob. p.d. is lower than any other attested salary for full-time work.

A fourth possibility that occurs to me is that there were *seven* epistatai (including the secretary), who were paid 4 ob. p.d. (like the Eleusinian epistatai), and that the assistant was paid 3 ob. p.d. This allocation of the 31 ob. p.d. fits better with contemporary figures than any of the earlier three, but all of these hypotheses are necessarily speculative.

2. c. 449–447? 4 ob. (p.d.) for 5 Eleusinian epistatai (one acting as secretary), apiece. As discussed in greater detail under "Public Officeholders" #4, the officials who were to be paid this amount (in *IG* I^3 32. 8–9) had a wide variety of responsibilites for finances and construction.

3. 447–432. Uncertain amount for Parthenon officials. The Parthenon accounts record payments for monthly salaries (καταμενί-

5. A. E. Raubitschek, "Greek Inscriptions," *Hesperia* 12 (1943) 12–88 at 15–16. He noted that "the same relation between the salary of the epistatai and that of their servant is found in" *IG* II^2 1673 (superseded by *SEG* XXXIV 122). 60–61 (quoted in n. 13 below). Actually, these salaries are for an *architect* (2 dr. p.d.) and an *elected scribe* (2 ob. p.d.), and in any event the figure for the scribe has been changed to 3 ob. p.d. by the join of a new fragment, which gives his annual salary as 195 dr.

6. But c. 10–20 years later the overseers of the public water supply may have received 1 dr. p.d. See "Public Officeholders" #6.

οις).[7] These are generally interpreted to include the epistatai, secretary and architect, presumably on the analogy of ##1 and 2 above, although that is not stated explicitly.[8] The gross amount of salaries is partially recoverable for 434/3,[9] but the number and pay of individual officials is not ascertainable.

4. 408/7. 1 dr. p.d. for Erechtheion architect, 5 ob. p.d. for undersecretary.[10] These payments are termed μισθοί, as in the Athena Promachos accounts (#1 above), but the absence of μισθοί for epistatai or other officials in these very detailed and well-preserved accounts suggests that there were no such μισθοί or that, if there were, they were administered by officials other than the epistatai themselves.

5. pre-mid 4th c. Uncertain amounts for Eleusis architect, assistant and secretary? In a very fragmentary account for work at Eleusis, possibly including a bridge, sums of 20 dr. (perhaps incomplete) and 120 dr. are recorded 3 and 4 lines, respectively, below words that have been restored as [ἀρχιτέκτο]νι καὶ ὑπ[η]ρέτηι, and 16 dr. 4 ob. is found in the line after the preserved part of [γρα]μματεῖ μισθ[ός].[11] Apart from the fragmentary state of key words, there is nothing to

---

7. *IG* I³ 436. 29; 443. 231; 446. 339; 447. 361; 449. 403. For this entry, see also "Public Officeholders" #5.

8. M-L 164: "monthly salaries (for architects, commissioners and their secretaries)." But in the Erechtheion accounts of 409–407 (#4 below) and the Eleusinian accounts of c. 333–329 (##7 and 8 below), there are no recorded payments to "commissioners" (epistatai).

9. *IG* I³ 449. 403: [Χ]𐅅ΗΗΗ[..]Δ⊦ΙΙ, i.e., 1,831 dr. 2 ob. to 1,961 dr. 2 ob.

10. *IG* I³ 476. 59–62:

[μ]-
ισθοί· ἀρχιτέκτονι Ἀρχ[ιλόχ]-
οι Ἀγρυλε͂θεν :ΔΔΔΓ⊦⊦: hυ[πογρ]-
αμματεῖ Πυργίονι :ΔΔΔΙΙΙ[ΙΙ:]

IG I³ 476. 266–269:

μισθοί· ἀρχιτέκτ-
ονι Ἀρχιλόχοι Ἀγρυλε͂θεν, ΔΔ
ΔΓ⊦, hυπογραμματεῖ Πυργίον-
ι hοτρυνεῖ :ΔΔΔ.

Pay in this account is by prytany (see lines 56–57, 66–67, 183–185, 281–282). The only reasonable way to account for the differences in pay between the first and second passages is to assume that the first prytany had 37 days, and the second 36, in each case with the architect being paid 1 dr. p.d. and the undersecretary 5 ob. p.d.

11. *IG* II² 1540. 46–50, 59–60:

[ἀρχιτέκτο]νι καὶ ὑπ[η]ρέτηι
[- γ]έφυραν ἐξεργασ-
[αμένωι -]ι ἐξεργασαμέν-
[ωι -] ΔΔ κατὰ ψήφισμ-
[α -]νι ΗΔΔ ἐπὶ Φορμ-
[ίωνος ἄρχοντος - - - - *a.* 396/5

[- γρα]μματεῖ μισθ-
[ὸς -]ρκωνι ΔΓ⊦ΙΙΙΙ

indicate that these odd figures are salaries or, even if they are, what the payment period is, so no useful information about salaries can be extracted from this inscription.

6. c. 337. 3 ob. p.d. apiece for [2 epistatai] to look after the repair of Long Walls and other Peiraieus fortifications and also [1 ob.?] p.? to look after harbor fortifications? This has been the editors' interpretation of a very fragmentary inscription.[12] Although most of it is restored, the inscription as a whole makes it clear that the repair of Peiraieus fortifications is the subject matter, and the words ἐξ Ἀθηναίων ἁπάντων, οἵτινες ἐπιμελήσονται τῶν ἔργων indicate that provision is being made for an election of persons who will oversee the works. Whether they were called epistatai (rather than ἐπιμεληταί) is less certain—they might have been inspectors of a *portion* of the repairs. The pay of 3 ob. p.d. probably, but not certainly, applies to them. The restoration of 1 obol for the second part of their work (καὶ τούτων τῶν ἔργων, line 43) has no basis on the stone, as the editors

---

12. *IG* II^2 244. 3, 28–31, 40–45:
[- - - - 17 - - - - κα]ὶ τὰ περὶ τὴν Ἠτιώνειαν καὶ τὸν ἄλλο[ν Πειραιᾶ] 3

[χειροτονῆσαι δὲ τὸν δῆμον αὐτίκα μάλα ἐπιστάτας δύο] 28
[ἄνδ]ρας ἐξ Ἀθηναίων ἁπάντων, οἵτινες ἐπιμελήσονται τῶν ἔργων [τῶν εἰς τὰ μακρὰ τείχη καὶ εἰς τὰ περὶ τὴν Ἠτιώνειαν καὶ τὸν ἄλλον Πειραιᾶ], 29
[ὅπ]ως ἂν ἐξεργάζωνται οἱ μισθωσάμενοι κατὰ τὸν ἐνιαυτὸν ἕκασ[τον - 48 - διδόναι δὲ] 30
[ἑκ]ατέρωι αὐτῶν τρεῖς ὀβολοὺς τῆς ἡμέρας ἐκ τῶν τειχοποιικῶν. . . . 31

. . . ὅπως δ' ἂν καὶ οἱ λιμένες κλείωνται [κλείθροις ὡς ἀσφαλεστά-τοις εἰσενεγκεῖν τοὺς ἀρχιτέκτονας τοὺς πα]- 40
ρὰ τῆς πόλεως μισθοφοροῦντας καὶ ἄλλον τὸμ βουλόμενον συγγραφὰ[ς συγγράψαντας- - - - - - - - - - - - - - - 37 - - - - - - - - - - - - - - - - τῆι βουλ]- 41
ῆι τῶν συγγραφῶν χειροτονῆσαι καθ' ἅστινας ἂν δοκῆι αὐτῆι ἐγδιδό[ναι τὰ ἔργα- - - - - - - - - - - - - - 31 - - - - - - - - - - - - - - τοὺς δὲ ἡιρημένους ἐ]- 42
πὶ τὴν ἐπιμέλειαν τῶν τειχῶν ἐπιμελεῖσθαι καὶ τούτων τῶν ἔργων ὅ[πως ἂν ἐξεργάζωνται οἱ μισθωσάμενοι, λαμβάνοντες ὀβολὸν (?) . . . 6 . . . παρ]- 43
[ὰ] τῆς πόλεως, τὸ δὲ ἀργύριον εἶναι εἰς ταῦ[τ]α ἐκ τῶν χρημάτων τῶν τει[χοποιικῶν. ἀποδιδόναι δὲ τὸ ἀργύριον τοὺς τειχοποιοὺς μετὰ τῶν κεχε]- 44
[ι]ροτονημένων ὑπὸ τοῦ δήμο τοῖς μισθωσαμένοις τὰ ἔργα λαμβάνον[τας ἐκ τῶν τει[χοποιικῶν] 45

For the date of c. 337 see Schwenk 24–26, and for further discussion of this entry see "Public Officeholders" #25.

confess with their question mark, and they do not hazard a guess as to the pay period to which the "obol" applies.

7. 333/2? 2 dr. p.d. for elected architect at Eleusis, 3 ob. p.d. for elected scribe, 1 2/3 ob. p.d. apiece for non-citizen treasurer who did the shopping for the public slaves and non-citizen epistatai of public slaves.[13] All of these payments are termed μισθός, except for the scribe's, but the implication is that his compensation (coming at the end of a list of μισθοί for other employees) also is μισθός. There is no payment recorded for the epistatai of these public works.

8. 329/8. 2 dr. p.d. for architect at Eleusis, c. 1 2/3 ob. p.d. for epistates of public slaves, 1 ob. p.d. for elected scribe.[14] Since the

---

13. *IG* II² 1673 + *SEG* XXXIV 122. 57–62:

ταμίαι τῶι [ἀγ]οράζοντι τοῖς δημοσίοις Ἀριστοκρίτωι Τροζη : μισθὸς : ΓͰͰͰΙΙ: τοῦ μη- 57
[νὸς : γί]γνεται τριῶν καὶ δέκα μηνῶ[ν :] ΗΓͰͰͰΙΙ : ἐπιστάτει τῶν δημ[ο]σίων [. .]ογένει Τροζηνί : μισθὸς ὁ ἴσος : ΗΓͰͰͰΙΙ : ἑτέρωι ἐπιστάτηι τῶμ μ- 58
[ὲν ὀκ]τ̣ὼ μηνῶν Ἀθηνίωνι ἐγ Κερα : οἰκ̣ [: γί]γνεται μισθὸς : 𐅄ΔΓͰΙΙΙΙ : τῶν δὲ π[έντε] μηνῶν Χρέμονι : Μεγαρεῖ : γίγνεται μισθὸς : ΔΔΔͰΙΙΙΙ : ἀρχιτέκτ- 59
[ονι Ἀ]θ̣ηνοδώρωι : Μέλι : τῶι κεχειροτ[ονη]μένωι ἐπὶ τὴν οἰκοδομίαν μισθὸς [τῆς ἡμ]έρας : ͰͰ : γίγνεται τριῶν καὶ δέκα μηνῶν : 𐅅ΗΗ vv 𐅄 ΔΔΔ : Εὐκλεῖ τῶι κ- 60
[εχε]ι̣ροτονημένω⟨ι⟩ ἀντιγράφεσθ[αι τὰ ἀ]ναλισκόμενα εἰς τὰ ἐπιτήδε[ια τρεῖς ὀβολ]οὶ τῆς ἡμέρας κατὰ τὸ ψήφισμα τὸ τοῦ δήμου : γίγνεται τριῶν καὶ 61
[δέκ]α̣ μηνῶν : Η𐅄ΔΔΔΔΓ: 62

For the date, see Clinton, "Ins. Eleusis" 107–113. In this year there were 13 months, each of 30 days, so that there were 390 days in the year. The architect therefore received 780 dr. (390 x 2 dr. p.d.) and the scribe 195 dr. (390 x 3 ob. p.d.), while the metic epistatai and treasurer were paid 8 dr. 2 ob. per month, which works out to 1 2/3 ob. p.d. (8 dr. 2 ob. = 50 ob. ÷ 30 days = 1 2/3 ob. p.d.). For this entry, see also "Public Officeholders" #27.

14. *IG* II² 1672. 5–6, 11–12, 43–44, 118–119,142–143 (all recording payments in individual prytanies):

ἐπιστάτηι δημ- 5
οσίων μισθὸς τῆς προτανεί[ας : Δ :] 6

Ἀ̣[θηνοδ]ώρωι ἀρχιτέκτονι, ὃ προέλαβεν Λυκούργου κελεύσαντος, τῆς προτ- 11
ανέας μισθὸς : 𐅄ΔΔͰͰ : Τηλοφίλωι τῶι κ[ε]χειροτονημένωι ἀντιγράφεσθαι τὰ ἀναλισκόμενα : ΓͰ : 12

ἐπιστάτηι δημοσίων μισθὸς : [Δ] · Τ[η]λοφίλωι τῶι [κ]εχειροτονημένωι ἀντιγράφ- 43
εσθαι τἀναλισκόμενα τῆς πρυτανείας : ΓͰ : 44

architect is the same as in #7, it is probable that he also was elected.[15] Again, these payments (including, almost certainly, the scribe's)[16] are termed μισθός, and there is no payment recorded for the epistatai of these public works.

Of these figures as a group, not all are secure, and of those even fewer are directly comparable.

(a) The earliest secure salary is 4 ob. p.d. in c. 449–447?, for the Eleusinian epistatai (#2), but the only other salary that we have for a (citizen) epistates is the much less secure 3 ob. p.d. for the "epistatai" of the rebuilding of the Peiraieus fortifications in c. 337 (#6), and this is not clearly comparable since the officials there may not have been epistatai and they may have been paid an additional sum for other daily work on the harbor fortifications.

(b) For architects, we have a very neat comparison: 1 dr. p.d. in 408/7 (#4) and 2 dr. p.d. in 333/2? and 329/8 (##7 and 8). It looks as if the salaries of architects on large public works projects had doubled in 75 years.

(c) There is no one in the later accounts who is precisely comparable to the citizen ὑπογραμματεύς who was paid 5 ob. p.d in 408/7 (#4); he seems to have had a higher status and/or more of a full-time

---

ἐπιστάτηι δημοσίων μισθὸς : Δ : Τηλοφίλωι τῶι κεχειροτονημένωι 118
[ἀντ]ιγράφεσθαι τἀναλισκόμενα : 𐅃IIIII : 119

ἐπιστάτηι μισθὸς τῆς προ- 142
τανείας : Δ : Τηλοφίλωι τῶι κεχειροτονημένωι ἀντιγράφεσθαι τἀναλισ- 143
κόμενα :𐅃IIIII:

Because the payments (recorded elsewhere in the inscription) of 3 ob. p.d. to 17 public slaves and their epistates (= 18 payees x 3 ob. p.d. = 9 dr. p.d., and see "Construction and Other Manual Workers" #8 with n. 27) resulted in prytany totals of 324 dr. and 315 dr., we know that the prytanies in lines 5–12 and 43–44 had 36 days, and that the prytanies in lines 118–119 and 142–143 had 35 days. The architect therefore was paid 2 dr. p.d. (72 dr. ÷ 36 days = 2 dr. p.d.) and the scribe was paid 1 ob. p.d. (6 dr. = 36 ob. ÷ 36 days = 1 ob. p.d., 5 dr. 5 ob. = 35 ob. ÷ 35 days = 1 ob. p.d.). The epistates was paid 10 dr. per prytany regardless of whether it was of 36 or 35 days (10 dr. = 60 ob. ÷ 36 = 1 2/3 ob. p.d., ÷ 35 = c. 1 2/3 ob. p.d.).

15. For the reading 'Α̣[θηνοδ]ώρωι in line 11, see Clinton, "Ins. Eleusis" 100. For this entry, see also "Public Officeholders" #29.

16. By even stronger implication than in #7, since the scribe's name is recorded four times, immediately after the μισθοί for the architect and the epistates of slaves.

job than the scribes who recorded expenditures in ##7 and 8 and were paid 3 ob. and 1 ob. p.d., respectively.

(d) The scribes themselves are puzzling. Why was there a drop from 3 to 1 ob. p.d. from 333/2? to 329/8? If anything, we should expect a salary *increase* since prices rose dramatically in those years, probably because of a grain shortage.[17] The jobs were the same in each case—the recording of expenditures—and both were probably part-time jobs since, in 329/8 at least, common laborers were earning 1 dr. 3 ob. and skilled workers 1 1/4 to 2 1/2 dr. for a day's work.[18] The only clue that I can discern is the fact that the scribe in #7 was paid κατὰ τὸ ψήφισμα τὸ τοῦ δήμου, while there is no mention of this for the scribe in #8. Did this decree perhaps provide for a "legal wage" in the absence of which the scribe was subject to a "market rate"?

(e) The non-citizen epistatai of public slaves in both #7 and #8 were paid c. 1 2/3 ob. p.d., and the non-citizen treasurer who did the shopping for the slaves was paid the same amount in #7. That suggests a "going rate" in c. 330 for what again must have been a part-time job; in this connection, it should be noted that in #8 the epistates of public slaves also received 3 ob. p.d. τροφή.[19]

---

17. The following are the price increases from 333/2? to 329/8 (parentheses after each figure enclose the line references in *SEG* XXXIV 122 and *IG* II^2 1672, respectively): baskets (κόφινοι) from 3 1/4 ob. (45) to 5 ob. or 1 dr. (65, 66, 168); felt hats (πῖλοι) from 3/4 ob. (48) to 1 3/4 ob. (71); leather jackets (διφθέραι) from 2 dr. 3 ob. or 3 dr. (47) to 4 dr. 3 ob. (104); shoes (ὑποδήματα) from 1 dr. 4 1/4 ob.–2 dr. 1 1/4 ob. (48–49) to 6 dr. (105); shoe repair (cobbler καττύσαντι) from 1 dr. 5 ob. (50) to 4 dr. (190). See also Clinton, "Ins. Eleusis" 111–112. For increases in grain prices in this period (range for a medimnos of wheat: 5–16 dr., for barley 3–18 dr., for σῖτος 10–32 dr.), most plausibly reflecting a shortage, see *IG* II^2 360. 9, 30, 56, 68; 408. 13–14; 1672. 283, 287–288, 297–298; [Dem.] xxxiv. 39; [Dem.] xlii. 20, 31; [Arist.] *Oec.* 1352b 15–20. For increases in livestock prices, presumably caused by the increase in grain prices, see *IG* II^2 1672. 120, 128, 289–290, and "Introduction" pp. 1–2 with n. 3.

18. See "Construction and Other Manual Workers" #7.

19. See "Construction and Other Manual Workers" #8.

Chapter 7
Construction and Other Manual Workers

These figures are organized and discussed in five categories: (1) "Workers Paid on the Basis of Time," (2) "Workers Paid on the Basis of Measure," (3) "Workers Paid on the Basis of Piece or Job," (4) "Labor and Material Costs Combined" and (5) "Labor and Transport Costs Combined." Inscribers are discussed separately in Chapter 8. Since Böckh's brief collection and discussion,[1] the principal detailed work has been done by scholars working on individual inscriptions (see notes 5, 12, 13 and 44 below).

Pay in the first category is usually for work per day, less often per prytany.

1. c. 450. [6,]600 dr. 2 ob. wages (μισθοί) for workers on the Athena Promachos statue in year (VI?), more than 10,100 dr. in year (VIII?).[2] Unfortunately only total figures for the entire work force are given, without any indication of the number of workers or days worked, so we can deduce nothing about individual wages.

---

1. Böckh, *SdA* I 148–151.
2. *IG* I^3 435. 76–77 (Year VI?):
   [𐅇X]𐅅HII　　μ[ισθοὶ κατ' ἐμέ]ραν, μισθοὶ κ[ατὰ πρυ]-
   　　　　　　τα̣[νείαν, μισθο]ὶ ἀπόπαχς·

IG I^3 435. 111–112 (Year VIII?):
   M - - - - -　　[μισθοὶ κατ' ἐμέραν], μισθοὶ κατ[ὰ]
   H - - - - -　　[πρυτανείαν, μισθ]οὶ ἀπόπαχς·

I suspect that the restoration κατ' ἐμέραν (rather than καθ' ἐμέραν) is based on preserved spellings in lines 18 and 25, but cf. *IG* I^3 475. 65–71 (quoted in n. 7 below), where both spellings appear in the same text. For this entry, see also "Actors, Artists, Musicians and Writers" #2.

2. pre-411? 4 ob. p.d. (p.d.) for Timon of Athens as a farm-worker.[3] It is not certain that Timon was a real person or, if he was, when precisely in the fifth century he lived.[4] Moreover, we do not know what evidence, if any, Lucian (writing in the second century A.D.) had for the 4 ob. wage. Finally, and most regrettably, we do not have *any* other Athenian wages for agricultural workers, with which we can compare this one. About all that can be said, therefore, is that, in relation to clearly attested wages of 1 dr. p.d. for manual workers in 409–407 (#3 below), and for soldiers and sailors as early as 432 ("Soldiers and Sailors" #5), this wage (if authentic) would fit best in an earlier period—cf. the 4 ob. (p.d.) for the Eleusinian epistatai in c. 449–447? ("Public Officeholders" #4), and the much less certain 4 ob. (p.d.?) for rowers or soldiers or officials in 450/49? ("Soldiers and Sailors" #2).

3. 409–407. 1 dr. or (in one instance) 5 ob. p.d. for Erechtheion workers. In the Erechtheion building accounts for the two years 409/8 and 408/7, there are about two dozen recorded payments of 1 dr., explicitly per day, to various workers. The payees include both skilled[5] workers (sawyers[6] and carpenters[7]) and laborers who did

---

3. Lucian *Tim.* 6 (Timon speaking): ἐργάζομαι τὴν γῆν ὑπόμισθος ὀβολῶν τεττάρων; *Tim.* 12 (Ploutos speaking): ἄθλιοι τέτταρας ὀβολοὺς ἀποφέροντες.

4. See testimonia collected in *PA* 13845 and more recent comments by J. Henderson, *Aristophanes Lysistrata* (Oxford 1987) 172, and A. H. Sommerstein, *Aristophanes Lysistrata* (Warminster 1990) 198, who both observe that Timon must have died before the production of the *Lysistrata* in 411.

5. I use the word "skilled" to refer to workers who are explicitly labeled "carpenters," "sawyers," "plasterers," etc., or who perform similarly specialized tasks, and the word "unskilled" to refer to workers who are explicitly labeled "hired laborers" (μισθωτοί) or who perform jobs that require only moving or lifting. On certain occasions (e.g., #3), at least some "unskilled" workers were paid the same as "skilled" workers, while at other times (e.g., #7) "skilled" workers were paid more. The differences, or lack of them, probably reflect a combination of market conditions (varying supply of and demand for "skilled" and "unskilled" workers) and social and political judgments, whether explicitly articulated or not (e.g., that all workers are entitled to the same "standard" wage, on which see pp. 117–119 below with n. 44 and "A Standard Athenian Wage?"). Those who could afford *not* to work with their hands, either as "skilled" or "unskilled" workers, frequently expressed disdain for all such workers as βάναυσοι, but it was recognized that training and apprenticeship were required for such "skilled" work as pot-making and stone-cutting, and "skilled" workers were proud of their skills. See literary and epigraphical sources collected by Burford, *Craftsmen* 11–12, 82–91, 129, 156–157. Cf. R. Mandolfo, "The Greek Attitude to Manual Labor," *P&P* 6 (1954) 1–5.

6. *IG* I^3 475. 54–57:

[πρίσ]ταις κα[illegible]ιμέ][illegible] ἐρheavy lifting, moving or unspecified work.[8] On one occasion, a carpenter was paid 5 ob. p.d.[9] There are a number of other instances

---

[γαζομένοις, ἀν]δρο[ῖ]ν δυοῖν, [hε]κατέρ-
[οι δραχμε̑ς, hε]μερο̑ν ⁝ΔΙΙ⁝ Ραιδίοι ⁝ ἐγ Κọ-
[λλ ⁝ οἱ ⁝ καὶ συνέρ]γο[ι]ς ⁝ΔΔ⊢⊢⊢⊢⁝

IG I³ 476. 33–46:
πρίσταις καθ' ἐμέραν hερ-
γαζομένοις, δυοῖν ἀνδροῖν, h-
εκκαίδεκα hεμερο̑ν, δραχμε̑ς
τε̑ς hεμέρας hεκάστες, hεκατ-
[έ]ροι, Ραιδίοι ἐν Κολλυτο̑ι hο-
ικο̑ντι καὶ συνέργοι, ΔΔΔ⊢⊢⁝ π-
ρίσταις καθ' ἐμέραν hεργαζο-
μένοις, τρίτες δοδεκεμέρο, κ-
αλύμματα εἰς τὲν hοροφέν, hε-
πτὰ hεμερο̑ν, δραχμὴν τῆς hεμ-
έρας hεκάστες, δυοῖν ἀνδροῖ-
ν, Ραιδίοι ἐν Κολλυτο̑ι hοικο̑-
ντι καὶ συνέργοι ⁝Δ⊢⊢⊢⊢⁝ κεφά-
λαιον πρίσταις ⁝ΔΔΔΔΠ⊢⁝

7. *IG* I³ 475. 65–71:
τέκτοσιν καθ' ἐ[μέ]ραν
ὀχετὸν ἐκποέσαντι καὶ hυποθέντι, hε-
μερο̑ν ⁝ΠΙΙΙΙ⁝ Κροίσοι Φιλοκλέος ⁝Π⊢⊢⊢⊢⁝ κ-
ανόνας ἀναχσέσαντι καὶ ἐργα[ζ]ομ-
ένοι κατ' ἐμέραν, hεμερο̑ν ⁝Δ⁝ Γέ[ρυι ⁝Δ⁝]
καθ' ἐμέραν κανόνα διαρρυ[θμίσαντι]
δυοῖν hεμέραιν Μικίονι [⁝ ⊢⊢⁝]

IG I³ 475. 250–251, 253–256:
τέκτοσι μισθόματα καὶ καθ-
εμερίσια. . . .
τὸσφεσκίσκος θε̑σι καὶ τὸς ἱ-
μάντας καθ' ἐμέραν, Γέρυι, hεμερ-
ο̑ν ⁝ΠΙ⁝Π⊢⁝ Μικίονι, hεμερο̑ν ⁝ΙΙΙ⁝ ⊢⊢⊢ ⁝ Κ-
ροίσοι, hεμερο̑ν ⁝Π⁝Π⁝

IG I³ 475. 288–291:
- - - - - - - - - - - - - hεμερο̑ν εἴκ-
[οσι τριο̑ν, δραχμὲν τε̑ς hε]μέρας ἐκάστ-
[ε]ς, Γέρυι Φιλοκλέο[ς ⁝ΔΔ⊢⊢]⊢⁝ πρίσταις καὶ τ-
έκτονι ἀργυρίο κ̣[εφάλ]αιον[⁝]𐅄⊢ *vacat*

8. *IG* I³ 475. 272–285:
[- - - - - - - - - δ]ε[υ]τέρα[ι τε̑ς πρυτα]-
[νείας ἀν]δράσιν ⁝ hενὸ[ς δέοσιν]
[εἴκοσιν ⁝Δ]Π⊢⊢⊢⊢ ⁝ τρίτει τ[ε̑ς πρυτ]-
[ανείας ⁝ ἀ]νδράσιν τριάκο[ντα καὶ]-
[hενὶ ⁝ ΔΔ]Δ⊢ ⁝ τετάρτει τε̑[ς πρυτα]-
[νείας ⁝ ἀ]νδράσιν τρισὶ καὶ τρ[ι]ά[κον]-
[τα ⁝ ΔΔ]Δ⟨⊢⊢⊢⟩ ⁝ πέμπτει τε̑ς π[ρυτανε]-
[ίας] ἀνδράσιν τρισὶ καὶ τρ[ιάκοντ]-

where the wage is not explicitly said to be 1 dr. *per day*, but the context suggests that it is, e.g., where numbers of men are paid 1 dr. apiece for unspecified work or unskilled work, such as placing ceiling beams on their beds, taking down scaffolding, or carrying up [paint pots?].[10] Finally, there are instances where one or more men are paid

---

[α ⁝ Δ]ΔΔ⟨⊢⊢⊢⟩ ⁝ hέ[κ]τει τε̑ς πρυτν[είας]
[ἀ]νδράσιν ἑνὸς δέοσι τριά[κοντα]
[Δ]ΔΠ⊢⊢⊢⊢ ⁝ hεβδόμει τε̑ς π[ρυτανε]-
ίας ἀνδράσιν τρισὶ καὶ εἴκο[σιν ⁝ΔΔ]
⊢⊢⊢ ⁝ hoγδόηι τε̑ς πρυτα[νείας ἀν]-
δράσιν ἑνὶ καὶ εἴκοσιν ⁝ΔΔ⊢ - - - - -

IG I³ 476. 124–134:

[huπoργoῖς καθ' hε]-
μέραν [h]εργ[αζομένοις, τε̑ν τρ]-
οχιλείαν [- - - - - 14 - - - - - Κ]-
εκροπίο h(?) [- - - - - 14 - - - - - Κ]-
εκροπικα [- - - - - 15 - - - - -]
ινας συνθε [- - - - - 14 - - - - -]
σασιν ἐν τε̑ι [- - - - 10 - - - - ἀνδ]-
ράσι[ν], δραχμ[ὲν τε̑ς ἑμέρας, Κό]-
νονι, ⊢ ⁝ 'Απολλο[δόροι ⁝ ⊢ ⁝ Πρέπον]-
τι ⁝ ⊢ ⁝ Μέδοι ⁝ ⊢ ⁝ [- - - - - 14 - - - - -]-
Μαμμάνοι ⁝ ⊢ ⁝ [- - - - 10 - - - - ⁝ ⊢ ⁝]

9. *IG* I³ 476. 104–109:

τέκ[τονι καθ' hεμέραν hεργα]-
ζομένοι μισ[θὸς ΠΙΙΙΙΙ τε̑ς τ]-
ρίτε[ς] δοδε[κεμέρο, πέντε ὀβο]-
λὸς τε̑[ς] hεμ[έρας hεκάστες hε]-
πτὰ hε[μ]ερο̑[ν . . . . 'Αλοπ]-
εκε̑σι hοικ[ο̑ντι, ΠΙΙΙΙΙ]

Why was this carpenter paid less than 1 dr. p.d.? Because we lack the immediately preceding lines, we cannot tell precisely what he was doing. His identification as a metic living in Alopeke indicates that he was *not* one of the higher-paid carpenters recorded in the passages quoted in n. 7 (Kroisos and Gerys were slaves, as shown by the genitive of the name of their owner Philokles [in lines 67 and 290], and Mikion seems to have been a metic living in Melite or Kollytos [*IG* I³ 475. 247, 260, 265]), so perhaps the 5-ob. carpenter was less skilled.

10. *IG* I³ 476. 5–25, 28–31:

[..]ε[.] τούτ[ο]ι[ν π]ροσλαβόντοι-
[ν] δυοῖν ἀνδροῖν, Σοσίαι 'Αλοπ-
εκε̑σι οἰκο̑ν ⁝ ⊢ ⁝ Σίνδρονι ⁝ ⊢ ⁝ τὲν
ὀροφὲν κατιστᾶσιν, τὲν καμπ-
ύλεν ⁝ σελίδα εἰς ἕδραν καὶ τὰ-
ς ἄλλας ἐπαγαγο̑σιν εἰς ἕδρα-
ν hεκάστεν, Μάνιδι ἐν Κολλυτ-
ο̑ι οἰκο̑ντι ⁝ ⊢ ⁝ Κροίσοι ἐν Σκαμ-
βονιδο̑ν hοικο̑ντι ⁝ ⊢ ⁝ 'Ανδρέαι
ἐμ Μελίτει hοικο̑ντι ⁝ ⊢ ⁝ Πρέπο-
ντι 'Αγρυλε̑σι οἰκο̑ντι ⁝ ⊢ ⁝ Μέδο-

3 ob. or 1 dr. 3 ob. apiece for similar unskilled work (putting up or taking down and carrying away scaffolding), and it seems likely that these jobs required a half day or a day and a half, respectively.[11] As discussed more fully by Randall, these payments are made without regard to the status of the payee, i.e., payments of 1 dr. p.d. are recorded for citizens, metics and slaves doing the same work, often side by side.[12]

4. 394. Aggregate μισθοί in one month for work by the day: 160 dr. for yokes (of oxen?) hauling stone and 53 dr. for (wages of ironworkers or rental of iron tools?).[13] Since the number of men

---

ι ἐμ Μελίτει hοικο͂ντι : ⊢: Ἀπολ-
λοδόροι ἐμ Μελίτει hοικο͂ντ-
ι : ⊢: hικριόματα καθελο͂σιν τὰ
ἀπὸ το͂ν κιόνον το͂ν hεν τε͂ι πρ-
οστάσει, hὲχς ἀνδράσιν, Τεῦκ-
ρος ἐν Κυδαθεναίοι hοικο͂ν : ⊢,
Κέρδον Ἀχσιοπείθος, ⊢: Κροῖσ-
ος ἐν Σκαμβονιδο͂ν : hοικο͂ν : ⊢: Π-
ρέπον Ἀγρυλε͂σι hοικο͂ν : ⊢: Κεφ-
ισόδορος : ⊢: Σποδίας: ⊢: . . . .

. . . . λ-
[εκάνας (?)] ἀναφορέσασιν Πρέπο-
[ντι Ἀ]γρυλε͂σι hοικο͂ντι : ⊢: Μέδ-
[ο]ι ἐμ Μελίτει : hοικο͂ντι : ⊢:

11. *IG* I^3 476. 134–140 (for immediately preceding payments to laborers who are explicitly paid 1 dr. p.d., see n. 8):

hίκ]-
ρια καθελο͂[σι καὶ ἀποκομίσα]-
σι hαπὸ το͂ το[ίχο το͂ πρὸς βορέ]-
ο hαφ' ο͂ν τὰ ζ[όιδια ἐτέθε, hεχς]
ἀνδράσι, Π[ρέποντι :III: Μέδοι :III: Α]-
πολλοδό[ροι :III: - - - 12 - - - -]
αίοι :III: [- - - - - - 17 - - - - - -]

IG I^3 476. 25–28:

hικριό-
σασι τοῖς ἐνκαυταῖς hεκ το͂ h-
[ε]ντὸς hυπὸ τὲν hοροφέν, Μάνι-
[δι ἐν Κ]ολλυτο͂ι : hοικο͂ντι : ⊢III:

In the first passage, three of the four 3 ob. payments are restored, but *IG* I^3 476. 18–25 (quoted in n. 10) suggests that men taking down scaffolding all would be paid the same amount. F. B. Jevons, "Work and Wages in Athens," *JHS* 15 (1895) 239–247 at 240, seems to have been the first to suggest that these men were paid for a half day or a day and a half.

12. Randall, "Erechtheum Workmen" 209.

13. *IG* II^2 1656:

ἐπὶ Διοφάντο ἄρχον- *a.* 395/4

working and, in the case of the yokes, the portion of the payment that was allocable to the drivers, is not stated, we can deduce nothing about individual wages.

5. 333/2? 4 dr. per yoke p.d. for yokes (of oxen), presumably plus driver(s), for hauling column drums from Mount Pentelikos to Eleusis, with a supplementary payment of 1 dr. per half-day for the yokes as a group. Since this supplementary payment may well have been a reimbursement for fixed expenses rather than compensation (and in any event amounted to only about 1/3 ob. p.d. per yoke),[14]

τος ⟨Σ⟩κιροφοριῶνος
μηνὸς ἐ̣[ς] τὰ κατ' ἡ̣-
μέραν ἔργα· ζεύγ-
εσι τὸς λίθος ἄγοσι
μισθὸς ⁝Η𐅄Δ·
σιδηρίων μι-
σθὸς ⁝𐅄⊢⊢⊢.

The words σιδηρίων μισθός are usually interpreted as "hire of stonemason's iron tools" (see LSJ *s.v.* σιδήριον and Maier no. 1 ["Werkzeugen"]), but 53 dr. seems too large a sum for only one month's rental of tools, even though their quantity is not stated, and in the context of other κατ' ἡμέραν ἔργα it might be more natural to take σιδηρίων as coming from σιδηρεύς "ironworker" even though this would require us to postulate a graphic mistake of *iota* for *epsilon*, i.e., σιδηρέων. As Clinton, "Ins. Eleusis" 105, observes, "there is nothing to indicate that the day rate [for yokes] was 4 drachmas" in 394, as it was in c. 330 (cf. ##5 and 6 below). (G. Glotz, "Un transport de marbre pour le portique d'Éleusis (333/2)," *REG* 36 [1923] 26–45 at 26, and A. K. Orlandos, Τὰ Ὑλικὰ Δομῆς II [Athens 1958] 100, had interpreted the 160 dr. as spread over 40 working days = 4 dr. p.d.)

14. *IG* II^2 1673 + *SEG* XXXIV 122. 64–90. The only entry with all figures preserved is found in lines 65–66:

κατὰ ψήφισμα δήμου ὃ Λυκοῦργος εἶπεν . . . 65
. . . ἕτερ̣ον σφόνδυλον ἠρξά̣[μεθα κομ]ι̣ζ̣ε̣ι̣ν̣ [παρὰ - - Quarrier c. 10 - -]Ο. 66
[- - Date c. 9 - - ἦγεν ζεύγη] : ΔΔΔΙΙΙ : ἐκομίσθη ἐν τρισὶν ἡμέραις,
μισθὸς τοῖς ζεύγεσιν : ΗΗΗΗ⊢⊢

402 dr. ÷ 3 days = 134 dr. p.d. ÷ 33 yokes = 4 dr. per yoke p.d. plus 2 dr. p.d. supplement. For 3 days the supplement works out to 6 dr. Five other, less well preserved, entries (in lines 64–66, 66, 67–68, 68, and 69), involving groups of 30, 32 and 33 yokes all delivering in three days, exhibit the same 6 dr. difference, so it is tempting to see the supplement as a 6 dr. *per trip* supplement. But in line 79, where the trip took two and one-half days, the supplement seems to have been 5 dr. ([24] teams x 4 dr. p.d. x 2 1/2 days = 240 dr. + 5 dr. = 245 dr.; if one assumes a 6 dr. per trip supplement and deducts that amount from 245 dr., the 239 dr. balance is not divisible by 4 dr. for a whole day or 2 dr. for a half day). Clinton, "Ins. Eleusis" 106–107, also worked out plausible restorations in lines 81 and 82 (4 dr. supplement for two days), and in lines 79, 84 and 86 (5 dr. supplement for two and one-half days), to which add the following possible restoration in line 83: [38] yokes x 4 dr. p.d. x [2] days = 304 dr. + 4 dr. supplement = [ΗΗ]ΗΓ⊢⊢⊢; in none of these six cases would the deduction of a 6 dr. per trip supplement from the gross wage result in a balance divisible by 4 dr. I therefore am inclined to agree with Clinton that the supplement is based on the number of half days taken to transport individual column drums. But I am not persuaded by his

for purposes of this study I am inclined to regard the compensation per yoke as a flat 4 dr. p.d. Because we are not told what portion of this was paid to the driver(s), this entry tells us nothing about daily wages for individuals.[15]

6. 330/29. 4 dr. p.d. for yokes (of oxen)?[16] Clinton interprets this honorary decree as indicating that a Plataian benefactor, Eude-

---

interpretation of this supplement as a bonus for delivery within three days, i.e., a kind of "express charge," for two reasons. First, since the supplement for delivery in three days (6 dr.) is greater than for delivery in two days (4 dr.) or two and one-half days (5 dr.), the "bonus" would provide a slight incentive to *delay* delivery. Second, since the "bonus" for a three-day delivery always was 6 dr. even though the number of yokes varied, the "bonus" per yoke would be different in each case and would be unevenly denominated (6 dr. = 36 ob. ÷ 33 yokes [lines 64–67] = 1 1/11 ob.; ÷ 32 yokes [line 68] = 1 1/8 ob.; ÷ 30 yokes [line 69] = 1 1/5 ob.; in each case, further divisible by 3 days to yield the per diem "bonus" per yoke). I suspect that Lykourgos' decree (line 65) laid down that the rate for this job was 4 dr. p.d. per yoke plus (for whatever reason, to us now impenetrable) an additional flat fee of 1 dr. per half day of the trip, without regard to how many yokes were involved or whether one or two drums (see lines 72–75) were being transported in the particular trip. E. Badian suggests to me that perhaps the supplement reimbursed the teams for a road toll or other fixed cost of transport. For more on the calculations, and for the date of "333/2?," see Clinton, "Ins. Eleusis" 102–113.

15. Burford ("Heavy Transport" 17, n. 3) states that a "day-wage of 4 . . . drachmai was much higher than the wages earned by skilled craftsmen; but it was only temporary, and irregular at that. Whether or not the driver of the beasts owned them or hired them from someone else, any money he received for this kind of transport would be *in addition to* this usual income." But this makes no allowance for the cost of maintaining or hiring the oxen and cart, and assumes (a) that only one man was involved in driving and handling each yoke, and (b) that he would not have been otherwise employed and earning money if he had not been hauling these columns. Although the Eleusis inscription sheds no light on the number of drivers, one piece of evidence collected by Burford suggests that at least two men may have been involved. Cato *Agr.* 22. 3, in speaking of the cost of transporting an olive press (which Burford calculates required three yokes), says: "vecturam boum, operas VI, homines VI cum bubulcis HS LXXII," i.e., six men plus an unstated number of drivers (*bubulcis*) for six work days (*operas*). Burford (at 9) comments: "Cato allows expenses for six day-wages, that is, presumably, two days' wages to each of the three yoke-drivers." See also T. Frank, *An Economic Survey of Ancient Rome* I (Baltimore 1933) 165–166: after translating "the fetching of it required six men, with six boys to drive the oxen, six days = 72 sesterces," Frank goes on to say that "the men count for 2 sesterces per day." But if there are six work days (*operas*) and the total cost is 72 sesterces, the gross wages per day are 12 sesterces, which have to be divided not only among the six *homines* but also among the unstated number of *bulbucis*, who (even if they were slaves) would have had to be maintained. Towards the end of the preserved part of the Eleusis inscription (*SEG* XXXIV 122. 92–96), there is insufficient context to permit interpretation of the 120 dr., 5 dr. and [- - - κον]τα καὶ ἑπτὰ τρι[ῶν] ὀβ[ολῶν - - - - -] Ọl μισθὸς τῆς ἡμέρας :Ͱ [.], although possibly they have something to do with the [ἀ]κολουθεῖ τοῖς ζεύγεσιν δυοῖν in line 90. In the end, we are forced to admit that neither the Eleusis inscription nor the Cato passage provide conclusive evidence as to how many men per yoke were employed, or what portion of the payment for transport went to them.

16. *IG* II^2 351. 11–20:

ἐπειδὴ *vacat*

mos, "in lieu of giving [4] thousand drachmas to the Athenians for military purposes, as he originally promised, made a gift of the use of one thousand teams for the construction of the Panathenaic stadium and spectator area. . . . This must of course mean day-teams; i.e., the number of teams multiplied by the number of days will equal one thousand. And since this gift in all probability was equivalent to his previous promise of 4000 drachmas, the rate will have been 4 drachmas per team per day."[17] But the restoration of [4,]000 dr. is no more than a guess (the number could be 𐅆XXX or MXXX), and the language makes it unlikely that the gift of the yokes was "in lieu of" the earlier promise,[18] so the interpretation of [4,]000 dr. as the equivalent of 1,000 day wages is very uncertain. In any event, even if Eudemos' yokes were paid 4 dr. p.d., as with #5, that would tell us nothing about individual wages.

7. 329/8. 1 dr. 1 1/2 ob. to 2 dr. 3 ob. p.d. for skilled workers (see n. 5 above) at Eleusis, 1 dr. 3 ob. p.d. for unskilled workers, in each case with the worker providing his own food. In the Eleusis building account for this year, there are a number of recorded payments of daily wages to workers, and in each case it is specified that the payee is οἰκόσιτος, i.e., that he provides his own food. This suggests that a different, presumably lower, wage scale would have been operating for any workers who were furnished food on the job, as public slaves had been in 333/2?.[19] For skilled workers, there are five

---

[Εὔδημ]ος πρότερον τε ἐπη[γ]γ[εί]-
[λατο τ]ῶι δήμωι ἐπιδώσει[ν εἰ]ς
[τὸν π]όλεμον εἴ τ[ι] δέ[οι]το [XXX]X
[δ]ραχμὰς καὶ νῦν [ἐπ]ι[δέδ]ω[κεν]
εἰς τὴν ποίησιν τοῦ σταδ[ί]ου
καὶ τοῦ θεάτρου τοῦ Παναθη[ναι]-
κοῦ χίλια ζεύγη καὶ ταῦτα
πέπομφεν ἅπαντα π[ρὸ Π]αναθη-
ναίων καθὰ ὑπέσχετο. . . .

17. Clinton, "Ins. Eleusis" 105, following Glotz (as in n. 13) 26 ("Eudèmos . . . ne voulut pas se tenir quitte de son engagement sous prétexte que la guerre n'avait pas éclaté"), and Orlandos (as in n. 13) 100.

18. The use of τε . . . καί (rather than μέν . . . δέ) indicates a plus b (rather than a as an alternative to b), and the ἐπί in the second form of ἐπιδίδωμι may suggest an additional gift.

19. See *IG* II² 1673 + *SEG* XXXIV 122. 57 (quoted in "Overseers, Architects and Other Salaried Construction Personnel" n. 13) for payments in 333/2? to the ταμίαι τῶι [ἀγ]οράζοντι τοῖς δημοσίοις. In 329/8, when the workers described in #7 were οικόσιτοι, the public slaves received a monetary allowance for food (see #8 below). Clinton, "Ins. Eleusis" 110–111,

recorded payments to οἰκόσιτοι: 2 dr. 3 ob. p.d. to carpenters laying bricks and working on wood;[20] 2 dr. p.d. to carpenters laying roof tiles and doing some other job (details lost);[21] 2 dr. to stonemasons smoothing door posts;[22] 1 dr. 3 ob. p.d. (probably) apiece to two sawyers (3 dr. p.d. for two);[23] and 1 dr. 1 1/2 ob. p.d. apiece (on average) to a mason finishing stone and a plasterer (2 dr. 3 ob. p.d. for the two of them).[24] This last payment looks suspiciously low, since unskilled workers were being paid 1 dr. 3 ob. p.d. (see below), and one wonders whether in fact *each* worker was paid 2 dr. 3 ob. p.d., but the payment of this wage to two workers together is confirmed by the total payment (2 dr. 3 ob. x 17 days = 42 dr. 3 ob.), so that the error (if there had been one) would have had to be repeated (there is no indication that each man worked half days). There are four instances of hired

---

attributes this new food allowance to the recent increase in grain prices, suggesting that the state preferred to provide a fixed food allowance rather than to incur an uncertain and potentially substantial liability for food furnished in kind. In the volatile grain market of 329/8 (with inflationary consequences for other prices, see "Overseers, Architects and Other Salaried Construction Personnel" n. 17), it is possible that the state declined to provide food in kind to *any* workers.

20. *IG* II[2] 1672. 26–28:

τέκτοσιν τοῖς πλινθοβολήσ- 26
ασιν τὰ περὶ τὸν πυλῶνα καὶ τὸν πύργον καὶ τὰ ξύλινα ἐργασαμένοις, 27
ἀνδράσιν τρισὶν τῆς ἡμέρας ἑκάσ-
τωι οἰκοσί : ⊢⊢ΙΙΙ : κεφά : Η𐅄ΔΔΔΠ⊢⊢ΙΙΙ 28

The total of 187 dr. 3 ob. indicates that the three men worked 25 days, like the μισθωτοί in lines 28–30 (quoted in n. 25 below), who also worked around the gateway and tower: 2 dr. 3 ob. x 3 men = 7 dr. 3 ob. aggregate wages p.d. x 25 days = 187 dr. 3 ob. total wages.

21. *IG* II[2] 1672. 110–111:

τέκτοσιν τρισὶν τοῖς τὴν πάροδον τοῦ τείχους ἀποκεραμώσασιν καὶ τοὺς θρ- 110
. . .[5]. . θεῖσιν, μισθὸς τῶι ἀνδρὶ οἰκοσίτωι : ⊢⊢ : δυοῖν ἡμέραιν κεφάλαιον Δ⊢⊢ : 111

22. *IG* II[2] 1672. 177–178:

τοῖς ἀποξέσασιν τὰς παραστάδας τὰς ἐν τῶι τοῦ Πλούτωνος, ἀνδράσ[ι]ν τέτταρσιν, τῶ- 177
ι ἀνδρὶ οἰκοσίτωι τῆς ἡμέρας : ⊢⊢ : δυοῖν ἡμέραιν : ΔΠ⊢ : 178

23. *IG* II[2] 1672. 159–160:

πρισ- 159
τῶν ζεύγει τοῖς τὰ ξύλα διαπρίσασιν, τῆς ἡμέρας οἰκοσίτ(ο)ις : ⊢⊢⊢ : ἡμερῶν : ΔΔΔΠ : κεφάλαιον : ΗΠ : 160

24. *IG* II[2] 1672. 31–32:

ἐπιξέστει καὶ ὑπαγωγεῖ τοῖς ἐργασαμένοις ἐπὶ τῶι πυλῶνι καὶ τῶι πύργωι τῶι παρὰ τὸ- 31
ν πυλῶνα, τῆς ἡμέρας δυοῖν οἰκοσίτοι[ν ⊢]⊢ΙΙΙ : ἡμερῶν : ΔΠΙΙ : κεφά : ΔΔΔΔ⊢⊢ΙΙΙ : 32

laborers, i.e., unskilled workers, being paid 1 dr. 3 ob. p.d. apiece for carrying bricks, wood, roof tiles, and earth, mixing mortar, breaking clods, sifting plaster, and doing unspecified work.[25]

8. 329/8. c. 1 1/4 (?) ob. to 1 dr. 2(?) ob. p.d. ration payments at Eleusis. In the same building account, there are a number of non-μισθός payments: σιτία (rations) of 1 dr. 1 ob. p.d. (or possibly, in one instance, 1 dr. 2 ob. p.d.) to (letter-) engravers on stone;[26] τροφή (here probably ration-money, as in "Soldiers and Sailors" ##29, 30) of 3 ob. p.d. to public slaves and their epistates;[27] and τροφή of (c. 1

---

25. *IG* II² 1672. 28–30, 32–34, 44–46, 60–62:
μισθωτοῖς *vvv* τοῖς ἐπὶ τὸν πύργον καὶ τὸν πυλῶνα πλινθοφοροῦσ- 28
ιν καὶ πηλοδευστοῦσιν καὶ τὰ ξύλα ἀνακομίσασιν καὶ τὸν κέραμον,
ἀνδράσιν ἕξ, τῶι ἀνδρὶ οἰκοσίτωι *v*
ͰΙΙΙ : ἡμερῶν : ΔΔΠ : κεφά : ΗΗΔΔΠ: 30

μισθωτοῖς τοῖς ἐργασαμέν- 32
οις ἐν τῶι ἱερῶι, ἀνδράσιν δέκα, ἀπὸ τῆς τετράδος ἱσταμένου τοῦ 33
Ἑκατονβαιῶνο : τῶι ἀνδρὶ οἰκοσίτωι : ͰΙΙΙ
ἡμερῶν : ΔΔΔΔ : κεφά : 𐅅Η : ἄχρι τῆς τρίτης ἐπὶ δέκα τοῦ Μεταγειτο : 34

εἰς τὸ τεῖχος κατὰ ψήφισμ[α βο]υ[λῆ]ς ἀπὸ τοῦ πύργου τοῦ παλαι- 44
οῦ τοῦ πεσόντος μισθωτοῖς τοῖς τὰς πλίνθους καὶ τὸγ χοῦν ἀπο[φ]ο[ρή- 45
σ]ασ[ι] εἰς τὸ θέατρον καὶ βωλοκοπή-
σασι, ἀνδράσιν : ΔΔΔ : τῆς ἡμέρας τεττάρων ἡμερῶν τῶι ἀνδρὶ οἰκοσίτωι 46
: ͰΙΙΙ : κεφάλαι Ḥ𐅄ΔΔΔ

μισθωτοῖς τοῖς τὴν γῆν βωλοκοπήσασι καὶ διαττήσασιν εἰς τ- 60
ὸν ἐπαγωγέα τοῦ τείχους καὶ εἰς τοὺς πύργους καὶ εἰς τὴν περιαλιφὴν τοὺ 61
τείχους ἀνδράσιν : Δ : τριῶν κ-
αὶ δέκα ἡμερῶν τῶι ἀνδρὶ : ͰΙΙΙ : οἰκοσίτωι κεφάλαι Η𐅄ΔΔΔΔΠ : 62

26. *IG* II² 1672 + *Hesperia* 64 (1995) 132, no. 2a. 6–8:
[τοῖς τὰ] γράμματα ἐπικολάψασιν ἐπὶ τὸ ἀνάθημα ἐν τῶι Ἐλευσιν- 6
ίωι σιτ-
ία : ΠͰͰ{Ͱ?} : καὶ ἐπὶ τῆς Λειωντ[ίδ]ος τῆς ἡμέρας : ͰΙ : ἡμερῶν : ΔΠΙΙ : 7
κεφάλαι : ΔΠͰͰͰͰΙΙΙΙΙ : καὶ ἐπὶ τῆς Οἰνηΐδος
δεκάτης προτανείας σιτία ΔΔ[ΔΔ]ͰͰͰͰΙΙ : 8

For the questionable drachma in line 7, see W. T. Loomis, "Eleusinian Inscriptions: Three Emendations," *Hesperia* 64 (1995) 131–134 at 132–133 (number of days worked is not stated; for six days the rate of 1 dr. 1 ob. p.d. attested two prytanies earlier in Leontis and restored for the immediately preceding (38-day) Oineis would work out to 7 dr., while 8 dr. would require an increased rate of 1 dr. 2 ob. p.d.). For this entry, see also "Inscribers" #112.

27. *IG* II² 1672. 4–5, 42–43, 117–118, 141–142, 233–234:
δημοσίοις τροφήν, 4
[ἀνδρ]άσιν δεκα[επτὰ καὶ] τῶι [ἐπιστάτηι] τῆς ἡμέρας τῶι ἀνδρὶ : ΙΙΙ : 5
κεφάλαιο[ν] : ΗΗΗΔΔͰͰͰͰ :

1/4 or 3?) ob. p.d. to another (private) slave.[28] As noted under "Overseers, Architects and Other Salaried Construction Personnel" p. 103 with n. 19, the epistates of the public slaves also received c. 1 2/3 ob. p.d. μισθός. In 332/3? public slaves had been furnished with food in kind, probably because food prices were more stable then (see n. 19 above).

9. c. 315? 1 dr. per night for grain grinders? Menedemos and Asklepiades, two young philosophers, are said to have worked in a grain mill, together (ἀμφότεροι) earning 2 dr. per night, i.e., 1 dr. apiece.[29] It is not known where Athenaios, writing c. A.D. 200, found

---

δημοσίοις τροφῆς ἀνδράσιν : ΔΠΙΙ{Ι}: [καὶ] τῶι ἐπιστάτηι, τῆς 42
ἡμέρας ἑκάστωι : ΙΙΙ εἰς τὴ
πρυτα : κεφάλαι : ΗΗΗΔΔ𐅂𐅂𐅂𐅂 : 43

τροφὴ δημοσίοις, ἀνδράσιν δεκαεπτὰ καὶ τῶι ἐπιστάτηι τῆς ἡ- 117
[μ]έρας [ἑκ]άστωι : ΙΙΙ, κεφάλαιον ΗΗΗ[Δ]Π : 118

δημοσίοις τροφή, ἀνδράσι δεκ- 141
αεπτὰ καὶ τῶι ἐπιστάτει, ἐ⟨π⟩ὶ τῆς ἡμέρας τῶι ἀνδρὶ : ΙΙΙ : κεφάλαιον : 142
ΗΗΗΔΠ :

[ἀν]- 233
δράσιν ΔΠΙ, τῆς ἡμέρας ΙΙΙ, ἡμερῶν ΔΙΙ, 𐅅ΔΔΔΠ𐅂 · 234

In lines 4–5 and 42–43, the payment period is a 36-day prytany (18 men x 3 ob. = 9 dr. x 36 days = 324 dr.), and in lines 118 and 142, the payment period is a 35-day prytany (18 men x 3 ob. = 9 dr. x 35 days = 315 dr.). In lines 233–234, not enough is preserved to make it certain that public slaves are the recipients, and indeed the fact that the payment period is only 12 days (x 16 men x 3 ob. = 96 dr.) may suggest that they are not.

28. *IG* II^2 1672. 100–101:

τροφὴ τῶι παιδὶ τῶι Κηφισοδώρου τοῦ τά 100
[.......................33.......................]τι δυοῖν προτανείαιν : ΔΠ : 101

K. Clinton (per epist.) comments as follows: "The lacuna urges caution. Yet the τροφή is most likely for the παῖς in 10[0], whose work is described in 10[1]. I would imagine that he received the same rate as the public slaves, 3 obols per day, and that in the course of the two prytanies he worked for only 30 days." The 1 1/4 ob. alternative is derived by dividing 15 dr. (= 90 ob.) by c. 72 days (2 c. 36-day prytanies); in the context of μισθοί of c. 1 2/3 ob. p.d. for epistatai and treasurers of public slaves in the same period ("Overseers, Architects and Other Salaried Construction Personnel" ##7, 8), 1 1/4 ob. p.d. τροφή might not be odd.

29. Athen. iv. 65 (168a–b): Μενέδημον γοῦν καὶ Ἀσκληπιάδην τοὺς φιλοσόφους νέους ὄντας καὶ πενομένους μεταπεμψάμενοι (sc. οἱ Ἀρεοπαγῖται) ἠρώτησαν πῶς ὅλας τὰς ἡμέρας τοῖς φιλοσόφοις συσχολάζοντες, κεκτημένοι δὲ μηδέν, εὐεκτοῦσιν οὕτω τοῖς σώμασι· καὶ οἳ ἐκέλευσαν μεταπεμφθῆναί τινα τῶν μυλωθρῶν. ἐλθόντος δ' ἐκείνου καὶ εἰπόντος ὅτι νυκτὸς ἑκάστης κατιόντες εἰς τὸν μυλῶνα καὶ ἀλοῦντες δύο δραχμὰς ἀμφότεροι λαμβάνουσι, θαυμάσαντες οἱ Ἀρεοπαγῖται διακοσίαις δραχμαῖς ἐτίμησαν αὐτούς.

this story, but its veracity (in all of its details) rightly has been doubted.[30]

Pay in the second and third categories ("Workers Paid on the Basis of Measure" and "Workers Paid on the Basis of Piece or Job") are best discussed together. Although the data for these categories are much more abundant than for "Workers Paid on the Basis of Time," they are much less useful because (a) we are not told how long the particular job took, and (b) the various jobs or items of piecework usually are not directly comparable with one another.

Workers Paid on the Basis of Measure include stonemasons who laid or finished stone and were paid by the tetrapody, foot or ὄργυα; carpenters and encaustic painters who were paid for their work by the foot; bricklayers and brickmakers who were paid by the 1,000 bricks; a grain measurer and grain carriers who were paid by the 100 medimnoi;[31] and (possibly) a ditchdigger who may have been paid by the square foot.[32] In most of these cases, there are no comparable figures because, e.g., the size of the stone differs or the carpentry task differs. There are, however, two types of work that do provide directly comparable figures:

(a) In 409/8, stonemasons were paid for laying blocks of Eleusinian stone 8 feet long by 2 feet high by (apparently) 1 foot thick. In one case, the work was priced at 5 dr. per tetrapody and the price for three blocks was 30 dr., i.e., 10 dr. per block. In another case, the

30. K. von Fritz, "Menedemos (9)," *RE* 15 (1932) 788–794, concludes (at 790) that Menedemos probably was born c. 339–337, but observes that since Asklepiades was much older, this story (which is attested only in Athenaios) "kann . . . nichts bedeuten" (at 789). That is perhaps an overly strong judgment but, in the absence of any other wages for "industrial" workers, it would not be prudent in this study to give much weight to these figures.

31. Clinton (per epist.) speculates that the 2 dr. charged by the grain measurer (προμετρητής) for measuring 80 1/6 medimnoi in *IG* II^2 1672. 299, as compared to the 1 dr. 1 1/2 ob. per 100 medimnoi in line 291 of the same account, may represent a minimum charge and/or may include the cost of the προμετρητής' journey to and from Eleusis. A minimum charge also might explain the different amounts paid to the men who brought out the grain: 4 ob. per 100 medimnoi in line 293 as compared to 1 dr. 5 1/4 ob. for the 80 1/6 medimnoi in line 299.

32. See Kirchner's commentary on *IG* II^2 1682. 16 (285/4 B.C.), where this theory is advanced. Of course, any ditch has three dimensions, so what really is involved is *cubic* feet, but in this case the depth was uneven, μέχρι τοῦ στερίφου (line 5).

work was priced by the block: four blocks for 40 dr., i.e., also 10 dr. per block.[33] The work appears to be identical, and it is interesting to see that the prices are the same even though their bases ostensibly are different, but because their dates also are the same there can be no diachronic comparison.

(b) From 394 to 328, bricklayers were paid 12 to 20 dr. for laying bricks, per 1,000 bricks. The figures per 1,000 bricks are as follows: in c. 394 12 dr. (twice, once restored), 13 dr. (twice), 15 dr. and 20 dr.,[34] in 392/1 15 dr.,[35] and in 329/8 17 dr.[36] The widest variation is in the earliest period, and the most likely explanation for the differences between a low of 12 dr. and a high of 20 dr. per 1,000 bricks is that the 20 dr. work involved greater time and difficulty, perhaps (in the Peiraieus fortifications) laying bricks in a high tower. It is possible, however, that the difference between all but one of the figures for the 390s (12–15 dr.) and that for 329 (17 dr., but cf. n. 36) is a reflection of the same rise in wages that is seen for Workers Paid on the Basis of Time (##3 and 7 above).

With respect to Workers Paid on the Basis of Piece or Job, I have only the following comments to add to the detailed summaries in the catalogue:

(a) 434/3. Parthenon Pediment Sculpture. It has been variously suggested that the 16,392 dr. paid in this year for pediment sculpture was divided among c. 20–25 sculptors working c. 300 days (i.e., 2–3 dr. per man p.d.), or c. 54 sculptors working the same number of days for 1 dr. p.d.[37] The former rate seems implausibly high in relation to

---

33. Cf. *IG* I^3 475. 1–3 (5 dr. per tetrapody, i.e., 10 dr. per block) with *IG* I^3 475. 29–31 (10 dr. per block).

34. *IG* II^2 1658. 7; 1659. 7 and 12; 1664. 6 and 10, *SEG* XIX 145. 3 (all Peiraieus fortifications).

35. *IG* II^2 1662. 5 (Peiraieus fortifications).

36. *IG* II^2 1672. 60 (Eleusis). If the 20 dr. 2 ob. for bricklaying in II^2 1672. 185 refers to the 1,600 bricks delivered in line 183, the cost of laying 1,000 bricks would be 12 dr. 4 1/4 ob. (20 dr. 2 ob. = 122 ob. ÷ 16 = 7.625 ob. for 100 bricks x 10 = 76.25 ob. or 12 dr. 4 1/4 ob. for 1,000 bricks).

37. For the text of the inscription, which gives the total figure, see "Actors, Artists, Musicians and Writers" #4 with n. 10. For the 20–25 sculptors, see Burford, *Craftsmen* 62 with notes 124 and 245. 16,392 dr. ÷ 300 days = 54.64 dr. gross wages p.d. ÷ 20 sculptors = 2.7 dr. p.d.

other figures discussed above, and in any event both figures are based on too many uncertain assumptions: we are not in fact told how many sculptors worked, or for how many days.

(b) 408/7. Erechtheion Frieze Sculpture.[38] Of the thirteen amounts paid for this sculpture, nine are effectively divisible by 60,

---

per sculptor (54.64 dr. gross wages ÷ 25 sculptors = 2.2 dr. p.d. per sculptor). I do not understand how Burford calculates, on the basis of her assumptions, that the pay was "1 1/2–2 dr. a day" (n. 124) or "a day-wage of 2 dr. per man" (n. 245, where, however, she notes the possibility that as many as *seventy* different sculptors may have been involved—this would result in .78 dr. p.d. per man if they all worked 300 days). Himmelmann, "Entlohnung" 139, suggests 1 dr. p.d. for "54 Bildhauer," while Stewart, *Greek Sculpture* 66, calculates "fifty-three carvers." At this early date, i.e. 434/3, 4 ob. p.d. might be a more typical wage (see "Public Officeholders" #4, "Soldiers and Sailors" #2), and that wage of 4 ob., when paired with the other assumption of 300 working days, yields 81–82 sculptors, which is more consistent with the stylistic evidence cited by Burford.

38. *IG* I^3 476. 144–181:

[. . . . .[17]. . . . . Φυρόμα]-
χ[ος Κεφισιεύς, τὸν τὲν ἅμαχσ]-
αν [σ . . . .[19]. . . . . β]-
άλλ[οντα 𐅄ΔΔΔ. Πραχσίας ἐμ Με]-
λίτε[ι hοικõν τὸν νεανίσκον]
τὸν τὸ σ[. . . . .[17]. . . . .]
[. .]ς τ[ὸγ γρ]άφοντα νεα[νίσ]κον
καὶ τ[ὸμ πρ]ο[σ]ε[στ]õτα hαυτõι : Η.
[Μ]υνν[ίον ἐν Κολλυτõι hοικ[õν]
[. . .]ο [. . κ]αὶ τὲν ἅμαχσαν πλ[ὲν]
[τοῖν ἐμιόν]οιν 𐅄ΔΔΔΔ. Ἀγ[α]θάν-
[ορ Ἀλοπεκε͂σι] hοικõν τὸ γυνα-
[ῖκε τὸ πρὸς τε͂ι ἁμ]άχσει καὶ τ-
[ὸ hεμιόνο ΗΗΔΔΔΔ . . .[6]. . .]ν ἐκ
lacuna
[. . . . .[22]. . . . . τ]-
[ὸν τὸ δ]όρυ hέχοντα, 𐅄Δ. Φυρόμα-
[χος Κ]εφισιεύς, τὸν νεανίσκο-
[ν τὸν] παρὰ τὸν θόρακα 𐅄Δ. Πραχ-
[σίας] ἐμ Μελίτει hοικõν, τὸν h-
[ίππο]ν καὶ τὸν hοπισθοφανε͂ τ-
[ὸν πα]ρακρόοντα, ΗΔΔ. Ἀντιφάν-
[ες hεκ] Κεραμέον, τὸ ἅρμα καὶ τ-
[ὸν νε]ανίσκον καὶ τὸ hίππο τὸ
[ζευγ]νυμένο, ΗΗΔΔΔΔ. Φυρόμαχ-
[ος Κε]φισιεύς, τὸν hάγοντα τὸ
[ν hί]ππον, 𐅄Δ: Μυννίον hαγρυλε͂-
[σι] hοικõν, τὸν hίππον καὶ τὸν
[hά]νδρα τὸν hεπικρόοντα καὶ
[τὲ]ν στέλεν hύστερον προσέθ-
[εκ]ε :ΗΔΔΠΗ. Σõκλος hαλοπεκε͂-
[σι] hοικõν, τὸν τὸν χαλινὸν hέ-
[χο]ντα, 𐅄Δ: Φυρόμαχος Κεφισιε-

and support the widely held notion[39] that the sculptors were paid 60 dr. per standard-sized figure (60 dr. for one figure, 120 dr. for two figures[40] and 240 dr. for four figures[41]); the other four amounts (of 80 dr. [twice], 90 dr. and 100 dr.) probably are for one normal-sized and one smaller figure of varying size. Presumably because of the other 1 dr. p.d. wages for Erechtheion workmen, Stewart recently stated that sculptural "carving time . . . on the Erechtheion was evidently estimated at sixty days per figure."[42] Although Randall had cast doubt on that theory,[43] it has an attractive plausibility. There is, to be sure, no explicit evidence as to how sculptors or other "artist" craftsmen were paid in relation to other workers, but at a time when it evidently seemed appropriate for carpenters and sawyers working on this public religious building to be paid no more than "unskilled" workers it might have seemed anomalous to put sculptors on a higher plane.[44] No doubt the epistatai knew how long it *ought* to take

---

[ύς], τὸν hάνδρα τὸν hεπὶ τε̂ς βα-
[κτ]ερίας εἱστεκότα τὸν παρὰ
[τὸ]ν βομὸν, 𐅄Δ: hίασος Κολλυτε-
[ύς], τὲγ γυναῖκα ἑ̂ι ἑ παῖς προσ-
[πέ]πτοκε, 𐅄ΔΔΔ ᵛκεφάλαιον hα-
[γα]λματοποϊκο̂, ΧΧΧΗΗΗΔΠᵛ

For this entry, see also "Actors, Artists, Musicians and Writers" #8.

39. See Randall, "Erechtheum Workers" 208–209; Stewart, *Greek Sculpture* 66.

40. The 127 dr. in *IG* I³ 476. 173 most probably is to be explained as 120 dr. for two standard-sized figures and 7 dr. for the stele (evidently shown in the sculpted scene), which was added later.

41. In *IG* I³ 476. 157, [240 dr.] are restored for "two women beside the wagon and two mules," i.e., five figures, perhaps on the theory that they overlapped on the metope and were deemed to be the equivalent of four standard-sized figures, but this is necessarily speculative.

42. Stewart, *Greek Sculpture* 66.

43. Randall, "Erechtheum Workmen" 209: "Since sculptors were not paid in any two consecutive prytanies, it might be argued that their wage of sixty drachmae per figure was based on a drachma per day. The wages paid to the masons, however, contradict this theory. For a mason received two drachmae four obols to lay a Pentelic backing stone, which was five and five-eighths cubic feet in volume, while receiving only one obol more for a block of the softer Aeginetan stone which was twelve cubic feet and must have taken considerably more time to lay." (For the backing stones, see *IG* I³ 475. 7–17, 35–41.) But the larger Aiginetan block may have been easier to lay because it was softer and therefore easier to work.

44. So Himmelmann, "Entlohnung." Contra B. Wesenberg, "Kunst und Lohn am Erechtheion," *AA* 1985 55–65. Wesenberg's main argument is that, since payments are made by prytany and some sculptors and stonemasons are paid more—often significantly more—for piecework than the 36–37 dr. per prytany paid to architects ("Overseers, Architects and Other Salaried Construction Personnel" #4), they must have been paid effectively more per day; but he acknowledges the

sculptors to carve a figure of a certain size, and they may well have set the rate on that basis.

(c) Other Erechtheion piecework. If the sculptors *were* paid on the estimated basis of 1 dr. p.d., then the other Erechtheion workers also probably were. Among the many miscellaneous amounts for piecework, one group of figures stands out, that for stonemasons fluting columns. Although the individual figures are fairly well preserved for only one column, their total—350 dr.—seems plausible for the other columns as well. If so, the epistatai may have determined that it *ought* to take 350 man-days to flute each column, and set the rate accordingly.[45]

(d) 333/2?→329/8. Cobblers raised from 1 dr. 5 ob. to 4 dr. per pair for repairing shoes.[46] As already observed ("Overseers, Architects and Other Salaried Construction Personnel" n. 17), this enormous increase is one of several examples of very severe inflation in these years, probably caused by a grain shortage, which in turn raised the price of cattle and (probably) of shoe leather, i.e., this raise probably reflects increases in the cost of materials more than in the cost of labor.[47]

---

possibilities that these payments are for work begun in earlier prytanies and/or completed in less time than that estimated by the architect and/or epistatai.

45. Wesenberg ("Kunst und Lohn" 61) argues instead that as skilled workers they may have been paid as much as 3 dr. 4 ob. p.d.!

46. *IG* II² 1673 + *SEG* XXXIV 122. 49–50:

καττύσαντι ταῦτα (28 pairs of shoes) ἅπαξ πλὴ- 49
[ν ἐννέα ζε]υγῶν τῶν λιθαγωγούντων, ταῦτα δὲ δὶς ἐν τῶι ἐνιαυτῶι, 50
τὸ ζε[ῦγ]ος : ͰİIIII : Χαρίαι 'Αγρυλῆ οἰκ : γίγνεται : 𐅄ΔΠͰͰIIII :

IG II² 1672. 190–191:

ὑποδημάτων δημοσίοις κάττυσις, τοῦ ζ[ε]ύγους 'Απολλọφάνηι 190
Τυρμείδει : ͰͰͰͰ : κεφάλαι
𐅄ΔΠͰͰͰ : 191

As observed by both Kirchner (ad *IG* II² 1673. 50) and Clinton ("Ins. Eleusis" 99), the total in the first entry should be 67 dr. 5 ob., viz., one obol *more* than recorded (28 pairs of shoes plus 9 that are repaired a second time = 37 x 1 dr. 5 ob. = 67 dr. 5 ob.), but Clinton remarks that the omitted obol may be reflected in the following line, where the total for shoe nails should be one obol *less* than recorded. The total in the second entry is for 17 pairs (68 dr. ÷ 4 dr. = 17), evidently for the 17 δημόσιοι mentioned in lines 141–142 (quoted in n. 27).

47. The 7 ob. μισθός for a cobbler who finished a pair of sandals (κρηπῖδα) in Lucian *Gall.* 22 seems to be for new shoes and is thus not precisely comparable to these figures for shoe repair, although both probably include materials as well as labor, and for that reason both are also listed in the catalogue under "L. Labor Costs—Labor and Materials Combined."

As a whole, what can be said about this material?[48] It is very abundant and provides a wealth of detailed information as to what workers were paid for various tasks. But the portion of this material that is clearly useful for comparative purposes is rather small: almost all of it comes from the first category, "Workers Paid on the Basis of Time," and within this category the useful information comes from only two building account inscriptions, without any direct corroboration by literary sources or other inscriptions. Although these inscriptions have been cited in support of the proposition that wages at Athens rose from 1 dr. p.d. in 409–407 to 1 1/2 to 2 1/2 dr. p.d. in 329/8,[49] this requires some qualification. Strictly speaking, all that these inscriptions tell us is that on two public works projects (a) in 409–407, 1 dr. p.d. was the wage for carpenters, sawyers and "unskilled" workers (and possibly most other workers as well, including sculptors and stonemasons), but (b) in 329/8, "skilled" workers were paid 1 1/4 to 2 1/2 dr. p.d. and "unskilled" workers were paid 1 1/2 dr. p.d. The inscriptions do not (at least by themselves) tell us explicitly (a) whether the same wage scale was operating in the private sector, (b) whether these wage scales were typical for the public sector, or (c) whether the wage scales recorded for "skilled" workers in these inscriptions were typical for other "skilled" workers. For the extent to which these increases were typical, see "Inflation and Deflation" pp. 241–242, 245–249.

---

48. The data in the last two categories, "Labor and Material Costs Combined" and "Labor and Transport Costs Combined," are difficult to use since it is impossible to separate labor costs from material and transport costs, and therefore to isolate what the worker took for himself.

49. Most recently by Gallo, "Salari" 29–34.

Chapter 8
Inscribers

Collected here are all sums appropriated for the inscription of documents on stone. Except as specifically stated otherwise, these are polis documents. Since Böckh's paragraph on this category,[1] the main work has been done by Drerup and Nolan,[2] with additional, very recent, contributions by Lawton and Clinton.[3] The payment formulas of many of the inscriptions discussed here also have been studied by Burstein and Henry, who have compiled useful lists.[4]

1. 408/7. 62 dr. for working, engraving and ἐ[λάσ]αντι (driving [into place], i.e., erecting?) stele showing accounts of Eleusinian epistatai.[5] It is worth noting that the comparatively specific description of this job does *not* include the cost of quarrying the stele, or of transporting it from the quarry to Eleusis.

2. c. 403/2. [20 dr.] for honorary decree, for sons of Theozotides?[6]

---

1. Böckh, *SdA* I 150–151, with Fränkel's additions in *SdA* II 34*, n. 204.

2. E. Drerup, "Über die Publicationskosten der attischen Volksbeschlüsse," *Neue Jahrbücher für Philologie und Paedogogik* 66 (1896) 227–257; "Zu den Publicationskosten der attischen Volksbeschlüsse: Nachtrag zu Jahrg. 1896 s. 227–57," *Neue Jahrbücher für Philologie und Paedogogik* 67 (1897) 871–873; Nolan, *Inscribing Costs*.

3. Lawton, *ADR*; Clinton, "Review."

4. S. M. Burstein, "Bithys, Son of Cleon from Lysimachia: a Reconsideration of the Date and Signficance of *IG* II^2, 808," *CSCA* 12 (1979) 39–50; A. S. Henry, "Provisions for the Payment of Athenian Decrees: A Study in Formulaic Language," *ZPE* 78 (1989) 247–295; A. S. Henry, "Bithys Son of Kleon of Lysimacheia: Formal Dating Criteria and *IG* ii^2. 808," in E. M. Craik, ed., *'Owls to Athens': Essays on Classical Subjects Presented to Sir Kenneth Dover* (Oxford 1990) 179–189.

5. *IG* I^3 386. 165–167:

σ[τέλε]ν Ἐλ[ε]υσῖνι ἐργασ[α]μένοι
𐅄Δ⊢⊢ καὶ [γρά]μμ[α]τα ἐγκολά[φσαν]τι 166
καὶ ἐ[λάσ]αντι

6. *IG* II^2 5 + *SEG* XXXII 39. 11–14:

[ἀναγράψαι τὸν γραμματέα τ]-
ῆς βολῆς ἐ[ν στήλῃι λιθίνηι καὶ καταθε͂ναι ἐν πόλει, τ]-
ὸς δὲ πωλη[τὰς ἀπομισθῶσαι, τὸς δὲ ταμίας δοῦναι ε]- 13
[ἴκ]ọσ[ι δραχμάς - - - -]

3. c. 402–post-385. [20 or 30?] dr. for honorary decree for Thasian exiles.[7]

4. 392/1. 2 dr. for stele showing account of repairs of Peiraieus fortifications.[8] The cost of inscribing is not said to be included, and the low price suggests that it is not. Unfortunately, the entire stele is not preserved, so it is not possible to use it to estimate the cost of the stele per square or cubic meter.

5. 390/89. [3]0 dr. for proxeny decree.[9]

6. 380s or earlier? [? dr.] for honorary decree for Boiotians.[10]

7. 389/8? 20 dr. for honorary decree for Thasian ambassadors.[11]

8. 388/7 or 375/4? [20] dr. for citizenship decree.[12]

For doubts about the identification of the honorees, and a slightly different restoration in lines 11–12, see *SEG* XIV 36. *SEG* XXXII 39 also reports the following alternative restoration for the last two lines:

[ἐς δὲ τὴν στήλην δοῦνα]- 13
[ι τ]ὸς [ταμίας - - - -]

7. *IG* II^2 33 + *SEG* XXXII 42. 0–3:
[- τ]-
[ὸ δ]ὲ ἀ[ργύριον εἰς τὴν ἀναγραφὴν τῆ]-
[ς] στ[ήλη]ς δõ[ναι τὸς ταμίας ^{v}ΔΔΔ^v δρ]- 2
[α]χμὰς [τ]ῶι γ[ραμματεῖ τ]ῆς βο[λῆς·]

For the date, see *SEG* XXXVII 67. *IG* II^2 33 had restored line 2 as [ς] στ[ήλη]ς δό[τω ὁ ταμίας τõ δήμο ΔΔ δρ]-.

8. *IG* II^2 1664 + *SEG* XIX 144. 16–18:
καταλιφῆς ἐπὶ Φιλοκλέος a. 392/1
[Δ]Π μισ Φάεννος Ἀχαρν.
⊦⊦ στήλης. 18

9. *IG* II^2 22 b. 8–10:
[ἐς δὲ τὴν ἀνα]-
[γρα]φὴν δõναι τ[ὸς ταμίας τῶν τῆς θεõ τρ]-
[ιά]κον[τ]α δραχμ[ὰς ἐκ τῶν δέκα ταλάντων]· 10

10. *IG* II^2 245. 4–5:
[τὸς δὲ ταμίας] τῆς [θ]εõ δõν[αι . .]
[. δραχμὰς ἐς τὴν ἀναγραφὴν] τῆς [σ]τήλ[ης·] 5

For the date, see *SEG* XXXII 48. In the period c. 403–330 (see pp. 163–164 below), with the sole exception of #18 (a stele that is atypical in other respects as well), the only attested figures for polis inscriptions are 20 dr. and 30 dr. In this stoichedon text, it is more likely that the three available letter spaces were filled by ΔΔΔ than the less typical ΔΔ: vel sim., on which see notes 60 and 106.

11. *IG* II^2 24 b. 8–10:
δõ[ναι δὲ . . . . ἐ]-
ς ἀναγραφὴν τῆς στήλ[ης τ]ῶι γρα[μματεῖ τὸν τ]-
αμίαν τῆς βολῆς εἴκο[σι] δραχμά[ς.] 10

For the date, see *SEG* XXXI 58.

12. *IG* II^2 25 + *Agora* XVI 40. 16–19:
[ἐς]

9. pre-387/6. 20 [dr.] for proxeny decree.[13]

10. pre-387/6. 20 dr. for proxeny decree.[14]

11. pre-387/6. [30 d]r. for decree (fragment).[15]

12. 386/5. [30 dr.] for honorary decree for King Hebryzelmis of the Odrysians.[16]

13. pre-378/7. 20 dr. for proxeny decree.[17]

14. pre-378/7. 20 dr. for honorary decree for Megarian.[18]

15. pre-378/7. [20] dr. for proxeny decree.[19]

δὲ τὴν ἀν[αγραφὴν δõναι]-
ι τὸν τα̣[μίαν εἴκοσι δρ]- 18
αχμάς.

For the date, see *Agora* XVI 40.

13. *IG* II^2 51. 13–15:
[τὸς δ]-
[ὲ τα]μ̣ίας δõ[ναι ἐς ἀναγραφὴ]-
[ν ε]ἴκοσ[ι δραχμάς·] 15

14. *IG* II^2 53. 7–9:
ἐς
δὲ τὴν στήλην δõναι τὸ[ν] ταμίαν ΔΔ δραχμὰς 8
[τῶ]ι [γ]ρ[αμματεῖ] τῆς βολῆς·

15. *IG* II^2 56. 3–5:
εἰς δὲ ἀναγ[ραφὴν τηστήλης δ]-
[õναι τὸν ταμίαν τ]õ δήμο τῶι [γραμματεῖ τῆς βο]-
[λῆς τριάκοντα δραχ]μάς. 5

16. *IG* II^2 31. 14–17:
[ἐς δ]ὲ τὴν ἀναγραφ[ὴν τῆς]
[σ]τή[λης μερίσαι] τὸς [ἀπ]οδέκτα[ς τριάκ]- 15
[ο]ν[τα] δ[ραχμὰς] τῶι γραμματεῖ τ[ῆς βολῆ]-
[ς·]

17. *IG* II^2 76. 17–22:
[ὁ] δὲ γ[ραμ]ματεὺς ὁ τῆ-
ς βολῆς ἀν[αγρ]αψάτω ἐν στ-
ήληι λιθ[ίνηι] καὶ θέτω ἐν
ἀκροπόλε[ι, τὸ] δὲ ἀργύριο-
ν δόντων ο[ἱ τα]μίαι τῶν τῆ-
[ς] θεõ εἴκο[σι δρ]αχμάς. 22

18. *IG* II^2 81 + *SEG* XXXII 51. 10–12:
[εἰς δ]-
[ὲ] τὴν ἀναγραφὴν δ[όντων οἱ ταμίαι τ]-
[ὰ]ς εἴκοσι δραχμ[άς.] 12

19. *IG* II^2 82. 16–19:
ἐς δὲ τὴν ἀνα-
[γραφὴν δõναι] τὸν ταμίαν τõ δήμ-
[ου ἐκ τῶν κατὰ] ψηφίσματα ἀναλι-
[σκομένων ΔΔ δ]ραχμάς. 19

16. pre-378/7. [3]0 dr. for honorary decree for foreigners.[20]
17. 378. [3]0 dr. for alliance with Thebes (2 stelai, apiece).[21]
18. 377. 60 dr. for charter of Second Athenian League.[22]
19. c. 377. 30 [dr.] for decree concerning Arethousa.[23]
20. c. 375–350 or 357/6? [30] dr. for citizenship decree.[24]
21. c. 375–350. [20 dr.] for decree (fragment).[25]
22. 372. 20 dr. for polis decree and agreements with Parians made by members of Second Athenian League.[26]

---

20. *IG* II^2 84. 4–7:
τὸ δ[ὲ] ἀργύρι-
[ον δõν]αι εἰς τὴν [σ]τήλην τ-
[ριάκ]οντα δραχμ[ὰ]ς ἐκ τῶν 6
[δέκ]α ταλάντων.

21. *IG* II^2 40. 21–23:
[ὑπὲρ δὲ τῆς ἀναγρα]φῆς τῶν στηλῶν μερίσ-
[αι τὸς ἀποδέκτας τριά]κοντα δραχμὰς ἑκατέ- 22
[ρας, καὶ ἀναγραψάτω ὁ γ]ραμματε[ὺς] τῆς [β]ολῆ[ς].

22. *IG* II^2 43. 66–69:
τὸ δὲ ἀρ[γύ]ριον δõναι εἰς τὴν ἀν-
αγραφὴν τῆς στ[ήλη]ς ἑξήκοντα δραχμὰς 67
ἐκ τῶν δέκα ταλ[άν]των τὸς ταμίας τῆς θε-
ᾶ

23. *Agora* XVI 43. 2–3:
ἐς δ[ὲ ἀναγραφὴν δõ]-
[ναι] τ̣ριάκ[οντα δραχμάς·] 3

24. *Agora* XVI 54. 17–20:
[δ]-
[οῦναι δὲ τὸν ταμία]ν τοῦ δήμου τ[ῶι γραμμ]-
[ατεῖ τῆς βουλῆς : ΔΔΔ :] δραχμὰς ἐ[κ τῶν κατ]- 19
[ὰ ψηφίσματα ἀναλισκ]ομένων τ[ῶι δήμωι. ^{v}]

For the date, cf. Osborne D13 (375–350) with *Agora* XVI 54 (357/6). Osborne leaves the numeral unrestored.

25. *IG* II^2 293 + *SEG* XXXVII 70. 21–26:
εις δὲ τὴν ἀναγ-
[ραφὴν] τῆς στήλης δο[ῦ]ν̣α̣ι̣ [τ]-
[ὸν ταμ]ίαν τοῦ δ[ήμου ΔΔ δρα]- 23
[χμὰς ἐ]κ τῶν κατ[ὰ ψηφίσματ]-
[α ἀναλ]ισκομέν[ων τῶι δήμω]-
[ι].

For the date, see *SEG* XXXVII 70, which also reports that this fragment cannot be part of *IG* II^2 64 + 425.

26. *SEG* XXXI 67. 7–11
ἀναγρ[ά]ψαι δὲ τὸ [ψ]ήφισμα καὶ τὰς διαλ-
λαγὰς [ἃ]ς ἐπ̣[οιήσ]αντο οἱ σύμμαχοι τοῖ-
[ς] Παρίο̣[ι]ς καὶ [σ]τ[ῆ]σαι στήλην ἐν Ἀκρο⟨π⟩-
[όλει· εἰς δὲ τὴν ἀν]αγραφὴν τῆς στήλης

23. c. 370–360. [30 dr.] for decree (fragment).[27]
24. 367. 20 d[r.] for proxeny decree.[28]
25. 367. 20 dr. for honorary decrees for Mytilenaians (2 decrees on one stele).[29]
26. 367? [30 dr.] for treaty with Dionysios I of Syracuse.[30]
27. 364? 30 dr. for honorary decree for King Strato of Sidon.[31]
28. 363. 20 dr. for citizenship decree.[32]
29. 362. 20 dr. for treaty with Keans.[33]

δο[ῦναι τὸν ταμίαν τõ δ]ήμου ΔΔ δραχμάς. . . . 11

27. *Hesperia* 7 (1938) 281, no. 15. 2–5:

[εἰς δὲ τὴν]
[ἀναγραφὴν τῆς] στήλ[ης δοῦναι τὸν ταμίαν τοῦ δή]-
[μου ᵛΔΔΔᵛ δραχμ]ὰς ἐ[κ τῶν κατὰ ψηφίσματα ἀναλι]- 4
σκομένων τῶι δή]μω[ι]

28. *IG* II^2 106. 17–19:

[εἰς δὲ τὴν ἀναγραφὴν ὁ]
[τα]μί[α]ς τõ δήμο δότω ΔΔ δ[ραχμὰς ἐκ τῶν ἐς τὰ κατὰ] 18
[ψ]ηφίσματα ἀναλ̣ισκ[ο]μέ[νων τῶι δήμωι].

29. *IG* II^2 107. 18–24:

ἀναγράψαι δ[ὲ τ]όδ-
[ε τὸ ψ]ή[φι]σμα τὸν γραμματέα τῆς [βου]λῆ[ς] ἐν στήληι λιθίνη-
[ι καὶ σ]τῆσαι ἐν ἀκροπόλει. [ἀν]αγράψαι δὲ κα[ὶ] τ[ὸ] ψήφι[σμα] ε-
[ἰς τὴν α]ὐτὴν στήλην ὃ ἀπε[κρ]ίνατο ὁ δῆμος τοῖς πρέσβεσι
[τοῖς Μυ]τιλην[αί]ων τοῖ[ς] μετὰ ['Ιε]ροίτ[α. εἰ]ς δὲ τὴν ἀναγραφ-
[ὴν δοῦναι τῆς στή]λης [τ]ὸν ταμίαν τοῦ δήμου τῶι γραμματεῖ τ-
[ῆς βου]λῆς ΔΔ δραχμάς. 24

30. *IG* II^2 105 + 523 + *Hesperia* 7 (1938) 627, no. 2. 42–44:

[εἰς] δὲ τ[ὴν ἀνα]-
[γραφὴν δοῦναι τὸν ταμίαν τοῦ δ]ήμ[ου ΔΔΔ δ]- 43
[ραχμάς .]

For doubts about the date, see *SEG* XXXII 58.

31. *IG* II^2 141. 15–18:

ἐς δὲ τὴν ἀ-
ναγραφὴν τῆς στήλης δοῦναι τοὺς
ταμίας τῶι γραμματεῖ τῆς βολῆς Δ 17
ΔΔ δραχμὰς ἐκ τῶν δέκα ταλάντων.

For the date, cf. *SEG* XXVI 73 ("364") with *SEG* XXXII 347 ("as late as 364").

32. *IG* II^2 109 b. 26–29:

εἰς [δὲ] τ-
ὴν ἀναγραφὴν τῆς στήλ[ης δ]õναι τὸν τα[μ]-
ίαν τõ δήμο ΔΔ δρα⟨χ⟩μὰς ἐκ [τ]ῶν [κα]τὰ ψηφί- 28
σματα ἀναλισκομένων τ[ῶι] δήμωι.

33. *IG* II^2 111. 25–27:

εἰς δὲ τὴν ἀναγραφὴν δõναι τὸν τ-
αμίαν τõ δήμο ΔΔ δραχμὰς ἐκ τῶν κατὰ ψηφίσματα ἀναλι- 26
σκομένων.

30. 361/0. 30 [dr.] for treaty with Thessalians.[34]
31. 361/0. [? dr.] for proxeny decree.[35]
32. 356/5. 20 dr. for treaty with Lokrians.[36]
33. pre-355 or 342? [20] dr. for proxeny decree.[37]
34. 354. [20] dr. for proxeny decree.[38]
35. 354. 20 dr. for proxeny decree.[39]
36. pre-353/2. 20 [dr.] for honorary decree for foreigner.[40]
37. pre-353/2. [30 dr.] for honorary decree (fragment).[41]

---

34. *IG* II^2 116. 44–45:

ε[ἰ]ς [δ]ὲ [τὴ]ν [ἀναγραφ]ὴν τῆς [σ]τ[ή]λη[ς] δõνα-
[ι] τὸν ταμίαν τõ δή[μο] ΔΔΔ [δρ]α[χμά]ς. 45

35. *IG* II^2 117. 16–19:

[εἰς δ]-
ὲ τὴν ἀναγ[ρα]φ[ὴν τῆς στήλης δõναι τ]-
ὸν ταμίαν τ[õ] δ[ήμο . . . . δραχμὰς τῶι] 18
γραμματεῖ [τῆς βολῆς.]

For the reasons stated in n. 10, of possible restorations :ΔΔ: is more likely than ΔΔΔ: vel sim.

36. *IG* II^2 148. 6–8:

εἰς δὲ τὴν ἀναγραφὴν τῶν συν[θη]-
[κῶν δ]οῦναι τὸν ταμίαν τοῦ δήμο τῶ[ι γρ]-
[αμμ]ατῆι τῆς βου[λ]ῆς ΔΔ ⁝ δραχμάς. . . . 8

37. *IG* II^2 149. 20–23:

εἰ-
[ς δὲ τὴν ἀναγραφὴν] τῆς στήλης δοῦναι τὸν ταμί-
[αν τοῦ δήμο . . .^{6}. . .] δραχμὰς ἐκ τῶν κατὰ ψηφίσ- 22
[ματα ἀναλισκομέν]ων τῶι δήμωι.

For the date, see *SEG* XXI 265. For the reasons stated in n. 10, in the six available spaces it is hard to see how any figure other than εἴκοσι can be restored.

38. *IG* II^2 132. 13–16:

[εἰς δὲ τὴν ἀναγραφ]ὴν δοῦνα[ι τὸν]
[ταμίαν τοῦ δήμο ΔΔ] δραχμὰς ἐ[κ τῶν] 14
[κατὰ ψηφίσματα ἀ]ν[α]λισκομ[ένων τ]-
[ῶι δήμωι]·

39. *IG* II^2 133. 17–20:

[εἰς]
δὲ τὴν ἀναγραφὴν [δοῦναι τὸν ταμίαν τ]-
οῦ δήμου ΔΔ δραχμ[ὰς ἐκ τῶν κατὰ ψηφίσ]- 19
ματα ἀναλισκ[ο]μ[ένων.]

40. *IG* II^2 151. -2 (*sic*)–3:

[. . .^{6}. . . εἰς δὲ τὴν ἀναγραφὴν τ]-
[ῆς στήλης δõναι τὸν ταμίαν τõ]
[δή]μο ΔΔ [δραχμὰς ἐκ τῶν κατὰ ψη]- 1
[φ]ίσματ[α ἀναλισκομένων τῶι δ]-
[ή]μωι·

41. *IG* II^2 173. 11–14:

ἐς δὲ

38. pre-353/2. [? dr.] for honorary decree for Kyrenaians.[42]
39. pre-353/2. [20 dr.] for proxeny decree.[43]
40. pre-353/2. [20] dr. for decree (fragment).[44]
41. pre-353/2. [30 dr.] for honorary decree for foreigners.[45]
42. pre-353/2. 20 dr. for honorary decree (fragment).[46]
43. pre-353/2. [? dr.] for decree (fragment).[47]
44. 353/2. 30 dr. for decree ordering inventory of Chalkotheke.[48]

[τὴν ἀναγραφὴν τῆς στήλης δο͂ναι] τὸς ταμ-
[ίας τῶν τῆς θεο͂ ΔΔΔ δραχμὰς ἐκ τῶν δ]έκα τ- 13
[αλάντων τῶι γραμματεῖ τῆς βολῆς·]

42. *IG* II^2 176. 11–14:
[. . .^{5}. . εἰς δὲ τὴν ἀναγραφὴν δο͂ν]αι . .
[. δραχμὰς τὸν ταμίαν τοῦ δήμ]ου ἐκ τ[ῶ]- 12
[ν κατὰ ψηφίσματα ἀναλ]ισ[κομ]ένω[ν τῶ]-
[ι δήμωι τῶι γραμματεῖ·]

For the reasons stated in n. 10, of possible restorations ΔΔΔ is more likely than ΔΔ: vel sim.

43. *IG* II^2 183. 11–14:
[ἐς δὲ τὴν ἀναγ]ραφὴ-
[ν τῆς στήλης δο͂ναι τὸν ταμί]αν τοῦ
[δήμο ΔΔ δραχμὰς ἐκ τῶν κατὰ ψ]ηφίσ- 13
[ματ' ἀναλισκομένων τῶι δήμω]ι ^{vvv}.

44. *IG* II^2 189. 3–6:
[εἰς δὲ τὴν ἀναγραφὴν τ]-
ῆς στήλη[ς δοῦναι τὸν ταμίαν τοῦ δήμο ΔΔ] 4
δραχμὰς ἐκ τ[ῶν κατὰ ψηφίσματα ἀναλισκο]-
μένων τῶι δήμ[ωι].

45. *IG* II^2 196. 8–11:
εἰς δὲ τὴν ἀνα[γραφὴν τῆς στήλης δο͂]-
ναι τὸν ταμίαν τ[ο͂ δήμου ΔΔΔ δραχμὰς ἐ]- 9
κ τῶν εἰς τὰ κατ[ὰ ψηφίσματ' ἀναλισκομ]-
ένων τῶι δήμω[ι]·

46. *IG* II^2 197 + *SEG* XXXII 69. 2–5:
[εἰς δὲ τὴ]-
ν ἀ̣ναγραφὴν δο͂ν[αι τὸν ταμίαν το͂ δή]-
μο Δ̣Δ δραχμὰς ἐ[κ τῶν κατὰ ψηφίσμ]- 4
ατα ἀ̣ναλισκομ[ένων·]

47. *IG* II^2 198. 3–5:
[εἰς δὲ τὴν ἀναγραφὴν τῆς στήλης δο͂να]-
[ι τ]ὸν ταμί[αν τοῦ δήμου . . . δραχμὰς ἐκ τῶν κατὰ ψηφί]- 4
[σμ]ατα ἀ[ναλισκομένων τῶι δήμωι].

For the reasons stated in n. 10, of possible restorations ΔΔΔ is more likely than ΔΔ: vel sim.

48. *IG* II^2 120. 20–22:
[ἐς] δὲ τὴν ἀναγραφὴν τῆς στήλης δοῦναι τοὺς ταμίας [τῆ]-
[ς] βουλῆς : ΔΔΔ : [δρ]αχμὰς ἐκ τῶγ κατὰ ψηφίσματα ἀναλ[ισ]- 21
[κο]μένων τῆι βουλῆι.

For the date, see *SEG* XXXII 68.

45. 353/2. <2>0 [dr.] for law on dedication of first fruits at Eleusis, on same stele as earlier law.[49]

46. 352. [20 dr.] for decree on Eleusinian orgas boundary dispute (2 stelai, apiece).[50]

47. pre-mid 4th c. [?] dr. for tribal honorary decree for tribal thesmothetes.[51]

48. pre-mid 4th c. 3[0 dr.] for decree (fragment).[52]

49. mid 4th c. 10 dr. for deme honorary decree for metic.[53]

50. mid 4th c. or c. 330–318? 30 dr. for deme honorary decree for deme financial official.[54]

---

49. *IG* II^2 140 + *Hesperia* 64 (1995) 131, no. 1. 31–38:

τὸν δὲ γραμμα[τέα τῆς βουλῆς]
προσαναγράψαι τ[ὸν νόμον τόνδε]
πρὸς τὸν πρότερο[ν τὸν Χαιρημον]-
ίδου εἰς τὴν στήλ[ην τὴν ἔμπροσθ]-
εν τοῦ Μητρώιου, ε[ἰς δὲ τὴν ἀναγρ]-
αφὴν τῆς στήλης δ[οῦναι τὸν ταμί]-
αν τοῦ δήμου ^{v} Δ⟨Δ̣⟩^{v} [δραχμὰς ἐκ τῶν] 37
εἰς τὰ κατὰ ψηφί[σματα].

For the second Δ, probably painted in a *vacat*, see W. T. Loomis, "Eleusinian Inscriptions: Three Emendations," *Hesperia* 64 (1995) 131–134 at 131–132.

50. *IG* II^2 204. 60–62:

δοῦ[ν]αι [δ]ὲ καὶ εἰς τὴν ἀναγρα-
φ[ὴν ταῖν στήλαιν :ΔΔ: δραχμὰς εἰς] ἑκ[α]τέραν ἐκ τῶν κατὰ ψη- 61
φ[ίσματα ἀναλισκομένων τῶι δή]μωι·

51. *IG* II^2 1148. 14–16:

[εἰς δ]ὲ τὴν ἀναγραφὴν τ-
[ῆς στήλης δôναι] τοὺς ἐπιμελητὰ-
[ς . . . . .⁹. . . . δρ]αχμάς. 16

52. *Agora* XVI 60. 1–5:

[ἐς δ]-
[ὲ τὴν ἀ̣ν̣αγραφὴν τῆς στήλης τὸν ταμίαν]
[τô δήμο δôνα]ι τ[ριάκοντα δραχμὰς ἐκ τῶ]- 3
[ν κατὰ ψηφί]σματ[α ἀναλισκομένων τῶι δ]-
[ήμωι·]

53. *IG* II^2 1186. 33–34:

εἰς δὲ τὴν ἀναγραφὴν δοῦναι Δ δρ- 33
[α]χμὰς τὸν δήμαρχον·

54. *IG* II^2 1182. 21–25:

εἰς δὲ τ[ὴ]ν ἀναγραφὴν τῆς
στήλης μερίσα[ι] τὸ ἀ[ν]ά[λωμ]-
[α] Φείδιππον καὶ τὸν ἀντιγ-
[ρα]φέα Μειξ[ί]αν ^{v}ΔΔΔ^v δραχ- 24
[μ]ὰς ἀπὸ τῆς προ[σ]όδου·

51. c. 350. [30] dr. for honorary decree.[55]

52. c. 350. [20 dr.] for citizenship decree.[56]

53. 350 or c. 343/2? 30 dr. for honorary decree for King Arybbas of the Molossians.[57]

54. post-mid 4th c. or 281/0? [20 d]r. for honorary decree for Tenians.[58]

55. c. 350–339? [? dr.] for proxeny decree.[59]

Kirchner's date of "med. s. IV" is based solely on the lettering, a criterion that is now impossible to test because the inscription has not been seen since c. 1887 (Kirchner himself never saw it), and it seems not to have been studied closely since c. 1871, when it was published by Koumanoudes. Köhler reported (*IG* II 575): "Titulum litteris bonae aetatis exaratum esse disserte prodit Kumanudis." Since the "good era" arguably continued until c. 318 (see n. 243 below), this inscription might be as late as that, and certainly the 30 dr. figure, the highest attested at any period for non-polis documents, would be more plausible after c. 330, when the prices of both polis and non-polis documents rose and for the first time we have securely dated non-polis documents in excess of 10 dr. Cf. ##49, 77, 95, 98, 132, 133, and 192.

55. *IG* II^2 257 + 300 + *SEG* XL 70. 4–7:

[εἰς δὲ τὴν ἀ]-
[ναγραφὴν τῆ]ς στήλης δ[ῶναι τὸν ταμίαν τõ]
[δήμο ΔΔΔ δρα]χμὰς ἐκ τῶν εἰς τ[ὰ κατὰ ψηφίσ]- 6
[ματα ἀναλισκ]ομέν[ων] τῶι δήμωι. . . .

Tracy, *ADIT* 70, attributes this inscription to "The Cutter of *IG* II^2 105," whom he dates "368–339."

56. *IG* II^2 282. 6–9:

[εἰς δὲ τὴν ἀν]αγραφὴν τῆς στ[ήλη]-
[ς δοῦναι τὸν τα]μίαν τοῦ δήμου [. . δ]- 7
[ραχμὰς ἐκ τῶν] κατὰ ψηφίσματα [ἀνα]-
[λισκομένων τ]ῶι δήμωι·

For the date, and the status of this fragment as a citizenship decree, see Osborne D20. For the reasons stated in n. 10, ΔΔ seems the only possible restoration in the two available spaces.

57. *IG* II^2 226. 21–26:

εἰς
δὲ τὴν ἀναγραφὴν τῆς στήλ-
ης δότω ὁ ταμίας τοῦ δήμου
ΔΔΔ δραχμὰς ἐκ τῶν κατὰ ψη- 24
φίσματα μεριζομένων τῶι
δήμωι.

Kirchner (followed by Osborne D14) dated this "c. a. 343/2." For the alternative date of 350, see *SEG* XXXVIII 62.

58. *IG* II^2 660. 22–24:

εἰς δὲ τὴν ἀναγραφὴν τ[ῆς στήλης δ]-
οῦναι τὸν ταμίαν τοῦ δή[μου ΔΔ δραχ]- 23
μάς.

For the alternative date of 281/0, see *SEG* XLII 97.

59. *IG* II^2 161 b. 1–3:

[- - - δραχμὰς ἐ]κ τῶ[ν ἐς τὰ κα]- 1
[τὰ ψηφίσματα ἀναλισ]κομέ[νων τῶι
[δήμωι·]

56. c. 350–330. [30 dr.] for proxeny decree.[60]

57. c. 350–325. [2]0 [dr.] for proxeny decree.[61]

58. 349/8. [20] or [30]? [d]r. for honorary decree for foreign ambassadors.[62]

59. 348. [20 dr.] for proxeny decree.[63]

60. 346. 30 dr. for honorary decree for sons of King Leukon of Bosporos.[64]

61. c. 345. [20 dr.] for proxeny decree or *no* appropriation for inscribing?[65]

Tracy, *ADIT* 69, attributes this inscription to "The Cutter of *IG* II^2 105," whom he dates "368–339." On the basis of the sculptural decoration, Lawton, *ADR* 143, dates it "mid–3rd q. 4th c." My date of c. 350–339 attempts to reconcile those two stylistic dates. In this period, the cost almost certainly was 20 or 30 dr. (see n. 10).

60. *Agora* XVI 66. 16–19:

[εἰς δὲ τὴν ἀ]ναγραφὴ[ν]
[τῆς στήλης δοῦναι τὸν τ]αμίαν [τοῦ]
[δήμου ΔΔΔ ἐκ τῶν κατὰ ψη]φίσ[ματα ἀ]- 18
[ναλισκομένων τῶν δήμωι. *vacat*]

Woodhead comments: "The numeral is restored *exempli gratia.* Numerals were not always inscribed in conformity with strict stoichedon requirements and are frequently distinguished by marks of punctuation. . . . The cost of the stele may thus have been twenty rather than thirty drachmas."

61. *IG* II^2 184 + *SEG* XXIV 92. 9–12:

[εἰς δὲ]
[τὴν ἀ]ναγραφὴν [τῆς στήλης δοῦναι τὸν ταμί]-
[αν τοῦ] δήμου Δ[Δ δραχμὰς ἐκ τῶν κατὰ ψηφίσμ]- 11
[α]τ' ἀ[να]λισκο[μένων τῶι δήμωι].

62. *IG* II^2 210 + 259 + *Hesperia* 6 (1937) 329, no. 6 (*SEG* XXIII 52). 18–20:

[εἰς δὲ τὴν ἀναγρα]φὴν δ̣-
[οῦναι τὸν ταμίαν τοῦ δήμου ΔΔΔΔ δραχμ]ὰς ἐκ τ- 19
[ῶν κατὰ ψηφίσματα ἀναλισκομένων τῶι] δήμωι.

For the reasons stated in n. 10, 40 dr. is unlikely at this date, and :ΔΔ: is more likely than ΔΔΔ: vel sim.

63. *IG* II^2 206. 30–34:

[εἰς]
δὲ τὴν ἀ]ναγραφὴ[ν τῆς στήλης δοῦνα]-
ι τὸν [τ]αμίαν τοῦ [δήμου ΔΔ δραχμὰς ἐ]- 32
κ τῶν κατὰ ψηφίσ[ματα ἀναλισκομέν]-
ων τῶι δήμωι.

64. *IG* II^2 212. 47–49:

ἐς δὲ τὴν ἀν[α]-
γραφὴν δοῦναι τὸν ταμίαν τοῦ δήμου τριά[κ]- 48
οντα δραχμάς.

65. *IG* II^2 272 + *Agora* XVI 45 d. 6–9:

[εἰς δὲ τὴν ἀναγ]-
[ραφὴν τῆς σ]τή[λης δοῦναι τὸν ταμίαν τοῦ δήμου εἴκοσι] 7
[δραχμὰς ἐκ τ]ῶ̣[ν κατὰ ψηφίσματα ἀναλισκομένων τῶι δή]-

62. c. 345–320. 30 [dr.] for proxeny decree.[66]
63. c. 345–320. 30 dr. for decree (fragment).[67]
64. c. 345–320. [3]0 d[r.] for decree (fragment).[68]
65. c. 345–320 or 307–301? [30 dr.] for proxeny decree.[69]
66. 344/3. [3]0 [dr.] for honorary decree for Pellanans.[70]
67. 344/3. [30 d]r. for honorary decree (fragment).[71]

[μωι. . . .]

Serious doubt recently has been cast on this text (and on its status as a proxeny decree) by Tracy, *ADIT* 70–72, who combines *IG* II^2 272 and *IG* II^2 274 to produce a text that makes *no* provision for inscribing costs. Nonetheless, for the sake of completeness I retain it in my catalogue of all published texts in this category, and assign it Tracy's date of "c. 345" for the combined *IG* II^2 272 and 274. Cf. *Agora* XVI's "*ca. a.* 375–360 *a.*"

66. *IG* II^2 285 + 414 d + *SEG* XXI 276. 0–5:

[- - - - εἰς δὲ τὴν ἀναγρα]-
[φὴν τῆς στήλης δ]ο[ῦναι τὸν]
[ταμίαν τοῦ δήμ]ου : ΔΔΔ[: δρ]- 2
[αχμὰς ἐκ τῶν κ]ατὰ ψηφί[σμα]-
[τα ἀναλισκο]μένων τῶι δ[ήμ]-
[ωι].

For the date, see Tracy, *ADIT* 77.

67. *IG* II^2 307. 1–5:

[- - - - - - - - - - - εἰς δὲ]
[τὴν ἀναγραφὴν τῆς στήλης δοῦνα]-
[ι τὸν ταμίαν τοῦ δήμου] ^{v} ΔΔΔ ^{v} δρα- 3
χμὰς ἐκ τῶν εἰς τὰ κατὰ ψηφίσματ-
α{τα} ἀναλισκομένων τῶι δήμωι·

For the date, and the braces in line 5, see Tracy, *ADIT* 84, 91.

68. *Agora* XVI 90. 7–10:

εἰς δὲ τ-
[ὴν ἀναγραφὴν τῆς στήλης] δοῦν[α]-
[ι τὸν ταμίαν τοῦ δήμου : Δ]ΔΔ : δ[ρ]- 9
[αχμὰς ἐκ τῶν - - - - - κτλ. - - - -]

For the date, see Tracy, *ADIT* 87 (Agora I 6434); cf. *Agora* XVI's "*vix post a.* 325 *a.*"

69. *IG* II^2 564 + *Agora* XVI 111. 20–23:

[εἰ]ς [δ]ὲ τὴν ἀναγ[ραφὴν τῆς]
[στήλης δοῦναι τὸν ταμίαν τοῦ] δήμ[ου : ΔΔΔ :] δρ[α]- 21
[χμὰς ἐκ τῶν κατὰ ψηφίσμα]τα ἀναλ[ισκομένω]ν ^{v}[^{v}]
[τῶι δήμωι·]

For the date, cf. *Agora* XVI's "*a.* 307/6–302/1 *a.* (*sed vix post a.* 306/5?)" with Tracy's (*ADIT* 77) "345–320".

70. *IG* II^2 220. 12–15:

[τὸν δὲ ταμίαν τ]οῦ δήμου [δοῦν]-
[αι εἰς τὴν ἀναγραφὴ]ν Δ[ΔΔ δραχμὰ]- 13
[ς ἐκ τῶν κατὰ ψηφίσματα ἀναλισκ]-
[ομένων τῶι δήμωι. . . .]

71. *IG* II^2 221. 5–8:

[εἰς δὲ τὴν ἀν]-

68. 342. 10 [dr.] (min. inc.) for honorary decree for bouleutes Phanodemos.[72]

69. 340/39. [2]0 [dr.] for honorary decree for Apelles of Byzantion.[73]

70. c. 340/39. [30 dr.] for honorary decree for (Hellespontine?) foreigner.[74]

71. c. (340 or 330?)–320. 50 d[r.] for decree (fragment).[75]

72. 339. [?] dr. for honorary decree for Aratos of Tenedos.[76]

73. 337. 30 dr. for honorary decree for Akarnanians.[77]

[αγραφὴν τῆ]ς στήλης δοῦναι τὸν [ταμίαν τοῦ δήμο]-
[υ : ΔΔΔ : δραχ]μὰς τῶι γραμματεῖ [ἐκ τῶν κατὰ ψηφί]- 7
[σματα ἀναλισ]κομένων.

72. *IG* II² 223 A. 15–16:
. . . . εἰς δὲ τὴν ἀνα[γραφὴν τῆς στ]ήλης δοῦναι τὸν ταμίαν τοῦ δήμου 15
Δ[- - δραχμὰς ἐκ τῶν κατὰ ψηφί]σματα
[ἀναλισκομ]ένων [τῶι δήμωι]. 16

For the reasons stated in n. 10, Δ[Δ] vel sim. or Δ[ΔΔ] vel sim. seem the most likely restorations.

73. *IG* II² 235. 29–34:
[εἰς]
[δὲ τὴ]ν ἀνα[γραφὴν τῆς στή]-
[λ]η[ς] δοῦνα[ι τὸν ταμίαν το]-
ῦ [δ]ήμου Δ[Δ δραχμὰς ἐκ τῶν] 32
[ε]ἰς τὰ κα[τὰ ψηφίσματα ἀν]-
[α]λισκο[μένων [τῶι δήμωι].

74. *SEG* XVI 51. 24–27:
εἰς [δὲ τὴν ἀναγραφὴν τῆς]
[στήλης δοῦν]αι τὸν [ταμίαν τοῦ δήμου ᵛ Δ] 25
[ΔΔ ᵛ δραχμὰς] ἐκ τῶ[ν εἰς τὰ κατὰ ψηφίσμα]-
[τ' ἀναλισκομ]ένω[ν τῶι δήμωι].

75. *IG* II² 306. 1–5:
εἰς δὲ [τὴν ἀνα]-
[γραφὴν τῆς] στήλης δο[ῦναι τὸ]-
[ν ταμίαν τ]οῦ δήμου : 𐅄 : δ[ραχμὰς] 3
[ἐκ τῶν κατ]ὰ ψηφίσματ[α ἀναλι]-
[σκομένω]ν τῶι δήμωι·

Tracy, *ADIT* 98, attributes this inscription to "The Cutter of *IG* II² 244," whom he dates "340/39–*ca.* 320." For the reasons stated in n. 10, it seems probable that the 50 dr. was appropriated after c. 330, and that #71 was therefore inscribed in the latter part of its letter-cutter's career.

76. *IG* II² 232. 23–27:
[εἰς]
δὲ τὴν ἀν[α]γρ[αφὴν τῆς στήλης δο]-
ῦναι τὸν ταμ[ίαν τοῦ δήμου . . . .] 25
δραχμὰς ἐκ [τῶν κατὰ ψηφίσματα]
ἀναλισκο[μένων τῶι δήμωι].

For the reasons stated in n. 10, of possible restorations :ΔΔ: is more likely than ΔΔΔ: vel sim.

77. *IG* II² 237 + *SEG* XXXI 76. 35–40:

74. 337. 20 dr. for proxeny decree.[78]

75. c. 337–324. 30 d[r.] for proxeny decree.[79]

76. c. 337–323. [20] dr. for honorary decree (fragment).[80]

77. c. (337 or 330?)–323. 20 dr. for decree of Mesogeians on proclamation of religious offerings.[81]

78. 336. 20 dr. for law against tyranny (2 stelai together).[82]

79. 336. 30 [dr.] for proxeny decree.[83]

εἰς δὲ τὴν ἀνα-
γ[ρ]αφὴν̣ τ̣ῆς σ̣τή[λης δοῦναι] τὸν ταμίαν τοῦ δήμου τῶι
γ[ρ]α̣μ̣μ̣α̣τ̣εῖ τ[ῆς βουλῆς τ]ρ[ιά]κοντα̣ δραχμὰς ἐκ τῶν κατ- 37
[ὰ ψ]η̣φίσ[μα]τ̣[α ἀ]-
[ναλισ]κ̣[ομέ]-
[νων τῶι δήμωι.]

78. *IG* II[2] 122 + 238. 17–20:
[εἰς δὲ τὴ]ν ἀναγραφὴν τῆς σ-
[τήλης δοῦνα]ι τὸν ταμίαν : ΔΔ : δρ- 18
[αχμὰς ἐκ τῶν] κατὰ ψηφίσματα ἀ-
[ναλισκομέν]ων τῶι δήμωι·

79. *IG* II[2] 426. 14–18:
εἰς δὲ
[τὴν ἀναγραφὴν τῆ]ς στήλης δοῦν-
[αι τὸν ταμίαν τοῦ] δήμου : ΔΔΔ : δ- 16
[ραχμὰς ἐκ τῶν κατὰ] ψηφίσματα ἀ-
[ναλισκομένων τῶι] δήμωι.

For the date, see Tracy, *ADIT* 106.

80. *IG* II[2] 434. 1–4:
[εἰς δὲ τὴν ἀναγραφὴν τ]-
[ῆς στή]λης δο[ῦναι τὸν ταμίαν τοῦ δή]-
[μου ΔΔ] δραχμὰ[ς ἐκ τῶν εἰς τὰ κατὰ ψη]- 3
[φίσμα]τα ἀναλισ[κομένων τῶι δήμωι]·

For the date, see Tracy, *ADIT* 114.

81. *IG* II[2] 1244. 8–11:
[εἰς δὲ ἀναγραφὴν δο]-
ῦνα⟨ι⟩ τὸν ταμ[ίαν - *(nomen proprium)* - εἴκ]-
οσι δραχμ[ὰς ἐκ τῶν κατὰ ψηφίσματ]- 10
α ἀναλισκο[μένων - - - - - - - - - - - -]

Tracy, *ADIT* 114, attributes this inscription to "The Cutter of *IG* II[2] 337," whom he dates "337–323." Because there is no clearly attested non-polis figure in excess of 10 dr. prior to c. 330 (see n. 54), it seems more likely than not that #77 was inscribed in the latter part of its letter-cutter's career.

82. *Agora* XVI 73. 27–29:
εἰς δὲ τὴν ἀναγραφὴν τῶν στηλῶν τὸν ταμίαν
δοῦναι τοῦ δήμου : ΔΔ : δραχμὰς ἐκ τῶν κατὰ ψη- 28
φίσματα ἀναλισκομένων τῶι δήμωι· *vacat*

83. *IG* II[2] 240. 23–25:
εἰς [δ]ὲ τὴν ἀναγρ[αφὴν τῆς σ]-
[τή]λης [δό]τω ὁ ταμίας τριά[κοντα δρ]- 24
[αχμ]ὰ[ς] κατὰ τὸν νόμον.

80. 336. 20 dr. for proxeny decree.[84]
81. 336. 20 dr. for isoteleia decree.[85]
82. pre-336/5. [20 dr.] for proxeny decree.[86]
83. pre-336/5. 30 dr. for decree (fragment).[87]
84. pre-336/5. 30 dr. for proxeny decree.[88]
85. pre-336/5. [20 dr.] for proxeny decree.[89]
86. pre-336/5. [20] dr. for proxeny decree.[90]

Lawton (*ADR* 25, n. 109) interprets this as "the treasurer is to pay the price (30 drachmai) dictated by law," but κατὰ τὸν νόμον, by itself, means only "in accordance with the law." As Nolan, *Inscribing Costs* 12, observes (citing a "[p]ersonal communication from A. G. Woodhead"), "[i]t may mean little more than that everything was done properly, according to the usual state procedures."

84. *IG* II^2 242 + 373 + *SEG* XL 74. 27–30:

εἰς δὲ τὴν ἀναγραφὴν τῆς στήλης δ-
οῦναι τὸν ταμίαν τοῦ δήμου :ΔΔ: δραχμὰς ἐκ 28
τῶν κατὰ ψηφίσματα ἀναλισκομένων τῶι δ-
[ή]μωι.

85. *IG* II^2 276. 20–23:

εἰς δὲ τὴν ἀναγραφὴν δ[ό]-
[τ]ω ὁ τα[μίας] τοῦ δήμου εἴκοσι δραχμὰς [ἐ]- 21
[κ] τῶν κ[ατὰ ψ]ηφίσματα ἀναλισκομένων [τ]-
[ῶ]ι δήμωι·

For the date, see Schwenk 62–63 and Tracy, *ADIT* 98.

86. *IG* II^2 250. 6–9:

[δõναι δὲ Δ]
[Δ δραχμὰς εἰς τὴν] ἀναγραφ[ὴν τῆς στήλ]- 7
[ης τὸν ταμίαν τõ δήμο]υ ἐκ τ[ῶν κατὰ ψηφ]-
[ίσματα ἀναλισκομένων τῶι δήμωι].

87. *IG* II^2 256. 4–6:

[εἰς δὲ τὴν ἀναγραφὴ]-
[ν τ]ῆς στήλη[ς δõναι τὸν ταμίαν τοῦ δήμ]-
ου ΔΔΔ δραχμ[ὰς - - - - - - - - - - -] 6

88. *IG* II^2 269. 6–9:

[εἰς δὲ τὴν ἀναγραφ]ὴν τῆς στήλης δ[ο]-
[ῦναι τὸν ταμίαν τοῦ δ]ήμου ΔΔΔ δραχμ[ὰ]- 7
[ς ἐκ τῶν κατὰ ψηφίσμ]ατα ἀναλισ[κ]ομέ[ν]-
[ων τῶι δήμωι·]

89. *IG* II^2 288. 12–16:

[εἰς δ]-
ὲ τὴν ἀναγρ[αφὴν τῆς στήλης δότω]
ὁ τοῦ δήμου [ταμίας ΔΔ δραχμὰς ἐκ] 14
τῶν κατὰ ψ[ηφίσματα ἀναλισκομέ]-
νων τῶι δή[μωι.]

90. *IG* II^2 290. 10–13:

[εἰς δὲ τὴν ἀναγραφ]ὴν δότω [ὁ τ]αμ-
[ίας τοῦ δήμου εἴκοσι] δ[ρ]αχ[μ]ὰ[ς] ἐκ [τ]- 11
[ῶν κατὰ ψηφίσματα ἀν]αλ[ι]σκομέ[νων]
[τῶι δήμωι].

87. pre-336/5. 20 dr. for decree (fragment).[91]

88. pre-336/5. 30 dr. for honorary decree for foreigner.[92]

89. post-336/5. 30 dr. for honorary decree (fragment).[93]

90. 335. [20] dr. for honorary decrees for ἱεροποιοί (3 decrees on one stele).[94]

91. c. 335–324. 30 dr. for proxeny decree.[95]

92. c. 334. 30 dr. for citizenship decree.[96]

93. c. 334–313. 20 dr. for honorary decree for foreigner Iatrokles.[97]

---

91. *IG* II² 299. 1–3:
[. εἰς δὲ τὴν ἀναγραφὴ]ν τῆς στήλ-
[ης δοῦναι τὸν ταμ]ίαν τῶι γραμμ-
[ατεῖ τῆς βουλῆς ε]ἴκοσι δραχμάς. 3

92. *IG* II² 302. 2–4:
εἰς δὲ τὴν ἀναγ[ραφὴν δοῦναι τὸν ταμίαν τοῦ δήμου]
ΔΔΔ : δραχμὰς ἐ[κ τῶν κατὰ ψηφίσματα ἀναλισκομέν]- 3
ων τῶι δήμωι·

93. *IG* II² 424. 14–16:
[εἰς δὲ τὴν ἀναγραφ]-
[ὴν τ]ῆς στήλης [δοῦναι τὸν ταμίαν τοῦ]
[δήμου] ΔΔΔ δρ[αχμὰς ἐκ τῶν κτλ. - -] 16

94. *IG* II² 330 + 445. 23–28:
[ἀναγράψαι δ]-
ὲ τόδε τὸ ψήφισμα τὸν γραμμα[τέα τὸν κατὰ πρυτανείαν ἐν σ]-
τήληι λιθίνηι καὶ τὸ τῆς βου[λῆς ὃ εἶπε Ἀγασίας καὶ τὸ τοῦ]
δήμου ὃ εἶπεν Ἱπποχάρης καὶ [στῆσαι ἐν ἀκροπόλει, εἰς δὲ τ]-
ὴν ἀναγραφὴν τῆς στήλης δοῦ[ναι τὸν ταμίαν τοῦ δήμου .. δ]- 27
ραχμὰς ἐκ τῶν κατὰ ψηφίσμα[τα ἀναλισκομένων τῶι δήμωι].
For the reasons stated in n. 10, ΔΔ seems the only possible restoration in the two available spaces.

95. *Hesperia* 43 (1974) 322, no. 3. 21–26:
εἰς δὲ τὴν ἀνα[γ]-
ρ⟨α⟩φὴν τῆς στήλης δοῦναι τὸ-
ν ταμίαν τοῦ δήμου : ΔΔΔ : δ̣ρ- 23
αχμὰς ἐκ τῶν εἰς τὰ κατὰ ψηφ-
ίσματα ἀναλισκομένων τῶι
δ̣ήμωι·
For the date, see Tracy, *ADIT* 34. In line 25, I correct the (mis)printed ἀναλισκομένον on the basis of Plate 64c.

96. *IG* II² 222. 29–31:
εἰς δὲ τὴν ἀναγραφὴ-
[ν τῆ]ς στ[ή]λης δότω ὁ ταμίας τοῦ δήμ-
[ου τ]ριά[κοντ]α δραχμάς. 31
For the date, see Osborne D22.

97. *IG* II² 264. 12–15:
[ἔτι δὲ εἰς τὴ]ν στήλην ΔΔ ἑτέρας τῶ- 12
[ι γραμματεῖ τῶ]ι κατὰ πρυτανείαν ἐκ
[τῶν κατὰ ψηφίσ]ματ᾽ ἀναλισκομένων τ-

94. c. 334–313. [20 dr.] for honorary decree for foreigner.[98]

95. c. (334 or 330?)–313. 20 dr. for deme honorary decree for deme choregos.[99]

96. 333. 20 dr. for honorary decrees for overseer of springs (2 stelai, each containing 2 decrees, apiece).[100]

97. c. 333. 30 [dr.] for prytany decree.[101]

98. 332. 10 dr. for deme decree regarding quarry lease.[102]

99. 332. [3]0 [dr.] for proxeny decree.[103]

[ῶι δήμωι·]

For the date, see Tracy, *ADIT* 122, 126. For more on this entry, see "Travel Allowances" #20.

98. *IG* II^2 292. 4–6:

[εἰς δὲ τὴν ἀναγραφὴν τῆς στ]ήλης δοῦναι τὸ-
[ν ταμίαν τοῦ δήμου ΔΔ δραχμὰς] ἐκ τῶν κατὰ ψηφ- 5
[ίσματα ἀναλισκομένων τῶι δή]μωι.

For the date, see Tracy, *ADIT* 122.

99. *SEG* XXXIV 103. 29–33:

Εἰς
δὲ τὴν ἀναγραφὴν τῆς στήλ-
ης δοῦναι τὸν ταμίαν τῶν θ-
[ε]ίων : ΔΔ : [δ]ραχμὰς καὶ λογίσ- 32
ασθαι τοῖς δημόταις - - -

Tracy, *ADIT* 124, attributes this inscription (EM 12807) to "The Cutter of EM 12807," whom he dates "334/3–314/3." Because there is no clearly attested non-polis figure in excess of 10 dr. prior to c. 330 (see n. 54), it seems more likely than not that #95 was inscribed in the latter part of its letter-cutter's career.

100. *IG* II^2 338. 28–31:

εἰς δὲ τὴν ἀναγραφὴν τῶν στηλῶν δότ-
ω ὁ ταμίας τοῦ δήμου : ΔΔ : δραχμὰς ἑκατέρας 29
τῆς στήλης ἐκ τῶν εἰς τὰ κατὰ ψηφίσματα ἀνα-
λισκομένων τῶι δήμωι.

101. *SEG* XXVIII 52. 26–29:

[εἰς δὲ τὴν ἀναγραφ]ὴν τῆς στήλ-
[ης δοῦναι τὸν ταμίαν το]ῦ δήμου ⁝ ΔΔΔ 27
[δραχμὰς ἐκ τῶν κατὰ ψηφίσματα] ἀναλισκομένων
[τῶι δήμωι. . . .]

102. *SEG* XXVIII 103. 49–51:

εἰς δὲ
τὴν ἀναγραφὴν τῆς στήλης δοῦναι τὸν δήμαρχον δέκα .·. 50
[δ]ραχμ[ὰς ἐ]κ τῆς τοῦ θεοῦ προσόδου.

For the date at the end of 333/2, see Schwenk 216–219.

103. *IG* II^2 344. 21–25:

εἰς δὲ [τὴν ἀ]-
[ναγρ]α[φ]ὴν τῆς στήλης δοῦ[ναι]
[τὸν] τα[μ]ίαν τοῦ δήμου ΔΔ[Δ δρα]- 23
[χμὰ]ς ἐκ τῶν κατὰ ψηφίσμ[ατα ἀ]-
[ναλι]σκομένω[ν].

100. 332. [20 dr.] for proxeny decree.[104]
101. 331. [?] d[r.] for proxeny decree.[105]
102. 331. [? d]r. for proxeny decree.[106]
103. 331. 20 dr. for honorary decree for god (Amphiareion).[107]
104. 331. 20 dr. for honorary decree for sanctuary nomothetes (Amphiareion).[108]
105. c. 330. [4]0 dr. for honorary decree for priest and ἱεροποιοί.[109]

For more on this text, see n. 106.

104. *IG* II^2 368. 15–18:

[εἰς δὲ τὴν ἀναγραφὴν τῆς]-
[στήλη]ς δοῦναι τ[ὸν ταμίαν τοῦ δήμου ΔΔ δρ]-
[αχμὰς] ἐκ τῶν κα[τὰ ψηφίσματα ἀναλισκομέ]-
[νων].

For more on this text, see n. 106.

105. *IG* II^2 347. 23–25:

- - - - - - - - - - - - - -
δρα[χμὰς] ἐκ τῶν κατ[ὰ ψηφίσμ]-
ατα ἀναλισκομέν[ω]ν [τῶι δήμ]-
[ωι].

106. *Agora* XVI 79. 21–24:

εἰ[ς δὲ τὴν ἀναγραφὴν τῆς στή]-
[λη]ς δοῦνα[ι τὸν ταμίαν τοῦ δήμου . . .]
[δρ]αχμὰς ἐ[κ τῶν κατὰ ψηφίσματα ἀναλ]-
[ισ]κομένων [τῶι δήμωι].

Woodhead comments: "Schweigert [the original editor] restored the cost of the stele as . . . [ΔΔΔ], without interruption of the stoichedon sequence, and the restoration was adopted by Schwenk [197]. For so brief a record, 20 drachmas might have been adequate, the inscribed figure being preceded and followed by marks of punctuation (:ΔΔ:). . . . [#99], of comparable length, affords no parallel, for although ΔΔ[Δ was restored in the *IG* text at line 23, the repetition of the same text in . . . [#100] allows for the restoration of no more than ΔΔ. Furthermore, sufficient of the stone survives in . . . [#99] to suggest that a blank space (or perhaps a single following mark of punctuation, for which compare, e.g., . . . [#123]) stood between ΔΔ and the concluding letters of the line." In this transitional period (see notes 10 and 113), it is difficult to know whether the minimum figure would have been 20 or 30 dr., so I agree with Woodhead that it should be left unrestored.

107. *IG* VII 4252 + B. C. Petrakos, Οἱ Ἐπιγραφὲς τοῦ Ὠρωποῦ (Athens 1997) 296. 34–38:

εἰς δὲ τ-
⟨ή⟩ν ἀναγραφὴν τῆς στήλης δοῦναι τὸ-
ν ταμίαν τοῦ δήμου : ΔΔ : δραχμὰς ἐ-
κ τῶν κατὰ ψηφίσμ[α]τα ἀναλισκομέ-
νων τῶι δήμωι.

108. *IG* VII 4253. 30–33:

εἰς δὲ τὴν
ἀναγραφὴν τῆς στήλης δοῦναι τὸν ταμ-
ίαν τοῦ δήμου : ΔΔ : δραχμὰς ἐκ τῶν κατ-
ὰ ψηφίσματα ἀναλισκομένων τῶι δήμωι.

109. *IG* II^2 410. 40–42:

εἰ[ς] δὲ τὴν ἀναγραφὴν τῆς στήλης δοῦναι τὸν τα-

106. c. 330? [40 d]r. for decree (fragment).[110]

107. c. 330/29. [? d]r. for decree (fragment).[111]

108. 320s. 30 dr. for citizenship decree.[112]

109. 320s or shortly afterwards. [20 dr.], [30 dr.], [40 dr.], or [50 dr.]? for citizenship decree (plural stelai?).[113]

110. 329. [?] dr. for honorary decree for Eudemos of Plataia.[114]

μίαν τοῦ δήμου : ΔΔΔ[Δ] : δραχμὰς ἐκ τῶν κατὰ ψηφίσματα [ἀ]ν- 41
αλισκομένων τῶι δήμωι.

110. *Agora* XVI 83. 1–4:

[. . . . .⁹. . . . · εἰς δὲ τὴν] ἀνα[γραφὴν καὶ τὴν]
[ποίησιν τῆς στήλης δ]οῦνα[ι τὸν ταμίαν τ]-
[οῦ δήμου ᵛ ΔΔΔΔ ᵛ δραχμ]ὰς ἐ[κ τῶν κατὰ ψηφ]- 3
[ίσματα ἀναλισκομένων ᵛ] *vacat*

For the unlikelihood of the restoration καὶ τὴν ποίησιν, see n. 248.

111. *IG* II^2 415. 3–6:

εἰς δὲ τὴν ἀνα[γραφὴν τῆς]
[στήλης δ]οῦναι τὸν ταμίαν τ[οῦ δήμου .]
[. . . δρα]χμὰς ἐκ τῶν κατὰ ψηφίσ[ματα ἀν]- 5
[αλισ]κομένων τῶι δήμωι.

Tracy, *ADIT* 84, attributes this inscription to "The Cutter of *IG* II^2 334," whom he dates "*ca.* 345–*ca.* 320." In this transitional period (see notes 10 and 113), restorations of :ΔΔ: vel sim., ΔΔΔ: vel sim., and ΔΔΔΔ all might be possible.

112. *IG* II^2 301. 4–7:

[εἰς δὲ τὴν ἀ]-
ναγραφὴν τῆς στ[ήλης μερίσαι τὸν ταμίαν]
ΔΔΔ δραχμὰς ἐκ τ[ῶν εἰς τὰ κατὰ ψηφίσματα] 6
ᵛ ἀναλισκο[μένων τῶι δήμωι].

For the date, and the status of this fragment as a citizenship decree, see Osborne D28.

113. *IG* II^2 575. 2–5:

εἰς [δὲ τὴν ἀναγραφὴν τῆ]-
[ς στήλης] δοῦναι τὸν ταμ[ίαν εἴκοσιν δραχμὰ]- 3
[ς ἐκ] τῶν κατὰ ψηφίσματα [ἀναλισκομένων τῶ]-
[ι δή]μωι.

For the date, see Osborne D41, where the following alternative is presented (vol. I, p. 108):

εἰς [δὲ τὴν ἀναγραφὴν τῶν]
[στηλῶν] δοῦναι τὸν ταμ[ίαν . . .⁶. . . δραχμὰς] 3
[ἐκ] τῶν κατὰ ψηφίσματα [ἀναλισκομένων τῶι]
[δή]μωι.

In vol. II, p. 113, Osborne offers a second alternative for the end of line 3: ταμ[ίαν τοῦ δήμου :𐅄:ᵛᵛ]. One could fill the six letter spaces in Osborne's first alternative with :ΔΔΔΔ: vel sim., and one could avoid the *vacats* in his second alternative by filling the five letter spaces with :ΔΔΔ: vel sim. Since there are no clearly attested polis figures below 30 dr. in the period c. 330–307 (see #144 with n. 149 and p. 164 below), the 20 dr. restoration seems unlikely.

114. *IG* II^2 351 + 624 (p. 660). 35–40:

εἰ[ς] δ[ὲ] τ[ὴν]
ἀναγραφὴν τῆς στήλη[ς δοῦ]να[ι]
τὸν ταμίαν τοῦ δήμ[ου - - -] 37

111. 329. 30 dr. for honorary decree for festival overseers (Amphiareion).[115]

112. 329/8. 1 dr. 1 ob. p.d. (or possibly, in one instance, 1 dr. 2 ob. p.d.) for σιτία (rations) for engravers of Eleusinian building account.[116]

113. 329/8. 3 5/7 dr. for σανίδες (wooden writing tablets), apiece, with γραφή (14 for 52 dr.).[117]

114. 327. [3]0 dr. for honorary decree for priest of Asklepios.[118]

115. c. 327–300. 50 dr. for honorary decree, for physicians?[119]

116. c. 326–318 (323–322?). [50] dr. for sacred law.[120]

δραχμὰς ἐκ τῶν εἰς τὰ κα[τὰ ψη]-
φίσμα[τα ἀναλισκομέ[νων τῶι]
δήμωι.

Kirchner reported that the number of letters per line in this inscription varies from 19 to 25, so, at this date (see n. 113) and in the 2–8 available spaces, restorations of ΔΔΔ, ΔΔΔΔ, : 𐅄 :, or differently punctuated versions of any of them all might be possible.

115. *IG* VII 4254. 48–52:
εἰς δὲ τὴν ἀναγρ-
αφὴν τῆς στήλης δοῦναι τὸν ταμία-
ν τοῦ δήμου :ΔΔΔ: δραχμὰς ἐκ τῶν κατ- 50
ὰ ψηφίσματα μεριζομένων τῶι δήμ-
ωι.

116. *IG* II² 1672 + *Hesperia* 64 (1995) 132, no. 2a. 6–8:
[τοῖς τὰ] γράμματα ἐπικολάψασιν ἐπὶ τὸ ἀνάθημα ἐν τῶι Ἐλευσινίωι σιτ- 6
ία : Π⊢⊢ {⊢ ?} : καὶ ἐπὶ τῆς Λειωντ[ίδ]ος τῆς ἡμέρας : ⊢Ι : ἡμερῶν : ΔΠΙΙ : κεφά- 7
λαι : ΔΠ⊢⊢⊢⊢ΙΙΙΙΙ : καὶ ἐπὶ τῆς Οἰνηΐδος
δεκάτης πρoτανείας σιτία ΔΔ[ΔΔ]⊢⊢⊢⊢ΙΙ : 8

For more on this entry, including the questionable drachma in line 7, see "Construction and Other Manual Workers" #8 (with n. 26).

117. *IG* II² 1672. 292: σανίδων ΔΙΙΙΙ τιμὴ καὶ γραφὴ 𐅄⊢⊢ ·

118. *IG* II² 354. 29–31:
εἰς δὲ τὴν ἀναγ[ραφὴν]
τῆς στήλης δοῦναι τὸν ταμίαν τοῦ δήμ[ου : Δ] 30
[Δ]Δ : δραχμὰς ὅθεν οἱ νόμοι κελεύουσι[ν].

119. *IG* II² 304 + 604 + *SEG* XVIII 11. 11–14:
εἰς δὲ τὴν ἀναγραφὴν τῆ-
ς στήλης δοῦναι [τ]ὸν ταμίαν τοῦ δήμου
𐅄 δραχμὰς ἐκ τῶν κατὰ ψηφίσματα ἀναλ- 13
ισκομένων τῶι δήμωι·

For the date, see Tracy, *ADIT* 152–153.

120. *IG* II² 620 + 1195 + *SEG* XLIV 42. 18–20:
εἰς δὲ τὴ̣ν [ἀναγραφὴν δοῦναι τὸν ταμίαν τ]-
οῦ δήμου [𐅄] ᵛ δραχ[μὰς ἐκ τῶν κατὰ ψηφίσματα ἀναλι]- 19
σκομένων τῶι δή[μωι *vacat*].

For the date, see Tracy, *ADIT* 134, and S. V. Tracy, "*IG* II² 1195 and Agathe Tyche in Attica," *Hesperia* 63 (1994) 241–244 at 242. M. B. Walbank, "A *Lex Sacra* of the State and of the Deme of Kollytos," *Hesperia* 63 (1994) 232–239 at 236, comments on the restored figure in line 19: "The nu-

117. c. 325. [? d]r. for decree (fragment).[121]

118. 325/4. 30 dr. for honorary decrees for Herakleides of Salamis (5 decrees on one stele).[122]

119. 323. 50 dr. for honorary decree for Euphron of Sikyon (2 stelai together).[123]

120. 323/2? [?] dr. for proxeny decree.[124]

---

meral has perished, but, since there is space for only one numeral, it is likely to have been the symbol for fifty; ten drachmai would be too small a sum for a stele such as this, and any other figure would be too large. The normal cost of a stele in the period under consideration was twenty or thirty drachmai [actually a minimum of 30 dr., see n. 113]. Possibly the stele was very large or, more likely, adorned with a relief."

121. *Agora* XVI 88. 3–8:

[εἰς δὲ τὴν ἀναγραφὴ]ν τῆς
[στήλης δοῦναι τὸν τ]αμία-
[ν τοῦ δήμου . . . . δρα]χμὰ[ς] 5
[ἐκ τῶν εἰς τὰ κατὰ ψη]φίσ[μ]-
[ατα ἀναλισκομένων τῶι δ]-
[ήμωι.]

Woodhead comments: "The exact cost of the stele (line 5) should remain unrestored. So narrow a text is unlikely, perhaps, to have been lengthy, but usage in the inscribing of numerals is variable, and : ΔΔΔ : would fill the available space no less than [the original editor] Schweigert's ^{v} ΔΔ ^{v}. It should also be noted that at this period 30 drachmas appear to represent the minimum expenditure." At this period (see n. 113), I think that 20 dr. is unlikely but another possibility, in addition to :ΔΔΔ:, might be ΔΔΔΔ; it is hard to see how any (even amply) punctuated version of 𐅄 could fill the four available letter spaces.

122. *IG* II^2 360. 21–27:

ἀναγράψαι δὲ τόδ-
ε τὸ ψήφισμα τὸν γραμματέα τὸν κατὰ πρυτανείαν
καὶ τοὺς ἄλλους ἐπαίνους τοὺς γεγενημένους αὐ-
τῶι ἐν στήλῃι λιθίνει καὶ στῆσαι ἐν ἀκροπόλει, ε-
ἰς δὲ τὴν ἀναγραφὴν τῆς στήλης δοῦναι τὸν ταμία-
ν ΔΔΔ δραχμὰς ἐκ τῶν εἰς τὰ κατὰ ψηφίσματ' ἀναλισ- 26
κομένων τῶι δήμωι.

123. *IG* II^2 448. 26–31:

ἀναγράψαι δὲ τὸ ψήφισμ[α ἐν στήλαις λ]-
ιθίναις καὶ στῆσαι τὴν μὲν μίαν παρὰ [τὸν Δία, τὴν δὲ]
ἑτέραν ἐν ἀ[κροπόλει παρὰ τὸν νεὼ τῆς Πολιάδος, εἰς]
δὲ τὴν ἀναγραφὴν [τῶν στηλῶν δοῦναι τὸν ταμίαν τοῦ]
δημου : 𐅄 : ἐκ τῶν κατὰ ψηφίσματα ἀναλι[σκομένων τῶι δ]- 30
ήμωι.

124. *IG* II^2 343 + *SEG* XXIV 103. 16–18:

εἰς δὲ τὴ[ν ἀναγραφὴν] τῆς στήλης δοῦν[αι τὸν]
ταμίαν τ[οῦ δήμου . . .] δραχμὰ[ς ἐκ] τῶν [εἰς τὰ κα]- 17
[τ]ὰ ψηφίσμα[τα ἀναλισκ]ομένων τῶι [δήμωι].

For the date, see *SEG* XXIV 103 and Schwenk 425–426. For the reasons stated in n. 113, ΔΔΔ or :𐅄: seem the most likely candidates for the 2–3 available letter spaces. See Schwenk 410–424 and notes 60, 106 and 121 above.

121. c. 321–319. [? dr.] for decree (fragment).[125]
122. c. 321–318. [? dr.] for citizenship decree.[126]
123. c. 321–318. 30 dr. for citizenship decree.[127]
124. c. 321–318. [? d]r. for citizenship decree.[128]
125. c. 321–318. [30?] dr. for proxeny decree.[129]
126. c. 321–318. [30 d]r. for honorary decree, for Milesian grain merchant?[130]

---

125. *IG* II² 397. 4–8:

[εἰς δὲ τὴν ἀναγρ]-
αφὴν τῆ[ς στήλης δοῦναι τὸν ταμί]-
αν τοῦ δ[ήμου . . . δραχμὰς ἐκ τῶν κ]- 6
ατὰ ψηφ[ίσματα ἀναλισκομένων τ]-
ῶι δήμω[ι].

For the reasons stated in n. 113, ΔΔΔ or :𐅄: seem the most likely restorations.

126. *IG* II² 392 + 586 + *SEG* XXVI 83. 17–20:

εἰς δὲ τὴν ἀν-
[αγραφὴν δοῦναι τ]ὸν ταμίαν τοῦ δήμ-
[ου . . . δραχμὰς ἐκ] τῶν κατὰ ψηφίσμα- 19
[τα ἀναλισκομένω]ν τῶι δήμωι.

For the reasons stated in n. 113, ΔΔΔ or :𐅄: seem the most likely restorations.

127. *IG* II² 393. 11–15:

εἰς δὲ τὴν ἀναγραφὴν τῆ-
ς στήλης δοῦναι τὸν ταμίαν τοῦ
δήμου ΔΔΔ: δραχμὰς ἐκ τῶν κατὰ ψ- 13
ηφίσματα ἀναλισκομένων τῶι δ-
ήμωι.

For more on this text, see n. 106.

128. *IG* II² 394. 18–20:

[εἰς δὲ τὴν ἀνα]-
[γραφὴ]ν τῆς στ[ήλης δοῦναι τὸν ταμίαν τοῦ δήμου]
[. . . . δρ]αχμ[ὰς - - - - - - - - - - - - - - -] 20

For the reasons stated in n. 113, ΔΔΔΔ might be the most likely restoration.

129. *IG* II² 396. 6–10:

[εἰς δὲ τὴν ἀν]-
[αγραφὴν τῆς σ]τήλης δοῦ[ναι τὸν ταμ]-
[ίαν τοῦ δήμου ΔΔΔ? δ]ραχμ[ὰς ἐκ τῶν εἰ]- 8
[ς τὰ κατὰ ψηφίσματα ἀναλισκομένω]-
[ν τῶι δήμωι].

In addition to ΔΔΔ, :𐅄: is a possible restoration (see n. 113).

130. *IG* II² 407 + *SEG* XL 79. 18–21:

εἰς δὲ [τὴν ἀναγραφὴν τῆς στήλ]-
[η]ς δοῦναι [τὸ]ν τα[μίαν τοῦ δήμου ΔΔΔ δρα]- 19
χμὰς ἐκ τῶν [κατὰ ψηφίσματα ἀναλισκομ]-
ένων τῶι δ[ήμωι].

For uncertainty about the join of the new fragment (which contains the quoted lines) with *IG* II² 407 (which contains the reference to the [Mile]sian), see *SEG* XXXVII 83, XL 79.

127. c. 320–296 (310/09?). 50 dr. for honorary decree for Carthaginian ambassadors.[131]

128. 318. [? dr.] for citizenship decree.[132]

129. 318. 30 d[r.] for citizenship decree.[133]

130. 318. 50 dr. for honorary decrees for Euphron of Sikyon (2 stelai together, each containing 2 decrees [this one and #119]).[134]

131. 318/17. [50 dr.] for honorary decree for ? of Herakleia.[135]

---

131. *IG* II^2 418. 7–11:

εἰς δὲ τὴν ἀναγ-
ραφὴν τῆς στήλης δοῦναι τὸν ταμία-
ν τοῦ δήμου 𐅄 δραχμὰς ἐκ τῶν εἰς τὰ κ- 9
ατὰ ψηφίσματ' ἀναλισκομένων τῶι δ-
ήμωι.

For the date, see Tracy, *ADIT* 36 (n. 2), 138.

132. *IG* II^2 391. 15–17:

[εἰς δ]-
[ὲ τὴ]ν ἀναγραφὴ[ν . . .⁵. . δοῦναι τὸν ταμ]-
[ίαν] τ[ο]ῦ δήμου [- - - δραχμάς]. 17

For the date, see Osborne D37.

133. *IG* II^2 398 b. 9–11:

[εἰς δὲ τὴν ἀναγραφ]ὴν τῆς στήλης δ-
[οῦναι τὸν ταμίαν τ]οῦ δήμου ΔΔΔ δρ- 10
[αχμάς].

For the date, see Osborne D36.

134. *IG* II^2 448. 85–87:

εἰς δὲ τὴν ἀναγραφὴν τῶν στηλῶν δοῦναι τὸν ταμίαν
τοῦ δήμου : 𐅄 : δρ⟨α⟩χμὰς ἐκ τῶν κατὰ ψηφίσματα ἀναλισκομ- 86
ένων τῶι δήμωι.

The circumstances of this decree and the reinscription of the earlier decree (#119) are given in lines 62–73:

νῦν δὲ ἐπειδὴ ὅ τε δῆμος [κατελ]-
ήλυθε καὶ τοὺς νόμους καὶ τὴν δημοκρατίαν ἀ[πείλη]-
φε, ἀγαθεῖ τύχει δεδόχθαι τῶι δήμωι, εἶναι τὰ[ς δωρε]-
ὰς κυρίας Εὔφρονι πάσας, αἷς ἐτίμησεν αὐτὸν ὁ [δῆμο]-
ς ὁ Ἀθηναίων, καὶ αὐτῶι καὶ ἐγγόνοις, καὶ τὰς σ[τήλας]
τὰς καθαιρεθείσας, ἐν αἷς αἱ δωρεαὶ ἦσαν γεγ[ραμμέν]-
αι καὶ τὸ ψήφισμα, ἀναγράψαι καὶ ἀναθεῖναι τ[ὸν γρα]-
μματέ⟨α⟩ τῆς βουλῆς τὴμ μὲν ἐν ἀκροπόλει τὴν δὲ πα[ρὰ τ]-
ὸν Δία τὸν Σωτῆρα καθάπερ ὁ δῆμος ἐψηφίσατο [πρότε]-
ρον, προσαναγράψαι δὲ καὶ τόδε τὸ ψήφισμα ἐν ἀ[μφοτ]-
έραις ταῖς στήλαις, συνεπιμεληθῆναι δὲ τῆς ἀν[αγρ]-
αφῆς τοὺς φίλους καὶ τοὺς οἰκείους τοὺς Εὔφρο[νος]·

135. *IG* II^2 535 + *Agora* XVI 104. 31–35:

[- - - - - - - - - - - -· ε]-
[ὶς δὲ τὴν ἀναγραφὴν δοῦναι τ]-
[ὸ]ν τ[αμίαν τοῦ δήμου 𐅄 δραχμὰ]- 33
[ς] ἐκ τῶ[ν κατὰ ψηφίσματα ἀναλ]-

132. 315/4. [20] dr. for deme honorary decree for deme treasurer.[136]

133. 315/4. 20 dr. for deme honorary decree for deme festival officials.[137]

134. c. 313/2. 30 dr. for decree (fragment).[138]

135. c. 310–300. [? d]r. for decree (fragment).[139]

136. 307. [?] dr. for honorary decree for Kolophonians.[140]

137. 307/6. 50 d[r.] for law on repair of Long Walls, etc.[141]

ι̣σκομέ[νων τῶι δήμωι].

Woodhead comments: "Schweigert [the original editor] restored Δ as the sum to be expended on the inscribing of the stele: but an expenditure of ten drachmas is, at this date, impossibly small."

136. *SEG* XLIII 26 A. 22–27:

ἀναγράψαι δὲ τόδε τὸ ψήφισμα ἐ στήληι
λιθίνει τὸν γραμματέα τῶν δημοτῶν κα-
ὶ στῆσαι ἐν τῶι ἱερῶι τῆς Ἀθηνᾶς τῆς Ἱππί-
ας, εἰς δὲ τὴν ἀναγραφὴν τῆς στήλης δοῦνα-
ι τὸν ταμίαν [: ΔΔ :] δραχμὰς καὶ λογίσασθ[α]- 26
ι τοῖς δημόται[ς].

137. *SEG* XLIII 26 B. 14–19:

[ἀναγράψαι δὲ τό]δε τὸ ψ[ή]φ[ι]σ[μ]α ἐν
στήληι λιθίνει [τὸν δήμαρ]χον Ο[ἰν]όφ[ιλ]ον
καὶ στ[ῆ]σα[ι] ἐ[ν τῶι ἱερῶι τῆ]ς Ἀθη[νᾶς τῆς] Ἱπ-
πίας [εἰς δὲ τὴν ἀναγραφὴν τῆς στήλης] δ[οῦ]-
ναι τὸ[ν] τ[αμ]ίαν Φανόμαχον : ΔΔ [:] δραχμὰς κα- 18
ὶ λογ[ίσασθαι τοῖς δη]μόταις·

138. *IG* II^2 530 + 590 + *SEG* XL 80. 5–7:

εἰς δὲ τὴν ἀναγραφὴν τῆστήλης δοῦναι τ-
ὸν ταμί[αν] τοῦ δήμου : ΔΔΔ : δραχμὰς ἐκ τῶν κατὰ ψηφίσμ- 6
ατα ἀν[αλι]σκομένων τοῖ δήμοι.

Until the republication of these fragments (announced in *SEG* XL 80), the foregoing composite text (with a stoichedon line length of 43 rather than 41 letters as announced) is obviously provisional.

139. *Hesperia* 7 (1938) 299, no. 23. 6–8:

[εἰς δὲ τὴν ἀναγραφὴν τῆς] στή[λης] δοῦναι τὸ]-
[ν ταμίαν τοῦ δήμου . . . δρ]αχ[μὰ]ς [ἐ]κ τῶν εἰ[ς] τ- 7
[ὰ κατὰ ψηφίσματα ἀναλισκ]ο̣[μένων] τῶι δήμωι.

Since this inscription may have been inscribed at the end of the century, when minimum appropriations for inscribing fell from 30 dr. to 10 or 20 dr. (p. 164 below), restorations of :Δ: vel sim., ΔΔ: vel sim., ΔΔΔ, :𐅄: vel sim., or even ΔΔΔΔ (see notes 60, 106 and 121) all might be possible.

140. *IG* II^2 456. 29–32:

[εἰς δὲ τὴν ἀν]-
αγραφὴν τῆς στήλης δοῦ[ναι] τὸν ταμ[ίαν τοῦ δήμου . .] 30
δραχμὰς ἐκ τῶν [κα]τὰ ψη[φίσμ]ατα ἀ[ναλισκομένων τῶι]
δήμωι.

In this period (see n. 113), 𐅄: vel sim. would be the most likely restoration.

141. *IG* II^2 463. 33–34:

[. . . εἰς δὲ τὴν ἀναγραφὴν] τ[ῆ]ς σ[τ]ή̣λ̣η̣ς δοῦναι τὸν ταμία[ν τ]οῦ δ[ήμ]ου 33
𐅄̣ δρα[χμὰς ἐ]-
[κ τῶν εἰς τὰ κατὰ ψηφίσματα ἀναλισκ]ο̣μένων [τ]ῶ[ι] δήμωι. 34

138. 307/6. [3]0 dr. for honorary decree for Tenians.[142]

139. 307/6. 50 dr. for posthumous inscription of all decrees of Lykourgos on plural stelai.[143] For so many decrees, the figure seems much too low, and the story is probably inaccurate or incomplete in one or more respects. The following possibilities, not necessarily mutually exclusive, occur to me: (a) the figure is wrong, i.e., too low; (b) the figure represents only the polis' contribution (which would have been supplemented by Lykourgos' sons); (c) the figure was to cover only two stelai; and (d) the figure was to cover only one decree, i.e., [Plutarch's] text is a slightly garbled copy of *IG* II[2] 457, a single decree that conferred posthumous honors on Lykourgos (Osborne suggests that #140 also is a copy of *IG* II[2] 457 and that 50 dr. is an appropriate sum for two copies, on two stelai, of a single decree).[144]

140. 307/6? 50 dr. for honorary decree (same as #139?), for Lykourgos and descendants?[145]

141. post-307/6. 30 dr. for honorary decree for polis magistrates.[146]

142. post-307/6. [? dr.] for honorary decree (fragment).[147]

---

142. *IG* II[2] 466. 49–52:
εἰς δὲ τ[ὴν ἀν]αγρ[αφ]ὴν δο[ῦν]-
[αι τὸν ταμίαν τοῦ] δήμο[υ : ΔΔ]Δ : [δ]ραχμ[ὰ]ς ἐκ [τῶν]
[εἰς τὰ κατὰ ψηφίσματα ἀνα]λισκομέν[ω]ν τῶ[ι δή]-
[μωι.]

143. [Plut.] *Mor.* 852e: ἀναθεῖναι δ' αὐτοῦ (sc. Λυκούργου)—καὶ εἶναι κύρια— πάντα τὰ ψηφίσματα τὸν γραμματέα τοῦ δήμου ἐν στήλαις λιθίναις καὶ στῆσαι ἐν ἀκροπόλει πλησίον τῶν ἀναθημάτων· εἰς δὲ τὴν ἀναγραφὴν τῶν στηλῶν δοῦναι τὸν ταμίαν τοῦ δήμου πεντήκοντα δραχμὰς ἐκ τῶν εἰς τὰ ⟨κατὰ⟩ ψηφίσματα ἀναλισκομένων τῷ δήμῳ.

144. M. J. Osborne, "Some Attic Inscriptions," *ZPE* 42 (1981) 171–178 at 172–174, who also raises the possibility that [Plutarch's] text should be emended to read ἐν στήλαιν λιθίναιν.

145. *IG* II[2] 513 + *SEG* XXXI 84. 11–14:
[εἰς δὲ τ]ὴν ἀναγραφὴν *vv*
[τῆς στήλης δοῦναι τὸν ταμίαν τοῦ] δήμου : 𐅄 *vvvvvv* 12
[δραχμὰς ἐκ τῶν εἰς τὰ κατὰ ψηφίσματα] ἀναλισκομένω[ν]
[τῶι δήμωι].

For the possible date and identification of the honorees, see *SEG* XXXI 84 and n. 144 above. For the possible identity of ##139 and 140, see #139.

146. *IG* II[2] 509. 11–13:
εἰς δὲ τὴν ἀναγρα[φὴν τῆς στήλης δοῦναι]
τὸν ταμίαν τοῦ δήμου : ΔΔΔ : δρ[αχμὰς ἐκ τῶν εἰς τὰ] 12
κατὰ ψηφίσματα ἀναλισκομ[ένων τῶι δήμωι].

147. *IG* II[2] 510. 9–12:
[εἰς δὲ τὴ]ν ἀναγραφὴ-
[ν τῆς στήλης δοῦναι τὸν ταμία]ν τοῦ δήμου
[. . . . δραχμὰς ἐκ τῶν εἰς τὰ κατὰ] ψηφίσματ- 11

143. c. 307–303. [30 dr.] for honorary decree for Asklepiades of Byzantion.[148]

144. c. 307–302. 10 dr. for citizenship decree.[149]

145. c. 307–302. [? dr.] for citizenship decree.[150]

146. c. 307–302. 50 dr. for citizenship decree.[151]

147. c. 307–302. [30 dr.] for citizenship decree.[152]

148. c. 307–302. 30 [dr.] for citizenship decree.[153]

[α ἀναλισκομένων τῶι δήμωι].

In the years immediately following 307/6, the most likely restorations are ΔΔΔ: vel sim. or ΔΔΔΔ, but towards the end of the century (see n. 139) δέκα and :ΔΔ: vel sim. also become possibilities.

148. *IG* II^2 555. 35–38:

[εἰς δὲ τὴ]-
[ν ἀναγρα]φὴν τῆς [στήλης δοῦναι τὸν ταμίαν]
[τοῦ δήμο]υ τρι[άκοντα δραχμὰς ἐκ τῶν εἰς τὰ] 37
[κατὰ ψηφ]ίσμ[ατα ἀναλισκομένων τῶι δήμωι].

149. *IG* II^2 508. 11–14:

εἰς δὲ τὴν ἀναγραφὴν τ-
ῆς στήλης δοῦναι τὸν ταμίαν τοῦ δή-
μου Δ δραχμὰς ἐκ [τῶ]ν κατὰ ψηφίσματ- 13
α ἀναλισκομένων [τ]ῶι δήμωι.

For the date, see Osborne D53. The low 10 dr. figure might suggest a date towards the end of this period, i.e., c. 302. See p. 164 below.

150. *IG* II^2 511. 9–12:

εἰς [δὲ τὴν ἀναγραφὴν τῆς στήλης δο]-
[ῦν]αι τὸν τα[μίαν τοῦ δήμου . . . .⁷. . . δραχμ]- 10
[ὰς] ἐκ τῶν κατ[ὰ ψηφίσματα ἀναλισκομένων]
[τῶι] δήμωι.

For the date, see Osborne D55. It is hard to see what restoration, of either numerals plus punctuation or a word like εἴκοσι (see n. 224), could have filled the seven letter spaces.

151. *IG* II^2 518 + Osborne D54. 5–9:

εἰς δὲ τ-
[ὴν ἀναγραφὴν τῆς σ]τήλη[ς δ]οῦναι
[τὸν ταμίαν τοῦ δήμ]ου ⁝ 𐅄 ⁝ δραχμὰ- 7
[ς ἐκ τῶν εἰς τὰ κατὰ ψ]ηφίσματα ἀν-
[αλισκομένων τῶι δή]μωι.

For the date, and the status of this fragment as a citizenship decree, see Osborne D54.

152. *IG* II^2 519. 5–9:

[εἰς δὲ τ]-
ὴν ἀναγ[ραφὴν τῆς στήλης δοῦναι τὸν τα]-
μίαν το[ῦ δήμου ΔΔΔ δραχμὰς ἐκ τῶν εἰς τ]- 7
ὰ κατὰ [ψηφίσματα ἀναλισκομένων τῶι]
δήμωι.

For the date, and the status of this fragment as a citizenship decree, see Osborne D56, where the figure is left unrestored.

153. *IG* II^2 696. 9-12:

[εἰς δὲ] τὴν ἀνα[γ]ραφὴν
[τῆς στήλης δοῦναι τὸν ταμίαν τ]οῦ δήμου ΔΔΔ 10

149. c. 307–301. 20 dr. for honorary decree for bouleutes.[154]
150. c. 306–302. [40 dr.] for citizenship decree.[155]
151. 305/4. [50 dr.] for honorary decree for ephebes.[156]
152. 305/4. [30 dr.] for prytany decree.[157]
153. c. 305/4. 50 dr. for honorary decree for Pyr? of Herakleia.[158]
154. 304/3. 30 dr. for citizenship decree.[159]
155. 304/3 or 303/2? [3]0 [dr.] for honorary decree for polis magistrates.[160]

[δραχμὰς ἐκ τῶν εἰς τὰ κατὰ ψηφ]ίσματα ἀναλισ[κο]-
[μένων τῶι δήμωι].

For the date, see Osborne D58.

154. *IG* II² 514 + *Agora* XVI 112. 8–12:

[. . . . · εἰ]ς δὲ [τὴν ἀναγραφὴν τῆς σ]-
[τήλη]ς δοῦνα[ι τὸν ταμίαν τοῦ δή]-
[μου] ΔΔ δραχμὰς ἐ[κ τῶν κατὰ ψηφί]- 10
[σματ]α ἀναλισκο[μένων τῶι δήμω]-
[ι. . . .]

The relatively low 20 dr. figure might suggest a date towards the end of this period, i.e., c. 302–301.

155. *RFIC* 70 (1942) 12, no. 6. 15–16:

[εἰς δὲ τὴ]ν ἀναγραφὴ[ν τῆς στήλης δοῦναι τὸν ταμίαν τοῦ δήμου 15
τετταράκοντα δραχμὰς]
[ἐκ τῶν εἰς τὰ ψηφί]σματα ἀνα[λισκομένων τῶι δήμωι.] 16

For the date, see Osborne D51, where the number is left unrestored.

156. *IG* II² 478. 30–31:

εἰς [δὲ τὴν ἀναγραφὴν τῆς στήλης δοῦναι τὸν τ]-
[αμίαν] τοῦ δήμου [𐅄 δραχμὰς ἐκ τῶν ε]ἰς τὰ κατὰ ψηφίσ[ματα ἀναλισκο- 31
μένων τῶι δήμωι].

O. Reinmuth, *The Ephebic Inscriptions of the Fourth Century B.C.* (*Mnemosyne* Supp. 14) (Leiden 1971) no. 17, leaves the numeral unrestored.

157. *Agora* XV 58. 6–9:

εἰς δὲ
[τὴν ἀναγραφὴν τῆς στήλης δοῦ]ναι τὸν ταμίαν τοῦ [δ]ήμ-
[ου : ΔΔΔ : δραχμὰς ἐκ τῶν εἰς τ]ὰ κατὰ ψηφίσματα [ἀν]αλι- 8
[σκομένων τῶι δήμωι]

158. *IG* II² 479. 27–29:

εἰς [δὲ τὴν ἀναγραφὴν δοῦναι τὸν τα]-
[μία]ν τοῦ δήμου ⁝ 𐅄 ⁝ [δραχμὰς ἐκ τῶν εἶς τὰ κατὰ ψηφί]- 28
[σμα]τ' ἀναλισκομ[ένων τῶι δήμωι].

159. *IG* II² 484 + 558 + *SEG* XL 83. 29–31:

εἰς δὲ τὴν ἀναγραφὴν τῆς στήλης
δοῦναι τὸν ταμίαν τοῦ δήμου ΔΔΔ δ- 30
ραχμὰς ἐκ τῶν κοινῶν χρημάτων. . . .

160. *IG* II² 488. 25–28 (dating the decree in 304/3):

[εἰς δὲ τὴν ἀναγραφὴν τῆς] στή-
[λης δοῦναι τὸν ταμίαν τοῦ δήμου : Δ]Δ[Δ] 26
[: δραχμὰς ἐκ τῶν εἰς τὰ κατὰ ψηφί]σματ-

156. pre-303/2. 30 d[r.] for proxeny decree.[161]
157. 303/2. [?] dr. for Athens-Sikyon alliance.[162]
158. c. 303/2. [? dr.] for citizenship decree.[163]
159. c. 303–301. [20] dr. for citizenship decree.[164]
160. c. 303–301. [30 dr.] for citizenship decree.[165]

[α ἀναλσκομένων τῶι δήμωι].
SEG XXXIV 75 (dating the decree in 303/2) reports that lines 26–27 can be restored as follows:
[λης δοῦναι τὸν ἐπὶ τῆι διοικήσει :] Δ[Δ]
[Δ δραχμὰς κτλ.]

161. *IG* II^2 542. 14–16:
[ε]ἰς δὲ τὴν ἀναγρ[αφὴν τῆς στήλης δοῦναι τὸν ταμί]-
[αν τ]οῦ δήμου ΔΔΔ δ[ραχμάς ἐκ τῶν εἰς τὰ κατὰ ψηφίσμ]-
[ατα] ἀναλισκομέν[ων τῶι δήμωι].

162. *Agora* XVI 115 c. 13–15:
[εἰ]ς δὲ τὴ[ν ἀναγραφὴν τῆς στήλης δοῦναι]
[τὸν ταμίαν τοῦ δήμου . . . .] δραχ[μὰς ἐκ τῶν εἰς τὰ κατὰ ψηφίσματ]-
[α ἀναλισκομένων τῶι δήμωι·]
I follow the date and precise line division (but not the line numbering) of *SEG* XLI 50, which Woodhead (Addendum on p. 186) indicates is now confirmed by an unpublished fragment, on which see also Tracy, *ADIT* 146 (Agora I 2636). If this inscription predates the reduction in minimum inscribing appropriations from 30 dr. to 10 or 20 dr. (see p. 164 below), ΔΔΔΔ or ΔΔΔ: vel sim. would be the most likely restorations.

163. *IG* II^2 806. 6–9:
[εἰς δ]ὲ τὴν ἀναγραφὴν τῆς στή-
[λης μερίσαι τὸν τ]αμίαν τῶν στρατιωτικῶν
[. . δραχμὰς ἐκ τῶν ε]ἰς τὰ κατὰ ψηφίσματα ἀνα-
[λισκομένων τῶι δήμω]ι.
For the date, see Osborne D48. For the reasons stated in n. 139, in this transitional period restorations of Δ: vel sim., ΔΔ, or 𐅄: vel sim. all might be possible, and perhaps ΔΔΔ also could be squeezed in.

164. *Agora* XVI 120. 10–13:
εἰς δ[ὲ τὴν ἀναγραφὴν τῆς στή]-
[λης] δοῦναι τ[ὸν ταμίαν τοῦ δήμου εἴκ]-
[οσι] δραχμὰς [ἐκ τῶν εἰς τὰ κατὰ ψηφί v]-
[σματ]α̣ ἀναλι[σκομένων τῶι δήμωι].
Woodhead comments: "Osborne [D63] observed that, if the disbursing officer be restored as ὁ ἐπὶ τῆι διοικήσει, other possibilities, showing ΔΔ or ΔΔΔ, are available; but this is a far less likely alternative. . . . A sum as small as twenty drachmas, though rare after *ca.* 332 . . ., is nevertheless a reasonable supposition at this period." It seems to me that 20 dr. would be likely only towards the end of this period, in c. 302 or later. See p. 164 below.

165. *Agora* XVI 121. 7–10:
[εἰς] δὲ τὴν ἀναγραφ-
[ὴν τῆς στήλης δοῦναι τὸν] ταμίαν τοῦ δήμ-
[ου v ΔΔΔ v δραχμὰς ἐκ τῶν εἰ]ς τὰ κατὰ ψηφί-
[σματα ἀναλισκομένων τῶ]ι δήμωι·
Woodhead comments: "The cost of the stele, as restored by [the original editor] Pritchett, was 30 drachmas. But the stone is thick and may have been sizable, and ; ΔΔΔΔ : in five letter spaces is also

161. 302. 30 dr. for citizenship decree.[166]

162. 302. [? dr.] for honorary decree for Adeimantos of Lampsakos.[167]

163. 302. [3]0 [dr.] for honorary decree for taxiarchs.[168]

164. 301. 30 dr. honorary decree for taxiarchs.[169]

165. 301. [4]0 dr. for honorary decree for generous metics.[170]

166. c. 301–297. [? dr.] for honorary decree for military commanders.[171]

167. c. 301–294. [e.g., 30 dr.] for proxeny decree.[172]

---

a possible restoration. . . . Osborne [D64] printed five letter spaces (. . . . .), remarking that 'Pritchett's supplement is not the only possibility.'"

166. *IG* II^2 496 + 507 + p. 661 + Osborne D61. 39–41:

εἰς δὲ τὴν
ἀναγραφὴν τῆ̣ς στήλης δοῦναι τὸν ἐ-
πὶ τῆι διοικήσει ^{v} ΔΔΔ ^{v} δραχμάς. 41

167. *Agora* XVI 122. 29–32:

[εἰς δὲ] τὴν ἀν[αγραφὴν τ]-
[ῆς στήλης δοῦναι τὸν ταμία]ν τῶν στ[ρατιωτι]-
[κῶν . . . . δραχμὰς ἐκ τῶν εἰς τὰ] κατ̣[ὰ ψηφίσμα]- 31
[τα ἀναλισκομένων τῶι δήμωι. *vacat*(?)]

For the reasons stated in n. 139, restorations of δέκα, :ΔΔ: vel sim., ΔΔΔ: vel sim., or ΔΔΔΔ all might be possible.

168. *Agora* XVI 123. 27–30:

[εἰς δὲ] τὴν ἀναγραφὴν τῆς στήλ-
[ης δοῦναι τὸν] ταμίαν τοῦ δήμου : Δ 28
[ΔΔ : δραχμὰς ἐκ τῶ]ν εἰς τὰ κατὰ ψηφ-
[ίσματα ἀναλισκομένων τῶι] δήμωι.

169. *IG* II^2 500. 40–43:

εἰς δὲ τὴν ἀναγρα[φὴ]ν τῆς στήλης μ-
ερίσαι τὸν ἐπὶ τῆι δ[ι]οι[κ]ήσει ΔΔΔ ^{v} 41
δραχμὰς ἐκ τῶν εἰς τ[ὰ] κα[τὰ] ψηφίσμα-
τα ἀναλισ[κ]ομένων τῶι δήμωι.

170. *IG* II^2 505. 62–64:

[εἰ]ς [δὲ] τὴν ἀναγραφὴν τῆς στήλης δοῦναι
[τὸν τα]μίαν τοῦ δήμου [: Δ]ΔΔΔ [:] δραχμὰς ἐκ τῶν εἰς τὰ 63
[κατὰ ψηφίσμα]τα ἀναλισκομένων τῶι δήμωι.

171. *Agora* XVI 129. 12–14:

[εἰς δὲ τὴ]ν ἀναγραφ[ὴν τῆς]
[στήλης δοῦναι τὸν ἐξ]εταστὴν κα[ὶ τοὺ]-
[ς τριττυάρχους . . . . δραχμ]άς. *vacat* 14

In line 14, the original editor Meritt had restored ^{v}ΔΔ^v, but Woodhead comments that "the vagaries in the recording of numerals in these decrees make it unwise to offer a restoration with any assurance."

172. *IG* II^2 722 + *SEG* XXIV 120. 11–13:

[εἰς δὲ τὴν ἀναγραφ]-
[ὴν μερίσαι τοὺς τριττ]υ̣άρ[χους καὶ τὸν ἐξεταστὴν (*e.g.*) ^{v}ΔΔΔ^v δραχμ]- 12

168. c. 300. 50 dr. for honorary decree (fragment).[173]
169. c. 300. [? d]r. for decree (fragment).[174]
170. late 4th c. [? dr.] for honorary decree for Paseas.[175]
171. late 4th c. [3]0 dr. for honorary decree (fragment).[176]
172. late 4th c. [30 dr.] for isoteleia decree.[177]
173. late 4th c. [? dr.] for honorary decree (fragment).[178]

[ὰς ἐκ τῶν εἰς τὰ κατὰ ψηφί]σ̣[ματα ἀναλισκομένων τῶι δήμωι.]
For a slightly narrower range of dates (298/7–295/4), see *SEG* XXIX 93. The restoration of ^{v}ΔΔΔ^{v} is based on a (not invariably observed) stoichedon line of 50 letters: δέκα or εἴκοσι also might be possible.

173. *IG* II^2 809. 4–8:

εἰς δὲ τὴν [ἀναγραφὴν τῆς στήλη]-
ς δοῦναι τὸν ταμ[ίαν τῶν στρατιωτικ]-
ῶν ^{vv} : 𐅄: ^{v} δραχμ[ὰς ἐκ τῶν εἰς τὰ κατὰ]
ψηφίσματα ἀν̣α̣{[ν]α}λισκομένων τῶι δή]-
[μ]ωι·

For the date of this entry, see *Agora* XVI 128.

174. *Agora* XVI 128 b. 1–5:

[εἰς δὲ τ]-
ὴν ἀν[αγραφὴν τῆς στήλης δ]ο̣[ῦναι]
[τ]ὸν ταμ[ίαν τῶν στρατιωτ]ικ̣[ῶν . .]
[. δ]ραχμ̣[ὰς ἐκ τῶν εἰς τὰ κ]ατὰ ψ[ηφί]-
[σματα ἀναλισκομένων τ]ῷ̣ι δή[μωι].

For the reasons stated in n. 139, restorations of :Δ: vel sim., ΔΔ: vel sim., ΔΔΔ, or : 𐅄: vel sim. all might be possible.

175. *IG* II^2 512. 11–14:

εἰς δὲ τὴν ἀναγραφ[ὴ]-
[ν τῆς στήλης δοῦνα]ι τὸν ταμίαν τοῦ δήμ-
[ου . . δραχμὰς ἐκ τῶν] κατὰ ψηφίσματα ἀν-
[αλισκομένων τῶι δήμ]ωι̣.

For the reasons stated in n. 139, restorations of Δ: vel sim., ΔΔ, or 𐅄: vel sim. all might be possible.

176. *IG* II^2 515. 6–9:

[εἰς δὲ τὴν ἀναγραφ]ὴν τῆς στήλης δ[οῦ]-
[ναι τὸν ταμίαν τοῦ] δήμου [ΔΔ]Δ δραχμ[ὰς]
[ἐκ τῶν κατὰ ψηφίσμα]τα ἀναλισκομέ[νω]-
[ν τῶι δήμωι. . . .]

177. *IG* II^2 516. 6–10:

[εἰς δὲ τὴν ἀ]-
[να]γραφὴν τῆ[ς στήλης δοῦναι τὸν ταμία]-
[ν το]ῦ δήμου [:ΔΔΔ: δραχμὰς ἐκ τῶν εἰς τὰ]
[κατ]ὰ ψηφίσμ[ατα ἀναλισκομένων τῶι δή]-
[μωι].

178. *IG* II^2 517. 11–14:

εἰς δὲ τὴν ἀναγ]ραφὴ-
[ν τῆς στήλης δοῦναι τὸν ταμία]ν τοῦ
[δήμου . . δραχμὰς ἐκ τῶν κατὰ ψ]ηφίσ-
[ματα ἀναλισκομένων τῶι δήμωι].

174. late 4th c. [? dr.] for decree (fragment).[179]
175. late 4th c. [30 dr.] for decree (fragment).[180]
176. late 4th c. [3]0 dr. for decree (fragment).[181]
177. late 4th c. 20 [dr.] for decree (fragment).[182]
178. late 4th c. [30 dr.] for decree (fragment).[183]
179. late 4th c. [? dr.] for decree (fragment).[184]
180. late 4th c. [? dr.] for honorary decree (fragment).[185]

For the reasons stated in n. 139, restorations of Δ: vel sim., ΔΔ, or 𐅄: vel sim. all might be possible.

179. *IG* II² 520. 7–11:

[εἰς δὲ]
[τὴ]ν ἀν[αγραφὴν τῆς στήλης μερίσα]-
[ι τ]ὸν τ[αμίαν τοῦ δήμου . . . . δραχμ]-
[ὰς] ἐκ τ[ῶν εἰς τὰ κατὰ ψηφίσματα ἀν]-
[αλι]σ[κομένων τῶι̣ δήμωι].

For the reasons stated in n. 139, restorations of δέκα, :ΔΔ: vel sim., ΔΔΔ: vel sim., or ΔΔΔΔ all might be possible.

180. *IG* II² 521. 5–9:

[εἰς δὲ]
[τὴ]ν ἀναγραφ[ὴν τῆστήλης δοῦναι τὸ]-
[ν τ]αμίαν τοῦ [δήμου ΔΔΔ δραχμὰς ἐκ τ]-
[ῶν] κατὰ ψηφί[σματα ἀναλισκομένων τῶ]-
[ι δήμωι].

181. *IG* II² 522. 3–7:

[εἰς δὲ τ]-
ὴ[ν] ἀναγραφὴν καὶ τὴν π[οίησι]ν τῆ[ς σ]τ[ή]-
λ[η]ς δοῦναι τὸν ταμίαν το[ῦ] δή[μου ΔΔ]Δ δ-
ρ[α]χμὰς ἐκ τῶν εἰς τὰ κατὰ [ψη]φί[σμ]α[τα]
ἀναλισκομένων τῶι δήμωι.

For the unlikelihood of the restoration καὶ τὴν π[οίησι]ν, see n. 248.

182. *IG* II² 524. 5–8:

[εἰς δὲ τὴν ἀναγραφὴ]ν τῆς σ[τήλη]-
[ς δοῦναι τὸν ταμίαν τοῦ δή]μου : ΔΔ : [δρα]-
[χμὰς ἐκ τῶν εἰς τὰ κατὰ ψηφί]σματα ἀ[ναλ]-
[ισκομένων τῶι δήμωι].

183. *IG* II² 526. 4–7:

[εἰς δὲ τὴν ἀναγρα]-
[φ]ὴν τ[ῆς στήλης δοῦναι τὸν ταμίαν τοῦ δήμο]-
υ τρι[άκοντα δραχμὰς ἐκ τῶν εἰς τὰ κατὰ ψηφ]-
[ί]σμ[ατα ἀναλισκομένων τῶι δήμωι].

184. *IG* II² 527. 3–6:

εἰς [δὲ τὴν ἀναγραφὴν τῆς στήλης δο]-
[ῦν]αι τὸν [ταμίαν τοῦ δήμου . . .⁵. . δραχμ]-
[ὰς] ἐκ τῶ[ν εἰς τὰ κατὰ ψηφίσματ' ἀναλισκ]-
[ομέ]νω[ν τῶι δήμωι].

If the other printed restorations are correct, the only restorations that would precisely fill the five available letter spaces are :ΔΔΔ: vel sim. and ΔΔΔΔ: vel sim., but see notes 60, 106 and 121.

185. *IG* II² 528. 0–3:

181. late 4th c. [? d]r. for decree (fragment).[186]
182. late 4th c. [20 dr.] for decree (fragment).[187]
183. late 4th c. [30 d]r. for decree (fragment).[188]
184. late 4th c. [? d]r. for decree (fragment).[189]
185. late 4th c. [20 dr.] for decree (fragment).[190]
186. late 4th c. [30 dr.] for honorary decree for Prieneans.[191]
187. late 4th c. 30 dr. for honorary decree for Prieneans.[192]

[- - - - - - - - - - - - - - - - εἰς]
[δὲ τὴν] ἀνα[γραφὴν τῆς στήλης δοῦναι τὸ]-
[ν ταμ]ίαν τ[οῦ δήμου . δραχμὰς ἐκ τῶν κατ]- 2
[ὰ ψη]φίσμα[τα ἀναλισκομένων τῶι δήμωι].

If the other printed restorations are correct, the only restorations that would precisely fill the single available letter space are Δ and 𐅄, but see notes 60, 106 and 121.

186. *IG* II^2 529. 2–5:
[εἰς δὲ τὴν ἀναγραφὴ]-
[ν] τῆς στήλη[ς δοῦναι τὸν ταμίαν τοῦ δήμου . . . δρ]- 3
[αχμ]ὰς ἐκ τῶν [εἰς τὰ κατὰ ψηφίσματα ἀναλισκομέ]-
[νων] τῶι δήμ[ωι].

For the reasons stated in n. 139, restorations of :Δ: vel sim., ΔΔ: vel sim., ΔΔΔ, or : 𐅄: vel sim. all might be possible.

187. *IG* II^2 531. 1–5:
[- - - - εἰς δὲ τὴν ἀναγραφὴν]
[τῆς στ]ήλη[ς δοῦναι τὸν ταμία]-
[ν τοῦ] δήμου [ΔΔ δραχμὰς ἐκ τῶν] 3
[εἰς] τὰ κατὰ [ψηφίσματ' ἀναλισκ]-
[ομέ]νων τῶι δ[ήμωι].

188. *IG* II^2 532. 1–4:
[- - - - - - - - - - - - εἰς δὲ τὴν ἀ]-
[ναγραφὴν τῆς στήλης] δοῦναι τὸ[ν] ταμ[ίαν]
[τοῦ δήμου : ΔΔΔ : δρα]χμὰς ἐκ τῶν εἰς [τὰ κα]- 3
[τὰ ψηφίσματα ἀναλι]σκομένων τῶ[ι δήμωι].

189. *IG* II^2 533. 1–3:
[. . . .^{7}. . . δοῦν]α[ι τὸν ταμίαν τοῦ δήμ]-
[ου . . . . δραχ]μὰς ἐκκτ[ῶν κατὰ ψηφίσ]- 2
[ματα ἀναλι]σκομένων τ[ῶι δήμωι].

For the reasons stated in n. 139, restorations of δέκα, :ΔΔ: vel sim., ΔΔΔ: vel sim., and ΔΔΔΔ all might be possible.

190. *IG* II^2 534. 2–4:
[εἰς δὲ τὴν ποίησιν καὶ τὴν ἀνάθεσιν τῆς στή]-
[λ]ης δοῦναι [τὸν ταμίαν τοῦ δήμου ΔΔ δραχμὰς ἐκ τῶν εἰς τὰ κατὰ ψηφ]- 3
[ί]σματ' ἀναλι[σκομένων τῶι δήμωι].

For the unlikelihood of the restoration εἰς δὲ τὴν ποίησιν, see n. 248.

191. *IG* II^2 565. 2–4:
[εἰς δὲ τὴν ἀναγραφὴν τῆ]ς στήλης δοῦνα-
[ι τὸν ταμίαν τοῦ δήμου ΔΔΔ δραχμὰς ἐκ τ]ῶν κατὰ ψηφίσμ- 3
[ατα ἀναλισκομένων τῶι δήμωι.]

192. *IG* II^2 567. 18–21:

188. late 4th c. [4]0 dr. for honorary decree (fragment).[193]
189. late 4th c. [? dr.] for honorary decree for Parians.[194]
190. late 4th c. [? d]r. for decree (fragment).[195]
191. late 4th c. 30 dr. (min. inc.) for decree (fragment).[196]
192. late 4th c. 20 dr. for deme decree on theatre leasing.[197]
193. late 4th c. [? d]r. for genos honorary decree for religious officials (two stelai).[198]
194. late 4th c. [20 d]r. for honorary decree (fragment).[199]

[εἰς δὲ τὴν ἀνα]-
γραφὴν τῆς [στήλης δοῦναι τὸν ταμίαν τοῦ δήμου]
ΔΔΔ: δραχμὰς ἐκ [τῶν κατὰ ψηφίσματα ἀναλισκομένων]
τῶι δήμωι.

193. *IG* II^2 571. 8–10:

μερίσαι [δὲ τὸν ἐπὶ τεῖ διοι]-
[κή]σει εἰς τὴν ἀναγρ[αφὴν τῆς στήλης : Δ]
[Δ]ΔΔ : δραχμάς.

Tracy, *ADIT* 166, attributes this inscription to "The Cutter of Agora I 4266," whom he dates "*ca.* 304–271."

194. *IG* II^2 573. 17–19:

[- - - - - - - - - - - - - - - - - - - δ]-
[ραχμὰς ἐκ τ]ῶν [κατὰ ψηφίσματ' ἀναλισκομέ]-
[νων τῶι δήμ]ωι.

Tracy, *ADIT* 139, attributes this inscription to "The Cutter of *IG* II^2 1262," whom he dates "*ca.* 320–*ca.* 296."

195. *IG* II^2 589. 4–7:

[εἰς δὲ τὴν ἀναγραφὴν τ]-
[ῆ]ς στήλης δ[οῦναι τὸν ταμίαν . . . .^{8}. . . . δρ]-
[α]χμὰς ἐκ τ[ῶν εἰς τὰ κατὰ ψηφίσματα ἀναλι]-
[σκ]ομέν[ων τῶι δήμωι].

It is hard to see what restoration, of either numerals plus punctuation or a word like τριάκοντα (see n. 224), could have filled the eight letter spaces.

196. *IG* II^2 600. 1–3:

- - - - - - - - - - - - ΔΔΔ . δρα-
χμὰς ἐκ τῶν εἰς τὰ κατὰ ψηφίσματ-
α {τὰ} ἀναλισκομένων τῶι δήμωι.

197. *IG* II^2 1206. 16–19:

[εἰς δ]ὲ τὴν ἀναγραφὴν τῆ[ς]
[στήλης δοῦ]ναι αὐτοῖς τὸν δήμ[α]-
[ρχον . . . .]ένην : ΔΔ : δραχμὰς κ[α]ὶ [λ]-
[ογισασθαι] τοῖς δημόταις.

198. *IG* II^2 1232. 24–25:

[εἰς δὲ τὴν ἀ]ναγραφὴν τῶν σ[τ]η[λ]ῶν δ[ο]ῦ-
[ναι - $^{c. 5}$ - δρα]χμάς. . . .

199. *Agora* XVI 137. 4–8:

[εἰ]ς δὲ τ[ὴν ἀναγραφὴν τ]-
[ῆς στήλης δοῦν]αι τὸν [ταμίαν τοῦ δή]-

195. late 4th c. [20 dr.] for decree (fragment).[200]
196. late 4th c. [30 dr.] for decree (fragment).[201]
197. late 4th c. [30 d]r. for decree (fragment) (plural stelai).[202]
198. c. 300–294. [3]0 dr. for citizenship decree.[203]
199. c. 300–294. 30 d[r.] for proxeny decree.[204]

[μου ᵛ ΔΔ ᵛ δραχμ]ὰς ἐκ τ[ῶν εἰς τὰ κατὰ] 6
[ψηφίσματα ἀνα]λισκο[μένων τῶι δήμ]-
[ωι. *vacat*]

For the possible association of this fragment with *IG* II² 540 b, and a date for the two fragments of c. 303/2, see Woodhead's commentary and *SEG* XL 68.

200. *Agora* XVI 138. 4–7:

εἰς δὲ τ[ὴν ἀναγραφ]-
[ὴν τῆς στήλης δοῦ]ναι τὸν ταμί[αν τοῦ δ]-
[ήμου: ΔΔ : δραχμὰς] ἐκ τῶν εἰς τὰ κατ[ὰ ψη]- 6
[φίσματ' ἀναλισκο]μένων τῶι δήμω[ι. ᵛᵛᵛ]

Tracy, *ADIT* 162, attributes this inscription (Agora I 4906) to "The Cutter of *IG* II² 495," whom he dates "304/3–303/2."

201. *Agora* XVI 139. 1–5:

[εἰς δὲ τὴν ἀναγ]-
[ραφὴν τῆ]ς στ[ήλης δοῦναι τὸν ταμί]-
[αν τοῦ δή]μου ᵛ [ΔΔΔ ᵛ δραχμὰς ἐκ τῶν] 3
[εἰς τὰ κα]τὰ ψη[φίσματ' ἀναλισκομέ]-
[νων τῶι δ]ήμωι.

For a slightly different text (not affecting the restored numerals), see *SEG* XVIII 17. Tracy, *ADIT* 140 (Agora I 5251), attributes this inscription to "The Cutter of *IG* II² 1262," whom he dates "*ca.* 320–*ca.* 296."

202. *Agora* XVI 140. 2–5:

[εἰς δὲ τὴν ἀναγραφὴν τῶν στή]λῶν δοῦ-
[ναι τὸν ταμίαν τοῦ δήμου ΔΔΔ δραχ]μὰς ἐκ τ- 3
[ῶν κατὰ ψηφίσματα ἀναλισκομένων] τῶι δή-
[μωι·]

Woodhead comments that the original editor Meritt "inserted two-dot punctuation before and after the numeral, but the stoichedon arrangement leaves no room for this as part of the pattern. If they were included, they were added *extra ordinem* between normally spaced letters; and there was indeed room for this."

203. *IG* II² 643 + *Agora* XVI 162. 20–23:

[εἰ]-
[ς δ]ὲ τ[ὴ]ν ἀναγραφὴν τηστήλης δ[οῦναι τ]-
[ὸν ἐ]ξε[τ]αστὴν καὶ τοὺς τριττ[υάρχου]-
[ς ᵛ ΔΔ]Δ ᵛ δραχμάς. 23

204. *Agora* XVI 164. 20–24:

εἰς δὲ τὴν ἀνα[γραφὴν τῆ]-
ς στήλης δοῦναι τοὺς τριτ[τυάρχους]
καὶ τὸν ἐξεταστὴν ᵛΔΔΔ: δ[ραχμὰς ἐκ] 22
τῶν εἰς τὰ κατὰ ψηφίσματ' ἀ[ναλισκομ]-
ένων τῶι δήμωι.

For a slightly narrower range of dates (298/7–295/4), see *SEG* XXIX 93.

200. early 3rd c. 20 dr. for decree (fragment).[205]

201. early 3rd c. 10 [dr.] (min. inc.) for decree (fragment).[206]

202. early 3rd c. [2]0 or [3]0 dr.? for honorary decree for foreigner.[207]

203. 299. 20 dr. for honorary decree for Athenian ambassador.[208]

204. c. 295/4. 30 dr. for citizenship decree (2 stelai, apiece).[209]

205. c. 295/4? [30] dr. for decree (fragment).[210]

206. c. 288–262. [? dr.] for honorary decree for archon.[211]

---

205. *IG* II^2 713. 6–8:

[εἰς δὲ τὴν ἀναγρ]-
[α]φὴν τῆς στήλης μερ[ίσαι τοὺς ἐπὶ τῆι δ]-
[ι]οικήσει ΔΔ δραχμά[ς]. 8

206. *IG* II^2 714. 3–5:

[εἰ]ς δὲ τὴν ἀναγρα[φὴν]
[τῆς στήλης μερίσαι τοὺς? ἐπὶ] τεῖ διοικήσει Δ - 4
[δραχμάς - - - - - - - - - - - - - -]

207. *IG* II^2 725. 9–10:

[εἰς δὲ τὴν ἀναγραφ]ὴν καὶ τὴν στάσιν μ-
[ερίσαι τὸν ἐπὶ τῆι διοικήσει ΔΔ]Δ δραχμάς. 10

SEG XXIV 124 reports that line 10 also can be restored as [ερίσαι τοὺς ἐπὶ τῆι διοικήσει Δ]Δ δραχμάς.

208. *IG* II^2 641. 29–32:

εἰς δὲ τὴν ἀν-
αγραφὴν τῆς στήλης δοῦναι τὸ-
ν ἐξεταστὴν καὶ τοὺς τριττυά-
ρχους ^{v} ΔΔ ^{v} δραχμάς. 32

209. *IG* II^2 648. 12–15:

ε[ἰς δὲ τὴν ἀν]-
[αγραφ]ὴ[ν] τῶν στηλῶν δοῦναι τὸν ἐ[πὶ τῆι διοι]-
[κήσει] : ΔΔΔ : εἰς ἑκατέραν ἐκ τῶν [εἰς τὰ κατὰ] 14
[ψηφίσ]ματα ἀναλισκομένων τῶι [δήμωι.]

210. *IG* II^2 709 + p. 665 + *SEG* XXXIV 80. 1–5:

[εἰς δὲ τὴν ἀναγραφὴν τ]-
[ῆς στήλης] δοῦναι τὸν ἐπὶ [τῆι διοική]-
[σει : ΔΔΔ :] δραχμὰς ἐκ τῶν [εἰς τὰ κατὰ] 3
[ψηφίσμα]τα ἀναλισκομένω[ν τῶι δήμω]-
[ι].

211. *Agora* XVI 174. 8–10:

[εἰς δὲ τὴν ἀναγραφὴν τῆς]
[σ]τήλης μερ[ίσαι τοὺς ἐπὶ τῆι διοικήσει . . . δραχ]- 9
[μάς]. *vacat*

Woodhead comments: "In lines 9–10, [the original editor] Meritt proposed διοικήσει ^{v} Δ ^{v} δραχ||μάς, but the figure should remain unrestored in view of the uncertainty concerning the arrangement of the present text on the stone and of numerals in general within the space available for them. Since [*Agora* XVI] 187 [#218 below] offers the latest certain instance of the statement of cost of a stele, this text should perhaps be assigned a date not later than 270."

207. c. 288–262. [?] for honorary decree (fragment).[212]

208. c. 286–262. 10 dr. for honorary decree for hipparchs and phylarchs.[213]

209. c. 286–262. [20 dr.] for honorary decree (fragment).[214]

210. c. 286–244. [20 dr.] for honorary decree (fragment).[215]

211. c. 284–280 or 239–229? 10 dr. for citizenship decree.[216]

212. 283. 20 dr. for honorary decree for Philippides the poet.[217]

213. 282. [10 dr.] for prytany decree.[218]

214. 281. 10 dr. for honorary decree for archon.[219]

---

212. *Agora* XVI 175. 4–5:

[εἰς δὲ τὴν ἀναγραφὴν τῆς σ]-
τήλης [- - - - - - - - - - ἐπὶ τῆι διοικήσει - - - - - - - - - (?)] 5

Woodhead reports that the original editor Meritt had restored μερίσαι τοὺς ἐπὶ τῆι διοικήσει - - - δραχμάς, but he remarks that "the sum expended might not have been expressed at all."

213. *SEG* XXI 357. 9–11:

[εἰς δὲ τὴ]-
ν ἀναγραφὴν τῆς στήλης μερίσαι τοὺς ἐπ[ὶ τεῖ διοκήσε]-
ι : Δ : δραχμάς. 11

For the date, see *SEG* XXXIV 260.

214. *SEG* XXXII 107. 10–13:

[εἰς δὲ τὴν ἀναγρα]-
φὴν [τῆς στήλης μερίσαι τοὺς ἐπὶ τῆι διοικήσ]-
ει [ΔΔ δραχμὰς ἐκ τῶν εἰς τὰ κατὰ ψηφίσματα ἀν]- 12
α[λισκομένων τῶι δήμωι.]

215. *IG* II^2 525 + 675 + *SEG* XXXIV 72. 5–7:

[εἰς δὲ τὴν ἀναγρα]φὴν τῆς στήλης
[δοῦναι τὸν ἐπὶ τεῖ διοκήσει ΔΔ δραχμὰ]ς ἐκ τῶν εἰς τ- 6
[ὰ κατὰ ψηφίσματα ἀναλισκομένων τῶι δήμω]ι.

For the date, see *SEG* XXXVIII 90.

216. *IG* II^2 808. 26–28:

[εἰς δὲ τὴν ἀν]-
αγραφὴν τῆς στήλ[ης μερίσαι τοὺς ἐπὶ τῆι διοική ^{v}]-
σει ^{v} Δ ^{v} δραχμάς. ^{vv} 28

For the date, see *SEG* XL 87.

217. *IG* II^2 657. 70–73:

εἰς
δὲ τὴν ἀναγραφὴν τῆς στήλης μερίσαι τοὺς ἐπὶ τῆι
διο[ι]κήσει ΔΔ δραχμὰς [ἐκ] τῶν εἰς τὰ κατὰ ψηφίσματ- 72
α ἀναλισκομένων τῶι δήμωι.

For the date, see *SEG* XXVIII 58.

218. *Agora* XV 71. 22–24:

[εἰς δὲ τὴν ἀναγρ]-
[αφὴν τῆς σ]τήλης μ[ερίσαι τοὺς ἐπὶ τῆι διοικήσει]
[Δ δραχμάς] *vacat* 24

219. *Agora* XVI 181. 40–42:

εἰς δὲ τὴν ἀναγραφὴν τῆς στήλης

215. 281. 10 dr. for honorary decree for taxiarchs.[220]
216. 278. 50 dr. for honorary decree for Komeas the hipparch.[221]
217. 272. [?] dr. for honorary decree for overseers of sacrifices.[222]
218. 271. 10 dr. for honorary decree for taxiarchs.[223]
219. 264/3. [20 dr.] for deme honorary decree (fragment).[224]
220. mid 3rd c. 10 [dr.] (min. inc.) for decree (fragment).[225]
221. mid 3rd c. 10 dr. for Mesogeians' honorary decree for religious official.[226]
222. mid 3rd c. [?] dr. for orgeones' honorary decree for officer.[227]

μερίσαι τοὺς ἐπὶ τῆι διοικήσει ᵛ Δ ᵛ δρ-
αχμάς.

220. *Agora* XVI 182. 30–32:

εἰς δὲ τὴν
ἀναγραφὴν τῆς στήλης μερίσαι τοὺς ἐπὶ ᵛᵛ
τῆι διοικήσει Δ δραχμάς. *vacat*

221. *IG* II² 672. 16–17:

[εἰς δὲ τὴν ἀναγρα]φὴν μερίσα[ι] τοὺς ἐπὶ τε[ῖ διοι]κήσει ἐκ τῶν εἰς τὰ [κατὰ ψ]-
[ηφίσματα ἀναλισκομένων τῶι δ]ήμωι : 𐅄 :

For the date, see *SEG* XXXVIII 74 and C. Habicht, *Untersuchungen zur politischen Geschichte Athens im 3. Jahrhundert v. Chr.* (Munich 1979) 140, n. 138.

222. *IG* II² 676. 36–37:

[εἰς δὲ τὴν ἀναγραφὴν] τῆς στή[λης μερίσαι το]-
[ὺς ἐπὶ τῆι διοικήσει - - -] : δραχ[μάς].

223. *Agora* XVI 187. 35–36:

εἰς δὲ τὴν ἀναγρα-
φὴν μερίσαι τοὺς ἐπὶ τεῖ διοικήσει : Δ : δραχμάς.

224. *Agora* XVI 192. 3–5:

[εἰς δὲ τὴν ἀναγραφὴν τῆς]
στήλης μερ[ίσαι τὸν δήμαρχον : ΔΔ : δραχμὰς καὶ λογίσασθαι τ]-
οῖς δημόταις.

Woodhead comments: "The assumed cost of twenty drachmas . . . is double that of the substantial stelai . . . [##214, 215 and 218]. The sum may have been expressed in full as δέκα: cf. . . . [##143, 47]."

225. *IG* II² 812. 4–5:

[εἰ]ς δὲ τὴν ἀναγρα[φὴν τῆς στήλης μερίσαι τὸν ἐ]-
[πὶ] τεῖ διοικήσει Δ[. δραχμάς].

226. *IG* II² 1247. 27–31:

εἰς δὲ τ-
ὴν ἀναγραφὴν τῆς στήλης δότω ὁ ἄρ-
χων Ἀδείμαντος : Δ : δραχμὰς ἐκ τῆς
κοινῆς προσόδου τῶν τοῦ θεοῦ χρη-
μάτων. . . .

227. *IG* II² 1284. 15–18:

[ἀ]-
ναγράψαι δὲ τόδε τὸ ψήφισμα τὸν γρα[μμ]-

223. mid 3rd c. [?] dr. for orgeones' honorary decree for secretary.[228]

224. c. 245? No figure or [20 dr.]? for honorary decree (fragment).[229]

225. 221. 8 dr. 3 ob. for decree on dedication to Hero Doctor.[230]

226. c. 210–170. [? dr.] for Asklepiastai honorary decree for benefactor.[231]

227. late 3rd c. [?] dr. for orgeones' honorary decree for benefactor and his priestess-wife.[232]

228. 74. [?] dr. for honorary decree for ἱεροποιοί to Lemnian Kabeirion.[233]

ατέα ἐν στήλει λιθίνει καὶ στῆσαι ἐν [τῶι]
ἱερῶι, τὸν δὲ ταμίαν μερίσαι δραχ[μὰς . .] 18

228. *IG* II^2 1284. 31–34:

ἀναγράψαι
δὲ τόδε τὸ ψήφισμα τὸν γραμματέα ἐ-
ν στήλει λιθίνει καὶ στῆσαι ἐν τῶι ἱ[ερ]-
ῶι, τὸν δὲ ταμίαν μερίσαι δραχμὰς . . . 34

229. *Agora* XVI 212 + *SEG* XIX 72 + *SEG* XXXIV 78. 7–9:

[- - - - - - - - - - - - - - - - - - - εἰς δὲ τὴν ποίησ]ιν κα[ὶ τὴν ἀνάθεσιν]
[τῆς στήλης δοῦναι τὸν ἐξεταστὴν καὶ τοὺς τριτ]τυά[ρχους ᵛ ΔΔ ᵛ δραχ]- 8
[μάς].

Woodhead declines to print *any* restoration in these lines and assigns the date of "*ca. a.* 245 *a.* (?)" on the basis of letter forms (cf. the date of c. 300 in earlier editions). At the later date of c. 245? (see #218 with n. 211), a polis inscription might not specify *any* sum for inscribing, but for the sake of completeness I retain it in my catalogue of all published texts in this category. For the unlikelihood of the restoration εἰς δὲ τὴν ποίησιν at the earlier date of c. 300, see n. 248.

230. *IG* II^2 839. 84–85:

καὶ εἰς ἀναγραφὴν τῆς στήλης
ΠHHHIII· 85

231. *IG* II^2 1293 + *SEG* XVIII 33. 18–20:

[εἰς δὲ τὴν ἀναγραφὴν]
[καὶ τὴν ποίη]σιν τῆς στή[λης μερίσαι τὸν ταμίαν]
[. . δραχμὰς ἀπὸ τοῦ] κο[ινοῦ]. 20

For the date, see Tracy, *ALC* 73. Because Kirchner reported that this text is non-stoichedon, it would be hazardous to speculate on possible restorations at the beginning of line 20.

232. *IG* II^2 1316. 23–24:

μ[ε]ρί[σ]αι [δ]ὲ τὸν ταμίαν ἀπὸ τ[οῦ κο]-
[ι]νοῦ ε[ἰς τὴν ἀνα]γραφὴν τῆς στήλης δρ[αχ]μὰ[ς -] 24

233. *ASAA* 3 (1941) 83, no. 6. 16–18:

[εἰς τὴν] ἀναγραφὴν [καὶ ἀ]-
[νάθεσιν τῆς στήλης ἐκ]τῶν ἱερῶν χρημάτων δραχμ-
[ὰς . . . . καὶ] λογίσασθαι τῶι δήμωι. 18

After collecting about 70% of the foregoing figures,[234] Nolan tested Drerup's (as in n. 2) theory that inscribing costs were determined by the number of letters in an inscription: 10 dr. for every 500 letters, but with a base price of 20 dr., i.e., 1,000 letters being the limit for 20 dr., 1,500 letters for 30 dr., 2,000 letters for 40 dr., 2,500 letters for 50 dr., and 3,000 letters for 60 dr., and with special rules for inscriptions containing more than one decree, a catalogue, or amendments to the orginal decree. Nolan demonstrated convincingly that neither the general rule nor the special rules of Drerup's theory are supported by the inscriptions themselves.[235] Nolan also showed that Drerup's notion that many inscriptions that did not fit his rules were "private copies of public decrees" was not supported by the language of the decrees.[236] As for Drerup's final point, that those decrees that are decorated with sculptural relief must be privately financed copies, Nolan observed that the reliefs on the treaty with the Thessalians (#30) and the law against tyranny (#78) certainly must have been paid for out of polis funds.[237]

Nolan then proceeded to ask the key questions:

> "What does the sum in the formula represent?" An upper limit for bids by competing masons? The actual payment to the mason? Or the amount the

---

234. Nolan, *Inscribing Costs*, omits all clearly fifth-century figures (##1–2), such special items as the 2 dr. stele, rations for the Eleusinian engravers and the σανίδες with γραφή (##4, 112, 113), the Amphiareion figures (##103, 104, 111), and all non-polis figures (##47, 50, 77, 95, 98, 132, 133, 192, 193, 219, 221–223, 226, 227). In addition, his chronological Table Five (*Inscribing Costs* 79–82) omits a great many polis figures (##22, 27, 37, 41, 48, 54, 55, 61, 72, 76, 84, 86, 91, 97, 107, 116, 126, 127, 135, 139, 149, 150, 152, 154, 157, 158, 163, 167, 168, 170, 196, 198, 201, 204, 205, 207, 209, 211, 220, 224, 225, 228), about two-thirds of which are uncertain.

235. Nolan, *Inscribing Costs* 18–36.

236. Nolan, *Inscribing Costs* 37–40.

237. Nolan, *Inscribing Costs* 40–44. In addition to the polis-financed reliefs in #30 and #78 (two stelai, each with a relief?), Clinton, "Review" 747, draws attention to #98, where the sculptural decoration of the deme lease probably was paid for by the deme. For further arguments against the theory that document reliefs were (as a rule) privately commissioned, see Lawton, *ADR* 22–25. Of course, as Nolan observes, private funds may have been used for the sculptural decoration of some honorary decrees, and the language of #130 (lines 72–73: συνεπιμεληθῆναι δὲ τῆς ἀν[αγρ]αφῆς τοὺς φίλους καὶ τοὺς οἰκείους τοὺς Εὔφρο[νος]) suggests that Euphron's friends and relatives were expected to help—their participation might also account for the fact that the figure (50 dr.) was the same as for #119, even though the text to be inscribed had more than doubled (87 lines as compared to the original 34). Lawton, *ADR* 23, notes two other instances of private participation in the costs of publication of decrees that had sculptural decoration (*IG* $I^3$101. 43–44 and *IG* $II^2$130. 18), to which Clinton, "Review" 746 (n. 2), adds *IG* II^2 1187. 27–28.

state was willing to contribute for inscribing, which did not necessarily cover all expenses? What was the money meant to pay for? Just the inscribing, or the whole process of quarrying, transport of the stone to Athens, and the making, inscribing and setting up of the stele?[238]

To answer these questions, Nolan took several different approaches. Parallels from Epidauros and Delos suggested to him that 20–30 dr. would be too much for inscribing alone. He also estimated that masons inscribed about 200 letters per day, which for a 20 dr. inscription of 1,000 letters (Drerup's rule!) would work out to five days of work at 4 dr. p.d., and he rightly judged that this was too high in relation to known wages for other manual workers.[239] He therefore concluded that the amount "must refer to the whole process, including the cost of the stele, layout of the text, and the inscribing itself."[240] He then tried to estimate the size and weight of an average stele, the time required to quarry and transport it, the cost of fodder for draft animals, and the time required to prepare the stele, and he concluded that the total cost of an uninscribed stele was 11.6 to 23.45 dr.[241] When he turned to the surviving stelai themselves, however, he found that "[i]n the 20 and 30 dr price ranges . . . there seems to be no significant correlation between the size of the stele and the price."[242] He also was "unable to find any correlation between the price and the quality of the lettering."[243] Finally, he considered the chronological order of the inscriptions, and reached the following conclusions:

ca. 390–368	Few inscriptions in general; fewer with prices for inscribing
368–332/1	Many inscriptions; all except one cost 20 or 30 dr

238. Nolan, *Inscribing Costs* 48.

239. See "Construction and Other Manual Workers" #3 (1 dr. p.d. in 409–407) and #7 (1 1/4–2 1/2 dr. p.d. in 329/8). See also "Inflation and Deflation" pp. 241–242.

240. Nolan, *Inscribing Costs* 54.

241. Nolan, *Inscribing Costs* 54–60.

242. Nolan, *Inscribing Costs* 65.

243. Nolan, *Inscribing Costs* 68. At 72–73, he remarks: "The only pattern observable in general is that the quality of inscribing begins to deteriorate after 318, and deteriorates rather rapidly after the restoration of the democracy in 307/6."

331–299	Many inscriptions; no 20 dr inscriptions; all inscriptions cost 30, 40, or 50 dr
318–307	Oligarchic rule; very few inscriptions
298–270	Many inscriptions; some 20 dr ones but after 2[9]8 10 dr becomes apparent norm.

The implications of the above chart are that the prices changed in the course of time. If there ever was a limit to the number of letters for any given price, it was also probably subject to change. The limits may also have varied within a given year, according to that year's budget, or have been different in different years. Thus, from 3[68] to 3[3]2, 20 or 30 dr were usually allotted for decrees—20 dr were allotted for the shorter decrees, 30 dr for the longer ones. After 332, however, 30 dr seems to have become the base price, at le[as]t until the turn of the century. 40 dr could be allotted for somewhat longer decrees and 50 dr for the longest of all. . . . In the first quarter of the third century, 10 dr began to be allotted for shorter decrees. . . . By this time, however, the practice of specifying the price seems to have fallen out of use, or at least was not used consistently.[244]

Nolan's final conclusions also deserve to be set out:

It seems to me that the sum in the publication formula, which is always in 10 dr increments, represents a standardized allottment of some kind for piece work; that is, the stele and the inscribing on it are considered to be a single piece of work (at least in Athens), for which standardized prices were allotted. Exactly how the price was determined is not clear—a combination of factors must have operated in determining the price: size of the stele, number of letters to be inscribed, whether or not there was to be a relief on the stele, or the stele was to be crowned by a molding or pediment. The financial condition of the state may also have influenced the allotments at any given time; if the state was short of money, less money may have been allotted for more inscribing. The allotment in some cases may have been more than enough to get a stele inscribed in which case the allotment may represent an upper limit for competing bids from masons; but we can only speculate about this. In other cases, where a particularly splendid stele with relief survives, it is likely that some money (perhaps a sizeable sum, at least equal to what the state had allotted) was contributed by a private party. In any

244. Nolan, *Inscribing Costs* 74–76 (notes omitted). The numbers and letters in square brackets are my corrections of obvious typographical errors.

> case, it seems clear that the allotment was meant to pay for both the stele and the inscribing of it.
>
> Two concepts go far to explain the prices for inscribing: "standardized prices" and "piece work." The prices are clearly standardized—the 10 dr increments attest to that. This means that the allotments bear only a rough correspondence to the actual work done; the sum does not represent a payment for the actual number of days worked in the making and inscribing of a particular stele. Rather it is the standard amount for a decree of that approximate length. The term "piece work" also implies this: a given amoun[t] was allotted for a stele, no matter how long it might take a particular mason to work it.[245]

It seems to me that Nolan has provided a convincing demonstration that these amounts were not determined by a fixed formula based on the number of letters, the size of the stele, or the quality of the lettering. I deal with the other possible explanations put forward by Nolan in order, beginning with what seems to me to be the least likely:

1. "An upper limit for bids by competing masons" is ruled out, I think, by the formulaic infinitive δοῦναι, which clearly directs the treasurer or other financial official(s) to pay out the specified sum, rather than "up to" that amount.

2. "The amount the state was willing to contribute for inscribing, which did not necessarily cover expenses" is unlikely because of the substantial number of public inscriptions with amounts in the typical (20–30 dr.) range.[246] If these amounts fully covered the cost of inscribing public laws and treaties, they also should have covered the costs of honorary decrees.

---

245. Nolan, *Inscribing Costs* 108–109 (notes omitted). Interpretation of the publicly appropriated sums as covering only part of the (entire) cost of a (quarried, transported, worked, inscribed and decorated) stele might be supported by the formulaic words εἰς τὴν ἀναγραφήν, which *could* (but need not) mean "*towards* the (cost of) inscribing" rather than "for (all) the (cost of) inscribing." See the discussion of the similar formula εἰς ἐφόδια in "Travel Allowances" n. 1.

246. Although most of figures collected here are for decrees that are clearly honorary (proxeny, citizenship, isoteleia) or potentially so (fragments) and thus *could* have been paid for by the honorees, there is a significant corpus of clearly public decrees, which could have been paid for only by the polis, and their figures are comparable to those for the honorary decrees: mostly 20 dr. (##22, 29, 32, 78, plus the restored #46) and 30 dr. (##19, 30, 44, plus the restored ##17, 26), with only three higher figures (50 dr. for #137 [plus the restored #116] and 60 dr. for #18).

3. "The whole process of quarrying, transport of the stone to Athens, and the making, inscribing and setting up of the stele" also is unlikely, for four reasons. First, the usual formulaic language (εἰς δὲ τὴν ἀναγραφήν) on its face refers only to inscribing.[247] Second, the rather specific language of #1 indicates that quarrying and transport were not covered by the 62 dr. appropriated there.[248] Third, since "there seems to be no significant correlation between the size of the stele and the price,"[249] the cost of the stele itself (quarrying) and its transport (a function of its weight) probably were not covered by the inscribing appropriation; this probability is made virtually certain by #45, where the stele already had been quarried, prepared and (partially) inscribed before the typical (for that period) sum of 20 dr. was appropriated for additional inscribing. Fourth, since the costs of sculptural decoration do not seem to have been covered by the inscribing appropriation,[250] sculpture must have been paid for separately, and if the state paid for sculpture separately, it would have been natural for it also to pay for other non-ἀναγραφή costs separately. Indeed, it would have been inefficient to

247. Clinton, "Review" 746 (n. 1), argues that this interpretation of ἀναγραφήν/ἀναγράψαι is refuted by *IG* II^2 2496. 24–25 (ἀναγράψαι δ[ὲ τ]άσδε τὰς συνθήκας Εὐκράτην ἐν στήλει λιθίνει), where the lessee Eukrates was required to inscribe the lease agreements (τὰς συνθήκας) on a stele that, when completed, included a relief, but the only thing that this language *requires* Eukrates to inscribe is the lease; the fact that the stele also included a relief means only that Eukrates or his letter-cutter *chose* to include a relief.

248. The (atypical) restorations of καὶ τὴν ποίησιν vel sim. in ##106, 176, 185 and 224 (if #224 is dated to c. 300 rather than c. 245) are not supported by any fully preserved text quoted in this chapter, and probably were suggested by preserved texts that first appear in 266/5 (see Henry, "Provisions" [as in n. 4] 259–260, 268, 273–275, and *IG* II^2 668. 36–37).

249. Nolan, *Inscribing Costs* 65.

250. The ἀναγραφή figures for the stelai with sculptural decoration ([?] dr. for ##55 and 101; 10 dr. for #98; 20 dr. for ##7, 35, 78 [2 stelai], and 80; 30 dr. for ##12 [restored], 30, 53, and 60; 50 dr. for #130 [2 stelai]) are also typical for stelai without sculptural decoration, and this suggests that the cost of sculptural decoration was not covered by these figures. This should not surprise us, since the figures are specified to be εἰς τὴν ἀναγραφήν. For a contrary view, see Lawton, *ADR* 25–26, and Clinton, "Review" 745–747, who both are inclined to see the cost of sculptural decoration as one of "a number of variable factors contributing to the total cost of the stele." On their hypothesis, I suppose, the secretary (or other official in charge of having the stele inscribed) could, on occasion, bargain for sculptural decoration for a single stele in exchange for an implicit or explicit promise to send quantities of stelai that would not require decoration to the same inscriber! The advantage of their hypothesis is that it does not require an explanation of how non-inscribing expenses (quarrying, transport, and sculptural decoration) were paid; the disadvantage is that it fails to account for the very narrow range of figures for ἀναγραφή. As to the former, I should think that the state paid (except to the extent that there were private contributions), in transactions that have not been recorded (as they were not in #1, and as μισθός was not in #112 [see n. 252]).

have the letter-cutter (the man who did the ἀναγραφή) go out to the quarry to cut out and carry away a stele each time he received an order; more likely, he had access in Athens to a supply of stelai that already had been quarried, transported, and (probably) roughly prepared in the sizes usually desired for decrees, etc.[251]

4. "The actual payment to the mason . . . [j]ust the inscribing" is the remaining, and most likely, alternative. When quarrying, transport and sculptural decoration are eliminated as cost elements, the relatively narrow variation in prices—20–30 dr. for shorter documents, 30–50 dr. for longer ones, depending on the period—becomes more plausible since non-inscribing elements (which might be expected to produce a much wider price variation) are not part of the price, although the letter-cutter's work could include *final* preparation of the stele and installation, as in #1.

Although these amounts covered inscribing costs only, they tell us nothing about per diem wages,[252] since (as Nolan observes) they obviously are piecework prices. But they do tell us something about price movements or, more accurately, what the state was willing to pay for this kind of work.

In the period c. 403–330, the normal rate for polis inscriptions was, as Nolan observed, 20 or 30 dr.; the only secure exception is the Charter of the Second Athenian League (#18), which cost 60 dr.[253] Deme and

---

251. See Lawton, *ADR* 26: "The varying quality of the stelai and the fact that so many inscriptions fall short of the amount of space provided on the stone suggest that the commissions were given out as piecework and that already roughly prepared rather than tailor-made stelai were used."

252. Here the most useful figure is #112 (σιτία for engravers of c. 1 dr. 1 ob. p.d. in 329/8), but it does not tell us whether or what the engravers were paid as μισθός in addition.

253. As observed under their respective entries, the 40 dr. originally restored in #58 could easily be restored as 20 dr. or (less likely) 30 dr., and the very high 50 dr. figure in #71 suggests that it was inscribed in the second half of its letter-cutter's career, i.e., after c. 330. The one other "anomalous" figure is the 62 dr. for the long and complicated Eleusinian building account in 408/6 (#1). The only later inscription of comparable complexity (the law on the repair of Long Walls for 50 dr. in 307/6 [#137]) we might have expected to cost more, since in the second half of the fourth century wages generally seem to have been higher than in the fifth (see n. 239), but the lower quality and smaller size of late fourth-century lettering may have enabled it to be inscribed in much less time than the Eleusinian account. In general, therefore, the higher figure of #1 seems reasonable in relation to later figures, which are for shorter (mostly formulaic) honorary decrees, or for less well inscribed stelai.

other local figures were lower—10 dr. for ##49 and 98.[254] There seems to have been no substantial change from c. 403 to c. 330, and this is surprising in the context of the other increases that we see in this period.[255]

In the period c. 330–300, although figures below 30 dr. have been restored (##109, 117, 159), only two are preserved (#144 for 10 dr. in c. 307–302 and #149 for 20 dr. in c. 307–301), both towards the end of the century, and this may suggest one or more of the following possibilities: (a) that the 10–20 dr. restorations are wrong (see notes under ##109, 117, 159), (b) that the restored inscriptions have been misdated, and (c) that the c. 300 dividing line is too late: a dividing line of c. 302 might accommodate ###144, 149 and (the restored) 159.[256] In any event, after c. 330 the normal base price seems to have become 30 dr., with occasional higher figures of 40 dr. (all restored—##105, 106, 109, 150, 165, 188) and 50 dr. (##71, 115, 119, 127, 130, 137, 139, 140, 146, 153, 168, plus the restored ##109, 116, 131, 151).[257] In this same period, deme and other local figures also rose, to 20 dr. (##77, 95, 133, 192 plus the restored #132) and 30 dr. (#50).[258]

In the period c. 300–250, polis base figures dropped to 10 or 20 dr., although they occasionally reached 30 dr. (#204 plus the restored ##198, 202 and 205) and once went as high as 50 dr. (#216). Local figures also fell, to 10 dr. (#221), although 20 dr. is restored once (#219). Towards the end of the century, in 221, we find the *much* smaller polis figure of 8 dr. 3 ob. (#225): this unevenly denominated sum (no longer a multiple of 10 dr.) surely represents a frugal and very precise determination of the actual costs of inscribing this decree.

As discussed in greater detail under "Inflation and Deflation" (at pp. 242, 249–250), the 50% increase in the base price of polis inscriptions from c. 330–300, and the 33 1/3 to 66 2/3% drop from c. 300–250, may

---

254. As observed under the respective entries for these non-polis inscriptions, the uniquely high 30 dr. in #50 may date from the period c. 330–318, and the relatively high 20 dr. figures in ##77 and 95 also could have been inscribed in the latter part of their respective letter-cutter's careers, i.e., after c. 330.

255. Summarized in "Inflation and Deflation" pp. 241–242 .

256. A number of 20 dr. figures (##166, 177, 182, 185, 194, 195—all restored except for #177), dated "late 4th c." vel sim., may indicate (a) that these inscriptions have been dated too early and/or (b) that the 20 dr. restorations are too low.

257. See #71 with n. 253 for its likely date after c. 330.

258. See ##50, 77 and 95 with n. 254 for their likely dates after c. 330.

reflect general trends for which evidence is lacking in most other categories.[259]

259. Although this chapter naturally has focused on inscribing *costs*, an incidental benefit has been the light it has cast on the date and restoration of a number of inscriptions: ##6, 31, 33, 38, 43, 50, 52, 55, 58, 68, 71, 72, 77, 90, 91, 95, 102, 106, 107, 109, 110, 117, 120, 121, 122, 124, 125, 134, 135, 136, 142, 144, 145, 149, 157, 158, 159, 162, 166, 167, 169, 170, 173, 174, 176, 177, 179, 180, 181, 182, 184, 185, 190, 194, 195, 224 and 226 (for ##166, 177, 182, 185, 194 and 195, see n. 256).

Chapter 9
Prostitutes and Pimps

Collected here are sums paid to female and male prostitutes, and to pimps and madams, for services rendered (usually on a single occasion), but excluding sums paid (a) as the purchase price of a slave intended for use as a prostitute or mistress or (b) as the private ransom of a prostitute or mistress.[1] Since Böckh's one-paragraph discussion,[2] there have been slightly longer treatments by Schneider and Halperin,[3] as well as by commentators on individual passages, notably Gomme and Sandbach on Menander (##26–28) and Gow on Machon (##13, 41–42).

1. c. 490–475. 2 ? for female and male prostitutes, apiece.[4] On these vase paintings, the number of coins may have been determined by considerations of artistic composition and, in any event, their denomination is unclear (at this period, and in comparison with later figures, obols would be most likely), so that it is impossible to say what the actual payments were.

2. c. 420. "Small change" for prostitutes (male, female or old man), together or separately?, at Kyzikos.[5] Although these payments are set in

---

1. For which see *Talents*, "H. Slaves: Individual Slaves" and "O. Individuals: Private Ransoms."

2. Böckh, *SdA* I 155–156, beginning "Wir schämen uns beinahe, von den Preisen der Buhlerei und Unzucht mit Weibern und Männern zu sprechen. . . ."

3. K. Schneider, "Hetairai," *RE* 8 (1913) 1331–1372 at 1343–1344; D. M. Halperin, *One Hundred Years of Homosexuality* (New York 1990) 107–112.

4. Makron, *ARV* nos. 148, 206 *bis* (four vase paintings, each showing a person receiving two coins). D. von Bothmer, "Notes on Makron," in D. Kurtz and B. Sparkes, eds., *The Eye of Greece: Studies in the Art of Athens* (Cambridge 1982) 29–52 at 42, describes and comments as follows: "On the exterior of no. 148 a man approaches, on one side, a seated woman with a flower in his left hand and two coins in his right, while on the other side of the cup the right-most reaches for the breasts of a blonde girl with his left hand and offers two coins with his right. On the Bochum cup (no. 206 *bis*), the central man on each half of the exterior offers two coins to a boy. Students of economics will be glad to learn that the fees paid are identical." J. Boardman, *Athenian Red Figure Vases: The Archaic Period* (London 1975) 140, places Makron "mainly in the 480's and a little later."

5. Eupolis fr. 247 (K-A):

Kyzikos, I include them here since they were paid by an Athenian in military service there. In this fictional and comic context, his boasts—both about his sexual adventures and their low cost—probably were exaggerations.

3. 411. 1 dr. for transvestite Euripides, agreed to by Scythian archer.[6] In this comic context, we might expect that Euripides was demanding a higher than usual fee: certainly the dialogue is funnier if a male in drag is able to exact more than a female normally would and a Scythian might be felt to be fair game for such an excessive demand!

4. pre-399. "Not much money" for Epichares, accepted from anyone who wanted him.[7] In this lawcourt attack on his own prosecutor, Andocides had every incentive to exaggerate all the "facts," not only the basic charge of prostitution (which if true would have deprived Epichares of all citizen rights, including the right to conduct a prosecution) but also the colorful details of making himself available to all comers and at a minimal charge, which in any event is unspecified.

5. 5th/4th c. 1 dr. for "god who bends backwards and thrusts hips forward," 3 ob. for "god who bends over."[8] In this comic catalogue of

---

ἡ δ' ὑστάτη [sc. πόλις] ποῦ 'σθ'; ἥδε Κύζικος πλέα στατήρων.
ἐν τῆιδε τοίνυν τῆι πόλει φρουρῶν ⟨ἐγώ⟩ ποτ' αὐτὸς
γυναῖκ' ἐκίνουν κολλύβου καὶ παῖδα καὶ γέροντα, 3
κἀξῆν ὅλην τὴν ἡμέραν τὸν κύσθον ἐκκορίζειν

For the date of the production of Eupolis' *Poleis* in c. 420, see K-A V 424.

6. Ar. *Thes.* 1193–1196 (Scythian Τοξότης and Euripides, dressed as a woman):

To. τί οὐ κατεύδει παρ' ἐμέ;
Ευ. χαῖρε, τοξότα·
οὐ γὰρ γένοιτ' ἂν τοῦτο.
To. ναί, ναί, γρᾴδιον,
ἐμοὶ κάρισο σὺ τοῦτο.
Ευ. δώσεις οὖν δραχμήν;
To. ναὶ, ναίκι, δῶσι.
Ευ. τἀργύριον τοίνυν φέρε.

7. Andoc. i. 100: εἶτα σὺ (sc. Ἐπιχάρης) περὶ ἑταιρείας ἐμοὶ μνείαν ποιῇ καὶ κακῶς τινας λέγεις; ὃς ἑνὶ μὲν οὐχ ἡταίρησας (καλῶς γὰρ ἄν σοι εἶχε), πραττόμενος δ' οὐ πολὺ ἀργύριον τὸν βουλόμενον ἀνθρώπων, ὡς οὗτοι ἴσασιν, ἐπὶ τοῖς αἰσχίστοις ἔργοις ἔζης, καὶ ταῦτα οὕτως μοχθηρὸς ὢν τὴν ἰδέαν. ἀλλ' ὅμως οὗτος ἑτέρων ἐτόλμα κατηγορεῖν, ᾧ κατὰ τοὺς νόμους τοὺς ὑμετέρους οὐδ' αὐτῷ ὑπὲρ αὑτοῦ ἔστιν ἀπολογεῖσθαι.

8. Plato Com. fr. 188. 17–18 (K-A) (in list of things to be offered by women who are fond of wine and sex):

Λόρδωνι δραχμή, Κυβδάσωι τριώβολον
ἥρωι Κέλητι δέρμα καὶ θυλήματα.

offerings to be made for Aphrodite's favors, it is not clear whether these sums are intended also to suggest typical fees for female and male prostitutes, although the 3 ob. would fit with #42.

6. 5th/4th c. 1 st. for middle-grade female prostitutes (apiece).[9] Although these staters are probably Athenian tetradrachms rather than Persian darics (= 20 dr.),[10] this still seems like a high figure for the middle grade (cf. ##3, 7, 9), and it is therefore probably exaggerated for comic effect.

7. 5th/4th c. "Staters" for Lais (the elder) of Corinth in her prime, 1 st. or 3 ob. as an older woman.[11] In this context, where the contrast is between the enormous fees of Lais' youth and the relative pittances of her old age, the "staters" are again probably tetradrachms rather than darics, but we are not told how many she received. At the other end of the scale, the single stater would be worth at least 4 dr., which is still eight times the 3 ob. fee of an average prostitute (#9). The point seems to be that a celebrated courtesan not only (a) in her prime commanded extraordinary fees, but even (b) in old age was paid at least an average, and sometimes more than an average, fee.

For Λόρδων and Κύβδασος, see J. Henderson, *The Maculate Muse: Obscene Language in Attic Comedy*² (New York 1991) 178–181. See also #42 with references in n. 66 to an illustration of the κύβδα position.

9. Theopomp. Com. fr. 22 (K-A) ap. Poll. ix. 59: τὰ δὲ στατῆρος ἄξια στατηριαῖα φαίης ἄν, ὡς Θεόπομπος ἐν Καλλαίσχρωι·

οὗ φησιν εἶναι τῶν ἑταιρῶν τὰς μέσας
στατηριαίας

10. See fifth-century sources cited in "Actors, Artists, Musicians and Writers" n. 19, to which add here Phot., στατήρ, and Kraay, *ACGC* 316–317. For 1 daric = 20 dr., see Xen. *Anab.* i. 7. 18; Harp., δαρεικός.

11. Epicrates fr. 3. 10–19 (K-A):

καὶ Λαῒς ὀρθῶς ⟨νῦν⟩ νομίζοιτ' ἂν τέρας.
αὕτη γὰρ οὖν ὁπότ' ἦν νεοττὸς καὶ νέα,
ὑπὸ τῶν στατήρων ἦν ἀπηγριωμένη,
εἶδες δ' ἂν αὐτῆς Φαρνάβαζον θᾶττον ἄν·
ἐπεὶ δὲ δόλιχον τοῖς ἔτεσιν ἤδη τρέχει
τὰς ἁρμονίας τε διαχαλᾶι τοῦ σώματος,
ἰδεῖν μὲν αὐτὴν ῥᾶιόν ἐστιν ἢ πτύσαι·
ἐξέρχεταί τε πανταχόσ' ἤδη πιομένη,
δέχεται δὲ καὶ στατῆρα καὶ τριώβολον,
προσίεται δὲ καὶ γέροντα καὶ νέον.

On the two Laises, see F. Geyer, "Lais (1), (2)," *RE* 12 (1925) 513–516.

8. post-394? 300 dr. for male Theodotos from Simon (long-term contract).[12] Although this is the amount that Simon alleged that he had paid,[13] the speaker suggests that the whole story of a contract and a contract price of 300 dr. that was paid and then refunded is a lie, and he observes that Simon had valued his own net worth at only 250 dr. But, even if the figure is accurate, we are not told what period it was intended to cover, so we cannot extrapolate a fee-per-service from it, which we could then compare with the other (mostly single-occasion) figures in our catalogue.

9. c. 391–355. 3 ob. for female prostitute.[14] In this long list of ways to get rid of things (wine with wine, a trumpet with a trumpet, a bawler with a herald, etc.), the humor is provided, right in the middle, by the unexpected and insulting equation of Kallistratos (the politician) with a cook! Since all the other pairs are either actual equivalents or close equivalents (e.g., the boxer who can be driven out with black eyes), the 3 ob. for an unnamed, and therefore probably *average*, πόρνη seems to be a well known equivalent, and I therefore am inclined to place some reliance on it.

---

12. Lys. iii. 22–25: ἐτόλμησε (sc. Σίμων) γὰρ εἰπεῖν ὡς αὐτὸς μὲν τριακοσίας δραχμὰς ἔδωκε Θεοδότῳ, συνθήκας πρὸς αὐτὸν ποιησάμενος, ἐγὼ δ' ἐπιβουλεύσας ἀπέστησα αὐτοῦ τὸ μειράκιον. . . . σκέψασθε δὲ ὡς ἄπιστα εἴρηκε. τὴν γὰρ οὐσίαν τὴν ἑαυτοῦ ἅπασαν πεντήκοντα καὶ διακοσίων δραχμῶν ἐτιμήσατο. καίτοι θαυμαστὸν εἰ τὸν ἑταιρήσοντα πλειόνων ἐμισθώσατο ὧν αὐτὸς τυγχάνει κεκτημένος. εἰς τοῦτο δ' ἥκει τόλμης ὥστε οὐκ ἐξαρκεῖ περὶ τούτου μόνον αὐτῷ ψεύσασθαι, περὶ τοῦ δεδωκέναι τὸ ἀργύριον, ἀλλὰ καὶ κεκομίσθαι φησί· καίτοι πῶς εἰκός ἐστι τότε μὲν ἡμᾶς τοιαῦτα ἐξαμαρτάνειν οἷα κατηγόρηκεν οὗτος, ἀποστερῆσαι βουλομένους τὰς τριακοσίας δραχμάς, ἐπειδὴ δὲ ἀπεμαχεσάμεθα, τηνικαῦτα ἀποδοῦναι τὸ ἀργύριον αὐτῷ, μήτε ἀφειμένους τῶν ἐγκλημάτων μήτε ἀνάγκης ἡμῖν μηδεμιᾶς γενομένης; Although Lysias iii was delivered after 394 (C. Carey, *Lysias Selected Speeches* [Cambridge 1989] 86), we are not told how recently the alleged payment had been made, and accordingly I assign a date of "post-394?"

13. As K. J. Dover, *Greek Homosexuality* (Cambridge, Massachusetts 1978) 33, observes, the speaker's report of Simon's allegation is "unlikely to be false, since Simon, as prosecutor, has already addressed the court."

14. Antiphanes fr. 293 (K-A):

οἴνωι ⟨ ⟩ τὸν οἶνον ἐξελαύνειν
σάλπιγγι τὴν σάλπιγγα, τῶι κήρυκι τὸν βοῶντα,
κόπωι κόπον, ψόφωι ψόφον, τριωβόλωι δὲ πόρνην,
αὐθαδίαν αὐθαδίαι, Καλλίστρατον μαγείρωι,
στάσιν στάσει, μάχηι μάχην, ὑπωπίοις δὲ πύκτην,
πόνωι πόνον, δίκην δίκηι, γυναικὶ τὴν γυναῖκα

I date this fragment to the years of Kallistratos' political activity, c. 391–355, for which see H. Swoboda, "Kallistratos (1)," *RE* 10 (1919) 1730–1735.

10. 388. 20 dr. for male (to buy ἱμάτιον?), from old woman.[15] Even if the 20 dr. in the second passage is the same as the 20 dr. in the first passage, the "gift" obviously is intended to be understood as recompense for services rendered. In this comic situation, the sum probably was meant to seem high,[16] in order to emphasize the ruinous, as well as ridiculous, position in which the old woman had placed herself. But since (a) in this very individual relationship we are not told (b) the gross amount of all payments and (c) the time period, the 20 dr. (even if it were accurate) would not tell us what she had paid per service.

11. c. 380–335. "Small change" for female prostitutes.[17] In the first, and possibly also in the second, of these passages, the cost of prostitutes is contrasted favorably with the costs (monetary and other) of illicit love affairs with married women. The "small change" (μικροῦ κέρματος, κερμάτων) may be intended to be accurate only in a relative (rather than an absolute) sense, and in any event its precise amount is not stated.

---

15. Ar. *Plut.* 980–983, 1018–1019 (Chremylos and old woman [Γραῦς] discussing her young lover):

Χρ. τί δ' ἦν ὅ τι σου μάλιστ' ἐδεῖθ' ἑκάστοτε;
Γρ. οὐ πολλά· καὶ γὰρ ἐκνομίως μ' ᾐσχύνετο.
ἀλλ' ἀργυρίου δραχμὰς ἂν ᾔτησ' εἴκοσιν
εἰς ἱμάτιον, ὀκτὼ δ' ἂν εἰς ὑποδήματα·

Γρ. καὶ τάς γε χεῖρας παγκάλας ἔχειν μ' ἔφη,—
Χρ. ὁπότε προτείνοιέν γε δραχμὰς εἴκοσιν.

16. As were the 8 dr. for shoes in line 983. See "Introduction" pp. 3, 5–6 with n. 12.

17. Eubulus fr. 67. 1–9 (K-A):

ὅστις λέχη γὰρ σκότια νυμφεύει λάθραι,
πῶς οὐχὶ πάντων ἐστὶν ἀθλιώτατος;
ἐξὸν θεωρήσαντι πρὸς τὸν ἥλιον
γυμνὰς ἐφεξῆς ἐπὶ κέρως τεταγμένας,
ἐν λεπτοπήνοις ὑμέσιν ἑστώσας, οἵας
Ἠριδανὸς ἁγνοῖς ὕδασι κηπεύει κόρας,
μικροῦ πρίασθαι κέρματος τὴν ἡδονήν,
καὶ μὴ λαθραίαν Κύπριν, αἰσχίστην νόσων
πασῶν, διώκειν, ὕβρεος οὐ πόθου χάριν.

Eubulus fr. 82 (K-A):

× τὰς φιλωιδοὺς κερμάτων παλευτρίας
× – ⏑ πώλους Κύπριδος ἐξησκημένας,
γυμνὰς ἐφεξῆς ἐπὶ κέρως τεταγμένας,
ἐν λεπτοπήνοις ὑμέσιν ἑστώσας, οἵας
Ἠριδανὸς ἁγνοῖς ὕδασι κηπεύει κόρας·
παρ' ὧν βεβαίως ἀσφαλῶς τ' ἔξεστί σοι
μικροῦ πρίασθαι κέρματος τὴν ἡδονήν

For c. 380–335 as Euboulos' floruit, see R. L. Hunter, "Eubulus (2)," *OCD* 564.

12. c. 366. 1 ob. for female prostitute.[18] The point here is the same as that in #11: the cheapness of visiting a prostitute as compared to affairs with married women, and thus the 1 ob. may be accurate more in a relative than an absolute sense, or it may even be an exaggeration downwards.

13. c. 350. 1 mn. demanded by Phryne, 2 gold pieces (= 40 dr.?) accepted by her when she is randy.[19] The point of this story, like many others in this collection (##7, 11, 12, 36, 39, 41) is the contrast between high and low fees. Here, even the low fee is pretty high, but I suppose that for a celebrated hetaira both fees (i.e., 40 and 100 dr.) are possible (cf. #41), and the whimsical remission of 60% of the higher fee certainly is plausible.

14. c. 350–300. 1 ob. for "Korydos" ("Lark") the (male) parasite, or price of bird?[20] Insofar as this story is true, Philoxenos obviously intends a double meaning: the price of larks (birds) may well have been 1 ob., while Korydos' rumored (ἐδόκει) price probably was much greater, but the pun allows Philoxenos to set it insultingly low.

15. c. 347–339. 10 T. Philosopher Speusippos offers to find more beautiful (male or female?) lover for this amount.[21] It is difficult to de-

---

18. Diog. Laert. vi. 4: ἰδών ποτε μοιχὸν φεύγοντα, "ὡς δυστυχής," εἶπε (sc. 'Αντισθένης), "πηλίκον κίνδυνον ὀβολοῦ διαφυγεῖν ἐδύνασο." For Antisthenes' floruit in c. 366, see Diod. Sic. xv. 76. 4.

19. Machon 450–455 (Gow):

Φρύνην ἐπείρα Μοίριχος τὴν Θεσπικήν·
κἄπειτεν αἰτήσασαν αὐτὸν μνᾶν μίαν
ὁ Μοίριχος, Μέγ', εἶπεν. οὐ πρῴην δύο
χρυσοῦς λαβοῦσα παραγένου ξένῳ τινί;
Περίμενε τοίνυν καὶ σύ, φησ', ἕως ἂν οὗ
βινητιάσω καὶ τοσοῦτον λήψομαι.

For the dates of Phryne of Thespiai, mistress of Praxiteles, see A. Raubitschek, "Phryne," *RE* 20 (1941) 893–907 at 895–897. These gold pieces cannot be (silver) tetradrachms, and most likely are Persian darics, worth 20 dr. apiece (see n. 10).

20. Athen. vi. 40 (241e): Φιλόξενος δ' ἡ Πτερνοκοπὶς ἐμπεσόντος λόγου ὅτι αἱ κίχλαι τίμιαί εἰσι καὶ τοῦ Κορύδου παρόντος, ὃς ἐδόκει πεπορνεῦσθαι, "ἀλλ' ἐγώ," ἔφη, "μνημονεύω ὅτε ὁ κόρυδος ὀβολοῦ ἦν." For the fourth-century date of "Korydos," see A. S. F. Gow and D. L. Page, *The Greek Anthology: Hellenistic Epigrams* II (Cambridge 1965) 494–495; Gow, *Machon* 10, 59.

21. Timotheus ap. Diog. Laert. iv. 4: οὗτος (sc. Σπεύσιππος), φησί (sc. Τιμόθεος), πρὸς τὸν ἐρῶντα πλούσιον ἀμόρφου ἔφη, "τί δέ σοι δεῖ τούτου; ἐγὼ γάρ σοι δέκα ταλάντων εὐμορφοτέραν εὑρήσω." For εὐμορφοτέραν, H. Richards (as reported in the Loeb edition) conjectured ἀμορφότερον; εὐμορφότερον also would be possible! For Speusippos' headship of the

cide whether Speusippos is volunteering to function here more as a matchmaker or a pimp. The difference in fact may really be one of price! In any event, his offer seems to have been a rhetorical one, and it is virtually certain that the amount was never paid.

16. pre-345. 20 dr. "spent on" hetaira Philoxene by Timarchos.[22] In this litigious context, the story (and the figure) may be distorted, but even if the sum is accurate, it may have gone for gifts as well as for fees, and for more than one occasion (albeit "in a short time"), and it is therefore difficult to compare with the other figures in this catalogue.

17. pre-345. 4 dr. for male Diophantos from foreigner.[23] Because it is said that Diophantos made this claim in court, it is probable that he did in fact make it. Whether the amount really was owed is another matter. Moreover, it may have been for more than one occasion (rather like a charge account that has been run up before the creditor decides to sue). Whether it was for one or more than one occasion, the specific figure of 4 dr. is neither very large nor very small, and it therefore seems credible.

18. c. 330–322. 3,000 dr. for male Melanopos.[24] No time period is stated for this fee, but even if one were, it would be suspect: in this rhetorically abusive passage by a late writer, all facts are likely to have been invented or distorted, and the enormous size of this figure suggests that it was highly exaggerated, if not wholly invented.

Academy from 347–339, see G. E. L. Owen and S. Hornblower, "Speusippus," *OCD* 1434–1435. For this entry, see also "Miscellaneous Workers" #4.

22. Aeschin. i. 115: εἰληφὼς ἠλέγχθη (sc. Τίμαρχος) παρὰ Λευκωνίδου τοῦ Φιλωτάδου κηδεστοῦ διὰ Φιλήμονος τοῦ ὑποκριτοῦ εἴκοσι μνᾶς, ἃς ἐν ὀλίγῳ χρόνῳ πρὸς Φιλοξένην ἀνήλωσε τὴν ἑταίραν. For 346 as the date of Aeschin. i, see E. M. Harris, "The Date of the Trial of Timarchus," *Hermes* 113 (1985) 376–380.

23. Aeschin. i. 158: τίς γὰρ ὑμῶν τὸν ὀρφανὸν καλούμενον Διόφαντον οὐκ οἶδεν, ὃς τὸν ξένον πρὸς τὸν ἄρχοντα ἀπήγαγεν ᾧ παρήδρευεν Ἀριστοφῶν ὁ Ἀζηνιεύς, ἐπαιτιασάμενος τέτταρας δραχμὰς αὐτὸν ὑπὲρ τῆς πράξεως ταύτης (prostitution) ἀπεστερηκέναι καὶ τοὺς νόμους λέγων οἳ κελεύουσι τὸν ἄρχοντα τῶν ὀρφανῶν ἐπιμελεῖσθαι, τοὺς ὑπὲρ τῆς σωφροσύνης κειμένους αὐτὸς ὑπερβεβηκώς;

24. [Aeschin.] *Epist.* vii. 3 (Aischines from exile [i.e., c. 330–322] to Melanopos): σοὶ δὲ τὸ μέχρι μὲν χθὲς καὶ πρώην θεσμοθετοῦντος ἤδη σοῦ προεστάναι τὴν μητέρα, τρὶς δὲ ἐμπεσεῖν εἰς τὸ δεσμωτήριον τὸν πατέρα σου, σὲ δὲ πραθέντα τρισχιλίων δραχμῶν τὴν ἀκμὴν ἡταιρηκέναι, τοῖς περὶ Τίμαρχον νέοις κοινὰ ταῦτ' εἶναι, οὐ τοῖς περὶ Θεμιστοκλέα ἢ Ἀριστείδην τὸν δίκαιον ὑπολαμβάνω. Although the reading of H is δισχιλίων, I presume that Böckh's identification of the purchaser (*SdA* I 156: "Timarch seine Keuschheit um zwanzig Minen verkauft haben") was a slip of the pen.

19. pre-324. "Many T." spent on sexual gratification, but not 1 dr. for rubbing of other parts of body, according to Diogenes.[25] This statement, while doubtless true (at least in its first part), tells us nothing about market rates for single occasions!

20. pre-322. 2 dr. max. for girls who play the reed-pipes, harp or lyre (per performance). As discussed in greater detail under "Actors, Artists, Musicians and Writers" #16, if they also were called on to provide sexual entertainment, I should think that that would be a matter of separate negotiation, i.e., the sumptuary limit (in Arist. *Ath. Pol.* l. 2) on payments to these girls as musicians says nothing at all about what they could have charged or did charge as prostitutes.

21. pre-322. 10,000 dr. demanded for the whole night by Lais (the younger?) of Corinth from Demosthenes, who refuses.[26] Scholars have noted the chronological incongruity of this story with the tradition that this Lais was already a young girl at the time of the Sicilian Expedition,[27] and the enormous amount casts further doubt on this story. Compare the identical (and equally implausible) amounts that Demosthenes is alleged to have paid to Isaios and Neoptolemos.[28]

22. c. 313. 3 ob. Philosopher Polemon had ready, to gratify his desires (the words ἑτοίμους λύσεις τῶν ἐπιθυμιῶν may suggest that it did not take long for him to do so!).[29] Although we are only told that a tri-

---

25. Dio Chrys. vi. 19: θαυμάζειν (sc. Διογένην) δὲ τῶν ἀνθρώπων τὸ τὸν μὲν πόδα μὴ θέλειν ἀργυρίου κνᾶσθαι μηδὲ τὴν χεῖρα μηδὲ ἄλλο μηδὲν τοῦ σώματος, μηδὲ τοὺς πάνυ πλουσίους ἀναλῶσαι ἂν μηδεμίαν ὑπὲρ τούτου δραχμήν· ἓν δὲ ἐκεῖνο τὸ μέρος πολλάκις πολλῶν ταλάντων, τοὺς δέ τινας ἤδη καὶ τὴν ψυχὴν παραβαλλομένους. For Diogenes' death in c. 324, see J. L. Moles, "Diogenes (2)," *OCD* 473–474.

26. Sotion ap. Gell. *N.A.* i. 8. 5–6: [Sotion inquit,] 'Ad hanc [sc. Laidem] ille Demosthenes clanculum adit et, ut sibi copiam sui faceret, petit. At Lais μυρίας δραχμὰς poposcit,' hoc facit nummi nostratis denarium decem milia. 'Tali petulantia mulieris atque pecuniae magnitudine ictus expauidusque Demosthenes auertitur et discedens "ego" inquit "paenitere tanti non emo."' Sed Graeca ipsa, quae fertur dixisse, lepidiora sunt: οὐκ ὠνοῦμαι, inquit, μυρίων δραχμῶν μεταμέλειαν. This story is repeated in Σ (*recent.*) Ar. *Plut.* 149d: Φωκίων (lege Σωτίων) δέ ὁ περιπατητικός, ἐν τῷ "κέρατι τῆς 'Αμαλθείας", Δημοσθένην ἱστορεῖ, Λαΐδος αὐτὸν μυρίας δραχμὰς αἰτησαμένης εἰς μισθὸν παννυχίδος, "οὐκ ὠνοῦμαι" φάναι "μυρίων δραχμῶν μεταμέλειαν".

27. Geyer (as in n. 11) 515.

28. "Doctors, Lawyers and Professors" ##17 and 18.

29. Diog. Laert. iv. 16: Πολέμων . . . νέος δ' ὢν ἀκόλαστός τε καὶ διακεχυμένος ἦν οὕτως ὥστε καὶ περιφέρειν ἀργύριον πρὸς τὰς ἑτοίμους λύσεις τῶν ἐπιθυμιῶν· ἀλλὰ καὶ ἐν τοῖς στενωποῖς διέκρυπτεν. καὶ ἐν 'Ακαδημείᾳ πρὸς κίονί τινι τριώβολον εὑρέθη προσπεπλασμένον αὐτοῦ διὰ [τὴν] ὁμοίαν τῇ προειρημένῃ πρόφασιν. Since this activity is said to have been

obol was found in one place, in the Academy, it is natural to suppose to that this was the coin that Polemon also hid in many other places, apparently to be used with many different prostitutes, and this suggests that it was the standard charge for an *average* prostitute.

23. c. 302. 250 T. given by Demetrios Poliorketes to Lamia and fellow courtesans for soap.[30] This enormous sum probably is an exaggerated detail in a generally hostile account of Demetrios, and, in any event, it tells us nothing about the charges of individual prostitutes.

24. 4th/3rd c. 2 dr. for Leme (Stratokles' hetaira), accepted from anyone who wanted her.[31] This excerpt appears in Athenaios' catalogue of miscellaneous gossipy details about individual courtesans, and it is impossible to evaluate its accuracy. On its face, however, 2 dr. is not implausible for what presumably was an above-average hetaira.

25. 4th/3rd c. 1 ob. for female prostitute.[32] In this passage, it is alleged that Solon founded public houses of prostitution to control the

---

especially prevalent in Polemon's youth, I assign it a date near the beginning of his headship of the Academy (c. 313–270), for which see D. N. Sedley, "Polemon (2)," *OCD* 1204.

30. Plut. *Demetr.* xxvii. 1: Πολλῶν δὲ γενομένων ἐν τῇ πόλει τότε πλημμελημάτων καὶ παρανομημάτων ἐκεῖνο μάλιστα λέγεται λυπῆσαι τοὺς Ἀθηναίους, ὅτι διακόσια καὶ πεντήκοντα τάλαντα πορίσαι ταχὺ καὶ δοῦναι προσταχθὲν αὐτοῖς, καὶ τῆς εἰσπράξεως συντόνου καὶ ἀπαραιτήτου γενομένης, ἰδὼν ἠθροισμένον τὸ ἀργύριον ἐκέλευσε Λαμίᾳ καὶ ταῖς περὶ αὐτὴν ἑταίραις εἰς σμῆγμα δοθῆναι.

31. Gorgias 351 *FGrH* 1 ap. Athen. xiii. 70 (596f): Στρατοκλῆς δ' ὁ ῥήτωρ ἐρωμένην εἶχε τὴν ἐπικληθεῖσαν Λήμην ἑταίραν, τὴν καλουμένην Παρόραμα * * διὰ τὸ καὶ δύο δραχμῶν φοιτᾶν πρὸς τὸν βουλόμενον, ὥς φησι Γοργίας ἐν τῶι Περὶ ἑταιρῶν. Kaibel observed that Δίδραχμον was a possible third name for this hetaira.

32. Philemo fr. 3 (K-A):

σὺ δ' εἰς ἅπαντας εὗρες ἀνθρώπους, Σόλων·
σὲ γὰρ λέγουσιν τοῦτ' ἰδεῖν πρῶτον, μόνον
δημοτικόν, ὦ Ζεῦ, πρᾶγμα καὶ σωτήριον,
(καί μοι λέγειν τοῦτ' ἐστὶν ἁρμοστόν, Σόλων)
μεστὴν ὁρῶντα τὴν πόλιν νεωτέρων
τούτους τ' ἔχοντας τὴν ἀναγκαίαν φύσιν
ἁμαρτάνοντάς τ' εἰς ὃ μὴ προσῆκον ἦν,
στῆσαι πριάμενόν τοι γυναῖκας κατὰ τόπους
κοινὰς ἅπασι καὶ κατεσκευασμένας.
ἑστᾶσι γυμναί, μὴ 'ξαπατηθῇς· πάνθ' ὅρα.
οὐκ εὖ σεαυτοῦ τυγχάνεις ἔχων, ἔχεις
× – ⏑ – † πῶς † ἡ θύρα 'στ' ἀνεῳγμένη.
εἷς ὀβολός· εἰσπήδησον. οὐκ ἔστ' οὐδὲ εἷς
ἀκκισμός, οὐδὲ λῆρος, οὐδ' ὑφήρπασεν,
ἀλλ' εὐθὺς ἣν βούλει σὺ χὤν βούλει τρόπον.
ἐξῆλθες· οἰμώζειν λέγ', ἀλλοτρία 'στί σοι

wild impulses of young men. Although it is possible that Solon also set the fee, the 1 ob. in this passage seems to be the *current* fee in the establishment run by the speaker, probably the pimp (see line 4). These are clearly slave girls (see line 8), offered with full prior inspection at bargain rates, although it is possible that their cost has been understated by the pimp ("our low, low prices!").

26. 4th/3rd. 12 dr. p.d. to pimp for hetaira Habrotonon.[33] Gomme and Sandbach comment:

> It is unfortunately not clear how extravagant this payment was, assuming that it was for the services of Habrotonon alone. According to Arist. *Ath. Pol.* 50. 2 [#20], a sumptuary law forbade the payment of a higher fee than 2 dr. for engaging a ψάλτρια. . . . *Samia* 392 [#28] speaks of *hetairai* going to dinner-parties for 'only 10 dr.', but these are free women, who may have been more expensive than slaves. Yet charges of this nature may not have been unheard of even for slaves. Plaut. *Asinaria* 230, 752 [#29] has a slave *hetaira* hired for a year for 2,000 dr., i.e. about 6 dr. a day, and a long contract would no doubt be at a cheaper rate than a short one; the prices paid for accomplished *hetairai* were high, ranging from 20 to 60 minae; (20 minae: *Pseudolus* 51; 30 minae: *Rudens* 45, *Mostellaria* 300, [Dem.] lix. 29; 40 minae: *Epidicus* 52, *Curculio* 343; 60 minae, *Persa* 662), whereas skilled male artisans might fetch much less, e.g. Demosthenes reckons his knife-makers as worth 'at least 3 minae on the average'. Even though prices of male slaves were somewhat higher fifty years later, to argue that it must have been extravagant to pay 12 dr. for a *hetaira* when a skilled man's wage was only 2 dr. is to think in terms of morals rather than economics. On the whole it seems likely that, as over the wine, Smikrines' indignation is a measure of his parsimony, rather than evidence that Charisios was really paying an excessive price.[34]

33. Men. *Epitr.* 134–137 (old man Smikrines complaining about relationship of his son-in-law Charisios with hetaira Habrotonon):

> προῖκα δὲ λαβὼν τάλαντα τέτταρ' ἀργύρου
> οὐ τῆς γυναικὸς νενόμιχ' αὑτὸν οἰκέτην·
> ἀπόκοιτός ἐστι· πορνοβοσκῶι δώδεκα
> τῆς ἡμέρας δραχμὰς δίδωσι.

34. G-S 298.

I quote this at length because it seems to me to misunderstand the economic, and the comic, situation. Everything in this passage is exaggerated:

(a) The 4 T. dowry far exceeds any of the dowries recorded in the orators, and even the highest amount recorded in Attic New Comedy (as distinct from Plautus and Terence).[35]

(b) The 12 dr. p.d.—which would work out to 4,320 dr. in a year of 360 days—would not be affordable for very long even on the exaggerated dowry (4 T. = 24,000 dr.).

(c) On its face, this enormous fee for one year—43 mnas—also would be disproportionately high in relation to (i) the prices of slave-prostitutes, even from the (mostly Roman comic)[36] sources cited by Gomme and Sandbach, or (ii) the 20 mn. fee for comparable (i.e., one-year) services reported in #29.

The explanation for both figures (the dowry and fee) is surely their comic effect: the old man asks why his son-in-law would give up a fabulously large dowry to pay an extravagantly large fee for a whore. There is a joke here, but we miss it if we fail to understand the figures.

27. 4th/3rd c. 3 mn. p.d. for female prostitute.[37] Gomme and Sandbach comment:

> Such a rate seems fantastically high, yet even modern experience shows that huge sums may be spent for a woman's favours. In an anecdote told by Machon . . . [#41] Gnathaina asks a rich foreign commander ten minae for Gnathainion for a single night, and compromises on five. But he, like Bias here, was paying an inflated price; see Gow's note.[38]

---

35. Cf. G-S 296–298, where they note that 3 T. is the next highest dowry in Attic New Comedy (the fragmentary 5 T. in Men. *Con.* 3 is not clearly a dowry, as G-S ad loc. concede). The highest fourth-century dowry recorded in the orators is 3 T. 40 mn. for the widow of Pasion, the richest man in Athens (Dem. xlv. 28). See also D. M. Schaps, *Economic Rights of Women in Ancient Greece* (Edinburgh 1979) 99: "Menander's dowries are hopelessly exaggerated."

36. More reliable are the Athenian sources: 300 dr. (= 3 mn.) for a slave girl in Hyp. *Athen.* col. I; 20 or 30 mn. for a slave girl-mistress in Isoc. xv. 288; and 20–30 mn. for the celebrated Neaira in [Dem.] lix. 29–32.

37. Men. *Col.* 128–130 (Πορνοβοσκός speaking):

ἢ μί' ἐλάμβανεν
ὅσον οὐχ]ὶ δέκα, τρεῖς μνᾶς ἑκάστης ἡμέρας
παρὰ τοῦ] ξένου.

38. G-S 430–431.

The sum of 3 mn. (= 300 dr.) is the equivalent of about 150 days' wages for a skilled construction worker in 329/8 (as Gomme and Sandbach recognize in their comments on ##26 and 28).[39] It is conceivable that an exceptional hetaira could exact such a sum for a single day, but it is unlikely. It is much more likely that here, as in #26, Menander has exaggerated, with his usual lack of subtlety, for comic effect.

28. 4th/3rd c. "only" 10 dr. for (free?) women (apiece) at dinner party.[40] Gomme and Sandbach comment:

> There is a difficulty in the word μόνας. It seems to imply that ten drachmae is poor pay, yet Charisios in *Epitrepontes* is called extravagant for giving twelve drachmae a day for Habrotonon. But it is argued in the note on *Epitr.* 139 [#26] that Charisios' 'extravagance' was solely in Smikrines' eye. Further a good payment for the services of a slave, even one trained in music, might be a poor one for a free woman of any pretensions. If ten drachmae is compared with the wage of a skilled workman, two drachmae a day at this time, it must be remembered that a *hetaira* could not count upon an invitation to dinner every day.[41]

Although Gomme and Sandbach do not cite any evidence for the free status of the 10 dr. women, I am inclined to agree with them since slave women might be less able to run off on their own to dinner parties. But I suspect that the 10 dr. here also is humorous: "only 10 dr." per dinner might seem like quite a lot to the audience, who would infer that the Samian concubine was giving up an even more lucrative situation as Demeas' concubine. The alternative is to take the sum quite seriously and to suppose that wages and prices had risen so dramatically after c. 330 that 10 dr. no longer seemed a large sum. If we could date ##26–33 more precisely, and (more importantly) if we had reliable evidence for

---

39. See "Construction and Other Manual Workers" #7.

40. Men. *Sam.* 390–396 (Demeas to Samian concubine Chrysis, whom he intends to eject):

ἐν τῆι πόλει
ὄψει σεαυτὴν νῦν ἀκριβῶς ἥτις εἶ.
οὐ κατά σε, Χρυσί, πραττόμεναι δραχμὰς δέκα
μόνας ἕτεραι τρέχουσιν ἐπὶ τὰ δεῖπνα καὶ
πίνουσ' ἄκρατον ἄχρι ἂν ἀποθάνωσιν, ἢ
πεινῶσιν ἂν μὴ τοῦθ' ἑτοίμως καὶ ταχὺ
ποῶσιν.

41. G-S 587–588.

wages and prices in c. 300, it would be easier to evaluate this possibility.[42] In the present state of the evidence, I am inclined to see all of the figures in ##26–33 as exaggerated.

29. 4th/3rd c.[43] 20 mn. for exclusive access to Philaenium (female) for one year.[44] (At one point, the madam offers Philaenium for one night for "free" subject to a gift of 2 T.!)[45] As Gomme and Sandbach note (see #26), this would work out to 6 dr. p.d., which is probably an exaggerated amount typical of Attic New Comedy. The 2 T. for one night is clearly intended as a joke.

30. 4th/3rd c. 20 mn. reduced to 10 mn. for Philematium (female).[46] The relative proportions (50% discount) are credible, but the absolute amount (= 1,000 dr., i.e., c. 500 wage days[47]) is not.

---

42. See "Inflation and Deflation" pp. 242, 249–250. Because Menander's plays began to be produced within a decade of Alexander's conquests, we might not expect them so soon to reflect any inflation caused by his capture of Persian bullion.

43. For purposes of this compilation, I assume that all passages from Plautus and Sextus Turpilius (## 29–33) are based on Attic New Comedy originals of the fourth or third centuries B.C. (some are explicitly said to be in their prologues, e.g., Plaut. *Asin.* 11).

44. Plaut. *Asin.* 229–231, 633–636, 751–754, 915–916 (lover Argyrippus, madam Cleareta, Parasite, rival Diabolus):

Arg. mane, mane, audi. dic, quid me aequom censes pro illa tibi dare,
annum hunc ne cum quiquam alio sit?
Cl. Tene? uiginti minas;
atque ea lege: si alius ad me prius attulerit, tu vale.

Arg. argenti uiginti minae med ad mortem appulerunt,
quas hodie adulescens Diabolus ipsi daturus dixit,
ut hanc ne quoquam mitteret nisi ad se hunc annum totum.
uidetin uiginti minae quid pollent quidue possunt?

Pa. 'Diabolus Glauci filius Clearetae
lenae dedit dóno argenti uiginti minas,
Philaenium ut secum esset noctes et dies
hunc annum totum.'
Di. neque cum quiquam alio quidem.

Pa. poste demum huc cras adducam ad lenam, ut uiginti minas
ei det, in partem hac amanti ut liceat ei potirier.

For other statements of the 20 mn. figure, see lines 89, 243, 364, 532, 579, 651, 653, 684, 725, 734 and 852.

45. Plaut. *Asin.* 193–194 (madam Cleareta to lover Argyrippus):

Cl. si mihi dantur duo talenta argenti numerata in manum,
hanc tibi noctem honoris caussa gratiis dono dabo.

46. Plaut. *Most.* 294–298 (lover Philolaches and courtesan Philematium):

Philol. sed, uoluptas mea,

31. 4th/3rd c. Less than 6 mn. for consumption, including prostitutes.[48] Here again, the total figure is probably exaggerated—and that in turn suggests that the higher figures for prostitutes alone in ##29–30, 32–33, 36 (1 T.), 37 and 40 are even more exaggerated. In any event, the figure here for prostitutes alone, and the number of trysts, are not stated, so the amount is not usable for comparative purposes.

32. 4th/3rd c. 6 mn. for Phronesium (female) from youth Diniarchus;[49] 20 mn., 1 mn. gold, 1 mn., 1 mn. gold, 1 T. silver from soldier Stratophanes;[50] and 20 mn. (= "mnas"?) from rustic Strabax.[51] Again, all of these sums seem to be enormous exaggerations for comic effect.

---

mea Philematium, potare tecum conlibitum est mihi.
Philem. ed edepol mihi tecum, nam quod tibi lubet idem míhi lubet,
mea uoluptas.
Philol. ém istuc verbum uile est uiginti minis.
Philem. cedo, amabo, decem: bene emptum tibi dare hoc uerbum uolo.

47. See n. 39.

48. Plaut. *Trin.* 402–412 (youth Lesbonicus and slave Stasimus):
Le. Minu' quindecim dies sunt quom pro hisce aedibus
minas quadraginta acceptisti a Callicle.
estne hoc quod dico, Stasime?
St. quom considero,
meminisse uideor fieri.
Le. quid factumst eo?
St. comessum, expotum; exussum: elotum in balineis,
piscator, pistor apstulit, lanii, coqui,
holitores, myropolae, aucupes: confit cito;
non hercle minu' diuorse distrahitur cito
quam si tu obicias formicis papauerem.
Le. minus hercle in istis rebus sumptumst sex minis.
St. quid quod dedisti scortis?
Le. ibidem una traho.
St. [quid] quod ego defrudaui?
Le. em, istaec ratio maxumast.

49. Plaut. *Truc.* 443–445, 579–580, 739–740 (youth Diniarchus and slave Cyamus):
Di. ego istí non munus mittam? ímmo ex hoc loco
iubebo ad istam quinque perferri minas,
praeterea opsonari una dumtaxat mina.

Cy. eru' meus, ocellus tuos, ád te ferre me haec iussit tibi
dona quae uides íllos ferre et has quinque argenti minas.

Di. dedi equidem hodie: <iussi> ei quinque argenti deferri minas,
praeterea unam in opsonatum.

50. Plaut. *Truc.* 542–544, 893–894, 899–900, 909–910, 934–936, 952 (soldier Stratophanes and courtesan Phronesium):

33. 4th/3rd c.? 1 T. for (female) prostitute?[52] That is the probable interpretation of this comic fragment, where the time period is not stated, and in any event the figure is likely to be a comic exaggeration.

Strat. nilne huic sat est?
ne bonum uerbum quidem unum dixit. uiginti minis 543
uenire illaec posse credo dona quae ei dono dedi.

Strat. Ego minam auri fero supplicium †damnis† ad amicam meam: 893
ut illud acceptum sit priu' quod perdidi, hoc addam insuper.

Strat. ego, mea uoluptas, si quid peccaui prius,
supplicium hanc minam fero auri. 900

Strat. respice ergo: áccipe hoc qui ístuc ecficias opus.
Ph. cedo, quamquam parum est.
Strat. addam unam minam istuc post.
Ph. parumst. 910

Strat. dedin ego aurum—
Ph. mihi? dedisti filio cibaria. 935
nunc, si hanc tecum esse speras, alia opust auri mina.

Strat. em tibi talentum argenti. 952

In 910, addam unam minam is Bothe's conjecture for the MS' †ad omnae manuc†

51. Plaut. *Truc.* 645–662, 947–948 (country youth Strabax):

Strab. Rus mane dudum hinc ire me iussit pater, 645
ut bubus glandem prandio depromerem.
post illoc quam ueni, aduenit, si dis placet,
ad uillam argentum meo qui debebat patri,
qui ouis Tarentínas erat mercatus de patre.
quaerit patrem. dico esse in urbe. interrogo 650
quid eum uelit * *
homo cruminam sibi de collo detrahit,
minas uiginti mi dat. accipio lubens,
condo in cruminam. ille abiit. ego †perpera† minas
ouis ín crumina hac <huc> in urbem detuli. 655
fuit edepol Mars meo periratus patri,
nam oues illius hau longe apsunt a lupis.
ne ego urbános istos mundulos amasios
hoc ictu exponam atque omnis eiciam foras.
eradicarest certum cumprimis patrem, 660
post id locorum matrem. nunc hoc deferam
argentum ad hanc, quam mage amo quam matrem meam.

Strab. at ego ouis et lanam et alia multa quae poscet dabo.
melius te minis certare mecum quam minaciis. 948

52. Sext. Turpilius 35–36 (Ribbeck):

34. 4th/3rd c.?[53] 1 mn. for virgin Korinna.[54] It is difficult to judge how closely this amount is modeled on New Comedy (see n. 53), or how exaggerated it might have been there. A hundred drachmas for a virgin is just possible, but it more likely is exaggerated.

35. 4th/3rd c.? 2 mn. offered to Mousarion (female) by Acharnian farmer, 1 mn. by Antiphanes, but neither accepted.[55] Here the point seems to be that, although a hetaira, this young woman was willing to forego enormous fees in order to bestow her favors for free on her lover—a credible enough story in its general outline, although the figures are probably exaggerated for dramatic effect.

36. 4th/3rd c.? Ampelis: 5 dr. max. from Demophantos, 10 dr. from Kallides, 1 T. from Demophantos (after jealousy aroused) for 8 months.[56] Here again the comic contrast is plausible, as are (possibly) the smaller figures, but the larger one—6,000 dr.—is certainly exaggerated.

37. 4th/3rd c.? 1 T. given and 1 T. promised to Pannychis by merchant Philostratos.[57] These figures are implausible on their face.

. . . . at étiam ineptus méus mi est iratús pater,
Quia sé talento argénti tetigi uéteri exemplo amántium.

53. For purposes of this compilation, I assume that Lucian's *D. Meretr.* (##34–40) is probably, though not certainly, also based on Attic New Comedy of the fourth and third centuries B.C. See M. D. Macleod, *Lucian* VII (Cambridge, Massachusetts 1961) 355 with references.

54. Lucian *D. Meretr.* vi. 1 (mother-madam Krobyle to new prostitute Korinna): Ὦ Κόριννα, ὡς μὲν οὐ πάνυ δεινὸν ἦν, ὃ ἐνόμιζες, τὸ γυναῖκα γενέσθαι ἐκ παρθένου, μεμάθηκας ἤδη, μετὰ μειρακίου μὲν ὡραίου γενομένη, μνᾶν δὲ τὸ πρῶτον μίσθωμα κομισαμένη, ἐξ ἧς ὅρμον αὐτίκα ὠνήσομαί σοι. In vi. 2, Korinna also refers to τὴν μνᾶν.

55. Lucian *D. Meretr.* vii. 3 (mother to Mousarion): καὶ πρῴην μὲν ὅτε ὁ γεωργὸς ὁ Ἀχαρνεὺς ἧκε δύο μνᾶς κομίζων, ἀγένειος καὶ αὐτός—οἴνου δὲ τιμὴν ἀπειλήφει τοῦ πατρὸς πέμψαντος—σὺ δὲ ἐκεῖνον μὲν ἀπεμύκτισας, καθεύδεις δὲ μετὰ τοῦ Ἀδώνιδος Χαιρέου. . . . τί καὶ Ἀντιφῶντα τὸν Μενεκράτους μνᾶν ὑπισχνούμενον οὐδὲ τοῦτον ἐδέξω;

56. Lucian *D. Meretr.* viii. 2–3 (Ampelis speaking): ἤρα μου Δημόφαντος ὁ δανειστὴς ὁ κατόπιν οἰκῶν τῆς Ποικίλης. οὗτος οὐδεπώποτε πλέον πέντε δραχμῶν δέδωκε καὶ ἠξίου δεσπότης εἶναι. ἤρα δέ, ὦ Χρυσί, ἐπιπόλαιόν τινα ἔρωτα οὔτε ὑποστένων οὔτε δακρύων οὔτε ἀωρὶ παραγιγνόμενος ἐπὶ τὰς θύρας, ἀλλ' αὐτὸ μόνον συνεκάθευδέ μοι ἐνίοτε, καὶ τοῦτο διὰ μακροῦ. ἐπειδὴ δὲ ἐλθόντα ποτὲ ἀπέκλεισα—Καλλίδης γὰρ ὁ γραφεὺς ἔνδον ἦν δέκα δραχμὰς πεπομφώς—τὸ μὲν πρῶτον ἀπῆλθέ μοι λοιδορησάμενος· ἐπεὶ δὲ πολλαὶ μὲν διῆλθον ἡμέραι, ἐγὼ δὲ οὐ προσέπεμπον, ὁ Καλλίδης δὲ ἔνδον ἦν, ὑποθερμαινόμενος ἤδη τότε ὁ Δημόφαντος καὶ αὐτὸς ἀναφλέγεται ἐς τὸ πρᾶγμα καὶ ἐπιστάς ποτε ἀνεῳγμένην τηρήσας τὴν θύραν ἔκλαεν, ἔτυπτεν, ἠπείλει φονεύσειν, περιερρήγνυε τὴν ἐσθῆτα, ἅπαντα ἐποίει, καὶ τέλος τάλαντον δοὺς μόνος εἶχεν ὀκτὼ ὅλους μῆνας.

57. Lucian *D. Meretr.* ix. 3–4: (Pannychis speaking) οὔτε γὰρ τοῦτον (sc. Φιλόστρατον) ἀποπέμψαι καλὸν τάλαντον ἔναγχος δεδωκότα καὶ τἆλλα ἔμπορον ὄντα καὶ πολλὰ

38. 4th/3rd c.? 5 dr. for Tryphaina from Charmides, who does not partake (he loves another).[58] As with the smaller figures in #36, this one is possible, but unverifiable.

39. 4th/3rd c.? Myrtale: 5 dr. from sailor Dorion over extended period (including 2 dr. for two nights), 2 mn. plus rent from Bithynian merchant.[59] Again, a comic contrast between a plausible lower figure and a less plausible higher one.

40. 4th/3rd c.? 2 T. demanded by Krokale from Aitolian soldier for exclusive access.[60] She may have demanded it, but it almost certainly could not have been paid.

41. c. 285. 1 mn. the usual fee for Gnathainion (female),[61] but on one occasion 1,000 dr. was demanded for one night and then reduced by negotiation to 5 mn.[62] Gow comments that the definite article (τὴν μνᾶν)

ὑπισχνούμενον, ... (Philostratos speaking) Παννυχὶς ἐμή ἐστι, καὶ τάλαντον εἴληφε, λήψεται δὲ ἤδη καὶ ἕτερον, ἐπειδὰν τὰ φορτία διαθώμεθα.

58. Lucian *D. Meretr.* xi. 1 (Tryphaina speaking): Ἑταίραν δέ τις (i.e., Χαρμίδης) παραλαβὼν πέντε δραχμὰς τὸ μίσθωμα δοὺς καθεύδει ἀποστραφεὶς δακρύων καὶ στένων;

59. Lucian *D. Meretr.* xiv. 2–3 (Myrtale to Dorion, after he reminds her that he gave her shoes worth δύο δραχμῶν): Ἀλλ' ἐκοιμήθης νύκτας δύο. . . . Πέντε ἴσως δραχμῶν, ὦ Δωρίων, πάντα ταῦτα (value of Dorion's gifts over a period of time: shoes, perfume, food and sandals). . . . (after mentioning the Bithynian's gifts of clothing and jewelry) καὶ πρῴην δύο μνᾶς, καὶ τὸ ἐνοίκιον κατέβαλεν ὑπὲρ ἡμῶν. . . . In xiv. 4, Dorion refers to διμναῖα μισθώματα.

60. Lucian *D. Meretr.* xv. 2: ἡ Κροκάλη δέ, οἶμαι, δύο τάλαντα αἰτήσασα, εἰ βούλεται (sc. ὁ Αἰτολὸς) μόνος ἔχειν αὐτήν. . . . Compare the 20 mn. for exclusive access for one year in #29, there demanded by the madam rather than the hetaira.

61. Lynceus ap. Athen. xiii. 47 (584c): ὡς δ' ὁ τὴν μνᾶν τῇ θυγατρὶ (sc. Γναθαινίῳ) δοὺς αὐτῆς οὐδὲν ἔτι ἔφερεν, ἀλλ' ἐφοίτα μόνον, "παιδίον," ἔφη (sc. Γνάθαινα), "ὥσπερ πρὸς Ἱππόμαχον τὸν παιδοτρίβην μνᾶν δοὺς οἴει αἰεὶ φοιτήσειν;" For the date, see "Doctors, Lawyers and Professors" #30 with n. 38.

62. Machon 333–348 (Gow):

Εἰς τὰς Ἀθήνας παρεπιδημήσας ξένος
σατράπης πάνυ γέρων ὡς ἐνενήκοντ' ⟨ὢν⟩ ἐτῶν
Κρονίοις ἀπιοῦσαν εἶδε τὴν Γναθαίνιον
μετὰ τῆς Γναθαίνης ἐξ Ἀφροδισίου τινός,
τό τ' εἶδος αὐτῆς τοὺς ῥυθμούς τε καταμαθών
ἐπυνθάνετο μίσθωμα πράττεται πόσον
τῆς νυκτός, ἡ Γνάθαινα δ' εἰς τὴν πορφύραν
καὶ τὰ δόρατ' ἀποβλέψασα δραχμὰς χιλίας
ἔταξεν. ὁ δ' ἄφνω καιρίμην πληγείς, Παπαῖ,
ζωγρεῖς, γύναι, φήσ', ἕνεκα τοῦ στρατιωτικοῦ,
μνᾶς πραξαμένη δὲ πέντε τὰς σπονδὰς ποιοῦ
καὶ στρῶσον ἡμῖν ἔνδον. ἡ δ' ἐπιδέξιον
βουλόμενον εἶναι τὸν σατράπην ἀπεδέξατο,

in the Lynkeus anecdote suggests that 1 mn. "was, at any rate at some period of Gnathaenium's life, a standard fee, as [line] 451 [#13] suggests it may have been Phryne's. The satrap had, if so, good reason to be shocked at Gnathaena's price [of 10 times that amount], and his offer of half ([in line] 343) was handsome."[63] But lines 339–342 suggest that Gnathaina raised the price to the level she thought the satrap could pay, and 1,000 dr. is just possible as the occasional "asking price" for the premiere hetaira of Athens.

42. pre-250. 3 ob. to male prostitute to service bent-over Gnathaina, or for bending over himself?[64] Gow comments:

> The butcher affects to misunderstand her question and, as Vollgraff saw, to suppose that she is making him an indecent proposition. The adv. κύβδα is as old as Archil. *fr.* 32, and is used, so far as the evidence goes, only in an obscene sense. The Aristophanic passages (*Equ.* 3[6]5, *Pax* 896, *Thesm.* 489) suggest that it refers to her position, not to his, and that he means στήσω σε κεκυφυῖαν. In other words he will treat her as Demetrius treats Mania in [line] 230, but in view of her age demands a fee, the amount of which reminds one, probably irrelevantly, of Plat. Com. . . . Λόρδωνι δραχμή, Κυβ-

---

εἶπεν δέ, ⟨   ⟩ δὸς ὅσον ἐπιθυμεῖς, πάτερ·
οἶδα γὰρ ἀκριβῶς καὶ πέποιθα τοῦθ' ὅτι
εἰς νύκτ' ἀποδώσεις τῷ θυγατρίῳ μου διπλοῦν.

Gow, *Machon* 121, translates ὅσον in line 346 "not *anything you like* (Gulick [*Athenaeus: The Deipnosophists* VI (Cambridge, Massachusetts 1937) 135]) but *the fee you wish to pay* (i.e. 5 minae)." Gow also reports "the *double entendre* discerned by Palmerius . . . σκώπτει εἰς τὸ ἄστυτον τοῦ γέροντος καὶ εἰς ἀναδίπλωσιν τοῦ αἰδοίου ὡς οὐ δυναμένου αὐτὸ ἁπλοῦν καὶ τείνειν," but thinks that if there is "a latent meaning, it is more likely to be δὶς συγγενήσει αὐτῇ."

63. Gow, *Machon* 120.

64. Machon 300–310 (Gow):

Ἐπεὶ προέβη τοῖς ἔτεσιν ἡ Γνάθαινα καί
ἤδη τελέως ἦν ὁμολογουμένως σορός,
εἰς τὴν ἀγορὰν λέγουσιν αὐτὴν ἐξίναι
καὶ τοὔψον ἐφορᾶν καὶ πολυπραγμονεῖν πόσου
πωλεῖθ' ἕκαστον, εἶτ' ἰδοῦσα κατὰ τύχην
ἱστῶντα κρεοπώλην τιν' ἀστεῖον πάνυ
τῇ θ' ἡλικίᾳ σφόδρα νέον, Ὦ πρὸς τῶν θεῶν
μειράκιον ὁ καλός, φησι, πῶς ἵστης φράσον.
ὁ δὲ μειδάσας, Κύβδ', ἔφη, τριωβόλου.
Τίς δ' οὐπιτρέψων ἐστί σοί, φησιν, τάλαν,
ὄντα γ' ἐν Ἀθήναις Καρικοῖς χρῆσθαι σταθμοῖς;

For the date, see "Doctors, Lawyers and Professors" #30 with n. 38.

> δάσῳ τριώβολον [#5].... Nothing is known of Carian perversions beyond what may be inferred from [line] 308. Σταθμοῖς means *scales*, *weights*, but Gnathaena implies a possible meaning *stance*, *position*.[65]

It may also be possible that Gnathaina is asking the lad what his normal charge is to submit (by bending over) to males,[66] although ἵστης (transitive) makes that less likely. In any event, this youth was not (at least yet) a celebrated prostitute and his stated fee of 3 ob. is plausible.

43. A.D. 2nd c.? 2 dr. offered to male cupbearer by Kleodemos.[67] This sum is plausible, but it is not verifiable by contemporary figures, and in any event it is not said whether any agreement has been reached: will the 2 dr. function as a partial deposit or a total advance payment for the hoped-for services?

As a group, these figures are not always easy to evaluate. It is in the nature of such charges that they vary considerably, depending on the attractions of the prostitute and the resources and urgency of the customer. Moreover, the nature of the services means that unimpeachable evidence is hard to come by: no inscriptions or Thucydides to help us here! The sources are overwhelmingly comedies, or comic fragments, where the usual tendency to exaggerate for comic effect is particularly tempting in a sexual context. After putting to one side the figures that are unusable, either because they are quite imprecise (##1, 19, 31), intention-

---

65. Gow, *Machon* 114.

66. As shown in the "Eurymedon oinochoe" published by K. Schauenburg, "ΕΥΡΥΜΕΔΩΝ ΕΙΜΙ," *MDAI(I)* 90 (1975) 97–121 at 103–104 with Taf. 25, and discussed further by G. F. Pinney, "For the Heroes are at Hand," *JHS* 104 (1984) 181–183 with Pl. VIII.

67. Lucian *Symp.* 15: ἐν τοσούτῳ δ' ἐγὼ τὸν παρεστῶτα τῷ Κλεοδήμῳ παῖδα οἰνοχόον ὄντα ὡραῖον ἰδὼν ὑπομειδιῶντα—χρὴ γάρ, οἶμαι, καὶ ὅσα πάρεργα τῆς ἑστιάσεως εἰπεῖν, καὶ μάλιστα εἴ τι πρὸς τὸ γλαφυρώτερον ἐπράχθη—μάλα ἤδη παρεφύλαττον ὅ τι καὶ μειδιάσειε. καὶ μετὰ μικρὸν ὁ μὲν προσῆλθεν ὡς ἀποληψόμενος παρὰ τοῦ Κλεοδήμου τὴν φιάλην, ὁ δὲ τόν τε δάκτυλον ἀπέθλιψεν αὐτοῦ καὶ δραχμὰς δύο, οἶμαι, συνανέδωκε μετὰ τῆς φιάλης· ὁ παῖς δὲ πρὸς μὲν τὸν δάκτυλον θλιβόμενον αὖθις ἐμεδίασεν, οὐ μὴν συνεῖδεν, οἶμαι, τὸ νόμισμα, ὥστε μὴ δεξαμένου ψόφον αἱ δύο δραχμαὶ παρέσχον ἐκπεσοῦσαι, καὶ ἠρυθρίασαν ἄμφω μάλα σαφῶς. ἠπόρουν δὲ οἱ πλησίον οὗτινος εἴη τὰ νομίσματα, τοῦ μὲν παιδὸς ἀρνουμένου μὴ ἀποβεβληκέναι, τοῦ δὲ Κλεοδήμου, καθ' ὃν ὁ ψόφος ἐγένετο, μὴ προσποιουμένου τὴν ἀπόρριψιν. ἠμελήθη οὖν καὶ παρώφθη τοῦτο οὐ πάνυ πολλῶν ἰδόντων πλὴν μόνου, ὡς ἐμοὶ ἔδοξε, τοῦ Ἀρισταινέτου· μετέστησε γὰρ τὸν παῖδα μικρὸν ὕστερον ἀφανῶς ὑπεξαγαγὼν καὶ τῷ Κλεοδήμῳ τινὰ παραστῆναι διένευσε τῶν ἐξώρων ἤδη καὶ καρτερῶν, ὀρεωκόμον τινὰ ἢ ἱπποκόμον.

ally vague (#11), not clearly applicable (##5, 20, 23), or unserious on their face (##15, 29 [2 T.]), and the three figures (##8, 16, 17) that unfortunately tell us nothing about rates for a single occasion, we are left with a motley collection. In most cases, the figure is pretty clearly an exaggeration, either upwards (##3, 5 [1 dr.], 6, 10, 18, 21, 26–28, 29 [20 mn.], 30, 32–35, 36 [1 T.], 37, 39 [2 mn.], 40: 1 dr. to 2 T.)[68] or downwards (##2, 4, 12, 14, 25: "small change" or "not much money" to 1 ob.). The remaining figures fall into three categories:

(a) 3 ob. for an average prostitute (##9, 22, 42 and possibly 5 [3 ob.]), with no apparent diachronic changes.

(b) 2 dr. to 1,000 dr. for a high-class and socially acceptable hetaira (##7, 13, 24, 41), depending on her age, attractions, mood at the moment, and the resources and urgency of the customer.

(c) 2 dr. to 10 dr. for named hetairai of late, possibly very late, date (see n. 53) (##36 [5–10 dr.], 38, 39 [5 dr.], 43).

---

68. Assuming that ##26 et seq. do not reflect an enormous increase in wages and prices after Alexander's conquests that is not attested by the (admittedly very meager) sober evidence for that period (see #28 with n. 42).

Chapter 10

Miscellaneous Workers

Collected here are wages, salaries and fees for all workers who do not fall clearly into the categories discussed in Chapters 1–9. Böckh discussed three of the figures in his chapter on "Lohn."[1]

1. 425. 8 dr. to Amphitheos ("divine on both sides") to make a private peace with Sparta?[2] In this fictional and humorous context, Aristophanes' audience would have regarded eight drachmas—only eight days' wages for a single soldier[3]—as an incredible bargain for peace. For the possibility that it was intended to be understood as a travel allowance, see "Travel Allowances" #5.

2. 422. 3 ob. to fuller to clean clothes sullied by diarrhea.[4] Because Philokleon is trying to make the unhappy consequences of his gastronomic excesses seem as great as possible, I suspect that this figure was exaggerated, but, in the absence of other figures for cleaning that we can compare to this one, we can do no more than regard it as a maximum.

3. 380/79. ? Aig. [st.] for λῶτις (= λοῦσις), i.e., ritual bathing of cult statue of Delphic Amphiktyons.[5] It is not certain that staters are

---

1. Böckh, *SdA* I 150–152, commenting on ##2, 6 and 14.
2. Ar. *Ach.* 130–32 (Dikaiopolis to Amphitheos):
   Δι. ἐμοὶ σὺ ταυτασὶ λαβὼν ὀκτὼ δραχμὰς
   σπονδὰς ποιῆσαι πρὸς Λακδαιμονίους μόνῳ
   καὶ τοῖσι παιδίοισι καὶ τῇ πλάτιδι·
3. See "Soldiers and Sailors" #5.
4. Ar. *Vesp.* 1125–1128 (Bdelykleon and Philokleon):
   Βδ. ἀγαθὸν ἔοικας οὐδὲν ἐπιθυμεῖν παθεῖν.
   Φι. μὰ τὸν Δί', οὐ γὰρ οὐδαμῶς μοι ξύμφορον.
   καὶ γὰρ πρότερον ἐπανθρακίδων ἐμπλήμενος
   ἀπέδωκ' ὀφείλων τῷ κναφεῖ τριώβολον.
5. *IG* II² 1126 + *CID* I 10. 26–27:
   . . . Λῶτις· ἁ λῶτις τᾶς Ἀμφι[κτιον . . . . . .c. 13. . . . . . . στατῆρες] 26
   Αἰγινα[ῖ]ọι·

See also *SEG* XXXII 139 for the restoration λῶτις τῆς (*sic*) Ἀμφι[κτιονίδος Ἀθάνας].

present in this passage, and, in any event, their number is not preserved, so this is not a usable figure.

4. c. 347–339. 10 T. For this amount, philosopher Speusippos offers to find a more beautiful (male or female?) lover, as a matchmaker or a pimp? As discussed in greater detail under "Prostitutes and Pimps" #15, Speusippos' offer is purely rhetorical, and in any event the amount (in Timotheus ap. Diog. Laert. iv. 4) was never paid.

5. Late 4th c. 4 dr. to cook.[6] Although the time period is not stated in this comic fragment, it probably was for a single feast, as in ##7 and 10. If so, this would be a very large wage—roughly twice the daily wage of skilled construction workers in 329/8[7] and also more than the figures in ##7 and 10—and the comic point would be that this pretentious cook would be willing to forego even this (exaggerated) sum if prevented from indulging his preferences.

6. 4th/3rd c. 6 ch. to 4 hired men, apiece.[8] In the absence of more context, it is impossible to say what their task was,[9] but the very low figure suggests either (a) that the task required very little time or (b) that their pay has been exaggerated downwards for comic effect.

7. 4th/3rd c. 3 dr. to cook, 1 dr. to waiter, for wedding.[10] These figures are stated rather matter-of-factly, and the proportional relation-

---

6. Strato fr. 1. 32–33 (K-A, Athenaios' [rather than papyrus'] version) (cook asking whether he is to abandon his scholarly pretensions, to which his employer objects):

"ἀλλὰ διὰ τὰς τέτταρας 32
δραχμὰς ἀποβαλῶ," φησί, "τὴν προαίρεσιν;"

7. See "Construction and Other Manual Workers" #7.

8. Philemo fr. 66 (K-A) ap. Poll. ix. 65–66: ὅτι δὲ τοὺς ἓξ χαλκοῦς τριτημόριον ὠνόμαζον, ἔστιν εὑρεῖν ἐν τῶι Φιλήμονος Σαρδίωι· . . . καὶ ἔτι σαφῶς (σαφέστερον? Kaibel) ἐν τῶι Πιττοκοπουμένῶι·

ἰδοὺ πάρεστιν, ὡς ὁρᾶις. τριτημόρου
ἕκαστος ὑμῶν ἦλθεν· εἰς ⟨τοὺς⟩ τέτταρας
εἴληφεν ὑμῖν οὑτοσὶ τριώβολον.

K-A quote Bentley's explanation: "conductor horum quat[t]uor mercenariorum debebat singulis sex chalcos: cum tot aenei chalci non essent ei ad manum, dedit uni illorum tres obolos argenteos, aequivalentes quater sex chalcis; quos ipsi postea κερματίζειν . . . possent."

9. Despite the play's title (see n. 8), this fragment is not long enough to guarantee Böckh's interpretation (*SdA* I 151): "für die edle Arbeit des Haarrupfens mit Pech, um eine weibliche Haut zu bekommen, zahlt ein feines Herrchen bei Philemon vier Personen, jedem sechs Chalkûs."

10. Men. *Asp.* 216–235 (Μάγειρος [cook], slave Δάος, and Τραπεζοποιός [waiter]):

Μα. ἂν καὶ λάβω ποτ' ἔργον, ἢ τέθνηκέ τις,
εἶτ' ἀποτρέχειν δεῖ μισθὸν οὐκ ἔχοντά με,
ἢ τέτοκε τῶν ἔνδον κυοῦσά τις λάθραι,
εἶτ' οὐκέτι θύουσ' ἐξαπίνης, ἀλλ' οἴχομαι

ship between them is plausible. Moreover, they fit well with the obvious exaggeration of 4 dr. in #5 and the 1 dr. for the run-of-the-mill cook in #10. So I am inclined to see 3 dr. for a first-class chef and 1 dr. for a waiter as plausible "background facts."

8. 4th/3rd c. 5 mn. for assailant of Olympic athlete?[11] The precise sense is not clear here, but since there probably was no "going rate" for this service I am inclined to see it as hypothetical—and high.

9. 4th/3rd c. 1 T. to anyone who will accept slave's punishment.[12] Again, in this comic context, this is a hypothetical figure, which on its face never was intended to be paid.

ἀπιὼν ἐγώ. τῆς δυσποτμίας.
Δα. πρὸς τῶν θεῶν,
μάγειρ', ἄπελθε.
Μα. νῦν δέ ⟨σοι⟩ τί δοκῶ ποιεῖν;
λαβὲ τὰς μαχαίρας, παιδάριον, θᾶττόν ποτε.
δραχμῶν τριῶν ἦλθον δι' ἡμερῶν δέκα
ἔργον λαβών· ᾤιμην ἔχειν ταύτας· νεκρὸς
ἐλθών τις ἐκ Λυκίας ἀφήιρηται βίαι
ταύτας. τοιούτου συμβεβηκότος κακοῦ
τοῖς ἔνδον, ἱερόσυλε, κλαούσας ὁρῶν
καὶ κοπτομένας γυναῖκας ἐκφέρεις κενὴν
τὴν λήκυθον; μέμνησο καιρὸν παραλαβὼν
τοιοῦτον. οὐ Σπινθῆρ', Ἀριστείδην δ' ἔχω,
ὑπηρέτην δίκαιον· ὄψομαί σ' ἐγὼ
ἄδειπνον. ὁ δὲ τραπεζοποιὸς καταμενεῖ
εἰς τὸ περίδειπνον τυχὸν ἴσως·
Τρ. δραχμὴν ἐγὼ
ἂν μὴ λάβω κοπτόμενος ὑμῶν οὐδὲ ἓν
αὐτὸς διοίσω.

11. Men. *Col.* 100–106:

]θ̣εν ὑ̣ιον Ἀστυάνακτος ὑ[πτίου
κατακειμένου δ̣οίδυ̣[κι
τὴν ῥῖνα συντριψαι μ[. . .] μ̣[. . . . .]α̣ν
ἀλλ' οὐχ ὁ πέντε μναῖς κα̣τ̣ε̣σ̣[κ]ε̣υ̣α̣[σμένος
ἐπ' αὐτὸ τοῦθ' ἥκων ἵν' ἐκειν[
οὐκ εὐπόρως ἂν τοῦτ' ἐποήσατ' [
φυλάττεται [

G-S 428 comment: "The general sense is: 'If Astyanax [winner of the pancratium] were lying flat on his back you could break his nose with a pestle; but a man secured for five minae, who came with the intention of killing (?) him, could not easily do it if he were looked out for.'"

12. Plaut. *Most.* 359–361 (slave Tranio speaking):

ego dabo ei talentum primus qui in crucem excucurrerit;
sed ea lege ut offigantur bis pedes, bis bracchia.
ubi id erit factum, a me argentum petito praesentarium.

10. 4th/3rd c. 1 dr. for average (cheap) cook, per feast.[13] At this time, one drachma for a job like this may well have been an average fee, and therefore a legitimate "background fact."

11. 4th/3rd c.?[14] 1 dr. plus 7 ob. to Syrian witch, to restore lover to hetaira.[15] We cannot be sure that Lucian, writing in the second century A.D., was accurately reproducing a figure from Attic New Comedy, but, even if he was, we lack the comparanda that would help us decide if these figures were reasonably accurate "background facts" of the period.

12. 4th/3rd c.? 2–4 ob. tip for hetaira's slave.[16] These very modest figures have an air of authenticity about them, but, as with #11, it is difficult to evaluate them with confidence.

13. pre-271. 4 T. for Epicurus' cook in less than 2 yrs. 10 mos.[17] In this comic context, this sounds like an exaggeration—almost 24 dr. p.d.!

---

13. Plaut. *Pseud.* 804–808 (cook speaking):
quia enim, quom extemplo ueniunt conductum coquom,
nemo illum quaerit qui optumus et carissimust:
illum conducunt potius qui uilissimust.
hoc ego fui hodie solus opsessor fori.
illi drachumissent miseri: me nemo potest
minoris quisquam nummo ut surgam subigere.

14. For the dates of ##11 and 12, and their possible Attic New Comedy models, see "Prostitutes and Pimps" n. 53.

15. Lucian *D. Meretr.* iv. 4 (hetairai Bacchis and Melitta): Βα. Ἔστιν, ὦ φιλτάτη, ὅτι χρησίμη φαρμακίς, Σύρα τὸ γένος, ὠμὴ ἔτι καὶ συμπεπηγυῖα, ἥ μοί ποτε Φανίαν χαλεπαίνοντα κἀκεῖνον εἰκῆ, ὥσπερ Χαρῖνος, διήλλαξε μετὰ μῆνας ὅλους τέτταρας, ὅτε ἐγὼ μὲν ἤδη ἀπεγνώκειν, ὁ δὲ ὑπὸ τῶν ἐπῳδῶν ἧκεν αὖθις ἐπ' ἐμέ. Με. Τί δὲ ἔπραξεν ἡ γραῦς, εἴπερ ἔτι μέμνησαι; Βα. Λαμβάνει μὲν οὐδὲ πολύν, ὦ Μέλιττα, τὸν μισθόν, ἀλλὰ δραχμὴν καὶ ἄρτον· ἐπικεῖσθαι δὲ δεῖ μετὰ τῶν ἁλῶν καὶ ὀβολοὺς ἑπτὰ καὶ θεῖον καὶ δᾷδα. ταῦτα δὲ ἡ γραῦς λαμβάνει, καὶ κρατῆρα κεκερᾶσθαι δεῖ καὶ πίνειν ἐκείνην μόνην. δεήσει αὐτοῦ μέντοι ⟨τι⟩ τοῦ ἀνδρὸς εἶναι, οἷον ἱμάτια ἢ κρηπῖδας ἢ ολίγας τῶν τριχῶν ἤ τι τῶν τοιούτων.

16. Lucian *D. Meretr.* xiv. 3 (lover Dorio to hetaira Myrtale): Ὦ Μυρτάλη, ὅσα ναύτης ἄνθρωπος ἐδυνάμην μισθοῦ ἐπιπλέων. νῦν γὰρ ἤδη τοίχου ἄρχω τοῦ δεξιοῦ καὶ σὺ ἡμῶν ὑπερορᾷς, πρῴην δὲ ὁπότε τὰ Ἀφροδίσια ἦν, οὐχὶ δραχμὴν ἔθηκα πρὸ τοῖν ποδοῖν τῆς Ἀφροδίτης σοῦ ἕνεκεν ἀργυρᾶν; καὶ πάλιν τῇ μητρὶ εἰς ὑποδήματα δύο δραχμὰς καὶ Λυδῇ ταύτῃ πολλάκις εἰς τὴν χεῖρα νῦν μὲν δύο, νῦν δὲ τέτταρας ὀβολούς. ταῦτα πάντα συντεθέντα οὐσία ναύτου ἀνδρὸς ἦν.

17. Damoxenus fr. 2. 1–4 (K-A, cook speaking):
Ἐπικούρου δέ με
ὁρᾶις μαθητὴν ὄντα τοῦ σοφοῦ, παρ' ὧι
ἐν δύ' ἔτεσιν καὶ μησὶν οὐχ ὅλοις δέκα
τάλαντ' ἐγώ σοι κατεπύκνωσα τέτταρα.

14. A.D. 2nd c. 2 ob. for bathhouse (establishment or attendant?).[18] Judging from the much lower non-Athenian amounts paid to bathhouse attendants, even in later periods,[19] I suspect that this amount went to the bathhouse, which in turn paid a salary to the attendant, in which case this is not a usable figure.

As a group, these figures are not very useful. In one case (#3), the figure is missing. Others lack sufficient context or detail to enable us tell precisely what they are for (##6, 14). Some on their face are not to be taken seriously (##1, 4, 8, 9). Most of the others are from comic sources whose context indicates that they may be exaggerated, either upwards (##2, 5, 13) or downwards (#6 [doubtful]). Although three *could* be plausible "background facts" (##6, 11, 12), we lack reliable comparanda that would enable us to make that judgment. The only figures that I am inclined to trust are the 3 dr. for a first-class chef (#7) and the 1 dr. for a waiter and an average cook (##7, 10), both uncertainly dated "4th/3rd c."

18. Lucian *Lex.* 2 (pretentious Atticist Lexiphanes reading to friend Lykinos): "Ἆιτα δειπνήσομεν," ἦ δ' ὃς ὁ Καλλικλῆς, "εἶτα τὸ δειλινὸν περιδινησόμεθα ἐν Λυκείῳ, νῦν δὲ ἤδη καιρός ἐστιν χρίεσθαι τὸ ἡλιοκαὲς καὶ πρὸς τὴν εἵλην θέρεσθαι καὶ λουσαμένους ἀρτοσιτεῖν. καὶ ἤδη γε ἀπιτητέα. σὺ δέ, ὦ παῖ, στελεγγίδα μοι καὶ βύρσαν καὶ φωσώνια καὶ ῥύμματα ναυστολεῖν ἐς τὸ βαλανεῖον καὶ τοὐπίλουτρον κομίζειν· ἔχεις δὲ χαμᾶζε παρὰ τὴν ἐγγυοθήκην δύ' ὀβολώ.

19. Stratonicus ap. Athen. viii. 45 (352a) (1 ch. extra fee for foreigners paid to Phaselis bathhouse attendant in c. 390–360); Lib. *Decl.* xxvi. 19 (1 ob. ± paid to Asia Minor bathhouse attendant in A.D. 4th c.?).

Chapter 11
Transport Costs

In this category are collected both passenger fares for individuals and freight costs for tangible personal property. These figures do not separate labor and non-labor costs, i.e., the wages of transport workers from the costs, e.g, of purchasing and maintaining a draft animal, wagon, or ship. Since Böckh's very brief initial collection and discussion,[1] Burford has referred to some of the freight figures, mostly in relation to non-Athenian freight costs.[2]

1. c. 446/5? [7 ob. or 1 dr.?] for individual from Oropos to Hestiaia [or to Dion or reverse of those trips]; 4 ob. from Chalkis to Hestiaia; [3 or 2 ob.?] from Chalkis to Oropos; half price on these three fares for passengers going to a certain festival?[3] The only figure that is secure is the 4

1. Böckh, *SdA* I 148–150.
2. Burford, "Heavy Transport" 15–18; *GTBE* 184–191.
3. *IG* I[3] 41. 67–74:

ΣΤΟΙΧ. 39?

ἔ̣[στο δὲ τᾶι πορθμεύοντι ἐκ Χ]-
[α]λκίδος ἐς Ὀροπὸν πρ̣[άττεσθαι τρε͂ς ὀβολός· ἐὰν δ]-
[έ] τις ἐχς Ὀροπο͂ ἐς hεστ̣[ίαιαν ε͂ ἐς Δῖον ε͂ ἐκεῖθεν ἐ]-
ς Ὀροπὸν πορθμεύει, πρ[αττέσθο hέπτ' ὀβολός· ἐὰν δ]-
έ τις ἐκ Χαλκίδος ἐς hε[στίαιαν πορθμεύει, πραττ]-
έσθο τέτταρας ὀβολό[ς ....21..........]
[.] μὲν hοι πομπεύοντε[ς ....18......... πομ]-
[π]εύεται, τελέτο τὸ hέ̣[μισυ.]

Lewis comments as follows on the restorations: "Supplementa nostra [Lewis'] sane audacissima exempli gratia dedimus, ut sensum textus difficillimi et nunquam re vera editi indicare possimus. Quantum in singulis a vero aberraverimus, cauti scrutentur lectores." On lines 72–74, he comments: "nauli pretium iis qui ad pompam quandam pergunt minuitur." *SEG* XXXII 3, positing a renumbered and shortened line, gives the following alternative text:

ΣΤΟΙΧ. 36

ἐ[ὰν δέ τις πορθμεύει ἐκ Χ]-
[α]λκίδος ἐς Ὀροπὸν πρ̣[αττέσθο δύο ὀβολό· ἐὰν δ]-
έ̣ τις ἐχς Ὀροπο͂ ἐς hεσ[τίαιαν ε͂ ἐχς Ἑστιαίας ἐ]-
ς̣ Ὀροπὸν πορθμεύει πρ[αττέσθο δραχμέν· ἐὰν δ]-
έ τις ἐκ Χαλκίδος ἐς hε[στίαιαν ἐκπλεῖ πρατт]-

ob. from Chalkis to Hestiaia. Since the distance from Chalkis to Hestiaia is more than three times the distance from Chalkis to Oropos, one might expect the fare from Chalkis to Oropos to be 2 ob. rather than 3 ob., and the fare from Oropos to Hestiaia [or Dion] to be at least 1 dr., but we cannot be sure that distance was the only factor in establishing these fares (fixed costs and competition also might have been influential). In any event, since destinations as well as fares are missing at crucial points, most of these figures are necessarily uncertain.

2. c. 415. ? dr. less 4 ob. κόμιστρον (porter charge), for what to where?[4] The absence of the complete figure and context make this partial figure (which may in any event have been exaggerated for comic purposes) impossible to evaluate or use.

3. 405. 2 ob. for Dionysos to be ferried by Charon across Acheron to Hades.[5] One obol seems to have been the standard amount, found in a wide variety of mythological texts,[6] so the 2 ob. here is clearly a comic exaggeration—a full doubling of what in any event is a fictional fare for a fictional trip!

4. 405. 2 dr. for Dionysos' baggage to Hades (his attempt to reduce cost to 9 ob. is unsuccessful).[7] Again, this is pure fiction, but Böckh

---

έσθο τέτταρας ὀβολός· [.........18.........]
[.] μὲν hoι πομπεύοντε[ς.........18.........]
[.]εύεται, τελέτο τὸ hέ[μισυ.]

For a defense of, and comments on, this second text, see M. F. McGregor, "Athens and Hestiaia," in *Studies in Attic Epigraphy, History, and Topography Presented to Eugene Vanderpool* (*Hesperia* Supp. 19) (Princeton 1982) 101–111 at 108–109. H. B. Mattingly, *The Athenian Empire Restored: Epigraphic and Historical Studies* (Ann Arbor 1996) 246–248 suggests a date of 424/3.

4. Ar. fr. 312 (K-A) ap. Poll. vii. 133 (ἀχθοφόροι): τὸ δὲ ἔργον αὐτῶν φορά, καὶ ὁ μισθὸς κόμιστρον . . . 'Αριστοφάνης δ' ἐν τοῖς "Ηρωσι δοκεῖ τὸ κόμιστρον κατὰ τὸ νῦν ἔθος εἰρηκέναι τὴν φοράν, ὅταν εἴπηι· "ὀβολῶν δεουσῶν τεττάρων καὶ τῆς φορᾶς." For the date of the *Heroes*, about the same time as the *Birds*, see K-A III.2 173.

5. Ar. *Ran.* 139–140, 270 (Herakles, Charon and Dionysos):

Ηρ. ἐν πλοιαρίῳ τυννουτῳί σ' ἀνὴρ γέρων
ναύτης διάξει δύ' ὀβολὼ μισθὸν λαβών.

Χα. ἔκβαιν', ἀπόδος τὸν ναῦλον.
Δι. ἔχε δὴ τὠβολώ.

6. See references in K. Dover, *Aristophanes Frogs* (Oxford 1993) 208, and additional figures in my Non-Athenian Catalogue. For this entry, see also "Priests, Oracles and Seers" #7 with n. 9.

7. Ar. *Ran.* 172–177 (Dionysos and corpse "Nekros"):

Δι. ἄνθρωπε, βούλει σκευάρ' εἰς "Αιδου φέρειν;
Νε. πόσ' ἄττα;

thought that these figures might have reflected actual porter charges, as well as negotiations.[8] At a time when public construction workers were getting 1 dr. p.d. and soldiers even less,[9] this seems highly unlikely to me, so I suspect that Aristophanes has exaggerated prevailing charges while retaining a realistic flavor for the negotiations (customer asks for a 25% discount!). How great the exaggeration was we cannot tell precisely, in the absence of contemporary porter charges, but to judge from the 1 dr. p.d. maximum paid to other manual workers it must have been doubled at least.

5. 395/4. 160 dr. p.m. aggregate daily wages for one month for yokes (of oxen?), presumably plus drivers, to haul stone for the Peiraieus fortifications.[10] Neither the length of the journey nor the amount of stone is stated, and, as discussed in greater detail under "Construction and Other Manual Workers" #4, there is no indication as to the number of yokes, so this is not a very useful figure for transport costs.

6. 392/1. 9 dr. for bricks, quan. unst., for Peiraieus fortifications.[11] Again, the number of bricks and distance traveled is not stated, so this figure is not very useful.

Δι. ταυτί.
Νε. δύο δραχμὰς μισθὸν τελεῖς;
Δι. μὰ Δί', ἀλλ' ἔλαττον.
Νε. ὑπάγεθ' ὑμεῖς τῆς ὁδοῦ.
Δι. ἀνάμεινον, ὦ δαιμόνι', ἐὰν ξυμβῶ τί σοι.
Νε. εἰ μὴ καταθήσεις δύο δραχμάς, μὴ διαλέγου.
Δι. λάβ' ἐννέ' ὀβολούς.
Νε. ἀναβιῴην νυν πάλιν.

8. Böckh, *SdA* I 149–150: "Wenn Dionysos in den Fröschen des Aristophanes von einem Lastträger seinen Bündel tragen lassen will, fordert dieser zwei Drachmen; als der Gott dem Schatten neun Obolen bietet, erklärt er, ehe er dieses thäte, müßte er wieder lebendig werden. Wenn diese Unterredung im Schattenreich nicht ein Auftritt aus dem wirklichen Leben ist, hat sie keine Spitze: ein lebender Lastträger zu Athen war wohl eben so unverschämt im Fordern, und wurde weniger geboten, mochte er sagen: 'Ich müßte sterben, ehe ich dieses thäte.'"

9. See "Construction and Other Manual Workers" #3; "Soldiers and Sailors" ##16–19.

10. *IG* II² 1656. 1–6:

ἐπὶ Διοφάντο ἄρχον- *a.* 395/4
τος ⟨Σ⟩κιροφοριῶνος
μηνὸς ἐ[ς] τὰ κατ' ἡ-
μέραν ἔργα· ζεύγ-
εσι τὸς λίθος ἄγοσι
μισθὸς ⁝Η𐅄Δ·

11. *SEG* XXXII 165. 1–3:

7. c. 385? 2 ob. for (individual alone or individual, children, baggage and women?) from Aigina to (Peiraieus); 2 dr. "at most" for individual, children, baggage and women from Egypt or Pontos to (Peiraieus).[12] Although, in this context (a favorable comparison of the power of the helmsman with that of the rhetorician), Plato's point is that the helmsman's compensation is modest, I doubt that he intentionally distorted these figures. But he may have been careless about details: in relation to #1 ([2–3 ob.] for one person from Chalkis to Oropos), 2 ob. could be plausible for one person from Aigina to Peiraieus, although in the intervening c. 60 years we might have expected an increase.[13] But 2 ob. for the entire family and luggage seems less plausible (possibly Plato was not thinking of them when he wrote 2 ob.), and 2 dr. for the transport of the entire family and baggage from Egypt or the Pontos to Peiraieus (a multiple of six for a distance that was at at least fifty times greater than the Aigina-Peiraieus trip) seems low in any event, especially if the 2 ob. for Aigina-Peiraieus is for one person only. Because of all of these uncertainties, I hesitate to place substantial reliance on these figures.

8. c. 379–377. 1 T. 700 dr. for (transport of theoroi and chorus?, quan. unst., from Peiraieus to Delos and back)?[14] This interpretation of a brief, and incompletely published, inscription is suggested by #9, but even if the interpretation is right, the gross figure tells us nothing about the cost per individual of a one-way or round trip to Delos.

ἐπὶ Φιλοκλέους ἄρχον(τος)· π̣λ̣ *a.* 392/1
ίνθος ἐς τὰς ἐπάλξες παρεν-
ενκόσι ΠΗΗΗ ·

12. Pl. *Gorg.* 511d–e: ἐὰν μὲν ἐξ Αἰγίνης δεῦρο σώσῃ [sc. ἡ κυβερνητική], οἶμαι δύ' ὀβολοὺς ἐπράξατο, ἐὰν δὲ ἐξ Αἰγύπτου ἢ ἐκ τοῦ Πόντου, ἐὰν πάμπολυ, ταύτης τῆς μεγάλης εὐεργεσίας, σώσασα ἃ νυνδὴ ἔλεγον, καὶ αὐτὸν καὶ παῖδας καὶ χρήματα καὶ γυναῖκας, ἀποβιβάσασ' εἰς τὸν λιμένα δύο δραχμὰς ἐπραξατο. Aelius Aristeides echoes this passage twice—ii. 370 (Behr): διὰ ταῦτα ὁ κυβερνήτης δύο ὀβολοὺς πραξάμενος, ἐὰν ἐξ Αἰγίνης, ἐὰν δὲ ἐξ Αἰγύπτου, φῄς, ἢ τοῦ Πόντου, δύο δραχμάς, ἐὰν πάμπολυ; iii. 184 (Behr): δύο, φῄς, ὀβολοὺς λαβὼν ἢ δραχμὰς ὁ κυβερνήτης ἀπήλλακται. For "c. 385?" as the "absolute date" of the *Gorgias*, see E. R. Dodds, *Plato Gorgias* (Oxford 1959) 24–25 (earlier observing, however [at 17–18], that the "dramatic date" is variously c. 428 to 405).

13. See "Inflation and Deflation" pp. 240–242.

14. *SEG* XXXIX 170. 22–23: Μαντίαι Θ[ο]ρι(κίωι) τριηράρχωι ΤΧΗΗ (numerals and line numbers derived from photograph published by O. Alexandri, "Χρονικά," *AD* 25 B.1 [1970] 40–91 at 60 with pl. 56a). For the date, see *SEG* XXXIX 170, XL 152.

9. 377/6–375/4. 1 T. 1,000 dr. for theoroi and chorus, quan. unst., (from Peiraieus?) to Delos (and back?), for how many times?[15] This large sum (recorded in the accounts of the Delian amphiktyons) must have covered a great many trips by sea, and for a great many individuals, but it is impossible, as with #8, to determine the cost per individual per (one-way or round) trip.

10. 372. 1,750 dr. freight (ναῦλον) for timber, quan. unst., from Macedon to Peiraieus.[16] Although this information comes from a lawsuit, many corroborating details are supplied, which, if they were false, easily could have been impeached by the defendant Timotheos, so it is likely that 1,750 dr. were in fact paid as ναῦλον, but we are not told how much timber was transported. The fact that only one shipowner (in the singular) is mentioned might suggest that only one shipload was involved,[17] but the figure seems rather high for a voyage that should not have taken much more than a week, so I suspect that more than one load was involved, perhaps in ships belonging to a single individual.[18] If so, the figure becomes less useful as an indication of transport costs.

---

15. *IG* II^2 1635. 34–35:

εἰς κομιδὴν τῶν θεωρῶν καὶ τῶν χορῶ-
[ν] Ἀντιμάχωι Φίλωνος Ἑρμείωι τριηράρχωι ΤΧ⁝

16. [Dem.] xlix. 28–30: ὁ δὲ Φιλώνδας, ᾧ συνέστησεν (sc. Timotheos) τὸν πατέρα τὸν ἐμόν, ἐπειδὰν ἀφίκτηται ἄγων τὰ ξύλα, τὸ ναῦλον παρασχεῖν, εἰς τὴν Μακεδονίαν τὴν πορείαν ἐποιεῖτο. καὶ οὗτοι οἱ χρόνοι ἦσαν περὶ θαργηλιῶνα μῆνα ἐπ' Ἀστείου ἄρχοντος [373/2]. τῷ δ' ὑστέρῳ ἔτει ἀφικομένου τοῦ Φιλώνδου ἐκ τῆς Μακεδονίας ἄγοντος τὰ ξύλα, ἀποδημοῦντος τούτου (Timotheos) παρὰ βασιλεῖ, καὶ προσελθόντος τῷ πατρὶ τῷ ἐμῷ καὶ κελεύοντος τὸ ναῦλον τῶν ξύλων παρασχεῖν ἵνα διαλύσῃ τὸν ναύκληρον, καθάπερ οὗτος (sc. Timotheos) ἐδεήθη ὅτε ἐξέπλει τοῦ πατρὸς καὶ συνέστησε τὸν Φιλώνδαν, προσαγαγὼν πρὸς τὴν τράπεζαν ὁ πατὴρ ἐκέλευσε δοῦναι τὸν Φορμίωνα τὸ ναῦλον τῶν ξύλων, χιλίας ἑπτακοσίας πεντήκοντα. καὶ ἠρίθμησε τὸ ἀργύριον ὁ Φορμίων· καὶ ἐγράψατο μὲν ὀφείλοντα Τιμόθεον (οὗτος γὰρ ἦν ὁ δεηθεὶς τοῦ πατρὸς παρασχεῖν τὸ ναῦλον τῶν ξύλων, καὶ τούτου ἦν), ὑπόμνημα δ' ἐγράψατο τήν τε χρείαν εἰς ἣν ἐλήφθη τὸ ἀργύριον καὶ τὸ ὄνομα τοῦ λαβόντος. καὶ οὗτος ὁ χρόνος ἦν Ἀλκισθένους ἀρχοντος [372/1].

17. So Böckh, *SdA* I 150, n. *b*.

18. Although R. Meiggs, *Trees and Timber in the Ancient Mediterranean World* (Oxford 1982) 208, describes this as "a substantial shipload of Macedonian timber," at 364 he compares the figures for #16: "If 14,040 drachmae was the cost of bringing timber for 100 triremes from Syria [see notes 37 and 38 below], 1,750 drachmae should imply sufficient timber for at least ten triremes. In the case brought against Timotheus the prosecutor charged him with having the timber taken to his house in the Piraeus for his own private building. The amount of timber was too large to make the charge plausible: Timotheos had more probably invested in a stock of ship-timber."

11. 367. 4 T. for Timagoras' journey from Sousa to (Aegean) sea by litter.[19] Because Timagoras also is said to have accepted some enormous bribes or gifts from Artaxerxes (40 T. and 10,000 darics are the sums mentioned),[20] it is possible—and indeed likely, given the amount—that the 4 T. also was a gift-bribe (notwithstanding that it is said to have been paid to the litter bearers), far in excess of the actual cost of paying and maintaining the bearers, so this figure is not a useful indication of actual transport costs.

12. pre-350. 1 ob. [per talent] of red ochre from Koresos (Keos) to (Peiraieus?).[21] The restoration of the quantity seems the only possible one, so I am inclined to accept this freight charge.

13. mid 4th c. 5 (dr.?) (inc.?) for ? from Delos to Athens.[22] This fragmentary line from an account of the Delian amphiktyons is too poorly preserved to give us any reliable information.

14. 333/2? Eleusinian freight:

(a) 228–402 dr. for one column drum from Pentelikos to Eleusis (charge based on 4 dr. per yoke [of oxen] p.d., with a supple-

---

19. Plut. *Pel.* xxx. 9–11: Τιμαγόραν γοῦν Ἀθηναῖοι κρίναντες ἀπέκτειναν, εἰ μὲν ἐπὶ τῷ πλήθει τῶν δωρεῶν, ὀρθῶς καὶ δικαίως· οὐ γὰρ μόνον χρυσίον οὐδὲ ἀργύριον ἔλαβεν, ἀλλὰ καὶ κλίνην πολυτελῆ καὶ στρώτας θεράποντας, ὡς τῶν Ἑλλήνων οὐκ ἐπισταμένων, ἔτι δὲ βοῦς ὀγδοήκοντα καὶ βουκόλους, ὡς δὴ πρὸς ἀρρωστίαν τινὰ γάλακτος βοείου δεόμενος. τέλος δὲ κατέβαινεν ἐπὶ θάλασσαν ἐν φορείῳ κομιζόμενος, καὶ τέσσαρα τάλαντα τοῖς κομίζουσι μισθὸς ἐδόθη παρὰ βασιλέως.

20. Dem. xix. 137: ἐξαπατηθεὶς [sc. Artaxerxes] ὑπὸ Τιμαγόρου καὶ τετταράκοντα τάλαντα, ὡς λέγεται, δεδωκὼς αὐτῷ; Plut. *Art.* xxii. 9–10: Τιμαγόρᾳ δὲ τῷ Ἀθηναίῳ, διὰ Βηλούριδος τοῦ γραμματέως εἰσπέμπψαντι γραμματίδιον ἀπόρρητον, ἡσθεὶς (sc. Artaxerxes) μυρίους τε δαρεικοὺς ἔδωκε, καὶ γάλακτος βοείου δεομένῳ δι' ἀσθενείαν ὀγδοήκοντα βοῦς ἀμέλγεσθαι παρηκολούθουν· ἔτι δὲ κλίνην καὶ στρώματα καὶ τοὺς στρωννύντας ἔπεμψεν, ὡς οὐ μεμαθηκότων Ἑλλήνων ὑποστρωννύναι, καὶ φορεῖς τοὺς κομίζοντας αὐτὸν μέχρι θαλάσσης μαλακῶς ἔχοντα.

21. *IG* II^2 1128. 11–14:

ὅπως δ' ἂν κύρια ἦι [τ]ὰ ψηφίσματα [τὰ πρότερον γεγενημένα Ἀθηναίων κ]- 11
αἱ Κορησίων τὰ περὶ τῆς μίλτου, ἐξάγειν ἐμ πλοίωι ὧι ἂν Ἀθηναῖοι ἀποδείξωσιν, ἐν ἄλλωι] 12
δὲ πλοίωι μηδενί, ναῦλλον δὲ τελεῖν ὀβολὸν τοῦ [ταλάντου ἑκάστου τοῖς ναυ-κλήροις το]- 13
[ὺ]ς ἐργαζομένους· 14

For the date, see Tod II p. 183.

22. *IG* II^2 1636 + *ID* 104-3 + *SEG* XXX 108. 14: π̣αγαγό̣ν̣τ[ι] Ἀθήναζε Π[.]. The Π need not be a number, or, it if is, it need not be a sum of money, or, if it is, it need not be a complete sum.

mentary payment of 1 dr. per half-day for the yokes as a group).[23]

(b) 9 dr. 3 ob. for (9 logs from Peiraieus?), to Eleusis?[24]

(c) Mule trips to Athens: 7 dr. 3 ob. for ? from ?; 4 dr. for thick ropes, quan. unst., from Peiraieus to the Pompeion (in Athens).[25] In each case, the number of mule loads is not stated, so we cannot extrapolate the cost of a single mule load.

15. 329/8. Freight (to Eleusis unless otherwise specified):

(a) Stone—60 dr. for 6 large blocks, from Skambonidai?;[26] 1 dr. 3 ob. for fieldstones, per stone, from Eleusis?[27]

(b) Brick—25 dr. 3 ob. for 1,500 bricks, from Eleusis?; 25 dr. for bricks, per 1,000, from Eleusis?; 15 dr. for bricks, per 1,000, from Melite? to Eleusis or to city Eleusinion?[28]

---

23. *IG* II^2 1673 + *SEG* XXXIV 122. 64–90. The only entry with all figures preserved is found in line 66: ἕτερον σφόνδυλον ἠρξά[μεθα κομ]ιζειν [παρὰ - - Quarrier c. 10 - -]Ο. [- - Date c. 9 - - ἦγεν ζεύγη] :ΔΔΔΙΙΙ: ἐκομίσθη ἐν τρισὶν ἡμέραις, μισθὸς τοῖς ζεύγεσιν : ΗΗΗΗΗ├├. The lowest figure, 228 dr., is recorded in line 81. For more on these figures, and for the date, see "Construction and Other Manual Workers" #5 with n. 14.

24. *IG* II^2 1673. 10–11:

τὰ ξύλα κομίσαι τὰ περιόντα ἐκ Πειραιέως εἰς τ[. .] 10
[- - - - - - - - - - - - - - - - - ων :ΠΙΙΙΙ: ἐμισθώθη :Π├├├├ΙΙΙ: 11

The ΠΙΙΙΙ may apply to something other than τὰ ξύλα.

25. *IG* II^2 1673. 18, 20:

[- - - - - - - - - - -] εἰς ἄστυ Σωσίαι ὀρεωκόμωι :Π├├ΙΙΙ: 18

[- - κομιδὴ τῶν ὑπ]οζωμάτων ἐκ Πειραιῶς εἰς τὸ πομπεῖον Κυπρίωι ὀρεωκόμωι 20
: ├├├├:

26. *IG* II^2 1672. 131–133 + p. 812:

[λ]ίθοι εἰς τὰς παραστάδας τέτταρες μῆκος πεντέποδες, πάχος 131
[ἑπτὰ παλαισταί], πλάτος τρεῖς πόδες, τιμὴ παρ' Ἡνύτου (ἐν) Σκανβωνιδῶν οἰ- 132
κοῦντ(ος) : ΔΔΔΔ : λίθοι δύο εἰς τὰ γεῖ
[σα δωδεκάποδες 𐅄]· κομιδὴ τῶν λί[θω]ν τούτων ἁπάντων Βίωνι : 𐅄Δ : 133

It is possible that both lots of stone—or neither of them—came from the deme where the (metic) seller of the first lot was registered.

27. *IG* II^2 1672. 48–51:

λίθοι ἀρουραῖοι εἰς τὸ στρῶμα τῶι πύργωι καὶ ἐκ τοῦ ἐντὸς ἀντιστρῶσαι ἄχρι 48
τοῦ ἐδάφους τῆς αὐλῆς, ἀ-
ρι⟨θ⟩μὸς :ΗΗΗΙΙΙΙ: τιμὴ τοῦ λίθου :├{Ι}: τούτους ἔτεμεν Δημήτριος, Ἐργασίων, 49
Κύπριος, Εὔαρχος, Μίλακος: κεφ
ΗΗΗΗΗ├├├ · ἀγωγὴ τῶν λίθων τούτων εἰς τὸ ἱερόν, τοῦ λίθου : ├ΙΙΙ : Φιλονίκωι, 50
Εὐξίππωι, Ἀρχίαι, Φερεκλείδε,
κεφάλαιον : ΗΗΗΗ𐅅Π├ : 51

The words ἐκ τοῦ ἐντός suggest that at least some of these stones came from Eleusis, and indeed, the epistatai would have little incentive to look for fieldstones outside of Eleusis!

28. *IG* II^2 1672. 57–59, 22–23:

(c) Lumber—7 dr. for moving 19 large pieces of lumber on rollers (across isthmus of Corinth?), 10 dr. for carrying this lumber down to the sea and loading it onto a boat, 56 dr. for ferrying the lumber from Corinth.[29]

(d) Roof tiles—40 dr. for 100 Corinthian tiles, from Lakiadai?; 6 dr. 4 ob. for 200 Corinthian tiles, from Corinth; 8 dr. for 25 "ordi-

---

πλίνθοι αἱ περιγενόμεναι 57
Χ𐅅 τῶν περυσινῶν, τῶι κομίσαντι :ΔΔΠΙΙΙ: ἀγωγὴ τῶν πλίνθων τῶν παρ' Εὐθίου: τῶν :Χ: ΔΔΠ : κεφάλαι:ΗΗΔΔΠ: ταύ- 58
τας ἤγαγε Καρίων, Ἀρτίμας, Κύπ[ρι]ος, Εὐκλῆς, Κόνων· 60

μισθωτεῖ τῶν πλίνθων τῆς ἀγω- 22
γῆς, ὧν εἵλκυσε Λυκοῦ⟨ρ⟩γος Μελιτεύς, τῶν χιλίων :ΔΠ, Φερεκλείδει Βοιωτίωι δι[ὰ] : ΜΜ𐅆Χ : ΗΗΗ𐅄ΔΔΔΔ : 23

Because the first lot of bricks is left over from the previous year, I suspect that it was moved within Eleusis, and, because in line 56 Euthias is described as Ἐλευσί, I suspect that the second lot also came from Eleusis. Since the seller of the third lot is a demesman of Melite (a city deme), one might expect transport of that lot to cost *more* than transport of the first two lots; because it costs less, I suspect either that Lykourgos of Melite's bricks (a) were already in Eleusis (perhaps he was living there) or (b) were transported from Melite to the city Eleusinion rather than to Eleusis.

29. *IG* II² 1672. 151–159:

[σ]ανίδες πτελείιναι ἑπτὰ εἰς ἀντίζυγα, μῆκος δεκάποδες, πλάτος δεκαδάκτυλοι, πάχος τριδάκτυλ- 151
οι, τιμὴ τῆς σανίδος :Δ⊦⊦⊦⊦: κεφάλαιον : 𐅄ΔΔΔΔΠ⊦⊦⊦: ἕτεραι σανίδες πτελείιναι τέτταρες, μῆκος δεκ- 152
άποδες, πλάτος ἡμιποδίου, πάχος παλαστιαῖαι, τιμὴ τῆς σανίδος :Δ⊦⊦⊦ΙΙΙ: κεφά : 𐅄⊦⊦⊦⊦: ἅτεραι σανίδ- 153
ες πτελείιναι τρεῖς, μῆκος ποδῶν :ΔΠΙ: πλάτος τριπάλαστοι, πάχος ἑγδάκτυλοι, τιμὴ τῆς σανίδ :ΔΔΙΙ: 154
κεφά :𐅄Δ⊦: σανίδες μελίιναι τρεῖς εἰς κανονῖδας καὶ ζυγὰ [τ]αῖς θύραις, τιμὴ τῆς σανίδος :ΔΠ⊦⊦: κεφά 155
𐅄⊦: σανίδες δύο πτελείιναι τοῖς τροχίλοις προσβαλεῖν, μῆκος πεντεκαιδεκάποδες, πλάτος τριπά- 156
λαστοι, πάχος παλαστιαῖοι, τιμὴ τῆς σανίδος :ΔΔ⊦⊦⊦ΙΙΙΙC: ταῦτα πάντα τὰ ξύλα παρ' Ἁγίου Κορινθίο, 157
κεφά :ΔΔΔΔΠ⊦⊦ΙΙΙ: μισθωτοῖς το[ῖς δ]ιακαλίσασιν τὰ ξύλα: Π⊦⊦: μισθωτοῖς τοῖς ἐπὶ θάλατταν κατακο- 158
μίσασιν καὶ εἰς τὸ πλοῖον ἐνθεῖσιν :Δ: ναῦλος τῶν ξύλων τούτων ἁπάντων Κλέωνι πορθμεῖ ᵛ 𐅄Π⊦: 159

Since line 150 ended with a purchase of wood παρὰ Φορμίωνος ἐγ Πειραιῶς, I am inclined to think that all of the wood described in lines 151–157 was purchased from Hagios the Corinthian, even though it might be possible to interpret ταῦτα πάντα τὰ ξύλα in line 157 as referring only to the last two boards. Meiggs, *Trees and Timber* 438, interprets the 10 dr. as going to "those who brought the timber across the isthmus to the port of Cenchreae and loaded it on board ship," but the transport across the isthmus more likely was done by το[ῖς δ]ιακαλίσασιν, since that phrase, as Meiggs says, "implies the use of rollers."

nary" tiles, from ?[30] Sea freight obviously was considerably cheaper than transport by land.

(e) Plaster, stone chips—40 dr. for 60 medimnoi of stone chips, from ?; 5 dr. for 30 medimnoi of black plaster dust (includes rental of sacks), from Ptelea?[31]

(f) Eumolpids (and/or their baggage?) "for the Mysteries"—24 dr. for yokes (of horses or mules?), quan. unst., from Athens?[32]

(g) Firewood, etc.—7 dr. 3 ob. for 67 talents of firewood and 60 faggots [by sea], from Peiraieus?[33]

(h) Miscellaneous—7 dr. 3 ob. for 10 talents of olive-wood wedges, 2 pots of pitch, 2 medimnoi of black pigment, and 25 staters of red ochre, from Athens?[34]

---

30. *IG* II² 1672. 71–73, 209–210:

κεραμίδες Κορίνθιαι παρὰ Δημητρίο ἐλ Λακι οἰκοῦ 71
Η : τιμὴ : Η· κομιδὴ τούτων Ἐλευσῖνάδε :ΔΔΔΔ: κεραμίδες Κορίνθιαι :ΗΗ: ἐκ 72
Κορίνθου, ἡ κεραμὶς :ΙΙΙΙΙ: κεφάλα
Η𐅄ΔΠ⊢ΙΙΙΙ: κομιδὴ τούτων Ἐλευσῖνάδε :Π⊢ΙΙΙΙ: 73

κεραμίδες ἀγελαῖαι προσειωνήθησαν ἐπὶ τὸν θησα- 209
υρὸ[ν παρὰ] Μοιροκλείους :ΔΔΠ: τιμὴ :ΔΔΠ[⊢⊢⊢⊢Ι]: κομιδὴ το[ύτων] Ἐλευσῖ- 210
νάδε Μοιροκλεῖ :Π⊢⊢⊢:

31. *IG* II² 1672. 207–208, 197–199:

λατύπης μέδιμνοι :𐅄Δ: ὁ μέδιμνος :⊦ΙΙΙ: κεφάλαιον :𐅄ΔΔΔΔ: κομιδὴ ταύ- 207
της Ἐλευσῖνάδε Θουδεῖ :ΔΔΔΔ: 208

κονίας με- 197
λαίνης μέδιμνοι :ΔΔΔ: ὁ μέδιμνος :⊦Ι: παρὰ Σωπόλιδος Πτε :ΔΔΔΠ: κομιδὴ τῆς 198
κονίας καὶ σάκκων μισθὸς
Π: 199

32. *IG* II² 1672. 41: ἐξηγηταῖς Εὐμολπιδῶν εἰς ζεύγη μυστηρίοις : ΔΔ⊢⊢⊢⊢ ·

33. *IG* II² 1672. 124–126:

ξύλα εἰς Ἁλῶια, τάλαντα :𐅄ΔΠΙΙ, 124
[τὸ τάλαντ]ον ⊢ΙΙΙ: παρὰ Κ[εφαλί]ωνος? ἐγ Πειραιῶς :ΗΙΙΙ: κληματίδας :𐅄Δ: δύο 125
τοὐβολοῦ, τιμὴ :Π: καταφορὰ τού-
[των ἐπὶ θάλαττα]ν μισθω[τοῖς. να]ῦ[λ]ος τούτων Ἐλευσῖνάδε Μελανθίωι 126
πορθμεῖ :Π⊢⊢ΙΙΙ:

The figure for the μισθωτοῖς who carried the wood to the sea seems to have been omitted.

34. *IG* II² 1672. 9–16:

ξύλα ἐλάϊνα εἰσφῆνας παρὰ Ἡρ- 9
ακλείδου ἐκ τοῦ Θησέου, εἰ[σ]φῆνα[ς τ]άλαντα : Δ : τὸ τάλαντον :⊦ΙΙ: κεφά : 10
Δ⊢⊢⊢Ι[Ι· πρ]ίσις σφηνῶν Ἀρίστωνι ἐν Κ-
ολλυτῶι οἰκοῦντι . . . 11

. . . μίλτου στ- 12
ατῆρες : ΔΔΠ ὁ στατὴρ :ΙΙΙC: κεφά : Δ⊢⊢⊢⊢ΙΙΙC: παρὰ Παμφίλου τοῦ σκην· πίττης 13

(i) Grain—4 ob. for bringing out grain, per 100 medimnoi; 1 dr. 5 1/4 ob. for (bringing out?) 80 1/6 medimnoi (minimum charge?).[35]

(j) Uncertain—12 dr. for ?, from ?[36]

16. 305. 702 gold (staters?) (= 14,040 dr.?) for pine (for 100 triremes?), from (Syria or Cyprus?) to (Peiraieus).[37] If all of Meiggs' premises are accurate,[38] that would work out to c. 140 dr. per load of timber

---

δύο κεράμια, τὰ ξύλα τὰ περὶ τ-
ὸ τεῖχος ἀλεῖψαι, παρὰ Παμφίλου σκη :Δ⊢⊢: μελαντηρίας δύο μέδιμνοι, τιμὴ 14
τοῦ μεδίμνου :Π⊢⊢⊢: κεφάλ ΔΠ⊢ ·
παρὰ Παμφίλου σκηνί : κηκῖδος τρία ἡμιεκτεῖα, ἡ χοῖνι⟨ξ⟩:III, κεφά : Π⊢ : παρὰ 15
Παμφίλου σκηνί: τῶι ἀπαγαγόν-
τι τοὺς σφῆνας καὶ τὴν πίττ[α]ν καὶ τὴν μελαντηρίαν καὶ τὴν μίλτον Ἐλευσῖ- 16
(νάδε) Διοκλείδαι μισθὸς : Π⊢⊢III ·

The mention of the Theseion and Kollytos in lines 10–11 suggest that this shipment came from Athens.

35. *IG* II² 1672 + *Hesperia* 64 (1995) 133, no. 2b. 292–293, 297–299:

μισθωτοῖς τοῖς ἐκφέρουσι 292
τὸν σῖτον, τῶν ἑκατὸν μεδίμνων IIII, κεφά Π⊢⊢⊢ · 293

πυρῶ[ν] μέδιμνοι ΔΔΔΠI , δέκα ἡμ[ι]- 297
εκτεῖα ἔχοντες τὴν ἐπιβολήν, τιμὴ τούτων ΗΗΔΔ⊢ · κριθῶν μέδιμνοι ΔΔΔΔIII, 298
ἡμιεκτε[ῖ]α τέτταρα ἔχοντες τὴν ἐπιβολήν, τιμὴ τούτων, τοῦ μεδίμνου
ἑκάστου ⊢⊢⊢IIIII · σύμπαν τιμῆς κεφάλαιον ΗΗΗ𐅄ΔΔ⟨Δ⟩Π⊢⊢[C] ·
ἀπὸ τούτου προμετρητεῖ ⊢⊢ · μισθωτοῖς ⊢IIIIIT · 299

For the possible minimum charge, see "Construction and Other Manual Workers" p. 115, n. 31.

36. *IG* II² 1672. 231–232: [- - 37 - -] I Ἐλευσῖνάδε Δ⊢⊢ ·

37. *IG* II² 1492 + *SEG* XXXII 159. 118–124:

[ἐ]πὶ [Κο]- *a.* 306/5
[ροίβο]υ ἄ[ρχ]οντος ἐπὶ τῆς Ἀντι[οχ]ίδος δωδεκάτης πρ[ύ]-
[τανε]ίας ἐνάτει φθίνοντ[ος ἐδώκ]αμεν εἰς τὴν τ[ῶ]ν [ξύ]- 120
[λω]ν κομιδ[ὴ]ν τῶν π[ιτ]ύ[ων] πα]ρὰ [βασιλ]έων [εἰ]ς τὰς ναῦς
[χρυσ]οῦς ἑπτακοσίους δύο κα[τὰ ψή]φ[ι]σμα δ[ή]μου, ὃ ἔ[γρ]-
[αψε]ν Φίλιππος Ἀχαρνεύς, ταμί[αι τῶν στρ]ατιωτικῶν Ἅ[β]ρω[νι]
[Βουτ]άδει ·

The archon's name, restored in lines 118–119, is preserved in line 97. Kirchner identifies the "kings" as Antigonos and Demetrios.

38. Meiggs, *Trees and Timber* 364 (quoted in n. 18 above), seems (without comment) to have converted the gold pieces to drachmas at an exchange rate of 20 dr. = 1 gold st. (this is the rate for Persian darics given by Xen. *Anab.* i. 7. 18 and Harp., δαρεικός). In line 121, I print his reading (*Trees and Timber* 145–146 with n. 87) of π[ιτ]ύ[ων] (pine) rather than Kirchner's π[ε]υ[κῶν] (fir). Meiggs suggests Cyprus rather than Syria as the source of this pine (*Trees and Timber* 145–146, 398 [citing Theophr. *H.P.* v. 7. 1 for an implied shortage of pine in Syria—in fact Theophrastos speaks explicitly only of an abundance of cedar and a shortage of fir]; cf. Meiggs 364, quoted in n. 18 above ["Syria"]). For the 100 triremes given by Demetrios to Athens, see Diod. Sic. xx. 46. 4: ἔδωκεν

sufficient for one trireme, but this conclusion would rest on a number of uncertain foundations.

17. A.D. 2nd c. 2 ob. for boatman on Eridanos, per customary trip?[39] Because we are not told the usual length, in time or distance, of this trip, this figure is difficult to use.

18. A.D. 2nd c. 4 ob. from (Peiraieus) to Aigina per person.[40]

What can be said about these figures as a whole?[41] Although there is a fairly large number of figures, they frequently are unaccompanied by the information we most want—the quantities transported, the number of trips, the time spent and/or the distance traveled.

For individuals, the only usable figures are ##1 and 7, and possibly 17 and 18. Of these, the only really secure figure is #1 (4 ob. from Chalkis to Hestiaia in c. 446/5?). To the extent that we can rely on #7, we can add, for c. 385, 2 ob. for Aigina to Peiraieus and 2 dr. for Egypt or the Pontos to Peiraieus. All of these figures suggest that individual fares were very modest in relation to daily wages of c. 3 ob. to 1 dr. p.d.[42] It may be that passengers simply went along as extra cargo on freight boats, without special accommodation or any provision for food; if so, their carriage would have added nothing to the shipowner's costs, and he therefore could have afforded to charge them very little.[43] Again, to the extent

---

αὐτοῖς . . . ὕλην δὲ τὴν ἱκανὴν ναυσὶν ἑκατόν. Since Diodoros assigns this gift to 307, can we be sure that his timber is the same as that in the inscription?

39. Lucian *Electr.* 3 (boatmen to narrator): εἰ δὲ ἦν τοιοῦτον (that the Eridanos river poplars wept tears of amber), οἴει ἡμᾶς δυοῖν ὀβολοῖν ἕνεκα ἐρέττειν ἂν ἢ ἕλκειν τὰ πλοῖα πρὸς ἐναντίον τὸ ὕδωρ. . . .;

40. Lucian *Nav.* 15: καίτοι πρῴην καὶ ἐς Αἴγιναν ἐπὶ τὴν τῆς Ἐνοδίας τελετὴν, οἶσθα, ἐν ἡλίκῳ σκαφιδίῳ πάντες ἅμα οἱ φίλοι τεττάρων ἕκαστος ὀβολῶν διεπλεύσαμεν. . . .;

41. The figures collected in the catalogue under "Tangible Personal Property with Transport Cost Specifically Included" are not useful for purposes of this discussion because the transport costs cannot be isolated. Four other figures, from *Talents*, "E. Building Materials: Building Materials with Transport Cost Specifically Included," are interesting: *IG* II^2 1672. 26, 183 (bricks per thousand, with transport, for 38 and 75 dr., respectively) suggest that the 75 dr. bricks had to travel a longer, or a more arduous, distance than the 38 dr. bricks, and *IG* II^2 1672. 195–196 (earth per load with transport—4 dr. 1 ob. for Skirad earth, 2 dr. 3 ob. for Lousiad earth) suggests that Skiras (in Phaleron) is farther from, and at a lower elevation than, the city Eleusinion than Lousia (west of the ἄστυ).

42. See "Inflation and Deflation" pp. 240–242.

43. Böckh, *SdA* I 150, makes the shipowner too charitable: "der Handel sehr einträglich war, sodaß man den Reisenden nicht viel abzunehmen nöthig fand."

we can rely on #7, it looks as if fares did not rise significantly from c. 446 to c. 385. On its face, #18 indicates that the fare from Peiraieus to Aigina had doubled between the fourth century B.C. and the second century A.D., but in the absence of other evidence for wage and price changes in that 500-year period I hesitate to draw any major conclusions. For the same reason—the absence of other wage and price information for second-century A.D. Athens—I hesitate to say anything about #17, which in any event is difficult to use.

Freight charges are even more uncertain. The first reliable figure that gives quantities and distance as well as cost is #12 (1 ob. [per talent] of red ochre from Keos to Peiraieus), but none of the figures that come after it gives the cost per talent for any commodity, so it is not usable for comparative purposes.[44] The freight charge for column drums in #14 (a) is based exclusively on time (rather than weight or distance). Within the year 329/8 (#15), we have a number of reliable figures, but often quantities, distance and/or time are uncertain or absent, and in any event we have nothing earlier or later with which we can compare these figures; the one thing that does seem to be clear (unsurprisingly) is that sea freight was cheaper than land transport (#15 [d]). There are too many uncertainties about the quantities in ##10 and 16 to permit a reliable comparison of the costs of a shipload of timber.

44. Unfortunately, #15 (h) does not give the net cost of transporting 25 staters of red ochre, which might then be compared with #12. Indeed, #12 provides our *only* net cost of transport based on weight; cf. ##15 (g) and (h).

Chapter 12

Travel Allowances

In this category are sums granted for travel expenses, usually by the state to ambassadors. There are three general uncertainties about these sums. First, none of them is accompanied by any (even general) indication of the kinds of expenses covered by the grants; I suspect that in most cases they were were intended to cover food, lodging, transport costs and incidentals, and that in any event the state (or other grantor) knew what expenses, and what standard of living, it intended to support. Second, for most sums the period of time covered by the grant is not stated; again, I suspect that in most such cases the state (or other grantor) knew how long a particular mission should take. Third, although it is natural to assume that the sums granted were intended to *cover* the first and second variables, we cannot always be certain that this was so: the frequently occurring phrase εἰς ἐφόδια could mean "*towards* travel expenses" rather than "for [all] such expenses."[1]

Apart from the lists collected by Böckh and Fränkel,[2] the only significant prior discussion of these figures has been Westermann's,[3] whose interpretation is discussed at the end of this chapter.

1. 480. 8 dr. distributed to each citizen embarking on ships before Salamis—μισθός, τροφή or ἐφόδια?[4] This whole story may well

---

1. LSJ s.v. εἰς V.2 categorizes this usage as "of Purpose or Object . . . freq. of expenditure *on* an object," citing *IG* II^2 102. 11 and *IG* II^2 116. 41 (quoted in notes 23 and 28 below). But the fact that money is granted *on* or *for* an object does not require that it be adequate to cover the *entire* cost of the object.

2. Böckh, *SdA* I 303–304, with Fränkel's additions in *SdA* II 67*, n. 442, collecting ##4, 6, 8, 10, 13, 15, 16, 18, 26 and 27.

3. Westermann, "Ephodia."

4. Cleidemus 323 *FGrH* 21(see Plut. below); Arist. *Ath. Pol.* xxiii. 1: τῶν γὰρ στρατηγῶν ἐξαπορησάντων τοῖς πράγμασι καὶ κηρυξάντων σώ[ι]ζειν ἕκαστον ἑαυτόν, [sc. ἡ ἐν Ἀρείωι πάγωι βουλὴ] πορίσασα δραχμὰς ἑκάστωι ὀκτὼ διέδωκε καὶ ἐνεβίβασεν εἰς τὰς ναῦς; Plut. *Them.* x. 6–7: οὐκ ὄντων δὲ δημοσίων χρημάτων τοῖς Ἀθηναίοις, Ἀριστοτέλης μέν φησι τὴν ἐξ Ἀρείου πάγου βουλὴν πορίσασαν ὀκτὼ δραχμὰς ἑκάστῳ τῶν

be legendary, but insofar as it is true, at this early date, before the introduction of military pay, the 8 dr. probably would not have been μισθός for military service, even if all the grantees did serve aboard triremes.[5] Notwithstanding Plutarch's use of the word ἐφοδίων, it also would not have been a travel allowance in the sense of most of the figures collected here, since the grantees were not one or a few individuals on a mission of known or predictable duration. Long before any of these categories had been regularized, the 8 dr. probably was intended as a cash allowance for food and other necessaries during a period of potentially great danger—a combination τροφή/ἐφόδιον for the entire body of citizen sailors. Because the time period was not stated, and indeed could not have been known at the time the grant was made, the 8 dr. figure may have been calculated simply by dividing the available funds by the number of grantees.[6] In any event, whether or not the story is true, the uncertainty of the time period means that this figure is not useful for comparative purposes.

2. 447/6 or 427/6? [1 dr.] or [4 ob.] p.d. [ἐφόδια] for Athenian οἰκισταί to Kolophon?[7] The preserved portions of the inscription as a whole (especially οἰκισταί in line 42 and references to Kolophon in

---

στρατευομένων αἰτιωτάτην γενέσθαι τοῦ πληρωθῆναι τὰς τριήρεις, Κλείδημος δὲ καὶ τοῦτο τοῦ Θεμιστοκλέους ποιεῖται στρατήγημα. . . . φησὶν . . . τὸν οὖν Θεμιστοκλέα . . . εὐπορῆσαι τοὺς ἐμβαίνοντας εἰς τὰς ναῦς ἐφοδίων. For this entry, see also "Welfare and Support Allowances and Distributions" #3.

5. The *Ath. Pol.*'s account gives no indication that the 8 dr. was μισθός, although Plutarch's loose discussion (πορίσασαν ὀκτὼ δραχμὰς ἑκάστῳ τῶν στρατευομένων αἰτιωτάτην γενέσθαι τοῦ πληρωθῆναι τὰς τριήρεις) shows how it could be so construed. But see "Soldiers and Sailors" #1 (with n. 17) for the introduction of military pay *after* the Battle of Salamis.

6. M. B. Wallace, "Herodotos and Euboia," *Phoenix* 28 (1974) 22–44 at 27, n. 16, observes "8 dr. = 24 days x 1/3 dr./day—a realistic maintenance figure for the period Athenian sailors were on duty at Salamis." This may be true, but the 24-day period could not have been known beforehand.

7. *IG* I^3 37. 20–21, 24–26:

οἱ δ' αἱρεθέντες πέ[ντε οἰκισταὶ οἱ ἐς Κο]-
[λοφôνα. . . .]

[τôν δὲ αἱρεθέντων λα]-
[μβανέτο] ἕκαστος τêς ἐμ[έρας ἑκάστες ἐς ἐφόδια δρ]-
[αχμέν· τὸ] δὲ ἀργύριον ὀφε[λόντον Κολοφόνιοι καὶ Λ]-
[εβέδιο]ι καὶ Διοσιρîται κ - - - - - - - - - - - - - - - - - -

For the alternative dates, see the Corpus commentary plus addenda at p. 939; M-L 125; *SEG* XLII 9.

lines 3, 9, 14, 17, 28 and 40) make it clear that it concerns an Athenian settlement in Kolophon, and the preserved portions of this passage (ἀργύριον ὀφε- and ἕκαστος τε̂ς ἐμ-) indicate that money is to be paid on a per diem basis, but the most important information for purposes of this study—the rate of 1 dr. and its character as ἐφόδια—has been wholly restored, so this "evidence" must be used with extreme caution. The restoration τε̂ς ἐμ[έρας ἐς ἐφόδια τέτταρας ὀ | βολός] would occupy the same number of letter spaces and would be more plausible for the earlier alternative date of 447/6. Cf. the 4 ob. p.d. for (a) the Athenian? officials? or rowers or soldiers? sent to Miletos? in 450/49? and (b) the Eleusinian epistatai in c. 449–447?.[8]

3. c. 440–425. 20 [dr. ἐφόδια?] for ἄποικοι.[9] This inscription is even more fragmentary than that in #2, so that, apart from the uncertainties as to (a) whether ἐφόδια are provided and (b) whether the figure is 20 *drachmas*, we cannot even be sure that (c) *any* payment is provided. In any event, the time period is not stated,[10] so that, even if εἴκοσι | [δραχμὰς ἐφόδια] is correctly restored, it is not a useful figure for comparative purposes.

4. 425. 2 dr. p.d. μισθός for ambassadors to Persian King for 11 years—μισθός or ἐφόδια?[11] In the fourth and third centuries, we hear only of ἐφόδια, and not of μισθός, for ambassadors and similar representatives (##8, 10, 12–18, 20, 22, 26, 27). It is possible that in the fifth century they *were* paid μισθός, but it is probably more likely that Aristophanes was using that word loosely, to reinforce the comic distinction between στρατωνίδεις and μισθαρχίδεις.[12] In any event, the 2 dr. p.d. rate probably, and the 11 year term certainly, are exaggerated for comic purposes: 2 dr. p.d. is twice what other public officials and soldiers were being paid as μισθός in the 430s and 420s.[13] Possi-

---

8. "Soldiers and Sailors" #2; "Public Officeholders" #4.

9. *IG* I^3 47 A. 10–11:

[?λαβόντον δ]ὲ hοι ἄποικοι εἴκοσι
[δραχμὰς ἐφόδια? - - - - -]

10. Scattered references to τριάκοντα ἐμερο̂ν, in lines A. 4 and B. 5–6 and 7–8, are not clearly related to the "payments" in A. 10–11.

11. Ar. *Ach.* 65–67, 90, quoted with discussion of chronology under "Public Officeholders" #8 with n. 13.

12. Ar. *Ach.* 596–597, quoted and discussed under "Public Officeholders" #9 with n. 14.

13. See "Public Officeholders" ##6, 13; "Soldiers and Sailors" ##3–5.

bly the exaggeration consisted of a simple doubling, i.e., perhaps the normal rate was 1 dr. p.d., but this is necessarily speculative since we have no trustworthy evidence for ambassadors' μισθός/ἐφόδια in this period.

5. 425. 8 dr. given by Dikaiopolis to Amphitheos for private peace mission to Sparta.[14] Since the 8 dr. in line 130 is not expressly called ἐφόδια, it may simply be a fanciful fee for peacemaking.[15] But Dikaiopolis' offer in line 130 may be a response to Amphitheos' earlier statement (in line 53) that he has no ἐφόδια. On that interpretation, Westermann estimated 3 days of travel each way, and 3 days of business, for a total of 9 days, which would work out to .9 dr. p.d.[16] In fact, we are not told how long Amphitheos' journey would have taken (as an immortal he could have gone instantaneously!), and it is hard to believe that Aristophanes went to the trouble of calculating the duration of the journey before selecting (i.e., creating) the 8 dr. figure. On the other hand, why did he select the specific figure of ὀκτώ, rather than (say) πέντε or δέκα δραχμάς?[17] Because we cannot be sure that Aristophanes intended this figure to represent ἐφόδια, or, if he did, that he intended it to be serious (usually he exaggerates figures), and because in any event we do not know the time period

---

14. Ar. *Ach.* 53 (Amphitheos speaking):

ἀλλ' ἀθάνατος ὤν, ἄνδρες, ἐφόδι' οὐκ ἔχω.

Ar. *Ach.* 130–132 (Dikaiopolis responding):

ἐμοὶ σὺ ταυτασὶ λαβὼν ὀκτὼ δραχμὰς
σπονδὰς ποιῆσαι πρὸς Λακεδαιμονίους μόνῳ
καὶ τοῖσι παιδίοισι καὶ τῇ πλάτιδι·

Note also line 137, where Dikaiopolis exclaims to an ambassador to Thrace (called Θέωρος!) that μισθόν . . . 'φερες πολύν. It is hard to square the passages referred to in notes 11 and 12 with Westermann's statement ("Ephodia" 204) that "[t]here is no indication in the *Acharnians* that money may be made by the *presbeis* out of ambassadorial work."

15. For which see "Miscellaneous Workers" #1.

16. Westermann, "Ephodia" 207–208. 2 days of business would yield the (neater) result of 1 dr. p.d., which would be consistent with the contemporary daily wages referred to in n. 13.

17. The final syllable of πέντε or δέκα could be long "by position" and therefore fit the meter. Westermann, "Ephodia" 207, suggests that ὀκτώ might have seemed funny to an "audience accustomed to . . . vote expense-money in multiples of ten," but we have no fifth-century evidence for such a custom.

and lack reliable comparative evidence for ἐφόδια rates in this period, it is difficult to evaluate this 8 dr. figure.[18]

6. 425. 3 dr. (p.d.) for ambassadors or taxiarchs? to Thrace, μισθοφοροῦντας (μισθός or ἐφόδια?).[19] As discussed in greater detail under "Public Officeholders" #9 (= "Soldiers and Sailors" #8), this passage could be interpreted as referring to the pay or ἐφόδια of an ambassador or a taxiarch, but it should not be taken seriously as independent evidence of any of these things. The 3 dr. figure is even more exaggerated than the 2 dr. figure in #4.

7. pre-422. 2 ob. (p.d.) for theoros or rower to Paros?, μισθός or ἐφόδιον?[20] As discussed in greater detail under "Public Officeholders" #12, I am inclined to view the 2 ob. here as a payment to a theoros rather than a rower, but there is no indication in the passage as to whether it is μισθός or ἐφόδιον, and no other evidence (so far as I am aware) as to whether theoroi received only one (or either) of these two kinds of payments. Even if the figure is accurately stated, we do not know how long before 422 it would have been paid. For all of these reasons, this is not a useful figure for comparative purposes.

8. 5th/4th c.? 1,000 dr. ambassador's ἐφόδιον.[21] Because the ultimate source for this figure is unknown, it is difficult to assess, and, in any event, the absence of the time period makes it useless for comparative purposes.

---

18. But Westermann, "Ephodia" 207, was surely right to see here a comic contrast between Amphitheos' modest allowance of 8 dr. for the entire mission and the extravagant 2–3 dr. p.d. for state ambassadors or taxiarchs in ##4 and 6.

19. Ar. *Ach.* 602, quoted under "Public Officeholders" #9, n. 14.

20. Ar. *Vesp.* 1188–1189 et Σa-b, d, quoted in "Public Officeholders" notes 29, 30 and 32.

21. Herm. *Stat.* ii. 140: μεταστάσεως μὲν παράδειγμα ὁ πρεσβευτής, ὃν εἴσω τριάκοντα ἡμέρων δέον ἐξιέναι λαβόντα παρὰ τοῦ ταμίου χιλίας δραχμὰς εἰς ἐφόδιον, μὴ λαβὼν καὶ διὰ τοῦτο μὴ ἐξελθών, εἶτα κρινόμενος; Σ Herm. *Stat.* (Walz IV 245, lines 29–30): τοῦ μὴ λαβόντος τὰς χιλίας δραχμὰς πρεσβευτοῦ; Σ Herm. *Stat.* (Walz IV 697–698, n. 12): τῆς δὲ μεταστάσεως ἡ μὲν τίς ἐστιν ἐπὶ ῥητὸν, ἧς παράδειγμα τὸ εἰρημένον ζήτημα, ἡ δὲ ἐπὶ πρώσωπον, ὡς τόδε, νόμος τὸν πρεσβευτὴν λαβόντα παρὰ τοῦ ταμίου χιλίας δραχμὰς εἰς ἐφόδιον ἐξιέναι, πρεσβευτής τις χειροτονηθεὶς καὶ μὴ λαβὼν παρὰ τοῦ ταμίου τὰ χρήματα οὐκ ἐξῆλθεν καὶ ὑπάγεται τῷ νόμῳ. I date this 1,000 dr. figure vaguely to the "5th/4th c.?" because Hermogenes' examples generally come from Attic court cases in the late fifth or the fourth centuries (cf. the immediately following reference [Herm. *Stat.* ii. 140] to συγγνώμης δὲ παράδειγμα οἱ δέκα στρατηγοὶ οἱ διὰ τὸν χειμῶνα μὴ ἀνελόμενοι τὰ σώματα καὶ κρινόμενοι, i.e., the generals at the Battle of Arginousai in 406). Hermogenes' source for the ambassadors who were granted but did not take 1,000 dr. ἐφόδιον is not preserved—it does not seem to fit with the 1,000 dr. in #18.

9. 395. 30 dr. for two citizens, apiece, given by Mantitheos as ἐφόδια (for τὰ ἐπιτήδεια?) to Battle of Haliartos in Boiotia.[22] We are not told precisely what constituted the ἐπιτήδεια. They may well have included arms as well as food. Nor are we told the time period. Haliartos is a very long day's walk from Athens, but Mantitheos had no way of knowing how long the citizen soldiers would be in Boiotia. His 30 dr. gift, like the 8 dr. grant to the citizens embarking for (what turned out to be) the Battle of Salamis in #1, necessarily was an estimate, perhaps with a generous cushion in this time of great public danger, for expenses that could not be known precisely in advance. But the dual uncertainties as to the expenses and time period mean that this figure is not useful for comparative purposes.

10. c. 375–373. 20 dr. for ambassadors to Macedon, apiece.[23] Their journey might have taken precisely 20 days, e.g., 5 days travel each way and 10 days for oathtaking and recording, in which case the grant would have been 1 dr. p.d.—but 10 days does seem a bit long for this (apparently) uncomplicated bit of diplomacy. Alternatively, it could have taken (say) 3 days by sea each way and 4 days of business, for a total of 10 days, or 2 dr. p.d. A third possibility was suggested by Westermann: 5 days travel each way and 3 days of business, for a total of 13 days, or "slightly over one and one-half drachmas per day for each man."[24] Since the ambassadors had returned from Macedon, the demos was in a position (a) to know precisely how long their

---

22. Lys. xvi. 14: Συλλεγέντων τοίνυν τῶν δημοτῶν πρὸ τῆς ἐξόδου (to the Battle of Haliartos), (Mantitheos, the defendant-speaker) εἰδὼς αὐτῶν ἐνίους πολίτας μὲν χρηστοὺς ὄντας καὶ προθύμους, ἐφοδίων δὲ ἀποροῦντας, εἶπον ὅτι χρὴ τοὺς ἔχοντας παρέχειν τὰ ἐπιτήδεια τοῖς ἀπόρως διακειμένοις. καὶ οὐ μόνον τοῦτο συνεβούλευον τοῖς ἄλλοις, ἀλλὰ καὶ αὐτὸς ἔδωκα δυοῖν ἀνδροῖν τριάκοντα δραχμὰς ἑκατέρῳ, οὐχ ὡς πολλὰ κεκτημένος, ἀλλ' ἵνα παράδειγμα τοῦτο τοῖς ἄλλοις γένηται.

23. *IG* II^2 102. 8–16:

ἐπαινέσαι [δὲ κ]αὶ τοὺς πρέσβε[ις]
τοὺς πεμφθέντ[ας ὑπ]ὸ τοῦ δήμου εἰς Μ[ακ]-
εδονίαν περὶ τ[ῆς συ]μαχίας· δοῦναι δ[ὲ]
το[ῖ]ς πρέσβεσ[ιν τοῖ]ς αἱρεθεῖσιν εἰ[ς]
[ἐφ]όδια ΔΔ δρ[αχμὰς ἑ]κάστωι τὸν ταμί[α]-
[ν τ]οῦ δήμο· κ[αλέσαι κ]αὶ ἐπὶ ξένια τοὺ[ς]
[πρέ]σβεις [τοὺς παρ' Ἀμ]ύντο καὶ τοὺς π[ε]-
[μφθ]έντα[ς ὑπὸ τõ δήμο] ἐπὶ δεῖπνον εἰς
[τὸ πρυτανεῖον εἰς αὔρ]ιον.

For the date, see Tod II, p. 92.

24. Westermann, "Ephodia" 205. But see n. 36.

journey had taken and (b) to set the ἐφόδια on a (roughly) per diem basis. Unfortunately, because *we* do not know how long the ambassadors' journey took, we cannot be sure what that basis was.

11. c. 368. 300 dr. given by Apollodoros to Deinon for trip from Athens to Aigina.[25] Aigina was only a few hours' sail from the Peiraieus, so much more than the costs of transport, food and lodging for c. 2 days must have been intended here. Perhaps bribes or "exit visas" also were included. Also, possibly, in this *lawsuit* the figure has been exaggerated. In any event, the absence of any specification of the time period or expenses makes this figure useless for comparative purposes.

12. 367. [30 drach]mas for herald sent to Aitolia to secure release of Eleusinian spondophoroi.[26] Since the first portion of the decree provides for the election of only one herald, the [30-drach]ma ἐφόδ[ια] probably applies to him alone. The duration of his mission into hostile territory and the scope of his expenses in that situation may not have been easy to estimate in advance, so the grant may have been intentionally liberal. Whether it was in fact *30* drachmas we cannot know for sure, but that restoration seems the most likely (of the usual multiples of 10 drachmas) in the context of a 32-letter stoichedon line.

---

25. [Dem.] liii. 6–8: (Nikostratos) ἁλίσκεται ὑπὸ τριήρους καὶ κατήχθη εἰς Αἴγιναν, καὶ ἐκεῖ ἐπράθη. . . . ἀποστέλλω τὸν Δείνωνα ιὸν ἀδελφὸν αὐτοῦ (Nikostratos) εὐθὺς ἐπὶ τοῦτον, δοὺς ἐφόδιον αὐτῷ τριακοσίας δραχμάς. . . . καὶ τάς τε τριακοσίας, ἃς τῷ ἀδελφῷ αὐτοῦ ἔδωκα ἐφόδιον ὅτε ἐπορεύετο ἐπὶ τοῦτον. . . . For the date, see L. Gernet, ed., *Démosthène, Plaidoyers Civils* III (Paris 1959) 86–87. The 300 dr. did not include Nikostratos' ransom, which was 26 mn., according to [Dem.] liii. 7.

26. *Agora* XVI 48. 14–18, 27–29:

ΣΤΟΙΧ. 32

ἑλέσθαι τὴμ βο-
[υ]λὴν αὐ[τ]ίκα μάλα κήρυκα ἐξ Ἀθηναίων ἀπ-
ά̣ντων ὅσ̣[τ]ις ἀφικόμενος πρὸς τὸ κοινὸν
[τὸ Αἰ]τ̣ω̣[λῶν] ἀ̣[παιτήσει τοὺς] ἄ̣ν̣δ̣ρ̣ας ἀφεῖ-
[ναι]

ἐς ἐφόδ[ια τὸν ταμίαν τοῦ δήμου ΔΔΔ δραχ]-
μὰς ἐκ τ[ῶν κατὰ ψηφίσματα ἀναλισκομέν]-
ω̣ν̣ τ̣ῶ̣ι̣ [δήμωι. *vacat* (?)]

For a slightly different version of the first part of this text, see Tod II, no. 137.

13. c. 364–362 or 349/8 or c. 341–339? 50 dr. for ambassadors sent to purchase grain from Orontes in Mysia, apiece.[27] Travel by sea should not have taken more than 2–3 days each way, for a total of c. 5 days, but the time necessary (to find and meet with Orontes, and to make the grain purchases) might have been difficult for the demos to predict, and in any event is difficult for us to estimate. Moreover, these ἐφόδια may have been intended to cover ambassadorial gifts, as well as food, lodging and travel. If the grant were based solely on an estimate of 2 dr. p.d., the time allowed for business would have been c. 20 days, but this is necessarily uncertain.

14. 361/0. 20 dr. for ambassadors to Thessaly, apiece.[28] As with #10, this could be based on an estimate of 5 days of travel each way (by land) and 10 days of preliminary discussions leading up to the oathtaking (for a total of 20 days at 1 dr. p.d.), or 2 days of travel each way (by sea) and 6 days of business (for a total of 10 days at 2 dr. p.d.), or some other calculation.[29]

---

27. *IG* II[2] 207 bcd + Osborne D12 (vol. II, p. 63). 7–10, 24:

ἐλέσθαι τὸν δῆμον αὐτίκα μ[ά]λ̣[α - c. 3 -]
[- - πρέσβεις - - · τοὺ]ς δὲ αἱρε[θέντας τὸ ἀρ]γύριον λαβόντας ὁπόθεν ἂν ὁ δῆμος [ψηφίσ]-
[ηται ἰέναι ὡς Ὀρόντην κ]αὶ ἀποδεῖξαι [τὰ σύμβολα] ἐν τῶι Θαργηλιῶνι μηνὶ καὶ ἀπάγειν ἀ̣[π' Ὀρ]-
[όντου τὸν σῖτον. . . .]

[- - c. 24–25 - - τὸν τα]μίαν τοῦ δήμου τὰ [ἐ]φόδια τῶν πρέσβεων ἑκάστωι 𐅄

For the date of c. 364–362, see Osborne II 61–80. For the other alternative dates, see *SEG* XXXI 70, XXXIII 79, XXXVII 71, XXXVIII 61, XXXIX 83, XL 71, XLI 43.

28. *IG* II[2] 116. 20–26, 40–42:

ὅπως δ' [ἂ]ν καὶ Θετταλοὶ ὀμόσωσι τῆι π-
[όλ]ει, ἑ[λ]έσθα[ι τ]ὸν δῆμον πέντε ἄν[δρ]ας ἐ[ξ] Ἀθηναίων ἁ-
πά[ν]των οἵτινες ἀφικόμενοι εἰς Θετταλία[ν] ἐξορκώ-
[σ]οσιν Ἀγέλαο[ν τ]ὸν ἄρχοντα καὶ τὸς [π]ολ[ε]μά[ρ]χος καὶ
τὸς ἱ[π]πάρχος καὶ τὸς ἱππέ[α]ς καὶ τὸ[ς ἱερ]ο[μν]ήμονας
καὶ τοὺς ἄλλο[ς] ἄρχοντας ὁπόσοι ὑπὲ[ρ] τô κοινô τô Θε-
τταλῶν ἄρχοσ[ι]ν τόνδε τὸν ὅρκον. . . .

τοῖς δὲ πρέσ-
[βεσι δ]ôναι τὸν [ταμί]αν τ[ο]ῦ [δήμ]ο εἰς ἐφόδια v ΔΔ δραχ-
[μὰς] ἑκάστωι.

29. Westermann, "Ephodia" 208–209, estimated 3 days for travel each way and 3 days for business, for a total of 9 days. Since he thought that there was a standard rate in this period of 1 1/2 dr. p.d. (see pp. 218–219 below), he thought that 20 dr. would result in an excessive rate and therefore restored v Δ v in line 41, yielding a rate of "1 1/10" dr. p.d. But the Corpus edition

15. c. 357. 10 or [2]0 dr. for ambassadors to Karystos (apiece)?, 20 dr. for ambassadors to Eretria, Chalkis and Hestiaia, apiece, and 10 dr. for ambassadors who negotiated alliance with Euboian cities, apiece.[30] The Euboian cities were even closer by sea than Thessaly, so travel time could have taken 1–2 days each way, and oathtaking, etc. could have been accomplished in about 2 days per city. For the ambassadors to Karystos, that would work out to about 5 days (= 2 or 4 dr. p.d., depending on whether the gross figure was 10 or 20 dr.). If, for the second grant, the same ambassadors went successively to Eretria, Chalkis and Hestiaia, the journey to Eretria might have taken 1 day, from there to Chalkis a couple of hours, from Chalkis to Hestiaia 1 day, and the return to Athens 2 days, for a total of about 4 days of travel time, to which could be added 6 days for business (2 days per city), for a total of 10 days; at 2 dr. p.d., this could account for their 20 dr. If the grant for the ambassadors to Karystos is 10 rather than 20 dr. and their trip took c. 5 days, the rate for both groups of ambassadors would be a uniform 2 dr. p.d.,[31] which could have been applied

---

(which was published in 1913, after Westermann's 1910 article) seems to be based on the stone itself and a squeeze, so the 20 dr. figure should be accepted. (20 dr. would be reconcilable with Westermann's postulated "usual" rate of 1 1/2 dr. p.d. if the mission lasted c. 13 days.) D. J. Mosley, *Envoys and Diplomacy in Ancient Greece* (*Historia* Einzelschrift 22) (Wiesbaden 1973) 75, thought that the journey might have taken 4 days each way, with c. 3 days for business, for a total of "about twelve days." As with all of these missions, we simply do not know the time period.

30. *IG* II^2 124. 4–6, 10–18:

[ἐλέσθ]-
[αι δὲ πέντε ἄνδρας οἵτινες ἥξουσ]ι ἀποληψό[μενοι τὸς ὅρ]-
[κος παρὰ τῶν Καρυστίων·]

ἐπαινέ[σαι] δὲ καὶ Μ[έ]νωνα τὸν στρατηγ[ὸν κ]-
[αὶ] τὸς πρέσβες τὸς πεμφ[θέ]ντας εἰ[ς] Κάρυστον καὶ καλ[έσα]-
[ι] επὶ δεῖπνον εἰς τὸ πρυτ[α]νεῖον ἐς [α]ὔριον· ἀποδôναι δ[ὲ α]-
[ὐ]τοῖς καὶ ἐφόδια τὸν ταμ[ία]ν τοῦ δή[μ]ο ^{v}Δ δραχμὰς ἐκ τῶν [ε]-
[ἰ]ς τὰ κατὰ ψηφίσματα ἀναλ[ι]σκομένω[ν τῶ]ι δήμωι· ἀποδοῦ[ν]-
[α]ι δὲ τὸν ταμίαν τô δήμο κα[ὶ τ]οῖς πρέ[σβεσ]ι τοῖς πρεσβεύ-
[σ]ασι εἰς Ἐρέτριαν καὶ Χαλ[κ]ίδα καὶ ἐς [Ἑστί]αιαν ΔΔ δραχμ-
ὰς ἑκάστωι· ἀποδôναι δὲ κα[ὶ] τοῖς τὴν συ[μμα]χίαν πρεσβε[ύ]-
σασι τὸν ταμίαν τô δήμο Δ δ[ρ]αχμὰς [ἑκάστωι.]

In line 13, B. Leonardos ("'Αττικὸν ψήφισμα τοῦ 320/9," *AD* 1 [1915] 195–224 at 213 [noted in *IG* II^2 124 (p. 658), and followed by Tod II, no. 153]) read [Δ]Δ, rather than the Corpus' ^{v}Δ, but both are possible. For the date, see *SEG* XXXVIII 59.

31. Cf. Westermann, "Ephodia" 206 with notes 3 and 5, who seems to have estimated 6 days at 1 dr. 4 ob. p.d. Both rates (6 days at 1 dr. 4 ob. p.d. and 5 days at 2 dr. p.d.) work only if the figure in line 13 is ^{v}Δ.

with some precision since the grants were voted *after* the ambassadors had returned. The ambassadors who negotiated the alliance with the Euboian cities ought to have been paid on the same basis as the other two groups. Two drachmas per day is plausible for all three groups, but, since the figure for the ambassadors to Karystos and the durations of all three trips are unknown, this is necessarily uncertain.

16. pre-355 or 342? 30 dr. for ambassadors to Euboian cities, apiece.[32] Because this figure is larger than the 10–20 dr. given to ambassadors to Euboia in #15, their missions probably lasted longer, and the demos no doubt took that fact into account when making its grant, after the ambassadors returned. 15 days at 2 dr. p.d. is plausible, but unverifiable, as the basis for the figure.

17. 352. [?] dr. for men sent to Delphi to inquire about cultivation of the Eleusinian sacred orgas, apiece; 5 dr. for men chosen to decide disputed boundaries of the sacred orgas, apiece.[33] We are not

---

32. *IG* II^2 149. 11–17:

ἐπαινέσαι
[δὲ τοὺς πρέσβεις τ]ῶν Ἀθηναίων τὸς πεμφθέντας
[καὶ τὸς πρέσβεις τὸ]ς ἐκ τῶν συμμάχων καὶ καλέ-
[σαι ἐπὶ δεῖπνον ἐς τ]ὸ πρυτανεῖον εἰς αὔριον. ἀ-
[ποδοῦναι δὲ εἰς ἐφό]δια τοῖς πρέσβεσι τὸν ταμ-
[ίαν τοῦ δήμου ἐκ τῶν] κατὰ ψηφίσματα ἀναλισκο-
[μένων τῶι δήμωι τρ]ιάκοντα δραχμὰς ἑκάστωι.

For the date, see *SEG* XXI 265.

33. *IG* II^2 204. 5–12, 42–49, 62–65:

[- ἑλέσθαι τὸν δῆμ]ον δέκα ἄνδρα-
[ς ἐξ Ἀθηναίων ἁπάντων αὐτίκα μάλα, πέντε δὲ] ἐκ τῆς βουλῆς· ν
[τοὺς δὲ αἱρεθέντες δικάζειν ἐν τῶι Ἐλευσ]ινίωι τῶι ἐν ἄστ-
[ει περὶ τῶν ὅρων τῶν ἀμφισβητουμένων] τῆς ἱερᾶς ὀργάδος ὀ-
[μόσαντας τὸν νόμιμον ὅρκον ἢ μὴν] μήτε χάριτος ἕνεκα μήτ' ἔ-
[χθρας ψηφιεῖσθαι, ἀλλὰ ὡς δι]καιότατα καὶ εὐσεβέστατα· τὰ
[ς δ' ἕδρας ποεῖν συνεχῶς ἀ]πὸ τῆς ἕκτης ἐπὶ δέκα τοῦ Ποσιδεῶ-
[νος ἕως ἂν διαδικασθῆι] ἐπὶ Ἀριστοδήμου ἄρχοντος. . . . (352/1 B.C.)

. . . ἑλέσθω
δὲ ὁ δ[ῆμ]ος [τρ]εῖς ἄνδρας ἕν[α] μ[ὲ]ν ἐκ τῆς βουλῆς, δύο δὲ ἐξ Ἀθην-
αίω[ν ἁ]πάντων, οἵτ[ιν]ες εἰ[ς Δ]ελφοὺς ἀφικόμενοι τὸν θεὸν ἐπ-
ερ[ήσ]ο[ν]τ[α]ι [κα]θ' ὁ[π]ότερα τὰ γρ[άμ]ματα ποιῶ[σ]ιν Ἀθηναῖοι περ-
ὶ τῆ[ς ἱ]ερ[ᾶ]ς ὀρ[γάδ]ος ε[ἴ]τ[ε] τ[ὰ] ἐκ τῆς [χ]ρυσῆς ὑδρίας εἴτε τὰ ἐκ
τῆ[ς ἀ]ρ[γ]υρ[ᾶς (i.e., whether it should be cultivated or not)· ἐπειδ]ὰν [δ]ὲ
[ἥκ]ωσιν παρὰ τοῦ θεοῦ, καθελόντωσα-
ν τὰ[ς] ὑδ[ρί]α[ς καὶ] ἀνα[γ]νωσθ[ήτ]ω τῶι δήμωι ἥ τε μαντεία καὶ τὰ
[ἐ]κ τῶ[ν κα]ττ[ι]τέρω[ν] γρ[ά]μματα. . . .

told how long the mission to Delphi would have taken, and indeed, because of unpredictable delays at Delphi, it may have been less easy (than for diplomatic missions) to estimate in advance. Even if we did know, that information would not help here since the sum granted has not been preserved. The 5 dr. for the fifteen Athenian citizens who were to determine the disputed boundaries of the orgas is not called ἐφόδια, properly, since these men were to remain in the ἄστυ. If they had homes in the city, or had access to free lodgings there, it would not have been necessary for any of the 5 dr. to go for the sort of "hotel" costs that ambassadors often might have incurred. The 5 dr. may, therefore, have been thought of as a kind of replacement wage, rather like our jury pay. How adequate it would have been would have depended, of course, on the length of their proceedings, which were potentially open-ended (lines 10–12): this clearly is a flat-rate grant that probably was set by the demos on the basis of how long they thought the job should take—two to five days at 1–2 dr. p.d.?

18. 346. 1,000 dr. for 10 ambassadors on the Second Embassy to Philip in Macedon for "3 whole months."[34] From Demosthenes' text, one might assume that the ambassadors were gone for c. 90 days. For 10 ambassadors, this would mean that c. 900 man-days were covered by the 1,000 dr. ἐφόδιον, or 1.1 dr. p.d. But the actual duration of their mission was only about 69 days,[35] which would work out to 690 man-days, or 1.45 dr. p.d. Obviously, Demosthenes exaggerated the length of the journey, in order to support his characterization of the embassy as intentionally dawdling. Did he also exaggerate the 1,000 dr.? I am inclined to think not, since that figure would be a

---

[δ]οῦναι δὲ καὶ τῶ̣ν αἱρεθ-
έ[ντων εἰς Δελφοὺς ἑκάστωι . . .] δρ[α]χμὰς εἰς ἐφόδια· δῶναι δὲ κα[ὶ]
το[ῖς αἱρεθεῖσιν ἐπὶ τὴν ἱερ]ὰν ὀργάδα : Π : δραχμὰς : ἑκάστ-
[ωι ἐκ τῶν εἰς τὰ κατὰ ψηφίσμα]τα ἀναλισκομένων τῶι δήμωι·

For the men chosen to decide the disputed boundaries, see also "Public Officeholders" #24.

34. Dem. xix. 158: ἀλλὰ τρεῖς μῆνας ὅλους ἀποδημήσαντες καὶ χιλίας λαβόντες δραχμὰς ἐφόδιον παρ' ὑμῶν. . . .

35. The ambassadors departed on 3 Mounychion, or immediately afterwards (Aeschin. ii. 91–92, Dem. xix. 154), returned on 13 Skirophorion (Dem. xix. 58), and thus were absent about 69 days (27 in Mounychion, 29 in Thargelion and 13 in Skirophorion). See W. W. Goodwin, *Demosthenes On the Crown* (Cambridge 1901) 258–261, 302, 307. This chronology also seems to have been followed recently by E. M. Harris, *Aeschines and Athenian Politics* (New York 1995) 79, 89.

matter of public record and his falsification of it would be easy to refute (unlike his statement about "three whole months," which, except for the "whole," was true!). If the figure was not exaggerated, what is its significance? Certainly that each ambassador was given 100 dr. as ἐφόδιον, and that when the mission was over, that figure turned out to be 1.45 dr. p.d. But if Demosthenes' charge is in effect correct (i.e., that the mission took longer than expected), and if (as seems likely from all of these figures except ##10, 15 and 16) the amount was voted in advance, the *intended* amount per day would have been greater. How much greater would have depended on the expected length of the mission. If we compare the grant here with #10, where ambassadors to Macedon were given 20 dr. apiece, it may be that this mission was expected to take five times as long, and if the earlier mission was expected to take c. 10 days, this one might be expected to take c. 50, which would work out to 2 dr. p.d.[36]

19. post-336/5. [?] dr. as πολιτῶν ἐφόδι[α]—for exiles?[37] Not enough of this decree is preserved for us to determine who received the ἐφόδια or for what purpose—and in any event the figure is not preserved.

20. c. 334–313. 20 dr. for ambassador to foreigner Iatrokles.[38] Because we do not know *who* this Iatrokes was, we have no idea *where*

---

36. In #10, I suggested that c. 10 days might have been its estimated length, and it certainly should not have been much less than 8 (3 days of travel each way and 2 days of business), in which case the rate in #10 would be 2 1/2 dr. p.d. Westermann, "Ephodia" 205–206, may have worked backwards from the 69-day duration of #18 (at 100 dr.) to arrive at his estimate of c. 13 days at c. 1 1/2 dr. p.d. for #10.

37. *IG* II^2 435. 3–5, 9–11:

[. . . .^{9}. . . . .] πολιτῶν ἐφόδι[α -]
[. . . .^{8}. . . .] δραχμὰς ἐκ τῶν κ[ατὰ ψηφίσματα ἀναλισκομένω]-
[ν τῶι δήμωι]·

[. . . ταῦτα δὲ εἶναι α]-
[ὐτοῖς ἕως ἂν τ]ὴν πατρίδα κομίσωνται καὶ . . . . . .^{12}. . . . . .]
[. . . . .^{10}. . . . . δι]ασεσωιμένους. . . .

I place square brackets around the lacunas at the beginnings of lines 3 and 4 of the Corpus text.

38. *IG* II^2 264. 3–6, 9–12:

[ἑλέσθαι δὲ κα]ὶ πρεσβευτὴν ἕ-
[να ἄνδρα ἐξ Ἀθηναί]ων ἁπάντων, ὅστις
[ἀπαγγελεῖ πρὸς Ἰ]ατροκλέα τὴν εὔνο-
[ιαν, ἣν ὁ δῆμος ἔχ]ει πρὸς αὐτόν. . . .

he was and therefore where the ambassador was sent, so this is not a useful figure for comparative purposes.[39]

21. 329/8. 250 dr. for Eleusinian σπονδοφόροι.[40] As discussed in greater detail under "Public Officeholders" #28, we are not told how many σπονδοφόροι there were, how long they were to be away, or whether the 250 dr. was ἐφόδια, τροφή, μισθός, other things or a combination thereof, so it is impossible to use this figure.

22. c. 328/7. 50 dr. for ambassador sent to Herakleia Pontica to recover sails of (metic) grain merchant Herakleides of (Cypriot) Salamis.[41] Travel by sea might have taken 5–6 days each way,[42] and negotiation should not have consumed more than 5–6 more days, for a maximum total of c. 15–18 days, and this would work out to an ἐφόδιον of c. 3 dr. p.d.

δ-
[ῶναι δὲ τῶι αἱρε]θέντι πρεσβευτῆι ἐ-
[φόδια τὸν ταμί]αν τοῦ δήμου ΔΔ δραχμ-
[άς, . . .]

For the date, and Iatrokles' status as a foreigner, see Tracy, *ADIT* 122, 126.

39. Cf. Westermann, "Ephodia" 205–206, who assumed that this Iatrokles was the Athenian who was held prisoner in Macedon in c. 348–346, and on that assumption calculated ἐφόδια at an assumed rate of c. 1 1/2 dr. p.d. for a journey lasting an assumed 13 days. As with #10 (see n. 36), Westermann may have been working backwards from #18.

40. *IG* II^2 1672. 4: [σ]πο[ν]δοφόροις ἐπὶ νή[σ]ων εἰς μυστήρια τὰ μεγάλα ΗΗ𐅄·

41. *IG* II^2 360 + p. 660. 35–44:

ἐπειδὴ δὲ καταχθεὶς ὑπὸ Ἡρακλεωτῶν πλέων Ἀθή-
ναζε παρειρέθη τὰ ἱστία ὑπ' αὐτῶν, ἑλέσθαι πρεσβ-
ευτὴν ἕνα ἄνδρα ἐξ Ἀθηναίων ἁπάντων, ὅστις ἀφικόμενος ε-
ἰς Ἡράκλειαν ὡς Διονύσιον ἀξιώσει ἀποδοῦναι τ-
ὰ ἱστία τὰ Ἡρακλείδου καὶ τὸ λοιπὸν μηδέν' ἀδικε-
ῖν τῶν Ἀθήναζε πλεόντων· καὶ ταῦτα ποιῶν τά τε δί-
καια ποιήσει καὶ οὐθενὸς ἀτυχήσει τοῦ δήμου τ[ο]ῦ Ἀ-
[θηναίων] τῶν δικαίων· δοῦναι δὲ τῶι αἱρεθέντι πρεσβευ-
τεῖ εἰς ἐφόδια τὸν ταμίαν τοῦ δήμου : 𐅄 : δραχμὰς ἐκ τῶ-
ν κατὰ ψηφίσματ' ἀναλισκομένων τῶι δήμωι.

For the date, see Schwenk, pp. 342–344. Kirchner identified the Dionysios in line 38 as tyrant of Herakleia Pontica, citing Diod. Sic. xvi. 88. 5, to which add xx. 77. 1. Westermann, "Ephodia" 209–212, estimated 6 days of sea travel each way plus about 10 days for business, for a total of 22 days, or c. 2 1/2 dr. p.d. Mosley (as in n. 29) 75–76, apparently relying on the misprint of Π in line 43 of the original Corpus publication (before correction by p. 660), reported that the amount granted was only 5 dr.

42. Herakleia was a long day's trireme row from Byzantion (Xen. *Anab.* vi. 4. 2), and Lampsakos could be a fast two-day sail from the Peloponnese (Xen. *Hell.* ii. 1. 30), so a voyage at normal speed from Athens to Herakleia should not have taken more than five or six days.

23. 328/7 or c. 321–319? [? dr. ἐφόδια] provided by Eurylochos of Kydonia to Athenians?[43] Since it is not certain that lines 19–20 contained *any* reference to ἐφόδια and since, in any event, there is no evidence as to the amount of the ἐφόδια, this text is not useful for purposes of this study.

24. pre-324. 8 dr. given to Aristogeiton by mistress Zobia for journey to Megara.[44] In this speech against Aristogeiton, we must be suspicious of any allegation that is made against him, but in this particular case, although the general allegation is that Aristogeiton exhibited callous ingratitude to his former protectress, the odd figure of 8 dr. seems a modest, i.e., uninflated, figure. Even if it is accurate, however, we are not told how long it was supposed to last: if only as far as Megara itself, it would have been a generous allowance for a day's journey!

25. pre-322. 1 dr. p.d. for amphiktyons to Delos, paid by Delos, probably ἐις σίτησιν.[45] If so, 1 dr. p.d. evidently was regarded as an appropriate amount for food. But what about lodging, i.e., to what extent was there an equivalence between σίτησις and ἐφόδιον?

26. c. 307–303. 50 dr. for 3 ambassadors sent to Byzantion to look after proclamation of gold crown and erection of bronze statue, apiece.[46] Apart from the journey to and from Byzantion (3–4 days

---

43. *IG* II^2 399 + *SEG* XXXIV 71. 5, 10, 15–20:
ἐπειδὴ . . . Εὐρύλοχος
. . . πολλοὺς Ἀθηναίων λ[υτρωσά]-
μενος ἐκ Κρήτης ἀπέστ[ειλε τοῖς]
αὐτοῦ ἀναλώ̣μασιν καὶ [αἴτιος ἐ]-
γένετο τοῦ σωθῆναι ἐ[κ τῶν πολ]-
[εμίω]ν εἰς τὴν ἰδίαν, συν[τάξας εἰς
[ἐφόδια . . . ^{5}. . ? δραχμάς . . .]
For the date, see *SEG* XXXIV 71, XXXIX 95.

44. Dem. xxv. 56: δοῦσα (Zobia) δραχμὰς ὀκτὼ ἐφόδιον καὶ χιτωνίσκον καὶ ἱμάτιον ἐξέπεμψεν εἰς Μέγαρα. For the date of this speech in 324, see G. Mathieu, *Démosthène, Plaidoyers Politiques* IV (Paris 1947) 132.

45. Arist. *Ath. Pol.* lxii. 2, quoted and discussed under "Public Officeholders" #30 (f) with notes 58 and 62.

46. *IG* II^2 555. 16–33:
ὅπως δ' ἂν ὅ τε στέφανος ἀναγορε-
[υθεῖ] ἐν Βυζαντίωι καὶ ἡ εἰκὼν σταθεῖ ἡ Ἀσκ-
[ληπι]άδου χειροτονῆσαι τὸν δῆμον τρεῖς ἄ-
[νδρα]ς ἐξ Ἀθηναίων ἁπάντων, οἵτινες ἀφικό-
[μενοι] εἰς Βυζάντιον ἀξιώσουσιν τὸν δῆμο-

each way, for a total of 6–8 days?; see n. 42), the business there might have taken more than the usual amount of time, because of the statue. A flat-rate grant based on an estimate of 3 dr. p.d. (cf. #22) would have allowed for c. 10 days of business.[47]

27. c. 286–244. [20 dr.] for ambassadors to ?, apiece.[48] Not enough of this decree survives to allow us to speculate where, for how long, or for what purpose these ambassadors were sent.

As a whole, what can be said about these figures?

The most promising figures for comparative purposes might be thought to be those that are per diem allowances (##2, 4, 6, 7 and 25). Unfortunately, the figure in #2 is uncertain, ##4 and 6 seem to be comic exaggerations, and in ##7 and 25 it is not clear that the figures are for ἐφόδια. So the per diem figures are not very helpful for comparative purposes.

A second criterion for comparison is destination. In ##10 and 18, it is Macedon, the figures being 20 and 100 dr. apiece. One might be tempted to to explain the increases between ##10 and 18 as caused by inflation, but there is no other attested fivefold increase from c. 375 to 346, so the most likely explanation is simply that the ambassadorial

---

[ν τὸν Βυ]ζαντίων ψηφίσασθαι τὸν στέφανον
[ἀναγορε]ῦσαι ἐν τῶι θεάτρωι Διονυσίων [τῶ]-
[ι ἀγῶνι κ]αὶ τὴν εἰκόνα στῆσαι τὴν Ἀσκλη[πι]-
[άδου ἐν τ]εῖ ἀγορᾶι ἣν ὁ δῆμος ὁ Ἀθηναίων . .
[. . . . . . . ε]ν αὐτοῦ καὶ διδάσκειν αὐτοὺς [ὅτι]
[ταῦτα πρ]άττοντες χαριοῦνται τῶι [δήμωι, τ]-
[ῆς δὲ ποι]ήσεως τοῦ στεφάνου καὶ τ[ῆς εἰκόν]-
[ος ἐπιμε]λη[θ]ῆναι τὸν ἐπὶ τεῖ διο[ικήσει με]-
[τὰ τῶν α]ἱρεθέντων πρέσβεων· δο[ῦναι δ' ἑκάσ]-
[τωι τῶν α]ἱρεθέντων πρέσβεω[ν ἐφόδιον τὸν]
[ταμίαν τ]οῦ δήμου πεντήκον[τα δραχμὰς ἐκ τ]-
[ῶν εἰς τὰ] κατὰ ψηφίσματα [ἀναλισκομένων τ]-
[ῶι δήμωι].

47. Westermann, "Ephodia" 209, 211, estimated 5 days for sea travel each way, and 10 days for business, for a total of 20 days, yielding a rate of 2 1/2 dr. p.d. Either rate would have allowed 10 days for the manufacture and erection of the statue.

48. *IG* II^2 525 + 675 cd + *SEG* XXXIV 72. 4–7:

δοῦναι δὲ ἐφόδ-
[ια τῶν αἱρεθέντων πρ]έσβε[ων ἑκάστ]ωι τὸν ταμίαν τοῦ
[δήμου ^{v} ΔΔ δραχμὰς] ἐκ τῶν εἰς τ[ὰ κατὰ] ψηφίσματα ἀναλ-
[ισκομένων τῶι δή]μωι

For the date, see *SEG* XXXVIII 90.

mission to Philip in 346 was expected to last longer. The 10–20 dr. differences in figures for ambassadors to various Euboian cities in the brief period of (at most) 357–342 (##15 and 16), and the 10 dr. difference(s) within #15, also suggest that it was the *duration* of these missions that determined the figures.

A third criterion for comparison are the various figures themselves. For the most part, they are flat-rate allowances in multiples of 10 dr. Prima facie, this suggests that they, like the figures for inscribers, were intended to be rough, but not precise, estimates of the ambassadors' actual travel expenses, probably based on the duration of their mission. This would explain the language εἰς ἐφόδια, "*towards* travel expenses," which might imply that everyone understood that the trip might cost more (see n. 1). Unlike other sums of money handled by public officials in Athens, the ambassadors evidently did not have to account for ἐφόδια,[49] but since the figure usually was set in advance, the ambassadors no doubt would have had an incentive to transact their business speedily.[50]

If these allowances were based on the expected length of the ambassador's journey, the key remaining question is, what was the (rough) per diem rate allowed by the demos? Westermann, after estimating the duration of the embassies in ##10, 15 and 20 (but see n. 39), concluded that there was a standard rate of c. 1 1/2 dr. p.d., for which he then found confirmation in #18.[51] He concluded:

> For the period from 370 to 340 B.C. . . . , the *ephodia* were evidently voted by the *Demos* on the following calculation. A rough estimate was made of the number of days needed to carry out the commission and return to Athens. The amount was then voted in some multiple of ten—ten, twenty, thirty, fifty, a thousand drachmas, on a basis of a necessary expense of about 1 1/2 drachmas per day. . . .[52]

---

49. E. Badian suggests to me that these ἐφόδια may have been like the per diem allowances for food, lodging and mileage expenses allowed by the United States Internal Revenue Code and the Regulations thereunder, without any requirement of detailed documention that the amounts were actually spent, only that the taxpayer was away from home during the days in question.

50. I am uncertain as to why a few amounts (##10, 15 and 16) were paid *after* the mission, but they do not seem to involve supplements to earlier grants.

51. Westermann, "Ephodia" 205–207. But see n. 36.

52. Westermann, "Ephodia" 207.

As indicated above, we really cannot tell how long the missions lasted, so this first part of Westermann's argument (that there was a standard rate of c. 1 1/2 dr. p.d.) is necessarily speculative and, indeed, it may be contradicted by the figures themselves in #14 (see n. 29). In the discussions of individual figures (##10, 13–16, 18), I have observed that a rate of 2 dr. p.d. would be consistent with all figures in the period c. 375–346, and I regard that as a likely, but necessarily unproveable, hypothesis. If this hypothesis is correct, it would indicate that the compensation of (at least some) public officeholders had risen from 1 dr. p.d. (the highest figure attested in the fifth century) to 2 dr. p.d. by c. 375.[53]

The second part of Westermann's argument (that the rate had risen to 2 1/2 dr. p.d. between 346 and 325)[54] is perhaps closer to the truth, at least for the period after c. 330, but 3 dr. p.d. also is possible (cf. ##22 and 26 with notes 41 and 47). The increase in the period c. 330–300 may be paralleled by a similar (50%) increase for inscribers.[55]

---

53. See "Public Officeholders" ##6, 13.
54. Westermann, "Ephodia" 209–212.
55. See "Inscribers" pp. 164–165.

Chapter 13

Welfare and Support Allowances and Distributions

Most of these figures were collected and discussed by Böckh.[1] Since then there has been a more up-to-date collection (of figures and scholarship) by Buchanan,[2] followed by brief but sensible comments by Pickard-Cambridge et al.[3]

1. 594/3 or 561–527? Dole, amount unstated, for those injured in war (and also war orphans, and persons maimed and disabled?), introduced by Solon or Peisistratos?[4] Since the amount is not stated by any of the sources, for purposes of this study the scope and date of this allowance need not be discussed.[5]

2. 483. 10 dr. available for distribution to each citizen (100 T. total) from Laureion mines, but used instead for triremes.[6] 100 T. (*Ath. Pol.*) =

---

1. Böckh, *SdA* I 274–287, 308–313.

2. Buchanan, *Theorika* 28–88; see also review thereof by G. E. M. de Ste. Croix, *CR* (n.s.) 14 (1964) 190–192.

3. Pickard-Cambridge, *DFA* 265–268.

4. Heracleides Pont. fr. 149 (Wehrli) (see Plut. below); Plut. *Sol.* xxxi. 3–4: καὶ νόμους αὐτὸς (Peisistratos) ἑτέρους ἔγραψεν, ὧν ἐστι καὶ ὁ τοὺς πηρωθέντας ἐν πολέμῳ δημοσίᾳ τρέφεσθαι κελεύων. τοῦτο δέ φησιν Ἡρακλείδης καὶ πρότερον ἐπὶ Θερσίππῳ πηρωθέντι τοῦ Σόλωνος ψηφισαμένου μιμήσασθαι τὸν Πεισίστρατον; Diog. Laert. i. 55: (Solon thought that it was) ἀπειρόκαλον γὰρ τὸ ἐξαίρειν τὰς τούτων (athletic victors) τιμάς, ἀλλὰ μόνων ἐκείνων τῶν ἐν πολέμοις τελευτησάντων, ὧν καὶ τοὺς υἱοὺς δημοσίᾳ τρέφεσθαι καὶ παιδεύεσθαι; Σ Aeschin. i. 103 (Dilts no. 223): . . . τῶν λελωβημένων καὶ ἀδυνάτων. νόμος γὰρ ἦν Σόλωνος ὁ κελεύων τοὺς τοιούτους ἐκ τῶν δημοσίων τρέφεσθαι. For war orphans receiving an allowance at least as early as 432, see Arist. *Ath. Pol.* xxiv. 3: ἔτι δὲ πρυτανεῖον καὶ ὀρφανοὶ καὶ δεσμωτῶν φύλακες· ἅπασι γὰρ τούτοις ἀπὸ τῶν κοινῶν ἡ διοίκησις ἦν.

5. For more on the origin of this allowance, see F. Jacoby on Philochorus 328 *FGrH* 197; R. S. Stroud, "Greek Inscriptions: Theozotides and the Athenian Orphans," *Hesperia* 40 (1971) 280–301 at 288 with n. 17.

6. Hdt. vii. 144. 1: ὅτε Ἀθηναίοισι γενομένων χρημάτων μεγάλων ἐν τῷ κοινῷ, τὰ ἐκ τῶν μετάλλων σφι προσῆλθε τῶν ἀπὸ Λαυρείου, ἔμελλον λάξεσθαι ὀρχηδὸν ἕκαστος δέκα δραχμὰς· τότε Θεμιστοκλέης ἀνέγνωσε Ἀθηναίους τῆς διαιρέσιος ταύτης παυσαμένους νέας τούτων τῶν χρημάτων ποιήσασθαι διηκοσίας ἐς τὸν πόλεμον; Arist. *Ath. Pol.* xxii. 7: ἔτει δὲ τρίτωι μετὰ

600,000 dr. ÷ 10 dr. (Hdt.) = 60,000 citizens, an improbably high number at this time, so the two traditions should not be merged. In any event, this distribution, which never was made, would have been a one-time windfall, for every citizen, and thus would not have been a support allowance.

3. 480. 8 dr. distributed to each citizen embarking on ships before Salamis—μισθός, τροφή or ἐφόδια?, for what period? As discussed in greater detail under "Travel Allowances" #1, this grant—if the story in Arist. *Ath. Pol.* xxiii. 1 and Plut. *Them.* x. 6–7 is true—probably was a combination τροφή/ἐφόδιον for the entire body of citizen sailors at a time of great public emergency, but because the effective per diem allowance could not have been known when the grant was made, the 8 dr. figure is not useful for comparative purposes.

4. 480. 2 ob. p.d. for each Athenian refugee, plus education costs for children, voted as support (τρέφειν) by Troizenians.[7] On its face, this seems to mean 2 ob. per individual, without regard to age or gender, i.e., 2 ob. apiece for each woman and child. The attribution of the decree to a certain Nikagoras of Troizen lends it an air of authenticity, but public support of education at this early date would be suspect, as would Troizen's ability to afford this very large outlay, so I follow Habicht in suspecting that it is a fourth-century reworking or fabrication.[8]

ταῦτα Νικοδήμου ἄρχοντος, ὡς ἐφάνη τὰ μέταλλα τὰ ἐν Μαρωνείαι καὶ περιεγένετο τῆι πόλει τάλαντα ἑκατὸν ἐκ τῶν ἔργων, συμβουλευόντων τινῶν τῶι δήμωι διανείμασθαι τὸ ἀργύριον Θεμιστοκλῆς ἐκώλυσεν, οὐ λέγων ὅ τι χρήσεται τοῖς χρήμασιν ἀλλὰ δανεῖσαι κελεύων τοῖς πλουσιωτάτοις Ἀθηναίων ἑκατὸν ἑκάστωι τάλαντον, εἶτ' ἐὰν μὲν ἀρέσκει τὸ ἀνάλωμα, τῆς πόλεως εἶναι τὴν δαπάνην, εἰ δὲ μή, κομίσασθαι τὰ χρήματα παρὰ τῶν δανεισαμένων. λαβὼν δ' ἐπὶ τούτοις ἐναυπηγήσατο τριήρεις ἑκατόν, ἑκάστου ναυπηγουμένου τῶν ἑκατὸν μίαν, αἷς ἐναυμάχησαν ἐν Σαλαμῖνι πρὸς τοὺς βαρβάρους.

7. Plut. *Them.* x. 5: οἱ πλεῖστοι τῶν Ἀθηναίων ὑπεξέθεντο γενεὰς καὶ γυναῖκας εἰς Τροιζῆνα, φιλοτίμως πάνυ τῶν Τροιζηνίων ὑποδεχομένων· καὶ γὰρ τρέφειν ἐψηφίσαντο δημοσίᾳ, δύο ὀβολοὺς ἑκάστῳ διδόντες, καὶ τῆς ὀπώρας λαμβάνειν ἐξεῖναι τοὺς παῖδας πανταχόθεν, ἔτι δ' ὑπὲρ αὐτῶν διδασκάλοις τελεῖν μισθούς. τὸ δὲ ψήφισμα Νικαγόρας ἔγραψεν.

8. C. Habicht, "Falsche Urkunden zur Geschichte Athens im Zeitalter der Perserkriege," *Hermes* 89 (1961) 1–35 at 18, 20–21. For other examples, see #5 and "Actors, Artists, Musicians and Writers" ##1, 5.

5. c. 467. 100 mn. and land, plus 4 dr. p.d., for Lysimachos, son of Aristeides.[9] I follow Davies in believing that this decree also is a fourth-century fabrication.[10]

6. 440s? Theorikon allowance for theatre seats, amount unstated, introduced by Perikles?[11] I am inclined to agree with Buchanan that, since "no extant Fifth Century document uses any such word as 'theorika' or 'theorikon,'"[12] Perikles probably did not initiate this allowance, although he did spend public funds on festivals and other public entertainments. In any event, since no *figure* is recorded for any allowance at this period, this evidence is not directly pertinent for this study.

7. 410–404. 2 ob. (p.d.) dole ("diobelia") instituted by Kleophon; in ?407/6 briefly reduced to 1 ob. or 1 ob. for war orphans?; at 2 ob. (p.d.) in 406 and 405; Kallikrates promised to add 1 ob. but then abolished; for at least part of 405/4 a grain distribution.[13] These are our first reliable

---

9. Dem. xx. 115: Λυσιμάχῳ δωρειάν, ἑνὶ τῶν τότε χρησίμων, ἑκατὸν μὲν ἐν Εὐβοίᾳ πλέθρα γῆς πεφυτευμένης ἔδοσαν, ἑκατὸν δὲ ψιλῆς, ἔτι δ' ἀργυρίου μνᾶς ἑκατόν, καὶ τέτταρας τῆς ἡμέρας δραχμάς. καὶ τούτων ψήφισμ' ἔστιν Ἀλκιβιάδου, ἐν ᾧ ταῦτα γέγραπται; Plut. *Arist.* xxvii. 2: (after Aristeides' death) Λυσιμάχῳ δὲ τῷ υἱῷ μνᾶς μὲν ἑκατὸν ἀργυρίου καὶ γῆς τοσαῦτα πλέθρα πεφυτευμένης ἔδωκεν ὁ δῆμος, καὶ ἄλλας δραχμὰς τέσσαρας εἰς ἡμέραν ἑκάστην ἀπέταξεν, Ἀλκιβιάδου τὸ ψήφισμα γράψαντος.

10. Davies, *APF* 51, who, after observing that the decree is inconsistent with evidence closer in time to the alleged grant, goes on to suggest that it may be one of "a series of . . . decrees which refer to events of the period 490–450, and which are at least in some sense forgeries," citing Habicht (as in n. 8) 17ff. For Aristeides' death in c. 467, see Davies, *APF* 49–50.

11. Plut. *Per.* ix. 1–3: ἄλλοι δὲ πολλοὶ πρῶτον ὑπ' ἐκείνου (Perikles) φασὶ τὸν δῆμον ἐπὶ κληρουχίας καὶ θεωρικὰ καὶ μισθῶν διανομὰς προαχθῆναι. . . . πρὸς τὴν Κίμωνος δόξαν ἀντιταττόμενος ὑπεποιεῖτο τὸν δῆμον, . . . Περικλῆς καταδημαγωγούμενος τρέπεται πρὸς τὴν τῶν δημοσίων διανομήν. . . . καὶ ταχὺ θεωρικοῖς καὶ δικαστικοῖς λήμμασιν ἄλλαις τε μισθοφοραῖς καὶ χορηγίαις συνδεκάσας τὸ πλῆθος; Σ Dem. i. 1f (Dilts 16. 8–13): Ἰστέον δὲ ὅτι τὰ χρήματα ταῦτα τὰ δημόσια θεωρικὰ ἐποίησεν ἐξ ἀρχῆς ὁ Περικλῆς δι' αἰτίαν τοιαύτην· ἐπειδὴ πολλῶν θεωμένων καὶ στασιαζόντων διὰ τὸν τόπον καὶ ξένων καὶ πολιτῶν, καὶ λοιπὸν τῶν πλουσίων ἀγοραζόντων τοὺς τόπους, βουλόμενος ἀρέσαι τῷ δήμῳ καὶ τοῖς πένησιν, ἵνα ἔχωσι καὶ αὐτοὶ πόθεν ὠνεῖσθαι τόπους, ἔγραψε τὰ προσοδευόμενα χρήματα τῇ πόλει γενέσθαι πᾶσι θεωρικὰ τοῖς πολίταις. For Theopompos as Plutarch's source, see H. T. Wade-Gery, *Essays in Greek History* (Oxford 1958) 237.

12. Buchanan, *Theorika* 31, n. 2. So too Rhodes, *CAAP* 492 (quoted under #11).

13. *IG* I^3 375 (410/9). 10, 12, 14, 22, 23 (five payments with preserved totals of 16 T. 4,787 dr. 3 1/4 ob. ἐς τὲν διοβελίαν); *IG* I^3 377 (407/6?) passim (the chronology is disputed, but it appears that there are fifteen payments, beginning 20 Hekatombaion and ending 18 Mounychion [i.e., c. July 407 to April 406, with a large gap for c. October to March], with preserved totals of 2 T. 3,044 dr. 4 3/4 ob. ἐς τὲν διοβελίαν, followed by six payments, from 27 Mounychion to 16 Skirophorion [i.e., c. April to June 406], with preserved totals of 2,370 dr. 2 ob. ἐς τὸν ὀβολὸν [interpreted (a) by B. D. Meritt, "The Choiseul Marble: The Text of 406 B.C.," in *Mélanges helléniques offerts à G. Daux* (Paris 1974) 255–267 at 262–264, as a temporary reduction in the diobelia, caused by extreme

figures, attested by inscriptions, Xenophon, Aristotle, and probably Aristophanes, although none of them tells us precisely what the διωβελία was. I am inclined to accept Tod's view: "The most probable theory is that which sees in it a measure of poor relief instituted by the state during the closing years of the Peloponnesian War, when the loss of Euboea and the Spartan occupation of Decelea brought widespread ruin to Athenian citizens."[14] Uncertainty remains as to whether the 1 ob. allowance in ?407/6 was for the poor generally or just for war orphans.

8. c. 403/2. 1 ob. p.d. dole for orphans of citizens who died fighting for the restoration of the Democracy; the same amount probably was then being paid to other war orphans.[15] As Stroud observes, there is no evi-

---

financial emergency, and (b) by W. K. Pritchett, "Loans of Athena in 407 B.C.," *AncSoc* 8 (1977) 33–47 at 45–46 (following a possibility raised by Stroud [as in n. 5] 292, n. 34) as an allowance for war orphans]); *IG* I³ 379 (405/4). 86–91 (distributions of [κριθῶν μέδιμνοι . . .]-εκτέα and πυρῶν μέδ[ιμνοι]; Xen. *Hell.* i. 7. 2: (immediately after the Battle of Arginousai in 406, general Erasinides accused by Ἀρχέδημος ὁ τοῦ δήμου τότε προεστηκὼς ἐν Ἀθήναις καὶ τῆς διωβελίας ἐπιμελόμενος; Ar. *Ran.* 139–141b (Herakles and Dionysos conversing, play produced in 405):

Ηρ. ἐν πλοιαρίῳ τυννουτῳί σ' ἀνὴρ γέρων
ναύτης διάξει δύ' ὀβολὼ μισθὸν λαβών.
Δι. φεῦ
ὡς μέγα δύνασθον πανταχοῦ τὼ δύ' ὀβολώ.

(Contrary to the scholiast to line 140 [quoted under "Public Officeholders" #11, n. 28], who interprets these 2 ob. as dikast pay [otherwise attested as 3 ob.], the "ubiquitously powerful two obols" probably are the diobelia, as first suggested by Böckh, *SdA* I 280, with the agreement most recently of K. Dover, *Aristophanes Frogs* [Oxford 1993] 208); Lys. *In Theozotidem*, lines 94–97 (Thalheim fr. lix. 42d): . . . ε̣πεισεν ὑμᾶς π̣ . . . | . . . κ̣η ἐξεῖναι̣ μ̣ . . . | . . . η̣ς̣ διωβελίας̣. . . | . . . α ⟨χ⟩ρήματα . . . (Stroud [as in n. 5] 292, n. 34, rightly observes that the context of this reference is "uncertain," but I am inclined to see it as referring to the diobelia [W. T. Loomis, "Pay Differentials and Class Warfare in Lysias' *Against Theozotides*: Two Obols or Two Drachmas?," *ZPE* 107 (1995) 230–236 at 233 with n. 17]); Arist. *Pol.* 1267a 41–b 3: ἔτι δ' ἡ πονηρία τῶν ἀνθρώπων ἄπληστον, καὶ τὸ πρῶτον μὲν ἱκανὸν διωβελία μόνον, ὅταν δ' ἤδη τοῦτ' ᾖ πάτριον, ἀεὶ δέονται τοῦ πλείονος, ἕως εἰς ἄπειρον ἔλθωσιν; Arist. *Ath. Pol.* xxviii. 3: . . . Κλεοφῶν ὁ λυροποιός, ὃς καὶ τὴν διωβελίαν ἐπόρισε πρῶτος· καὶ χρόνον μέν τινα διεδίδου, μετὰ δὲ ταῦτα κατέλυσε Καλλικράτης Παιανιεὺς πρῶτον ὑποσχόμενος ἐπιθήσειν πρὸς τοῖν δυοῖν ὀβολοῖν ἄλλον ὀβολόν. The διωβελία defined in *Et. Magn.*, διωβελία (Gaisford 280. 24–25), and *Lex. Seg.* 237. 15–16, διωβελία (both quoted in n. 21), seems in fact to have been the theorikon.

14. Tod I 206, followed verbatim by M-L 260. See also Rhodes, *CAAP* 356: "the διωβελία should be regarded as a subsistence grant available to citizens not otherwise in receipt of money from the state."

15. *SEG* XXVIII 46. 4–19:

. . . ὁπόσοι Ἀθηναίω[ν] ἀ[πέθαν]ον [β]ιαί̣
ωι θανάτωι ἐν τῆι ὀλιγ[αρχίαι β]ο̣[ηθ]ῶντ-
ε̣ς τῆι δημοκρατίαι, τοῖς [παισ]ὶ̣ τότω̣ν ε-
[ὐ̣]ε̣ρ̣γεσ:ίας ἕν[εκ]α τῶμ πατ[έρων] α[ὐ̣]τῶν ἐς
[τ]ὸ̣[ν δῆμ]ον τὸν Ἀ̣θ̣[ην]αίω[ν καὶ ἀνδ]ραγαθ[ί]-

dence (except, possibly, #7) for the amount paid to war orphans in earlier periods, and the allowance was eliminated in the fourth century.[16]

9. late 5th c.? 2 ob. (p.d.) dole (diobelia) or soldier's pay? As discussed in greater detail under "Soldiers and Sailors" #20, the lack of context and precise date make it impossible to know whether the 2 ob. in Theopomp. Com. fr. 56 (K-A) refers to soldier's pay, the diobelia, or something else, although the diobelia is perhaps the likeliest interpretation.

10. late 5th c.? 1 ob. (p.d.) dole for ἀδύνατοι.[17] These seem to be the same physically disabled and relatively impecunious individuals

---

α[ς, ...]σ̣αι τοῖς π̣[α]ισὶ α[. . .6. . .] τ̣[ότ]ω[ν] ὀ-
[β]ο̣λ̣ὸν [τῆς] ἡμέρας τ[ροφὴν . . .7. . . .] δ̣ὲ̣ το-
ῖς ὀρφανο[ῖς] ἀποδίδω[σι . . . . .10. . . . .]το
Πρυτανει̣[ο . . . .]ο αὐτὸς [. . .6. . .]η[. . .]ιν
[. .5. . .]α̣ε̣σο̣[. . . . .10. . . . .]ο̣[. . . . .10. . . . .]σ
[. . .7. . . .]την οσ[. . . . . .19. . . . .]
δ[οκι]μασά̣τω αὐ[τ]ὸ̣[ς . . . . .16. . . . .]
διδόναι αὐτ[οῖς . . . . . . .15. . . . . κα]θ-
ά̣περ [τ]ῶν ἐν τῶι [. . . . . .18. . . . . τ]-
[ὸ]ς Ἑλληνοταμίας το [.]α̣[. . . . . .13. . . . . . .]
[. καθά]περ τὸς ὀρφανὸ[ς. . . .

Stroud (as in n. 5) 287–288 suggests as a possible restoration in lines 10–11 [καθάπερ] δ̣ὲ̣ τοῖς ὀρφανο[ῖς] ἀποδίδω[σιν . . . . ἐκ] τõ Πρυτανεί̣[ο], commenting "the beneficiaries of the decree are to receive an obol per day just as the war-orphans are paid their obol." Similarly, in lines 14–18, Stroud 294–295 suggests the following illustrative restoration (which he concedes is one letter too long in line 17):

[τὴν δὲ τροφὴν]
δ[οκι]μασά̣τω αὐ[τ]ὸ̣[ς ἡ βολή· τὸν δὲ ὀβολὸν]
διδόναι αὐτ[οῖς . . . . [officials]. . . . . . . κα]θ-
ά̣περ [τ]ῶν ἐν τῶι [πολέμωι τοῖς ὀρφανοῖς τ] -
[ὸ]ς Ἑλληνοταμίας. . .,

conjecturing that "'[t]he sons' are to be paid by some unknown official(s) just as the Hellenotamiai paid the sons of those who fell in the war."

16. Stroud (as in n. 5) 289–290.

17. Lys. xxiv. 13, 26 (invalid plaintiff speaking): (My opponent) ὑμᾶς πειρᾶται πείθειν, τοσούτους ὄντας εἷς ὤν, ὡς οὐκ εἰμὶ τῶν ἀδυνάτων ἐγώ. καίτοι εἰ τοῦτο πείσει τινὰς ὑμῶν, ὦ βουλή, τί με κωλύει κληροῦσθαι τῶν ἐννέα ἀρχόντων, καὶ ὑμᾶς ἐμοῦ μὲν ἀφελέσθαι τὸν ὀβολὸν ὡς ὑγιαίνοντος, τούτῳ δὲ ψηφίσασθαι ἐλεήσαντας ὡς ἀναπήρῳ; οὐ γὰρ δήπου τὸν αὐτὸν ὑμεῖς μὲν ὡς δυνάμενον ἀφαιρήσεσθε τὸ διδόμενον, οἱ δὲ ⟨θεσμοθέται⟩ ὡς ἀδύνατον ὄντα κληροῦσθαι κωλύσουσιν; . . . ἀλλὰ τὴν αὐτὴν ψῆφον θέσθε περὶ ἐμοῦ ταῖς ἄλλαις βουλαῖς, ἀναμνησθέντες ὅτι οὔτε χρήματα διαχειρίσας τῆς πόλεως δίδωμι λόγον αὐτῶν, οὔτε ἀρχὴν ἄρξας οὐδεμίαν εὐθύνας ὑπέχω νῦν αὐτῆς, ἀλλὰ περὶ ὀβολοῦ μόνον ποιοῦμαι τοὺς λόγους; Arist. fr. 470 (Rose) (quoted in n. 35); *Suda* α 540 (Adler), ἀδύνατοι (quoted in n. 35). For the date of Lysias xxiv, see L. Gernet and M. Bizos, *Lysias* II (Paris 1926) 102: "ne fut pas prononcé très longtemps après la tyrannie?"

who were receiving 2 ob. p.d. by 322 (#22). One wonders whether they had been receiving 2 ob. when the diobelia was in force.

11. 395/4? 1 dr. theorikon, introduced by Agyrrhios?[18] Whether the fund for this allowance originally was earmarked for military purposes and/or whether the allowance arose from discontent by poor citizens who could not afford theatre seats (see also the sources quoted in notes 11 and 21) need not be resolved in this study. Harpokration ascribes its introduction to Agyrrhios, and Hesychios gives an archon date of 395/4, but Rhodes rightly observes: "Aristophanes and other contemporaries are suspiciously silent on the theoric fund in the late fifth and early fourth centuries, and I prefer to believe that the fund was created by Diophantus [of the same name as Hesychios' archon] and Eubulus in the 350's."[19] As for the 1 dr. figure, this also is not attested by contemporary sources, but perhaps, as Pickard-Cambridge et al. suggest, it "represents three days of tragedies"[20] at the 2 ob. p.d. rate that is found later (##12, 15, 16).

12. c. 355? 2 ob. theorikon.[21] All of these late sources (including the fictional declamation of Libanios, which uses the 2 ob. theorikon as

---

18. Philoch. 328 *FGrH* 33 (see Harp. below); *Com. Adesp.* fr. *950 (K-A): Zenob. . . . iii. 27 [*CPG*] = Hesych. δ 2351 [Latte] δραχμὴ χαλαζῶσα· ἐπὶ Διοφάντου (a. 395/4) τὸ θεωρικὸν ἐγένετο δραχμή; Σ Lucian *Tim.* 49 (in C. Jacobitz, *Lucianus* IV [Leipzig 1841] 50, but not in H. Rabe, *Scholia in Lucianum* [Leipzig 1906] 118): [sc. τὸ θεωρικὸν] δραχμὴ δὲ ἦν τὸ διδόμενον, καὶ οὔτε πλέον ἐξῆν δοῦναι δραχμῆς οὔτε ἔλαττον; Harp., θεωρικά: . . . θεωρικὰ ἦν τινὰ ἐν κοινῷ χρήματα, ἀπὸ τῶν τῆς πόλεως προσόδων συναγόμενα· ταῦτα δὲ πρότερον μὲν εἰς τὰς τοῦ πολέμου χρείας ἐφυλάττετο καὶ ἐκαλεῖτο στρατιωτικά, ὕστερον δὲ κατετίθετο εἴς τε τὰς δημοσίας κατασκευὰς καὶ διανομάς τῶν πολιτῶν, ὧν πρῶτος ἤρξατο Ἀγύρριος ὁ δημαγωγός. Φιλόχορος δὲ ἐν τῇ ϝ´ τῆς Ἀτθίδος φησὶ "τὸ δὲ θεωρικὸν ἦν τὸ πρῶτον νομισθὲν δραχμὴ τῆς θέας, ὅθεν καὶ τοὔνομα ἔλαβε," καὶ τὰ ἑξῆς (see Jacoby's commentary ad loc. for emendation of γ´ to ϝ´); Phot., θεωρικά (repeated by *Suda* θ 218 [Adler], θεωρικά): ἐν ταῖς λεγομέναις Διονυσίαις θεωρίαις ἀγώνων τελουμένων φιλοτίμων συνέβαινέ τινας τῶν πολιτῶν εἰς ὕβρεις καὶ τραύματα διαφέρεσθαι. ἔδοξεν οὖν τῷ δήμῳ μηκέτι προῖκα θεωρεῖν, ἐκμισθοῦν δὲ ταῖς θέαις τοὺς τόπους. πλεονεκτουμένων δὲ τῶν πενήτων διὰ τὸ ῥᾳδίως τοῖς πλουσίοις πλείονος τιμῆς τοῦτο γίνεσθαι, ἐψηφίσαντο ἐπὶ δραχμῇ καὶ μόνον εἶναι τὸ τίμημα, θεωρικὸν αὐτῇ θέντες ὄνομα.

19. Rhodes, *CAAP* 492, referring to 514–515, where Rhodes identifies Diophantos as "Δ. Σφήττιος (*P.A.* 4438), an associate of Eubulus in the 350's and 340's . . . and . . . the institution [of the theorikon] was created by these men, probably soon after 355. . . ." This conclusion is further supported by (a) Philochoros' location of this event in his Book 6 (see n. 18) and (b) the words ἔναγχος αὐτὰ πεποιήκασι θεωρικά in Σ Dem. i. 1f (Dilts 15. 28) (quoted in n. 21).

20. Pickard-Cambridge, *DFA* 267. So too Böckh, *SdA* I 283–284, and Buchanan, *Theorika* 50, n. 2.

21. Σ Ar. *Vesp.* 1189d: ⟨ἀπ'⟩ ἰκρίων θεωροῦντες τοὺς δύο ὀβολοὺς παρεῖχον τοῖς ἀρχιτέκτοσιν; Σ Dem. i. 1f (Dilts 15. 27–31): ἐπειδήπερ χρήματα ἔχοντες στρατιωτικὰ οἱ Ἀθηναίοι ἔναγχος αὐτὰ πεποιήκασι θεωρικά, ὥστε λαμβάνειν ἐν τῷ θεωρεῖν ἕκαστον τῶν ἐν τῇ πόλει δύο ὀβολούς, ἵνα τὸν μὲν ἕνα κατάσχῃ εἰς ἰδίαν τροφήν, τὸν δὲ ἄλλον παρέχειν ἔχωσι τῷ ἀρχιτέκ-

an authentic historical "background fact") seem to be based on orations that probably date from the fourth century, and Rhodes further narrows the date to the period after c. 355 (see n. 19). The statement by the scholiast to Demosthenes that the allowance was one-half for private sustenance and one-half for theatre seats should be rejected because of the statement by Demosthenes himself that the cost of a theatre seat was 2 ob. (#16).[22]

13. 355. 3 ob. p.d. projected yield per citizen from proposed eisphora for mine development.[23] This allowance is merely a projection by

τονι τοῦ θεάτρου (οὐδὲ γὰρ εἶχον τότε θέατρον διὰ λίθων κατεσκευασμένον); Lib. *Decl.* xxxii. 15–16: διὸ κἂν θεωρῇ, φησί, τὼ δύ' ὀβολὼ λαμβανέτω, ἵνα μὴ οἴκοθεν θέαν πριάμενος πλέον δάκνηται ζημιούμενος ἢ θεώμενος τέρπεται. . . . Ταύταις οὖν ταῖς προσόδοις οὐ παρέργως προσέσχον, ὦ βουλή, ἀλλ' ὁσάκις θεωρικοῦ διανομὴν ἡ πόλις ἐποίει, ὁ μὲν γείτων ἐκάθευδεν ἂν καὶ ὑετὸν ἢ κρύος ἀντὶ τῆς ἀργίας ἐμποδὼν εἶναι φήσας ὑπερεφρόνει τοῖν δυοῖν ὀβολοῖν καὶ σεμνότερος ἦν τῶν νόμων, ἐμοὶ δὲ οὐδὲ ὕπνος ἐπῄει οὐδ' ἦν τὰ ἐκ τοῦ οὐρανοῦ δεινὰ φοβερώτερα τοῦ μὴ λαβεῖν, ἀλλὰ μέσων νυκτῶν ἀναστὰς ἐφεστήκειν ἂν τῷ διανέμοντι καὶ κατὰ σχολὴν τἀργύριον καταριθμηθείς, ὅπερ οὐκ ἂν ὑπῆρξε μετὰ πολλοὺς ἐληλυθότι, ἀλλὰ προέρριψεν ἂν ἐν τῷ ὄχλῳ τὸ ἥμισυ, ἀπῄειν οἴκαδε τὸ πᾶν ἔχων καὶ πρίν τινα κινηθῆναι τῆς εὐνῆς ἡ κιβωτὸς εἶχε τὼ δύ' ὀβολώ. θέαν δ' οὐκ ἂν ἔτ' ἐπριάμην, ἀλλ' ἐρρῶσθαι φράσας τῷ ἀρχιτέκτονι καὶ τῷ σεμνῶς καθῆσθαι θεώμενος ἑστὼς ἐθεώμην παρενείρας που τοῖς μετοίκοις ἐμαυτὸν ἢ τοῖς ξένοις. καὶ οὕτως ἡ τέρψις ἦν οὐκ ἐλάττων καὶ τἀργύριον πλέον; *Arg.* i. 8: οὐκ ὄντος τὸ παλαιὸν θεάτρου λιθίνου παρ' αὐτοῖς, ἀλλὰ ξυλίνων συμπηγνυμένων ἰκρίων καὶ πάντων καταλαμβάνειν τόπον σπευδόντων πληγαί τε ἐγίνοντο καί που καὶ τραύματα. τοῦτο κωλῦσαι βουληθέντες οἱ προεστῶτες τῶν Ἀθηναίων ὠνητοὺς ἐποιήσαντο τοὺς τόπους καὶ ἕκαστον ἔδει διδόναι δύο ὀβολοὺς καὶ καταβαλόντα θέαν ἔχειν. ἵνα δὲ μὴ δοκῶσιν οἱ πένητες τῷ ἀναλώματι λυπεῖσθαι, ἐκ τοῦ δημοσίου λαμβάνειν ἕκαστον ἐτάχθη τοὺς δύο ὀβολούς; Phot., θεωρικόν καὶ θεωρική (repeated by *Suda* θ 220 [Adler], θεωρικόν καὶ θεωρική): Ἀθήνησιν ἦν χρήματα κοινά, ἃ θεωρικὰ ἐκαλεῖτο, διδόμενα τοῖς Ἀθηναίοις εἰς διανομήν. προήχθη δὲ οὕτως. τὸ παλαιὸν ὄχλου γενομένου ἐν τοῖς θεάτροις κὰι τῶν ξένων τὰς θέας προκαταλαμβανόντων, διεδίδοτο τοῖς πολίταις τὸ θεωρικόν, ὅπερ ἦσαν δύο ὀβολοί, ἵνα τοῦτο λαμβάνοντες οἱ πολῖται διδῶσιν αὐτὸ τῇ πόλει μισθὸν τῆς θέας; *Et. Magn.*, διωβελία (Gaisford 280. 24–25) (substantially repeated by *Lex. Seg.* 237. 15–16, διωβελία): ὀβελοὶ δύο· οὓς ὁ δῆμος καθήμενος ἐμισθοφόρει; *Et. Magn.*, θεωρικὸν ἀργύριον (Gaisford 448. 47–56): . . . ἦν τοίνυν κοινὰ χρήματα Ἀθήνῃσιν, ἃ ἐκάλουν θεωρικά, εἰς διανομὴν διδόμενα τοῖς Ἀθηναίοις· ἐπειδὴ φασὶ τὸ παλαιὸν ὄχλου γενομένου ἐν τῷ θεάτρῳ, κὰι τῶν ξένων προκαταλαμβανόντων τὰς θέας, καὶ ἐκκλειομένων τῶν ἀστῶν, ἔδοξε δίδοσθαι θεωρικόν, ἵνα τοῦτο λαμβάνοντες παρὰ τῆς πόλεως οἱ πολῖται διδῶσιν αὐτοῖς τὸν τόπον τῆς θέας. ἦν δὲ τοῦτο ὀβολοὶ δύο.

22. As Böckh seems to have been the first to observe (*SdA* I 278–279). Pickard-Cambridge et al., however, at one point seem to accept the scholiast's remarks at face value (*DFA* 268): "The θεωρικόν . . . seems to have covered more than the price of the ticket and contributed to a citizen's festival expenses"; but cf. n. 27 below.

23. Xen. *Vect.* iii. 9–10: ᾧ μὲν γὰρ ἂν δέκα μναῖ εἰσφορὰ γένηται, ὥσπερ ναυτικόν, σχεδὸν ἐπίπεμπτον αὐτῷ γίγνεται, τριώβολον τῆς ἡμέρας λαμβάνοντι· ᾧ δέ γ' ἂν πέντε μναῖ, πλέον ἢ ἐπίτριτον. οἱ δέ γε πλεῖστοι Ἀθηναίων πλείονα λήψονται κατ' ἐνιαυτὸν ἢ ὅσα ἂν εἰσενέγκωσιν. οἱ γὰρ μνᾶν προτελέσαντες ἐγγὺς δυοῖν μναῖν πρόσοδον ἕξουσι. . . .

Xenophon of a scheme that never was realized, and thus cannot be used here.[24]

14. c. 355–322. 4 ob. theorikon?, for 2 performances? or ekklesiast pay at normal Ekklesia?[25] As discussed in greater detail under "Public Officeholders" #23, the 4 ob. in Dem. *Prooem.* lii. 4 possibly refers to a theoric distribution of 2 ob. for each of two days of performances, but any interpretation of this brief passage is necessarily uncertain.

15. c. 349. 2 ob. theorikon.[26] The two obols here are generally taken to be the theorikon—the earliest surviving evidence as to the amount of that allowance.

16. 346. 2 ob. theatre seat,[27] paid for by theorikon? This is the earliest—and the only—explicit testimony that the cost of the theatre seat was two obols—the same, apparently, as the theorikon allowance.

17. c. 344/3 or 334? 1 dr. p.d. τροφή for Peisitheides of Delos until he returns to Delos (payable each prytany).[28] This is an individual allow-

---

24. Gallo, "Salari" 21–24, 54–60, argues (a) that Xenophon's "utopistico" proposal indicates (a) that by 355 the polis no longer had revenues or a treasury surplus that permitted it to support priests, public officeholders and cavalrymen at their fifth-century levels, (b) that the salaries of these individuals, even if nominally at fifth-century levels, must therefore have been inadequate by fifth-century standards, and thus (c) that the cost of living must have increased since the fifth century.

25. Dem. *Prooem.* lii. 4: νῦν δὲ δραχμῇ καὶ χοῖ καὶ τέτταρσιν ὀβολοῖς ὥσπερ ἀσθενοῦντα τὸν δῆμον διάγουσιν.

26. Dem. xiii. 10: ὃ δέ μοι πλείστην ἀθυμίαν παρέσχεν ἁπάντων, ἐρῶ πρὸς ὑμᾶς καὶ οὐκ ἀποκρύψομαι, ὅτι πολλῶν καὶ μεγάλων καὶ καλῶν ὄντων τούτων ἁπάντων, τῶν μὲν ἄλλων οὐδενὸς οὐδεὶς μέμνηται, τοῖν δυοῖν δ' ὀβολοῖν ἅπαντες. καίτοι τοὺς μὲν οὐκ ἔστι πλείονος ἢ δυοῖν ὀβολοῖν ἀξίους εἶναι, τἄλλα δὲ μετὰ τούτων ὧν εἶπον τῶν βασιλέως ἄξι' ἐστὶ χρημάτων, πόλιν τοσούτους ὁπλίτας ἔχουσαν καὶ τριήρεις καὶ ἵππους καὶ χρημάτων πρόσοδον συντετάχθαι καὶ παρεσκευάσθαι. For the date, see M. Croiset, *Démosthène Harangues* I (Paris 1924) 71. As Pickard-Cambridge et al. observe (*DFA* 266 with n. 2), this text "points the same way . . . [as Dem. xvii. 28, quoted in n. 27] treating two obols as the unit of the theorikon."

27. Dem. xviii. 28: ἀλλὰ τί ἐχρῆν με ποιεῖν; μὴ προσάγειν γράψαι τοὺς (Philip's ambassadors) ἐπὶ τοῦθ' ἥκοντας, ἵν' ὑμῖν διαλεχθῶσιν; ἢ θέαν μὴ κατανεῖμαι τὸν ἀρχιτέκτον' αὐτοῖς κελεῦσαι; ἀλλ' ἐν τοῖν δυοῖν ὀβολοῖν ἐθεώρουν ἄν, εἰ μὴ τοῦτ' ἐγράφη. Pickard-Cambridge et al. (*DFA* 265–266, n. 9) note that one of the scholia ad loc. (Dilts 209. 14–15, no. 74a: δύο γὰρ ὄντων πρέσβεων δύο ἦσαν οἱ ὀβολοί) "is impossible as an interpretation of the text, but there was in later times a belief that of the two obols only one was paid to the lessee of the theatre, and the other was for refreshments"; cf. n. 22 above. The other scholion ad loc. (Dilts 209. 17–20, no. 74b) had a better understanding: τὸ διώβολον παρεῖχον οἱ θεωροῦντες, ὡς ἤδη ἔγνωμεν. ὥστε οὖν γνωστέον ὅτι οἱ δύο πρέσβεις, Ἀντίπατρος καὶ Παρμενίων, τοὺς δύο ὀβολοὺς ἐδίδοσαν, ὁ εἷς πρὸς ἕνα, ἀλλ' οὐ πρὸς δύο. διὰ τοῦτο εἶπε "τοῖν δυοῖν ὀβολοῖν ἐθεώρουν."

28. *IG* II^2 222. 35–41, 46–48:

ὅπως ἂν δὲ μὴ ἀπορῆται τ[ρ]-
[οφῆς Πει]σιθείδης, ἕως ἂν κατέλθ[η]-
[ι εἰς Δῆ]λον, τὸν ταμίαν τοῦ δήμου [τ]-

ance for a Delian partisan of Athens, whom Athens evidently felt obliged to support during his exile. His allowance is three times the 2 ob. p.d. theorikon or ἀδύνατοι allowances (see #22), which evidently were thought to be inadequate for a person of Peisitheides' station (inter alia, he would have had to support a slave).

18. c. 338–325. 50 dr. or 1 mn.?, per citizen, provided by Lykourgos from 160 T. judgment against Diphilos.[29] These figures are implausible on their face: 160 T. = 960,000 dr. ÷ 50 dr. = 19,200 citizens; ÷ 100 dr. [i.e., 1 mn.] = 9,600 citizens—in each case far too few. Apart from the inaccuracy of the figures, I am inclined *not* to follow Jones and de Ste. Croix in connecting this with #20, since the distribution there was made at the instigation of Demades rather than Lykourgos.[30] To the extent that this story is true, it was obviously a one-time windfall distribution, made to every citizen, rather than a support allowance.

19. c. 338–325. 18,900 T. total distributions under Lykourgos.[31] In the absence of any indication as to per capita and per diem figures, this gross figure (possibly exaggerated by this late souce) is not very useful for this study.

20. 331. 1/2 mn. distribution by Demades to each citizen for Choes festival.[32] As with #18, this seems to have been made to every citizen, and thus is a distribution rather than a support allowance.

[ὸν ἀεὶ τ]αμ[ι]εύοντα διδόναι Πεισ[ι]-
[θείδηι] δραχμὴν τῆς ἡμέρας ἐκ τῶ[ν]
[κατὰ ψηφί]σματα ἀναλισκομένων [τ]- 40
[ῶι δήμωι]·

ὁ δὲ τ-
[αμίας ἀπ]οδότω Πει[σι]θείδει κατὰ 47
[τὴν πρυτ]ανείαν ἑκάστην.

For the date 334, see Osborne D22.

29. [Plut.] *Mor.* 843d: ἔκρινε [sc. Λυκοῦργος] δὲ καὶ Δίφιλον, ἐκ τῶν ἀργυρείων μετάλλων τοὺς μεσοκρινεῖς, οἳ ἐβάσταζον τὰ ὑπερκείμενα βάρη, ὑφελόντα καὶ ἐξ αὐτῶν πεπλουτηκότα παρὰ τοὺς νόμους· καὶ θανάτου ὄντος ἐπιτιμίου ἁλῶναι ἐποίησε, καὶ πεντήκοντα δραχμὰς ἐκ τῆς οὐσίας αὐτοῦ ἑκάστῳ τῶν πολιτῶν διένειμε, τῶν πάντων συναχθέντων ταλάντων ἑκατὸν ἑξήκοντα· ἤ, ὥς τινες, †μνᾶν†.

30. Jones, *Ath. Dem.* 34; de Ste. Croix (as in n. 2) 191.

31. [Plut.] *Mor.* 852b: καὶ γενόμενος τῆς κοινῆς προσόδου ταμίας τῇ πόλει ἐπὶ τρεῖς πενταετηρίδας καὶ διανείμας ἐκ τῆς κοινῆς προσόδου μύρια καὶ ὀκτακισχίλια καὶ ἐνακόσια τάλαντα. . . .

32. Plut. *Mor.* 818e: (The people) ὡρμημένων γὰρ ἐκπέμπειν τριήρεις βοηθοὺς τοῖς ἀφισταμένοις Ἀλεξάνδρου καὶ χρήματα κελευόντων παρέχειν ἐκεινον, "ἔστιν ὑμῖν" ἔφη (sc.

21. pre-323. 5 dr. theorikon,[33] p.a.? One year is the period suggested by Ste. Croix.[34] If the theorikon was still 2 ob. per performance, this distribution would have been for fifteen performances, but this is necessarily speculative.

22. pre-322. 1, 2 or 3 ob. p.d.? (almost certainly 2 ob. p.d.), dole for citizens possessing less than 3 mnas and physically unable to work (ἀδύνατοι).[35] In the face of the *Ath. Pol.*'s preserved statement that this allowance was 2 ob., the report by Harpokration that the *Ath. Pol.* said that it was 1 ob. obviously must be rejected (possibly there was an error in Harpokration's copy of the *Ath. Pol.*). The 1 ob. allowance reported by the *Suda* presumably either copies Harpokration or refers to the situation at the end of the fifth century attested by Lysias (#10). Similarly, in reporting the figure as 3 ob., the scholiast to Aischines is probably con-

---

Δημάδης) "χρήματα· παρεσκευασάμην γὰρ εἰς τοὺς Χόας, ὥσθ' ἕκαστον ὑμῶν λαβεῖν ἡμιμναῖον· εἰ δ' εἰς ταῦτα βούλεσθε μᾶλλον, αὐτοὶ καταχρῆσθε τοῖς ἰδίοις." καὶ τοῦτον τὸν τρόπον, ὅπως μὴ στεροῖντο τῆς διανομῆς, ἀφέντων τὸν ἀπόστολον, ἔλυσε τὸ πρὸς Ἀλέξανδρον ἔγκλημα τοῦ δήμου.

33. Hyp. *Dem.* col. XXVI: καὶ Κόν[ων] μὲν ὁ Παι⟨α⟩νιεύς, [ὅτι] ὑπὲρ τοῦ ὑοῦ ἔλαβ[εν] τὸ θεωρικὸν ἀπ[οδη]μοῦντος, πέντ[ε δρα]χμῶν ἕνεκεν [ἱκε]τεύων ὑμᾶς τάλαντον ὦφλεν ἐν τῶι δικαστηρίωι. . . .; Dinarch. i. 56: πάλιν τὸν τὴν πεντεδραχμίαν ἐπὶ τῷ τοῦ μὴ παρόντος ὀνόματι λαβεῖν ἀξιώσαντα, καὶ τοῦτον ὑμῖν ἀπέφηνε [sc. the Areopagos]. . . . For doubts as to whether Deinarchos' culprit also was Konon, see I. Worthington, *A Historical Commentary on Dinarchus* (Ann Arbor 1992) 220.

34. Ste. Croix (as in n. 2) 191: "it looks as if they [the distributions] must have reached at least 5 drachmae per head per year . . . for at least some years, for the use of the expression ἡ πεντεδραχμία in Deinarch. . . . proves that Conon cannot have drawn his 5 dr. 'over several years'."

35. Arist. *Ath. Pol.* xlix. 4: Δοκιμάζει δὲ καὶ τοὺς ἀδυνάτους ἡ βουλή· νόμος γάρ ἐστιν ὃς κελεύει τοὺς ἐντος τριῶν μνῶν κεκτημένους καὶ τὸ σῶμα πεπηρωμένους ὥστε μὴ δύνασθαι μηδὲν ἔργον ἐργάζεσθαι δοκιμάζειν μὲν τὴν βουλήν, διδόναι δὲ δημοσίαι τροφὴν δύο ὀβολοὺς ἑκάστωι τῆς ἡμέρας; Arist. fr. 470 (Rose) (see Harp. and Phot. below); Σ Aeschin. i. 103 (Dilts no. 222b): τοῖς ἀδυνάτοις τοῖς σώμασιν ἐχορηγεῖτο ἑκάστης ἡμέρας ἐκ τοῦ δημοσίου εἰς τροφὴν τριώβολον; Harp., ἀδύνατοι: . . . οἱ ἐντὸς τριῶν μνῶν κεκτημένοι καὶ τὸ σῶμα πεπηρωμένοι. ἐλάμβανον δὲ οὗτοι δοκιμασθέντες ὑπὸ τῆς βουλῆς β´ ὀβολοὺς τῆς ἡμέρας ἑκάστης, ἢ ὀβολόν, ὥς φησιν Ἀριστοτέλης ἐν Ἀθηναίων πολιτείᾳ, ὡς δὲ Φιλόχορός φησιν, θ´ δραχμὰς κατὰ μῆνα. ἔστι δὲ καὶ λόγος τις, ὡς λέγεται, Λυσίου περὶ τοῦ ἀδυνάτου, ἐν ᾧ ὡς ὀβολὸν λαμβάνοντος μέμνηται; Hesych. α 1217 (Latte), ἀδύνατοι: οἱ ἐντὸς κεκτημένοι τριῶν ⟨μνῶν⟩ παρὰ Ἀττικοῖς. ἐλάμβανον δὲ παρὰ τῆς βουλῆς δύο ὀβολούς; Phot. α 393 (Theodoridis), ἀδύνατοι (substantially repeated by *Lex. Seg.* 345. 15–22, ἀδύνατοι): οἱ μέρος τι βεβλαμμένοι τοῦ σώματος, ὡς μηδὲ ἐργάζεσθαι, οἳ καὶ ἐχορηγοῦντο τὰ πρὸς τὸ ζῆν παρὰ τῆς πόλεως, μισθοφορούντων αὐτοῖς τῶν ἐντὸς τριῶν μνῶν περιουσίαν κεκτημένων. ἐδοκιμάζοντο δὲ οἱ ἀδύνατοι ὑπὸ τῆς τῶν πεντακοσίων βουλῆς καὶ ἐλάμβανον τῆς ἡμέρας, ὡς μὲν Λυσίας λέγει, ὀβολὸν ἕνα, ὡς δὲ Φιλόχορος, πέντε· Ἀριστοτέλης δὲ δύο ἔφη; *Suda* α 540 (Adler), ἀδύνατοι: οἱ πεπηρωμένοι τὸ σῶμα· ἐλάμβανον δὲ οὗτοι δοκιμασθέντες ὑπὸ τῆς βουλῆς, οἱ μέν φασιν, ἑκάστης ἡμέρας ὀβολοὺς δύο, οἱ δὲ ὀβολόν. Φιλόχορος δέ φησιν ἐννέα δραχμὰς κατὰ μῆνα.

fusing this dole with the dikastic triobol.[36] In any event, the more contemporary authority of the *Ath. Pol.* is to be preferred. For Philochoros' report that the allowance was 9 dr. per month, see #24.

23. c. 317–307. Allowance for mother and maternal aunt of Lysimachos raised from 3 ob. to 1 dr. p.d.[37] I follow Davies in believing that this Lysimachos cannot, on chronological grounds, be the grandson of the famous Aristeides (cf. #5), but that a grant probably was made to relatives of a fourth-century Lysimachos of Alopeke.[38]

24. post-306/5. 9 dr. p.m. (i.e., c. 1.8 ob. p.d.) dole for ἀδύνατοι.[39] Jacoby explained the difference between (a) the πέντε in Photios and the *Lexica Segueriana* and (b) the θ´ in Harpokration, as a palaeographical confusion of E with Θ, further compounded by the misunderstanding of 5 *obols* in Photios and the *Lexica Segueriana*, and he observed that 2 ob. p.d. "yield about 9 drachmas per month," with a resulting "reduction of between eight and eighteen drachms in the year," attributable to the fact that "in the bourgeois republic the sense of social obligation continued to dwindle." But because Philochoros is transmitted by late (and evidently confused) sources, this figure is not certain, and Jacoby's explanation is, in any event, speculative: *if* there was a cut from 2 ob. to c. 1.8 ob. p.d., it may reflect a decline in living costs generally, or at least in Athens' public financial resources.[40]

25. 72. Lucullus gives 200 dr. apiece to Athenian refugees at Amisos, to return home.[41] This is a one-time allowance, not linked to a particular time period or standard of living.

---

36. As Böckh seems to have been the first to observe (*SdA* I 310).

37. Dem. Phal. 228 *FGrH* 45: ὁ δὲ Φαληρεὺς ἐν τῶι Σωκράτει φησὶ μνημονεύειν Ἀριστείδου θυγατριδοῦν εὖ μάλα πένητα Λυσίμαχον . . ., τῆι δὲ μητρὶ καὶ τῆι ταύτης ἀδελφῆι ψήφισμα γράψας ἔπεισε τὸν δῆμον τροφὴν διδόναι τριώβολον ἑκάστης ἡμέρας. αὐτὸς μέντοι φησὶν ὁ Δημήτριος νομοθετῶν ἀντὶ τριωβόλου δραχμὴν ἑκατέραι τάξαι τῶν γυναικῶν.

38. Davies, *APF* 51–52.

39. Philoch. 328 *FGrH* 197a (Harp.), b (Phot., *Lex. Seg.*), quoted in n. 35, with Jacoby ad loc., who also discusses the date.

40. See "Inflation and Deflation" pp. 242, 249–250.

41. Plut. *Luc.* xix. 6–8: . . . καὶ τοὺς φεύγοντας Ἀμισηνῶν ἐδέξατο (sc. Λεύκολλος). . . . ἦν δ' ἡ πόλις Ἀθηναίων ἄποικος . . ., καὶ διὰ τοῦτο πολλοὶ τῶν τὴν Ἀριστίωνος τυραννίδα βουλομένων φεύγειν ἐκπλεύσαντες αὐτοῦ κατῴκουν καὶ μετεῖχον τῆς πολιτείας, οἷς συνέβη τὰ οἰκεῖα κακὰ φεύγουσιν ἀπολαῦσαι τῶν ἀλλοτρίων. ἀλλά τούς γε σωθέντες αὐτῶν ὁ Λεύκολλος ἀμφιέσας καλῶς καὶ διακοσίας ἑκάστῳ δραχμὰς ἐπιδοὺς ἀπέστειλε.

26. A.D. 2nd c. 100 dr. p.m. (= c. 3 1/3 dr. p.d.) proposed dole (διανομαί) for citizens, 50 dr. p.m. (= c. 1 2/3 dr. p.d.) for metics.[42] Like Xenophon's proposal (#13), this does not reflect actual payments, but it may reflect an increase in living costs from the fourth century B.C. to the second century A.D.

What can be said about these figures as a whole? The 2 ob. p.d. διωβελία allowance, probably for poor citizens who were not necessarily disabled (#7), is attested for only a few years in the last decade of the fifth century. The allowance for war orphans, although in existence earlier in the fifth century and possibly also the sixth (##1, 8) has a clearly attested figure (1 ob. p.d.) only in c. 403/2.[43] The only per diem figure that is (fairly) reliably attested for the theorikon distribution is 2 ob. (##12, 15) in the mid fourth century, and other figures, of 1 dr., 4 ob. and 5 dr. (##11, 14, 21), may well represent payments for three to fifteen days of performances at 2 ob. p.d. The only useful figures for comparative purposes, therefore, are the doles for the ἀδύνατοι, which rose from 1 ob. p.d. in the late fifth century (#10) to 2 ob. p.d. sometime before 322 (#22), and may have declined very slightly to c. 1.8 ob. p.d. after 306/5 (#24). As discussed in greater detail under "Inflation and Deflation" (pp. 241–242, 248–250), these changes in ἀδύνατοι allowances parallel general trends in wage levels.[44]

---

42. Lucian *Nav.* 24: τῇ πόλει δὲ ταῦτα ἐξαίρετα παρ' ἐμοῦ ὑπῆρξεν ἄν, αἱ μὲν διανομαὶ κατὰ μῆνα ἕκαστον δραχμαὶ τῷ μὲν ἀστῷ ἑκατόν, τῷ δὲ μετοίκῳ ἥμισυ τούτων....

43. If the 1 ob. in *IG* I^3 377 is for war orphans rather than a reduced diobelia allowance (see n. 13), that would indicate only that the war orphan allowance was stable in the last decade of the fifth century.

44. Gallo, "Salari" 24–29, plausibly argues that the increase from 1 to 2 ob. in the period c. 400–322 reflects a 200% increase in the minimum cost of living. For more on this, see the evidence collected in *Talents*, "O. Individual Finances: Support Costs."

Chapter 14
A Standard Athenian Wage?

One frequently reads, not only in the older handbooks, but also in the more recent specialized literature, that the standard wage at Athens was one drachma per day.[1] Archaeologists have used this "fact" to calculate the number of sculptors who worked on the Parthenon pediments,[2] and advocates of a "primitive" or "embedded" model of the Ancient Economy have used it to support their view that market factors, especially the demand for and supply of various kinds of workers, had no effect at all on their wages, which were merely "conventional" or "nominal."[3]

What is meant by a "standard wage"? For purposes of this discussion, it does not mean a uniform wage within a particular job class, e.g., 3 ob. p.d. for all dikasts, or 1 dr. p.d. for all soldiers. These are *job-based* pay rates—a familiar phenomenon in our own society, where we have uniform salaries for all (United States) G-12 civil servants, for all army privates, and sometimes even (within a particular university) for all professors of the same rank. But when scholars say that there was a standard wage of 1 dr. p.d. at Athens, they usually mean that this was the wage for all (or at least most) categories and fields of workers, and they point to soldiers and sailors, and to a wide variety of "skilled" and "unskilled"

---

1. E.g., Burford, *Craftsmen* 138; Himmelmann, "Entlohnung" 139–140; Gallo, "Salari" 47, 58; Stewart, *Greek Sculpture* xii, 66.

2. See "Construction and Other Manual Workers" pp. 116–117 with n. 37.

3. The most influential proponent of the view that wages were merely "conventional" or "nominal" has been M. I. Finley, e.g., in *The Ancient Economy*^{2} (Berkeley 1985) 23 (with n. 19), 80 (all passages quoted in "An Embedded or a Market Economy?" n. 9). For an example of his influence, see Stewart, *Greek Sculpture* 65: "The amount that a man is paid for his work both helps to determine his self-esteem, and testifies to society's valuation of his services. Yet there may be distorting factors. Wage levels may be fixed by *convention*, and therefore become unrealistic with time, or be *purely nominal*; or monetary compensation itself may be regarded as demeaning in certain cases or by certain recipients. Wages are but a segment of a wider social context, and must be treated accordingly" (italics mine).

workers on the Erechtheion, viz., architects, sawyers, carpenters and laborers—all of whom were paid 1 dr. p.d.[4]

It turns out that these figures, when subjected to critical scrutiny, are both unrepresentative and misleading.

First of all, these figures are drawn only from the last third of the fifth century. Before then, a majority of attested wages were lower, and afterwards many attested wages were higher.[5]

Second, these figures are drawn only from the "public sector"—soldiers, sailors and employees on a public works project. Unfortunately, we have almost no evidence from the private sector: a second century A.D. account has Timon of Athens getting 4 ob. p.d. as an agricultural laborer 600 years earlier, in the fifth century B.C.,[6] and we have a few figures for (usually atypical) lawyers, professors and prostitutes;[7] in addition, there are scattered references that suggest that the "going rate" for an *average* prostitute was 3 ob. per *occasion*, but (if this is true) it certainly should have been possible for an energetic prostitute to earn much more than 1 dr. per *day*.[8] In any event, the lack of adequate evidence from the "private sector" means that the discussion has to be based on public wages alone—and it is important to realize this limitation.

Third, even within the public sector, it is clear that per diem pay rates were different for different job classifications, at least in the second half of the fourth century, when dikasts were paid 3 ob., archons were paid 4 ob., bouleutai were paid 5–6 ob., and ekklesiasts were paid 6–9 ob.[9] A similar variation in per diem pay rates, evidently based on skills, is attest-

---

4. "Soldiers and Sailors" ##5, 12, 13, 15; "Overseers, Architects and Other Construction Personnel" #4; "Construction and Other Manual Workers" #3.

5. For the three wages arguably attested before c. 433, see "Public Officeholders" ##4 (4 ob. [p.d.]), 6 (1 dr. p.d.); Soldiers and Sailors #2 (4 ob. [p.d.?]). For wages higher than 1 dr. p.d. after c. 400, see "Public Officeholders #30 (a) (9 ob. p.d.); "Overseers, Architects and Other Salaried Construction Personnel" ##7, 8 (2 dr. p.d.); "Construction and Other Manual Workers" #7 (1 1/4–2 1/2 dr. p.d.).

6. "Construction and Other Manual Workers" #2.

7. "Doctors, Lawyers and Professors" ##4, 7, 12, 13, 14, 19, 27; "Prostitutes and Pimps" ##7, 13, 24, 41.

8. "Prostitutes and Pimps" ##9, 22, 42, and possibly 5.

9. "Public Officeholders" #30 (a)–(d).

ed for public construction workers at Eleusis, who were paid 1 1/4 to 2 1/2 dr. p.d.[10]

Fourth, even in the late fifth century, the period from which the 1 dr. p.d. figures are drawn, the evidence does not support the standard wage theory. We may leave to one side the fact that during the years c. 425–412, when soldiers and sailors were paid 1 dr. p.d., dikasts were being paid only half as much—3 ob. p.d.—since that difference plausibly might be explained by the fact that dikasts were not on call 24 hours per day, and in any event were sitting rather than actively working.[11] But the more crucial alleged correspondence—between soldiers and sailors on the one hand and Erechtheion workers on the other—is not, on closer inspection, attested. In 409–407, when Erechtheion workmen were being paid 1 dr. p.d.,[12] soldiers and sailors were getting only 3 ob. p.d.,[13] so that even in those years there certainly was *not* a standard wage that applied to workers in quite different fields.[14]

In the end, the only evidence that points to something like a standard wage is the 1 dr. p.d. that was paid to many categories of Erechtheion workers, i.e., to workers *within* a field. It *is* remarkable that 1 dr. was the daily wage not only of skilled workers like carpenters and sawyers (and also, possibly, of sculptors), but also of day laborers who did heavy lifting and moving.[15] For us, this may seem surprising, since we are used to paying more to skilled workers, who usually are in shorter supply than unskilled workers.

---

10. "Construction and Other Manual Workers" #7.

11. "Soldiers and Sailors" ##4, 5, 12, 13, 15; "Public Officeholders" #11.

12. "Construction and Other Manual Workers" #3.

13. "Soldiers and Sailors" ##16–18. Strictly speaking, "Soldiers and Sailors" ##16–18 refer only to sailors, the most active category of military personnel in c. 412–403, but there is no reason to suppose that after c. 412 the Athenians departed from their long-attested practice of paying the same wage to both soldiers and sailors. See also "Soldiers and Sailors" #19.

14. As far as I can determine, all scholars who have considered this question have assumed that soldiers and construction workers were being paid 1 dr. p.d. at the same time. See Gallo, "Salari" 47 and n. 73 with references. For the possibility that 1 dr. p.d. had been the wage of soldiers, sailors and construction workers *before* 412, see notes 16 and 22.

15. See "Construction and Other Manual Workers" #3 and further discussion at pp. 117–119. But the Erechtheion undersecretary and one carpenter were paid 5 ob. p.d. ("Overseers, Architects and Other Salaried Construction Personnel" #4; "Construction and Other Manual Workers" #3).

Why would the Athenians have made a different judgment? Several scholars have suggested that it had to do with politics, taking as their point of departure Plutarch's report that Perikles instituted public works projects to give employment and money to the non-military masses.[16] This view has a certain plausibility. The argument, in more developed form, might run along the following lines:

First, every Athenian citizen was entitled to vote, and every citizen's vote was worth as much as his fellow citizen's. This is a view that we moderns also share.

Second, every Athenian citizen also had a statistically equal chance to be allotted to public office, e.g., to serve in the Boule or as eponymous archon.[17] This is a view that we do not share—we agree that everyone is eligible to run, but we have elections rather than lotteries to determine who actually shall hold office.

Third, the Athenians took these (already extreme?) democratic notions one step further and said that, insofar as the polis was the employer, every citizen was entitled to the same daily wage regardless of the job performed. This would have been a logical extension of political equality: just as no man's vote was worth more than any other man's, so too his labor should not have been worth more than any other man's. After the economic (as well as the military) disasters in Sicily, Dekeleia, Chios, etc., and the consequent austerity of the oligarchical regimes of

---

16. Stewart, *Greek Sculpture* 66: "A remark of Plutarch's suggests that it was Perikles who instituted the 1-dr. wage for public projects, for political and/or ideological reasons: . . . [Plut. *Per.* xii. 5: τοῖς μὲν γὰρ ἡλικίαν ἔχουσι καὶ ῥώμην αἱ στρατεῖαι τὰς ἀπὸ τῶν κοινῶν εὐπορίας παρεῖχον, τὸν δ' ἀσύντακτον καὶ βάναυσον ὄχλον οὔτ' ἄμοιρον εἶναι λημμάτων βουλόμενος, οὔτε λαμβάνειν ἀργὸν καὶ σχολάζοντα, μεγάλας κατασκευασμάτων ἐπιβολὰς καὶ πολυτέχνους ὑποθέσεις ἔργων διατριβὴν ἐχόντων ἐνέβαλε φέρων εἰς τὸν δῆμον, ἵνα μηδὲν ἧττον τῶν πλεόντων καὶ φρουρούντων καὶ στρατευομένων τὸ οἰκουροῦν ἔχῃ πρόφασιν ἀπὸ τῶν δημοσίων ὠφελεῖσθαι καὶ μεταλαμβάνειν]. Hoplite pay in classical Athens was indeed 1 dr. per day (Thucydides 3. 17. 3). If *this standard day-wage was extended to craftsmen to better their lot*, as Plutarch hints, then it is ironic that less than a century later inflation and increasing demand from other sources should have turned it into at best a bare minimum, at worst a detriment to the work at hand" (italics mine). Himmelmann, "Entlohnung" 139–140, also had speculated that 1 dr. p.d. had been the wage for the Periklean building program. There is no positive evidence for this, and indeed the figures collected in n. 5 suggest that the Periklean wage might have been closer to 4 ob. p.d.

17. As a practical matter, even citizens who were thetes (members of the lowest property class) were eligible to serve (Arist. *Ath. Pol.* vii. 4), although Lys. xxiv. 13 (quoted in "Welfare and Support Allowances and Distributions" n. 17) indicates that poor citizens who also were physically disabled (ἀδύνατοι) were not eligible.

411,[18] the people needed work and money, and the restored democratic regime would have had the political incentive to give it to them, on a strictly equal and democratic basis.

Now, if all of this were true, it would say something about Athenian Democracy that has not been noticed before—that it embraced an ideal of economic as well as political equality, at least as far as public employment was concerned.

Enticing as this argument might be, it does not work. The problem with it is that the 1 dr. p.d. Erechtheion wage was paid to metics and slaves, as well as to citizens. Since political equality was confined to citizens (and strictly so), the democratic regime would have had *no* political incentive to pay metics and slaves the same wage as citizens, so the putative political rationale for the 1 dr. p.d. Erechtehion wage collapses.

Closely connected with the question of why wages were equal for most Erechtheion workers, regardless of skill or civil status, is a second question. In 409–407, when many Erechtheion workmen were paid 1 dr. p.d., soldiers and sailors were being paid only half as much—3 ob. p.d. How could the polis have justified *this* politically, i.e., how could it justify paying citizens who were risking their lives for their country one-half the wage that was being paid to construction workers at home, many of whom were metics and slaves?[19]

I have tried to think of an answer to both of these questions by asking what is special about the Erechtheion. That is, is there anything special about this public religious building that would (a) excuse a higher wage rate for construction workers than for soldiers and sailors and (b) justify

18. "Public Officeholders" ##17, 18; "Soldiers and Sailors" ##16, 17; "Inflation and Deflation" pp. 240–241, 244– 245.

19. Although some soldiers may have had income (whether in cash or in kind, from farms or other assets) that would have brought their aggregate daily income up to the 1 dr. p.d. for Erechtheion workers, their much lower wages remain puzzling, for three reasons. First, some of the Erechtheion workers (those who were citizens, and perhaps some of the metics) may also have had such "outside" income. Second, some of the soldiers, and most of the sailors (the more numerous category at this time [see n. 13]), would *not* have had such income. Third, and most important, what needs to be explained here are the (explicitly very different) levels of wages for labor, not the (possibly less different) levels of aggregate income from all sources, so the question remains: how could Athens justify paying citizen soldiers and sailors one-half the wage that was being paid to citizen, metic and slave construction workers?

the same wage rate for all construction workers, regardless of their skill or civil status? The following arguments might be relevant:

First, one might argue that considerations of religious piety required the polis to build the highest quality building, and that the polis was therefore justified in paying whatever was required to get the best craftsmen possible—but surely that would not justify paying "unskilled" workmen as much as "skilled" workers.

Second, one could argue that the Erechtheion, as a public works project, was intended to confer an economic, as well as a religious and aesthetic, benefit on the polis, and that by paying 1 dr. p.d. to every worker, even if he was a slave or metic, that money got into circulation in the community, as it would not have in the hands of soldiers, who would have spent much of their pay abroad. But if that were the objective, the polis could have raised the pay of dikasts, or the diobelia dole itself, to 1 dr. p.d., and thereby restricted the entire economic benefit to resident *citizens*.

Third, one might point to the fact that the Erechtheion workmen were paid only for the days that they worked, while soldiers and sailors presumably were paid for every day that they were on duty, including festival days, so that over the course of the year they might actually have earned more money. But there is no evidence that during the active period of construction Erechtheion workmen were employed less than half the year, so they should in any event have been paid more per *year* than soldiers who were paid only half as much per *day*.[20]

Fourth, one might speculate that there was competition from the private sector, i.e., that the polis had to match a 1 dr. p.d. wage in the private construction industry. But how much of a large-scale construction industry could there have been after the Sicilian disaster and during the Dekeleian War, and, even if there was one, what incentive—or economic possibility—would *it* have had, while the diobelia was in force (i.e., when many unemployed workers were available), to pay unskilled workers the same wage as skilled workers?

Fifth, one might wonder whether Athenian soldiers had any choice in the matter, i.e., were they not obliged to serve no matter how low their

20. I.e., an Erechtheion worker who is paid 1 dr. p.d. needs to work only 183 days in a given year in order to earn more money than a soldier who is paid 3 ob. for every one of the 365 days in that year.

pay was? Thucydides certainly does tell us of citizens who were obliged to serve as soldiers and sailors, just as he also tells us of foreign mercenaries who served alongside these citizens as soldiers and sailors.[21] But even if these citizen soldiers and sailors were obliged, after 412, to accept the reduced military pay of 3 ob. p.d., why would the polis choose to pay 1 dr. p.d.—twice as much—to other citizens, and to metics and slaves as well, who were engaged in labor on the Erechtheion that frequently was unskilled, and in all cases was safe from the dangers of war?

Sixth, one could also speculate that if 1 dr. p.d. had been the rate for public construction workers before 412,[22] it might have persisted as the "legal" construction wage even though soldiers' and sailors' pay had been cut—but how could the polis have justified this (well publicized) retention to soldiers and sailors and their families? (It surely would be too facile to suggest that soldiers and sailors never had the votes to change this legal wage because, at any given time, most of them were away from Athens!)

Seventh and finally, one might wonder whether every Erechtheion worker was deemed to be in the service of Athena Polias, and entitled to equal treatment by her, in the construction of an offering that many hoped would deliver Athens from her military and economic woes.

Although these last two considerations—the possibility that the 1 dr. p.d. Erechtheion wage may be a vestige of a pre-412 "legal" wage, and the possibility that there was a religious motivation to treat all Erechtheion workmen equally—may point to a solution of the two Erechtheion questions, they do not, in my view, provide a full and convincing explanation. At our distance, and with our relatively meager evidence, we cannot always understand why the Athenians made the judgments that they did on questions of social valuc and comparability.[23] But the mere

21. Thuc. iii. 16. 1, 18. 3–4, vii. 48. 5, viii. 24. 2 (Athenian citizens obliged to serve as soldiers and sailors); Thuc. i. 143. 1, vi. 43, vii. 63. 3, viii. 73. 5 (foreign mercenaries serving alongside Athenian soldiers and sailors.).

22. See n. 16 for the absence of positive evidence for a per diem construction wage during the Periklean building program (4 ob. p.d. is perhaps more likely than 1 dr. p.d.). In the immediately following period (i.e., c. 429–412), when pay for soldiers and sailors was 1 dr. p.d., construction wages may also been 1 dr. p.d., although again there is no positive evidence.

23. As E. Badian points out to me, we have trouble enough understanding our own judgments in these matters, e.g., why we pay teachers so much *less* than auto workers. Here, the question is slightly different: why were all Erechtheion workers paid the *same* amount?

asking of these questions does clarify the initial question about a standard wage: there is *no* evidence of a standard wage that applied to all workers in all fields. As far as we can tell, the Erechtheion was the exception, not the rule, in paying the same wage, within a single field, to workers of widely differing tasks and skills.

Do we know how serving hoplites, rowers etc: were victualled? did they have to spend their pay on food as they went, or was it additional to actual costs of maintenance?? How practical would it have been for troops on campaign to get daily supplies for themselves?? — does anyone consider this?

[Bakers ⇒ Sicily ?]

Chapter 15
Inflation and Deflation?

The second general question that arises out of this study concerns inflation. To what extent *was* there inflation and deflation in Athens, and what were the causes and effects in each case? These questions have been considered recently by Gallo, although only with respect to period #4 discussed below.[1]

The evidence comes almost entirely from the "public sector." From the various categories that comprise that sector we have evidence of certainly three, and perhaps as many as six, periods of wage movements:

1. c. 450–432. Around 450, 4 ob. p.d. was the pay of epistatai of Eleusinian funds and possibly of officials or soldiers who were involved in Athens' arrangements with Miletos, but the dates for both figures are controversial. By c. 432, there is fragmentary evidence that another supervisory official was drawing 1 dr. p.d., which also is the clearly attested rate for soldiers and sailors in that year.[2] So the very limited evidence that we have suggests that there was a broad 50% rise in public wages in the 20 years or so before the outbreak of the Peloponnesian War—but again, the uncertain dates for the first two figures, as well as the small number of figures, mean that this conclusion is far from certain.

2. c. 432–412. In this period, public wages for the most part were stable: 1 dr. p.d. for soldiers and sailors, 1 dr. p.d. for a public prosecutor, and a raise, exceptionally, for dikasts, from 2 to 3 ob. p.d. in 425.[3]

3. c. 412–403. In c. 412, the wages of soldiers and sailors were cut very sharply, from 1 dr. to 3 ob. p.d., and in 411 the pay of most public

1. Gallo, "Salari" passim, esp. 60–63. Inflation in period #4 had been detected much earlier by F. B. Jevons, "Work and Wages in Athens," *JHS* 15 (1895) 239–247 at 244–245.

2. "Public Officeholders" ##3–4, 6; "Soldiers and Sailors" ##2, 4–5.

3. "Soldiers and Sailors" ##5, 12–13, 15; "Public Officeholders" ##10–11, 13. As discussed at pp. 244 and 250 below, I attribute the raise for dikasts primarily to political pressures at a time when the state could ill afford it, even though the dikasts may have needed it.

officeholders was eliminated altogether. In 410, the 2 ob. p.d. dole for citizens was introduced, but it may have been cut to 1 ob. p.d. in 407/6, and for at least part of 405/4 it was a grain distribution. In 403/2, cavalrymen and mounted archers suffered a 33 1/3% cut, which may also have been shared by soldiers and sailors.[4] The aggregate reductions in this period, therefore, range from 50 to 100%.[5]

4. c. 403–330. In the 10 years after 403, dikasts probably were restored to 3 ob. p.d., ekklesiasts were raised in stages from nothing to 1 ob. to 2 ob. to 3 ob. p.d., and soldiers probably were restored to 1 dr. p.d. (μισθός + σιτηρέσιον).[6] By c. 375, ambassadors may have been drawing travel allowances of 2 dr. p.d.—twice the highest well-attested rate for higher public officials before 412.[7] By 322, at the latest, public officeholders other than dikasts (and, apparently, public lawyers) all had received a per diem raise—ekklesiasts from 3 ob. to 1 dr. for most sessions, prytaneis from 3 ob. to 1 dr., and archons from 3 ob. to 4 ob.—and the doles for ἀδύνατοι had been increased from 1 ob. to 2 ob. p.d.[8] Meanwhile, for public construction workers there was a raise from 1 dr. p.d. in the years 409–407 to 1 1/4–2 1/2 dr. p.d. in 329/8 (1 1/2 dr. for unskilled workers, 2 1/2 dr. top wage for skilled workers),[9] and in this same period architects' salaries went from 1 dr. to 2 dr. p.d.[10] Contemporaneous with these clear jumps are apparent increases in fees for professors (from 300–500 dr. to 500–1,000 dr., presumably for a course of instruction),[11] and possibly also for artists and musicians (from 1 dr. to 2 dr. p.d.).[12] For soldiers and sailors, however, 1 dr. p.d. seems to have remained the base

---

4. "Soldiers and Sailors" ##16–19 with further discussion at pp. 56–57; "Public Officeholders" ##17–18; "Welfare and Support Allowances and Distributions" #7.

5. As discussed in greater detail under "A Standard Athenian Wage?" (at p. 238 with n. 22), we do not know whether the 1 dr. p.d. wage for the Erechtheion workmen in 409–407 reflected a cut from earlier levels, the retention of an earlier "legal wage," or something else. M. N. Tod, "The Economic Background of the Fifth Century," *CAH* V^1 (1927) 1–32 at 24–25, apparently relying only on the Erechtheion wages, saw a *rise* in wages at the end of the fifth century.

6. "Public Officeholders" ##11, 19; "Soldiers and Sailors" ##21–24 with further discussion at pp. 57–58.

7. "Travel Allowances" #10 with further discussion at p. 219.

8. "Public Officeholders" ##30 (a)–(d), 31; "Welfare and Support Allowances and Distributions" ##10, 22.

9. "Construction and Other Manual Workers" ##3, 7.

10. "Overseers, Architects and Other Salaried Construction Personnel" ##4, 7, 8.

11. "Doctors, Lawyers and Professors" ##12, 13, 19, and possibly 23.

12. "Actors, Artists, Musicians and Writers" ##8, 16.

compensation (but with possibilities of increases by booty or in other special circumstances), and 20 dr. continued to be the base cost of public inscriptions.[13] Thus, in this (relatively long) period, there was a general, but by no means uniform, increase: from 0% (dikasts, public lawyers, soldiers and inscribers) to 33 1/3% (archons) to 50% (unskilled workers) to 100% (ekklesiasts, prytaneis, architects, dole recipients; also, apparently, ambassadors and professors, and perhaps artists and musicians as well) to 150% (the most skilled construction workers). The median increase seems to have been 100%.[14]

5. c. 330–300. In this period, the base price for public inscriptions rose from 20 to 30 dr., and the per diem travel allowance for public officials may have risen from 2 to 2 1/2 or 3 dr. p.d.—a 25 to 50% increase.[15]

6. c. 300–250. In this period, the ἀδύνατοι dole may have declined from 2 ob. to c. 1.8 ob. p.d., and the base price for public inscriptions dropped from 30 dr. to 20 dr. or less, i.e., a drop of 10 to 33 1/3% or more.[16]

As for the *causes* of these upward and downward movements—attested, it must again be emphasized, almost exclusively in the public sector[17]—the sources only rarely offer us explicit help, but it is possible to speculate with varying degrees of confidence.

---

13. "Soldiers and Sailors" ##26, 29–32 with further discussion at pp. 57–58; "Inscribers" with discussion at pp. 163–164.

14. I exclude the ekklesiasts' early rapid jumps (0 to 3 ob. p.d. in c. 403–393) from this general summary of percentage increases because it seems to me that those increases—more than 300% in 10 years—are wholly unrepresentative, reflecting not so much *general* inflationary pressures as a "catch-up" designed to put ekklesiasts on an equal footing with dikasts. Like the later increases for ekklesiasts, however, these early increases evidently reflected a "demand" for ekklesiasts whose "supply," in the numbers needed for a quorum, required something approaching a market wage. See "Public Officeholders" #19 with further discussion at pp. 30–31; see also p. 248 with n. 49 below.

15. "Inscribers" with discussion at p. 164; "Travel Allowances" ##22, 26 with further discussion at p. 219.

16. "Welfare and Support Allowances and Distributions" #24; "Inscribers" with discussion at 164. See also "Doctors, Lawyers and Professors" #33 for an apparent drop for professors in the second century B.C.

17. Apparently untouched by these fluctuations were "Priests, Oracles and Seers" (##2, 6), "Prostitutes and Pimps" (##9, 22, 42 and possibly 5 [average prostitutes]), and "Transport Costs" (##1, 7, with further discussion at pp. 201–202). Payments to priests may have been ossified by religious conservatism (see pp. 86–87 with n. 29), while the supply of average prostitutes may have been adequate for the demand.

1. The possible c. 50% rise in wages from c. 450 to 432 would be the natural result of enormous tribute revenues pouring into Athens year after year. With the transfer of the treasury of the Delian League from Delos to Athens by 453 and the elimination of the Persian military threat by the Peace of Kallias in 449, more money was available for expenditure in Athens itself, for (the raw materials for) public works, and for the wages of public officeholders, soldiers and sailors, and public construction workers.[18] The increasing amount and circulation of this money, in the context of a (presumably) less rapidly increasing labor supply, would have been the cause of the wage increases in this period.

2. The period c. 432 to 412 was not an easy time to maintain these wage levels. Thucydides tells us that the siege of Poteidaia (432–430) cost 2,000 talents, primarily because of wages for soldiers and sailors,[19] and these military wages would have continued to be the primary drain on the public treasury for the rest of the Archidamian War. In addition to military expenditures, the war must have disrupted trade, at least to some extent,[20] and this in turn would have reduced revenues from harbor duties.[21] Finally, the plague (430–426)[22] must have taken an economic as well as a human toll. To meet these rising expenses, Athens resorted to a number of extraordinary measures. First, the Hellenotamiai as early as 433/2 had begun to borrow heavily from the Treasurers of Athena and the Other Gods, and they borrowed every year thereafter until 422.[23] Second, the eisphora property tax was introduced in 428.[24] Third, the

---

18. *IG* I^3 259. 3; Plut. *Per.* xii. 1–6; E. Badian, *From Plataea to Potidaea* (Baltimore 1993) 1–72, 103; D. M. Lewis, "The Thirty Years Peace," *CAH* V^2 (1992) 121–146 at 126.

19. Thuc. ii. 70. 2; iii. 17. 3–4.

20. Thuc. ii. 69. 1 (in 430/29, Melesander sent as strategos to Caria and Lycia, ὅπως ταῦτά τε ἀργυρολογῶσι καὶ τὸ λῃστικὸν τῶν Πελοποννησίων μὴ ἐῶσιν αὐτόθεν ὁρμώμενον βλάπτειν τὸν πλοῦν τῶν ὁλκάδων τῶν ἀπὸ Φασήλιδος καὶ Φοινίκης καὶ τῆς ἐκεῖθεν ἠπείρου), iv. 53. 3 (before Athenian capture of Kythera in 424, the Spartans used to garrison it, ἦν γὰρ αὐτοῖς τῶν τε ἀπ' Αἰγύπτου καὶ Λιβύης ὁλκάδων προσβολή, καὶ λῃσταὶ ἅμα τὴν Λακωνικὴν ἧσσον ἐλύπουν ἐκ θαλάσσης, ᾗπερ μόνον οἷόν τε ἦν κακουργεῖσθαι).

21. For the existence of these prior to 413, see Böckh, *SdA* I 388–395.

22. Thuc. ii. 47. 3, iii. 87. 1–3.

23. *IG* I^3 369 passim. See summary in M-L 217, showing estimated total borrowings of 5,598 T.

24. Thuc. iii. 19. 1. On the question of whether the eisphora was levied for the first time ever, or only for the first time in the war, see L. Kallet-Marx, *Money, Expense, and Naval Power in Thucydides' History 1–5.24* (Berkeley 1993) 134–136. As D. M. Lewis, "The Archidamian War,"

tribute assessment was more than doubled in 425.[25] Although in these increasingly difficult circumstances it might have been prudent to *reduce* public expenditures, the Athenians evidently made a conscious determination to *maintain* wages, presumably to bolster domestic morale and to impress the Athenians' enemies with their resources. I suggest that these considerations also motivated the *increase* for dikasts in 425, from 2 to 3 obols per day. As discussed in greater detail under "Public Officeholders" #10, the very specific statement of the scholiast that Kleon as strategos was responsible for this increase, "when the war was going well," is a credible detail. With the capture of Pylos and the Spartan hostages, and the expected increase in tribute revenues as a result of the reassessment (proposed by Thoudippos, who may have been Kleon's son-in-law),[26] Kleon would have been able to argue that victory—and prosperity—were just around the corner, and that his (actual or potential) supporters among the dikasts deserved a raise. This turned out to be premature: peace did not come until 421, but the Athenians were in fact able to maintain the new raise, as well as the earlier wage levels for soldiers and sailors.

3. The ultimate cause of the sharp cuts in 412–411 was the Sicilian Expedition (415–413), which had been enormously costly in money, as well as lives.[27] The Spartan occupation of Dekeleia followed (413), with a consequent loss of agricultural wealth and production, the desertion of 20,000 slaves, the closing of the silver mines at Laureion, and the blocking of the overland grain route from Euboia.[28] All of this naturally reduced private wealth, and hence (the possibility of) public revenues from the eisphora. Tribute revenues also must have become inadequate, for in 413 a 5% harbor tax was imposed in their place,[29] but the effectiveness of

---

CAH V² (1992) 370–432 at 420, n. 126, observes, Ar. *Eq.* 923–926 suggests that the eisphora had become a familiar institution by 424.

25. *IG* I³ 71 (= M-L no. 69) passim.

26. See M-L 196–197.

27. For the financial cost, see Thuc. vi. 12. 1, 31. 5, 94. 4, vii. 16. 2, viii. 1. 2; *IG* I³ 370. 73–76, 371. 8.

28. Thuc. vii. 19. 1, 27. 3–28. 1. At vi. 91. 7, Alcibiades had said that the occupation of Dekeleia would result in the closing of the mines, and the substitute gold and bronze coinage issued in 407–405 (see n. 33) indicates that they were in fact closed.

29. Thuc. vii. 28. 4: δι' ἃ καὶ τότε ὑπό τε τῆς Δεκελείας πολλὰ βλαπτούσης καὶ τῶν ἄλλων ἀναλωμάτων μεγάλων προσπιπτόντων ἀδύνατοι ἐγένοντο τοῖς χρήμασιν. καὶ τὴν εἰκοστὴν ὑπὸ τοῦτον τὸν χρόνον τῶν κατὰ θάλασσαν ἀντὶ τοῦ φόρου τοῖς ὑπηκόοις ἐποίησαν,

this new tax was put in jeopardy by the revolts of Chios, Miletos, Rhodes and other allies in the Eastern Mediterranean (412–411),[30] which obviously ended Athens' firm control of the sea, and consequently disrupted trade.[31] As a result, the Athenians had recourse in 411, for the first time in the war, to their thousand-talent reserve, and they were forced to do what they had resisted doing in the Archidamian War, namely, to cut public salaries: the wages of soldiers and sailors already had been cut in half in c. 412, and in 411 pay for most other public officeholders was eliminated altogether.[32] Part of these savings were offset by the introduction in 410 of the new diobelia dole—itself an indication of the hard times on which the citizenry had fallen—but even this may have been cut to 1 ob. in 407/6, when the Athenians also were forced to melt down the golden statues of the goddess Nike for an emergency issue of gold coins. In 406/5, they had to issue silver-plated token bronze coins, and in 405/4 the diobelia was converted to a grain distribution.[33] Finally, in 403/2, cavalrymen and mounted archers (and possibly also soldiers and sailors) took a 33 1/3% pay cut.[34] As discussed in greater detail under "A Standard Athenian Wage?" (at pp. 235–239), the difficult fact to fit into the earlier years of this period (409–407) is the construction of the Erechtheion, whose workers were paid 1 dr. p.d. when soldiers and sailors were getting 3 ob. p.d. and many citizens were on the dole: perhaps this was a vestige of an earlier "legal" construction wage and/or equal payment of all workers was somehow required for religious reasons.

4. In the fourth century, where we lack evidence of decade-by-decade changes, it is harder to pinpoint the causes of the rebound in

---

πλείω νομίζοντες ἂν σφίσι χρήματα οὕτω προσιέναι· αἱ μὲν γὰρ δαπάναι οὐχ ὁμοίως καὶ πρίν, ἀλλὰ πολλῷ μείζους καθέστασαν, ὅσῳ καὶ μείζων ὁ πόλεμος ἦν· αἱ δὲ πρόσοδοι ἀπώλλυντο.

30. Thuc. viii. 14. 2–3, 17. 3, 44. 2.

31. Thuc. vii. 28. 1, viii. 35. 2. For the likelihoood that the tribute was reintroduced, see A. Andrewes, "The Peace of Nicias and the Sicilian Expedition," *CAH* V^2 (1992) 433–463 at 458 with n. 44 and references therein.

32. Thuc. viii. 15. 1; "Soldiers and Sailors" ##16–18; "Public Officeholders" ##17, 18.

33. "Welfare and Other Support Allowances and Distributions" #7; Ar. *Ran.* 720; Σ Ar. *Ran.* 725; Hellanicus 323a *FGrH* 26; Philochorus 328 *FGrH* 141. For the chronology and background, see Kraay, *ACGC* 68–70; A. Andrewes, "The Spartan Resurgence," *CAH* V^2 (1992) 464–498 at 492 with n. 57; K. Dover, *Aristophanes Frogs* (Oxford 1993) 281–282. The token bronze coins were outlawed sometime before c. 392 (Ar. *Eccl.* 815–822).

34. "Soldiers and Sailors" #19.

wages after 403, and their (median) doubling by c. 330. There are at least three possibilities:

(a) *Famine*. Two inscriptions carrying building accounts for public works projects at Eleusis around 330[35] also show that between 333/2? and 329/8 there was a very significant rise in prices, notably for grain but also for clothing and livestock. The rise in grain prices is confirmed by other sources, which collectively establish pretty clearly that there was a severe grain shortage in Athens around 330, probably caused by drought or other adverse conditions in the usual (overseas) sources of supply.[36] Are the increases that we see in wages also caused by the jump in grain prices, and if so, are they to be seen as rapid (but temporary) jumps around the year 330? Almost certainly not, because the earlier inscription, which shows the *lower* costs of clothing and livestock, also shows that architects' salaries already had increased to 2 dr. p.d., i.e., before the rise in clothing and livestock prices.[37]

(b) *Bullion*. Another possible reason for the increase in wages evident in c. 330 is the enormous quantity of gold and silver that had been captured by Alexander the Great from the Persian treasuries.[38] Westermann suggested that this bullion flooded into Greece from the East, reducing the value of the precious metals that already were there, and inflating the price of all goods and services that one could buy with these metals—and he pointed to a parallel for this in the five years following the discovery of gold in California in 1849, when (he reported) prices as well as wages rose dramatically in the United States and Europe.[39] To the extent that Alexander's booty consisted of silver that reached Greece before the attested wage increases in

---

35. "Overseers, Architects and Other Salaried Construction Personnel" ##7, 8; "Construction and Other Manual Workers" ##7, 8.

36. For these price increases, see "Introduction" n. 3; "Overseers, Architects and Other Salaried Construction Personnel" p. 103 with n. 17.

37. "Overseers, Architects and Other Salaried Construction Personnel" #7. See also n. 42 below for even earlier increases in architects' salaries at Delphi.

38. Diod. Sic. xvii. 66. 1–2, 71. 1, 74. 5, 80. 3; Plut. *Alex.* xxxvi. 1; Strabo xv. 3. 9; Arrian *Anab.* iii. 16. 7; Curtius v. 2. 11, v. 6. 9–10, vi. 2. 10; Justin xi. 14. 9.

39. Westermann, "Ephodia" 215–216.

Athens, there might be some plausibility to this theory, although most of his booty seems to have consisted of gold (the usual Persian metal for coins and bullion), and its principal immediate effect, therefore, would have been to reduce the value of gold as against silver, rather than to increase wages and prices normally payable in silver.[40] But since Alexander's bullion was captured in Persia no earlier than 331,[41] it is chronologically impossible that this bullion could have been responsible for the wage levels attested at Athens in 333/2.[42]

(c) *Gradual Inflation.* If neither famine nor a massive infusion of bullion caused a sudden doubling of wage levels around 330, this increase was probably a very gradual phenomenon,[43] fueled by a similarly gradual increase in the silver supply (caused by the revival of the Laureion mines),[44] as well as by the expansion of commercial and banking activity during a long period of sustained prosperity.[45] We see jumps as early as the 390s for ekklesiasts, and possibly in the 370s and 360s for ambassadors and top professors, and by c. 330 large raises are attested for ekklesi-

---

40. Xen. *Vect.* iv. 10 explicitly recognized that an increased supply of gold would reduce its price and raise the price of silver: ἐκεῖνο μέντοι οἶδα, ὅτι καὶ χρυσίον ὅταν πολὺ παραφανῇ, αὐτὸ μὲν ἀτιμότερον γίγνεται, τὸ δὲ ἀργύριον τιμιώτερον ποιεῖ. See also J. R. Melville-Jones, "The Value of Gold at Athens in 329/8," *AJAH* 3 (1978) 184–187, esp. n. 7; D. M. Lewis, "New Evidence for the Gold-Silver Ratio," in C. M. Kraay and G. K. Jenkins, eds., *Essays in Greek Coinage Presented to Stanley Robinson* (Oxford 1968) 105–110.

41. Arrian *Anab.* iii. 16. 10 tells us that in December 331, precisely (see P. A. Brunt, *Arrian* I [Cambridge, Massachusetts 1976] 483), Alexander sent up to 3,000 T. of silver to Antipater for the Lacedaimonian War. Most of this would have gone to mercenaries, some to civilian workers, all of them in the Greek-Macedonian area. How much of it would have reached Athens, and how early, we do not know.

42. "Overseers, Architects and Other Salaried Construction Personnel" #7. Gallo, "Salari" 61–63, also rejected bullion as the cause of the wage increases evident in c. 330 because (a) architects' salaries of 2–4 Aiginetan dr. already had been attested in the 340s at Delphi ("Salari" 31), and (b) Xen. *Vect.* iii. 9–10 ("Welfare and Support Allowances and Distributions" #13 with n. 24) indicated to Gallo that the cost of living already had risen by 355.

43. Inflation of much less than 1% per year would result in a doubling of wages in c. 70 years.

44. See M. Langdon, "Poletai Records," *Agora* XIX (Princeton 1991) 57–143; R. J. Hopper, "The Attic Silver Mines in the Fourth Century B.C.," *ABSA* 48 (1953) 200–254; R. J. Hopper, "The Laureion Mines: A Reconsideration," *ABSA* 63 (1968) 293–326.

45. See E. E. Cohen, *Athenian Economy and Society: A Banking Perspective* (Princeton 1992) 219, with references. See also Gallo, "Salari" 62, who points to the increase in attested banking and trade activities, and the theorikon, as probable indications of an increased circulation of money that might gradually have raised wages and prices.

asts, prytaneis, architects, construction workers and dole recipients.[46] But side by side with these increases there are no changes at all for dikasts, soldiers, and inscribers, and only a negligible increase for archons.[47] What accounts for these discrepancies?[48]

(i) In the case of ekklesiasts, the sources are very explicit: ekklesiasts were not showing up in numbers sufficient to constitute a quorum, so pay of 1 ob. was introduced, but the turnout was still too small, so the pay was increased to 2 ob., and finally to 3 ob.[49] In other words, there was a high *demand* for a (large number of) ekklesiasts, but the required *supply* of these ekklesiasts would respond to this demand only if their wages were raised significantly.

(ii) I suggest that supply and demand also were responsible for the other changes in public wages, i.e., that the polis paid more only when it had to, and only as much as it had to: relatively small increases for archons (who may have been honored to serve) and unskilled construction workers (of whom there were always a fair number available); more to ekklesiasts (to persuade enough of them to show up to constitute a quorum), to prytaneis (to induce them to devote an uninterrupted 35–36 days to the polis), to dole recipients (who could not have sur-

46. "Public Officeholders" ##19, 30 (a) and (c); "Travel Allowances" #10 with further discussion at p. 219; "Doctors, Lawyers and Professors" ##19, 23; "Overseers, Architects and Other Salaried Construction Personnel" ##7, 8; "Construction and Other Manual Workers" #7; "Welfare and Support Allowances and Distributions" #22.

47. "Public Officeholders" #11, 30 (b) and (d); "Soldiers and Sailors" ##26, 29–32 with further discussion at pp. 57–58; "Inscribers" with discussion at pp. 163–164.

48. Gallo, "Salari" 24–54, suggests that the 100 to 150% increases for skilled workers and architects reflects increased demand for their increasingly scarce services and that the 100% increase in the dole for ἀδύνατοι reflects an increase in the basic cost of living, while lesser increases for soldiers and (some) public officeholders indicate that the "public sector" was not keeping up with the cost of living—but that ignores the facts (a) that public construction workers and dole recipients also were part of the public sector and (b) that ekklesiasts and prytaneis also had 100% increases. Nonetheless, his larger point—that some workers stayed ahead of cost-of-living increases and others fell behind—seems correct.

49. Ar. *Eccl.* 183–188, 300–310, esp. 302b and 309; Arist. *Ath. Pol.* xli. 3 (both quoted in "Public Officeholders" notes 44 and 45).

vived—and who would have created an unacceptable social and political problem—without an increase), to ambassadors (to enable them to represent the state in a respectable fashion), and to architects and some skilled construction workers (whose supply of specialized skills was in varying demand and accordingly received varying compensation); and the largest increase to construction workers whose specialized skills were in the greatest demand. The fact that dikasts, soldiers, and inscribers received no increase suggests that their supply was adequate for the demand—something that we might have suspected already in the case of soldiers, from the growth of mercenary armies in the fourth century. This wide range—and very different pace of change—in public wages indicates that these wages were set, and modified, as they needed to be in order to secure workers, and thus that there was in some sense a "labor market."

(iii) Because wages in the "private sector" are much less well attested, it is difficult to speak with similar confidence about them, but it is worth noting that the apparent increases for professors, and possibly also for artists and musicians, might suggest that their "performances" were in great demand, while the fact that 3 ob. per occasion seems to have remained the charge of average prostitutes (even into periods ##5 and 6) suggests that *their* supply was adequate for the demand.[50]

5 and 6. For the periods after c. 330, the evidence becomes much more meager. It is certainly plausible, though unverifiable, that inscribing costs and travel allowances rose in the period c. 330–300 because of general inflation caused by Alexander's bullion (see n. 15). But if there was substantial inflation in the last 30 years of the fourth century, what caused the *drop* in inscribing costs, and possibly in welfare allowances as well, in the third century (see n. 16)? I suspect that in the third century

50. "Doctors, Lawyers and Professors" ##12, 13, 19, and possibly 23; "Actors, Artists, Musicians and Writers" ##8, 16; "Prostitutes and Pimps" ##9, 22, 42, and possibly 5.

Athens was in an economic (as well as a political) slump and that wealth and skills gravitated to the new centers of the Hellenistic world, i.e., that this was a local, rather than a global, depression.

One may speculate also about the *effects* of the ups and downs in wages. In general, upward movements in wages (in c. 450–432, c. 403–330 and c. 330–300) also should have increased prices—and public expenditures—and, indeed, it may be that the (chronologically) unique increases for dikasts in 425 and for ekklesiasts in c. 403–393 were "catch-up" raises,[51] prompted by the fact that everyone else already was earning more, and having more to spend, on goods that now cost more. Similarly, the abrupt drop in wages in c. 412–403 should have decreased prices (and public expenditures, though not for the diobelia) since there was less money available for goods. Unfortunately, most surviving prices are not as precisely comparable with one another as surviving wages and allowances, so it is not possible to confirm this (reasonable but hypothetical) correlation of prices with labor costs.[52]

51. "Public Officeholders" ##10, 19.
52. See "Introduction" pp. 1–2.

Chapter 16

An Embedded or a Market Economy?

One of the most hotly debated questions in ancient history today concerns the nature of the ancient economy generally,[1] and more particularly of the Athenian economy: was it primitive or modern, an embedded or a market economy? In the earliest phase of this debate, which has been going on since the late nineteenth century, the "primitivists" (led by Karl Bücher) held that the ancient economy was a "closed household economy," while the "modernists" (led by Eduard Meyer) argued that by the fifth century B.C. industrial production, international commerce and monetary exchange had replaced aristocratic landholdings as the dominant forces in the economy. Later, under the leadership of Max Weber, Johannes Hasebroek and Karl Polanyi, the primitivist position was modified and replaced by those who saw the ancient economy as "embedded" in society and for *that* reason not subject to independent market forces. Similarly, the modernists have been succeeded by those who concede that the ancient economy was significantly different from the large-scale industrial economies of the nineteenth and twentieth centuries, but nonetheless see it as subject to independent market forces.[2]

An embedded economy is one in which goods and services are distributed on the basis of personal and political relationships (with relatives, friends, dependents, patrons and fellow citizens generally), with no independent weight being given to market conditions. It has been described very recently as follows: "Polanyi called himself a 'substantivist,' arguing that in Europe before 1800 production and exchange had been 'embedded' in other institutions. He did not deny that there had been a profit

1. For the view that the economy in the Graeco-Roman world remained essentially unchanged for a very long time (1000 B.C.–A.D. 500), notwithstanding very significant political changes, see M. I. Finley, *The Ancient Economy*² (Berkeley 1985) 27–34; K. Hopkins, "Introduction," in P. Garnsey, K. Hopkins and C. R. Whittaker, eds., *Trade in the Ancient Economy* (Berkeley 1983) ix–xxv at xiv.

2. For a brief history of the debate, with references, see M. M. Austin and P. Vidal-Naquet, *Economic and Social History of Ancient Greece: An Introduction* (Berkeley 1977) 3–8. For the proponents of a "market" model of the Athenian economy, see n. 7.

motive in earlier societies, but argued that it had been a means to other ends, not an end in itself. Goods circulated through reciprocity and redistribution rather than through impersonal markets. Social relationships fixed values, not abstract laws of supply and demand; and these relationships made the rational choices of the isolated actor of economic theory irrelevant."[3]

A market economy, on the other hand, is one in which goods and services are distributed on the basis of negotiations by unrelated individuals who are motivated less by personal and political relationships than by such considerations as supply, demand, quality and price. These are also characteristics of a "modern economy, which is an independent sphere of activity, governed by its own laws and capable of being studied in isolation."[4]

These models of an embedded and market economy are not necessarily mutually exclusive: even we, who think that we live in a modern market economy, often choose to do business (more expensively than we might otherwise) with persons with whom we have some sort of personal, political or (other) business relationship. But frequently—and usually quite explicitly—our purchases and employment decisions are influenced very significantly by market factors, e.g., we pay more to plumbers (whom we often do not know at all) than to office workers (with whom we may have a closer personal relationship), primarily because the former have more specialized skills and are in shorter supply.

The most prominent modern proponent of the embedded model of the ancient economy was Moses Finley,[5] and his eloquently argued views have attained a kind of orthodoxy over the past 40 years.[6]

Recently, however, there have been a number of dissents in individual areas.[7] The most sustained challenge has come from Edward Cohen, writing about Athenian banking in the fourth century: "The Athenians functioned through a market process in which unrelated indivi-

3. I. Morris, "The Athenian Economy Twenty Years after *The Ancient Economy*," *CPh* 89 (1994) 351–366 at 352.

4. E. M. Burke, "The Economy of Athens in the Classical Era: Some Adjustments to the Primitivist Model," *TAPhA* 122 (1992) 199–226 at 199–200.

5. Most notably in *The Ancient Economy* (as in n. 1), passim.

6. See, e.g., Hopkins (as in n. 1) xi, describing Finley's views as the "new orthodoxy."

7. E.g., Burke (as in n. 4) 199–226; E. E. Cohen, *Athenian Economy and Society: A Banking Perspective*, (Princeton 1992).

duals, often in the city only transiently, sometimes even operating from abroad, sought monetary profit through commercial exchange. . . . Not only were these transactions 'disembedded from' society: they were seen by theoreticians in their writings and litigants in their court cases as threatening traditional social and familial methods of handling production and consumption."[8]

I do not wish, in this book, to enter into this debate in any detail. But I do want to note the implications for that debate of my conclusions (a) that there was not a standard Athenian wage and (b) that there were periods of marked inflation and deflation in public wages in classical Athens.

Both of these conclusions had been denied by Finley.[9] If wages were indeed "nominal" or "conventional" (e.g., a drachma a day for everyone, regardless of the work performed),[10] and if they did not change significantly over time, that would support Finley's model of an embedded economy in which wages were merely token exchanges among members of a status-ordered society, who engaged in a variety of reciprocal transactions without any recognition of the "market" value of the particular labor being compensated.

While it might be possible to argue that this view of wages finds (at least) partial support in Athens prior to c. 412, when most attested wages were 4 ob. p.d. (before c. 432) or 1 dr. p.d. (c. 432–412), it is clear that after c. 412 wages were very different for different categories of workers, and that over time these wages changed at different rates for different

---

8. Cohen (as in n. 7) 4.

9. Finley (as in n. 1) 23 with n. 19: "The economic language and concepts we are all familiar with, even the laymen among us, the 'principles', whether they are Alfred Marshall's or Paul Samuelson's, the models we employ, tend to draw us into a false account. For example, wage rates and interest rates in the Greek and Roman worlds were both fairly stable locally over long periods (allowing for sudden fluctuations in moments of intense political conflict or military conquest), so that to speak of a 'labour market' or a 'money market' is immediately to falsify the situation. For Rome, where the evidence about wage rates is even more skimpy than for Greece, the dominance of a conventional, rather than a market-determined, figure is shown by M. H. Crawford, *Roman Republican Coinage* (2 vols., Cambridge 1974) II chap. 6." At 80, Finley added: "Wage rates in antiquity generally remained remarkably stable and undifferentiated."

10. Finley (as in n. 1) 79-80 drew this (generalized) conclusion from the Erechtheion wages ("Construction and Other Manual Workers #3) even though he conceded that slaves (who under his view of the Ancient Economy would not be eligible participants in reciprocal exchanges) also were paid 1 dr. p.d. His remark at 80 that "Simias, of course, pocketed both his own pay and that of his slaves" may be true (although it is unprovable), but the metics (who also would not have been fully eligible for reciprocal exchanges) presumably pocketed their own pay.

categories of workers.[11] Status does *not* seem to have been the determining factor: in c. 412–403, rowers were paid more than public officials, and metic and slave construction workers were paid more than citizen rowers,[12] while in c. 330 ekklesiasts were paid more than archons.[13] Independent economic forces of supply and demand are a more likely explanation, for four reasons: (a) although modern scholars have not always taken notice, the concept of "disembedded" supply and demand *was* recognized by at least one Athenian writer on the basis of his own practical, everyday experience;[14] (b) we are told explicitly that it was the demand for a large number of ekklesiasts that kept pushing up their wages;[15] (c) varying demand in relation to varying supply most plausibly accounts for the wide variety of construction wages at Eleusis;[16] and (d) large supply also would explain why dikasts, soldiers, and (for a long time) inscribers failed to share in the increases paid to other categories of workers.[17] From all the evidence at our disposal, it now seems, at least for public wages and at least for the years after c. 412, that there was in some sense a "labor market," with wages being set, and modified, as they needed to be, in order to secure workers. To that extent, classical Athens resembles a market economy more closely than the modern orthodoxy has held.

---

11. See "A Standard Athenian Wage?" at pp. 233–234; "Inflation and Deflation" at pp. 240–242, 244–249.

12. "Public Officeholders" ##17–19; "Soldiers and Sailors" ##16–18; "Construction and Other Manual Workers" #3.

13. "Public Officeholders #30 (a) and (d).

14. Xen. *Vect.* iv. 10 (quoted in "Inflation and Deflation" n. 40, where detailed references are also given to the declining price of gold as its supply increased). As an Athenian citizen with wide practical experience of politics, war, agriculture and economic realities generally, Xenophon is more likely to be representative of Athenian views on economic matters than either Plato or Aristotle—both of them detached intellectuals, and the latter a metic.

15. "Public Officeholders" #19 with further discussion at pp. 30–31, and in "Inflation and Deflation" at pp. 248, 250.

16. "Construction and Other Manual Workers" #7 with further discussion at p. 120, and in "Inflation and Deflation" at pp. 248–249.

17. "Public Officeholders" ##11, 30 (b) with further discussion at pp. 30–31, and in "Inflation and Deflation" at pp. 248–249; "Soldiers and Sailors" pp. 57–58, with further discussion in "Inflation and Deflation" at pp. 248–249.

Conclusions

The results of this study may be summarized briefly.

First, all of the evidence for Athenian wages, salaries, transport costs, and travel and welfare allowances has been collected, categorized, dated and summarized in tabular form in Appendix 1, so that it is now possible to review all of this evidence in one place.

Second, each item of evidence has been evaluated critically. Where necessary, there have been detailed discussions of the textual authority,[1] interpretation[2] and date[3] of the particular item, and in all cases the credibility[4] and utility[5] of the item have been discussed.

1. See especially "Public Officeholders" #33; "Soldiers and Sailors" ##14, 32; "Priests, Oracles and Seers" #4; "Actors, Artists, Musicians and Writers" ##1 (with n. 7), 13, 18; "Overseers, Architects and Other Salaried Construction Personnel" #1 (with n. 3); "Construction and Other Manual Workers" ##1, 4, 5 (with n. 14), 6; "Inscribers" ##6, 31, 33, 38, 43, 52, 55, 58, 68, 72, 90–91, 102, 106–107, 109–110, 117, 120–122, 124–125, 134–136, 142, 145, 157–159, 162, 167, 169–170, 173–174, 176, 179–181, 184–185, 190, 224, 226; "Prostitutes and Pimps" #18; "Miscellaneous Workers" #3; "Travel Allowances" ##2, 12, 14, 19; "Welfare and Support Allowances and Distributions" #24. See also W. T. Loomis, "Eleusinian Inscriptions: Three Emendations," *Hesperia* 64 (1995) 131–134 (for "Construction and Other Manual Workers" #8 [with n. 26]; "Inscribers" ##45 [with n. 49], 112 [with n. 116]; "Transport Costs" #15 [i] [with n. 35]); W. T. Loomis, "Pay Differentials and Class Warfare in Lysias' *Against Theozotides*: Two Obols or Two Drachmas?," *ZPE* 107 (1995) 230–236 (for "Soldiers and Sailors" #19).

2. See especially "Public Officeholders" ##8–9, 17, 19, 22–23, 30; "Soldiers and Sailors" ##2–3, 7, 14, 16, 19–20, 28–29, 32; "Priests, Oracles and Seers" ##2, 5–6, 9, 14–17; "Actors, Artists, Musicians and Writers" ##4, 8, 16–18; "Overseers, Architects and Other Salaried Construction Personnel" ##1, 3–8, and p. 103; "Construction and Other Manual Workers" ##2, 3 (with n. 9), 4, 5 (with n. 14), 6–7, 8 (with n. 28), and pp. 116–119; "Inscribers" ##79, 139; "Prostitutes and Pimps" ##3–9, 13–14, 22, 25–28, 41–42; "Transport Costs" ##8, 13, 14 (with n. 24), 15 (with notes 26–29, 34); "Travel Allowances" ##5, 10, 13–18, 22, 26 with pp. 217–219; "Welfare and Support Allowances and Distributions" ##22, 24.

3. See especially "Public Officeholders" #22; "Soldiers and Sailors" ##22–24; "Doctors, Lawyers and Professors" ##2, 5, 8, 17–23, 25–26, 30–31, 33; "Actors, Artists, Musicians and Writers" ##9, 15, 19–20; "Inscribers ##50, 55, 71, 77, 95, 144, 149, 166 (with n. 256), 177 (with n. 256), 182 (with n. 256), 185 (with n. 256), 194 (with n. 256), 195 (with n. 256); "Prostitutes and Pimps" ##8–9, 16, 22 and notes 43 and 53.

4. In addition to the frequent unreliability of monetary figures in comic poets, orators and late writers (for which see "Introduction" pp. 5–8 with examples cited), see "Doctors, Lawyers and Professors" passim and pp. 74–75; "Actors, Artists, Musicians and Writers" passim and p. 96;

From the great mass of figures, many of which are either unreliable or impossible to use for comparative purposes (or both), I have isolated those figures that tell us what people really were paid for various kinds of work and allowances at various periods.[6] Most of the evidence comes from the classical period (c. 450–320 B.C.), and of this evidence most of the useful figures come from the "public sector"—public officeholders, soldiers and sailors, public construction employees (overseers, architects and manual workers), inscribers of public documents, travel allowances for ambassadors, and public welfare allowances. There is also a small amount of useful evidence for lawyers, professors and prostitutes, and even less for artists, musicians, cooks and transport costs. The evidence for physicians, priests, oracles, seers, actors, writers and pimps is either not reliable or not useful for comparative purposes.

Third, in addition to the critical discussions that have elucidated individual figures, there are three that have resulted in conclusions of broader importance:

(a) In fifth-century Athens, the words μισθός and τροφή, when applied to soldiers and sailors, mean gross pay (pay plus ration-money), i.e., the *sum* of what later came to be known as μισθός and σιτηρέσιον, and it is likely that the word σῖτος, as used in the Athens-Argos-Mantineia-Elis alliance of 420, also means gross pay, even though it means only food, grain or horse-rations in other contexts.[7]

(b) Military pay was introduced in Athens no later than 441, and possibly as early as the 460s or 450s.[8]

(c) The frequent public appropriations for the inscribing of documents on stone covered only the actual inscribing of letters,

---

"Prostitutes and Pimps" passim and pp. 174–178, 184–185; "Transport Costs" ##3–4; "Travel Allowances" #5; "Welfare and Support Allowances and Distributions" ##2, 4–5, 18, 23.

5. See especially "Introduction" p. 8; "Construction and Other Manual Workers" pp. 115, 120; "Miscellaneous Workers" p. 190; "Transport Costs" pp. 201–202; "Welfare and Support Allowances and Distributions" p. 231.

6. Summarized for each category of worker or allowance recipient at the ends of Chapters 1–13.

7. See "Soldiers and Sailors" pp. 33–36, 55–58, ##11 (with n. 36), 15, 19 (with notes 54, 59).

8. See "Soldiers and Sailors" ##1, 3.

and possibly also the final preparation and installation of the inscribed stelai, but not the quarrying, transport and sculptural decoration of those stelai.[9]

Fourth, on the basis of all of these critical discussions, it has been possible to address three general questions:

(a) *A Standard Athenian Wage?* The frequently repeated statement that the "standard wage at Athens was one drachma per day" is not supported by the evidence. Wages and welfare allowances varied from period to period, and within individual periods there is no evidence that one drachma (or any other single sum) was paid to all (or most) workers in all (or most) fields. It is true that many of the Erechtheion workers in 409–407 were paid one drachma per day, regardless of skill or civil status, but in those years soldiers and sailors were paid only half as much—three obols per day.

(b) *Inflation and Deflation?* There were at least three, and perhaps as many as six, periods of wage movements in Athens, attested almost exclusively in the "public sector":

1. c. 450–432. 50% possible rise in wages, probably caused by the influx of tribute and other revenues from the Athenian Empire.
2. c. 432–412. Stable wage levels during the first years of the Peloponnesian War, probably attributable to a political determination to maintain those levels despite the heavy costs of the war.
3. c. 412–403. 50 to 100% cuts in wages, after the Sicilian disaster and the Spartan occupation of Dekeleia, when Athens no longer had the resources to support the earlier wage levels.
4. c. 403–330. Uneven rises in wages and allowances (with a median increase of 100%), which I have interpreted as very slight and gradual inflation during a long period of sustained prosperity and growth in the silver supply, with the greatest increases for workers in short supply and high demand.

9. See "Inscribers" pp. 158–163.

5. c. 330–300. 25 to 50% possible increase (attested for inscribers, and possibly also for travel allowances), perhaps caused by Persian bullion flowing into Greece after the conquests of Alexander the Great.
6. c. 300–250. 10 to 33 1/3% possible drop (attested for inscribers, and possibly also for welfare allowances), perhaps caused by a local economic slump.

(c) *An Embedded or Market Economy?* The answers to the first two general questions suggest that, at least in the fourth century, Athens had more of a market economy than the modern orthodoxy has held.

Wages and welfare allowances are illuminating for Athenian history as a whole. Because our sources emphasize military and political developments, it is easy to lose sight of the economic developments that accompanied them. But it is now clear that, just as Athens' military and political power rose and fell in the fifth century, so too its economic power—and the wages of its public employees—rose and fell. During the Archidamian War, it was difficult for Athens to maintain public wages and during the Ionian War it was impossible, and as a result public wages declined along with Athens itself. In the fourth century, public wages and allowances recovered, and in some cases increased, but selectively, and this is probably a reflection of Athens' ability to pay and the labor market: certain public officeholders, public construction workers and allowance recipients (for whom payments were regarded as either necessary or desirable) fared well, while soldiers and dikasts (whose supply evidently exceeded the demand for their services) fared much less well. The tantalizing indications of public wage increases at the end of the fourth century, and decreases in the third century, may help to clarify those less well documented periods of Athenian history.

Appendices
Labor, Transport and Welfare Costs

The following catalogues, one for Athenian and one for non-Athenian labor, transport and welfare costs, are excerpted from larger catalogues (which I shall publish separately in *Talents*[1]) of all monetary figures that I have found in Greek and Latin literature, Attic inscriptions on stone, and graffiti and dipinti on Greek vases.[2]

The figures from Greek literary and epigraphical sources were collected by means of Ibycus computer word searches for talents, mnas, drachmas, obols, chalkoi, kollyboi, kermata, chrysoi, staters, darics, sigloi, litras, hexantes, noummoi, tesserakosts, and acrophonic numerals in (a) the Greek literary texts (other than those by Christian and Jewish writers) recorded on the *Thesaurus Linguae Graecae* (*TLG*) compact disk C (1987) and (b) the Attic inscriptions recorded on the Packard Humanities Institute (PHI) Greek inscriptions compact disk 4 (1990). The same words (excluding litras [= librae], noummoi [= nummi] and acrophonic numerals) were collected from the Latin literary texts recorded on the PHI Latin compact disk 3 (1990). There are some significant omissions in this collection:

1. Not all Greek literary texts were included on *TLG* disk C. Although most authors whose texts survive in continuous form were included, some important fragments and grammarians (notably Jacoby's *FGrH* and Pollux), as well as most scholia, were excluded. I was

1. Footnote cross-references that are not prefaced by the labels "L. Labor Costs," "M. Transport Costs," or "N. Travel, Welfare and Other Support Allowances and Distributions" (e.g., the cross-reference at p. 273 (n. 2) to "T. Religious Finances: Religious Charges") are advance references to sections of *Talents*.

2. Graffiti and dipinti on vases give prices only for the vases and/or their contents, and thus they do not appear in these excerpts.

able to have the *FGrH* searched on an unpublished disk, and I picked up figures in many of the other fragments through searches in authors like Plutarch and Athenaios, and in (necessarily unsystematic) searches by non-computer methods, through which I also picked up many figures in scholia.

2. Since the search in all sources was confined to the foregoing (mostly) Greek monetary terms, no explicitly Roman figures (such as denarii and sesterces) are included, and Roman figures that have been converted (e.g., denarii to drachmas) are given in their Greek form.

3. Obviously the non-Athenian catalogue does not include any of the numerous figures from non-Attic papyri and inscriptions.

4. I have noticed a (very) few instances where, unaccountably, the Ibycus program failed to pick up a key word even though that word correctly appeared in the text recorded on the compact disk.

I hope to eliminate most of these omissions in the *Talents* book, for which I shall undertake a fresh search through the (then) latest compact disks, using a different search program.[3] At that time, sections L, M and N of the two catalogues in *Talents* will supersede these appendices.

3. As of 1 August 1997, they were compact disks D (1992) for the *TLG*, 7 (1996) for the PHI Greek inscriptions, and 5.3 (1991) for the PHI Latin texts. In my new search, I shall use the Pandora search program.

Appendix 1

Athenian Labor, Transport and Welfare Costs

L. Labor Costs

Public Officeholders[1]

late 460s	1 or 2 ob. p.d.?	Dikast, pay introduced by Perikles	Ar. *Nub.* 863; Pl. *Gorg.* 515e; Arist. *Pol.* 1274a 8–9; Arist. *Ath. Pol.* xxvii. 3–4; Σ Ar. *Vesp.* 88a, 300b; Σ Ar. *Av.* 1541e; Σ Ar. *Ran.* 140; Plut. *Per.* ix. 1–3; Ael. Arist. iii. 98 (Behr) Poll. viii. 113; Hesych. δ 1813 (Latte), δικαστικόν; *Com. Adesp.* fr. 941 (K-A)
c. 450	1–9 ob. p.d.?	Athena Promachos statue officials (aggregate annual salaries [μισθοί] of 1,963 dr. 2 ob. [= 31 ob. p.d. for year of 380 days?], for epistatai [quan. unst.], secretary and assistant, i.e., 4, 6 or 9 ob. p.d. for 2–7 epistatai and secretary, apiece, and 1 or 3 ob. p.d. for assistant?)—Year VI?	*IG* I³ 435. 81–82
"	Same?	Same—1,[963 dr. 2 ob.]? in Year VIII?	" 114–115
450/49?	4 ob. (p.d.?)	Athenian? officials? (or rowers or soldiers?), sent to Miletos, or Milesian soldiers?	*IG* I³ 21. 13
c. 449–447?	4 ob. (p.d.)	5 Eleusinian epistatai (including secretary), apiece	*IG* I³ 32. 8–9

1. See also "Labor Costs: Priests, Oracles and Seers"; "N. Travel, Welfare and Other Support Allowances: Travel Allowances."

447–432	?	Parthenon officials? ([1,]8[3]1 dr. 2 ob. [min. inc.] aggregate annual salaries [in 434/3] for personnel paid by the month [καταμενίοις] include elected epistatai [quan. unst.], secretaries and architect?); no individual amts.	*IG* I^3 436. 29; *IG* I^3 443. 231; *IG* I^3 446. 339; *IG* I^3 447. 361; *IG* I^3 449. 403
c. 440–432	1 dr. p.[d.]	Overseers of public water supply, apiece?	*IG* I^3 49. 3–4
pre-431	?	Before war, >20,000 men supported (τρέφεσθαι) by the state, including 6,000 dikasts, 500 bouleutai, 500 dockyard guards, 50 Akropolis guards, 700 local officials, 700? overseas officials; just before? war began, this number was increased by 2,000 (rowers?) selected by lot; also prison guards (quan. unst.); no amts.	Arist. *Ath. Pol.* xxiv. 3
425	2 dr. p.d.	Ambassadors to Persian King, μισθός for 11 years—pay or ἐφόδια?	Ar. *Ach.* 66–67, 90
425	3 dr. (p.d.)	Ambassadors or taxiarchs? to Thrace, pay (μισθοφοροῦντας) or ἐφόδια?	Ar. *Ach.* 602
425	2→ 3 ob. (p.d.)	Dikast (raised by Kleon as στρατηγός)	Σ Ar. *Vesp.* 88a, 300b; Σ Ar. *Av.* 1541e; Σ Ar. *Ran.* 140; Σ (*vet.*) Ar. *Plut.* 330b; Poll. viii. 113
424	3 ob. (p.d.)	Dikast	Ar. *Eq.* 51, 255, 800
post-424	5 ob. (p.d.)	Athenian dikast sitting in Arkadia in the future, predict "oracles"	Ar. *Eq.* 798
pre-422	2 ob. (p.d.)	Theoros (member of state delegation) or rower? to Paros; μισθός or ἐφόδιον?	Ar. *Vesp.* 1189; Σ Ar. *Vesp.* 1189 a–b, d
422	3 ob. (p.d.)	Dikast	Ar. *Vesp.* 609, 684, 690, 788, 791, 1121; Σ Ar. *Vesp.* 300 b–c, 389c, 663, 684a–b
422	1 dr. (p.d.)?	Dikast	Σ Ar. *Vesp.* 658
422	150 T. p.a.	6,000 dikasts (Σ says 3 ob. p.d. apiece)	Ar. *Vesp.* 663 et Σ

422	1 dr. (p.d.)	Public prosecutor (συνηγορικόν fee)	Ar. *Vesp.* 691 et Σa–b
421/0	?	Hieropoioi of Hephaistia (μισθοφορόντον)	*IG* I^3 82. 20
c. 421–414	3 ob. (p.d.)	Dikast	Ar. fr. 588 (K-A)
c. 420	1,000 dr. (yielding 120 dr. p.a.?)	Demarch of Plotheia, salary or (more likely) allowance for deme cult expenses? (for amt. see Whitehead, *Demes* 166–169)	*IG* I^3 258. 2
414	3 ob. (p.d.)	Dikast	Ar. *Av.* 1541 et Σd
pre-411	? p.d.	Bouleutai drawing pay	Thuc. viii. 69. 4
411	3 ob. p.d.	Nine archons and prytaneis, apiece; pay abolished for other officials under 400	Thuc. viii. 65. 3, 67. 3; Arist. *Ath. Pol.* xxix. 5
411	Nothing	No pay for public officials under 5,000 (except nine archons and prytaneis?)	Thuc. viii. 97. 1; Arist. *Ath. Pol.* xxxiii. 1
pre-405?	3 ob. (p.d.)	Dikast	Phryn. Com. fr. 70 (K-A)
405	?	Dikast being paid	Ar. *Ran.* 1466
405	2 ob., 3 ob., 1 dr. (p.d.)?	Dikast	Σ Ar. *Ran.* 140
pre-403/2	Nothing	Ekklesiast	Ar. *Eccl.* 305b
c. 403–393	1 ob. (p.d.)	Ekklesiast, pay introduced by Agyrrhios or Kallistratos?	Ar. *Eccl.* 184, 302b; Arist. *Ath. Pol.* xli. 3; *Com. Adesp.* fr. 941 (K-A)
c. 403–393	2 ob. (p.d.)	Ekklesiast, pay increased by Herakleides of Klazomenai	Arist. *Ath. Pol.* xli. 3
4th c.?	3 ob. (p.d.)	Dikast (Lucian: per *case*)	Lucian *Bis Acc.* 12; Poll. viii. 20, 113; Lib. *Decl.* xxxiii. 5; *Suda* β 49 (Adler), βακτήρια καὶ σύμβολον, η 214 (Adler) ἡλιασταί; Eust. ad *Il.* xviii. 490–540 (van der Valk IV 229. 5) ad *Od.* i. 156 (Stallbaum I 41. 21)

4th c.?	3 ob. p.d.	Hero Lykos as dikast	Zenob. v. 2 (*CPG*), Λύκου δεκάς
4th c.?	4 ob. (p.d.)?	Dikast	Eust. ad *Od.* i. 156 (Stallbaum I 41. 21–23); Phot., τετρωβολίζων
pre-c. 393	3 ob. (p.d.)	Ekklesiast, pay increased by Agyrrhios (Ar. *Eccl.* 188: μισθοφορεῖν)	Ar. *Eccl.* 186, 292b, 309, 380, 392; Arist. *Ath. Pol.* xli. 3
388	3 ob. (p.d.)	Ekklesiast	Ar. *Plut.* 329; Σ (*vet.*) Ar. *Plut.* 171bα, 330b
c. 379–377	40 dr. (min. inc.)	Secretary (of board having something to do with Delos?), μισθός, for what period?	*SEG* XXXIX 170. 5
pre-c. 360	2–3 dr. (p.m. or p.pr.?)	Young Aischines, as junior clerk (ὑπογραμματεύοντα) in public offices	Dem. xix. 200
c. 355–322	1 dr. (p.d.)	Ekklesiast?, at regular or principal (κυρία) ekklesia?	Dem. *Prooem.* lii. 4; [Lucian] *Dem. Enc.* 36
c. 355–322	4 ob. (p.d.)	Ekklesiast at regular ekklesia or theorikon for two days?	Dem. *Prooem.* lii. 4
c. 355–322	3 ob. (p.d.)	Dikast?	[Lucian] *Dem. Enc.* 36
352/1	5 dr.	Men chosen to decide disputed boundaries of Eleusinian sacred orgas, apiece	*IG* II^2 204. 64
350/49	Nothing	Dikast pay, and jury trials, suspended during financial crisis	Dem. xxxix. 17
c. 337	3 ob. p.d.	Elected officials (epistatai?) of Peiraieus fortifications, apiece—for looking after repair of Long Walls, etc.	*IG* II^2 244. 31
"	[1 ob. (?)] p.?	Same—for looking after repair of harbor fortifications?	" 43
c. 335–322	1 dr. p.d.	Sophronistes of ephebes, apiece, εἰς τροφ[ήν] or μισθός?	Arist. *Ath. Pol.* xlii. 3; Phot., σωφρονισταί; *Lex. Seg.* 301. 10, σωφρονισταί
c. 335–322	4 ob. (p.d.)	Ephebes, apiece, εἰς τροφ[ήν]	Arist. *Ath. Pol.* xlii. 3

333/2?	2 dr. p.d.	Eleusis, salary (μισθός) for year of 13 months—elected architect, 2 dr. p.d., 780 dr. p.a.	*IG* II^2 1673 + *SEG* XXXIV 122. 60
"	3 ob. p.d.	Same—elected scribe of expenditures, 3 ob. p.d., 195 dr. p.a. κατὰ τὸ ψήφισμα τὸ τοῦ δήμου (not explicitly μισθός)	" 61–62
329/8	?	Eleusis—250 dr. for σπονδοφόροι, quan. unst., for what period?; pay or ἐφόδια ?	*IG* II^2 1672. 4
"	2 dr. p.d.	Eleusis, salary (μισθός) for prytany—(probably elected) architect (72 dr. for 36-day prytany)	" 12
"	1 ob. p.d.	Same—elected scribe of expenditures (6 dr. per 36-day prytany, 5 dr. 5 ob. per 35-day prytany)	" 12, 44, 119, 143
pre-322	1 dr. (p.d.)	Ekklesiast, μισθοφοροῦσι	Arist. *Ath. Pol.* lxii. 2
"	9 ob. (p.d.)	Ekklesiast at principal (κυρία) ekklesia, μισθοφοροῦσι	"
"	3 ob. (p.d.)	Dikast, μισθοφοροῦσι	"
"	5 ob. (p.d.)	Bouleutes, μισθοφοροῦσι	"
"	6 ob. (p.d.)	Bouleutes who serves as prytaneus (extra ob. εἰς σίτησιν)	"
"	4 ob. (p.d.)	Nine archons, apiece, εἰς σίτησιν, but collectively they must support a herald and a piper (out of these funds?)	"
"	1 dr. p.d.	Governor of Salamis, εἰς σίτησιν?	"
"	1 dr. p.d.	Amphiktyons to Delos, paid by Delos, probably εἰς σίτησιν	"
"	?	εἰς σίτησιν ἀργύριον for whatever officers were sent to Samos, Skyros, Lemnos or Imbros	"
pre-322	1 dr.	Arbitrator, paid (a) as deposit by prosecuting party and (b) by party seeking (for reasons sworn to under oath) to postpone arbitrator's judgment	Dem. Phal. 228 *FGrH* 7; Men. fr. 278 (K-T); Harp., παράστασις; Poll. viii. 39, 127;

			Phot., παρακατά-στασις; *Suda* π 443 (Adler), παράστασις; *Lex. Seg.* 290. 19, παρακατάστασις
late 4th c.?	1 dr. p.d.	Bouleutes	Hesych. β 931 (Latte), βουλῆς λαχεῖν
161/0	1 dr. p.d.?	Bouleutes' καθέσιμον (fee for attendance) at Theseia—1,200 dr. for two sittings of 600 bouleutai?	*IG* II² 956. 15
157/6	1 dr. p.d.?	Same—600 dr. for one sitting?	*IG* II² 957. 10
153/2 or 149/8?	1 dr. p.d.?	Same—1,200 dr. for two sittings?	*IG* II² 958. 12
109/8	?	Same—? dr.	*IG* II² 959 + 1014 + *SEG* XL 121. 19

Soldiers and Sailors

480	?	8 dr. distributed to each citizen embarking on ships before Salamis—μισθός, τροφή or ἐφόδια? (Plut. says ἐφόδια), for what period?	Cleidemus 323 *FGrH* 21; Arist. *Ath. Pol.* xxiii. 1; Plut. *Them.* x. 6–7
480	?	Themistokles gives 1 T. to Athenian trierarch Architeles—bribe to remain at Artemision or wages for crew (of 200 sailors?, for what period?)	Phanias Eres. *FHG* II 295, fr. 7 ap. Plut. *Them.* vii. 7
c. 477–441	?	Pay (τροφή/μισθός) for soldiers and sailors introduced by Aristeides, Kimon or Perikles? (amt. unspecified)	[Xen.] *Ath. Pol.* i. 13; Ion Chius 392 *FGrH* 13; Arist. *Ath. Pol.* xxiv. 1, xxvii. 2; Plut. *Cim.* xi. 2, *Per.* xi. 4, xii. 5; Σ Dem. xiii (Dilts 167. 24–25)
450/49?	4 ob. (p.d.?)	Athenian? rowers, soldiers or officials? sent to Miletos, or Milesian soldiers?	*IG* I³ 21. 13
441–439	1 dr. p.d.?	Sailors in the Samian War—appropriations of 128 T. (min.) for 40 ships for c. 3 mos.?, 368 T. (min.) for 60–160 ships for 1 to 3 1/2 mos.?, 908 T. (min.)	*IG* I³ 363. 5, 12, 17, 19; Thuc. i. 115. 3, 116. 1–2, 117. 2; Isoc. xv. 111;

		for 160 ships for c. 5 1/2 mos.?, i.e., c. 1 T. per ship (of 200 men?) p.m.?	Diod. Sic. xii. 28. 3; Nep. *Timoth.* i. 2
433	1 dr. p.d.?	Sailors on Kerkyraian Expedition—appropriations of [2]6 T. (min.) for 10 ships and [50] T. (min.) for 20 ships, i.e., c. 1 T. per ship (of 200 men?) p.m. for c. 2 1/2 mos.?	*IG* I[3] 364. 12, 23; Thuc. i. 45. 1, 50. 5, 51. 4
432–430	2 dr. p.d.	Hoplite at Poteidaia, 1 dr. μισθός for himself and 1 dr. for his servant (ὑπηρέτῃ)	Thuc. iii. 17. 4; Poll. iv. 165
432–430	1 dr. p.d.	Sailor at Poteidaia, μισθός	Thuc. iii. 17. 4
pre-431	?	Before war, >20,000 men supported (τρέφεσθαι) by the state, including 1,600 archers, 1,200 cavalrymen; just before? war began, this number was increased by 2,500 hoplites, (4,000 rowers on?) 20 guard ships and 2,000 (rowers?) selected by lot on other ships; no amts.	Arist. *Ath. Pol.* xxiv. 3
425	2 dr. (p.d.)	Thracian mercenaries, proposed μισθός	Ar. *Ach.* 159, 161
425	3 dr. (p.d.)	Taxiarchs or ambassadors to Thrace? pay (μισθοφοροῦντας) or ἐφόδια ?	Ar. *Ach.* 602
pre-422	3 ob. (p.d.)	Rower/soldier or (more likely) dikast?	Ar. *Vesp.* 684 et Σa
pre-422	2 ob. (p.d.)	Rower or (more likely) theoros? to Paros; pay or ἐφόδιον ?	Ar. *Vesp.* 1189 Σ Ar. *Vesp.* 1189a–b, d
420	3 Aig. ob. p.d.	Treaty with Argos, Elis and Mantineia, σῖτος (ration-money or gross pay?)—hoplites, light-armed soldiers and archers, apiece	*IG* I[3] 83. 23–24; Thuc. v. 47. 6
"	1 Aig. dr. p.d.	Same—cavalrymen, apiece	"
415	1 dr. p.d.?	1 T. p.m. μισθός for trireme (crew of 200?)	Thuc. vi. 8. 1
415	1 dr. p.d.	Sailor ἐκ δημοσίου μισθῷ	Thuc. vi. 31. 3, 5
415	1 dr.+ p.d.	*Thranites* (rower with longest oar), 1 dr. ἐκ δημοσίου μισθῷ plus extra amt. from trierarch	"

415	4 ob. (p.d.?)	Sicilian Expedition—μισ[θ for (mercenary?) peltasts and/or archers?	*IG* I^3 93. 32
413	1 dr. p.d.	Thracian peltasts, apiece	Thuc. vii. 27. 2
411	3 ob. (p.d.)	Sailor, μισθοφορά	Thuc. viii. 45. 2
411	?	Soldiers and sailors paid (μισθοφορητέον), unlike most other public employees	Thuc. viii. 65. 3; Arist. *Ath. Pol.* xxix. 5
c. 408	3 ob. (p.d.)	Alcibiades' μισθός to sailors, apiece (cf. 4 ob. [p.d.] paid by Lysander)	Xen. *Hell.* i. 5. 4–7; Plut. *Alc.* xxxv. 5, *Lys.* iv. 5–6
403/2	1 dr. → 4 ob. (p.d.)	Cavalrymen (ἱππέας), μισθοφορεῖν, apiece	Lys. *In Theozotidem*, lines 75–76 (Gernet-Bizos fr. vi)
403/2	2 [dr.] → 8 ob. (p.d.)	Mounted archers (ἱπποτοξότας), μισθοφορεῖν, apiece	Lys. *In Theozotidem*, lines 78–79 (Gernet-Bizos fr. vi + *ZPE* 107 [1995] 230–236)
late 5th c.?	2 or 4 ob. (p.d.)?	Soldier or dole recipient?	Theopomp. Com. fr. 56 (K-A)
4th c.?	4 ob. (p.d.)	στρατιωτικὸς/στρατιώτου μισθός	Paus. Att. τ 25 (Erbse), τετρωβόλου βίος; Eust. ad *Il.* xiii. 637 (van der Valk III 529. 18–19), ad *Od.* i. 156 (Stallbaum I 41. 23–24)
4th c.?	4 ob. (p.d.)	Rowers on Paralos, throughout year	Harp., Πάραλος
395	?	220 T. (partial?) arrearages for (15 mos.?) μισθός, paid by Tithraustes to Konon's sailors, quan. unst.; 700 T. left for war expenses	*Hell. Oxy.* 555–563
393	?	100 mn. spent by Aristophanes (for sailors, quant. unst.?) on Sicilian expedition	Lys. xix. 43
390	?	30,000 dr. for μισθός for sailors and peltasts, quant. unst., and for arms, quant. unst., furnished by Aristophanes for Cyprus expedition	Lys. xix. 22, 32, 43

375	?	13 T. for 50 or 60 triremes?, for what period?	Xen. *Hell.* v. 4. 63; Isoc. xv. 109
374/3	?	Rowers, quan. unst., ἐμισθοδότησαν >60 T.	Diod. Sic. xv. 47. 7
373	?	7 mn. per trierarch for τροφήν, for 200 men?, for what period?	[Dem.] xlix. 11
373	?	1,000 dr. for καθ' ἡμέραν τροφήν for Boiotian fleet, quan. unst.	[Dem.] xlix. 14–15
pre-368	1 dr. p.d.	Treaty with Alexander II of Macedon—[ὑ]πασπιστῆς (shield-bearing footsoldier), to be paid by Athens, in addition to σῖτος (rations in kind)	*IG* II^2 329. 9
360s	?	<40 T. p.a. spent on cavalry, quan. unst.—pay for cavalrymen or σῖτος (ration-money) for horses? (if σῖτος, 4 ob. p.d. for 1,000 horses?)	Xen. *Hipparch.* i. 19
c. 359	?	Sailors, 30 dr., for what period?	Dem. li. 11
351	?	5 T. pay for 10 ships sent to Thrace, i.e., 3,000 dr. per ship (of 200 sailors = 15 dr. apiece?), for what period?	Dem. iii. 4
351	2 ob. p.d.	τροφή, σιτηρέσιον μόνον, i.e., ration-money only, *not* μισθὸν ἐντελῆ—rowers, apiece (20 mn. per ship [of 200 rowers] p.m.)	Dem. iv. 28
"	1 dr. p.d.	Same—cavalrymen, apiece (30 dr. p.m.)	"
"	2 ob. p.d.	Same—infantry, apiece (10 dr. p.m.)	"
c. 335–322	4 ob. (p.d.)	Ephebes, apiece, εἰς τροφ[ήν]	Arist. *Ath. Pol.* xlii. 3
314/3	4 ob. p.d.	Sailor serving with admiral Aristoteles	Men. fr. 297 (K-T)
4th/3rd c.	4 ob. (p.d.)	Soldier (mercenary?)	Men. *Peric.* 380, 393
4th/3rd c.	4 dr. (p.d.)	Mercenary? officer?	Men. *Peric.* 381

Military Bonuses

335	5 T.	Mercenaries, quan. unst., to give up citadel of Thebes (not paid by	Aeschin. iii. 240

		Demosthenes)	
335	9 T. or 10 T.?	Arkadian mercenaries, quan. unst., to liberate Thebes (not paid by Demosthenes)	Aeschin. iii. 240; Dinarch. i. 20–21

Doctors, Lawyers and Professors

pre-c. 522	100 mn. p.a.	Physician Demokedes, from Athenians	Hdt. iii. 131. 2
c. 470–420	100 mn.	Protagoras for instruction (per student)	Diog. Laert. ix. 52; Σ Pl. *Rep.* 600c; Quintilian iii. 1. 10
c. 450	100 mn.	Zeno, for teaching Pythodoros and and Kallias, apiece	Pl. *Alc.* I 119a; Ael. Arist. iv. 31 (Behr)
c. 450–395	1/2 dr., 1 dr., 2 dr., 4 dr., 50 dr.	Prodikos' lessons, apiece	Pl. *Crat.* 384b; [Pl.] *Ax.* 366c; Arist. *Rhet.* 1415b 16–17; Anon. Comm. ad Arist. *Rhet.* 1415b 16; *Suda* π 2366 (Adler), Πρόδικον; Σ (Tzetzes) Ar. *Nub.* 358a
post-427?	100 mn.	Gorgias for instruction in rhetoric, per (single?) student	Diod. Sic. xii. 53. 2; *Suda* γ 388 (Adler), Γοργίας
pre-423	1 T.	Sokrates?, from Hyperbolos, for instruction in forensic speaking	Ar. *Nub.* 876
422	1 dr. (p.d.)	Public prosecutor (συνηγορικόν fee)	Ar. *Vesp.* 691 et Σa–b
c. 410–399	20 mn.	Sokrates, sent by Aristippos (in gratitude for prior instruction?) but not accepted	Phanias Eres. *FHG* II 299, fr. 21 ap. Diog. Laert. ii. 65
5th/4th c.	1 T.	Illness—weight or fee for curing?	Alcaeus Com. fr. 12 (K-A)
5th/4th c.	3 ob.	Fever—negligible value or fee for curing?	Nicophon fr. 20. 3 (K-A)
5th/4th c.?	3 ob.	Common advocate	Lucian *Bis Acc.* 15
pre-399	5 mn.	Euenos of Paros for instruction (for one student or two?)	Pl. *Apol.* 20b

c. 390	3–4 mn.	Sophists for instruction (per student)	Isoc. xiii. 3
388	3 T.	Advocates for Ergokles	Lys. xxix. 6
c. 373	20 T.	Isokrates from Nikokles for speech—fee or patronage gift?	Plin. *N.H.* vii. 110; [Plut.] *Mor.* 838a
c. 367–360	>80 T.	Plato from Dionysios (II) of Syracuse (in gratitude for prior instruction?)	Satyrus *FHG* III 163–164, fr. 16 ap. Diog. Laert. iii. 9
c. 366–364	10,000 dr.	Isaios from Demosthenes for instruction in public speaking	[Plut.] *Mor.* 839f
c. 366–364	10,000 dr.	Actor Neoptolemos from Demosthenes for teaching him to speak whole paragraphs (periods) without taking a breath	[Plut.] *Mor.* 844f
c. 366–338	10 mn.	Isokrates' usual fee for instruction in public speaking	Dem. xxxv. 42; Plut. *Demosth.* v. 6; [Plut.] *Mor.* 837d, 838e
c. 366–338	10,000 mn.	Isokrates would give for instruction in self-confidence and a good voice	[Plut.] *Mor.* 838e
c. 365	1 T.	Isokrates from Timotheos for writing letters to the Athenians—fee or gift?	[Plut.] *Mor.* 837c
pre-360	1 T.	Aristippos for teaching one student rhetoric and philosophy	Alexis fr. 37.7 (K-A)
pre-360	500 or 1,000 dr.?	Aristippos for instruction, per student	Plut. *Mor.* 4f; Diog. Laert. ii. 72
335	5 T.	Demades, from Demosthenes et al. to negotiate with Alexander for their safety (advocacy or bribe?)	Diod. Sic. xvii. 15. 3; Plut. *Demosth.* xxiii. 6
c. 335–323	800 T.	Aristotle from Alexander for research on animals—patronage gift?	Athen. ix. 58 (398e)
c. 335–323	50 T. (or 30 gold T?) → 30 mn.	Philosopher Xenokrates from Alexander (50 T. sent, 30 mn. accepted)—patronage gift	Cic. *Tusc.* v. 91; Val. Max. iv. 3. ext. 3; Plut. *Alex.* viii. 5, *Mor.* 181e, 331e, 333b; Themistius xxi. 252a; *Suda* ξ 42 (Adler), Ξενοκράτης
pre-322	1 dr.	Arbitrator, paid (a) as deposit by	Dem. Phal. 228 *FGrH* 7;

		prosecuting party and (b) by party seeking (for reasons sworn to under oath) to postpone arbitrator's judgment	Men. fr. 278 (K-T); Harp., παράστασις; Poll. viii. 39, 127; Phot., παρακατά-στασις; *Suda* π 443 (Adler), παράστασις; *Lex. Seg.* 290. 19, παρακατάστασις
c. 307–270	120 dr. p.a.	Epicurus, from each (student?)	Epicurus *Ep.* fr. 121. 6–7 (Arrighetti)
c. 300–250	7 dr.	"Philosopher" (i.e., actor) hired for one show	Lucian *Icar.* 29
c. 285	1 mn.	Hippomachos the gymnastic trainer—normal course fee?	Lynceus ap. Athen. xiii. 47 (584c)
c. 270–226	9 ob. p.m.	Tuition at Lyceum under Lykon (inadequate for extravagant entertainment costs)	Antigonus Carystius ap. Athen. xii. 69 (547e)
c. 232–207	1 T.	Sophist will even turn three somersaults for this amount	Chrysippus *SVF* III fr. 688 ap. Plut. *Mor.* 1047f
c. 160–152	1 mn.	Customary fee for teaching Stoic dialectic	Cic. *Acad.* ii. 98
A.D. 2nd c.	2 ob.–2 T.	Various philosophies or philosophers (Cynic 2 ob., Sceptic 1 mn., Epicurean 2 mn., Pythagorean 10 mn., Stoic 12 mn., Peripatetic 20 mn., Academic 2 T.)	Lucian *Vit. Auct.* 6, 11, 18–19, 25–27, *Pisc.* 15, 23, 27, 48
A.D. 2nd c.	2 mn., 2 T.	2 mn. proposed for every self-proclaimed philosopher, 2 T. claimed by Academic	Lucian *Pisc.* 41–43
A.D. late 2nd c.	1 T. (p.a.?)	Apollonios for chair of political oratory	Philostr. *V.S.* 600
c. A.D. 190–230	100 dr.	Proklos for lectures for all time, per auditor	Philostr. *V.S.* 604

Priests, Oracles and Seers[2]

450–430	3 ob.	Paiania deme—ἀπόμετρα (priestly emoluments)	*IG* I³ 250 A. 28, B. 32
"	[4 dr.?]	Same—hιερ[ε]όσυνα (priestly emoluments)	" B. 22
c. 448	50 dr. (p.a.)	Priestess of Athena Nike	*IG* I³ 35. 10
c. 440–430?	1 dr.	Lunch for Thorikos deme (priest or guard?, and attendants?), apiece	*IG* I³ 256 bis (= *SEG* XXXIII 147). 4
c. 440–430 or c. 400–375?	[1 dr.] p.d.	Polis priest ἐς σιτία	*IG* I³ 48 bis. 5
c. 430	10 dr.	Local (trittys?) cults—ἀπόμετρα	*IG* I³ 255 B. 10
"	1 dr.	Same—for priestess?	" 12
"	1 dr.	Same—for (priest or priestess?)	" 22
424/3	50 dr. (p.a.)	Priestess of Athena Nike	*IG* I³ 36. 6
422	2 ob. (p.d.?)	Dream interpreter	Ar. *Vesp.* 52
408/7	3 dr. 3 ob. (inc.)	Eumolpids (for Eleusinian Mysteries)—emoluments or expenses?	*IG* I³ 386. 162
c. 403–399	10 dr.	Polis sacred calendar amounts—ἀπόμετρα for priestess of Athena Polias	*IG* II² 1357 b. 3
"	2 ob. (inc.)	Same—ἱερεώσυνα for (priest of?) Hermes in Lykeion	" 6
"	100 dr.	Same—ἀπόμετρα for priestess of Demeter	*Hesperia* 4 (1935) 19, no. 2. 76 (= *SEG* XL 146. 259)
"	16 dr.	Same—tribal ἱερεώσυνα	" 52
"	4 dr. 2 ob.	Same—tribal ἱερεώσυνα	" 39
early 4th c.	5 dr.	(Deme or tribe?) priestesses—ἱερεώσυνα (amt. restored 3 of 6 times)	*IG* II² 1356. 5, 10, 12, 16, 20, 24

2. See also "T. Religious Finances: Religious Charges," "Religious Outlays (General)" and "Religious Outlays (Miscellaneous)."

"	3 dr.	Same—in lieu of skin of singed victim	" 6, 13
4th c.?	1 dr.	Apollo's oracles, apiece	*Com. Adesp.* fr. 1062. 9, 11 (K-A)
c. 400–350	1 dr. 2 ob.	Teithras deme ἱερειώσυνα	*SEG* XXI 542 A. 6
396/5	3 ob.	Demotionidai phratry priest's ἱερεώσυνα	*IG* II^2 1237 + *SEG* XL 132. 6
"	1 dr.	Same	" 8
377/6–375/4	1 T.	Delian ἀρχεθέωροι (emoluments or expenses?)	*IG* II^2 1635. 34
363/2	30 dr.	Salaminioi clan priests—ἱερεώσυνα	*SEG* XXI 527. 29
"	3 dr.	Same—for πελανός (sacrificial cake)	" 30
"	6 dr.	Same—ἱερεώσυνα	" 34
"	7 dr.	Same—for πελανός (two cults)	" 35
"	13 dr.	Same—in lieu of leg and skin of victim	" 36
352	[30 dr.]	Hierophant and priestess of Demeter (apparently together), (emoluments or expenses?) for performing sacrifices in connection with Eleusinian orgas boundary dispute	*IG* II^2 204. 60
pre-350	22 dr.	Eleusinian priestess for favorable sacrifices? (emoluments or expenses?)	*IG* II^2 1540. 58
c. 350	1 1/2 ob.– 7 dr. 1 1/2 ob.	Marathon deme ἱερώσυνα (20 preserved or partially preserved amts.)	*IG* II^2 1358. 9, 12, 15, 16, 18, 21, 22, 28, 29, 31, 32, 33, 36, 37, 42, 45, 46, 47, 49, 50, 52
c. 350–300	[3 ob.]	ἱερειώσυνα include καταρχήν (sacrifice charge?)?—[adult victim]	*IG* II^2 1359 + *SEG* XXV 166. 6
"	1 1/2 ob.	Same—[suck]ling victim	" 7
334/3	4 dr.	Priestess at Cholargos deme Thesmophoria (emoluments or expenses?)	*IG* II^2 1184. 17
c. 330–270	1 dr. 3 ob.	Eleusis sacred calendar amounts—lunch for hierophant and herald, together	*IG* II^2 1363 + *SEG* XXIII 80 A. 7

"	20 dr.	Same—ἱερεώσυνα and other items (same amt. in A. 34 and A. 41)	" A. 9
"	10 dr.	Same—ἀπόμετρα for priestess	" B. 23
329/8	49 dr. 2 ob.	Eleusinian priest for πελανός	*IG* II^2 1672. 291

Actors, Artists, Musicians and Writers[3]

c. 475	10,000 dr.	Pindar for line of poetry praising Athens	Isoc. xv. 166
c. 450	<[6,]600 dr. 2 ob.; <10,100 dr.	Sculptors of Athena Promachos statue—sums are gross wages for *all* workers, including sculptors, in two years (VI and VIII?)	*IG* I^3 435. 76–77, 111–112
c. 430s	100 T.	Eleans agree to return Pheidias to Athens, or pay this sum	Sen. *Contr.* viii. 2
434/3	16,392 dr.	Parthenon pediment sculptors (number unstated), annual wages	*IG* I^3 449. 401–402
pre-425	10 T.	Herodotos for flattering Athens	Diyllus 73 *FGrH* 3
421/0–416/5	<5 T. 3,310 dr.	Bronze workers on statues of Athena and Hephaistos—sum is gross cost of statues, including labor and materials	*IG* I^3 472. 166
413	50 dr.	Hegemon of Thasos, for singing epic parody of Gigantomachia at Athens	Hegemon fr. 1. 17 (Brandt) ap. Athen. xv. 55 (698f)
408/7	60 dr. per standard-sized figure or 1 dr. p.d.?	Erechtheion sculptors, paid on the basis of piece, or by the day (on assumption that 60 days at 1 dr. p.d. were required for a standard-sized figure)? See prices below for individual figures and groups.	*IG* I^3 476. 147–180
"	[240 dr.]	Erechtheion sculpture—2 women [beside wa]gon and [2 mules]	" 157
"	240 dr.	Same—chariot, youth, 2 horses	" 167
"	127 dr.	Same—horse, man striking horse, stele added later (i.e., figures 120 dr.,	" 173

3. See also "C. Tangible Personal Property: Pottery Containers," "Sculpture" and "Paintings"; "L. Labor Costs: Pay Based on Piece or Job."

		stele 7 dr.?)	
"	120 dr.	Same—h[orse] and man striking it	" 164
"	100 dr.	Same—youth writing and man [standing beside] him (i.e., one standard and one smaller figure?)	" 151
"	90 dr.	Same—? and wagon, except its [2 mules] (i.e., one standard and one smaller figure?)	" 154
"	[80 dr.]	Same—[man s]trik[ing wag]on? (i.e., one standard and one smaller figure?)	" 147
"	80 dr.	Same—woman and little girl (i.e., one standard and one smaller figure?)	" 180
"	60 dr.	Same—man holding spear	" 159
"	60 dr.	Same—youth beside breast plate	" 161
"	60 dr.	Same—man leading horse	" 169
"	60 dr.	Same—man holding bridle	" 175
"	60 dr.	Same—man leaning on staff beside altar	" 178
c. 407–400?	1 gold st.	Choirilos for poem celebrating Athenian victories over Xerxes, per line	*Suda* χ 595 (Adler), Χοιρίλος, Σάμιος
post-403/2	7 ob.	μισθός, for trumpeter-fish or musician?	Archippus fr. 16. 2 (K-A)
c. 366–364	10,000 dr.	Actor Neoptolemos from Demosthenes for teaching him to speak whole paragraphs (periods) without taking a breath	[Plut.] *Mor.* 844f
365	<16 mn.	Leochares for "Apollo" and one other statue (sum also used for food and *eisphorai*)	Pl. *Epist.* xiii 361b
350–320	[160?] dr.	Sculptor for restoring Athena Nike	*IG* II^2 403 + *SEG* III 85. 26–27
pre-336	1 T. or "sufficient change"?	(60?) Athenian humorists, to write down and send humorous sayings to Philip of Macedon	Telephanes 371 *FGrH* 1; Hegesander *FHG* IV 413, fr. 3 ap.

			Athen. vi. 76 (260b)
pre-323	3,000 dr.	Portrait statue (bronze?)—how much for sculptor?	Diog. Laert. vi. 35
pre-322	2 dr. max.	Girls who play the reed-pipes, harp or lyre (apiece and per performance?)	Arist. *Ath. Pol.* l. 2
pre-322	1 T.	Actor (Aristodemos or Polos?), for one play or two days?	Critolaus *FHG* IV 373, fr. 3 ap. Gell. *N.A.* xi. 9. 2; C. Gracchus fr. 44. 20–23 (Malcovati); [Plut.] *Mor.* 848b
c. 307–303	3,000 dr.	Bronze statue of Asklepiades of Byzantion—how much for sculptor?	*IG* II^2 555. 15–16
4th/3rd c.	60 T.	Offered to painter Nikias for painting: (Attalos' or Ptolemy's?) offer declined	Plin. *N.H.* xxxv. 132; Plut. *Mor.* 1093e
c. 300–250	7 dr.	"Philosopher" (i.e., actor) hired for one show	Lucian *Icar.* 29
mid 3rd c.	1 T.	Amoibeus the citharode, for one day's performance	Aristeas ap. Athen. xiv. 17 (623d)
A.D. 2nd/3rd c.	1,000 dr.	Painter for finest painting (rhetorical example)	Σ Herm. *Stat.* (Walz V 3. 9–10)
Date?	1, 4 dr.	Arabian flute player plays for 1 dr., stops for 4!	*Com. Adesp.* fr. *920 (K-A); Steph. Byz. *Ethn.* (Meineke 108. 1), Ἀραβία; Zenob. ii. 58 (*CPG*), Ἀράβιος ἄγγελος

Overseers, Architects and Other Salaried Construction Personnel (paid every day of the year, including holidays)

c. 450	1–9 ob. p.d.?	Athena Promachos statue, aggregate annual salaries (μισθοί) of 1,963 dr. 2 ob. (= 31 ob. p.d. for year of 380 days?) for epistatai, quan. unst., secretary and assistant, i.e., 4, 6 or 9 ob. p.d. for 2–7 epistatai (including secretary), apiece, and 1 or 3 ob. p.d. for assistant?—Year VI?	*IG* I^3 435. 81–82

"	Same?	Same (1,[963 dr. 2 ob.]?)—Year VIII?	" 114–115
c. 449–447?	4 ob. (p.d.)	5 epistatai (including secretary) of Eleusinian funds (including for construction), apiece	*IG* I^3 32. 8–9
434/3	?	Parthenon, [1,]8[3]1 dr. 2 ob. (min. inc.) aggregate annual salaries for personnel paid by the month (καταμενίοις) include epistatai, quan. unst., secretary, and architect?; no individual amts.	*IG* I^3 449. 403
408/7	1 dr. p.d.	Erechtheion, salaries (μισθοί) paid by 36–37 day prytany—36–37 dr. for architect	*IG* I^3 476. 61, 267–268
"	5 ob. p.d.	Same—30 dr.–30 dr. 5 ob. for undersecretary	" 62, 269
pre-mid 4th c.	?	Eleusis—20 dr. (min. inc.), 120 dr. for architect and assistant (ὑπ[η]ρέτηι)?, for work on bridge?, salaries?, for what period?	*IG* II^2 1540. 49, 50
"	?	Same—16 dr. 4 ob. μισθ[ός] for secretary?, for what period?	" 60
c. 337	3 ob. p.d.	Epistatai? of Peiraieus fortifications, apiece—for looking after repair of Long Walls, etc.	*IG* II^2 244. 31
"	[1 ob. (?)] p.?	Same—for looking after repair of harbor fortifications?	" 43
333/2?	2 dr. p.d.	Eleusis, salary (μισθός) for year of 13 months—elected architect, 2 dr. p.d., 780 dr. p.a.	*IG* II^2 1673 + *SEG* XXXIV 122. 60
"	3 ob. p.d.	Same—elected scribe of expenditures, 3 ob. p.d., 195 dr. p.a. κατὰ τὸ ψήφισμα τὸ τοῦ δήμου (not explicitly μισθός)	" 61–62
"	1 2/3 ob. p.d.	Same—non-citizen treasurer doing shopping for public slaves (8 dr. 2 ob. p.m., 108 dr. 2 ob. p.a.)	" 57–58
"	1 2/3 ob. p.d.	Same—non-citizen epistatai of public slaves, apiece (8 dr. 2 ob. p.m., 108 dr. 2 ob. p.a.)	" 58–59

329/8	2 dr. p.d.	Eleusis, salary (μισθός) for prytany—(probably elected) architect (72 dr. for 36-day prytany)	*IG* II^2 1672. 12
"	c. 1 2/3 ob. p.d.	Same—epistates of public slaves (10 dr. [amt. restored twice] per prytany, whether of 35 or 36 days); also receives 3 ob. p.d. τροφή	" 6, 43, 118, 143
"	1 ob. p.d.	Same—elected scribe of expenditures (6 dr. per 36-day prytany, 5 dr. 5 ob. per 35-day prytany)	" 12, 44, 119, 143

Construction and Other Manual Workers Paid on the Basis of Time[4]

c. 450	?	Athena Promachos statue, aggregate wages (μισθοί) paid by day or prytany for quan. unst.—[6,]600 dr. 2 ob. (Year VI?)	*IG* I^3 435. 76–77
"	?	Same—10,100 + dr. (inc.) (Year VIII?)	" 111–112
pre-411	4 ob. (p.d.)	Timon as farmworker	Lucian *Tim.* 6, 12
409/8	1 dr. p.d	Erechtheion, men paid by the day—sawyers (πρῖσται)	*IG* I^3 475. 54–57
"	"	Same—carpenter{s} (τέκτονες) making a strut (?) and placing it under	" 66–67
"	"	Same—(carpenter) making and trimming straight edges	" 69
"	"	Same—(carpenter) truing up straight edge	" 71
"	"	Same—(carpenters) laying rafters and crosspieces	" 255–256
"	"	Same—carpenter	" 289–290
"	"	Same—laborers (ἄνδρες) doing unspecified work (19–33 men on 7 days)	" 274–285
408/7	1 dr. p.d.	Erechtheion, men paid by the day—sawyers	*IG* I^3 476. 35–38

4. See also "J. Interest Rates and Other Investment Yields and Penalties: Income from Slaves."

"	"	Same—sawyers making coffer lids	"	42–45
"	"	Same—laborers, using block and tackle?	"	124–134
"	[5] ob. p.d.	Same—carpenter	"	105–109
408/7	1 dr. (p.d.?)	Erechtheion, men paid by the day, or on the basis of piece or job? (paid 1 dr. unless otherwise specified)—(laborers?) doing ? (2 men, apiece)	*IG* I^3 476. 7	
"	"	Same—(laborers?) laying ceiling and placing ceiling beams on bed (6 men, apiece)	"	12–18
"	"	Same—(laborers?) taking down scaffolding (6 men, apiece)	"	21–25
"	"	Same—(laborers?) carrying up [paint pots?] (2 men, apiece)	"	30–31
"	"	Same—(laborers?) taking down and carrying away scaffolding (6 men apparently paid 3 ob., apiece, for 1/2 day or job?)	"	138–140
"	"	Same—(laborer?) putting up scaffolding for encaustic painters paid 1 dr. 3 ob. for 1 1/2 days or for job?	"	28
"	"	Same—sculptors (if standard-sized figure is priced at 60 dr., calculated on the basis of 60 days' work)? [for details, see below under "Construction and Other Manual Workers Paid on the Basis of Piece or Job"]	"	147–180
"	"	Same—(stonemasons) fluting columns of east pediment (if price per column is 350 dr., calculated on the basis of 350 man-days)? [for details, see below under "Construction and Other Manual Workers Paid on the Basis of Piece or Job"]	"	76–100, 196–248, 310–326
"	"	Same—other workers?	"	passim
394	?	Peiraieus fortifications, aggregate μισθοί in one month for work by the day—160 dr. for yokes (of oxen?)	*IG* II^2 1656. 6	

		hauling stone, presumably including drivers, quan. unst.; what portion is attributable to drivers?	
"	?	Same—53 dr. for σιδηρίων (wages of ironworkers or rental of stoneworking tools?), quan. unst.	" 8
333/2?	?	Eleusis—yoke (of oxen?), presumably plus driver(s), paid 4 dr. p.d. (2 dr. per half day) for hauling column drums from Mount Pentelikos to Eleusis, with 1 dr. per half-day supplement (possibly reimbursement for fixed costs rather than compensation) for yokes as a group	*IG* II^2 1673 + *SEG* XXXIV 122. 64–90
"	?	Same—payments of 120 dr., 5 dr., ?3 ob. and 1 dr. (min. inc.) for men working with yokes, quan. and time period unst.	" 92–96
330/29	?	[4,]000 dr. = 4 dr. p.d. for 1,000 yokes? (of oxen?), presumably plus driver(s); what portion is attributable to driver?	*IG* II^2 351. 14–18
329/8	2 dr. 3 ob. p.d. οἰκόσιτος (man provides own food)	Eleusis, men paid by the day—carpenters laying bricks around gate and tower and working on the wood	*IG* II^2 1672. 28
"	2 dr. p.d. οἰκόσιτος	Same—carpenters putting roof tiles on passageway and ?	" 111
"	"	Same—(stonemasons) smoothing door posts	" 178
"	1 dr. 3 ob. p.d. οἰκόσιτος	Same—sawyers splitting wood (pair of sawyers paid 3 dr. p.d.)	" 160
"	c. 1 dr. 1 1/2 ob. p.d. οἰκόσιτος	Same—mason who finishes stone (ἐπιξέστης) and plasterer (ὑπαγωγεύς) together paid 2 dr. 3 ob. p.d.	" 32
"	1 dr. 3 ob. p.d. οἰκόσιτος	Same—hired laborers (μισθωτοί) carrying bricks, mixing mortar, bringing up wood and roof tiles	" 29–30
"	"	Same—hired laborers working in the sanctuary	" 33–34

"	"	Same—hired laborers carrying away bricks and earth, breaking clods	" 46
"	"	Same—hired laborers breaking clods, sifting earth for plaster coat and whitewash	" 62
329/8	1 dr. 1 ob.–1 dr. 2 ob. (?) p.d.	Eleusis, σιτία ("rations")—engravers of dedicatory inscription: 7 or {8} dr.? [i.e., 1 dr. 1 ob. or 1 dr. 2 ob. p.d. for 6 days?] in one prytany, [6]4 dr. 1 ob. at 1 dr. 1 ob. p.d. for 55 days in two other prytanies	*IG* II^2 1672 + *Hesperia* 64 (1995) 132, no. 2a. 7–8
329/8	3 ob. p.d.	Eleusis, τροφή ("ration-money")—17 public slaves and 1 epistates, apiece; epistates also receives c. 1 2/3 ob. p.d. μισθός	*IG* II^2 1672. 5–6, 42–43, 118, 142–143, 234(?)
"	c. 1 1/4 or 3 ob. p.d.?	Same—15 dr. for παῖς (private slave) doing what?, for 2 prytanies (i.e., c. 72 days) or 30 days spread over those prytanies?	" 101
c. 315?	1 dr. per night	Menedemos and Asklepiades, philosophers, for grinding grain, per night—together (ἀμφότεροι) they receive 2 dr.	Athen. iv. 65 (168b)

Construction and Other Manual Workers Paid on the Basis of Measure

409/8	5 dr.	Erechtheion, (stonemason) laying Eleusinian stone [cf. similar work in "Construction and Other Manual Workers Paid on the Basis of Piece or Job" below], per tetrapody—(stone 8 feet long x 2 feet high, i.e., 2 tetrapodies, for 10 dr.)	*IG* I^3 475. 2–3
409/8	3 dr. 3 1/3 ob.	Erechtheion, (stonemasons) finishing stone, per tetrapody—(1 1/2 tetrapodies for 5 dr. 2 ob.)	*IG* I^3 475. 28
"	3 dr. 3 ob.	Same—14 tetrapodies, apiece	" 18–20
"	"	Same—(14 tetrapodies for [4]9 dr.)	" 42–43
409/8	5 dr.	Erechtheion, (carpenters) ?ing coffer frames, per foot (20 dr. per frame)	" 231–235
409/8	4 ob.	Erechtheion, (carpenters) turning	" 293–294

		astragal in ceiling beams, per foot	
408/7	5 ob.	Erechtheion, (encaustic painter) painting kymatia in encaustic, per foot	*IG* I^3 476. 49–50, 272–273
394/3	13 dr.	Peiraieus fortifications, (bricklayer) laying bricks, per 1,000	*IG* II^2 1658. 7
394/3	12 dr.	Peiraieus fortifications, (bricklayer) laying bricks, per 1,000	*IG* II^2 1659. 7
"	15 dr.	Same	" 12
394/3	[12 dr.]	Peiraieus fortifications, (bricklayer) laying bricks, per 1,000	*IG* II^2 1664. 6
"	13 dr.	Same	" 10
c. 394–391	20 dr.	Peiraieus fortifications, (bricklayer) laying bricks, per 1,000	*SEG* XIX 145. 3
392/1	15 dr.	Peiraieus fortifications, (bricklayer) laying bricks, per 1,000	*IG* II^2 1662. 5
380–375	[3? dr.]	Erechtheion, (carpenters or stone-masons?) making new ὀχετός (struts or water channels?), per 20 feet	*IG* II^2 1654 + *SEG* X 299. 37–38; *IG* I^3 479 (comm.)
329/8	40 dr.	Eleusis—(brickmakers) making bricks 1 1/2 feet (long?), incl. γεώνιον (price of clay), per 1,000	*IG* II^2 1672. 57
"	36 dr.	Same—same (γεώνιον not mentioned)	" 56
"	17 dr.	Same—(bricklayer) laying bricks, per 1,000	" 60
"	12 dr. 4 1/4 ob.	Same—(bricklayer) laying bricks, per 1,000? (quan. unst., but 22 dr. for possibly 1,600 bricks)	" 185
"	8 dr.	Same—(stonemason) furnishing and laying foundation stones, per ὄργυα	" 9
"	1 dr.	Same—(stonemason) laying Aktitan and Aiginetan stone in round tower retaining wall, per tetrapody	" 21
"	?	Same—(stonemason) laying un-worked foundation stones, per ὄργυα	" 98

"	1 dr. 1 1/2 ob.	Same—grain measurer (προμε-τρητής) measuring grain, per 100 medimnoi	"	291
"	4 ob.	Same—hired laborers bringing out grain, per 100 medimnoi	"	293
285/4	1 dr. 3 ob.?	Eleusis—(laborer) ditchdigging, per "square" foot? (x 240 sq. ft. = 360 dr. plus presumed 40 dr. ἐπιδέκατον = 400 dr.?) or for job?	*IG* II^2 1682. 16	

Construction and Other Manual Workers Paid on the Basis of Piece or Job[5]

447/6	?	Parthenon, various amts. (all inc.) as aggregate wages for year for marble quarriers and transporters, carpenters, and road builders	*IG* I^3 436. 23–26, 28	
446/5	?	Parthenon, various amts. (all inc.) for ?	*IG* I^3 437. 52–58	
434/3	?	Parthenon—1,[92]6 dr. 2 ob. for workmen and stone loaders at Pentelikos, quan. unst.	*IG* I^3 449. 398–400	
"	?	Same—16,392 dr. for pediment sculptors, quan. unst.	"	401–402
409/8	10 dr.	Erechtheion, (stonemasons) laying stone (Eleusinian unless otherwise stated) [cf. similar work, explicitly priced by measure, in "Construction and Other Manual Workers Paid on the Basis of Measure" above], per block—8 (feet long) x 2 (feet high or wide) x 1 (foot thick)	*IG* I^3 475. 31	
"	7 dr. 3 ob.	Same—6 x 2 x 1 ([5] blocks for 37 dr. <3> ob.)	"	5
"	[7] dr. [3] ob.	Same—6 x 2 x 1	"	23
"	?	Same—5 x 3 x 1 1/4	"	83
"	?	Same—4 x 3 x 1 1/4 (6 blocks)	"	81
"	?	Same—? x ? x 1, 4 dr. (inc.?) for	"	49

5. See also "L. Labor Costs: Labor and Material Costs Combined," "Labor and Transport Costs Combined" and "Inscribers"; "M. Transport Costs."

		? blocks?	
"	[3 dr.]	Same—4 x 2 x 3/4 (backers) (2 for [6 dr.])	" 26
"	[3 dr.]	Same—4 x 2 x 3/4 (Pentelic backers)	" 34–35
"	2 dr. 5 ob.	Same—4 x 2 x 1 1/2 (Aiginetan backers)	" 15–17, 39–40
"	2 dr. 4 ob.	Same—3 3/4 x 2 x 3/4 (Pentelic backers)	" 10–12
"	2 dr. 3 ob.	Same—2 x 2 x [1]	" 6
409/8	20 dr.	Erechtheion, (stonemasons) doing "remaining work" on east pediment, per block(s)—central block and its backer, 5 x 3 1/2 x 1	*IG* I^3 475. 103
"	16, 10 dr.	Same—adjacent block and backer, 7 x 3 x 1 (16 dr. for block, 10 dr. for backer)	" 108, 110
"	15 dr.	Same—other adjacent block *and* backer, 7 x 3 x 1	" 107
"	10 dr.	Same—wedge-shaped block and backer, 5 x 1 1/2 x 1	" 113
"	8 dr.	Same—other wedge-shaped block and backer	" 114
409/8	40 dr.	Erechtheion, (stonemasons) shaping blocks on west pediment, per block(s)—central block 4 x 4 x 1 1/2	*IG* I^3 475. 121
"	10 dr. (min. inc.)	Same—adjacent block and backer, 7 x 3 x 1	" 125
"	8 dr.	Same—wedge-shaped block and backer, 5 x 1 1/2 x 1	" 129
409/8	?	Erechtheion, (stonemason) shaping corner blocks, per block—7 1/2 x 3 1/2 x 1 1/4	*IG* I^3 475. 90
"	?	Same—6 x 3 1/2 x 1 1/4	" 87
409/8	10 dr.	Erechtheion, carpenters gluing, smoothing and/or truing up—	*IG* I^3 475. 214–15

		mouldings of two "ladders" (coffer frames), apiece	
"	6 dr.	Same—box-wood frames, apiece	" 209
"	5 dr.	Same—kymatia, apiece	" 183
"	3 dr.	Same—mouldings of square frames, apiece	" 194, 219
"	3 dr.	Same—small kymatia, apiece	" 222
409/8	37 dr.	Erechtheion, carpenters doing misc. work—doweling lathe-turned astragal [for similar work, see lines 148, 160, 197, 203, 224, where amts. are missing]	*IG* I^3 475. 211
"	30 dr.	Same—making "ladder" and two small box-wood frames	" 200
"	24 dr.	Same—laying roof tiles	" 253
"	10 dr.	Same—placing grilles in inter-columniations, apiece (40 dr. for 4)	" 257–259
"	5 dr. 3 ob.	Same—building up wall of workshop	" 265
"	3 dr. 1 ob.	Same—turning bosses for coffer lids, quan. unst.	" 260
409/8	5 dr.	Erechtheion, sawyers—sawing rafter into coffer lids, quan. unst.	*IG* I^3 475. 262
"	5 dr.	Same—sawing timber 24 feet long, 5 cuts, 1 dr. per cut [= 2 ob. for 8 foot cut x 3, see following entry]	" 63
"	2 dr.	Same—sawing timbers 8 feet long, apiece (2 ob. per cut, 6 cuts per timber, 28 dr. for 14 timbers)	" 59–61
"	1 dr. 2 ob.	Same—sawing wood for struts, quan. unst.	" 65
409/8	1 1/2 ob.	Erechtheion, woodworkers planing crosspieces for roof, 7 palms long by 10 fingers wide, apiece	*IG* I^3 475. 243
409/8	4 dr.	Erechtheion, painter painting coffer lids, apiece	*IG* I^3 475. 270–271

409/8	150 dr. (inc.?)	Erechtheion, ? doing ?	*IG* I³ 475. 301
"	6 dr. (inc.?)	Same	" 286
409/8	1,100 dr. (inc.?)	Erechtheion, aggregate prytany wages—(carpenters) making all coffer frames	*IG* I³ 475. 239
"	500 dr.	Same—(carpenters) making small coffer frames	" 237
"	347 dr. 2 ob.	Same—(stonemasons) laying and finishing [18] Eleusinian stones, [6] Pentelic backers and [2]7 Aiginetan backers	" 51
"	[1]89 dr.	Same—carpenters doing ceiling work	" 205
"	150 dr. (inc.?)	Same—carpenter dowelling astragal, smoothing ?, etc.	" 153
"	121 dr. + (inc.)	Same—carpenters doing ceiling work	" 185
"	97 dr.	Same—woodworkers planing crosspieces for roof	" 249–250
"	91 dr. 4 ob.	Same—carpenters and sawyer doing variety of work	" 267
"	7[9 dr. 3 ob.] (inc.?)	Same—sawyers working by the day, piece or job	" 72
"	79 dr.	Same—(stonemasons) doing "remaining work" on east pediment (5 blocks, 5 backers)	" 117
"	[60 dr.] (inc.)	Same—(stonemasons) shaping blocks on west pediment (3 blocks, 2 backers)	" 132
"	51 dr.	Same—sawyers and carpenters	" 291
408/7	[260] dr.	Erechtheion, (stonemasons) fluting columns of east pediment, total of preserved or restored amts. (actual total for each column = 350 dr.?, if so, paid by the day, on assumption that 350 man-days were required for each column at 1 dr. p.d.?)—Column I	*IG* I³ 476. 76–78, 224–227, 310
"	[260] dr.	Same—Column II	" 80–83, 228–231, 310

"	[350] dr.	Same—Column III	" 85–87, 196–199, 233–235, 317
"	[300] dr.	Same—Column IV	" 88–92, 201–205, 237–242, 321
"	[209] dr. [4] ob.	Same—Column V	" 207–212, 244–248
"	[250] dr.	Same—Column VI	" 95–100, 213–218, 326
408/7	35 dr.	Erechtheion, (stonemason) smoothing 2 orthostates	*IG* I[3] 476. 221
408/7	[240 dr.]	Erechtheion, (sculptors) sculpting (paid on the basis of piece, or by the day [i.e., standard-sized figure priced at 60 dr. on assumption that 60 days were required]?)—2 women [beside wa]gon and [2 mules]	*IG* I[3] 476. 157
"	240 dr.	Same—chariot, youth, 2 horses	" 167
"	127 dr.	Same—horse, man striking horse, stele added later [i.e., figures 120 dr., stele 7 dr.?]	" 173
"	120 dr.	Same—h[orse] and man striking it	" 164
"	100 dr.	Same—youth writing and man [standing beside] him (i.e., one standard and one smaller figure?)	" 151
"	90 dr.	Same—? and wagon, except its [2 mules] (i.e., one standard and one smaller figure?)	" 154
"	[80 dr.]	Same—[man s]trik[ing wag]on? (i.e., one standard and one smaller figure?)	" 147
"	80 dr.	Same—woman and little girl (i.e., one standard and one smaller figure?)	" 180
"	60 dr.	Same—man holding spear	" 159
"	60 dr.	Same—youth beside breastplate	" 161
"	60 dr.	Same—man leading horse	" 169
"	60 dr.	Same—man holding bridle	" 175

"	60 dr.	Same—man leaning on staff beside altar	"	178
408/7	?	Erechtheion, (goldsmith) gilding rosettes, quan. unst.	*IG* I³ 476.	54–59
408/7	2 dr.	Erechtheion, carpenters gluing around openings—per coffer opening	*IG* I³ 476.	111–112
"	2 dr.	Same—per kymatia opening	"	116–117, 121–122
408/7	14 dr.	Erechtheion, carpenters—making rosettes, apiece	*IG* I³ 476.	329–341
"	2 dr.	Same—making? coffer lids, apiece	"	250–251, 256–257
408/7	8 dr.	Erechtheion, wax modelers modeling—rosette for coffer lids	*IG* I³ 476.	261
"	8 dr.	Same—acanthus for coffer lids	"	265, 345
408/7	1 dr.	Erechtheion, men paid by the day, or on the basis of piece or job? (paid 1 dr. unless otherwise specified)—(laborers?) doing ? (2 men, apiece)	*IG* I³ 476.	7
"	"	Same—(laborers?) laying ceiling and placing ceiling beams on bed (6 men, apiece)	"	12–18
"	"	Same—(laborers?) taking down scaffolding (6 men, apiece)	"	21–25
"	"	Same—(laborers?) carrying up [paint pots?] (2 men, apiece)	"	30–31
"	3 ob.	Same—(laborers?) taking down and carrying away scaffolding (6 men apparently paid 3 ob., apiece, for job or for 1/2 day?)	"	138–140
"	1 dr. 3 ob.	Same—(laborer?) putting up scaffolding for encaustic painters paid 1 dr. 3 ob. for job or for 1 1/2 days?	"	28
408/7	5 dr.	Erechtheion, ? doing ?	*IG* I³ 476.	104
"	2 dr.	Same—apiece	"	347–348

"	?	Same—various amts.	" 367–460
408/7	1,790 dr. 3 1/2 ob.	Erechtheion, aggregate wages—Prytany 6 (includes 84 dr. 4 1/2 ob. for day? laborers, 46 dr. for sawyers, 30 dr. for encaustic painter, ? for goldsmith, 67 dr. 5 ob. for architect and undersecretary)	*IG* I^3 476. 32–33, 46, 54 59, 63, 65
"	[4,]302 dr. 1 ob.	Same—Prytany 7 (includes 52 dr. 4 ob. for carpenters, 3,315 dr. for sculptors, other amts. lost)	" 124, 181, 182–183
"	1,237 dr. 1 ob.	Same—Prytany 8 (includes [914 dr. 4 ob.] min. for stoneworkers, 16 dr. for wax modelers, 66 dr. for architect and undersecretary, 44 dr. 1 ob. for encaustic painters [in addition to 50 dr. already paid], other amts. lost; 2 dr. for purchases deducted from total given of 1,239 dr. 1 ob.)	" 192, 266, 270, 279–281
"	[2,]300 dr. max.	Same—Prytany 9 (includes 500 dr. for stonemasons, 372 dr. (min.) for wood-carvers, other amts. lost; 189 dr. 1 ob. for purchases and 4 dr. 3 ob. for sacrifices deducted from maximum of less than 2,500 dr.)	" 285, 288, 303–304, 327
"	[3,795 dr.] (min.)	Same—Prytany 10 (includes [2,90]6 dr. for sculptors)	" 422–426
408/7	2 dr.	Eleusis—(laborer?) putting tile(s) in order by sacred fig	*IG* I^3 386. 163
"	1 dr. 3 ob.	Same—? doing ?	" 170
c. 407–405	?	Erechtheion—various amts. for ?	*IG* I^3 477. 1, 3
c. 406	?	Erechtheion—3 ob. (twice), 21 dr. for ?	*IG* I^3 478. 1–4
394/3	?	Peiraieus fortifications—8 dr. for ?	*IG* II^2 1664. 4
c. 394–391	?	Peiraieus fortifications—various amts. for?	*SEG* XIX 145. 6, 8
393/2	?	Peiraieus fortifications—2 dr. (inc.?), 2 dr. 3 ob., 2 dr. 4 ob. for ?	*IG* II^2 1663. 1, 3, 5
393/2	30 dr.	Peiraieus fortifications—(plasterer)	*IG* II^2 1664. 13

		for plastering, quan. unst.		
"	6 dr. 5 ob.	Same—(carpenter or stone mason?) for repair of stairs	"	14–15
392/1	[1]5 dr.	Peiraieus fortifications—(plasterer) for plastering, quan. unst.	*IG* II^2 1664 + *SEG* XIX 144. 14	
392/1	18 dr.	Peiraieus fortifications—(bricklayer) for laying bricks, quan. unst.	*SEG* XXXII 165. 3–4	
380–375	?	Erechtheion—various amts. (all inc.?) for ?	*IG* II^2 1654 + *SEG* X 299 passim; *IG* I^3 479 (comm.)	
pre-mid 4th c.	16 dr.	Eleusis—[μισ]θός for (laborer) oiling and cleaning?	*IG* II^2 1540. 56	
"	5 dr. (inc.?)	Same—?	"	57
post-mid 4th c.	448 dr.	Temple of Zeus Soter in Peiraieus—(stonemason) ?ing Hymettan stones?, quan. unst.	*IG* II^2 1669. 13	
"	428 dr. 4 ob.	Same—(stonemason) finishing 51 stylobate blocks?	"	24
"	240 dr. 3 ob.	Same—?	"	15
"	160 dr.	Same—? (money or number?) (min. inc.)?	"	32
"	[8]0 dr.+ (inc.)	Same—(stonemason) finishing 25 stones	"	10
"	30 dr. (inc.?)	Same—?	"	13
"	5 dr.?	Same—? (money or number?)	"	18
"	3 dr. (inc.?)	Same—?	"	33
"	1 dr. (inc.?)	Same—?	"	39
"	3 ob. (inc.)	Same—?	"	29
350–320	[160?] dr.	Sculptor for restoring Athena Nike?	*IG* II^2 403 + *SEG* III 85. 26–27	
c. 334	5–40 dr.	(Goldsmith) making 7 gold crowns, apiece	*IG* II^2 1496. 52–64 et comm.	

333/2?	120 dr.	(Stonemason?) building wall	*IG* II² 1673. 25
333/2?	22 dr. 4 ob. (inc.)	(Smiths?) sharpening cutting edges—total pay for year (4 men)	*IG* II² 1673 + *SEG* XXXIV 122. 36–38
"	>1 ob.	Same—(large) drill bits, apiece	" 3
"	1 ob.	Same—τύχοι (instruments for dressing stone), apiece	" 37
"	1 ob.	Same—(small) drill bits, for 3	" 36
"	2 dr. 3 ob.	(Smith?) repairing bronze kettle	" 39
"	6 dr.	(Cart maker?)—replacing broken parts of wagons, quan. unst.	" 55
"	6 dr.	Same—sawing ἐπωτίδες (metal ?), quan. unst., from axles	" 35
"	5 dr.	Same—installing new axles, apiece	" 32
"	[2] dr.	Same—removing old axle rings, apiece	" 32
333/2?	8 dr.	(Sawyer?) sawing ? of μεσ[όμνων?] (tie beams)	*IG* II² 1673. 24
"	4 dr.	(Sawyer) sawing and ?	" 23
333/2?	3 dr. 3 ob.	Rope maker repairing broken ropes—(ἀρτήματα), quan. unst.	*IG* II² 1673 + *SEG* XXXIV 122. 41
"	2 dr.	Same—(σειρῶν), quan. unst. (min. inc.?)	" 41
"	2 dr.	(Carpenter?) boring and joining δόκοι (bearing beams), apiece (4 for 8 dr.)	" 36
"	1 dr. 5 ob.	(Cobbler) repairing shoes, per pair (includes materials?)	" 50
"	1 dr. + (inc.)	(Laborer) cleaning road through Phlya	" 63
"	?	(Laborers?) removing and repairing sacred σκεύη paid >1 dr. (inc.)	" 45
331/0	? dr.	(Metalworkers?) making processional equipment?	*IG* II² 1496. 212, 228
c. 330	30 dr.	(Stonemason) for portion of portico steps and stylobate?	*IG* II² 1670. 34

329/8	16[9] dr.	(Stonemasons)—making "the stone things" (2 ?, 4 doorjamb blocks, 2 geison blocks)	*IG* II^2 1672.	134
"	150 dr. (min. inc.?)	Same—building foundation for new house for priestess	"	78
"	50 dr.	Same—working the ἐπίκρανα (capitals) on doorposts, quan. unst.	"	186
"	5 dr.	Same—laying foundation for kitchen	"	190
"	1 dr.	Same—cutting fieldstone, per stone	"	49
"	1 dr.	Same—laying fieldstone, per stone	"	51
"	20 dr. 2 ob.	(Bricklayers)—laying bricks, quan. unst. (possibly 1,600 bricks, in which event cost is 12 dr. 4 1/4 ob. per 1,000)	"	185
"	10 dr.	Same—making? 4 πλινθεῖα (brick window frames?) for towers	"	204
"	100 dr.	(Carpenter)—building? τροχιλεία (block and tackle) for towers?	"	236
"	86 dr.	Same—making doors, quan. unst.	"	166
"	85 dr.	Same—making and installing doors, quan. unst., in gates	"	164
"	78 dr. (inc.?)	Same—making? ἱματιοθήκη (wardrobe)	"	229
"	65 dr.	Same—making doors, quan. unst.	"	68
"	60 dr.	Same—making θυροκλινκλίδες (lattice doors), quan. unst.	"	172
"	5 dr.	Same—repairing θακεῖον (seat) and gluing 3 feet	"	145
"	23 dr.	(Sawyers)—sawing 3 Macedonian (boards?) into lintels, 2 into doorframes	"	67
"	10 dr.	Same—sawing olive wood into wedges, quan. unst. (for amt. see *SEG* XXXIV 121)	"	11
"	100 dr.	(Plasterers)—amount due to for ?	"	239

"	80 dr.	Same—plastering, painting city Eleusinion	"	203
"	45 dr.	Same—plastering Epistasion	"	107
"	27 dr.	Same—plastering and whitewashing 3 altars	"	141
"	40 dr. 1 1/4 ob.	(Encaustic painters)—? and encaustic work	"	238
"	40 dr.	Same—encaustic work, quan. unst.	"	186
"	5 dr.	(Painter)—painting kymatia, quan. unst.	"	188
"	26 dr.	(Roofers?)—smearing roof with pitch	"	180
"	4 dr.	(Cobbler)—repairing shoes, per pair (includes materials?)	"	190
"	?	Same—repairing shoes (41 dr. [inc.?] for quan. unst.; includes materials?)	"	230
"	1 dr.+ (inc.)	(Smith)—sharpening iron tools, quan. unst.	"	122
"	2 dr.	Grain measurer (προμετρητής) measuring 80 1/6 medimnoi? [minimum charge?, includes journey to Eleusis and back?]	"	299
"	2 dr.	[δη]μοσίωι (public slave) for ?	"	235
"	300 dr.	(Laborers)—removing damaged stone, quan. unst., from walls	"	25
"	270 dr.+ (inc.)	Same—removing stones, quan. unst.	"	52
"	125 dr.	Same—clearing foundations for Sacred House	"	75
"	115 dr.	Same—clearing foundations of retaining wall	"	19
"	70 dr.	Same—preparing tower for grain	"	292
"	67 dr.	Same—clearing old foundations and cleaning down to bedrock	"	77
"	60 dr.	Same—hauling away earth, quan. unst.	"	76

"	[50 dr.]	Same—erecting scaffolding for stonemasons and roofers	" 179
"	48 dr.	Same—clearing and cleaning tower foundation down to bedrock	" 47
"	23 dr. (inc.?)	Same—clearing sanctuary and threshing floor	" 233
"	6 dr.	Same—cleaning Rharia	" 120
"	4 dr.	Same?—opening 2 treasure chests	" 302
"	2 dr.	Same—purifying ?	" 128
"	1 dr. 5 1/4 ob.	Same—bringing out 80 1/6 medimnoi of grain	" 299
"	150 dr. 3 ob.	(Laborers?) doing work whose description is missing—includes 12 dr. for ?	" 99
"	80 dr.	Same	" 96
"	72 dr.	Same	" 100
"	50 dr.	Same	" 84
"	40 dr. (inc.?)	Same—[μισθ]ὸς	" 227
"	14 dr.	Same	" 95
late 4th c.	?	Eleusis repairs—various amts. for ?	*IG* II^2 1673a passim
285/4	2,000 dr.	Eleusis—various works on portico	*IG* II^2 1682. 32
"	400 dr.	Same—(laborer) ditchdigging, 400 dr. for job or 1 dr. 3 ob. per "square" foot?	" 16
"	16 dr.	Same—(stonemason) finishing columns, per column	" 20
221/0	12 dr.	(Silversmith) making silver oinochoe for Hero Doctor (weight 183 dr. 3 ob.)	*IG* II^2 839. 85
A.D. 2nd c.?	7 ob.	Cobbler making pair of sandals, μισθός includes materials? (Athens?)	Lucian *Gall.* 22

Labor and Material Costs Combined

421/0–	<5 T. 3,310 dr.	Bronze workers on statues of Athena	*IG* I^3 472. 166

416/5		and Hephaistos—sum is gross cost of statues, including all labor and materials	
377/6–375/4	1,500 dr.	(Goldsmith)—gold crown	*IG* II² 1635. 33
"	1,000 dr.+ (inc.)	Same—victory tripod	" 34
"	125 dr.+ (inc.)	Same—gold petals	" 37
333/2?	3 dr. 3 ob.	(Smith)—replacing στομώματα (cutting edges) of τύχοι, apiece (each weighs 1 stater and price is per stater)	*IG* II² 1673 + *SEG* XXXIV 122. 56–57
"	2 dr.	Same—adding iron to δικέλλας (2-pronged hammers?), 1 1/2 staters of iron to each at 1 dr. 2 ob. per stater	" 51
"	1 dr. 5 ob.	(Cobbler) repairing shoes, per pair	" 50
329/8	462 dr.	(Carpenter)—14 doorways, including weights, lintels, wood, nails, glue and labor (quantities and individual amts . not specified), i.e., 33 dr. per doorway	*IG* II² 1672. 295
"	60 dr.	Same—making προσβάθραι (steps?), quan. unst., and furnishing wood for same	" 144
"	45 dr.	Same—propping up νεωκόριον (sacristy), furnishing wood and removing same	" 182
"	17 dr.	Same—making kymatia and κανονίς (doorframe), also furnishing the wood	" 187
"	40 dr.	(Brickmaker) making bricks 1 1/2 feet (long?), including γεώνιον (price of clay), per 1,000	" 57
"	8 dr.	(Stonemason) furnishing and laying foundation stones, per ὄργυα	" 9
"	4 dr.	(Cobbler)—repairing shoes, per pair (includes materials?)	" 190
"	?	Same—repairing shoes (41 dr. for quan. unst.) (includes materials?)	" 230
"	3 5/7 dr.	(Scribes?) supplying σανίδες, with γραφή (?), apiece (14 for 52 dr.)	" 292

A.D. 2nd c.?	7 ob.	Cobbler making pair of sandals, μισθός includes materials? (Athens?)	Lucian *Gall.* 22

Labor and Transport Costs Combined

394/3	790 dr.	Peiraieus fortifications, builder of section of wall, including transport of stones	*IG* II^2 1657. 6
333/2?	5 ob.	Eleusis, transport [and clearing] of 20 stones, apiece	*IG* II^2 1673. 6
329/8	25 dr.	(Stonemason) installing thresholds, quan. unst., for lattice doors, including delivery, boring holes and pouring lead for door sockets	*IG* II^2 1672. 176
"	4 dr.	(Sand dealer?) sifting and transporting sand, quan. unst., from?	" 110
"	3 dr.	Same—sifting and transporting sand from ?, per load (5 loads for 15 dr.)	" 197
"	4 dr.	(Basket maker) for basket, including transport from (Boiotia?) to Eleusis	" 117
"	3 dr. 1 ob.	(Stonemason) cutting, transport (from ?) and placement of stones, per stone—foundation stone	" 18
"	3 dr. 1 ob.	Same—fieldstone	" 22

Inscribers
(of polis documents unless otherwise stated)

408/7	62 dr.	Eleusinian epistatai accounts—working, engraving and ἐ[λάσ]αντι (erecting?) stele	*IG* I^3 386. 166
c. 403/2	[20 dr.]	Honorary decree, for sons of Theozotides?	*IG* II^2 5 + *SEG* XXXII 39. 13–14
c. 402–post-385	[20 or 30?] dr.	Honorary decree for Thasian exiles	*IG* II^2 33 + *SEG* XXXII 42. 2–3
392/1	2 dr.	Stele showing account of repairs of Peiraieus fortifications (probably does *not* include inscribing)	*IG* II^2 1664 + *SEG* XIX 144. 18

390/89	[3]0 dr.	Proxeny decree	*IG* II^2 22 b. 9–10
380s or earlier?	[? dr.]	Honorary decree for Boiotians	*IG* II^2 245. 4–5
389/8?	20 dr.	Honorary decree for Thasian ambassadors	*IG* II^2 24 b. 10
388/7 or 375/4?	[20] dr.	Citizenship decree	*IG* II^2 25 + *Agora* XVI 40. 18–19
pre-387/6	20 [dr.]	Proxeny decree	*IG* II^2 51. 15
pre-387/6	20 dr.	Proxeny decree	*IG* II^2 53. 8
pre-387/6	[30 d]r.	Decree (fragment)	*IG* II^2 56. 5
386/5	[30 dr.]	Honorary decree for King Hebryzelmis of the Odrysians	*IG* II^2 31. 15–16
pre-378/7	20 dr.	Proxeny decree	*IG* II^2 76. 22
pre-378/7	20 dr.	Honorary decree for Megarian	*IG* II^2 81 + *SEG* XXXII 51. 12
pre-378/7	[20] dr.	Proxeny decree	*IG* II^2 82. 19
pre-378/7	[3]0 dr.	Honorary decree for foreigners	*IG* II^2 84. 5–6
378	[3]0 dr.	Alliance with Thebes (2 stelai, apiece)	*IG* II^2 40. 22
377	60 dr.	Charter of Second Athenian League	*IG* II^2 43. 67
c. 377	30 [dr.]	Decree concerning Arethousa	*Agora* XVI 43. 3
c. 375–350 or 357/6?	[30] dr.	Citizenship decree	*Agora* XVI 54. 19
c. 375–350	[20 dr.]	Decree (fragment)	*IG* II^2 293 + *SEG* XXXVII 70. 23–24
372	20 dr.	Polis decree and agreements with Parians made by members of Second Athenian League	*SEG* XXXI 67. 11
c. 370–360	[30 dr.]	Decree (fragment)	*Hesperia* 7 (1938) 281, no. 15. 4
367	20 d[r.]	Proxeny decree	*IG* II^2 106. 18
367	20 dr.	Honorary decrees for Mytilenaians	*IG* II^2 107. 24

		(2 decrees on one stele)	
367?	[30 dr.]	Treaty with Dionysios I of Syracuse	*IG* II^2 105 + 523 + *Hesperia* 7 (1938) 627, no. 2. 43–44
364?	30 dr.	Honorary decree for King Strato of Sidon	*IG* II^2 141. 17–18
363	20 dr.	Citizenship decree	*IG* II^2 109 b. 28
362	20 dr.	Treaty with Keans	*IG* II^2 111. 26
361/0	30 [dr.]	Treaty with Thessalians	*IG* II^2 116. 45
361/0	[? dr.]	Proxeny decree	*IG* II^2 117. 18
356/5	20 dr.	Treaty with Lokrians	*IG* II^2 148. 8
pre-355 or 342?	[20] dr.	Proxeny decree	*IG* II^2 149. 22
354	[20] dr.	Proxeny decree	*IG* II^2 132. 14
354	20 dr.	Proxeny decree	*IG* II^2 133. 19
pre-353/2	20 [dr.]	Honorary decree for foreigner	*IG* II^2 151. 1
pre-353/2	[30 dr.]	Honorary decree (fragment)	*IG* II^2 173. 13
pre-353/2	[? dr.]	Honorary decree for Kyrenaians	*IG* II^2 176. 11–12
pre-353/2	[20 dr.]	Proxeny decree	*IG* II^2 183. 13
pre-353/2	[20] dr.	Decree (fragment)	*IG* II^2 189. 4–5
pre-353/2	[30 dr.]	Honorary decree for foreigners	*IG* II^2 196. 9
pre-353/2	20 dr.	Honorary decree (fragment)	*IG* II^2 197 + *SEG* XXXII 69. 4
pre-353/2	[? dr.]	Decree (fragment)	*IG* II^2 198. 4
353/2	30 dr.	Decree ordering inventory of Chalkotheke	*IG* II^2 120. 21
353/2	<2>0 [dr.]	Law on dedication of first fruits at Eleusis, on same stele as earlier law	*IG* II^2 140 + *Hesperia* 64 (1995) 131, no. 1. 37
352	[20 dr.]	Decree on Eleusinian orgas boundary	*IG* II^2 204. 61

		dispute (2 stelai, apiece)	
pre-mid 4th c.	[?] dr.	Tribal honorary decree for tribal thesmothetes	*IG* II^2 1148. 16
pre-mid 4th c.	3[0 dr.]	Decree (fragment)	*Agora* XVI 60. 3
mid 4th c.	10 dr.	Deme honorary decree for metic	*IG* II^2 1186. 33–34
mid 4th c. or c. 330–318?	30 dr.	Deme honorary decree for deme financial official	*IG* II^2 1182. 24–25
c. 350	[30] dr.	Honorary decree	*IG* II^2 257 + 300 + *SEG* XL 70. 6
c. 350	[20 dr.]	Citizenship decree	*IG* II^2 282. 7–8
350 or c. 343/2?	30 dr.	Honorary decree for King Arybbas of the Molossians	*IG* II^2 226. 24
post-mid 4th c. or 281/0?	[20 d]r.	Honorary decree for Tenians	*IG* II^2 660. 23–24
c. 350–339?	[? dr.]	Proxeny decree	*IG* II^2 161 b. 1
c. 350–330	[30 dr.]	Proxeny decree	*Agora* XVI 66. 18
c. 350–325	[2]0 [dr.]	Proxeny decree	*IG* II^2 184 + *SEG* XXIV 92. 11
349/8	[20] or [30]? [d]r.	Honorary decree for foreign ambassadors	*IG* II^2 210 + 259 + *Hesperia* 6 (1937) 329, no. 6 (*SEG* XXIII 52). 19
348	[20 dr.]	Proxeny decree	*IG* II^2 206. 32
346	30 dr.	Honorary decree for sons of King Leukon of Bosporos	*IG* II^2 212. 48–49
c. 345	[20 dr.] or no figure?	Proxeny decree?	*IG* II^2 272 + *Agora* XVI 45 d. 7–8; Tracy, *ADIT* 70–72
c. 345–320	30 [dr.]	Proxeny decree	*IG* II^2 285 + 414 d + *SEG* XXI 276. 2–3
c. 345–320	30 dr.	Decree (fragment)	*IG* II^2 307. 3–4

c. 345–320	[3]0 d[r.]	Decree (fragment)	*Agora* XVI 90. 9–10
c. 345–320 or 307–301?	[30 dr.]	Proxeny decree	*IG* II^2 564 + *Agora* XVI 111. 21–22
344/3	[3]0 [dr.]	Honorary decree for Pellanans	*IG* II^2 220. 13–14
344/3	[30 d]r.	Honorary decree (fragment)	*IG* II^2 221. 7
342	10 [dr.] (min. inc.)	Honorary decree for bouleutes Phanodemos	*IG* II^2 223 A. 15
340/39	[2]0 [dr.]	Honorary decree for Apelles of Byzantion	*IG* II^2 235. 32
c. 340/39	[30 dr.]	Honorary decree for (Hellespontine?) foreigner	*SEG* XVI 51. 25–26
c. (340 or 330?)–320?	50 d[r.]	Decree (fragment)	*IG* II^2 306. 3
339	[?] dr.	Honorary decree for Aratos of Tenedos	*IG* II^2 232. 25–26
337	30 dr.	Honorary decree for Akarnanians	*IG* II^2 237 + *SEG* XXXI 76. 37
337	20 dr.	Proxeny decree	*IG* II^2 122 + 238. 18–19
c. 337–324	30 d[r.]	Proxeny decree	*IG* II^2 426. 16–17
c. 337–323	[20] dr.	Honorary decree (fragment)	*IG* II^2 434. 3
c. (337 or 330?)–323?	20 dr.	Mesogeians' decree on religious offerings	*IG* II^2 1244. 9–10
336	20 dr.	Law against tyranny (2 stelai together)	*Agora* XVI 73. 28
336	30 [dr.]	Proxeny decree	*IG* II^2 240. 24–25
336	20 dr.	Proxeny decree	*IG* II^2 242 + 373 + *SEG* XL 74. 28
336	20 dr.	Isoteleia decree	*IG* II^2 276. 21
pre-336/5	[20 dr.]	Proxeny decree	*IG* II^2 250. 6–7
pre-336/5	30 dr.	Decree (fragment)	*IG* II^2 256. 6
pre-336/5	30 dr.	Proxeny decree	*IG* II^2 269. 7–8

pre-336/5	[20 dr.]	Proxeny decree	*IG* II^2 288. 14
pre-336/5	[20] dr.	Proxeny decree	*IG* II^2 290. 11
pre-336/5	20 dr.	Decree (fragment)	*IG* II^2 299. 3
pre-336/5	30 dr.	Honorary decree for foreigner	*IG* II^2 302. 3
post-336/5	30 dr.	Honorary decree (fragment)	*IG* II^2 424. 16
335	[20] dr.	Honorary decrees for ἱεροποιοί (3 decrees on one stele)	*IG* II^2 330 + 445. 27–28
c. 335–324	30 dr.	Proxeny decree	*Hesperia* 43 (1974) 322, no. 3. 23–24
c. 334	30 dr.	Citizenship decree	*IG* II^2 222. 31
c. 334–313	20 dr.	Honorary decree for foreigner Iatrokles	*IG* II^2 264. 12
c. 334–313	[20 dr.]	Honorary decree for foreigner	*IG* II^2 292. 5
c. (334 or 330?)–313?	20 dr.	Deme honorary decree for deme choregos	*SEG* XXXIV 103. 32
333	20 dr.	Honorary decrees for overseer of springs (2 stelai, each containing 2 decrees, apiece)	*IG* II^2 338. 29
c. 333	30 [dr.]	Prytany decree	*SEG* XXVIII 52. 27–28
332	10 dr.	Deme decree regarding quarry lease	*SEG* XXVIII 103. 50–51
332	[3]0 [dr.]	Proxeny decree	*IG* II^2 344. 23–24
332	[20 dr.]	Proxeny decree	*IG* II^2 368. 16–17
331	[?] d[r.]	Proxeny decree	*IG* II^2 347. 23
331	[? d]r.	Proxeny decree	*Agora* XVI 79. 22–23
331	20 dr.	Honorary decree for god (Amphiareion)	*IG* VII 4252. 36
331	20 dr.	Honorary decree for sanctuary nomothetes (Amphiareion)	*IG* VII 4253. 32
c. 330	[4]0 dr.	Honorary decree for priest and ἱεροποιοί	*IG* II^2 410. 41

c. 330?	[40 d]r.	Decree (fragment)	*Agora* XVI 83. 3
c. 330/29	[? d]r.	Decree (fragment)	*IG* II^2 415. 4–5
320s	30 dr.	Citizenship decree	*IG* II^2 301. 6
320s or shortly afterwards	[20 dr.], [30 dr.] [40 dr.] or [50 dr.]?	Citizenship decree (plural stelai?)	*IG* II^2 575 + Osborne D41. 3–4
329	[?] dr.	Honorary decree for Eudemos of Plataia	*IG* II^2 351 + 624 (p. 660). 37–38
329	30 dr.	Honorary decree for festival overseers (Amphiareion)	*IG* VII 4254. 50
329/8	1 dr. 1 ob.– 1 dr. 2 ob. (?) p.d.	σιτία ("rations") for engravers of Eleusis building account: 7 or {8} dr.? [i.e., 1 dr. 1 ob. or 1 dr. 2 ob. p.d. for 6 days?] in one prytany, [6]4 dr. 1 ob. at 1 dr. 1 ob. p.d. for 55 days in two other prytanies	*IG* II^2 1672 + *Hesperia* 64 (1995) 132, no. 2a. 7–8
329/8	3 5/7 dr.	σανίδες (wooden writing tablets), apiece with γραφή (14 for 52 dr.)	*IG* II^2 1672. 292
327	[3]0 dr.	Honorary decree for priest of Asklepios	*IG* II^2 354. 30–31
c. 327–300	50 dr.	Honorary decree, for physicians?	*IG* II^2 304 + 604 + *SEG* XVIII 11. 13
c. 326–318 (323–322?)	[50] dr.	Sacred law	*IG* II^2 620 + 1195 + *SEG* XLIV 42. 19
c. 325	[? d]r.	Decree (fragment)	*Agora* XVI 88. 5
325/4	30 dr.	Honorary decrees for Herakleides of of Salamis (5 decrees on one stele)	*IG* II^2 360. 26
323	50 dr.	Honorary decree for Euphron of Sikyon (2 stelai together)	*IG* II^2 448. 30
323/2?	[?] dr.	Proxeny decree	*IG* II^2 343 + *SEG* XXIV 103. 17
c. 321–319	[? dr.]	Decree (fragment)	*IG* II^2 397. 6
c. 321–318	[? dr.]	Citizenship decree	*IG* II^2 392 + 586 + *SEG* XXVI 83. 19

c. 321–318	30 dr.	Citizenship decree	*IG* II^2 393. 13
c. 321–318	[? d]r.	Citizenship decree	*IG* II^2 394. 20
c. 321–318	[30?] dr.	Proxeny decree	*IG* II^2 396. 8
c. 321–318	[30 d]r.	Honorary decree, for Milesian grain merchant?	*IG* II^2 407 + *SEG* XL 79. 19–20
c. 320–296 (310/09?)	50 dr.	Honorary decree for Carthaginian ambassadors	*IG* II^2 418. 9
318	[? dr.]	Citizenship decree	*IG* II^2 391. 17
318	30 d[r.]	Citizenship decree	*IG* II^2 398 b. 10–11
318	50 dr.	Honorary decrees for Euphron of Sikyon (2 stelai together, each containing 2 decrees)	*IG* II^2 448. 86
318/17	[50 dr.]	Honorary decree for ? of Herakleia	*IG* II^2 535 + *Agora* XVI 104. 33–34
315/4	[20] dr.	Deme honorary decree for deme treasurer	*SEG* XLIII 26 A. 26
"	20 dr.	Deme honorary decree for deme festival officials	" B. 18
c. 313/2	30 dr.	Decree (fragment)	*IG* II^2 530 + 590 + *SEG* XL 80. 6
c. 310–300	[? d]r.	Decree (fragment)	*Hesperia* 7 (1938) 299, no. 23. 7
307	[?] dr.	Honorary decree for Kolophonians	*IG* II^2 456. 30–31
307/6	50 d[r.]	Law on repair of Long Walls, etc.	*IG* II^2 463. 33
307/6	[3]0 dr.	Honorary decree for Tenians	*IG* II^2 466. 50
307/6	50 dr.	(All?) decrees of Lykourgos (plural stelai)	[Plut.] *Mor.* 852e
307/6?	50 dr.	Honorary decree, for Lykourgos and descendants? (same as preceding?)	*IG* II^2 513 + *SEG* XXXI 84. 12–13
post-307/6	30 dr.	Honorary decree for polis magistrates	*IG* II^2 509. 12
post-307/6	[? dr.]	Honorary decree (fragment)	*IG* II^2 510. 11

c. 307–303	[30 dr.]	Honorary decree for Asklepiades of Byzantion	*IG* II² 555. 37
c. 307–302	10 dr.	Citizenship decree	*IG* II² 508. 13
c. 307–302	[? dr.]	Citizenship decree	*IG* II² 511. 10–11
c. 307–302	50 dr.	Citizenship decree	*IG* II² 518 + Osborne D54. 7–8
c. 307–302	[30 dr.]	Citizenship decree	*IG* II² 519. 7
c. 307–302	30 [dr.]	Citizenship decree	*IG* II² 696. 10–11
c. 307–301	20 dr.	Honorary decree for bouleutes	*IG* II² 514 + *Agora* XVI 112. 10
c. 306–302	[40 dr.]	Citizenship decree	*RFIC* 70 (1942) 12, no. 6. 15
305/4	[50 dr.]	Honorary decree for ephebes	*IG* II² 478. 31
305/4	[30 dr.]	Prytany decree	*Agora* XV 58. 8
c. 305/4	50 dr.	Honorary decree for Pyr? of Herakleia	*IG* II² 479. 28
304/3	30 dr.	Citizenship decree	*IG* II² 484 + 558 + *SEG* XL 83. 30–31
304/3 or 303/2?	[3]0 [dr.]	Honorary decree for polis magistrates	*IG* II² 488 + *SEG* XXXIV 75. 26–27
pre-303/2	30 d[r.]	Proxeny decree	*IG* II² 542. 15
303/2	[?] dr.	Athens-Sikyon alliance	*Agora* XVI 115 c. 14
c. 303/2	[? dr.]	Citizenship decree	*IG* II² 806. 8
c. 303–301	[20] dr.	Citizenship decree	*Agora* XVI 120. 11–12
c. 303–301	[30 dr.]	Citizenship decree	*Agora* XVI 121. 9
302	30 dr.	Citizenship decree	*IG* II² 496 + 507 + p. 661 + Osborne D61. 41
302	[? dr.]	Honorary decree for Adeimantos of Lampsakos	*Agora* XVI 122. 31
302	[3]0 [dr.]	Honorary decree for taxiarchs	*Agora* XVI 123. 28–29

301	30 dr.	Honorary decree for taxiarchs	*IG* II^2 500. 41–42
301	[4]0 dr.	Honorary decree for generous metics	*IG* II^2 505. 63
c. 301–297	[? dr.]	Honorary decree for military commanders	*Agora* XVI 129. 14
c. 301–294	[e.g., 30 dr.]	Proxeny decree	*IG* II^2 722 + *SEG* XXIV 120. 12
c. 300	50 dr.	Honorary decree (fragment)	*IG* II^2 809. 6
c. 300	[? d]r.	Decree (fragment)	*Agora* XVI 128 b. 3–4
late 4th c.	[? dr.]	Honorary decree for Paseas	*IG* II^2 512. 13
late 4th c.	[3]0 dr.	Honorary decree (fragment)	*IG* II^2 515. 7
late 4th c.	[30 dr.]	Isoteleia decree	*IG* II^2 516. 8
late 4th c.	[? dr.]	Honorary decree (fragment)	*IG* II^2 517. 13
late 4th c.	[? dr.]	Decree (fragment)	*IG* II^2 520. 9–10
late 4th c.	[30 dr.]	Decree (fragment)	*IG* II^2 521. 7
late 4th c.	[3]0 dr.	Decree (fragment)	*IG* II^2 522. 5–6
late 4th c.	20 [dr.]	Decree (fragment)	*IG* II^2 524. 6–7
late 4th c.	[30 dr.]	Decree (fragment)	*IG* II^2 526. 6
late 4th c.	[? dr.]	Decree (fragment)	*IG* II^2 527. 4–5
late 4th c.	[? dr.]	Honorary decree (fragment)	*IG* II^2 528. 2
late 4th c.	[? d]r.	Decree (fragment)	*IG* II^2 529. 3–4
late 4th c.	[20 dr.]	Decree (fragment)	*IG* II^2 531. 3
late 4th c.	[30 d]r.	Decree (fragment)	*IG* II^2 532. 3
late 4th c.	[? d]r.	Decree (fragment)	*IG* II^2 533. 2
late 4th c.	[20 dr.]	Decree (fragment)	*IG* II^2 534. 3
late 4th c.	[30 dr.]	Honorary decree for Prieneans	*IG* II^2 565. 3
late 4th c.	30 dr.	Honorary decree for Prieneans	*IG* II^2 567. 20
late 4th c.	[4]0 dr.	Honorary decree (fragment)	*IG* II^2 571. 9–10

late 4th c.	[? dr.]	Honorary decree for Parians	*IG* II^2 573. 17–18
late 4th c.	[? d]r.	Decree (fragment)	*IG* II^2 589. 5–6
late 4th c.	30 dr. (min. inc.)	Decree (fragment)	*IG* II^2 600. 1–2
late 4th c.	20 dr.	Deme decree on theatre leasing	*IG* II^2 1206. 18
late 4th c.	[? d]r.	Genos honorary decree for religious officials (two stelai)	*IG* II^2 1232. 25
late 4th c.	[20 d]r.	Honorary decree (fragment)	*Agora* XVI 137. 6
late 4th c.	[20 dr.]	Decree (fragment)	*Agora* XVI 138. 6
late 4th c.	[30 dr.]	Decree (fragment)	*Agora* XVI 139. 3
late 4th c.	[30 d]r.	Decree (fragment) (plural stelai)	*Agora* XVI 140. 3
c. 300–294	[3]0 dr.	Citizenship decree	*IG* II^2 643 + *Agora* XVI 162. 23
c. 300–294	30 d[r.]	Proxeny decree	*Agora* XVI 164. 22
early 3rd c.	20 dr.	Decree (fragment)	*IG* II^2 713. 8
early 3rd c.	10 [dr.] (min. inc.)	Decree (fragment)	*IG* II^2 714. 4–5
early 3rd c.	[2]0 or [3]0 dr.?	Honorary decree for foreigner	*IG* II^2 725 + *SEG* XXIV 124. 10
299	20 dr.	Honorary decree for Athenian ambassador	*IG* II^2 641. 32
c. 295/4	30 dr.	Citizenship decree (2 stelai, apiece)	*IG* II^2 648. 14
c. 295/4?	[30] dr.	Decree (fragment)	*IG* II^2 709 + p. 665 + *SEG* XXXIV 80. 3
c. 286–262	[? dr.]	Honorary decree for archon	*Agora* XVI 174. 9–10
c. 286–262	[?]	Honorary decree (fragment)	*Agora* XVI 175. 5
c. 286–262	10 dr.	Honorary decree for hipparchs and phylarchs	*SEG* XXI 357. 11
c. 286–262	[20 dr.]	Honorary decree (fragment)	*SEG* XXXII 107. 12
c. 286–244	[20 dr.]	Honorary decree (fragment)	*IG* II^2 525 + 675 + *SEG* XXXIV 72. 6

c. 284–280 or 239–229?	10 dr.	Citizenship decree	*IG* II^2 808. 28
283	20 dr.	Honorary decree for Philippides the poet	*IG* II^2 657. 72
282	[10 dr.]	Prytany decree	*Agora* XV 71. 24
281	10 dr.	Honorary decree for archon	*Agora* XVI 181. 41–42
281	10 dr.	Honorary decree for taxiarchs	*Agora* XVI 182. 32
278	50 dr.	Honorary decree for Komeas the hipparch	*IG* II^2 672. 17
272	[?] dr.	Honorary decree for overseers of sacrifices	*IG* II^2 676. 37
271	10 dr.	Honorary decree for taxiarchs	*Agora* XVI 187. 36
264/3	[20 dr.]	Deme honorary decree (fragment)	*Agora* XVI 192. 4
mid 3rd c.	10 [dr.] (min. inc.)	Decree (fragment)	*IG* II^2 812. 5
mid 3rd c.	10 dr.	Mesogeians' honorary decree for religious official	*IG* II^2 1247. 29
mid 3rd c.	[?] dr.	Orgeones' honorary decree for officer	*IG* II^2 1284. 18
mid 3rd c.	[?] dr.	Orgeones' honorary decree for secretary	" 34
c. 245?	no figure or [20 dr.]?	Honorary decree (fragment)	*Agora* XVI 212 + *SEG* XIX 72 + *SEG* XXXIV 78. 8–9
221	8 dr. 3 ob.	Decree on dedication to Hero Doctor	*IG* II^2 839. 85
c. 210–170	[? dr.]	Asklepiastai honorary decree for benefactor	*IG* II^2 1293 + *SEG* XVIII 33. 20
late 3rd c.	[?] dr.	Orgeones' honorary decree for benefactor and his priestess-wife	*IG* II^2 1316. 24
74	[?] dr.	Honorary decree for ἱεροποιοί to Lemnian Kabeirion	*ASAA* 3 (1941) 83, no. 6. 17–18

Prostitutes and Pimps (per occasion, unless otherwise specified)[6]

c. 490–475	2 ?	Female prostitutes, 2 coins apiece	Makron, *ARV* no. 148
c. 490–475	2 ?	Male prostitutes, 2 coins apiece	Makron, *ARV* no. 206 *bis*
c. 420	"small change"	Prostitutes (male, female, old man), together or separately?, at Kyzikos	Eupolis fr. 247. 3 (K-A)
411	1 dr.	Transvestite Euripides, from Scythian	Ar. *Thes.* 1195
pre-399	"not much money"	Epichares, from anyone who wants him	Andoc. i. 100
5th/4th c.	1 dr.	Prostitute fee or religious offering?—"God who bends backwards and thrusts hips forward"	Plato Com. fr. 188. 17 (K-A)
"	3 ob.	Same—"God who bends over"	"
5th/4th c.	1 st.	Middle-grade female prostitutes (apiece)	Theopomp. Com. fr. 22. 2 (K-A)
5th/4th c.	"staters"	Lais (the elder) of Corinth, in her prime	Epicrates fr. 3. 12 (K-A)
"	1 st. or 3 ob.	Lais (the elder), as an older woman	" 18
post-394?	300 dr.	Theodotos (male) from Simon (long-term contract)	Lys. iii. 22, 25
c. 391–355	3 ob.	Female prostitute	Antiphanes fr. 293. 3 (K-A)
388	20 dr.	Male (to buy ἱμάτιον?)	Ar. *Plut.* 982, 1019
c. 380–335	"small change"	Female prostitutes (apiece)	Eubulus fr. 67. 7 (K-A) 82. 1, 7
c. 366	1 ob.	Female prostitute	Diog. Laert. vi. 4
c. 350	1 mn.	Phryne demands	Machon 451 (Gow)
"	2 gold pieces (= 40 dr.?)	Phryne accepts, when she is randy	" 452–453
c. 350–300	1 ob.	"Korydos" the parasite, or price of bird?	Athen. vi. 40 (241e)
c. 347–339	10 T.	Philosopher Speusippos offers to find	Timotheus ap.

6. See also "H. Slaves"; "O. Individuals: Private Ransoms."

		more beautiful (male or female?) lover for this amount—pimp or matchmaker?	Diog. Laert. iv. 4
pre-345	20 dr.	Hetaira Philoxene from Timarchos, "spent in a short time"	Aeschin. i. 115
pre-345	4 dr.	Diophantos, male prostitute, from foreigner (for one occasion or more?)	Aeschin. i. 158
c. 330–322	3,000 dr.	Melanopos, male prostitute, for what period?	[Aeschin.] *Epist.* vii. 3
pre-324	"many T."	Spent on sexual gratification, but not 1 dr. for rubbing of other parts of body	Dio Chrys. vi. 19
pre-322	2 dr. max.	Girls who play the reed-pipes, harp or lyre (per performance)—also for sex?	Arist. *Ath. Pol.* l. 2
pre-322	10,000 dr.	Lais (the younger?) of Corinth demands for whole night from Demosthenes (he refuses)	Sotion ap. Gell. *N.A.* i. 8. 5–6; Σ (*recent.*) Ar. *Plut.* 149d
c. 313	3 ob.	Polemon has ready, to gratify his desires	Diog. Laert. iv. 16
c. 302	250 T.	Demetrios Poliorketes gives to Lamia and fellow courtesans for soap	Plut. *Demetr.* xxvii. 1
4th/3rd c.	2 dr.	Leme (Stratokles' hetaira) accepts from anyone who wants her	Gorgias 351 *FGrH* 1 ap. Athen. xiii. 70 (596f)
4th/3rd c.	1 ob.	Female prostitute	Philemo fr. 3. 13 (K-A)
4th/3rd c.	12 dr. p.d.	Pimp for Habrotonon (female)	Men. *Epitr.* 136–137
4th/3rd c.	3 mn. p.d.	Female prostitute	Men. *Col.* 129
4th/3rd c.	"only" 10 dr.	(Free?) women, at dinner party (apiece)	Men. *Sam.* 392
4th/3rd c.	20 mn.	Philaenium (female)—exclusive use for one year	Plaut. *Asin.* 89, 230, 243, 364, 532, 579, 633, 636, 651, 653, 684, 725, 734, 752, 852, 915
"	2 T.	Same—for one night "for free"	" 193
4th/3rd c.	20→ 10 mn.	Philematium (female)	Plaut. *Most.* 297–298
4th/3rd c.	<6 mn.	Consumption, including prostitutes	Plaut. *Trin.* 411

4th/3rd c.	6 mn.	Phronesium (female) from Diniarchus	Plaut. *Truc.* 444–445, 580, 739–740
"	20 mn., 1 mn. gold, 1 mn., 1 mn. gold, 1 T.	Phronesium from Stratophanes	" 543, 893, 900, 910, 935, 936, 952
"	20 mn. (= "mnas"?)	Phronesium from Strabax	" 653–654, 948
4th/3rd c.	1 T.	(Female) prostitute	Sext. Turpilius 36 (Ribbeck)
4th/3rd c.?	1 mn.	Virgin Korinna	Lucian *D. Meretr.* vi. 1–2
4th/3rd c.?	2 mn., 1 mn.	Mousarion (female), offered but not accepted	Lucian *D. Meretr.* vii. 3
4th/3rd c.?	5 dr. max.	Ampelis from Demophantos	Lucian *D. Meretr.* viii. 2
"	10 dr.	Ampelis from Kallides	" 3
"	1 T.	Ampelis from Demophantos (after jealousy aroused) for 8 months	" 3
4th/3rd c.?	1 T. + 1 T.	Pannychis from Philostratos (1 T. given, 1 T. promised)	Lucian *D. Meretr.* ix. 3–4
4th/3rd c.?	5 dr.	Tryphaina from Charmides, who does not partake (he loves another)	Lucian *D. Meretr.* xi. 1
4th/3rd c.?	5 dr.	Myrtale from Dorion over extended period (includes 2 dr. for 2 nights)	Lucian *D. Meretr.* xiv. 2
"	2 mn.	Myrtale from Bithynian merchant	" 3–4
4th/3rd c.?	2 T.	Demanded by Krokale from Aitolian for exclusive access	Lucian *D. Meretr.* xv. 2
c. 285	1 mn.	Gnathainion (female)—usual fee	Lynceus ap. Athen. xiii. 47 (584c)
c. 285	1,000 dr.→ 500 dr.	Same—demanded for one night but reduced by negotiation	Machon 340–348 (Gow)
pre-250	3 ob.	Male prostitute's charge for servicing bent-over Gnathaina or for bending over himself?	Machon 308 (Gow)
A.D. 2nd c.	2 dr.	Male wine-server, offered by	Lucian *Symp.* 15

Kleodemos

Miscellaneous Workers

425	8 dr.	Amphitheos for private peace with Sparta, or as ἐφόδια to Sparta?	Ar. *Ach.* 130
422	3 ob.	Fuller, to clean clothes sullied by diarrhea	Ar. *Vesp.* 1128
380/79	? Aig. st.	Ritual bathing of Delphic cult statue	*IG* II^2 1126 + *CID* I 10. 26–27
c. 347–339	10 T.	Philosopher Speusippos offers to find more beautiful (male or female?) lover for this amount—matchmaker or pimp?	Timotheus ap. Diog. Laert. iv. 4
late 4th c.	4 dr.	Cook's pay (for feast?)	Strato fr. 1. 32–33 (K-A)
4th/3rd c.	6 ch.	4 men, apiece, for ?	Philemo fr. 66 (K-A)
4th/3rd c.	3 dr.	Cook, for wedding	Men. *Asp.* 223
"	1 dr.	Waiter, for wedding	" 233
4th/3rd c.	5 mn.	Assailant of Olympic victor	Men. *Col.* 103
4th/3rd c.	1 T.	Anyone who will accept slave's punishment	Plaut. *Most.* 359
4th/3rd c.	1 dr.	Average (cheap) cook, per feast	Plaut. *Pseud.* 808
4th/3rd c.?	1 dr. + 7 ob.	Syrian witch, to restore lover	Lucian *D. Meretr.* iv. 4
4th/3rd c.?	2–4 ob.	Tip for hetaira's slave	Lucian *D. Meretr.* xiv. 3
pre-271	4 T.	Epicurus' cook in less than 2 yrs. 10 mos.	Damoxenus fr. 2. 4 (K-A)
A.D. 2nd c.	2 ob.	Bathhouse (establishment or attendant?)	Lucian *Lex.* 2

M. Transport Costs

Transport Costs[7]

c. 446/5?	[7 ob. or 1 dr.?]	Individual—from Oropos to Hestiaia [or to Dion or reverse of those trips]	*IG* I^3 41. 70; *SEG* XXXII 3. 56
"	4 ob.	Same—Chalkis to Hestiaia	*IG* I^3 41. 72; *SEG* XXXII 3. 58
"	[3 or 2 ob.?]	Same—Chalkis to Oropos	*IG* I^3 41. 68; *SEG* XXXII 3. 54
"	Half Price?	Same—on these three fares if passenger going to a festival?	*IG* I^3 41. 74; *SEG* XXXII 3. 60
c. 415	?	Porter charge, for what to where?, is ? less 4 ob.	Ar. fr. 312 (K-A)
405	2 ob.	Dionysos, across Acheron to Hades	Ar. *Ran.* 140, 270
405	2 dr.	Dionysos' baggage to Hades (his attempt to reduce charge to 9 ob. is unsuccessful)	Ar. *Ran.* 173, 176, 177
395/4	160 dr. p.m.	Stone, quan. unst., for Peiraieus fortifications, from ? (aggregate daily wages for yokes [of oxen?], quan. unst.)	*IG* II^2 1656. 6
392/1	9 dr.	Bricks, quan. unst., for Peiraieus fortifications, from ?	*SEG* XXXII 165. 3
c. 385?	2 ob.	(Individual alone or individual plus children, baggage and women?) from Aigina to (Peiraieus)	Pl. *Gorg.* 511d–e; Ael. Arist. ii. 370, iii. 184 (Behr)
"	2 dr. "at most"	Individual, children, baggage and women from Egypt or Pontos to (Peiraieus)	"
c. 379–377	1 T. 700 dr.	Theoroi and chorus?, quan. unst., from Peiraieus to Delos and back?, how many times?	*SEG* XXXIX 170. 23
377/6–375/4	1 T. 1,000 dr.	Theoroi and chorus, quan. unst., (from Peiraieus?) to Delos (and back?), how many times?	*IG* II^2 1635. 35

7. See also "E. Building Materials: Building Materials with Transport Costs Specifically Included"; "L. Labor Costs: Labor and Transport Costs Combined"; "M. Transport Costs: Tangible Personal Property with Transport Cost Specifically Included."

372	1,750 dr.	Timber freight (ναῦλον), from Macedon to Peiraieus, for how many shiploads?	[Dem.] xlix. 29
367	4 T.	Timagoras, from Sousa to (Aegean?) Sea by litter—actual cost or gift-bribe?	Plut. *Pel.* xxx. 11
pre-350	1 ob.	Red ochre from Koresos (Keos) to (Peiraieus?), [per talent]	*IG* II^2 1128. 13
mid 4th c.	5 (dr.?) (inc.?)	? from Delos to Athens	*IG* II^2 1636 + *ID* 104-3 + *SEG* XXX 108. 14
333/2?	228–402 dr.	Column drum from Pentelikos to Eleusis (charge based on 4 dr. per yoke [of oxen] p.d., with a supplementary payment of 1 dr. per half-day for the yokes as a group)	*IG* II^2 1673 + *SEG* XXXIV 122. 64–90
333/2?	9 dr. 3 ob.	9 logs from Peiraieus? to Eleusis?	*IG* II^2 1673. 11
"	7 dr. 3 ob.	? by mule from ? to Athens	" 18
"	4 dr.	Thick ropes, quan. unst., by mule from Peiraieus to the Pompeion (Athens)	" 20
329/8	60 dr.	Freight (to Eleusis unless otherwise stated)—6 large stone blocks, from Skambonidai?	*IG* II^2 1672. 133 + p. 812
"	1 dr. 3 ob.	Same—fieldstones per stone, from Eleusis?	*IG* II^2 1672. 50
"	25 dr. 3 ob.	Same—1,500 bricks, from Eleusis?	" 58
"	25 dr.	Same—bricks per 1,000, from Eleusis?	" 58
"	15 dr.	Same—bricks per 1,000, from Eleusis or Melite?, to Eleusis or to city Eleusinion?	" 23
"	7 dr.	Same—moving 19 large pieces of lumber on rollers (across isthmus of Corinth?)	" 158
"	10 dr.	Same—carrying said lumber down to sea and loading it onto boat	" 159
"	56 dr.	Same—ferrying said lumber from Corinth	" 159

"	40 dr.	Same—100 Corinthian roof tiles, from Lakiadai?	"	72
"	6 dr. 4 ob.	Same—200 Corinthian roof tiles, from Corinth	"	73
"	8 dr.	Same—25 ordinary roof tiles, from ?	"	210
"	40 dr.	Same—60 medimnoi of stone chips,, from?	"	208
"	5 dr.	Same—30 medimnoi of black plaster dust, from Ptelea? (includes rental of sacks)	"	199
"	24 dr.	Same—Eumolpids (and/or their baggage?) "for the Mysteries," by yokes (of horses or mules?), quan. unst., from Athens?	"	41
"	7 dr. 3 ob.	Same—67 T. of firewood and 60 faggots [by sea], from Peiraieus?	"	126
"	7 dr. 3 ob.	Same—10 T. of olive-wood wedges, 2 pots of pitch, 2 medimnoi of black pigment, and 25 staters of red ochre, from Athens?	"	16
"	4 ob.	Same—bringing out grain, per 100 medimnoi	"	293
"	1 dr. 5 1/4 ob.	Same—(bringing out?) grain, 80 1/6 medimnoi (minimum charge?)	"	299
"	12 dr.	Same—? from ?	"	232
305	702 gold (sts.?) (= 14,440 dr.?)	Pine for ships (100 triremes?) (from Syria or Cyprus?) to (Peiraieus)	*IG* II^2 1492 + *SEG* XXXII 159. 122	
A.D. 2nd c.	2 ob.	Boatman on Eridanos, per trip?	Lucian *Electr.* 3	
A.D. 2nd c.	4 ob.	Individual (from Peiraieus) to Aigina	Lucian *Nav.* 15	

Tangible Personal Property with Transport Cost Specifically Included[8]

329/8	20 dr.	κιβωτός (chest?) for τἀπὸ τῶν κιόνων delivered from (Athens?) to	*IG* II^2 1672. 193

8. See also "E. Building Materials: Building Materials with Transport Cost Specifically Included."

		Eleusis		
"	4 dr.	κανοῦν (basket), including transport from ? to Eleusis	"	117
"	3 dr.	σχενδύλη (blacksmith's tool, perhaps pinchers or tongs), including delivery from ? to Eleusis	"	102

N. Travel, Welfare and Other Support Allowances and Distributions

Travel Allowances
(unless otherwise stated, period covered not specified)

480	8 dr.	Citizens embarking on ships before Salamis, apiece—μισθός, τροφή or ἐφόδια?	Cleidemus 323 *FGrH* 21; Arist. *Ath. Pol.* xxiii. 1; Plut. *Them.* x. 6–7
447/6 or 427/6?	[1 dr.] or [4 ob.] p.d.?	[ἐφόδια?] for Athenian οἰκισταί to Kolophon?	*IG* I^3 37. 25–26
c. 440–425	20 [dr.]	ἐφόδια? for ἄποικοι	*IG* I^3 47 A. 10–11
425	2 dr. p.d.	Ambassadors to Persian King, μισθός for 11 years—μισθός or ἐφόδια?	Ar. *Ach.* 66–67, 90
425	8 dr.	Amphitheos from Dikaiopolis for private peace mission to Sparta—ἐφόδια or fee for peacemaking?	Ar. *Ach.* 53, 130
425	3 dr. (p.d.)	Ambassadors or taxiarchs? to Thrace, pay (μιθοφοροῦντας) or ἐφόδια?	Ar. *Ach.* 602
pre-422	2 ob. (p.d.)	Theoros (member of state delegation) or rower? to Paros; μισθός or ἐφόδιον?	Ar. *Vesp.* 1189 et Σa–b, d
5th/4th c.?	1,000 dr.	Ambassador's ἐφόδιον	Herm. *Stat.* ii. 140; Σ Herm. *Stat.* (Walz IV 245. 29–30, 697–698 [n. 12])
395	30 dr.	Two citizens, apiece, given by Mantitheos as ἐφόδια for Battle of Haliartos	Lys. xvi. 14
c. 375–373	20 dr.	Ambassadors to Macedon, apiece	*IG* II^2 102. 12

c. 368	300 dr.	Deinon for trip to Aigina, given by Apollodoros	[Dem.] liii. 7, 8
367	[30 dr.]	Herald sent to Aitolia to secure release of Eleusinian spondophoroi	*Agora* XVI 48. 27
c. 364–362 or 349/8 or c. 341–339?	50 dr.	Ambassadors sent to purchase grain from Orontes in Mysia, apiece	*IG* II^2 207 bcd + Osborne D12. 24 (vol. II, p. 63)
361/0	20 dr.	Ambassadors to Thessaly, apiece	*IG* II^2 116. 41–42
c. 357	10 or [2]0 dr.?	Ambassadors to Karystos (apiece)	*IG* II^2 124 + p. 658. 13
"	20 dr.	Ambassadors to Eretria, Chalkis and Hestiaia, apiece	*IG* II^2 124. 16
"	10 dr.	Ambassadors who negotiated alliance with Euboian cities, apiece	" 18
pre-355 or 342?	30 dr.	Ambassadors to Euboian cities, apiece	*IG* II^2 149. 17
352	[?] dr.	Men sent to Delphi to inquire about cultivation of Eleusinian sacred orgas, apiece	*IG* II^2 204. 63
"	5 dr.	Men chosen to decide disputed boundaries of Eleusinian sacred orgas, apiece (not ἐφόδια)	" 64
346	1,000 dr.	10 ambassadors for "3 whole months" (actually c. 69 days, so c. 1.45 dr. p.d.)	Dem. xix. 158
post-336/5	[?] dr.	πολ̣ιτῶν ἐφόδι[α]—for exiles?	*IG* II^2 435. 4
c. 334–313	20 dr.	Ambassador to Iatrokles	*IG* II^2 264. 11–12
329/8	250 dr.	Eleusinian σπονδοφόροι, quan. unst.—ἐφόδια, τροφή, μισθός or something else?	*IG* II^2 1672. 4
c. 328/7	50 dr.	Ambassador to Herakleia Pontica	*IG* II^2 360 + p. 660. 43
328/7 or c. 321–319?	[? dr.]	[ἐφόδια] provided by Eurylochos of Kydonia to Athenians?	*IG* II^2 399 + *SEG* XXXIV 71. 20
pre-324	8 dr.	Aristogeiton for journey to Megara, given by mistress Zobia	Dem. xxv. 56
pre-322	1 dr. p.d.	Amphiktyons to Delos, paid by Delos,	Arist. *Ath. Pol.* lxii. 2

		probably εἰς σίτησιν, not ἐφόδιον	
c. 307–303	50 dr.	3 ambassadors to Byzantion, apiece	*IG* II^2 555. 31
c. 286–244	[20 dr.]	Ambassadors to ?, apiece	*IG* II^2 525 + 675 cd + *SEG* XXXIV 72. 6

Welfare and Support Allowances and Distributions[9]

594/3 or 561–527?	?	Dole for those injured in war (and also also war orphans, and persons maimed and disabled?), introduced by Solon or Peisistratos?	Heracleides Pont. fr. 149 (Wehrli) ap. Plut. *Sol.* xxxi. 4; Plut. *Sol.* xxxi. 3; Diog. Laert. i. 55; Σ Aeschin. i. 103 (Dilts no. 223)
483	10 dr.	Available for distribution to each citizen (100 T. total) from Laureion mines, but used instead for triremes	Hdt. vii. 144. 1; Arist. *Ath. Pol.* xxii. 7
480	8 dr.	Distributed to each citizen embarking on ships before Salamis—μισθός, τροφή or ἐφόδια?, for what period?	Cleidemus 323 *FGrH* 21; Arist. *Ath. Pol.* xxiii. 1; Plut. *Them.* x. 6–7
480	2 ob. p.d.	Troizenians vote as support (τρέφειν) for each Athenian (female and child) refugee	Plut. *Them.* x. 5
c. 467	100 mn. plus 4 dr. p.d.	Lysimachos, son of Aristeides	Dem. xx. 115; Plut. *Arist.* xxvii. 2
440s?	?	Theorikon (allowance for theatre seats), introduced by Perikles?	Plut. *Per.* ix. 1–3; Σ Dem. i. 1f (Dilts 16. 8–13)
pre-431	?	War orphans	Arist. *Ath. Pol.* xxiv. 3
410–404	2 ob. (p.d.) → 1 ob.? → 2 ob. → grain	Diobelia (dole) instituted by Kleophon; in ?407/6 briefly reduced to 1 ob. or 1 ob. for war orphans?; 2 ob. in 406 and 405; Kallikrates promised to add 1 ob. but then abolished; for at least part of 405/4 a grain distribution	*IG* I^3 375. 10–23 *IG* I^3 377 passim *IG* I^3 379. 86–91 Ar. *Ran.* 141b; Xen. *Hell.* i. 7. 2; Lys. *In Theozotidem*, line 96 (Thalheim fr. lix. 42d); Arist. *Pol.* 1267b 2; Arist. *Ath. Pol.* xxviii. 3

9. See also "O. Individuals: Support Costs."

c. 403/2	1 ob. p.d.	Dole for orphans of citizens who died fighting for the restoration of the Democracy (and probably also for other war orphans)	*SEG* XXVIII 46. 9–10
late 5th c.?	2 ob. (p.d.)	Diobelia, soldier's pay or something else?	Theopomp. Com. fr. 56 (K-A)
late 5th c.?	1 ob. (p.d.)	Dole for ἀδύνατοι (for probable definition, see entry under "pre-322" below)	Lys. xxiv. 13, 26; Arist. fr. 470 (Rose); *Suda* α 540 (Adler), ἀδύνατοι
395/4?	1 dr.	Theorikon, introduced by Agyrrhios? (1 dr. for 3 days of performances, i.e., 2 ob. p.d. apiece?)	Philoch. 328 *FGrH* 33; *Com. Adesp.* fr. *950 (K-A); Zenob. iii. 27 (*CPG*), δραχμὴ χαλαζῶσα; Σ Lucian *Tim.* 49 (Jacobitz); Harp., θεωρικά; Hesych. δ 2351 (Latte), δραχμὴ χαλαζῶσα; Phot., θεωρικά; *Suda* θ 218 (Adler), θεωρικά
c. 355?	2 ob.	Theorikon: 2 ob. for theatre seat (rather than 1 ob. for theatre seat and 1 ob. εἰς ἰδίαν τροφήν)	Σ Ar. *Vesp.* 1189d; Σ Dem. i. 1f (Dilts 15. 29–30); Lib. *Decl.* xxxii. 15–16, *Arg.* i. 8; Phot., θεωρικόν καὶ θεωρική; *Suda* θ 220 (Adler), θεωρικόν καὶ θεωρική; *Et. Magn.*, διωβελία, θεωρικὸν ἀργύριον (Gaisford 280. 24, 448. 56); *Lex. Seg.* 237. 15, διωβελία
355	3 ob. p.d.	Projected yield per citizen from proposed eisphora for mine development	Xen. *Vect.* iii. 9
c. 355–322	4 ob.	Theorikon?, for 2 performances?, or ekklesiast pay at normal Ekklesia?	Dem. *Prooem.* lii. 4
c. 349	2 ob.	Theorikon	Dem. xiii. 10

346	2 ob.	Theatre seat, paid for by theorikon?	Dem. xviii. 28 et Σ 74a, 74b (Dilts 209. 14–20)
c. 344/3 or 334?	1 dr. p.d.	Peisitheides of Delos, for τροφή, until he returns to Delos (payable each prytany)	*IG* II^2 222. 39
c. 338–325	50 dr. or 1 mn.?	Per citizen, provided by Lykourgos from 160 T. judgment against Diphilos	[Plut.] *Mor.* 843d
c. 338–325	?	18,900 T. total distributions under Lykourgos	[Plut.] *Mor.* 852b
331	1/2 mn.	Distribution by Demades to each citizen for Choes festival	Plut. *Mor.* 818e
pre-323	5 dr.	Theorikon, for what period? (15 performances at 2 ob.?)	Hyp. *Dem.* col. XXVI; Dinarch. i. 56
pre-322	1, 2 or 3 ob. p.d.? (most likely 2 ob. p.d.)	Dole for citizens possessing less than 3 mnas and physically unable to work (ἀδύνατοι)	Arist. *Ath. Pol.* xlix. 4; Arist. fr. 470 (Rose); Σ Aeschin. i. 103 (Dilts no. 222b); Harp., ἀδύνατοι; Hesych. α 1217 (Latte), ἀδύνατοι; Phot. α 393 (Theodoridis), ἀδύνατοι; *Suda* α 540 (Adler), ἀδύνατοι; *Lex. Seg.* 345. 20–22, ἀδύνατοι
c. 317–307	3 ob. → 1 dr. p.d.	Mother and maternal aunt of Aristeides' grandson	Dem. Phal. 228 *FGrH* 45
post-306/5	c. 1.8 ob. p.d.?	Dole for ἀδύνατοι (9 dr. p.m.—fr. 197b says 5 ob. p.d.)	Philoch. 328 *FGrH* 197a, b
72	200 dr.	Lucullus to Athenian refugees at Amisos, to return home, apiece	Plut. *Luc.* xix. 8
A.D. 2nd c.	c. 3 1/3 dr., 1 2/3 dr. p.d.	100 dr. p.m. proposed dole (διανομαί) for citizens, 50 dr. p.m. for metics	Lucian *Nav.* 24

Appendix 2

Non-Athenian Labor, Transport and Welfare Costs in Literary Sources

L. Labor Costs

Soldiers and Sailors

c. 519	?	140 T. p.a. for cavalry in Cilicia, quan. unst.	Hdt. iii. 90. 3
420	3 Aig. ob. p.d.	Athens-Argos-Mantineia-Elis treaty, σῖτος (ration-money or gross pay?)—hoplites, light-armed and archers, apiece	*IG* I[3] 83. 23–24; Thuc. v. 47. 6
"	1 Aig. dr. p.d.	Same—cavalrymen, apiece	"
412	1 Attic dr. (p.d.)	Tissaphernes to each sailor in Peloponnesian fleet as τροφή for 1 (prior) month	Thuc. viii. 29. 1
412	3 ob.+/ 1 Attic dr. (p.d.)	Tissaphernes gives 3 ob.+ apiece to sailors in Peloponnesian fleet as τροφή/μισθός for future, subject to increase to 1 dr. by Persian King	Thuc. viii. 29. 1–2
411	1 dr. or 3 ob.+? →3 ob. (p.d.)	Tissaphernes cuts μισθοφορά for sailors in Peloponnesian fleet, apiece	Thuc. viii. 45. 2
411	?	Chians to Peloponnesian sailors: 3 Chian tessarakostai apiece, for what period?	Thuc. viii. 101. 1
c. 408	3→4 ob. (p.d.)	Cyrus' μισθός to Peloponnesian sailors—at first 30 mn. per ship p.m., i.e., 3 ob. per sailor p.d., but raised to 4 ob. p.d. (Lysander wanted 1 dr. p.d. to lure Athenian rowers, who were being paid 3 ob. p.d.)	Xen. *Hell.* i. 5. 4–7; Plut. *Alc.* xxxv. 5, *Lys.* iv. 5–6
406	?	Chios to Peloponnesian sailors: 5 dr. apiece travel expenses (ἐφοδιασάμενος), for what period?	Xen. *Hell.* i. 6. 12
406	"double pay"	(διπλοῦς μισθούς) Dionysios I of	Diod. Sic. xiii. 93. 2

		Syracuse promises from booty	
401	1→1 1/2 darics p.m.	Cyrus promises μισθός to Greek mercenaries, apiece, after negotiation (Asia)	Xen. *Anab.* i. 3. 21
c. 400	1 Kyz. st. p.m.	Timasion promises μισθοφορά (Asia)	Xen. *Anab.* v. 6. 23
c. 400	?	Greek mercenaries demand of Herakleia Pontica >3,000–>10,000 Kyz. st., for σιτία, for what period? (not paid)	Xen. *Anab.* vi. 2. 4
399	1–4 Kyz. st. (p.m.)	Seuthes promises μισθός: 1 to each soldier, 2 to each captain (λοχαγός), and 4 to each general, soldiers to take σῖτα and ποτά "from country," but Seuthes pays only 1 T. of 30 T. owed (Thrace)	Xen. *Anab.* vii. 2. 36 3. 10 7. 25 7. 53–54
399	1–4 darics p.m.	Thibron offers μισθός: 1 to each soldier, 2 to each captain, and 4 to each general (Asia)	Xen. *Anab.* vii. 6. 1, 7
383	3 Aig. ob. (p.d.)	Contribution of Sparta's allies in lieu of sending army—μισθός per soldier	Xen. *Hell.* v. 2. 21
"	2 Aig. dr. (p.d.)	Same—μισθός per cavalryman	"
"	1 [Aig.] st. [= 2 Aig. dr.] p.d.	Fine of Sparta's allies for not paying foregoing contributions, per soldier	Xen. *Hell.* v. 2. 22
377/6	"2 ψιλοί" (light-armed)	Contribution of Sparta's allies for military pay in lieu of sending army—hoplite	Diod. Sic. xv. 31. 2
"	"4 hoplites"	Same—cavalryman	"
"	?	Same—ψιλός (light-armed soldier)	"
374	2–4 x normal	Jason of Pherai to each able mercenary	Xen. *Hell.* vi. 1. 6
c. 360	?	20 T. owed to mercenaries, quan. unst. (Klazomenai)	[Arist.] *Oec.* 1348b 23
355/4	"1 1/2 pay"	(μισθοὺς ἡμιολίους) Philomelos to mercenaries	Diod. Sic. xvi. 25. 1
354/3	"1 1/2 pay"	(μισθοὺς ἡμιολίους) Philomelos to mercenaries	Diod. Sic. xvi. 30. 1
353/2	"double pay"	(διπλασιάσας μισθούς) Phaullos to mercenaries	Diod. Sic. xvi. 36. 1
pre-347/6	?	Phokians spend >10,000 T. on	Diod. Sic. xvi. 56. 5–6

		μισθοφορά for soldiers, quan. unst., in Sacred War	
331	?	Alexander gives 1,000 T., or <3,000 T.?, to recruit soldiers, quan. unst.	Diod. Sic. xvii. 64. 5-6 Curtius v. 1. 43; Arrian *Anab.* iii. 16. 10
pre-323	5 gold mn. or 1 gold st.?, p.m.	Alexander to Amazon cavalry, apiece (1 gold st. supplemented by σιτηρέσια [ration-money])	*Hist. Alex. Magni* (α) iii. 26. 4; (β) iii. 26; (γ) iii. 26
323	?	Alexander gives 500 T. as μισθός to recruit or buy sailors, quan. unst.	Aristobulus 139 *FGrH* 55 ap. Arrian *Anab.* vii. 19. 5
323	"10 stater," "double pay" men	Alexander's higher-paid soldiers (δεκα-στάτηρον, διμοιρίτην) receive more μισθοφορά than ordinary soldiers	Arrian *Anab.* vii. 23. 3
319	?	600 T. μισθοφορία for Antigonos' mercenaries, quan. unst.	Diod. Sic. xviii. 52. 7
315	?	1,000 T. to recruit Antigonos' Peloponnesian mercenaries, quan. unst.	Diod. Sic. xix. 57. 5
315	?	500 T. from Antigonos to Alexander, to recruit mercenaries (quan. unst.)?	Diod. Sic. xix. 61. 5
early 3rd c.	4 ob. (p.d.)	Soldier (but not a Spartan) in Lysimachos' army	Plut. *Mor.* 233c
277	?	Antigonos Gonatas' μισθός to Gauls, quant. unst.: 1 Macedonian gold (st.?) apiece (30 T. total), for what period?	Polyaenus iv. 6. 17
241	?	Carthaginian mercenaries, quan. unst.: 1 gold (st.?) εἰς τὰ κατεπείγοντα ("pressing expenses" = ration-money?), for what period?	Polyb. i. 66. 6
222	?	Ptolemy gives 24 T. p.a. σύνταξις to Kleomenes for himself and his soldiers, quan. unst. (Egypt)	Plut. *Agis et Cleom.* liii. 5
218	<c. 3 ob. p.d.?	Achaians vote 50 T. for 3 months, and thereafter 17 T. p.m., to Philip V's 7,200 soldiers, plus σῖτος	Polyb. v. 1. 11–12 2.11
205	10 mn. p.d.	Skopas the general, ὀψώνιον (Egypt)	Polyb. xiii. 2. 3
"	1 mn. p.d.	Skopas' soldiers, ὀψώνιον apiece	"

		(Egypt)	
202	?	1,000 T. paid by Carthaginians for Scipio's army, quan. unst. (for 150 days?), ἐς δαπάνην, plus ἀγοράν	App. *Lib.* 238
pre-184	?	3,000 T. spent by Scipio for soldiers, quan. unst.	Diod. Sic. xxix. 21. 1
171	c. 1 2/3 or 6 2/3 dr. p.d.?	200 T. half year's *stipendium* for all 4,000 of Perseus' cavalrymen, or only the 1,000 contributed by Cotys?	Liv. xlii. 51. 10–11 67. 5
169	?	>120 T. needed for 5,000 Peloponnesian soldiers in Epiros, i.e., c. 145 dr. apiece, for what period?	Polyb. xxviii. 13. 13
168	5–1,000 gold (sts.?)	Perseus promises to Gauls but does not pay: 5 gold (sts.?) apiece to foot-soldiers, 10 to cavalrymen, 1,000 to leader Gentius/Kloilios, for what period? (total is >150,000 gold st. or 500 T.?; Perseus brought 10,000 st.)	Diod. Sic. xxx. 19. 1; Liv. xliv. 26. 4; App. *Mac.* 18. 2
pre-146	2 ob. p.d.	ὀψώνιον *less* deductions for food, clothing and arms—Roman foot soldier	Polyb. vi. 39. 12–15
"	4 ob. p.d.	Same—Roman centurion	"
"	1 dr. p.d.	Same—Roman cavalryman	"
85/4	16 dr. p.d.	Roman soldiers quartered with families in Asia, apiece, from hosts (Sulla orders)	Plut. *Sull.* xxv. 5
"	50 dr. p.d.	Roman tribunes quartered with families in Asia, apiece, from hosts (Sulla orders)	"
52	?	1,000 T. p.a. to Pompey's troops, quan. unst.	Plut. *Caes.* xxviii. 8, *Pomp.* lv. 12
A.D. 14	1 dr. p.d.	Pannonian legions demand	Dio Cass. lvii. 4. 2
A.D. 83	75→100 dr. (p.a.?)	Soldier's pay increased by Domitian	Dio Cass. lxvii. 3. 5

Military Bonuses[1]

c. 534–509	5 mn.	Tarquin to each soldier after taking Suessa (Italy)	Dion. Hal. *A.R.* iv. 50. 5, vi. 74. 2

1. See also "P. Public Revenues: War Booty."

5th c.?	10 dr.	Discharged soldiers, apiece (Egypt)	Heliodorus vii. 8. 4
480	1,000 T.	Drako the far-sighted, by Xerxes, to report distant events, including Battle of Salamis	Ptol. Chennus ap. Phot. *Bibl.* 148b. 7
461	1 mn.	Syracusans to 600 elite soldiers, apiece	Diod. Sic. xi. 76. 2
401	5 mn.+	Cyrus promises to Greek mercenaries: 5 mn. at Babylon, full pay during return trip to Ionia	Xen. *Anab.* i. 4. 13; Diod. Sic. xiv. 21. 6
397	100 mn.	Dionysius gives to Archylos as first to mount wall of Motya (Sicily)	Diod. Sic. xiv. 53. 4
c. 397	100 T.	Persian satraps to Spartan captors of Kisthene (Asia Minor)	Isoc. iv. 153
349/8	100 T.	Persian King to Mentor for generalship against Egyptians	Diod. Sic. xvi. 52. 2
331	2–6 mn.+	Alexander to soldiers, apiece: 2 mn. to Macedonians in phalanx, 5 to allied cavalry, 6 to companion cavalry, plus 2 months' pay (διμήνου μισθοφοραῖς) to mercenaries	Diod. Sic. xvii. 64. 6; Curtius v. 1. 45
330	10 mn.–1 T.	Alexander to Greek mercenaries on discharge, apiece: 10 mn. to foot-soldiers, 1 T. to cavalry (2,000 T. total)	Diod. Sic. xvii. 74. 3; Curtius vi. 2. 17; Plut. *Alex.* xlii. 5; Arrian *Anab.* iii. 19. 5
330	12,000 or 13,000 T.?	Alexander's gross bonuses	Diod. Sic. xvii. 74. 5; Curtius vi. 2. 10
330	3 T.	Alexander to troops remaining with him, apiece	Diod. Sic. xvii. 74. 4
329	3,000 dr.–2 T.	Alexander to discharged troops, apiece: 3,000 dr. to infantry, 2 T. to cavalry	Curtius vii. 5. 27
324	9,870, <10,000 or 20,000 T.?	Total debts of discharged, or marrying?, soldiers paid by Alexander	Diod. Sic. xvii. 109. 2; Curtius x. 2. 9–11; Plut. *Alex.* lxx. 3; Arrian *Anab.* vii. 4. 8, 5. 3; Justin xii. 11. 3
324	1 T.	Alexander to discharged soldiers, apiece	Arrian *Anab.* vii. 12. 2
323	3 gold T.	Older and weaker veterans, apiece (provided in Alexander's will)	*Hist. Alex. Magni* (α) iii. 33. 1

317	"6 mos. pay"	Eumenes to soldiers—extra or advance pay?, as incentive? (Persia)	Diod. Sic. xix. 15. 5
306	2 mn.–1 T.	Ptolemy offers to deserters from Antigonos: 2 mn. to each ordinary soldier, 1 T. to each officer (Egypt)	Diod. Sic. xx. 75. 1
302	"3 mos. pay"	Antigonos to soldiers—extra or advance pay?, as incentive? (Cilicia)	Diod. Sic. xx. 108. 2
243	60 T.	Aratos of Sikyon to 4 mercenaries, together, to betray Corinth (1 T. and house per man if attempt unsuccessful)	Plut. *Arat.* xix. 1–2
229	50 T.	Aristomachos of Argos asks from Aratos to discharge soldiers, quan. unst.	Plut. *Arat.* xxxv. 2
216	500 dr.	Marcellus to Bantius for past services (Italy)	Plut. *Marc.* x. 9
214	10 T.	Sosibios to Bolis to secure release of Achaios (Alexandria)	Polyb. viii. 15. 7 16. 7
c. 203	"2 mos. pay"	(διμήνου . . . ὠψωνίασε) Agathokles to soldiers—extra or advance pay?, as incentive? (Egypt)	Polyb. xv. 25. 11
192	<100 or 120 T.?	Spartans to Philopoimen for protection against Romans	Plut. *Phil.* xv. 6; Paus. viii. 51. 2
168	50 T.	Perseus to Cretan soldiers, quan. unst., in plate (Macedon)	Liv. xliv. 45. 13; Plut. *Aem.* xxiii. 8
168	60 T.	Perseus gives to soldiers but later takes back	Diod. Sic. xxx. 21. 1
64	50 dr.–6,000 T.	Tigranes of Armenia to Pompey: 6,000 T. for Pompey, and for his army 50 dr. per soldier, 1,000 dr. per centurion and 6,000 (or 10,000?) dr. per tribune and cavalry prefect	Strabo xi. 14. 10; App. *Mith.* 490
63	950 dr.	Soldiers, apiece, at Lucullus' triumph over Mithradates (Rome)	Plut. *Luc.* xxxvii. 6
61	1,500 Att. dr., etc.	Pompey to his army: 1,500 Attic dr. per soldier, proportionate amts. for officers (16,000 T. total)	Plut. *Pomp.* xlv. 4; App. *Mith.* 565
50	250 dr.	Caesar to each soldier recalled by Pompey	Plut. *Caes.* xxix. 4; App. *B.C.* ii. 115

pre-49	5 mn.	Caesar promises to each soldier at Brundisium	App. *B.C.* ii. 191
47	1,000 dr.	Caesar to each soldier	Plut. *Caes.* li. 2; App. *B.C.* ii. 387
46	5,000–20,000 dr.	Caesar on triumph: 5,000 per soldier, 10,000 per centurion, 20,000 per tribune and cavalry prefect	App. *B.C.* ii. 422; Dio Cass. xliii. 21. 3
44	500 dr.	Octavian to each soldier on enlisting	App. *B.C.* iii. 165; Nic. Damas. 90 *FGrH* 130. 136
44	100 dr.	Antony promises to each soldier going to Gaul	App. *B.C.* iii. 177, 181
44	500 dr.	Antony to each soldier	App. *B.C.* iii. 187
44	500 dr.	Octavian to each soldier from two legions that deserted from Antony	App. *B.C.* iii. 197
44–43	5,000 dr.	Octavian promises to each soldier if victorious; confirmed by Senate, but made payable in 2 equal installments; 1st installment paid, balance promised	App. *B.C.* iii. 197, 303, 353, 370, 387
43	2,500 dr.	Octavian gives to soldiers, apiece	Dio Cass. xlvi. 46. 6
42	1,500–7,500 + Italian dr., etc.	Cassius promises before Philippi: 1,500 per soldier, 7,500 per centurion, proportionate amt. per tribune	App. *B.C.* iv. 422
42	1,000 dr., etc. or 2,000 dr.?	Brutus at Philippi: 1,000 per soldier with proportionately larger amts. for officers	Plut. *Brut.* xliv. 3; App. *B.C.* iv. 497
42	5,000–50,000 dr.	Antony and Octavian promise at Philippi: 5,000 per soldier, 25,000 per centurion, 50,000 per tribune	Plut. *Ant.* xxiii. 1; App. *B.C.* iv. 507; Dio Cass. xlvii. 42. 5
36	500 dr.	Octavian to each soldier	App. *B.C.* v. 536; Dio Cass. xlix. 14. 2
36	100 dr., etc.	Antony gives to each foot soldier, with proportionately larger amts. for officers	Dio Cass. xlix. 31. 4
30	1,500 dr.	Antony promises to Octavian's soldiers, apiece (Egypt)	Dio Cass. li. 10. 2
30	250 dr.	Augustus gives to soldiers, apiece, for	Dio Cass. li. 17. 7

		not plundering (Egypt)	
A.D. 5	5,000 dr.	Praetorian guards, apiece, after 16 years of service (Rome)	Dio Cass. lv. 23. 1
"	3,000 dr.	Other soldiers, apiece, after 20 years of service (Rome)	"
A.D. 14	75–250 dr.	Augustus' bequests: 250 to praetorian guards, 125 to city soldiers and 75 to other soldiers, apiece	Dio Cass. lvi. 32. 2
A.D. 37	500 dr.	Gaius to praetorian guards, apiece (includes Tiberius' bequests of 250 dr. apiece)	Dio Cass. lix. 2. 1
A.D. 37	75–125 dr.	Tiberius' bequests, paid by Gaius, 125 to city soldiers, 75 to others, apiece (Rome)	Dio Cass. lix. 2. 3
A.D. 38–42	25 dr.	Gaius to praetorian guards, annually	Dio Cass. lx. 12. 4
A.D. 68	7,500 dr.	Sabinus promises—to praetorians	Plut. *Galb.* ii. 2
"	1,250 dr.	Same—to other soldiers	"
A.D. 69	25 dr.	Mucianus to each soldier (Rome)	Dio Cass. lxv. 22. 2
A.D. 69	1,250 dr.	Otho to each soldier	Plut. *Oth.* iii. 12
A.D. 193	3,000 dr.	Pertinax to praetorians, apiece	Dio Cass. lxxiii. 1. 2, 5. 4
A.D. 193	250 dr.	Severus to soldiers, apiece (Rome)	Dio Cass. xlvi. 46. 7
A.D. 193	5,000→ 6,250 dr.	Sulpicianus and Julianus "bid" for support, per soldier, Julianus winning (Rome)	Dio Cass. lxxiv. 11. 4–5
A.D. 202	10 gold pieces	Septimius Severus to recipients of grain dole and praetorian guards, apiece (total 50,000,000 dr.)	Dio Cass. lxxvi. 1. 1
A.D. 212	2,500 Att. dr.	Caracalla promises to praetorian guards, apiece	Herodian *Hist.* iv. 4. 7
A.D. 217	750 dr.	Macrinus promises to soldiers, apiece (Rome)	Dio Cass. lxxviii. 19. 2
A.D. 218	5,000 dr.	Macrinus promises to soldiers, apiece (Rome)	Dio Cass. lxxviii. 34. 2

A.D. 218	1,000 dr.	Macrinus gives to soldiers, apiece (Rome)	Dio Cass. lxxviii. 34. 3
A.D. 218	500 dr.	Elagabalus promises to soldiers, apiece (Antioch)	Dio Cass. lxxix. 1. 1
A.D. 6th c.	5 gold st.	Each soldier every fourth year (Byzantion)	Procop. *Anec.* xxiv. 28
		Doctors, Lawyers and Professors	
pre-531	3 ob.	Pythagoras to student per mathematics lesson, at first; thereafter, student to Pythagoras per lesson (Samos)	Iambl. *V.P.* v. 22–24, *Protr.* 108. 12, 125. 2 (Pistelli)
pre-c. 522	1 T. p.a.	Physician Demokedes, from Aiginetans	Hdt. iii. 131. 2
pre-c. 522	2 T. p.a.	Physician Demokedes, from Polykrates (Samos)	Hdt. iii. 131. 2; *Suda* δ 442 (Adler), Δημοκήδης
post-c. 522	"gold staters"	Physician Demokedes, from Darius' wives for curing Darius (Persia)	Hdt. iii. 130. 5
pre-450?	1,000 dr.	Korax charges Teisias for rhetorical instruction (Sicily)	Planudes *Proleg. Rhet.* 215 (Rabe 67. 9)
c. 450–415	>150 mn.	Hippias in Sicily (>20 mn. from small town Inykos)	Pl. *Hp. Ma.* 282e
c. 450–400	"many" T.	Hippokrates offered by Persian King (not accepted)	Plut. *Cat. Mai.* xxiii. 4
c. 450–400	10 T.	Hippokrates, potential fees from Abdera rejected	Hipp. *Epist.* xi, xvi
c. 400	1 T.	Rhodian asks for float system to convey Greek mercenaries across river (Asia)	Xen. *Anab.* iii. 5. 8
4th c.	1 T.	Pamphilos for instruction in painting, 500 dr. p.a. (for 12 years?) (Sikyon)	Plin. *N.H.* xxxv. 76
c. 370	100 or 500 T.?	Demokritos, for reading aloud from his works (Abdera)	Antisthenes 508 *FGrH* 14; Diog. Laert. ix. 39–40
361	1 T.	Helikon of Kyzikos from Dionysios II for predicting solar eclipse (Syracuse)	Plut. *Dion* xix. 6
c. 356–336	300, 400 and 500 T.	Aristotle, promised by individual sons of Philip (except Alexander),	*Hist. Alex. Magni* (ε) 3. 6

		in each case if he should become king	
c. 335–323	100 T.	Philosopher Anaxarchos of Abdera from Alexander	Plut. *Mor.* 179f
c. 323–301	1 dr., 1 T.	Thrasyllos the Cynic from Antigonos (who would not give so little or so much)	Sen. *Ben.* ii. 17. 1; Plut. *Mor.* 182e, 531f
c. 323–301	1 T.	Bion from Antigonos	Plut. *Mor.* 531e
4th/3rd c.	1 dr.	Doctor (Thebes?)	Crates Theb. fr. 362. 1 (*Supp. Hell.*)
4th/3rd c.	3 ob.	Philosopher (Thebes?)	Crates Theb. fr. 362. 3 (*Supp. Hell.*)
c. 300	2,000 gold st.	Anyte from Phalysios for bringing Asklepios' cure for blindness (Naupaktos)	Paus. x. 38. 13
c. 285–246	50 T.	Phoenix for engineering scheme to transport obelisk blocks (Egypt)	Plin. *N.H.* xxxvi. 68
c. 281–261	100 T.	Physician Kleombrotos of Keos or Erasisitratos?, for saving life of Antiochos	Plin. *N.H.* vii. 123 xxix. 5
c. 246–221	12 T. p.a.	Panaretos the philosopher from Ptolemy (Egypt)	Polemon *FHG* III 141, fr. 84 ap. Athen. xii. 77 (552c)
62	1 T.	Rhodian sophists, apiece, from Pompey	Plut. *Pomp.* xlii. 10
c. 27–A.D. 14	1 T.	Rhetorician Kraton from Augustus	Sen. *Contr.* x. 5. 21
A.D. 1st c.	?	Medical expenses 1 dr. more if miser survives than if he dies (Italy?)	*Anth. Pal.* xi. 171. 5 (Lucilius)
A.D. 2nd c.	2, 4, 5 or "a few ob."	Greek tutors in wealthy Roman households	Lucian *Merc. Cond.* 11, 24, 38
A.D. 2nd c.	200 dr.	Rhetorician for dinner speech at Roman banquet	Lucian *Merc. Cond.* 35
A.D. 2nd c.	1 ob.→ "fortunes"	Philosophers demand (Roman Empire)	Lucian *Fug.* 20
A.D. 2nd c.	2 T.	Polemon for advocacy (Sardis)	Philostr. *V.S.* 525
A.D. 2nd c.	10 T.	Polemon from Bosporan King (Smyrna)	Philostr. *V.S.* 535

A.D. 2nd c.	150,000→ 250,000 dr.	Polemon from Herodes Atticus for three days of declamation lessons—150,000 rejected, 250,000 accepted (Smyrna)	Philostr. *V.S.* 538
A.D. 2nd c.	10 T.	Herakleides' accumulated teaching fees (Smyrna)	Philostr. *V.S.* 615
A.D. late 2nd c.	8 gold pieces	Medical fee, to cure Leukippe of madness in 2 installments of 4 gold pieces (Egypt)	Ach. Tat. iv. 15. 5, 16. 1, 2, 5
A.D. 2nd/ 3rd c.	20 mn.	Physician Eudoxos for death potion (Asia)	Xen. Eph. iii. 5. 9

Priests, Oracles and Seers

pre-546	"not a few" T.	Ambiguous oracles, paid by Croesus (Asia Minor, Delphi, etc.)	Lucian *J. Tr.* 43
5th c.	5 uncias– 1 litra	Wicked female seers (Syracuse)	Epicharmus fr. 9 (Kaibel)
401	3,000 darics = 10 T.	Silanos, paid by Cyrus for correct prediction that Artaxerxes would not fight for 10 days	Xen. *Anab.* i. 7. 18, v. 6. 18
323	1 T. p.a.	Priest of Alexander at Alexandria, as provided in Alexander's wil	*Hist. Alex. Magni* (α) iii. 33. 19
3rd/2nd c.	1 dr.	Seers (Rome?)	Enn. *Scen.* 322–3 (Vahlen)
2nd c.	1 ob.	Seer (loc. unst.)	Dion. Thrax fr. 51 (Linke)
A.D. 2nd c.	2 ob.	Amphilochos, per prophecy (Cilicia)	Lucian *Alex.* 19, *Deor. Conc.* 12
c. A.D. 150–170	1 dr. 2 ob.	Alexander, per prophecy (Paphlagonia) (8 dr. + τὸ γιγνόμενον for 8)	Lucian *Alex.* 23, 54
"	1 Attic T.	Interpreters of Alexander's oracles to Alexander (one-time license fee?) (Paphlagonia)	Lucian *Alex.* 49
A.D. 4th c.	1 ob.	Apollo's oracles, apiece (Roman Empire)	Lib. *Decl.* xxxiv. 49

Actors, Artists, Musicians and Writers[2]

c. 483	3 or 3,000 dr.?	Pindar for victory ode for Pytheas of Aigina (bronze portrait statue would have cost the same)	Σ Pind. *Nem.* v. 1a
450s	?	"Talents" for wages (including Pheidias'), gold, ivory, wood, etc., for statue of Zeus (Olympia)	Dio Chrys. xii. 49
c. 450–400	100 T.	Polykleitos for sculpture of "Diadumenos" (Sikyon)	Plin. *N.H.* xxxiv. 55
c. 413–399	4 mn. p.d.	Poet Choirilos, from Archelaos (Macedon)	Istrus 334 *FGrH* 61
5th/4th c.	"gold sigloi"	Timotheos for Hymn to Artemis (Ephesos)	Alex. Aetol. fr. 4. 3–4 (Powell)
4th c.	500 dr. p.a., 1 T. total	Pamphilos for instruction in painting, for 12 years? (Sikyon)	Plin. *N.H.* xxxv. 76
c. 400–350	1 T.	Kitharode from Dionysios, promised but not given (Syracuse)	Plut. *Mor.* 333f
331	10 T.	Alexander to actor Lykon of Skarpheia, in response to request inserted into comedy	Plut. *Alex.* xxix. 6, *Mor.* 334e
pre-323	10,000 gold pieces	Pyrrhon for poem for Alexander	Plut. *Mor.* 331e; Sext. Emp. *Math.* i. 282
302	>200 T.	Antigonos to athletes and artists after games cancelled (Syria)	Diod. Sic. xx. 108. 1
4th/3rd c.	1 T.	Apelles pays to be admitted to society of artists (Sikyon)	Plut. *Arat.* xiii. 1
4th/3rd c.	20 gold T.	Apelles for painting of "Alexander Hurling Thunderbolt" (Ephesos)	Plin. *N.H.* xxxv. 92
4th/3rd c.	50 T.	Protogenes of Rhodes for paintings, offered by Apelles	Plin. *N.H.* xxxv. 88
4th/3rd c.	1,000 mn.	Aristides of Thebes for painting of "Alexander's Battle with Persians" (100 human figures at 10 mn. per figure)	Plin. *N.H.* xxxv. 99
4th/3rd c.	3,600 mn.	Asclepiodorus for painting of	Plin. *N.H.* xxxv. 107

2. See also "C. Tangible Personal Property: Sculpture" and "Paintings."

		"Twelve Gods" (300 mn. per god)	
early 3rd c.	300 T., "talents"	Colossos of Rhodes (gross cost)—how much for sculptors?	Plin. *N.H.* xxxiv. 41; Lucian *J. Tr.* 11
3rd c.	1 T.	Prize for poets praising hair of Stratonike, wife of Seleukos	Lucian *Pro Imag.* 5
200–A.D. 200?	200 Parian dr.	Arkesilaos for statue of Artemis (Paros)	"Simonides" lxiii. 1–2 (Page)
200–A.D. 200?	1 dr.	(Sculptor) for wax model of Eros (Ionia?)	Anacreontea 11. 13 (West)
pre-73	500 T.	"Apollo" statue (cost of manufacture)—how much for sculptor? (Pontic Apollonia)	Plin. *N.H.* xxxiv. 40
pre-56	1 T.	Arcesilaus for plaster model of wine bowl (Rome)	Plin. *N.H.* xxxv. 156
53	1 T.	Parthian king to actor Iason	Plut. *Crass.* xxxiii. 7
A.D. 1st c.	6 dr.	Painter for "Child with Dog's Head" (Italy?)	*Anth. Pal.* xi. 212. 5 (Lucilius)
A.D. 1st c.	500 or 1,000 dr.	Portrait statues —how much for sculptor? (Rhodes)	Dio Chrys. xxxi. 59
pre-A.D. 2nd c.?	1 dr.	Sculptor for statues (loc. unst.)—Zeus	Aesop 90 (Hausrath)
"	>1 dr.	Same—Hera	"
"	free	Same—Hermes (if bought with Zeus and Hera)	"

Architects

91?	5→10 T.	Livius Drusus to make house more open instead of less (Rome)	Plut. *Mor.* 800f

Construction and Other Manual Workers Paid on the Basis of Time

450s	?	"Talents" for wages, gold, ivory, wood, etc., for statue of Zeus (Olympia)	Dio Chrys. xii. 49
c. 224	c. 3 ob. p.d. apiece?	100 master builders (οἰκοδόμους) and 350 masons (ὑπουργούς) paid 14 T.	Polyb. v. 89. 3

		p.a. εἰς ὀψώνιον (Rhodes)	
A.D. 2nd c.	4 ob. p.d.	Daily wage or cost of daily food? (Asia Minor?)	Lucian *Sat.* 21

Construction and Other Manual Workers Paid on the Basis of Piece or Job

pre-12th c.	>30 Trojan dr.	Owed to Apollo and Poseidon for making bricks and working on Trojan Wall	Lucian *Sacr.* 4

Inscribers

99	200 dr. max.	Decree, etc. for Athena Lindia (Rhodes)	(Timachidas Rhod.) 532 *FGrH* 1A. 19

Prostitutes and Pimps (per occasion unless otherwise specified)[3]

7th c.?	"small change"	Male or female prostitute	[Archilochus] fr. 328. 2 (West)
c. 420	"small change"	Prostitutes (male, female or old man), together or separately? (Kyzikos)	Eupolis fr. 247. 3 (K-A)
5th/4th c.	"staters"	Lais (the elder) of Corinth, in her prime	Epicrates fr. 3. 12 (K-A)
"	1 st. or 3 ob.	Lais (the elder), as an older woman	" 18
pre-367?	"chalkoi"	Owed by Dionysios the Younger to brothel (Syracuse)	Nicias Nicaeensis *FHG* IV 464 ap. Athen. x. 50 (437f)
pre-322	10,000 dr.	Lais (the younger?) of Corinth demands for whole night from Demosthenes (he refuses)	Sotion ap. Gell. *N.A.* i. 8. 5–6; Σ (*recent.*) Ar. *Plut.* 149d
4th/3rd c.	1 T.	Female prostitute (Thebes?)	Crates Theb. fr. 362. 3 (*Supp. Hell.*)
4th/3rd c.	2 ob.	Female prostitute (Sikyon) (*diobolares meretrices*)	Plaut. *Cist.* 407; Varro *Ling. Lat.* vii. 64; Festus 74M
4th/3rd c.	1 T. gold	Male prostitute (*miles gloriosus*) (Ephesos)	Plaut. *Mil.* 1061
4th/3rd c.	2 ob.	Prostitutes at Kalydon—cheap female	Plaut. *Poen.* 270
"	"not even 3 ob."	Same—female from pimp's slave	Plaut. *Poen.* 868

3. See also "H. Slaves."

	(i.e., free)		
"	1 mn.	Same—pimp for Anterastilis from soldier	Plaut. *Poen.* 467, 1280, 1287, 1353 1359, 1399, 1414
3rd c.	2 ob., "chalkoi"	Female prostitutes (Megalopolis)	Cercidas frs. 5. 31, 17. 41 (Powell)
1st c.	100 gold pieces	Danae from Zeus	*Anth. Pal.* v. 31. 6 (Antipater Thess.)
"	1 dr.	"Attic Europa" (Italy?)	*Anth. Pal.* v. 109. 1 (Antipater Thess.)
1st c.	5 T.	Prostitutes (Italy?)—ugly female for one time	*Anth. Pal.* v. 126. 1 (Philodemus)
"	5 dr.	Same—better-looking female for 12 times	" 3
c. 60	1 ch.? (1 quadrans)	Clodia from a lover	Plut. *Cic.* xxix. 5
c. 30	5 T.	Demanded by woman (prostitute?) (Rome)	Hor. *Sat.* ii. 7. 89
A.D. 1st c.	2 ob.	Korinna (Italy?)	*Anth. Pal.* v. 125. 4 (Bassus)
A.D. 2nd c.	5 dr.→ 1 gold piece	Female prostitute?, after negotiation	*Anth. Pal.* xii. 239. 1–2 (Strato)
A.D. 2nd c.?	1 dr.–"talents"	Prostitute v. true love (loc. unst.)	Plut. *Mor.* 759e–f
A.D. 2nd c.?	20 dr.	Chrysis (married woman), "to go to Hyperboreans," i.e., to do anything	Lucian *Philops.* 15
A.D. 2nd c.?	2 T.	Kiss of Charmoleos (male) of Megara	Lucian *D. Mort.* xx. 3
A.D. late 2nd c.	50 gold pieces	Offered to Menelaos to procure Leukippe (Egypt)	Ach. Tat. iv. 6. 2
A.D. 4th c.?	20 mn.?	Female prostitute (Asia Minor?)	Lib. *Decl.* xxxii. 38, 41
A.D. 5th c.?	30 (lepta?)	Female prostitute	Hesych. τ 41 (Latte), τριᾶντος πόρνη
A.D. 6th c.	3 ob.	Female prostitute (Constantinople)	Procop. *Anec.* xvii. 5

Miscellaneous Workers

8th c.?	1,000 st.	Kerses to murder Ardys (not carried out) (Lydia and Kyme)	Nic. Damas. 90 *FGrH* 44. 4
5th c.	10 litras	μισθός for ? (Syracuse)	Sophron fr. 37 (Kaibel)
c. 390–360	1 ch.	Bathhouse attendant (extra fee for foreigners) (Phaselis)	Stratonicus ap. Athen. viii. 45 (352a)
pre-367	1 T.	Dionysios to man pretending to reveal names of conspirators (Syracuse)	Plut. *Mor.* 176a
326	80 T.	Alexander promises to old man to serve as guide up Mt. Aornus (India)	Curtius viii. 11. 4
302	>200 T.	Antigonos to athletes and artists after games cancelled (Syria)	Diod. Sic. xx. 108. 1
4th/3rd c.	5 T.	Flatterer (Thebes)	Crates Theb. fr. 362. 2 (*Supp. Hell.*)
"	10 mn.	Cook (Thebes)	Crates Theb. fr. 362. 1 (*Supp. Hell.*)
3rd c.	4 ob.	Sharpener of millstone (Ionia)	Herodas vi. 84
A.D. 1st/2nd c.	5 T.	Olympic victors hired by public office seekers (Rome?)	Dio Chrys. lxvi. 11
A.D. 2nd c.	4→20 mn.	Magician to obtain married woman for suitor: 4 mn. down (for sacrificial victims) plus 16 mn. if successful (Roman Empire)	Lucian *Philops.* 14–15
A.D. 2nd c.	5 dr.	Slave bringing dinner invitation (tip) (Roman Empire)	Lucian *Merc. Cond.* 14
A.D. 2nd c.	10,000 dr.	Sisinnes to serve as gladiator (Amastris)	Lucian *Tox.* 59
A.D. 4th c.?	1 ob.±	Bathhouse attendant (Asia Minor?)	Lib. *Decl.* xxvi. 19

M. Transport Costs

Transport Costs

19th c.	50 T. min.	To open or close canal between Nile and Lake Moeris (Egypt)	Diod. Sic. i. 52. 2
6th c.?	2 ob.	Across Acheron—1 ob. for Aiakos as as toll-collector, and 1 for Charon (underworld)	Lucian *Cont.* 2, 11, 20
4th/3rd c.?	1 ob.	Across Acheron (underworld)	*Anth. Pal.* vii. 67. 6 (Leonidas Tar.)
3rd c.?	>1 ob.	Across Acheron (underworld)	*Et. Magn.*, δανάκης (Gaisford 247. 41)
early 1st c.	1 ob.	Across Acheron (underworld)	*Anth. Pal.* vii. 68. 6 (Archias)
1st c.?	1 ob.	Across Acheron (underworld)	*Anth. Pal.* xi. 168. 6 (Antiphanes)
c. 50	[1 ob.]	To underworld, according to Egyptians	Diod. Sic. i. 96. 8
43	1 dr.	Toll per man levied by Gauls on Decimus Brutus fleeing Mutina	Strabo iv. 6. 7
A.D. 2nd c.	1 ob.	Across Acheron (underworld)	*Anth. Pal.* xi. 209. 3 (Ammianus)
A.D. 2nd c.	1 ob.	Entry fee (κατιτήριον) to underworld	Herodian Gram. vol. 3.2 (Lenz 531. 13)
A.D. 2nd c.	1 ob.	Across Acheron (underworld)	*Scol. Alph.* vii. 34 (Heitsch)
A.D. 2nd c.?	1 ob.	Across Acheron (underworld)	Lucian *Cat.* 1, 18, 19, 21
A.D. 2nd c.?	1 ob.	Across Acheron (underworld) (Attic, Aiginetan or Macedonian ob.?)	Lucian *Luct.* 10
A.D. 2nd c.?	12 T. min.	Annual receipts (μισθοφορίαν) of enormous grain ship on Egypt-Italy run	Lucian *Nav.* 13
A.D. 2nd c.?	1 ob.	Across Acheron (underworld)	Lucian *D. Mort.* ii. 1–2, xxi. 4
A.D. 6th c.	1 gold st.	Across Ister River, per person	Procop. *Bell.* viii. 25. 5

N. Travel, Welfare and Other Support Allowances and Distributions

Travel Allowances
(unless otherwise stated, period covered not specified)

406	5 dr.	Chios' ἐφόδια to Spartan sailors, apiece	Xen. *Hell.* i. 6. 12
395	?	30 T. ἐφόδιον for Agesilaos' troops (number unstated) or bribe from Tissaphernes to leave Lydia?	Plut. *Ages.* x. 8
c. 370	50 dr. or "much gold"	Epameinondas borrows from fellow citizen for ἐφόδιον to Peloponnese	Plut. *Mor.* 193b–c, 583f; Ael. *V.H.* xi. 9
334	?	70–200 T. for Alexander's troops (number unstated) for Asian campaign (Douris says 70 T. for 30 days)	Duris 76 *FGrH* 40; Onesicritus 134 *FGrH* 2; Aristobulus 139 *FGrH* 4
A.D. late 2nd c.	100 gold pieces	Gift/ἐφόδιον (Ephesos)	Ach. Tat. vi. 1. 4
"	10 gold pieces	Gift/ἐφόδιον or bribe? (Ephesos)	Ach. Tat. vi. 2. 5

Welfare and Support Allowances and Distributions[4]

405	1 gold st.	Pharnabazos to Milesian refugees, apiece, before resettlement	Diod. Sic. xiii. 104. 6
330/29	3,000, 2,000 or 1,000 dr.?	Alexander to Darius' mutilated Greek prisoners, apiece	Diod. Sic. xvii. 69. 8; *Hist. Alex. Magni* (α) ii. 18. 3 (β) ii. 18 (γ) ii. 18; Curtius v. 5. 24
224	6→12 T.	Pension for Aratos of Sikyon (6 T. from Ptolemy doubled by Kleomenes)	Plut. *Arat.* xli. 5
147	10 T.	Gulussa offers to Hasdrubal, together with 100 slaves and asylum, for 10 Carthaginian families (Africa)	Polyb. xxxviii. 8. 4; Diod. Sic. xxxii. 22. 1
133	9 ob. p.d.	Tiberius Gracchus from Senate	Plut. *Gracch.* xiii. 3

4. See also "O. Individuals: Support Costs."

		εἰς ἀνάλωμα	
72	200 dr.	Lucullus to Athenian refugees to return home, apiece (Amisos)	Plut. *Luc.* xix. 8
63	?	1,250 T. p.a. grain distributions to quan. unst. (Rome)	Plut. *Cat. Min.* xxvi. 1, *Caes.* viii. 7
52	?	1,000 T. p.a. to Pompey's troops, quan. unst.	Plut. *Caes.* xxviii. 8, *Pomp.* lv. 12
49	75 dr.	Caesar promises to each citizen (Rome)	Dio Cass. xli. 16. 1
46	100 dr.	Caesar gives to each dole recipient; includes 75 dr. promised in 49 (Rome)	App. *B.C.* ii. 422; Dio Cass. xliii. 21. 3
44	30, 70 or 75 dr.?	Caesar bequeaths to each citizen (Rome)	Nic. Damas. 90 *FGrH* 130. 48; Plut. *Ant.* xvi. 2, *Brut.* xx. 3, *Mor.* 206f; App. *B.C.* ii. 596; Dio Cass. xliv. 35. 3
44	500 dr.	Octavian gives to Campanians, apiece	Dio Cass. xlv. 12. 2
44	100 dr.	Antony promises to citizens, apiece (Rome)	Dio Cass. xlv. 13. 2
43	2,500 dr.	Senate gives to certain citizens (but not others), apiece (Rome)	Dio Cass. xlvi. 40. 6
post-40	25 dr.	Lucius Cornelius Balbus bequeaths to each Roman citizen	Dio Cass. xlviii. 32. 2
29	100 dr.	Augustus gives to each citizen (Rome)	Dio Cass. li. 21. 3
24	100 dr.	Augustus promises to each citizen (Rome)	Dio Cass. liii. 28. 1
12	100 dr.	Augustus gives to each citizen on death of Agrippa (Rome)	Dio Cass. liv. 29. 4
2	60 dr.	Augustus gives to each grain recipient (Rome)	Dio Cass. lv. 10. 1
A.D. 14	10,000,000 dr.	Augustus' bequest to people, quant. unst. (Rome)	Dio Cass. lvi. 32. 2
A.D. 15	65 dr.	Tiberius to each citizen in satisfaction of Augustus' bequest (Rome)	Dio Cass. lvii. 14. 2

A.D. 37	75 dr.+	Gaius to each citizen (payment of 11,250,000 dr. bequest by Tiberius, plus 60 dr. apiece from Gaius, plus 15 dr. interest from his assumption of toga virilis) (Rome)	Dio Cass. lix. 2. 2
A.D. 45	75–312 1/2 dr.	Claudius to dole receivers, apiece (Rome)	Dio Cass. lx. 25. 7
A.D. 68	"obols"	Galba gives as presents rather than drachmas (Rome)	Dio Cass. lxiv. 2. 1
A.D. 145–147	2–3 ob. p.d.	Dole? (Pergamon)	Ael. Arist. xxviii. 139 (Keil)
A.D. 176	200 dr.	Marcus Aurelius to citizens, apiece	Dio Cass. lxxi. 32. 1
A.D. 192	140 dr.	Commodus to citizens, apiece	Dio Cass. lxxii. 16. 2
A.D. 193	100 dr.	Pertinax to citizens, apiece	Dio Cass. lxxiii. 5. 4
A.D. 202	10 gold pieces	Septimius Severus to grain recipients and praetorian guards, apiece—total is 50,000,000 dr.	Dio Cass. lxxvi. 1. 1
pre-A.D. 565	1 gold st. p.d.	Justinian to daughter of Anatolios (Constantinople)	Procop. *Anec.* xxix. 25

Bibliography

Alexandri, O. "Χρονικά," *AD* 25 B.1 (1970) 40–91.

Anderson, J. K. *Xenophon* (New York 1974).

Andrewes, A. "The Peace of Nicias and the Sicilian Expedition," *CAH* V² (1992) 433–463.

———. "The Spartan Resurgence," *CAH* V² (1992) 464–498.

Annas, J. "Chrysippus," *OCD* 329.

———. "Diogenes (3)," *OCD* 474.

Austin, M. M. and Vidal-Naquet, P. *Economic and Social History of Ancient Greece: An Introduction* (Berkeley 1977).

Badian, E. *From Plataea to Potidaea* (Baltimore 1993).

Beazley, J. D. *Attic Red-figure Vase Painters²* (Oxford 1963).

———. *Paralipomena* (Oxford 1971).

Boardman, J. *Athenian Red Figure Vases: The Archaic Period* (London 1975).

Böckh, A. *Die Staatshaushaltung der Athener³* (M. Fränkel rev.), 2 vols. (Berlin 1886).

Bogaert, R. "Le cours du statère de Cyzique à Athènes aux Vᵉ et IVᵉ siècles avant J.-C.: état de la question," *RBN* 123 (1977) 17–39.

Bothmer, D. von "Notes on Makron," in D. Kurtz and B. Sparkes, eds., *The Eye of Greece: Studies in the Art of Athens* (Cambridge 1982) 29–52.

Bowen, A. J. *Plutarch: The Malice of Herodotus* (Warminster 1992).

Bradeen, D. W. "An Athenian Peltast?," ΦΟΡΟΣ 29–35.

Bradeen, D. W. and McGregor, M. F. *Studies in Fifth-Century Attic Epigraphy* (Norman, Oklahoma 1973).

Brunt, P. A. *Arrian*, 2 vols. (Cambridge, Massachusetts 1976–1983).

Buchanan, J. J. *Theorika: A Study of Monetary Distributions to the Athenian Citizenry during the Fifth and Fourth Centuries* B.C. (Locust Valley, New York 1962).

Bugh, G. R. *The Horsemen of Athens* (Princeton 1988).

Burford, A. *Craftsmen in Greek and Roman Society* (London 1972).

———. *The Greek Temple Builders at Epidauros* (Liverpool 1969).

———. "Heavy Transport in Antiquity," *Economic History Review* (2nd ser.) 13 (1960) 1–18.

Burke, E. M. "The Economy of Athens in the Classical Era: Some Adjustments to the Primitivist Model," *TAPhA* 122 (1992) 199–226.

Burstein, S. M. "Bithys, Son of Cleon from Lysimachia: a Reconsideration of the Date and Signficance of *IG* II², 808," *CSCA* 12 (1979) 39–50.

Busolt, G. *Griechische Staatskunde*, 2 vols. (vol. 2 with H. Swoboda) (Munich 1920–1926).

Carey, C. *Lysias Selected Speeches* (Cambridge 1989).

Carpenter, T. H. *Beazley Addenda*^{2} (Oxford 1989).

Chambers, M. *Aristoteles Staat der Athener* (Berlin 1990).

Classen, J. and Steup, J. *Thucydides*$^{3-5}$ (Berlin 1892–1922).

Clinton, K. "Inscriptions from Eleusis," *AE* (1971) 81–136.

———. Review of C. L. Lawton, *Attic Document Reliefs*, *BMCRev* 7 (1996) 743–751.

Cohen, E. E. *Athenian Economy and Society: A Banking Perspective* (Princeton 1992).

Croiset, M. *Démosthène Harangues*, 2 vols. (Paris 1924–1925).

Davies, J. K. *Athenian Propertied Families, 600–300 B.C.* (Oxford 1971).

Develin, R. *Athenian Officials, 684–321 B.C.* (Cambridge 1989).

Dodds, E. R. *Plato Gorgias* (Oxford 1959).

Dover, K. J. *Aristophanes Clouds* (Oxford 1968).

———. *Aristophanes Frogs* (Oxford 1993).

———. *Greek Homosexuality* (Cambridge, Massachusetts 1978).

Dow, S. "The Athenian Calendar of Sacrifices," *Historia* 9 (1960) 270–293.

———. "The Law Codes of Athens," *Proceedings of the Massachusetts Historical Society* 71 (1953–57) [1959] 3–36.

———. "Six Athenian Sacrificial Calendars," *BCH* 92 (1968) 170–186.

Drerup, E. "Über die Publicationskosten der attischen Volksbeschlüsse," *Neue Jahrbücher für Philologie und Paedogogik* 66 (1896) 227–257.

———. "Zu den Publicationskosten der attischen Volksbeschlüsse: Nachtrag zu Jahrg. 1896 s. 227–57," *Neue Jahrbücher für Philologie und Paedogogik* 67 (1897) 871–873.

Edelstein, L. *Plato's Seventh Letter* (Leiden 1966).

Edmonds, J. M. *The Fragments of Attic Comedy*, 3 vols. (Leiden 1957–1961).

Ehrenberg, V. *The People of Aristophanes*^{2} (Oxford 1951).

Finley, M. I. *The Ancient Economy*^{2} (Berkeley 1985).

Fornara, C. W. "The Date of the 'Regulations for Miletus'," *AJPh* 92 (1971) 473–475.

———. "On the Chronology of the Samian War," *JHS* 99 (1979) 7–19.

Frank, T. *An Economic Survey of Ancient Rome*, 6 vols. (Baltimore 1933–1940).

Fritz, K. von. "Menedemos (9)," *RE* 15 (1932) 788–794.

Furley, D. J. "Epicurus," *OCD* 532–534.

Gabrielsen, V. *Financing the Athenian Fleet: Public Taxation and Social Relations* (Baltimore 1994).

———. *Remuneration of State Officials in Fourth Century B.C. Athens* (Odense 1981).

Gallo, L. "Salari e inflazione: Atene tra V e IV sec. A.C.," *ASNP* (ser. 3) 17 (1987) 19–63.

Gauthier, P. "Les clérouques de Lesbos et la colonisation athénienne au Ve siècle," *REG* 79 (1966) 64–88.

Gernet, L. *Démosthène Plaidoyers Civils*, 4 vols. (Paris 1954–1960).
Gernet, L. and Bizos, M. *Lysias Discours*, 2 vols. (Paris 1924–1926).
Geyer, F. "Lais (1), (2)," *RE* 12 (1925) 513–516.
Glotz, G. "Un transport de marble pour le portique d'Éleusis (333/2)," *REG* 36 (1923) 26–45.
Glucker, J. and Sharples, R. W. "Lyco," *OCD* 895.
Gomme, A. W., Andrewes, A. and Dover, K. J. *A Historical Commentary on Thucydides*, 5 vols. (Oxford 1945–1981).
Gomme, A. W. and Sandbach, F. W. *Menander: A Commentary* (Oxford 1973).
Goodwin, W. W. *Demosthenes On the Crown* (Cambridge 1901).
Gow, A. S. F. *Machon* (Cambridge 1965).
Gow, A. S. F. and Page, D. L. *The Greek Anthology: Hellenistic Epigrams*, 2 vols. (Cambridge 1965).
Griffith, G. T. *The Mercenaries of the Hellenistic World* (Cambridge 1935).
Gulick, C. B. *Athenaeus: The Deipnosophists*, 7 vols. (Cambridge, Massachusetts 1927–1941).
Guthrie, W. K. C. *A History of Greek Philosophy*, 6 vols. (Cambridge 1962–1981).
Habicht, C. "Falsche Urkunden zur Geschichte Athens im Zeitalter der Perserkriege," *Hermes* 89 (1961) 1–35.
———. *Untersuchungen zur politischen Geschichte Athens im 3. Jahrhundert v. Chr.* (Munich 1979).
Halperin, D. M. *One Hundred Years of Homosexuality* (New York 1990).
Hansen, M. H. *The Athenian Assembly* (Oxford 1987).
———. *The Athenian Democracy in the Age of Demosthenes* (Oxford 1991).
———. *Demography and Democracy: The Number of Athenian Citizens in the Fourth Century B.C.* (Copenhagen 1986).
———. "Misthos for Magistrates in Classical Athens," *SO* 54 (1979) 5–22.
Hanslik, R. "Proklos (1)," *RE* 23 (1957) 183.
Hardwick, N. "The Solution to Thucydides VIII 101.1: The 'Chian Fortieths'," *NAC* 25 (1996) 59–69.
Harris, E. M. *Aeschines and Athenian Politics* (New York 1995).
———. "The Date of the Trial of Timarchus," *Hermes* 113 (1985) 376–380.
———. "When was Aeschines Born?," *CPh* 83 (1988) 211–214
Hedrick, C. W., Jr. *The Decrees of the Demotionidai* (Atlanta 1990).
Heisserer, A. J. *Alexander the Great and the Greeks: The Epigraphic Evidence* (Norman, Oklahoma 1980).
Henderson, J. *Aristophanes Lysistrata* (Oxford 1987).
———. *The Maculate Muse: Obscene Language in Attic Comedy*[2] (New York 1991).
Henry, A. S. "Bithys Son of Kleon of Lysimacheia: Formal Dating Criteria and *IG* ii^2. 808," in E. M. Craik, ed.,*'Owls to Athens': Essays on Classical Subjects Presented to Sir Kenneth Dover* (Oxford 1990) 179–189.
———. "Provisions for the Payment of Athenian Decrees: A Study in Formulaic Language," *ZPE* 78 (1989) 247–295.

———. "The Sigma Enigma," *ZPE* 120 (1998) 45–48.
Himmelmann, N. "Zur Entlohnung künsterlischer Tätigkeit in klassischen Bauinschriften," *JDAI* 94 (1979) 127–142.
Hopper, R. J. "The Attic Silver Mines in the Fourth Century B.C.," *ABSA* 48 (1953) 200–254.
———. "The Laureion Mines: A Reconsideration," *ABSA* 63 (1968) 293–326.
Hopkins, K. "Introduction," in P. Garnsey, K. Hopkins and C. R. Whittaker, eds., *Trade in the Ancient Economy* (Berkeley 1983) ix–xxv.
Hornblower, S. *A Commentary on Thucydides* (Oxford 1991–).
Hunter, R. L. "Eubulus (2)," *OCD* 564.
Jacobitz, C. *Lucianus*, 4 vols. (Leipzig 1836–1841).
Jevons, F. B. "Work and Wages in Athens," *JHS* 15 (1895) 239–247.
Jones, A. H. M. *Athenian Democracy* (Oxford 1957).
Jordan, B. *The Athenian Navy in the Classical Period* (*University of California Publications: Classical Studies* 13) (Berkeley 1975).
Kallet-Marx, L. *Money, Expense, and Naval Power in Thucydides'* History *1–5.24* (Berkeley 1993).
Kirchhoff, A. "Über die Rede 'vom trierarchischen Kranze'," *Philologische und historische Abhandlungen der Königlichen Akademie der Wissenschaften zu Berlin aus dem Jahre 1865* (1866) 65–108.
Kirchner, I. *Propographia Attica*, 2 vols. (Berlin 1901–1903).
Körte, A. "Hegemon (3)," *RE* 7 (1912) 2595–2596.
Kraay, C. M. *Archaic and Classical Greek Coins* (London 1976).
Krentz, P. *Xenophon, Hellenika I–II.3.10* (Warminster 1989).
Kroll, J. H. "An Archive of Athenian Cavalry," *Hesperia* 46 (1977) 83–140.
Langdon, M. "Poletai Records," *Agora* XIX (Princeton 1991) 57–143.
Larsen, J. A. O. "The *Acharnians* and the Pay of Taxiarchs," *CPh* 41 (1946) 91–98.
Lawton, C. L. *Attic Document Reliefs* (Oxford 1995).
Leonardos, B. "'Αττικὸν ψήφισμα τοῦ 320/9," *AD* 1 (1915) 195–224.
Lewis, D. M. "The Archidamian War," *CAH* V² (1992) 370–432.
———. "Chronological Notes," *CAH* V² (1992) 498–505.
———. "New Evidence for the Gold-Silver Ratio," in C. M. Kraay and G. K. Jenkins, eds., *Essays in Greek Coinage Presented to Stanley Robinson* (Oxford 1968) 105–110.
———. Review of V. Gabrielsen, *Remuneration of State Officials in Fourth Century Athens*, *JHS* 102 (1982) 269.
———. "The Thirty Years Peace," *CAH* V² (1992) 121–146.
Loomis, W. T. "Eleusinian Inscriptions: Three Emendations," *Hesperia* 64 (1995) 131–134.
———. "Pay Differentials and Class Warfare in Lysias' *Against Theozotides*: Two Obols or Two Drachmas?," *ZPE* 107 (1995) 230–236.
MacDowell, D. M. *Aristophanes Wasps* (Oxford 1971).
———. *The Law in Classical Athens* (London 1978).
Macleod, M. D. *Lucian*, 2 vols. (vols. 7–8) (Cambridge, Massachusetts 1961).

MacMullen, R. "The Epigraphic Habit in the Roman Empire," *AJPh* 103 (1982) 233–246.

Maier, F. G. *Griechische Mauerbauinschriften*, 2 vols. (Heidelberg 1959–1961).

Mandolfo, R. "The Greek Attitude to Manual Labor," *P&P* 6 (1954) 1–5.

Marchetti, P. "Les cours de l'attique et l'éginétique et les rapports or-argent dans les comptes de Delphes," in D. Knoepfler, ed., *Comptes et inventaires dans la cité grecque (Actes du colloque international d'epigraphie tenu à Neuchâtel du 23 au 26 septembre 1986 en l'honneur de Jacques Tréheux)* (Neuchâtel 1988) 103–110.

Markle, M. M. "Jury Pay and Assembly Pay at Athens," in P.A. Cartledge and F. D. Harvey, eds., *Crux: Essays in Greek History presented to G. E. M. de Ste. Croix on his 75th Birthday* (Exeter 1985) 265–297.

Mathieu, G. *Démosthène Plaidoyers Politiques*, 2 vols. (vols. 3–4) (Paris 1947).

Mathieu, G. and Brémond, E. *Isocrate Discours*, 4 vols. (Paris 1929–1962).

Mattingly, H. B. *The Athenian Empire Restored: Epigraphic and Historical Studies* (Ann Arbor 1996).

McGregor, M. F. "Athens and Hestiaia," in *Studies in Attic Epigraphy, History and Topography Presented to Eugene Vanderpool* (*Hesperia* Supp. 19) (Princeton 1982) 100–111.

Meiggs, R. *Trees and Timber in the Ancient Mediterranean World* (Oxford 1982).

Meiggs, R. and Lewis, D., eds. *A Selection of Greek Historical Inscriptions to the End of the Fifth Century* B.C., rev. ed. (Oxford 1988).

Melville-Jones, J. R. "The Value of Gold at Athens in 329/8," *AJAH* 3 (1978) 184–187.

Meritt, B. D. "The Choiseul Marble: The Text of 406 B.C.," in *Mélanges helléniques offerts à G. Daux* (Paris 1974) 255–267.

———. "Greek Inscriptions," *Hesperia* 5 (1936) 355–430.

Moles, J. L. "Diogenes (2)," *OCD* 473–474.

Morris, I. "The Athenian Economy Twenty Years after *The Ancient Economy*," *CPh* 89 (1994) 351–366.

Mosley, D. J. *Envoys and Diplomacy in Ancient Greece* (*Historia* Einzelschrift 22) (Wiesbaden 1973).

Nolan, B. T. *Inscribing Costs at Athens in the Fourth Century* B.C. (Ph.D. diss., Ohio State University, 1981) (Ann Arbor 1981).

Orlandos, A. K. Τὰ Ὑλικὰ Δομῆς, 2 vols. (Athens 1955–1958).

Osborne, M. J. *Naturalization in Athens*, 4 vols. (Brussels 1981–1983).

———. "Some Attic Inscriptions," *ZPE* 42 (1981) 171–178.

Owen, G. E. L. and Hornblower, S. "Speusippus," *OCD* 1434–1435.

Peppa-Delmousou, D. "Χαλκῆ ἐπιγραφὴ τοῦ Μουσείου Ἀκροπόλεως," *AE* (1971) 137–145.

Petrakos, B.C. Οἱ Ἐπιγραφὲς τοῦ Ὠρωποῦ (Athens 1997).

Pickard-Cambridge, A. *The Dramatic Festivals of Athens* ^{2} (1968 rev. 2nd ed. with 1988 supp., both by J. Gould and D. M. Lewis) (Oxford 1988).

Pinney, G. F. "For the Heroes are at Hand," *JHS* 104 (1984) 181–183.
Pritchett, W. K. "The Attic Stelai, Part II," *Hesperia* 25 (1956) 178–328.
———. *The Greek State at War,* 5 vols. (Berkeley 1974–1991).
———. "Loans of Athena in 407 B.C.," *AncSoc* 8 (1977) 33–47.
Quinn, G. M. "The Sacrificial Calendar of the Marathonian Tetrapolis" (Ph.D. diss., Harvard University, 1971).
Rabe, H. *Scholia in Lucianum* (Leipzig 1906).
Randall, R. H. Jr. "The Erechtheum Workmen," *AJA* 57 (1953) 199–210.
Raubitschek, A. E. "Greek Inscriptions," *Hesperia* 12 (1943) 12–88.
———. "Phryne," *RE* 20 (1941) 893–907.
Reger, G. *Regionalism and Change in the Economy of Independent Delos, 314–167 B.C.* (Berkeley 1994).
Reinmuth, O. *The Ephebic Inscriptions of the Fourth Century B.C.* (*Mnemosyne* Supp. 14) (Leiden 1971).
Rhodes, P. J. *A Commentary on the Aristotelian* Atheniaion Politeia (Oxford 1981).
Roy, J. "The Mercenaries of Cyrus," *Historia* 16 (1967) 287–323.
Ste. Croix, G. E. M. de. Review of J. J. Buchanan, *Theorika*, *CR* (n.s.) 14 (1964) 190–192.
Sandys, J. E. *Aristotle's Constitution of the Athenians*[2] (London 1912).
Schaps, D. M. *Economic Rights of Women in Ancient Greece* (Edinburgh 1979).
Schauenburg, K. "ΕΥΡΥΜΕΔΩΝ ΕΙΜΙ," *MDAI(A)* 90 (1975) 97–121.
Schneider, K. "Hetairai," *RE* 8 (1913) 1331–1372.
Schulthess, O. "Σιτηρέσιον," *RE* (2. Reihe) 3 (1927) 382–388.
Schweigert, E. "Inscriptions from the North Slope of the Acropolis," *Hesperia* 7 (1938) 264–310.
Schwenk, C. J. *Athens in the Age of Alexander: The Dated Laws & Decrees of 'the Lykourgan Era,' 338–322 B.C.* (Chicago 1985).
Seager, R. "Thrasybulus, Conon and Athenian Imperialism, 396–386 B.C.," *JHS* 87 (1967) 95–115.
Sedley, D. N. "Polemon (2)," *OCD* 1204.
Sommerstein, A. H. *The Comedies of Aristophanes* (Warminster 1980–).
Spence, I. G. *The Cavalry of Classical Greece* (Oxford 1993).
Starkie, W. J. M. *The Acharnians of Aristophanes* (London 1909).
Stewart, A. *Greek Sculpture*, 2 vols. (New Haven 1990).
Striker, G. "Carneades," *OCD* 293–294.
Stroud, R. S. "Theozotides and the Athenian Orphans," *Hesperia* 40 (1971) 280–301.
Swoboda, H. "Kallistratos (1)," *RE* 10 (1919) 1730–1735.
Tod, M. N. "The Economic Background of the Fifth Century," *CAH* V[1] (1927) 1–32.
———. *A Selection of Greek Historical Inscriptions*, 2 vols. (vol. 1[2]) (Oxford 1946–1948).
Todd, S. "*Lady Chatterley's Lover* and the Attic Orators: The Social Composition of the Athenian Jury," *JHS* 110 (1990) 146–173.

Tracy, S. V. *Athenian Democracy in Transition: Attic Letter-Cutters of 340–290 B.C.* (Berkeley 1995).

———. *Attic Letter Cutters of 229 to 86 B.C.* (Berkeley 1990).

———. "Hands in Fifth-Century B.C. Attic Inscriptions," in *Studies Presented to Sterling Dow on His Eightieth Birthday* (*Greek, Roman and Byzantine* Monograph 10) (Durham, North Carolina 1984) 277–282.

———. "*IG* II^2 1195 and Agathe Tyche in Attica," *Hesperia* 63 (1994) 241–244.

Tronson, A. "The Relevance of *IG* II^2 329 to the Hellenic League of Alexander the Great," *AncW* 12 (1985) 15–19.

Ussher, R. G. *Aristophanes Ecclesiazusae* (Oxford 1973).

Wade-Gery, H. T. *Essays in Greek History* (Oxford 1958).

Walbank, M. B. *Athenian Proxenies of the Fifth Century B.C.* (Toronto 1978).

———. "A *Lex Sacra* of the State and of the Deme of Kollytos," *Hesperia* 63 (1994) 232–239.

Wallace, M. B. "Herodotos and Euboia," *Phoenix* 28 (1974) 22–44.

Wesenberg, B. "Kunst und Lohn am Erechtheion," *AA* 1985 55–65.

Westermann, W. L. "Notes upon the Ephodia of Greek Ambassadors," *CPh* 5 (1910) 203–216.

Whitehead, D. *The Demes of Attica 508/7–ca. 250 B.C.: A Political and Social Study* (Princeton 1986).

Will, E. "Notes sur ΜΙΣΘΟΣ," in J. Bingen, G. Cambier and G. Nachtergael, eds., *Le monde grec: hommages à Claire Préaux* (Brussels 1975) 426–438.

Worthington, I. *A Historical Commentary on Dinarchus* (Ann Arbor 1992).

[no author stated] "Apollonios (88)," *RE* 2 (1896) 144.

Index Locorum

Parenthetical references to entry numbers signify that the passage may be cited under that number; e.g., *Agora* XV 58. 6–9 is cited on p. 146 as "*Agora* XV 58. 6–9," while on p. 158 it is cited as "'Inscribers' #152." Spurious works, e.g., [Xen.] *Ath. Pol.,* are listed without distinction under the author to whom they were ascribed in antiquity.

Inscriptions

Literary Texts

Vases

Index of Greek Words

General Index